Anonymous

The Prose Epitome

Anonymous

The Prose Epitome

ISBN/EAN: 9783744696463

Printed in Europe, USA, Canada, Australia, Japan

Cover: Foto ©Thomas Meinert / pixelio.de

More available books at **www.hansebooks.com**

THE

PROSE EPITOME;

OR,

ELEGANT EXTRACTS ABRIDGED

FROM THE LARGER VOLUME,

FOR

The Improvement of Scholars at Claſſical and other Schools,

IN THE ART OF SPEAKING;
IN READING, THINKING, COMPOSING;
AND IN THE CONDUCT OF LIFE.

Happy they who love to read!

LONDON:

TO THE

PROSE EXTRACTS.

THE Value and Utility of this Volume for the Purposes of Education are evident on Inspection. So large a Quantity of excellent Matter has never been presented to studious Youth in so small a Form.

The original Octavo Volume, printed also by MR. DILLY, *has met with general Approbation. Its Bulk was, in some Cases, an Objection to it. An* Abridgment *of it is therefore here published; and both the Conductors of Education and young Persons who delight in Reading, may now furnish themselves with ELEGANT EXTRACTS IN PROSE, or ELEGANT EXTRACTS IN POETRY, in the* large Octavo Volumes, *or in the EPITOMES, as may best suit their own Convenience.*

MR. DILLY *begs leave to observe, that the genuine and original Editions of ELEGANT EXTRACTS, which have been so long and so much patronized by the Public, are published with* his Name only *at the Bottom of the Title Page; and that he has no Concern whatever with any* IMITATION *which the good Success of the genuine and original Work may have occasioned.*

INTRODUCTION.

ON

PRONUNCIATION, OR DELIVERY.

FROM DR. BLAIR'S LECTURES.

I.

HOW much ſtreſs was laid upon Pronunciation, or Delivery, by the moſt eloquent of all orators, Demoſthenes, appears from a noted ſaying of his, related both by Cicero and Quinctilian; when being aſked, What was the firſt point in oratory? he anſwered Delivery; and being aſked, What was the ſecond? and afterwards, What was the third? he ſtill anſwered, Delivery. There is no wonder, that he ſhould have rated this ſo high, and that for improving himſelf in it, he ſhould have employed thoſe aſſiduous and painful labours, which all the Ancients take ſo much notice of; for, beyond doubt, nothing is of more importance. To ſuperficial thinkers, the management of the voice and geſture, in public ſpeaking, may appear to relate to decoration only, and to be one of the inferior arts of catching an audience. But this is far from being the caſe. It is intimately connected with what is, or ought to be, the end of all public ſpeaking, Perſuaſion; and therefore deſerves the ſtudy of the moſt grave and ſerious ſpeakers, as much as of thoſe, whoſe only aim it is to pleaſe.

For, let it be conſidered, whenever we addreſs ourſelves to others by words, our intention certainly is to make ſome impreſſion on thoſe to whom we ſpeak; it is to convey to them our own ideas and emotions. Now the tone of our voice, our looks and geſtures, interpret our ideas and emotions no leſs than words do; nay, the impreſſion they make on others, is frequently much ſtronger than any that words can make. We often ſee that an expreſſive look, or a paſſionate cry, unaccompanied by words, conveys to others more forcible ideas, and rouſes within them ſtronger paſſions, than can be communicated by the moſt eloquent diſcourſe. The ſignification of our ſentiments, made by tones and geſtures, has this advantage above that made by words, that it is the language of nature. It is that method of interpreting our mind, which nature has dictated to all, and which is understood by all; whereas, words are only arbitrary, conventional symbols of our ideas; and, by consequence, must make a more feeble impression. So true is this, that, to render words fully significant, they must, almost in every case, receive some aid from the manner of Pronunciation and Delivery; and he who, in speaking, should employ bare words, without enforcing them by proper tones and accents, would leave us with a faint and indistinct impression, often with a doubtful and ambiguous conception of what he had delivered. Nay, so close is the connection between certain sentiments and the proper manner of pronouncing them, that he who does not pronounce them after that manner, can never persuade us, that he believes, or feels, the sentiments themselves. His delivery may be such, as to give the lie to all that he asserts. When Marcus Callidius accused one of an attempt to poison him, but enforced his accusation in a languid manner, and without any warmth or earnestness of delivery, Cicero, who pleaded for the accused person, improved this into an argument of the falsity of the charge, "An tu, M. "Callidi nisi fingeres, sic ageres?" In Shakespeare's Richard II. the Duchess of York thus impeaches the sincerity of her husband:

Pleads he in earnest?—Look upon his face,
His eyes do drop no tears; his prayers are jest;
His words come from his mouth; ours, from our breast:
He prays but faintly, and would be denied;
We pray with heart and soul.

But, I believe it is needless to say any more, in order to shew the high importance of a good Delivery. I proceed, therefore, to such observations as appear to me most useful to be made on this head.

The great objects which every public speaker will naturally have in his eye in forming his Delivery, are, first, to speak so as to be fully and easily understood by all who hear him; and next, to speak with grace and force, so as to please and to move his audience. Let us consider what is most important with respect to each of these *.

In order to be fully and easily understood, the four chief requisites are, A due degree of loudness of voice; Distinctness; Slowness; and, Propriety of Pronunciation.

The first attention of every public speaker, doubtless, must be, to make himself be heard by all those to whom he speaks. He must endeavour to fill with his voice the space occupied by the assembly. This power of voice, it may be thought, is wholly a natural talent. It is so in a good measure; but, however, may receive considerable assistance from art. Much depends for this purpose on the proper pitch, and management of the voice. Every man has three pitches in his voice; the high, the middle, and the low one. The high, is that which he uses in calling aloud to some one at a distance. The low is, when he approaches to a whisper. The middle is, that which he employs in common conversation, and which he should generally use in public discourse. For it is a great mistake, to imagine that one must take the highest pitch of his voice, in order to be well heard by a great assembly. This is confounding two things which are different, loudness, or

* On this whole subject, Mr. Sheridan's Lectures on Elocution are very worthy of being consulted; and several hints are here taken from them.

strength

ſtrength of ſound, with the key, or note on which we ſpeak. A ſpeaker may render his voice louder, without altering the key; and we ſhall always be able to give moſt body, moſt perſevering force of ſound, to that pitch of voice, to which in converſation we are accuſtomed. Whereas, by ſetting out on our higheſt pitch or key, we certainly allow ourſelves leſs compaſs, and are likely to ſtrain our voice before we have done. We ſhall fatigue ourſelves, and ſpeak with pain; and whenever a man ſpeaks with pain to himſelf, he is always heard with pain by his audience. Give the voice therefore full ſtrength and ſwell of ſound; but always pitch it on your ordinary ſpeaking key. Make it a conſtant rule never to utter a greater quantity of voice, than you can afford without pain to yourſelves, and without any extraordinary effort. As long as you keep within theſe bounds, the other organs of ſpeech will be at liberty to diſcharge their ſeveral offices with eaſe; and you will always have your voice under command. But whenever you tranſgreſs theſe bounds, you give up the reins, and have no longer any management of it. It is an uſeful rule too, in order to be well heard, to fix our eye on ſome of the moſt diſtant perſons in the aſſembly, and to conſider ourſelves as ſpeaking to them. We naturally and mechanically utter our words with ſuch a degree of ſtrength, as to make ourſelves be heard by one to whom we addreſs ourſelves, provided he be within the reach of our voice. As this is the caſe in common converſation, it will hold alſo in public ſpeaking. But remember, that in public as well as in converſation, it is poſſible to offend by ſpeaking too loud. This extreme hurts the ear, by making the voice come upon it in rumbling indiſtinct maſſes; beſides its giving the ſpeaker the diſagreeable appearance of one who endeavours to compel aſſent, by mere vehemence and force of ſound.

In the next place, to being well heard, and clearly underſtood, diſtinctneſs of articulation contributes more, than mere loudneſs of ſound. The quantity of ſound neceſſary to fill even a large ſpace, is ſmaller than is commonly imagined; and with diſtinct articulation, a man of a weak voice will make it reach farther, than the ſtrongeſt voice can reach without it. To this, therefore, every public ſpeaker ought to pay great attention. He muſt give every ſound which he utters its due proportion, and make every ſyllable, and even every letter in the word which he pronounces, be heard diſtinctly; without ſlurring, whiſpering, or ſuppreſſing any of the proper ſounds.

In the third place, in order to articulate diſtinctly, moderation is requiſite with regard to the ſpeed of pronouncing. Precipitancy of ſpeech confounds all articulation, and all meaning. I need ſcarcely obſerve, that there may be alſo an extreme on the oppoſite ſide. It is obvious, that a lifeleſs, drawling pronunciation, which allows the minds of the hearers to be always outrunning the ſpeaker, muſt render every diſcourſe inſipid and fatiguing. But the extreme of ſpeaking too faſt is much more common, and requires the more to be guarded againſt, becauſe, when it has grown up into a habit, few errors are more difficult to be corrected. To pronounce with a proper degree of ſlowneſs, and with full and clear articulation, is the firſt thing to be ſtudied by all who begin to ſpeak in public; and cannot be too much recommended to them. Such a pronunciation gives weight and dignity to their diſcourſe. It is a great aſſiſtance to the voice, by the pauſes and reſts which it allows it more eaſily to make; and it enables the ſpeaker to ſwell all his ſounds, both with more

more force and more music. It assists him also in preserving a due command of himself; whereas a rapid and hurried manner, is apt to excite that flutter of spirits, which is the greatest enemy to all right execution in the way of oratory. "Promptum sit os," says Quinctilian, "non præceps, moderatum, non lentum."

After these fundamental attentions to the pitch and management of the voice, to distinct articulation, and to a proper degree of slowness of speech, what a public speaker must, in the fourth place, study, is Propriety of Pronunciation; or the giving to every word, which he utters, that sound, which the most polite usage of the language appropriates to it; in opposition to broad, vulgar, or provincial pronunciation. This is requisite, both for speaking intelligibly, and for speaking with grace or beauty. Instructions concerning this article, can be given by the living voice only. But there is one observation, which it may not be improper here to make. In the English language, every word which consists of more syllables than one, has one accented syllable. The accent rests sometimes on the vowel, sometimes on the consonant. Seldom, or never, is there more than one accented syllable in any English word, however long; and the genius of the language requires the voice to mark that syllable by a stronger percussion, and to pass more slightly over the rest. Now, the same word; from a mistaken notion, that it gives gravity and force to their discourse, and adds to the pomp of public declamation. Whereas, this is one of the greatest faults that can be committed in pronunciation; it makes what is called a theatrical or mouthing manner; and gives an artificial affected air to speech, which detracts greatly both from its agreeableness, and its impression.

I proceed to treat next of those higher parts of Delivery, by studying which, a speaker has something farther in view than merely to render himself intelligible, and seeks to give grace and force to what he utters. These may be comprised under four heads, Emphasis, Pauses, Tones, and Gestures. Let me only premise in general, to what I am to say concerning them, that attention to these articles of Delivery, is by no means to be confined, as some might be apt to imagine, to the more elaborate and pathetic parts of a discourse; there is, perhaps, as great attention requisite, and as much skill displayed, in adapting emphases, pauses, tones, and gestures, properly, to calm and plain speaking: and the effect of a just and graceful delivery will, in every part of a subject, be found of high importance for commanding attention, and enforcing what is spoken.

First, let us consider Emphasis; by this is meant a stronger and fuller sound of voice, by which we distinguish the accented syllable of

and lifeless, but the meaning left often ambiguous. If the emphasis be placed wrong, we pervert and confound the meaning wholly. To give a common instance; such a simple question as this: "Do you ride to town today?" is capable of no fewer than four different acceptations, according as the emphasis is differently placed on the words. If it be pronounced thus: Do *you* ride to town today? the answer may naturally be, No; I send *my servant* in my stead. If thus; Do you *ride* to town to-day? Answer, No; I intend to *walk*. Do you ride *to town* today? No; I ride out into *the fields*. Do you ride to town *to-day?* No; but I shall *to-morrow*. In like manner, in solemn discourse, the whole force and beauty of an expression often depend on the accented word; and we may present to the hearers quite different views of the same sentiment, by placing the emphasis differently. In the following words of our Saviour, observe in what different lights the thought is placed, according as the words are pronounced. "Judas, betrayest thou the Son of Man with a kiss?" *Betrayest* thou—makes the reproach turn, on the infamy of treachery.—Betrayest *thou*—makes it rest, upon Judas's connection with his master. Betrayest thou the *Son of Man*—rests it, upon our Saviour's personal character and eminence. Betrayest thou the Son of Man *with a kiss?* turns it upon his prostituting the signal of peace and friendship, to the purpose of a mark of destruction.

In order to acquire the proper management of the emphasis, the great rule, and indeed the only rule possible to be given, is, that the speaker study to attain a just conception of the force and spirit of those sentiments which he is to pronounce. For to lay the emphasis with exact propriety, is a constant exercise of good sense and attention. It is far from being an inconsiderable attainment. It is one of the greatest trials of a true and just taste; and must arise from feeling delicately ourselves, and from judging accurately of what is fittest to strike the feelings of others. There is as great a difference between a chapter of the Bible, or any other piece of plain prose, read by one who places the several emphases every where with taste and judgment, and by one who neglects or mistakes them, as there is between the same tune played by the most masterly hand, or by the most bungling performer.

In all prepared discourses, it would be of great use, if they were read over or rehearsed in private, with this particular view, to search for the proper emphases before they were pronounced in public; marking, at the same time, with a pen, the emphatical words in every sentence, or at least the most weighty and affecting parts of the discourse, and fixing them well in memory. Were this attention oftener bestowed, were this part of pronunciation studied with more exactness, and not left to the moment of delivery, as is commonly done, public speakers would find their care abundantly repaid, by the remarkable effects which it would produce upon their audience. Let me caution, at the same time, against one error, that of multiplying emphatical words too much. It is only by a prudent reserve in the use of them, that we can give them any weight. If they recur too often; if a speaker attempts to render every thing which he says of high importance, by a multitude of strong emphases, we soon learn to pay little regard to them. To crowd every sentence with emphatical words, is like crowding all the pages of of a book with italic characters, which, as to the effect, is just the same with using no such distinctions at all.

Next to emphasis, the Pauses in speaking demand attention. These are of two kinds; first, emphatical pauses; and next, such as mark the distinctions of sense. An emphatical pause is made, after something has been said of peculiar moment, and on which we want to fix the hearer's attention. Sometimes, before such a thing is said, we usher it in with a pause of this nature. Such pauses have the same effect as a strong emphases, and are subject to the same rules; especially to the caution just now given, of not repeating them too frequently. For, as they excite uncommon attention, and of course raise expectation, if the importance of the matter be not fully answerable to such expectation, they occasion disappointment and disgust.

But the most frequent and the principal use of pauses, is to mark the divisions of the sense, and at the same time to allow the speaker to draw his breath; and the proper and graceful adjustment of such pauses, is one of the most nice and difficult articles in delivery. In all public speaking, the management of the breath requires a good deal of care, so as not to be obliged to divide words from one another, which have so intimate a connection, that they ought to be pronounced with the same breath, and without the least separation. Many a sentence is miserably mangled, and the force of the emphasis totally lost, by divisions being made in the wrong place. To avoid this, every one, while he is speaking, should be very careful to provide a full supply of breath for what he is to utter. It is a great mistake to imagine, that the breath must be drawn only at the end of a period, when the voice is allowed to fall. It may easily be gathered at the intervals of the period, when the voice is only suspended for a moment; and, by this management, one may have always a sufficient stock for carrying on the longest sentence, without improper interruptions.

If any one, in public speaking, shall have formed to himself a certain melody or tune, which requires rest and pauses of its own, distinct from those of the sense, he has, undoubtedly, contracted one of the worst habits into which a public speaker can fall. It is the sense which should always rule the pauses of the voice; for wherever there is any sensible suspension of the voice, the hearer is always led to expect something corresponding in the meaning. Pauses in public discourse, must be formed upon the manner in which we utter ourselves in ordinary, sensible conversation; and not upon the stiff, artificial manner which we acquire from reading books according to the common punctuation. The general run of punctuation is very arbitrary; often capricious and false; and dictates an uniformity of tone in the pauses, which is extremely disagreeable; for we are to observe, that to render pauses graceful and expressive, they must not only be made in the right place, but also be accompanied with a proper tone of voice, by which the nature of these pauses is intimated; much more than by the length of them, which can never be exactly measured. Sometimes it is only a slight and simple suspension of voice that is proper; sometimes a degree of cadence in the voice is required; and sometimes that peculiar tone and cadence, which denotes the sentence finished. In all these cases, we are to regulate ourselves, by attending to the manner in which nature teaches us to ſpeak when engaged in real and earneſt diſcourſe with others.

When we are reading or reciting verſe, there is a peculiar difficulty in making the pauſes juſtly. The difficulty ariſes from the melody of verſe, which dictates to the ear pauſes or reſts of its own; and to adjuſt and compound theſe properly with the pauſes of the ſenſe, ſo as neither to hurt the ear, nor offend the underſtanding, is ſo very nice a matter, that it is no wonder we ſo ſeldom meet with good readers of poetry. There are two kinds of pauſes that belong to the muſic of verſe; one is, the pauſe at the end of the line; and the other, the cæſural pauſe in the middle of it. With regard to the pauſe at the end of the line, which marks that ſtrain or verſe to be finiſhed, rhyme renders this always ſenſible, and in ſome meaſure compels us to obſerve it in our pronunciation. In blank verſe, where there is a greater liberty permitted of running the lines into one another, ſometimes without any ſuſpenſion in the ſenſe, it has been made a queſtion, Whether, in reading ſuch verſe with propriety, any regard at all ſhould be paid to the cloſe of a line? On the ſtage, where the appearance of ſpeaking in verſe ſhould always be avoided, there can, I think, be no doubt, that the cloſe of ſuch lines as make no pauſe in the ſenſe, ſhould not be rendered perceptible to the ear. But on other occaſions, this were improper: for what is the uſe of melody, or for what end has the poet compoſed in verſe, if, in reading his lines, we ſuppreſs his numbers; and degrade them, by our pronunciation, into mere proſe? We ought, therefore, certainly to read blank verſe ſo as to make every line ſenſible to the ear. At the ſame time, in doing ſo, every appearance of ſing-ſong and tone muſt be carefully guarded againſt. The cloſe of the line, where it makes no pauſe in the meaning, ought to be marked, not by ſuch a tone as is uſed in finiſhing a ſentence, but without either letting the voice fall or elevating it, it ſhould be marked only by ſuch a ſlight ſuſpenſion of ſound, as may diſtinguiſh the paſſage from one line to another, without injuring the meaning.

The other kind of muſical pauſe, is that which falls ſomewhere about the middle of the verſe, and divides it into two hemiſtichs; a pauſe, not ſo great as that which belongs to the cloſe of the line, but ſtill ſenſible to an ordinary ear. This, which is called the cæſural pauſe, in the French heroic verſe falls uniformly in the middle of the line, in the Engliſh, it may fall after the 4th, 5th, 6th, or 7th ſyllables in the line, and no other. Where the verſe is ſo conſtructed that this cæſural pauſe coincides with the ſlighteſt pauſe or diviſion in the ſenſe, the line can be read eaſily; as in the two firſt verſes of Mr. Pope's Meſſiah,

> Ye nymphs of Solyma! begin the ſong;
> To heavenly themes, ſublimer ſtrains belong;

But if it ſhall happen that words, which have ſuch a ſtrict and intimate connection, as not to bear even a momentary ſeparation, are divided from one another by this cæſural pauſe, we then feel a ſort of ſtruggle between the ſenſe and the ſound, which renders it difficult to read ſuch lines gracefully. The rule of proper pronunciation in ſuch caſes is, to regard only the pauſe which the ſenſe forms; and to read the line accordingly. The neglect of the cæſural pauſe may make the line ſound ſomewhat unharmoniouſly; but the effect would be much worſe, if the ſenſe were ſacrificed to the ſound. For inſtance, in the following line of Milton,

—What

——What in me is dark,
Illumine; what is low, raise and support.

The sense clearly dictates the pause after "illumine," at the end of the third syllable, which, in reading, ought to be made accordingly; though, if the melody only were to be regarded, "illumine" should be connected with what follows, and the pause not made till the 4th or 6th syllable. So in the following line of Mr. Pope's (Epistle to Dr. Arbuthnot):

I sit, with sad civility I read:

The ear plainly points out the cæsural pause as falling after "sad," the 4th syllable. But it would be very bad reading to make any pause there, so as to separate "sad" and "civility." The sense admits of no other pause than after the second syllable "sit," which therefore must be the only pause made in the reading.

I proceed to treat next of Tones in pronunciation, which are different both from emphasis and pauses; consisting in the modulation of the voice, the notes or variations of sound which we employ in public speaking. How much of the propriety, the force and grace of discourse, must depend on these, will appear from this single consideration; that to almost every sentiment we utter, more especially to every strong emotion, nature hath adapted some peculiar tone of voice; insomuch, that he who should tell another that he was very angry, or much grieved, in a tone which did not suit such emotions, instead of being believed, would be laughed at. Sympathy is one of the most powerful principles by which persuasive discourse works its effect. The speaker endeavours to transfuse into his hearers his own sentiments and emotions; which he can never be successful in doing, unless he utters them in such a manner as to convince the hearers that he feels them *. The proper expression of tones, therefore, deserves to be attentively studied by every one who would be a successful orator.

The greatest and most material instruction which can be given for this purpose is, to form the tones of public speaking upon the tones of sensible and animated conversation. We may observe that every man, when he is much in earnest in common discourse, when he is engaged in speaking on some subject which interests him nearly, has an eloquent or persuasive tone and manner. What is the reason of our being often so frigid and unpersuasive in public discourse, but our departing from the natural tone of speaking, and delivering ourselves in an affected, artificial man-

* "All that passes in the mind of man may be "reduced to two classes, which I call, Ideas, and "Emotions. By Ideas, I mean all thoughts "which rise and pass in succession in the mind: "By Emotions, all exertions of the mind in arranging, combining, and separating its ideas, "as well as all the effects produced on the mind "itself by those ideas, from the more violent "agitation of the passions, to the calmer feelings "produced by the operation of the intellect and "the fancy. In short, thought is the object of "the one, internal feeling of the other. That "which serves to express the former, I call the "Language of Ideas; and the latter, the Language of Emotions. Words are the signs of the "one, tones of the other. Without the use of "these two sorts of language, it is impossible to "communicate through the ear all that passes in "the mind of man."

SHERIDAN on the Art of Reading.

ner? Nothing can be more abſurd than to imagine, that as ſoon as one mounts a pulpit, or riſes in a public aſſembly, he is inſtantly to lay aſide the voice with which he expreſſes himſelf in private; to aſſume a new, ſtudied tone, and a cadence altogether foreign to his natural manner. This has vitiated all delivery; this has given riſe to cant and tedious monotony, in the different kinds of modern public ſpeaking, eſpecially in the pulpit. Men departed from nature; and ſought to give a beauty or force, as they imagined, to their diſcourſe, by ſubſtituting certain ſtudied muſical tones, in the room of the genuine expreſſions of ſentiment, which the voice carries in natural diſcourſe. Let every public ſpeaker guard againſt this error. Whether he ſpeak in a private room, or in a great aſſembly, let him remember that he ſtill ſpeaks. Follow nature: conſider how ſhe teaches you to utter any ſentiment or feeling of your heart. Imagine a ſubject of debate ſtarted in converſation among grave and wiſe men, and yourſelf bearing a ſhare in it. Think after what manner, with what tones and inflexions of voice, you would on ſuch an occaſion expreſs yourſelf, when you were moſt in earneſt, and ſought moſt to be liſtened to. Carry theſe with you to the bar, to the pulpit, or to any public aſſembly; let theſe be the foundation of your manner of pronouncing there; and you will take the ſureſt method of rendering your delivery both agreeable and perſuaſive.

I have ſaid, Let theſe converſation tones be the *foundation* of public pronunciation; for, on ſome occaſions, ſolemn public ſpeaking requires them to be exalted beyond the ſtrain of common diſcourſe. In a formal, ſtudied oration, the elevation of the ſtyle, and the harmony of the ſentences, prompt, almoſt neceſſarily, a modulation of voice more rounded, and bordering more upon muſic, than converſation admits. This gives riſe to what is called, the Declaiming Manner. But though this mode of pronunciation runs conſiderably beyond ordinary diſcourſe, yet ſtill it muſt have, for its baſis, the natural tones of grave and dignified converſation. I muſt obſerve, at the ſame time, that the conſtant indulgence of a declamatory manner, is not favourable either to good compoſition, or good delivery; and is in hazard of betraying public ſpeakers into that monotony of tone and cadence, which is ſo generally complained of. Whereas, he who forms the general run of his delivery upon a ſpeaking manner, is not likely ever to become diſagreeable through monotony. He will have the ſame natural variety in his tones, which a perſon has in converſation. Indeed, the perfection of delivery requires both theſe different manners, that of ſpeaking with livelineſs and eaſe, and that of declaiming with ſtatelineſs and dignity, to be poſſeſſed by one man; and to be employed by him, according as the different parts of his diſcourſe require either the one or the other. This is a perfection which is not attained by many; the greateſt part of public ſpeakers allowing their delivery to be formed altogether accidentally, according as ſome turn of voice appears to them moſt beautiful, or ſome artificial model has caught their fancy; and acquiring, by this means, a habit of pronunciation, which they can never vary. But the capital direction, which ought never to be forgotten, is, to copy the proper tones for expreſſing every ſentiment from thoſe which nature dictates to us, in converſation with others; to ſpeak always with her voice; and not to form to ourſelves a fantaſtic public manner, from an an absurd fancy of its being more beautiful than a natural one *.

It now remains to treat of Gesture, or what is called Action in public discourse. Some nations animate their words in common conversation, with many more motions of the body than others do. The French and the Italians are, in this respect, much more sprightly than we. But there is no nation, hardly any person so phlegmatic, as not to accompany their words with some actions and gesticulations, on all occasions, when they are much in earnest. It is therefore unnatural in a public speaker, it is inconsistent with that earnestness and seriousness which he ought to shew in all affairs of moment, to remain quite unmoved in his outward appearance; and to let the words drop from his mouth, without any expression of meaning, or warmth in his gesture.

The fundamental rule as to propriety of action, is undoubtedly the same with what I gave as to propriety of tone. Attend to the looks and gestures, in which earnestness, indignation, compassion, or any other emotion, discovers itself to most advantage in the common intercourse of men; and let these be your model. Some of these looks and gestures are common to all men; and there are also certain peculiarities of manner which distinguish every individual. A public speaker must take that manner which is most natural to himself. For it is here just as in tones. It is not the business of a speaker to form to himself a certain set of motions and gestures, which he thinks most becoming and agreeable, and to practise these in public, without their having any correspondence to the manner which is natural to him in private. His gestures and motions ought all to carry that kind of expression which nature has dictated to him; and, unless this be the case, it is impossible, by means of any study, to avoid their appearing stiff and forced.

However, although nature must be the ground-work, I admit that there is room in this matter for some study and art. For many persons are naturally ungraceful in the motions which they make; and this ungracefulness might, in part at least, be reformed by application and care. The study of action in public speaking, consists chiefly in guarding against awkward and disagreeable motions, and in learning to perform such as are natural to the speaker, in the most becoming manner. For this end, it has been advised by writers on this subject, to practice before a mirror, where one may see, and judge of his own gestures. But I am afraid, persons are not always the best judges of the gracefulness of their own motions: and one may declaim long enough before a mirror, without correcting any of his faults. The judgment of a friend, whose good taste they can trust, will be found of much greater advantage to beginners, than any mirror they can use. With regard to particular rules concerning action and gesticulation, Quinctilian has delivered a great many, in the last chapter of the 11th Book of his Institutions;

* "Loquere," (says an author of the last century, who has written a Treatise in Verse, de Gestu et Voce Oratoris)

——"Loquere; hoc vitium commune, loquatur
"Ut nemo; at tensâ declamaret omnia voce.
"Tu loquere, ut mos est hominum; Boat & latrat ille:
"Ille ululat; rudit hic (fari si talia dignum est);
"Non hominem vox ulla sonat ratione loquentem."

JOANNES LUCAS, de Gestu et Voce, Lib. II. Paris 1675.

stitutions; and all the modern writers on this subject have done little else but translate them. I am not of opinion, that such rules, delivered either by the voice or on paper, can be of much use, unless persons saw them exemplified before their eyes*.

I shall only add further on this head that in order to succeed well in delivery, nothing is more necessary than for a speaker to guard against a certain flutter of spirits, which is peculiarly incident to those who begin to speak in public. He must endeavour above all things to be recollected, and master of himself. For this end, he will find nothing of more use to him, than to study to become wholly engaged in his subject; to be possessed with a sense of its importance or seriousness; to be concerned much more to persuade than to please. He will generally please most, when pleasing is not his sole nor chief aim. This is the only rational and proper method of raising one's self above that timid and bashful regard to an audience, which is so ready to disconcert a speaker, both as to what he is to say, and as to his manner of saying it.

I cannot conclude, without an earnest admonition to guard against all affectation, which is the certain ruin of good delivery. Let your manner, whatever it is, be your own; neither imitated from another, nor assumed upon some imaginary model, which is unnatural to you. Whatever is native, even though accompanied with several defects, yet is likely to please; because it shows us a man; because it has the appearance of coming from the heart. Whereas a delivery attended with several acquired graces and beauties, if it be not easy and free, if it betray the marks of art and affectation, never fails to disgust. To attain any extremely correct, and perfectly graceful delivery, is what few can expect; so many natural talents being requisite to concur

* The few following hints only I shall adventure to throw out, in case they may be of any service. When speaking in public, one should study to preserve as much dignity as possible in the whole attitude of the body. An erect posture is generally to be chosen: standing firm, so as to have the fullest and freest command of all his motions; any inclination which is used, should be forwards towards the hearers, which is a natural expression of earnestness. As for the countenance, the chief rule is, that it should correspond with the nature of the discourse, and when no particular emotion is expressed, a serious and manly look is always the best. The eyes should never be fixed close on any one object, but move easily round the audience. In the motions made with the hands, consists the chief part of gesture in speaking. The Ancients condemned all motions performed by the left hand alone; but I am not sensible, that these are always offensive, though it is natural for the right hand to be more frequently employed. Warm emotions demand the motion of both hands corresponding together. But whether one gesticulates with one or with both hands, it is an important rule, that all his motions should be free and easy. Narrow and straightened movements are generally ungraceful; for which reason, motions made with the hands are directed to proceed from the shoulder, rather than from the elbow. Perpendicular movements too with the hands, that is, in the straight line up and down, which Shakespeare, in Hamlet, calls, "sawing the air with the hand," are seldom good. Oblique motions are, in general, the most graceful. Too sudden and nimble motions should be likewise avoided. Earnestness can be fully expressed without them. Shakespeare's directions on this head, are full of good sense; "use all gently," says he, "and in the very torrent and tempest of passion, acquire a temperance that may give it smoothness."

in

in forming it. But to attain, what as to the effect is very little inferior, a forcible and persuasive manner, is within the power of most persons; if they will only unlearn false and corrupt habits; if they will allow themselves to follow nature, and will speak in public, as they do in private, when they speak in earnest, and from the heart. If one has naturally any gross defects in his voice or gestures, he begins at the wrong end, if he attempts at reforming them only when he is to speak in public: he should begin with rectifying them in his private manner of speaking; and then carry to the public the right habit he has formed. For when a speaker is engaged in a public discourse, he should not be then employing his attention about his manner, or thinking of his tones and his gestures. If he be so employed, study and affectation will appear. He ought to be then quite in earnest; wholly occupied with his subject and his sentiments; leaving nature, and previously formed habits, to prompt and suggest his manner of delivery.

II.

Means of improving in Eloquence.

I have now treated fully of the different kinds of public speaking, of the composition, and of the delivery of a discourse. Before I finish this subject, it may be of use to suggest some things concerning the properest means of improvement in the art of public speaking, and the most necessary studies for that purpose.

To be an eloquent speaker, in the proper sense of the word, is far from being either a common or an easy attainment. Indeed to compose a florid harangue on some popular topic, and to deliver it so as to amuse an audience, is a matter not very difficult. But though some praise be due to this, yet the idea, which I have endeavoured to give of eloquence, is much higher. It is a great exertion of the human powers. It is the art of being persuasive and commanding; the art, not of pleasing the fancy merely, but of speaking both to the understanding and to the heart; of interesting the hearers in such a degree, as to seize and carry them along with us; and to leave them with a deep and strong impression of what they have heard. How many talents, natural and acquired, must concur for carrying this to perfection! A strong, lively, and warm imagination; quick sensibility of heart, joined with solid judgment, good sense, and presence of mind; all improved by great and long attention to style and composition; and supported also by the exterior, yet important qualifications, of a graceful manner, a presence not ungainly, and a full and tuneable voice. How little reason to wonder, that a perfect and accomplished orator should be one of the characters that is most rarely to be found!

Let us not despair, however. Between mediocrity and perfection there is a very wide interval. There are many intermediate spaces, which may be filled up with honour; and the more rare and difficult that complete perfection is, the greater is the honour of approaching to it, though we do not fully attain it. The number of orators who stand in the highest class is, perhaps, smaller than the number of poets who are foremost in poetic fame; but the study of oratory has this advantage above that of poetry, that, in poetry, one must be an eminently

eminently good performer, or he is not supportable;

> ———— Mediocribus esse poëtis
> Non homines, non Di, non concessêre columnæ*.

In Eloquence this does not hold. There, one may possess a moderate station with dignity. Eloquence admits of a great many different forms; plain and simple, as well as high and pathetic; and a genius that cannot reach the latter, may shine with much reputation and usefulness in the former.

Whether nature or art contribute most to form an orator, is a trifling enquiry. In all attainments whatever, nature must be the prime agent. She must bestow the original talents. She must sow the seeds; but culture is requisite for bringing those seeds to perfection. Nature must always have done somewhat; but a great deal will always be left to be done by art. This is certain, that study and discipline are more necessary for the improvement of natural genius in oratory, than they are in poetry. What I mean is, that though poetry be capable of receiving assistance from critical art, yet a poet, without any aid from art, by the force of genius alone, can rise higher than a public speaker can do, who has never given attention to the rules of style, composition, and delivery. Homer formed himself; Demosthenes and Cicero were formed by the help of much labour, and of many assistances derived from the labour of others.

After these preliminary observations, let us proceed to the main design of this lecture; to treat of the means to be used for improvement in eloquence.

In the first place, what stands highest in the order of means, is personal character and disposition. In order to be a truly eloquent or persuasive speaker, nothing is more necessary than to be a virtuous man. This was a favourite position among the ancient rhetoricians: "Non posse oratorem esse nisi virum "bonum." To find any such connection between virtue and one of the highest liberal arts, must give pleasure; and it can, I think, be clearly shewn, that this is not a mere topic of declamation, but that the connection here alledged, is undoubtedly found in truth and reason.

For, consider first, Whether any thing contributes more to persuasion, than the opinion which we entertain of the probity, disinterestedness, candour, and other good moral qualities of the person who endeavours to persuade? These give weight and force to every thing which he utters; nay, they add a beauty to it; they dispose us to listen with attention and pleasure; and create a secret partiality in favour of that side which he espouses. Whereas if we entertain a suspicion of craft and disingenuity, of a corrupt, or a base mind, in the speaker, his eloquence loses all its real effect. It may entertain and amuse; but it is viewed as artifice, as trick, as the play only of speech; and, viewed in this light, whom can it persuade? We even read a book with more pleasure, when we think favourably of its author; but when we have the living speaker before our eyes, addressing us personally on some subject of importance, the opinion we entertain of his character must have a much more powerful effect.

But, lest it should be said, that this relates only to the character of virtue, which one may

* For God and man, and lettered post denies,
That poets ever are of middling size.
FRANCIS.

may maintain, without being at bottom a truly worthy man, I muſt obſerve farther, that, beſides the weight which it adds to character, real virtue operates alſo in other ways, to the advantage of eloquence.

Firſt, nothing is ſo favourable as virtue to the proſecution of honourable ſtudies. It prompts a generous emulation to excel; it inures to induſtry; it leaves the mind vacant and free, maſter of itſelf, diſencumbered of thoſe bad paſſions, and diſengaged from thoſe mean purſuits, which have ever been found the greateſt enemies to true proficiency. Quinctilian has touched this conſideration very properly: "Quod ſi agrorum nimia "cura, et ſollicitior rei familiaris diligentia, "et venandi voluptas, et dati ſpectaculis dies, "multum ſtudiis auferunt, quid putamus "facturas cupiditatem, avaritiam, invidiam? "Nihil enim eſt tam occupatum, tam multi-"forme, tot ac tam variis affectibus conci-"ſum, atque laceratum, quam mala ac im-"proba mens. Quis inter hæc, literis, aut "ulli bonæ arti, locus? Non hercle magis "quam frugibus, in terra ſentibus ac rubis "occupata *."

* "If the management of an eſtate, if anxious "attention to domeſtic œconomy, a paſſion for "hunting, or whole days given up to public "places and amuſements, conſume ſo much time "that is due to ſtudy, how much greater waſte "muſt be occaſioned by licentious deſires, avarice, "or envy! Nothing is ſo much hurried and agi-"tated, ſo contradictory to itſelf, or ſo violently "torn and ſhattered by conflicting paſſions, as a "bad heart. Amidſt the diſtractions which it "produces, what room is left for the cultivation "of letters, or the purſuit of any honourable art? "No more, aſſuredly, than there is for the growth "of corn in a field that is over-run with thorns "and brambles."

But, beſides this conſideration, there is another of ſtill higher importance, though I am not ſure of its being attended to as much as it deſerves; namely, that from the fountain of real and genuine virtue, are drawn thoſe ſentiments which will ever be moſt powerful in affecting the hearts of others. Bad as the world is, nothing has ſo great and univerſal a command over the minds of men as virtue. No kind of language is ſo generally underſtood, and ſo powerfully felt, as the native language of worthy and virtuous feelings. He only, therefore, who poſſeſſes theſe full and ſtrong, can ſpeak properly, and in its own language, to the heart. On all great ſubjects and occaſions, there is a dignity, there is an energy in noble ſentiments, which is overcoming and irreſiſtible. They give an ardour and a flame to one's diſcourſe, which ſeldom fails to kindle a like flame in thoſe who hear; and which, more than any other cauſe, beſtows on eloquence that power, for which it is famed, of ſeizing and tranſporting an audience. Here art and imitation will not avail. An aſſumed character conveys nothing of this powerful warmth. It is only a native and unaffected glow of feeling, which can tranſmit the emotion to others. Hence the moſt renowned orators, ſuch as Cicero and Demoſthenes, were no leſs diſtinguiſhed for ſome of the high virtues, as public ſpirit and zeal for their country, than for eloquence. Beyond doubt, to theſe virtues their eloquence owed much of its effect; and thoſe orations of theirs, in which there breathes moſt of the virtuous and magnanimous ſpirit, are thoſe which have moſt attracted the admiration of ages.

Nothing, therefore, is more neceſſary for thoſe who would excel in any of the higher kinds of oratory, than to cultivate habits of the

the ſeveral virtues, and to refine and improve all their moral feelings. Whenever theſe become dead, or callous, they may be aſſured, that on every great occaſion, they will ſpeak with leſs power, and leſs ſucceſs. The ſentiments and diſpoſitions particularly requiſite for them to cultivate, are the following; the love of juſtice and order, and indignation at inſolence and oppreſſion; the love of honeſty and truth, and deteſtation of fraud, meanneſs, and corruption; magnanimity of ſpirit; the love of liberty, of their country and the public; zeal for all great and noble deſigns, and reverence for all worthy and heroic characters. A cold and ſceptical turn of mind is extremely adverſe to eloquence; and no leſs ſo, is that cavilling diſpoſition which takes pleaſure in depreciating what is great, and ridiculing what is generally admired. Such a diſpoſition beſpeaks one not very likely to excel in any thing; but leaſt of all in oratory. A true orator ſhould be a perſon of generous ſentiments, of warm feelings, and of a mind turned towards the admiration of all thoſe great and high objects which mankind are naturally formed to admire. Joined with the manly virtues, he ſhould, at the ſame time, poſſeſs ſtrong and tender ſenſibility to all the injuries, diſtreſſes, and ſorrows, of his fellow-creatures; a heart than can eaſily relent; that can readily enter into the circumſtances of others, and can make their caſe his own. A proper mixture of courage, and of modeſty, muſt alſo be ſtudied by every public ſpeaker. Modeſty is eſſential; it is always, and juſtly, ſuppoſed to be a concomitant of merit; and every appearance of it is winning and prepoſſeſſing. But modeſty ought not to run into exceſſive timidity. Every public ſpeaker ſhould be able to reſt ſomewhat on himſelf; and to aſſume that air, not of ſelf-complacency, but of firmneſs, which beſpeaks a conſciouſneſs of his being thoroughly perſuaded of the truth or juſtice, of what he delivers; a circumſtance of no ſmall conſequence for making impreſſion on thoſe who hear.

CONTENTS.

BOOK I. *Moral and Religious.*

CATECHETICAL LECTURES.

BOOK II. *Classical and Historical.*

BOOK III. *Orations, Characters, &c.*

75 Another

BOOK IV.

Narratives, Dialogues, &c. with other humorous, facetious, and entertaining Pieces; and with Specimens of Natural History.

36 Distempers

NATURAL HISTORY.

FISHES.

THE

THE
PROSE EPITOME;
OR,
ELEGANT EXTRACTS ABRIDGED, &c.

BOOK I. MORAL AND RELIGIOUS.

§ 1. *The Vision of Mirza, exhibiting a Picture of Human Life.*

ON the fifth day of the moon, which, according to the custom of my forefathers, I always keep holy, after having washed myself, and offered up my morning devotions, I ascended the high hills of Bagdat, in order to pass the rest of the day in meditation and prayer. As I was here airing myself on the tops of the mountains, I fell into a profound contemplation on the vanity of human life; and, passing from one thought to another, Surely, said I, man is but a shadow, and life a dream. Whilst I was thus musing, I cast my eyes towards the summit of a rock that was not far from me, where I discovered one in the habit of a shepherd, with a little musical instrument in his hand. As I looked upon him, he applied it to his lips, and began to play upon it. The sound of it was exceeding sweet, and wrought into a variety of tunes that were inexpressibly melodious, and altogether different from any thing I had ever heard: they put me in mind of those heavenly airs that are played to the departed souls of good men upon their first arrival in Paradise, to wear out the impressions of the last agonies, and qualify them for the pleasures of that happy place. My heart melted away in secret raptures.

I had been often told, that the rock before me was the haunt of a genius; and that several had been entertained with that music, who had passed by it, but never heard that the musician had before made himself visible. When he had raised my thoughts, by those transporting airs which he played, to taste the pleasures of his conversation, as I looked upon him like one astonished, he beckoned to me, and, by the waving of his hand, directed me to approach the place where he sat. I drew near with that reverence which is due to a superior nature; and as my heart was entirely subdued by the captivating strains I had heard, I fell down at his feet, and wept. The genius smiled upon me with a look of compassion and affability that familiarized him to my imagination, and at once dispelled all the fears and apprehensions with which I approached him. He lifted me from the ground, and taking me by the hand, Mirza, said he, I have heard thee in thy soliloquies; follow me.

He then led me to the highest pinnacle of the rock, and placing me on the top of it, Cast thy eyes eastward, said he, and tell me what thou seest. I see, said I, a huge valley, and a prodigious tide of water rolling through it. The valley that thou seest, said he, is the vale of misery; and the tide of water that thou seest, is part of the great tide of eternity. What is the reason, said I, that the tide I see rises out of a thick mist at one end, and again loses itself in a thick mist at the other? What thou seest, said he, is that portion of eternity which is called Time, measured out by the sun, and reaching from the beginning of the world to its consummation. Examine now, said he, this sea that is bounded with darkness at both ends, and tell me what thou discoverest in it. I see a bridge, said I, standing in the midst of the tide. The bridge thou seest, said he, is human life; consider it attentively. Upon a more leisurely survey of it, I found that it consisted of threescore and ten entire arches, with several broken arches, which, added to those that were entire, made up the number about an hundred. As I was counting the arches, the genius told me that this bridge consisted at first of a thousand arches; but that a great flood swept away the rest, and left the bridge in the ruinous condition I now beheld it: but tell me further, said he, what thou discoverest on it. I see multitudes of people passing over it, said I, and a black cloud hanging on each end of it. As I looked more attentively, I saw several of the passengers dropping through the bridge into the great tide that flowed underneath it; and upon further examination, perceived there were innumerable trap-doors that lay concealed in the bridge, which the passengers no sooner trod upon, but they fell through them into the tide, and immediately disappeared. These hidden pit-falls were set very thick at the entrance of the bridge, so that throngs of people no sooner broke through the cloud, but many of them fell into them. They grew thinner towards the middle, but multiplied and lay closer together towards the end of the arches that were entire.

There were indeed some persons, but their number was very small, that continued a kind of hobbling march on the broken arches, but fell through one after another, being quite tired and spent with so long a walk.

I passed some time in the contemplation of this wonderful structure, and the great variety of objects which it presented. My heart was filled with a deep melancholy, to see several dropping unexpectedly in the midst of mirth and jollity, and catching at every thing that stood by them, to save themselves. Some were looking up towards the heavens in a thoughtful posture, and, in the midst of a speculation, stumbled and fell out of sight. Multitudes were very busy in the pursuit of bubbles, that glittered in their eyes, and danced before them; but often, when they thought themselves within the reach of them, their footing failed, and down they sunk. In this confusion of objects, I observed some with scimitars in their hands, and others with urinals, who ran to and fro upon the bridge, thrusting several persons on trap-doors which did not seem to lie in their way, and which they might have escaped had they not been thus forced upon them.

The genius seeing me indulge myself in this melancholy prospect, told me I had dwelt long enough upon it: Take thine eyes off the bridge, said he, and tell me if thou seest any thing thou dost not comprehend. Upon looking up, What mean, said I, those great flights of birds that are perpetually hovering about the bridge, and settling upon it from time to time? I see vultures, harpies, ravens, cormorants, and, among many other feathered creatures, several little winged boys, that perch in great numbers upon the middle arches. These, said

ſaid the genius, are envy, avarice, ſuperſtition, deſpair, love, with the like cares and paſſions that infeſt human life.

I here fetched a deep ſigh: Alas, ſaid I, man was made in vain! how is he given away to miſery and mortality! tortured in life, and ſwallowed up in death! The genius being moved with compaſſion towards me, bid me quit ſo uncomfortable a proſpect. Look no more, ſaid he, on man in the firſt ſtage of his exiſtence, in his ſetting out for eternity; but caſt thine eye on that thick miſt into which the tide bears the ſeveral generations of mortals that fall into it. I directed my ſight as I was ordered, and (whether or no the good genius ſtrengthened it with any ſupernatural force, or diſſipated part of the miſt that was before too thick for the eye to penetrate) I ſaw the valley opening at the farther end, and ſpreading forth into an immenſe ocean, that had a huge rock of adamant running through the midſt of it, and dividing it into two equal parts. The clouds ſtill reſted on one half of it, inſomuch that I could diſcover nothing in it: but the other appeared to me a vaſt ocean, planted with innumerable iſlands, that were covered with fruits and flowers, and interwoven with a thouſand little ſhining ſeas that ran among them. I could ſee perſons dreſſed in glorious habits, with garlands upon their heads, paſſing among the trees, lying down by the ſides of fountains, or reſting on beds of flowers; and could hear a confuſed harmony of ſinging birds, falling waters, human voices, and muſical inſtruments. Gladneſs grew in me at the diſcovery of ſo delightful a ſcene. I wiſhed for the wings of an eagle, that I might fly away to thoſe happy ſeats; but the genius told me there was no paſſage to them, except through the gates of death that I ſaw opening every moment upon the bridge. The iſlands, ſaid he, that lie ſo freſh and green before thee, and with which the whole face of the ocean appears ſpotted as far as thou canſt ſee, are more in number than the ſands on the ſea-ſhore; there are myriads of iſlands behind thoſe which thou here diſcovereſt, reaching further than thine eye, or even thine imagination, can extend itſelf. Theſe are the manſions of good men after death, who, according to the degree and kinds of virtue in which they excelled, are diſtributed among theſe ſeveral iſlands, which abound with pleaſures of different kinds and degrees, ſuitable to the reliſhes and perfections of thoſe who are ſettled in them; every iſland is a paradiſe accommodated to its reſpective inhabitants. Are not theſe, O Mirza, habitations worth contending for? Does life appear miſerable, that gives thee opportunities of earning ſuch a reward? Is death to be feared, that will convey thee to ſo happy an exiſtence? Think not man was made in vain, who has ſuch an eternity reſerved for him.—I gazed with inexpreſſible pleaſure on theſe happy iſlands. At length, ſaid I, Shew me now, I beſeech thee, the ſecrets that lie hid under thoſe dark clouds, which cover the ocean on the other ſide of the rock of adamant. The genius making me no anſwer, I turned about to addreſs myſelf to him a ſecond time, but I found that he had left me: I then turned again to the viſion which I had been ſo long contemplating; but inſtead of the rolling tide, the arched bridge, and the happy iſlands, I ſaw nothing but the long hollow valley of Bagdat, with oxen, ſheep, and camels, grazing upon the ſides of it.

Spectator.

§ 2. *The Voyage of Life; an Allegory.*

'Life,' ſays Seneca, 'is a voyage, in the progreſs of which we are perpetually changing our scenes: 'we first leave childhood behind us, then youth, then the years of ripened manhood, then the better or more pleasing part of old age.'—The perusal of this passage having excited in me a train of reflections on the state of man, the incessant fluctuation of his wishes, the gradual change of his diposition to all external objects, and the thoughtlessness with which he floats along the stream of time, I sunk into a slumber amidst my meditations, and, on a sudden, found my ears filled with the tumult of labour, the shouts of alacrity, the shrieks of alarm, the whistle of winds, and the dash of waters.

My astonishment for a time repressed my curiosity; but soon recovering myself so far as to enquire whither we were going, and what was the cause of such clamour and confusion; I was told that they were launching out into the ocean of Life; that we had already passed the streights of infancy, in which multitudes had perished, some by the weakness and fragility of their vessels, and more by the folly, perverseness, or negligence of those who undertook to steer them; and that we were now on the main sea, abandoned to the winds and billows, without any other means of security than the care of the pilot, whom it was always in our power to chuse, among great numbers that offered their direction and assistance.

I then looked round with anxious eagerness ... pause of waters violently agitated, and covered with so thick a mist, that the most perspicacious eyes could see but a little way. It appeared to be full of rocks and whirlpools, for many sunk unexpectedly while they were courting the gale with full sails, and insulting those whom they had left behind. So numerous, indeed, were the dangers, and so thick the darkness, that no caution could confer security. Yet there were many, who, by false intelligence, betrayed their followers into whirlpools, or by violence pushed those whom they found in their way against the rocks.

The current was invariable and insurmountable; but though it was impossible to sail against it, or to return to the place that was once passed, yet it was not so violent as to allow no opportunities for dexterity or courage, since, though none could retreat back from danger, yet they might often avoid it by oblique direction.

It was, however, not very common to steer with much care or prudence; for, by some universal infatuation, every man appeared to think himself safe, though he saw his consorts every moment sinking round him; and no sooner had the waves closed over them, than their fate and their misconduct were forgotten; the voyage was pursued with the same jocund confidence; every man congratulated himself upon the soundness of his vessel, and believed

rushed upon destruction failed, when he was sinking, to call loudly upon his associates for that help which could not now be given him: and many spent their last moments in cautioning others against the folly by which they were intercepted in the midst of their course. Their benevolence was sometimes praised, but their admonitions were unregarded.

The vessels in which we had embarked, being confessedly unequal to the turbulence of the stream of life, were visibly impaired in the course of the voyage, so that every passenger was certain, that how long soever he might, by favourable accidents, or by incessant vigilance, be preserved, he must sink at last.

This necessity of perishing might have been expected to sadden the gay, and intimidate the daring, at least to keep the melancholy and timorous in perpetual torments, and hinder them from any enjoyment of the varieties and gratifications which nature offered them as the solace of their labours; yet in effect none seemed less to expect destruction than those to whom it was most dreadful; they all had the art of concealing their danger from themselves; and those who knew their inability to bear the sight of the terrors that embarrassed their way, took care never to look forward, but found some amusement of the present moment, and generally entertained themselves by playing with Hope, who was the constant associate of the voyage of Life.

Yet all that Hope ventured to promise, even to those whom she favoured most, was, not that they should escape, but that they should sink last; and with this promise every one was satisfied, though he laughed at the rest for seeming to believe it. Hope, indeed, apparently mocked the credulity of her companions; for, in proportion as their vessels grew leaky, she redoubled her assurances of safety; and none were more busy in making provisions for a long voyage, than they whom all but themselves saw likely to perish soon by irreparable decay.

In the midst of the current of Life, was the gulph of Intemperance, a dreadful whirlpool, interspersed with rocks, of which the pointed crags were concealed under water, and the tops covered with herbage, on which Ease spread couches of repose; and with shades, where Pleasure warbled the song of invitation. Within sight of these rocks, all who sailed on the ocean of Life must necessarily pass. Reason indeed was always at hand to steer the passengers through a narrow outlet, by which they might escape; but very few could, by her entreaties or remonstrances, be induced to put the rudder into her hand, without stipulating that she should approach so near unto the rocks of Pleasure, that they might solace themselves with a short enjoyment of that delicious region, after which they always determined to pursue their course without any other deviation.

Reason was too often prevailed upon so far by these promises as to venture her charge within the eddy of the gulph of Intemperance, where, indeed, the circumvolution was weak, but yet interrupted the course of the vessel, and drew it, by insensible rotations, towards the centre. She then repented her temerity, and with all her force endeavoured to retreat; but the draught of the gulph was generally too strong to be overcome; and the passenger, having danced in circles with a pleasing and giddy velocity, was at last overwhelmed and lost. Those few whom Reason was able to extricate, generally suffered so many shocks upon the points which shot out from the rocks of Pleasure, that they were unable to continue their course with the same strength and facility as as before, but floated along timorously and feebly, endangered by every breeze, and shattered by every ruffle of the water, till they sunk, by slow degrees, after long struggles, and innumerable expedients, always repining at their own folly, and warning others against the first approach of the gulph of intemperance.

There were artists who professed to repair the breaches and stop the leaks of the vessels which had been shattered on the rocks of Pleasure. Many appeared to have great confidence in their skill, and some, indeed, were preserved by it from sinking, who had received only a single blow; but I remarked, that few vessels lasted long which had been much repaired, nor was it found that the artists themselves continued afloat longer than those who had least of their assistance.

The only advantage which, in the voyage of Life, the cautious had above the negligent, was, that they sunk later, and more suddenly; for they passed forward till they had sometimes seen all those in whose company they had issued from the streights of infancy, perish in the way, and at last were overset by a cross breeze, without the toil of resistance, or the anguish of expectation. But such as had often fallen against the rocks of Pleasure, commonly subsided by sensible degrees, contended long with the encroaching waters, and harrassed themselves by labours that scarce Hope herself could flatter with success.

As I was looking upon the various fate of the multitude about me, I was suddenly alarmed with an admonition from some unknown power, 'Gaze not idly upon others when thou thyself art sinking. Whence is this thoughtless tranquillity, when thou and they are equally endangered?' I looked, and, seeing the gulph of Intemperance before me, started and awaked. *Rambler.*

§ 3. *Motives to Piety and Virtue, drawn from the Omniscience and Omnipresence of the Deity.*

In one of your late papers, you had occasion to consider the ubiquity of the Godhead, and at the same time to shew, that as he is present to every thing, he cannot but be attentive to every thing, and privy to all the modes and parts of its existence: or, in other words, that his omniscience and omnipresence are co-existent, and run together through the whole infinitude of space. This consideration might furnish us with many incentives to devotion, and motives to morality; but as this subject has been handled by several excellent writers, I shall consider it in a light in which I have not seen it placed by others.

First, How disconsolate is the condition of an intellectual being, who is thus present with his Maker, but at the same time receives no extraordinary benefit or advantage from this his presence!

Secondly, How deplorable is the condition of an intellectual being, who feels no other effects from this his presence, but such as proceed from divine wrath and indignation!

Thirdly, How happy is the condition of that intellectual being, who is sensible of his Maker's presence from the secret effects of his mercy and loving-kindness!

First, How disconsolate is the condition of an intellectual being, who is thus present with his Maker, but at the same time receives no extraordinary benefit or advantage from this his presence! Every particle of matter is actuated by this Almighty Being which passes through it. The heavens and the earth, the

the ſtars and planets, move and gravitate by virtue of this great principle within them. All the dead parts of nature are invigorated by the preſence of their Creator, and made capable of exerting their reſpective qualities. The ſeveral inſtincts, in the brute creation, do likewiſe operate and work towards the ſeveral ends which are agreeable to them, by this divine energy. Man only, who does not co-operate with his holy ſpirit, and is unattentive to his preſence, receives none of theſe advantages from it, which are perfective of his nature, and neceſſary to his well-being. The divinity is with him, and in him, and every where about him, but of no advantage to him. It is the ſame thing to a man without religion, as if there were no God in the world. It is indeed impoſſible for an infinite Being to remove himſelf from any of his creatures; but though he cannot withdraw his eſſence from us, which would argue an imperfection in him, he can withdraw from us all the joys and conſolations of it. His preſence may perhaps be neceſſary to ſupport us in our exiſtence; but he may leave this our exiſtence to itſelf, with regard to its happineſs or miſery. For, in this ſenſe, he may caſt us away from his preſence, and take his holy ſpirit from us. This ſingle conſideration one would think ſufficient to make us open our hearts to all thoſe infuſions of joy and gladneſs which are ſo near at hand, and ready to be poured in upon us; eſpecially when we conſider, Secondly, the deplorable condition of an intellectual being, who feels no other effects from his Maker's preſence, but ſuch as proceed from divine wrath and indignation!

We may aſſure ourſelves, that the great Author of nature will not always be as one who is indifferent to any of his creatures. Thoſe who will not feel him in his love, will be ſure at length to feel him in his diſpleaſure. And how dreadful is the condition of that creature, who is only ſenſible of the being of his Creator by what he ſuffers from him! He is as eſſentially preſent in hell as in heaven; but the inhabitants of thoſe accurſed places behold him only in his wrath, and ſhrink within the flames to conceal themſelves from him. It is not in the power of imagination to conceive the fearful effects of Omnipotence incenſed.

But I ſhall only conſider the wretchedneſs of an intellectual being, who, in this life, lies under the diſpleaſure of him, that at all times, and in all places, is intimately united with him. He is able to diſquiet the ſoul, and vex it in all its faculties. He can hinder any of the greateſt comforts of life from refreſhing us, and give an edge to every one of its ſlighteſt calamities. Who then can bear the thought of being an out-caſt from his preſence, that is, from the comforts of it, or of feeling it only in its terrors? How pathetic is that expoſtulation of Job, when for the real trial of his patience, he was made to look upon himſelf in this deplorable condition! 'Why haſt thou ſet me as a mark 'againſt thee, ſo that I am become a burden 'to myſelf?' But, thirdly, how happy is the condition of that intellectual being, who is ſenſible of his Maker's preſence from the ſecret effects of his mercy and loving-kindneſs:

The bleſſed in heaven behold him face to face, that is, are as ſenſible of his preſence as we are of the preſence of any perſon whom we look upon with our eyes. There is doubtleſs a faculty in ſpirits, by which they apprehend one another, as our ſenſes do material objects; and there is no queſtion but our souls, when they are disembodied, or placed in glorified bodies, will by this faculty, in whatever part of space they reside, be always sensible of the divine presence. We, who have this veil of flesh standing between us and the world of spirits, must be content to know the spirit of God is present with us by the effects which he produceth in us. Our outward senses are too gross to apprehend him; we may however taste and see how gracious he is, by his influence upon our minds, by those virtuous thoughts which he awakens in us, by those secret comforts and refreshments which he conveys into our souls, and by those ravishing joys and inward satisfactions which are perpetually springing up, and diffusing themselves among all the thoughts of good men. He is lodged in our very essence, and is as a soul within the soul, to irradiate its understanding, rectify its will, purify its passions, and enliven all the powers of man. How happy therefore is an intellectual being, who by prayer and meditation, by virtue and good works, opens this communication between God and his own soul! Though the whole creation frowns upon him, and all nature looks black about him, he has his light and support within him, that are able to cheer his mind, and bear him up in the midst of all those horrors which encompass him. He knows that his helper is at hand, and is always nearer to him than any thing else can be, which is capable of annoying or terrifying him. In the midst of calumny or contempt, he attends to that Being who whispers better things within his soul, and whom he looks upon as his defender, his glory, and the lifter-up of his head. In his deepest solitude and retirement, he knows that he is in company with the greatest of beings; and perceives within himself such real sensations of his presence, as are more delightful than any thing that can be met with in the conversation of his creatures. Even in the hour of death, he considers the pains of his dissolution to be nothing else but the breaking down of that partition, which stands betwixt his soul, and the sight of that being who is always present with him, and is about to manifest itself to him in fulness of joy.

If we would be thus happy, and thus sensible of our Maker's presence, from the secret effects of his mercy and goodness, we must keep such a watch over all our thoughts, that in the language of the scripture, his soul may have pleasure in us. We must take care not to grieve his holy spirit, and endeavour to make the meditations of our hearts always acceptable in his sight, that he may delight thus to reside and dwell in us. The light of nature could direct Seneca to this doctrine, in a very remarkable passage among his epistles: *Sacer inest in nobis spiritus, bonorum malorumque custos et observator; et quemadmodum nos illum tractamus, ita et ille nos.* 'There is a 'holy spirit residing in us, who watches and 'observes both good and evil men, and will 'treat us after the same manner that we 'treat him.' But I shall conclude this discourse with those more emphatical words in divine revelation; 'If a man love me, he will 'keep my words; and my Father will love 'him, and we will come unto him, and make 'our abode with him.' *Spectator.*

§ 4. *On the Immortality of the Soul.*

I was yesterday walking alone in one of my friend's woods, and lost myself in it very agreeably, as I was running over in my mind the several arguments that establish this great point, which is the basis of morality, and the source of all the pleasing hopes and

secret

secret joys that can arise in the heart of a reasonable creature. I considered those several proofs drawn,

First, from the nature of the soul itself, and particularly its immateriality; which, though not absolutely necessary to the eternity of its duration, has, I think, been evinced to almost a demonstration.

Secondly, from its passions and sentiments, as particularly from its love of existence, its horror of annihilation, and its hopes of immortality, with that secret satisfaction which it finds in the practice of virtue, and that uneasiness which follows in it upon the commission of vice.

Thirdly, from the nature of the Supreme Being, whose justice, goodness, wisdom, and veracity, are all concerned in this point.

But among these and other excellent arguments for the immortality of the soul, there is one drawn from the perpetual progress of the soul to its perfection, without a possibility of ever arriving at it; which is a hint that I do not remember to have seen opened and improved by others who have written on this subject, though it seems to me to carry a very great weight with it. How can it enter into the thoughts of man, that the soul, which is capable of such immense perfections, and of receiving new improvements to all eternity, shall fall away into nothing almost as soon as it is created? Are such abilities made for no purpose? A brute arrives at a point of perfection that he can never pass: in a few years he has all the endowments he is capable of; and were he to live ten thousand more, would be the same thing he is at present. Were a human soul thus at a stand in her accomplishments, were her faculties to be full blown, and incapable of farther enlargements, I could imagine it might fall away insensibly, and drop at once into a state of annihilation. But can we believe a thinking being, that is in a perpetual progress of improvements, and travelling on from perfection to perfection, after having just looked abroad into the works of its Creator, and made a few discoveries of his infinite goodness, wisdom, and power, must perish at her first setting out, and in the very beginning of her enquiries?

A man, considered in his present state, seems only sent into the world to propagate his kind. He provides himself with a successor, and immediately quits his post to make room for him.

——————————— *Hæres*
Hæredem alterius, velut unda supervenit undam.
HOR. Ep. ii. l. 2. v. 175.

—— Heir crowds heir, as in a rolling flood
Wave urges wave. CREECH.

He does not seem born to enjoy life, but to deliver it down to others. This is not surprising to consider in animals, which are formed for our use, and can finish their business in a short life. The silk-worm, after having spun her task, lays her eggs and dies. But a man can never have taken in his full measure of knowledge, has not time to subdue his passions, establish his soul in virtue, and come up to the perfection of his nature, before he is hurried off the stage. Would an infinitely wise being make such glorious creatures for so mean a purpose? Can he delight in the production of such abortive intelligences, such short-lived reasonable beings? Would he give us talents that are not to be exerted? capacities that are never to be gratified? How can we find that wisdom which shines through all his works, in the formation of man, without looking on this world as only a nursery for the next, and believing that the several generations of rational creatures, which rise up and disappear in such quick successions, are only to receive their first rudiments of existence here; and afterwards to be transplanted into a more friendly climate, where they may spread and flourish to all eternity?

There is not, in my opinion, a more pleasing and triumphant consideration in religion, than this of the perpetual progress which the soul makes towards the perfection of its nature, without ever arriving at a period in it. To look upon the soul as going on from strength to strength, to consider that she is to shine for ever with new accessions of glory, and brighten to all eternity; that she will be still adding virtue to virtue, and knowledge to knowledge; carries in it something wonderfully agreeable to that ambition which is natural to the mind of man. Nay, it must be a prospect pleasing to God himself, to see his creation for ever beautifying in his eyes, and drawing nearer to him, by greater degrees of resemblance.

Methinks this single consideration, of the progress of a finite spirit to perfection, will be sufficient to extinguish all envy in inferior natures, and all contempt in superior. That cherubim, which now appears as a God to a human soul, knows very well that the period will come about in eternity, when the human soul shall be as perfect as he himself now is: nay, when she shall look down upon that degree of perfection as much as she now falls short of it. It is true, the higher nature still advances, and by that means preserves his distance and superiority in the scale of being; but he knows that, how high soever the station is of which he stands possessed at present, the inferior nature will at length mount up to it, and shine forth in the same degree of glory.

With what astonishment and veneration may we look into our own souls, where there are such hidden stores of virtue and knowledge, such inexhausted sources of perfection! We know not yet what we shall be, nor will it ever enter into the heart of man to conceive the glory that will be always in reserve for him. The soul, considered with its Creator, is like one of those mathematical lines that may draw nearer to another for all eternity without a possibility of touching it: and can there be a thought so transporting as to consider ourselves in these perpetual approaches to him, who is not only the standard of perfection, but of happiness! *Spectator.*

§ 5. *The Duty of Children to their Parents.*

I am the happy father of a very towardly son, in whom I do not only see my life, but also my manner of life renewed. It would be extremely beneficial to society, if you would frequently resume subjects which serve to bind these sort of relations faster, and endear the ties of blood with those of good-will, protection, observance, indulgence, and veneration. I would, methinks, have this done after an uncommon method; and do not think any one, who is not capable of writing a good play, fit to undertake a work wherein there will necessarily occur so many secret instincts and biasses of human nature, which would pass unobserved by common eyes. I thank Heaven I have no outrageous offence against my own excellent parents to answer for; but when I am now and then alone, and look back upon my past life, from my earliest infancy to this time, there are many faults which I committed that did not appear to me, even

even until I myself became a father. I had not until then a notion of the yearnings of heart, which a man has when he sees his child do a laudable thing, or the sudden damp which seizes him when he fears he will act something unworthy. It is not to be imagined what a remorse touched me for a long train of childish negligences of my mother, when I saw my wife the other day look out of the window, and turn as pale as ashes upon seeing my younger boy sliding upon the ice. These slight intimations will give you to understand, that there are numberless little crimes, which children take no notice of while they are doing, which, upon reflection, when they shall themselves become fathers, they will look upon with the utmost sorrow and contrition, that they did not regard, before those whom they offended were to be no more seen. How many thousand things do I remember, which would have highly pleased my father, and I omitted for no other reason but that I thought what he proposed the effect of humour and old age, which I am now convinced had reason and good sense in it! I cannot now go into the parlour to him, and make his heart glad with an account of a matter which was of no consequence, but that I told it and acted in it. The good man and woman are long since in their graves, who used to sit and plot the welfare of us their children, while, perhaps, we were sometimes laughing at the old folks at another end of the house. The truth of it is, were we merely to follow nature in these great duties of life, though we have a strong instinct towards the performing of them, we should be on both sides very deficient. Age is so unwelcome to the generality of mankind, and growth towards manhood so desirable to all, that resignation to decay is too difficult a task in the father; and deference, amidst the impulse of gay desires, appears unreasonable to the son. There are so few who can grow old with a good grace, and yet fewer who can come slow enough into the world, that a father, were he to be actuated by his desires, and a son, were he to consult himself only, could neither of them behave himself as he ought to the other. But when reason interposes against instinct, where it would carry either out of the interests of the other, there arises that happiest intercourse of good offices between those dearest relations of human life. The father, according to the opportunities which are offered to him, is throwing down blessings on the son, and the son endeavouring to appear the worthy offspring of such a father. It is after this manner that Camillus and his first-born dwell together. Camillus enjoys a pleasing and indolent old age, in which passion is subdued and reason exalted. He waits the day of his dissolution with a resignation mixed with delight, and the son fears the accession of his father's fortune with diffidence, lest he should not enjoy or become it as well as his predecessor. Add to this, that the father knows he leaves a friend to the children of his friends, an easy landlord to his tenants, and an agreeable companion to his acquaintance. He believes his son's behaviour will make him frequently remembered, but never wanted. This commerce is so well cemented, that without the pomp of saying, Son, be a friend to such a one when I am gone; Camillus knows, being in his favour is direction enough to the grateful youth who is to succeed him, without the admonition of his mentioning it. These gentlemen are honoured in all their neighbourhood, and the same effect which the court has on the manners of a kingdom, their characters have on all who live within the influence of them.

My ſon and I are not of fortune to communicate our good actions or intentions to ſo many as theſe gentlemen do; but I will be bold to ſay, my ſon has, by the applauſe and approbation which his behaviour towards me has gained him, occaſioned that many an old man, beſides myſelf, has rejoiced. Other men's children follow the example of mine; and I have the inexpreſſible happineſs of overhearing our neighbours, as we ride by, point to their children, and ſay, with a voice of joy, "There they go." *Spectator.*

§ 6. *The Importance of Time, and the proper Methods of ſpending it.*

We all of us complain of the ſhortneſs of time, ſaith Seneca, and yet have much more than we know what to do with. Our lives, ſays he, are ſpent either in doing nothing at all, or doing nothing to the purpoſe, or in doing nothing that we ought to do. We are always complaining our days are few, and acting as though there would be no end of them. That noble philoſopher has deſcribed our inconſiſtency with ourſelves in this particular by all thoſe various turns of expreſſion and thought which are peculiar in his writings.

I often conſider mankind as wholly inconſiſtent with itſelf, in a point that bears ſome affinity to the former. Though we ſeem grieved at the ſhortneſs of life, in general, we are wiſhing every period of it at an end. The minor longs to be at age, then to be a man of buſineſs, then to make up an eſtate, then to arrive at honours, then to retire. Thus, although the whole of life is allowed by every one to be ſhort, the ſeveral diviſions of it appear long and tedious. We are for lengthening our ſpan in general, but would fain contract the parts of which it is compoſed. The uſurer would be very well ſatisfied to have all the time annihilated that lies between the preſent moment and the next quarter-day. The politician would be contented to loſe three years in his life, could he place things in the poſture which he fancies they will ſtand in after ſuch a revolution of time. The lover would be glad to ſtrike out of his exiſtence all the moments that are to paſs away before the happy meeting. Thus, as faſt as our time runs, we ſhould be very glad, in moſt parts of our lives, that it ran much faſter than it does. Several hours of the day hang upon our hands; nay, we wiſh away whole years, and travel through time, as through a country filled with many wild and empty waſtes which we would fain hurry over, that we may arrive at thoſe ſeveral little ſettlements or imaginary points of reſt which are diſperſed up and down in it.

If we divide the life of moſt men into twenty parts, we ſhall find that at leaſt nineteen of them are mere gaps and chaſms, which are neither filled with pleaſure nor buſineſs. I do not however include in this calculation the life of thoſe men who are in a perpetual hurry of affairs, but of thoſe only who are not always engaged in ſcenes of action; and I hope I ſhall not do an unacceptable piece of ſervice to theſe perſons, if I point out to them certain methods for the filling up their empty ſpaces of life. The methods I ſhall propoſe to them are as follow:

The firſt is the exerciſe of virtue, in the moſt general acceptation of the word. That particular ſcheme which comprehends the ſocial virtues, may give employment to the moſt induſtrious temper, and find a man buſineſs more than the moſt active ſtation of life.

To advise the ignorant, relieve the needy, comfort the afflicted, are duties that fall in our way almost every day of our lives. A man has frequent opportunities of mitigating the fierceness of a party; of doing justice to the character of a deserving man; of softening the envious, quieting the angry, and rectifying the prejudiced; which are all of them employments suitable to a reasonable nature, and bring great satisfaction to the person who can busy himself in them with discretion.

There is another kind of virtue that may find employment for those retired hours in which we are altogether left to ourselves, and destitute of company and conversation; I mean that intercourse and communication which every reasonable creature ought to maintain with the great Author of his being. The man who lives under an habitual sense of the divine presence, keeps up a perpetual chearfulness of temper, and enjoys every moment the satisfaction of thinking himself in company with his dearest and best of friends. The time never lies heavy upon him: it is impossible for him to be alone. His thoughts and passions are the most busied at such hours when those of other men are the most unactive. He no sooner steps out of the world but his heart burns with devotion, swells with hope, and triumphs in the consciousness of that presence which every-where surrounds him; or, on the contrary, pours out its fears, its sorrows, its apprehensions, to the great Supporter of its existence.

I have here only considered the necessity of a man's being virtuous, that he may have something to do; but if we consider further, that the exercise of virtue is not only an amusement for the time it lasts, but that its influence extends to those parts of our existence which lie beyond the grave, and that our whole eternity is to take its colour from those hours which we here employ in virtue or in vice, the argument redoubles upon us, for putting in practice this method of passing away our time.

When a man has but a little stock to improve, and has opportunities of turning it all to good account, what shall we think of him if he suffers nineteen parts of it to lie dead, and perhaps employs even the twentieth to his ruin or disadvantage?—But because the mind cannot be always in its fervours, nor strained up to a pitch of virtue, it is necessary to find out proper employments for it, in its relaxations.

The next method therefore that I would propose to fill up our time, should be useful and innocent diversions. I must confess I think it below reasonable creatures to be altogether conversant in such diversions as are merely innocent, and have nothing else to recommend them, but that there is no hurt in them. Whether any kind of gaming has even thus much to say for itself, I shall not determine; but I think it is very wonderful to see persons of the best sense passing away a dozen hours together in shuffling and dividing a pack of cards, with no other conversation but what is made up of a few game phrases, and no other ideas but those of black or red spots ranged together in different figures. Would not a man laugh to hear any one of this species complaining that life is short.

The stage might be made a perpetual source of the most noble and useful entertainments, were it under proper regulations.

But the mind never unbends itself so agreeably as in the conversation of a well-chosen friend. There is indeed no blessing of life that is any way comparable to the enjoyment

of

of a discreet and virtuous friend. It eases and unloads the mind, clears and improves the understanding, engenders thought and knowledge, animates virtue and good resolution, soothes and allays the passions, and finds employment for most of the vacant hours of life.

Next to such an intimacy with a particular person, one would endeavour after a more general conversation with such as are capable of edifying and entertaining those with whom they converse, which are qualities that seldom go asunder.

There are many other useful amusements of life, which one would endeavour to multiply, that one might, on all occasions, have recourse to something rather than suffer the mind to lie idle, or run adrift with any passion that chances to rise in it.

A man that has a taste in music, painting, or architecture, is like one that has another sense, when compared with such as have no relish of those arts. The florist, the planter, the gardener, the husbandman, when they are only as accomplishments to the man of fortune, are great reliefs to a country life, and many ways useful to those who are possessed of them. *Spectator.*

§ 7. *Mis-spent Time, how punished.*

I was yesterday comparing the industry of man with that of other creatures; in which I could not but observe, that notwithstanding we are obliged by duty to keep ourselves in constant employ, after the same manner as inferior animals are prompted to it by instinct, we fall very short of them in this particular. We are here the more inexcusable, because there is a greater variety of business to which we may apply ourselves. Reason opens to us a large field of affairs, which other creatures are not capable of. Beasts of prey, and I believe of all other kinds, in their natural state of being, divide their time between action and rest. They are always at work or asleep. In short, their waking hours are wholly taken up in seeking after their food, or in consuming it. The human species only, to the great reproach of our natures, are filled with complaints, that "The day hangs heavy on them," that "They do not know what to do with themselves," that "They are at a loss how to pass away their time," with many of the like shameful murmurs, which we often find in the mouths of those who are stiled reasonable beings. How monstrous are such expressions among creatures who have the labours of the mind, as well as those of the body, to furnish them with proper employments; who, besides the business of their proper callings and professions, can apply themselves to the duties of religion, to meditation, to the reading of useful books, to discourse; in a word, who may exercise themselves in the unbounded pursuits of knowledge and virtue, and every hour of their lives make themselves wiser or better than they were before!

After having been taken up for some time in this course of thought, I diverted myself with a book, according to my usual custom, in order to unbend my mind before I went to sleep. The book I made use of on this occasion was Lucian, where I amused my thoughts for about an hour among the dialogues of the dead, which in all probability produced the following dream.

I was conveyed, methought, into the entrance of the infernal regions, where I saw Rhadamanthus, one of the judges of the dead, seated on his tribunal. On his left-hand stood the keeper of Erebus, on his right the

keeper

keeper of Elysium. I was told he sat upon women that day, there being several of the sex lately arrived, who had not yet their mansions assigned them. I was surprised to hear him ask every one of them the same question, namely, "What they had been doing?" Upon this question being proposed to the whole assembly, they stared one upon another, as not knowing what to answer. He then interrogated each of them separately. Madam, says he to the first of them, you have been upon the earth about fifty years; what have you been doing there all this while? Doing! says she, really I do not know what I have been doing: I desire I may have time given me to recollect. After about half an hour's pause, she told him that she had been playing at crimp; upon which Rhadamanthus beckoned to the keeper on his left hand, to take her into custody. And you, madam, says the judge, that look with such a soft and languishing air; I think you set out for this place in your nine-and-twentieth year, what have you been doing all this while? I had a great deal of business on my hands, says she, being taken up the first twelve years of my life in dressing a jointed baby, and all the remaining part of it in reading plays and romances. Very well, says he, you have employed your time to good purpose. Away with her. The next was a plain country-woman: Well, mistress, says Rhadamanthus, and what have you been doing? An't please your worship, says she, I did not live quite forty years; and in that time brought my husband seven daughters, made him nine thousand cheeses, and left my eldest girl with him to look after his house in my absence, and who, I may venture to say, is as pretty a housewife as any in the country. Rhadamanthus smiled at the simplicity of the good woman, and ordered the keeper of Elysium to take her into his care. And you, fair lady, says he, what have you been doing these five-and-thirty years? I have been doing no hurt, I assure you, sir, said she. That is well, said he, but what good have you been doing? The lady was in great confusion at this question, and not knowing what to answer, the two keepers leaped out to seize her at the same time; the one took her by the hand to convey her to Elysium, the other caught hold of her to carry her away to Erebus. But Rhadamanthus observing an ingenuous modesty in her countenance and behaviour, bid them both let her loose, and set her aside for a re-examination when he was more at leisure. An old woman, of a proud and sour look, presented herself next at the bar, and being asked what she had been doing? Truly, said she, I lived threescore-and-ten years in a very wicked world, and was so angry at the behaviour of a parcel of young flirts, that I passed most of my last years in condemning the follies of the times; I was every day blaming the silly conduct of people about me, in order to deter those I conversed with from falling into the like errors and miscarriages. Very well, says Rhadamanthus; but did you keep the same watchful eye over your own actions? Why truly, says she, I was so taken up with publishing the faults of others, that I had no time to consider my own. Madam, says Rhadamanthus, be pleased to file of to the left, and make room for the venerable matron that stands behind you. Old gentlewoman, says he, I think you are fourscore: you have heard the question, what have you been doing so long in the world? Ah, Sir! says she, I have been doing what I should not have done, but I had made a firm resolution to have changed my life, if I had not been snatched

ſnatched off by an untimely end. Madam, ſays he, you will pleaſe to follow your leader: and ſpying another of the ſame age, interrogated her in the ſame form. To which the matron replied, I have been the wife of a huſband who was as dear to me in his old age as in his youth. I have been a mother, and very happy in my children, whom I endeavoured to bring up in every thing that is good. My eldeſt ſon is bleſt by the poor, and beloved by every one that knows him. I lived within my own family, and left it much more wealthy than I found it. Rhadamanthus, who knew the value of the old lady, ſmiled upon her in ſuch a manner, that the keeper of Elyſium, who knew his office, reached out his hand to her. He no ſooner touched her, but her wrinkles vaniſhed, her eyes ſparkled, her cheeks glowed with bluſhes, and ſhe appeared in full bloom and beauty. A young woman obſerving that this officer, who conducted the happy to Elyſium, was ſo great a beautifier, longed to be in his hands; ſo that preſſing through the crowd, ſhe was the next that appeared at the bar. And being aſked what ſhe had been doing the five-and-twenty years that ſhe had paſſed in the world? I have endeavoured, ſaid ſhe, ever ſince I came to years of diſcretion, to make myſelf lovely and gain admirers. In order to it, I paſſed my time in bottling up May-dew, inventing white waſhes, mixing colours, cutting out patches, conſulting my glaſs, ſuiting my complexion, tearing off my tucker, ſinking my ſtays— Rhadamanthus, without hearing her out, gave the ſign to take her off. Upon the approach of the keeper of Erebus, her colour faded, her face was puckered up with wrirkles, and her whole perſon loſt in deformity.

I was then ſurpriſed with a diſtant ſound of a whole troop of females, that came forward laughing, ſinging, and dancing. I was very deſirous to know the reception they would meet with, and withal was very apprehenſive, that Rhadamanthus would ſpoil their mirth: But at their nearer approach the noiſe grew ſo very great that it awakened me.

I lay ſome time, reflecting in myſelf on the oddneſs of this dream, and could not forbear aſking my own heart, what I was doing? I anſwered myſelf that I was writing *Guardians*. If my readers make as good a uſe of this work as I deſign they ſhould, I hope it will never be imputed to me as a work that is vain and unprofitable.

I ſhall conclude this paper with recommending to them the ſame ſhort ſelf-examination. If every one of them frequently lays his hand upon his heart, and conſiders what he is doing, it will check him in all the idle, or, what is worſe, the vicious moments of life, lift up his mind when it is running on in a ſeries of indifferent actions, and encourage him when he is engaged in thoſe which are virtuous and laudable. In a word, it will very much alleviate that guilt which the beſt of men have reaſon to acknowledge in their daily confeſſions, of 'leaving undone thoſe things which they ought to have done, and of doing thoſe things which they ought not to have done.'

Guardian.

§ 8. *A Knowledge of the Uſe and Value of Time very important to Youth.*

There is nothing which I more wiſh that you ſhould know, and which fewer people do know, than the true uſe and value of time. It is in every body's mouth; but in few people's practice. Every fool who flatterns away his whole time in nothings, utters, however, ſome trite common-place ſentence, of which there are millions, to prove, at once, the value and the

the fleetneſs of time. The ſun-dials, likewiſe, all over Europe, have ſome ingenious inſcription to that effect; ſo that nobody ſquanders away their time, without hearing and ſeeing, daily, how neceſſary it is to employ it well, and how irrecoverable it is if loſt. But all theſe admonitions are uſeleſs, where there is not a fund of good ſenſe and reaſon to ſuggeſt them, rather than receive them. By the manner in which you now tell me that you employ your time, I flatter myſelf, that you have that fund: that is the fund which will make you rich indeed. I do not, therefore, mean to give you a critical eſſay upon the uſe and abuſe of time; I will only give you ſome hints, with regard to the uſe of one particular period of that long time which, I hope, you have before you; I mean the next two years. Remember then, that whatever knowledge you do not ſolidly lay the foundation of before you are eighteen, you will never be maſter of while you breathe. Knowledge is a comfortable and neceſſary retreat and ſhelter for us in an advanced age; and if we do not plant it while young, it will give us no ſhade when we grow old. I neither require nor expect from you great application to books, after you are once thrown out into the great world. I know it is impoſſible; and it may even, in ſome caſes, be improper: this, therefore, is your time, and your only time, for unwearied and uninterrupted application. If you ſhould ſometimes think it a little laborious, conſider, that labour is the unavoidable fatigue of a neceſſary journey. The more hours a day you travel, the ſooner you will be at your journey's end. The ſooner you are qualified for your liberty, the ſooner you ſhall have it; and your manumiſſion will entirely depend upon the manner in which you employ the intermediate time. I think I offer you a very good bargain, when I promiſe you, upon my word, that, if you will do every thing that I would have you do, till you are eighteen, I will do every thing that you would have me do, ever afterwards.

Lord Cheſterfield.

§ 9. *On Truth and Sincerity.*

Truth and reality have all the advantages of appearance, and many more. If the ſhew of any thing be good for any thing, I am ſure ſincerity is better: for why does any man diſſemble, or ſeem to be that which he is not, but becauſe he thinks it good to have ſuch a quality as he pretends to? for to counterfeit and diſſemble, is to put on the appearance of ſome real excellency. Now the beſt way in the world for a man to ſeem to be any thing, is really to be what he would ſeem to be. Beſides, that it is many times as troubleſome to make good the pretence of a good quality, as to have it; and if a man have it not, it is ten to one but he is diſcovered to want it, and then all his pains and labour to ſeem to have it is loſt. There is ſomething unnatural in painting, which a ſkilful eye will eaſily diſcern from native beauty and complexion.

It is hard to perſonate and act a part long; for where truth is not at the bottom, nature will always be endeavouring to return, and will peep out and betray herſelf one time or other. Therefore, if any man think it convenient to ſeem good, let him be ſo indeed, and then his goodneſs will appear to every body's ſatisfaction; ſo that, upon all accounts, ſincerity is true wiſdom. Particularly as to the affairs of this world, integrity hath many advantages over all the fine and artificial ways of diſſimulation and deceit; it is much the plainer and eaſier, much the ſafer and more ſecure way of dealing in the world; it it has leſs of trouble and difficulty, of entanglement and perplexity, of danger and hazard in it; it is the ſhorteſt and neareſt way to our end, carrying us thither in a ſtrait line, and will hold out and laſt longeſt. The arts of deceit and cunning do continually grow weaker and leſs effectual and ſerviceable to them that uſe them; whereas integrity gains ſtrength by uſe; and the more and longer any man practiſeth it, the greater ſervice it does him, by confirming his reputation, and encouraging thoſe with whom he hath to do to repoſe the greateſt truſt and confidence in him, which is an unſpeakable advantage in the buſineſs and affairs of life.

Truth is alwaye conſiſtent with itſelf, and needs nothing to help it out; it is always near at hand, and ſits upon our lips, and is ready to drop out before we are awafe; whereas a lie is troubleſome, and ſets a man's invention upon the rack, and one trick needs a great many more to make it good. It is like building upon a falſe foundation, which continually ſtands in need of props to ſhore it up, and proves at laſt more chargeable than to have raiſed a ſubſtantial building at firſt upon a true and ſolid foundation; for ſincerity is firm and ſubſtantial, and there is nothing hollow or unſound in it, and becauſe it is plain and open, fears no diſcovery; of which the crafty man is always in danger, and when he thinks he walks in the dark, all his pretences are ſo tranſparent, that he that runs may read them; he is the laſt man that finds himſelf to be found out, and whilſt he takes it for granted that he makes fools of others, he renders himſelf ridiculous.

Add to all this, that ſincerity is the moſt compendious wiſdom, and an excellent inſtrument for the ſpeedy diſpatch of buſineſs; it creates confidence in thoſe we have to deal with, ſaves the labour of many inquiries, and brings things to an iſſue in few words; it is like travelling in a plain beaten road, which commonly brings a man ſooner to his journey's end than bye-ways, in which men often loſe themſelves. In a word, whatſoever convenience may be thought to be in falſhood and diſſimulation, it is ſoon over; but the inconvenience of it is perpetual, becauſe it brings a man under an everlaſting jealouſy and ſuſpicion, ſo that he is not believed when he ſpeaks truth, nor truſted perhaps when he means honeſtly. When a man has once forfeited the reputation of his integrity, he is ſet faſt, and nothing will then ſerve his turn, neither truth nor falſhood.

And I have often thought that God hath, in his great wiſdom, hid from men of falſe and diſhoneſt minds the wonderful advantages of truth and integrity to the proſperity even of our worldly affairs; theſe men are ſo blinded by their covetouſneſs and ambition, that they cannot look beyond a preſent advantage, nor forbear to ſeize upon it, though by ways never ſo indirect; they cannot ſee ſo far as to the remote conſequences of a ſteady integrity, and the vaſt benefit and advantages which it will bring a man at laſt. Were but this ſort of men wiſe and clear-ſighted enough to diſcern this, they would be honeſt out of very knavery, not out of any love to honeſty and virtue, but with a crafty deſign to promote and advance more effectually their own intereſts; and therefore the juſtice of the divine providence hath hid this trueſt point of wiſdom from their eyes, that bad men might not be upon equal terms with the juſt and upright, and ſerve their own wicked deſigns by honeſt and lawful means.

Indeed, if a man were only to deal in the world for a day, and ſhould never have occaſion

ſion to converſe more with mankind, never more need their good opinion or good word, it were then no great matter (ſpeaking as to the concernments of this world) if a man ſpent his reputation all at once, and ventured it at one throw: but if he be to continue in the world, and would have the advantage of converſation whilſt he is in it, let him make uſe of truth and ſincerity in all his words and actions; for nothing but this will laſt and hold out to the end: all other arts will fail, but truth and integrity will carry a man through, and bear him out to the laſt.

Spectator.

§ 10. *The Neceſſity of forming religious Principles at an early Age.*

As ſoon as you are capable of reflection, you muſt perceive that there is a right and wrong in human actions. You ſee that thoſe who are born with the ſame advantages of fortune, are not all equally proſperous in the courſe of life. While ſome of them, by wiſe and ſteady conduct, attain diſtinction in the world, and paſs their days with comfort and honour; others of the ſame rank, by mean and vicious behaviour, forfeit the advantages of their birth, involve themſelves in much miſery, and end in being a diſgrace to their friends, and a burden on ſociety. Early, then, you may learn that it is not on the external condition in which you find yourſelves placed, but on the part which you are to act, that your welfare or unhappineſs, your honour or infamy, depend. Now, when beginning to act that part, what can be of greater moment, than to regulate your plan of conduct with the moſt ſerious attention, before you have yet committed any fatal or irretrievable errors? If, inſtead of exerting reflection for this valuable purpoſe, you deliver yourſelves up, at ſo critical a time, to ſloth and pleaſure; if you refuſe to liſten to any counſellor but humour, or to attend to any purſuit except that of amuſement; if you allow yourſelves to float looſe and careleſs on the tide of life, ready to receive any direction which the current of faſhion may chance to give you; what can you expect to follow from ſuch beginnings? While ſo many around you are undergoing the ſad conſequences of a like indiſcretion, for what reaſon ſhall not theſe conſequences extend to you? Shall you only attain ſucceſs without that preparation, and eſcape dangers without that precaution, which is required of others? Shall happineſs grow up to you of its own accord, and ſolicit your acceptance, when, to the reſt of mankind, it is the fruit of long cultivation, and the acquiſition of labour and care? — Deceive not yourſelves with ſuch arrogant hopes. Whatever be your rank, Providence will not, for your ſake, reverſe its eſtabliſhed order. By liſtening to wiſe admonitions, and tempering the vivacity of youth with a proper mixture of ſerious thought, you may enſure chearfulneſs for the reſt of your life; but by delivering yourſelves up at preſent to giddineſs and levity, you lay the foundation of laſting heavineſs of heart. *Blair.*

§ 11. *The Acquiſition of virtuous Diſpoſitions and Habits a neceſſary Part of Education.*

When you look forward to thoſe plans of life, which either your circumſtances have ſuggeſted, or your friends have propoſed, you will not heſitate to acknowledge, that in order to purſue them with advantage, ſome previous diſcipline is requiſite. Be aſſured, that whatever is to be your profeſſion, no education is more neceſſary to your ſucceſs, than the

the acquirement of virtuous dispositions and habits. This is the universal preparation for every character, and every station in life. Bad as the world is, respect is always paid to virtue. In the usual course of human affairs it will be found, that a plain understanding, joined with acknowledged worth, contributes more to prosperity, than the brightest parts without probity or honour. Whether science, or business, or public life, be your aim, virtue still enters, for a principal share, into all those great departments of society. It is connected with eminence, in every liberal art; with reputation, in every branch of fair and useful business; with distinction, in every public station. The vigour which it gives the mind, and the weight which it adds to character; the generous sentiments which it breathes; the undaunted spirit which it inspires, the ardour of diligence which it quickens, the freedom which it procures from pernicious and dishonourable avocations, are the foundations of all that is high in fame or great in success among men. Whatever ornamental or engaging endowments you now possess, virtue is a necessary requisite, in order to their shining with proper lustre. Feeble are the attractions of the fairest form, if it be suspected that nothing within corresponds to the pleasing appearance without. Short are the triumphs of wit, when it is supposed to be the vehicle of malice. By whatever arts you may at first attract the attention, you can hold the esteem and secure the hearts of others only by amiable dispositions and the accomplishments of the mind. These are the qualities whose influence will last, when the lustre of all that once sparkled and dazzled has passed away. *Blair.*

§ 12. *The Happiness and Dignity of Manhood depend upon the Conduct of the youthful Age.*

Let not the season of youth be barren of improvements, so essential to your felicity and honour. Your character is now of your own forming; your fate is in some measure put into your own hands. Your nature is as yet pliant and soft. Habits have not established their dominion. Prejudices have not preoccupied your understanding. The world has not had time to contract and debase your affections. All your powers are more vigorous, disembarrassed and free, than they will be at any future period. Whatever impulse you now give to your desires and passions, the direction is likely to continue. It will form the channel in which your life is to run; nay, it may determine an everlasting issue. Consider then the employment of this important period as the highest trust which shall ever be committed to you; as, in a great measure, decisive of your happiness, in time and in eternity. As in the succession of the seasons, each, by the invariable laws of nature, affects the productions of what is next in course; so, in human life, every period of our age, according as it is well or ill spent, influences the happiness of that which is to follow. Virtuous youth gradually brings forward accomplished and flourishing manhood; and such manhood passes of itself, without uneasiness, into respectable and tranquil old age. But when nature is turned out of its regular course, disorder takes place in the moral, just as in the vegetable world. If the spring put forth no blossoms, in summer there will be no beauty, and in autumn no fruit: So, if youth be trifled away without improvement, manhood will be contemptible, and old age miserable. *Ibid.*

§ 13.

§ 13. *Religion never to be treated with Levity.*

Impress your minds with reverence for all that is sacred. Let no wantonness of youthful spirits, no compliance with the intemperate mirth of others, ever betray you into profane sallies. Besides the guilt which is thereby incurred, nothing gives a more odious appearance of petulance and presumption to youth, than the affectation of treating religion with levity. Instead of being an evidence of superior understanding, it discovers a pert and shallow mind; which, vain of the first smatterings of knowledge, presumes to make light of what the rest of mankind revere. At the same time, you are not to imagine, that when exhorted to be religious, you are called upon to become more formal and solemn in your manners than others of the same years; or to erect yourselves into supercilious reprovers of those around you. The spirit of true religion breathes gentleness and affability. It gives a native unaffected ease to the behaviour. It is social, kind, and chearful; far removed from that gloomy and illiberal superstition which clouds the brow, sharpens the temper, dejects the spirit, and teaches men to fit themselves for another world, by neglecting the concerns of this. Let your religion, on the contrary, connect preparation for heaven with an honourable discharge of the duties of active life. Of such religion discover, on every proper occasion, that you are not ashamed; but avoid making any unnecessary ostentation of it before the world.

Blair.

§ 14. *Temperance in Pleasure recommended.*

Let me particularly exhort youth to temperance in pleasure. Let me admonish them, to beware of that rock on which thousands, from race to race, continue to split. The love of pleasure, natural to man in every period of his life, glows at this age with excessive ardour. Novelty adds fresh charms, as yet, to every gratification. The world appears to spread a continual feast; and health, vigour, and high spirits, invite them to partake of it without restraint. In vain we warn them of latent dangers. Religion is accused of insufferable severity, in prohibiting enjoyment; and the old, when they offer their admonition, are upbraided with having forgot that they once were young.—And yet, my friends, to what do the constraints of religion, and the counsels of age, with respect to pleasure, amount? They may all be comprized in a few words—not to hurt yourselves, and not to hurt others, by your pursuit of pleasure. Within these bounds, pleasure is lawful; beyond them it becomes criminal, because it is ruinous. Are these restraints any other than what a wise man would choose to impose on himself? We call you not to renounce pleasure, but to enjoy it in safety. Instead of abridging it, we exhort you to pursue it on an extensive plan. We propose measures for securing its possession, and for prolonging its duration. *Ibid.*

§ 15. *Irregular Pleasures.*

By the unhappy excesses of irregular pleasures in youth, how many amiable dispositions are corrupted or destroyed! How many rising capacities and powers are suppressed! How many flattering hopes of parents and friends are totally extinguished! Who but must drop a tear over human nature, when he beholds that morning, which arose so bright, overcast with such untimely darkness; that good-humour, which once captivated all

hearts,

hearts, that vivacity which ſparkled in every company, thoſe abilities which were fitted for adorning the higheſt ſtations, all ſacrificed at the ſhrine of low ſenſuality; and one who was formed for running the fair career of life in the midſt of public eſteem, cut off by his vices at the beginning of his courſe; or ſunk for the whole of it into inſignificancy and contempt!—Theſe, O ſinful Pleaſure, are thy trophies! It is thus that, co-operating with the foe of God and man, thou degradeſt human honour, and blaſteſt the opening proſpects of human felicity! *Blair.*

§ 16. *Induſtry and Application.*

Diligence, induſtry, and proper improvement of time, are material duties of the young. To no purpoſe are they endowed with the beſt abilities, if they want activity for exerting them. Unavailing, in this caſe, will be every direction that can be given them, either for their temporal or ſpiritual welfare. In youth, the habits of induſtry are moſt eaſily acquired: in youth the incentives to it are ſtrongeſt, from ambition and from duty, from emulation and hope, from all the proſpects, which the beginning of life affords. If, dead to theſe calls, you already languiſh in ſlothful inaction, what will be able to quicken the more ſluggiſh current of advancing years? Induſtry is not only the inſtrument of improvement, but the foundation of pleaſure. Nothing is ſo oppoſite to the true enjoyment of life, as the relaxed and feeble ſtate of an indolent mind. He who is a ſtranger to induſtry, may poſſeſs, but he cannot enjoy. For it is labour only which gives the reliſh to pleaſure. It is the appointed vehicle of every good man. It is the indiſpenſable condition of our poſſeſſing a ſound mind in a ſound body. Sloth is ſo inconſiſtent with both, that it is hard to determine, whether it be a greater foe to virtue, or to health and happineſs. Inactive as it is in itſelf, its effects are fatally powerful. Though it appear a ſlowly-flowing ſtream, yet it undermines all that is ſtable and flouriſhing. It not only ſaps the foundation of every virtue, but pours upon you a deluge of crimes and evils. It is like water which firſt putrefies by ſtagnation, and then ſends up noxious vapours, and fills the atmoſphere with death. Fly, therefore, from idleneſs, as the certain parent both of guilt and of ruin. And under idleneſs I include, not mere inaction only, but all that circle of trifling occupations, in which too many ſaunter away their youth; perpetually engaged in frivolous ſociety, or public amuſements; in the labours of dreſs, or the oſtentation of their perſons.—Is this the foundation which you lay for future uſefulneſs and eſteem? By ſuch accompliſhments do you hope to recommend yourſelves to the thinking part of the world, and to anſwer the expectations of your friends and your country? —Amuſements youth requires; it were vain, it were cruel, to prohibit them. But, though allowable as the relaxation, they are moſt culpable as the buſineſs, of the young. For they then become the gulph of time, and the poiſon of the mind. They foment bad paſſions. They weaken the manly powers. They ſink the native vigour of youth into contemptible effeminacy. *Ibid.*

§ 17. *The Employment of Time.*

Redeeming your time from ſuch dangerous waſte, ſeek to fill it with employments which you may review with ſatisfaction. The acquiſition of knowledge is one of the moſt honourable occupations of youth. The deſire of it diſcovers a liberal mind, and is connected

nected with many accomplishments and many virtues. But though your train of life should not lead you to study, the course of education always furnishes proper employments to a well-disposed mind. Whatever you pursue, be emulous to excel. Generous ambition, and sensibility to praise, are, especially at your age, among the marks of virtue. Think not that any affluence of fortune, or any elevation of rank, exempts you from the duties of application and industry. Industry is the law of our being; it is the demand of nature, of reason, and of God. Remember always, that the years which now pass over your heads, leave permanent memorials behind them. From your thoughtless minds they may escape; but they remain in the remembrance of God. They form an important part of the register of your life. They will hereafter bear testimony, either for or against you, at that day when, for all your actions, but particularly for the employments of youth, you must give an account to God. Whether your future course is destined to be long or short, after this manner it should commence; and, if it continue to be thus conducted, its conclusion, at what time soever it arrives, will not be inglorious or unhappy. *Blair.*

§ 18. *The Necessity of an early and close Application to Wisdom.*

It is necessary to habituate our minds, in our younger years, to some employment which may engage our thoughts, and fill the capacity of the soul at a riper age. For, however we may roam in youth from folly to folly, too volatile for rest, too soft and effeminate for industry, ever ambitious to make a splendid figure; yet the time will come when we shall outgrow the relish of childish amusements; and, if we are not provided with a taste for manly satisfactions to succeed in their room, we must of course become miserable, at an age more difficult to be pleased. While men, however unthinking and unemployed, enjoy an inexhaustible flow of vigorous spirits; a constant succession of gay ideas, which flatter and sport in the brain, makes them pleased with themselves, and with every frolic as trifling as themselves: but, when the ferment of their blood abates, and the freshness of their youth, like the morning dew, passes away, their spirits flag for want of entertainments more satisfactory in themselves, and more suited to a manly age; and the soul, from a sprightly impertinence, from quick sensations, and florid desires, subsides into a dead calm, and sinks into a flat stupidity. The fire of a glowing imagination (the property of youth) may make folly look pleasing, and lend a beauty to objects, which have none inherent in them: just as the sun-beams may paint a cloud, and diversify it with beautiful stains of light, however dark, unsubstantial, and empty in itself. But nothing can shine with undiminished lustre, but religion and knowledge, which are essentially and intrinsically bright. Take it therefore for granted, which you will find by experience, that nothing can be long entertaining, but what is in some measure beneficial; because nothing else will bear a calm and sedate review.

You may be fancied for a while, upon the account of good-nature, the inseparable attendant upon a flush of sanguine health, and a fulness of youthful spirits: but you will find, in process of time, that among the wise and good, useless good-nature is the object of pity, ill-nature of hatred; but nature beautified and improved by an assemblage of moral and intellectual endowments, is the only object of a solid and lasting esteem. *Seed.*

§ 19.

§ 19. *The Unhappiness consequent on the Neglect of early improving the Mind.*

There is not a greater inlet to misery and vices of all kinds, than the not knowing how to pass our vacant hours. For what remains to be done, when the first part of their lives, who are not brought up to any manual employment, is slipt away without an acquired relish for reading, or taste for other rational satisfactions? That they should pursue their pleasures? — But, religion apart, common prudence will warn them to tie up the wheel as they begin to go down the hill of life. Shall they then apply themselves to their studies? Alas! the seed-time is already past: The enterprizing and spirited ardour of youth being over, without having been applied to those valuable purposes for which it was given, all ambition of excelling upon generous and laudable schemes quite stagnates. If they have not some poor expedient to deceive the time, or, to speak more properly, to deceive themselves, the length of a day will seem tedious to them, who, perhaps, have the unreasonableness to complain of the shortness of life in general. When the former part of our life has been nothing but vanity, the latter end of it can be nothing but vexation. In short, we must be miserable, without some employment to fix, or some amusement to dissipate our thoughts: the latter we cannot command in all places, nor relish at all times; and therefore there is an absolute necessity for the former. We may pursue this or that new pleasure; we may be fond for a while of a new acquisition; but when the graces of novelty are worn off, and the briskness of our first desire is over, the transition is very quick and sudden, from an eager fondness to a cool indifference. Hence there is a restless agitation in our minds, still craving something new, still unsatisfied with it, when possessed; till melancholy increases, as we advance in years, like shadows lengthening towards the close of day.

Hence it is, that men of this stamp are continually complaining that the times are altered for the worse: Because the sprightliness of their youth represented every thing in the most engaging light; and, when men are in high good-humour with themselves, they are apt to be so with all around; the face of nature brightens up, and the sun shines with a more agreeable lustre: but when old-age has cut them off from the enjoyment of false pleasures, and habitual vice has given them a distaste for the only true and lasting delights; when a retrospect of their past lives presents nothing to view but one wide tract of uncultivated ground; a soul distempered with spleen, remorse, and an insensibility of each rational satisfaction, darkens and discolours every object; and the change is not in the times, but in them, who have been forsaken by those gratifications which they would not forsake.

How much otherwise is it with those, who have laid up an inexhaustible fund of knowledge! When a man has been laying out that time in the pursuit of some great and important truth, which others waste in a circle of gay follies, he is conscious of having acted up to the dignity of his nature; and from that consciousness there results that serene complacency, which, though not so violent, is much preferable to the pleasures of the animal life. He can travel on from strength to strength: for, in literature as in war, each new conquest which he gains, impowers him to push his conquests still farther, and to enlarge the empire of reason: thus he is ever in in a progressive state, still making new acquirements, still animated with hopes of future discoveries. *Seed.*

§ 20. *Riches or Fortune no Excuse to exempt any from Study.*

Others there are, who plead an exemption from study, because their fortune makes them independent of the world, and they need not be beholden to it for a maintenance—that is, because their situation in life exempts them from the necessity of spending their time in servile offices and hardships, therefore they may dispose of it just as they please. It is to imagine, because God has empowered them to single out the best means of employing their hours, viz. in reading, meditation; in the highest instances of piety and charity; therefore they may throw them away in a round of impertinence, vanity, and folly. The apostle's rule, 'that if any man will not work, neither should he eat,' extends to the rich as well as the poor; only supposing, that there are different kinds of work assigned to each. The reason is the same in both cases, viz. that he who will do no good, ought not to receive or enjoy any. As we are all joint traders and partners in life, he forfeits his right to any share in the common stock of happiness, who does not endeavour to contribute his quota or allotted part to it: the public happiness being nothing but the sum total of each individual's contribution to it. An easy fortune does not set men free from labour and industry in general; it only exempts them from some particular kinds of labour: it is not a blessing, as it gives them liberty to do nothing at all; but as it gives them liberty wisely to chuse, and steadily to prosecute, the most ennobling exercises, and the most improving employments, the pursuit of truth, the practice of virtue, the service of God who giveth them all things richly to enjoy, in short, the doing and being every thing that is commendable; though nothing merely in order to be commended. That time which others must employ in tilling the ground (which often deceives their expectation) with the sweat of their brow, they may lay out in cultivating the mind, a soil always grateful to the care of the tiller.—The sum of what I would say, is this: That, though you are not confined to any particular calling, yet you have a general one; which is, to watch over your heart, and to improve your head; to make yourself master of all those accomplishments—an enlarged compass of thought, that flowing humanity and generosity, which are necessary to become a great fortune; and of all those perfections, viz. moderation, humility, and temperance, which are necessary to bear a small one patiently; but especially it is your duty to acquire a taste for those pleasures, which, after they are tasted, go off agreeably, and leave behind them a grateful and delightful flavour on the mind. *Ibid.*

§ 21. *The justly valuing and duly using the Advantages enjoyed in a Place of Education.*

One considerable advantage is, that regular method of study, too much neglected in other places, which obtains here. Nothing is more common elsewhere, than for persons to plunge, at once, into the very depth of science, (far beyond their own) without having learned the first rudiments: nothing more common, than for some to pass themselves upon the world for great scholars, by the help of universal Dictionaries, Abridgements, and Indexes; by which means they gain an useless smattering in every branch of literature, just

 enough

enough to enable them to talk fluently, or rather impertinently, upon most subjects; but not to think justly and deeply upon any: like those who have a general superficial acquaintance with almost every body. To cultivate an intimate and entire friendship with one or two worthy persons, would be of more service to them. The true genuine way to make a substantial scholar, is what takes place here, ——to begin with those general principles of reasoning, upon which all science depends, and which give a sight to every part of literature; to make gradual advances, a slow but sure process; to travel gently, with proper guides to direct us, through the most beautiful and fruitful regions of knowledge in general, before we fix ourselves in, and confine ourselves to any particular province of it; it being the great secret of education, not to make a man a complete master of any branch of science, but to give his mind that freedom, openness, and extent, which shall empower him to master it, or indeed any other, whenever he shall turn the bent of his studies that way; which is best done, by setting before him, in his earlier years, a general view of the whole intellectual world: whereas, an early and entire attachment to one particular calling, narrows the abilities of the mind to that degree, that he can scarce think out of that track to which he is accustomed.

The next advantage I shall mention is, a direction in the choice of authors upon the most material subjects. For it is perhaps a great truth, that learning might be reduced to a much narrower compass, if one were to read none but original authors, those who write chiefly from their own fund of sense, without treading servilely in the steps of others.

Here, too, a generous emulation quickens our endeavours, and the friend improves the scholar.' The tediousness of the way to truth is insensibly beguiled by having fellow-travellers, who keep an even pace with us: each light dispenses a brighter flame by mixing its social rays with those of others. Here we live sequestered from noise and hurry, far from the great scene of business, vanity, and idleness; our hours are all our own. Here it is, as in the Athenian torch-race, where a series of men have successively transmitted from one to another the torch of knowledge; and no sooner has one quitted it, but another equally able takes the lamp, to dispense light to all within its sphere *. *Seed.*

§ 22. *Discipline of the Place of Education not to be relaxed.*

May none of us complain, that the discipline of the place is too strict: may we rather reflect, that there needs nothing else to make a man completely miserable, but to let him, in the most dangerous stage of life, carve out an happiness for himself, without any check upon the sallies of youth! Those to whom you have been over indulgent, and perhaps could not have been otherwise, without proceeding to extremities, never to be used but in desperate cases, those have been always the most liberal of their censures and invectives against you: they put one in mind of Adonijah's rebellion against David his father; because his father had not displeased him at any time, in saying, Why hast thou done so?—It is a certain sign men want restraints, when they are impatient under any; too headstrong to be governed by authority, too weak to be conducted by reason. *Ibid.*

* —Quasi cursores, vita lampada tradunt. *Lucretius.*

§ 23.

§ 23. *The Beginnings of Evil to be resisted.*

Think not, as I am afraid too many do, that because your passions have not hurried you into atrocious deeds, they have therefore wrought no mischief, and have left no sting behind them. By a continued series of loose, though apparently trivial gratifications, the heart is often as thoroughly corrupted, as by the commission of any one of those enormous crimes which spring from great ambition, or great revenge. Habit gives the passions strength, while the absence of glaring guilt seemingly justifies them; and, unawakened by remorse, the sinner proceeds in his course, till he wax bold in guilt, and become ripe for ruin: for, by gradual and latent steps, the destruction of our virtues advances. Did the evil unveil itself at the beginning; did the storm which is to overthrow our peace, discover, as it rose, all its horrors, precautions would more frequently be taken against it. But we are imperceptibly betrayed; and from one licentious attachment, one criminal passion, are, by a train of consequences, drawn on to another, till the government of our minds is irrecoverably lost. The enticing and the odious passions are, in this respect, similar in their process; and, though by different roads, conduct at last to the same issue.

Blair.

§ 24. *A due Regard to Order necessary in Business, Time, Expence, and Amusements.*

Throughout your affairs, your time, your expence, your amusements, your society, the principle of order must be equally carried, if you expect to reap any of its happy fruits. For if into any one of those great departments of life you suffer disorder to enter, it will spread through all the rest. In vain, for instance, you purpose to be orderly in the conduct of your affairs, if you be irregular in the distribution of your time. In vain you attempt to regulate your expence, if into your amusements, or your society, disorder has crept. You have admitted a principle of confusion which will defeat all your plans, and perplex and entangle what you sought to arrange. Uniformity is above all things necessary to order. If you desire that any thing should proceed according to method and rule, 'let all things be done in order.'

I must also admonish you, that in small, as well as in great affairs, a due regard to order is requisite. I mean not, that you ought to look on those minute attentions, which are apt to occupy frivolous minds, as connected either with virtue or wisdom: but I exhort you to remember, that disorder, like other immoralities, frequently takes rise from inconsiderable beginnings. They who, in the lesser transactions of life, are totally negligent of rule, will be in hazard of extending that negligence, by degrees, to such affairs and duties as will render them criminal. Remissness grows on all who study not to guard against it; and it is only by frequent exercise, that the habits of order and punctuality can be thoroughly confirmed.

Ibid.

§ 25. *Idleness avoided by the Observation of Order.*

By attending to order, you avoid idleness, that most fruitful source of crimes and evils. Acting upon a plan, meeting every thing in its own place, you constantly find innocent and useful employment for time. You are never at a loss how to dispose of your hours, or to fill up life agreeably. In the course of human action, there are two extremes equally dangerous to virtue; the multiplicity of affairs,

fairs, and the total want of them. The man of order stands in the middle between these two extremes, and suffers from neither: he is occupied, but not oppressed. Whereas the disorderly, overloading one part of time, and leaving another vacant, are at one period overwhelmed with business, and at another, either idle through want of employment, or indolent through perplexity. Those seasons of indolence and idleness, which recur so often in their life, are their most dangerous moments. The mind, unhappy in its situation, and clinging to every object which can occupy or amuse it, is then aptest to throw itself into the arms of every vice and folly.

Farther; by the preservation of order, you check inconstancy and levity. Fickle by nature is the human heart. It is fond of change; and perpetually tends to start aside from the straight line of conduct. Hence arises the propriety of bringing ourselves under subjection to method and rule; which, though at first it may prove constraining, yet by degrees, and from the experience of its happy effects, becomes natural and agreeable. It rectifies those irregularities of temper and manners to which we give the name of caprice; and which are distinguished characteristics of a disorderly mind. It is the parent of steadiness of conduct. It forms consistency of character. It is the ground of all the confidence we repose in one another. For, the disorderly we know not where to find. In him only can we place any trust, who is uniform and regular; who lives by principle, not by humour; who acts upon a plan, and not by desultory motions.

Blair.

§ 26. *The Beginnings of Passion to be opposed.*

Oppose early the beginnings of passion. Avoid particularly all such objects as are apt to excite passions which you know to predominate within you. As soon as you find the tempest rising, have recourse to every proper method, either of allaying its violence, or of escaping to a calmer shore. Hasten to call up emotions of an opposite nature. Study to conquer one passion by means of some other which is of less dangerous tendency. Never account any thing small or trivial, which is in hazard of introducing disorder into your heart. Never make light of any desire which you feel gaining such progress as to threaten entire dominion. Blandishing it will appear at the first. As a gentle and innocent emotion, it may steal into the heart; but as it advances, is likely to pierce you through with many sorrows. What you indulged as a favourite amusement, will shortly become a serious business, and in the end may prove the burden of your life. Most of our passions flatter us in their rise: but their beginnings are treacherous; their growth is imperceptible; and the evils which they carry in their train, lie concealed, until their dominion is established. What Solomon says of one of them, holds true of them all, 'that their beginning is as 'when one letteth out water.' It issues from a small chink, which once might have been easily stopped; but being neglected, it is soon widened by the stream, till the bank is at last totally thrown down, and the flood is at liberty to deluge the whole plain.

Ibid.

§ 27. *The Government of Temper, as included in the Keeping of the Heart.*

Passions are quick and strong emotions which by degrees subside. Temper is the disposition which remains after these emotions are past, and which forms the habitual propensity of the soul. The one are like the stream

ſtream when it is ſwoln by the torrent, and ruffled by the winds; the other reſembles it when running within its bed, with its natural force and velocity. The influence of temper is more ſilent and imperceptible than that of paſſion; it operates with leſs violence; but as its operation is conſtant, it produces effects no leſs conſiderable. It is evident, therefore, that it highly deſerves to be conſidered in a religious view.

Many, indeed, are averſe to behold it in this light. They place a good temper upon the ſame footing with a healthy conſtitution of body. They conſider it as a natural felicity which ſome enjoy; but for the want of which, others are not morally culpable, nor accountable to God: and hence the opinion has ſometimes prevailed, that a bad temper might be conſiſtent with a ſtate of grace. If this were true, it would overturn that whole doctrine, of which the goſpel is ſo full, 'that regeneration, or change of nature, is the eſſential characteriſtic of a Chriſtian.' It would ſuppoſe that grace might dwell amidſt malevolence and rancour, and that heaven might be enjoyed by ſuch as are ſtrangers to charity and love.—It will readily be admitted that ſome, by the original frame of their mind, are more favourably inclined than others, towards certain good diſpoſitions and habits. But this affords no juſtification to thoſe who neglect to oppoſe the corruptions to which they are prone. Let no man imagine, that the human heart is a ſoil altogether unſuſceptible of culture! or that the worſt temper may not, through the aſſiſtance of grace, be reformed by attention and diſcipline. Settled depravity of temper, is always owing to our own indulgence. If, in place of checking, we nouriſh that malignity of diſpoſition to which we are inclined, all the conſequences will be placed to our account, and every excuſe, from natural conſtitution, be rejected at the tribunal of Heaven. *Blair.*

§ 28. *That Diſcipline which teaches to moderate the Eagerneſs of worldly Paſſions, and to fortify the Mind with the Principles of Virtue, is more conducive to true Happineſs that the Poſſeſſion of all the Goods of Fortune.*

That diſcipline which corrects the eagerneſs of worldly paſſions, which fortifies the heart with virtuous principles, which enlightens the mind with uſeful knowledge, and furniſhes to it matter of enjoyment from within itſelf, is of more conſequence to real felicity, than all the proviſion which we can make of the goods of fortune. To this let us bend our chief attention. Let us keep the heart with all diligence ſeeing out of it are the iſſues of life. Let us account our mind the moſt important province which is committed to our care; and if we cannot rule fortune, ſtudy at leaſt to rule ourſelves. Let us propoſe for our object, not worldly ſucceſs, which it depends not on us to obtain, but that upright and honourable diſcharge of our duty in every conjuncture, which, through the divine aſſiſtance, is always within our power. Let our happineſs be ſought where our proper praiſe is found; and that be accounted our only real evil, which is the evil of our nature; not that which is either the appointment of Providence, or which ariſes from the evil of others. *Ibid.*

§ 29. *The Difference between true and falſe Politeneſs.*

It is evident enough, that the moral and Chriſtian duty, of preferring one another in honour, reſpects only ſocial peace and charity, and terminates in the good and edification of our Chriſtian brother. Its uſe is, to ſoften the

the minds of men, and to draw them from that ſavage ruſticity, which engenders many vices, and diſcredits the virtues themſelves. But when men had experienced the benefit of this complying temper, and further ſaw the ends, not of charity only, but of ſelf-intereſt, that might be anſwered by it; they conſidered no longer its juſt purpoſe and application, but ſtretched it to that officious ſedulity, and extreme ſervility of adulation, which we too often obſerve and lament in poliſhed life.

Hence, that infinite attention and conſideration, which is ſo rigidly exacted, and ſo duly paid, in the commerce of the world: hence, that proſtitution of mind, which leaves a man no will, no ſentiment, no principle, no character; all which diſappear under the uniform exhibition of good manners: hence, thoſe inſidious arts, thoſe ſtudied diſguiſes, thoſe obſequious flatteries, nay, thoſe multiplied and nicely-varied forms of inſinuation and addreſs, the direct aim of which may be to acquire the fame of politeneſs and good-breeding, but the certain effect, to corrupt every virtue, to ſoothe every vanity, and to inflame every vice of the human heart.

Theſe fatal miſchiefs introduce themſelves under the pretence and ſemblance of that humanity, which the ſcriptures encourage and enjoin: but the genuine virtue is eaſily diſtinguiſhed from the counterfeit, and by the following plain ſigns.

other. It reſpects, in a word, the credit and eſtimation of his neighbour.

The mimic of this amiable virtue, falſe politeneſs, is, on the other hand, ambitious, ſervile, timorous. It affects popularity: is ſolicitous to pleaſe, and to be taken notice of. The man of this character does not offer, but obtrude his civilities; becauſe he would merit by this aſſiduity; becauſe, in deſpair of winning regard by any worthier qualities, he would be ſure to make the moſt of this; and laſtly, becauſe of all things, he would dread, by the omiſſion of any punctilious obſervance, to give offence. In a word, this ſort of politeneſs reſpects, for its immediate object, the favour and conſideration of our neighbour.

2. Again; the man who governs himſelf by the ſpirit of the Apoſtle's precept, expreſſes his preference of another in ſuch a way, as is worthy of himſelf: in all innocent compliances, in all honeſt civilities, in all decent and manly condeſcenſions.

On the contrary, the man of the world, who reſts in the *letter* of this command, is regardleſs of the means by which he conducts himſelf. He reſpects neither his own dignity, nor that of human nature. Truth, reaſon, virtue, all are equally betrayed by this ſupple impoſtor. He aſſents to the errors, though the moſt pernicious; he applauds the follies, though the moſt ridiculous; he ſoothes the vices, though the moſt flagrant, of other men. He

sued, and by so different *means*, must also lie wide of each other.

Accordingly, the true polite man would, by all proper testimonies of respect, promote the credit and estimation of his neighbour; *because* he sees that, by this generous consideration of each other, the peace of the world is, in a good degree, preserved; *because* he knows that these mutual attentions prevent animosities, soften the fierceness of men's manners, and dispose them to all the offices of benevolence and charity; *because*, in a word, the interests of society are best served by this conduct; and *because* he understands it to be his duty to love his *neighbour*.

The falsely polite, on the contrary, are anxious, by all means whatever, to procure the favour and consideration of those they converse with; *because* they regard, ultimately, nothing more than their private interest; *because* they perceive, that their own selfish designs are best carried on by such practices: in a word, *because* they *love themselves*.

Thus we see, that genuine virtue consults the honour of others by worthy means, and for the noblest purposes; the counterfeit solicits their favour by dishonest compliances, and for the basest end. *Hurd.*

§ 30. *The Temple of virtuous Love.*

The structure on the right hand was (as I afterwards found) consecrated to virtuous Love, and could not be entered, but by such as received a ring, or some other token, from a person who was placed as a guard at the gate of it. He wore a garland of roses and myrtles on his head, and on his shoulders a robe like an imperial mantle white and unspotted all over, excepting only, that where it was clasped at his breast, there were two golden turtle doves that buttoned it by their bills, which were wrought in rubies: he was called by the name of Hymen, and was seated near the entrance of the temple, in a delicious bower, made up of several trees that were embraced by woodbines, jessamines, and amaranths, which were as so many emblems of marriage, and ornaments to the trunks that supported them. As I was single and unaccompanied, I was not permitted to enter the temple, and for that reason am a stranger to all the mysteries that were performed in it. I had, however, the curiosity to observe, how the several couples that entered were disposed of; which was after the following manner: there were two great gates on the backside of the edifice, at which the whole crowd was let out. At one of these gates were two women, extremely beautiful, though in a different kind; the one having a very careful and composed air, the other a sort of smile and ineffable sweetness in her countenance: the name of the first was Discretion, and of the other Complacency. All who came out of this gate, and put themselves under the direction of these two sisters, were immediately conducted by them into gardens, groves, and meadows, which abounded in delights, and were furnished with every thing that could make them the proper seats of happiness. The second gate of this temple let out all the couples that were unhappily married; who came out linked together by chains, which each of them strove to break, but could not. Several of these were such as had never been acquainted with each other before they met in the great walk, or had been too well acquainted in the thicket. The entrance to this gate was possessed by three sisters, who joined themselves with these wretches, and occasioned most of their miseries. The youngest of the sisters was known by the name of Levity; who, with the innocence of a virgin, had the drefs and behaviour of a harlot: the name of the fecond was Contention, who bore on her right arm a muff made of the fkin of a porcupine, and on her left carried a little lap-dog, that barked and fnapped at every one that paffed by her. The eldeft of the fifters, who feemed to have an haughty and imperious air, was always accompanied with a tawny Cupid, who generally marched before her with a little mace on his fhoulder, the end of which was fafhioned into the horns of a ftag: her garments were yellow, and her complexion pale: her eyes were pierceing, but had odd cafts in them, and that particular diftemper which makes perfons who are troubled with it fee objects double. Upon enquiry, I was informed that her name was Jealoufy. *Tatler.*

§ 31. *The Temple of Luft.*

Having finifhed my obfervations upon this temple, and its votaries, I repaired to that which ftood on the left hand, and was called the Temple of Luft. The front of it was raifed on Corinthian pillars, with all the meretricious ornaments that accompany that order; whereas that of the other was compofed of the chafte and matron-like Ionic. The fides of it were adorned with feveral grotefque figures of goats, fparrows, heathen gods, fatyrs, and monfters, made up of half men, half beaft. The gates were unguarded, and open to all that had a mind to enter. Upon my going in, I found the windows were blinded, and let in only a kind of twilight, that ferved to difcover a prodigious number of dark corners and apartments, into which the whole temple was divided. I was here ftunned with a mixed noife of clamour and jollity: on one fide of me I heard finging and dancing; on the other, brawls and clafhing of fwords: in fhort, I was fo little pleafed with the place, that I was going out of it; but found I could not return by the gate where I entered, which was barred againft all that were come in, with bolts of iron and locks of adamant; there was no going back from this temple through the paths of pleafure which led to it: all who paffed through the ceremonies of the place, went out at an iron wicket, which was kept by a dreadful giant called Remorfe, that held a fcourge of fcorpions in his hand, and drove them into the only outlet from that temple. This was a paffage fo rugged, fo uneven, and choaked with fo many thorns and briars, that it was a melancholy fpectacle to behold the pains and difficulties which both fexes fuffered who walked through it: the men, though in the prime of their youth, appeared weak and infeebled with old age: the women wrung their hands, and tore their hair, and feveral loft their limbs, before they could extricate themfelves out of the perplexities of the path in which they were engaged.—The remaining part of this vifion, and the adventures I met with in the two great roads of Ambition and Avarice, muft be the fubject of another paper. *Ibid.*

§ 32. *The Temple of Virtue.*

With much labour and difficulty I paffed through the firft part of my vifion, and recovered the centre of the wood, from whence I had the profpect of the three great roads. I here joined myfelf to the middle-aged party of mankind, who marched behind the ftandard of Ambition. The great road lay in a direct line, and was terminated by the Temple of Virtue. It was planted on each fide with laurels, which were intermixed with marble trophies, carved pillars, and ftatues of lawgivers, heroes, ftatefmen, philofophers, and poets. The

The perſons who travelled up this great path, were ſuch whoſe thoughts were bent upon doing eminent ſervices to mankind, or promoting the good of their country. On each ſide of this great road, were ſeveral paths that were alſo laid out in ſtraight lines, and ran parallel with it: theſe were moſt of them covered walks, and received into them men of retired virtue, who propoſed to themſelves the ſame end of their journey, though they choſe to make it in ſhade and obſcurity. The edifices, at the extremity of the walk, were ſo contrived, that we could not ſee the temple of Honour, by reaſon of the temple of Virtue, which ſtood before it: at the gates of this temple, we were met by the goddeſs of it, who conducted us into that of Honour, which was joined to the other edifice by a beautiful triumphal arch, and had no other entrance into it. When the deity of the inner ſtructure had received us, ſhe preſented us in a body, to a figure that was placed over the high altar, and was the emblem of Eternity. She ſat on a globe, in the midſt of a golden zodiac, holding the figure of a ſun in one hand, and a moon in the other: her head was veiled, and her feet covered. Our hearts glowed within us, as we ſtood amidſt the ſphere of light which this image caſt on every ſide of it. *Tatler.*

§ 33. *The Temple of Vanity.*

Having ſeen all that happened to the band of adventurers, I repaired to another pile of buildings that ſtood within view of the temple of Honour, and was raiſed in imitation of it, upon the very ſame model; but, at my approach to it, I found that the ſtones were laid together without mortar, and that the whole fabric ſtood upon ſo weak a foundation, that it ſhook with every wind that blew. This was called the Temple of Vanity. The goddeſs of it ſat in the midſt of a great many tapers, that burned day and night, and made her appear much better than ſhe would have done in open day-light. Her whole art was to ſhew herſelf more beautiful and majeſtic than ſhe really was. For which reaſon ſhe had painted her face, and wore a cluſter of falſe jewels upon her breaſt: but what I more particularly obſerved, was the breadth of her petticoat, which was made altogether in the faſhion of a modern fardingal. This place was filled with hypocrites, pedants, free-thinkers, and prating politicians, with a rabble of thoſe who have only titles to make them great men. Female votaries crowded the temple, choaked up the avenues of it, and were more in number than the ſand upon the ſea-ſhore. I made it my buſineſs, in my return towards that part of the wood from whence I firſt ſet out, to obſerve the walks which led to this temple; for I met in it ſeveral who had begun their journey with the band of virtuous perſons, and travelled ſome time in their company: but, upon examination, I found that there were ſeveral paths, which led out of the great road into the ſides of the wood, and ran into ſo many crooked turns and windings, that thoſe who travelled through them, often turned their backs upon the temple of Virtue, then croſſed the ſtraight road, and ſometimes marched in it for a little ſpace, till the crooked path which they were engaged in again led them into the wood. The ſeveral alleys of theſe wanderers, had their particular ornaments: one of them I could not but take notice of, in the walk of the miſchievous pretenders to politics, which had at every turn the figure of a person, whom, by the inscription, I found to be Machiavel, pointing out the way, with an extended finger, like a Mercury.

Tatler.

§ 34. *The Temple of Avarice.*

I was now returned in the same manner as before, with a design to observe carefully every thing that passed in the region of Avarice, and the occurrences in that assembly, which was made up of persons of my own age. This body of travellers had not gone far in the third great road, before it led them insensibly into a deep valley, in which they journied several days, with great toil and uneasiness, and without the necessary refreshments of food and sleep. The only relief they met with, was in a river that ran through the bottom of the valley on a bed of golden sand: they often drank of this stream, which had such a particular quality in it, that though it refreshed them for a time, it rather inflamed than quenched their thirst. On each side of the river was a range of hills full of precious ore; for where the rains had washed off the earth, one might see in several parts of them long veins of gold, and rocks that looked like pure silver. We were told that the deity of the place had forbad any of his votaries to dig into the bowels of these hills, or convert the treasures they contained to any use, under pain of starving. At the end of the valley stood the Temple of Avarice made after the manner of a fortification, and surrounded with a thousand triple-headed dogs, that were placed there to keep off beggars. At our approach they all fell a barking, and would have much terrified us, had not an old woman, who had called herself by the forged name of Competency, offered herself for our guide. She carried under her garment a golden bow, which she no sooner held up in her hand, but the dogs lay down, and the gates flew open for our reception. We were led through an hundred iron doors before we entered the temple. At the upper end of it, sat the god of Avarice, with a long filthy beard, and a meagre starved countenance, inclosed with heaps of ingots and pyramids of money, but half naked and shivering with cold: on his right hand was a fiend called Rapine, and on his left a particular favourite, to whom he had given the title of Parsimony; the first was his collector, and the other his cashier. There were several long tables placed on each side of the temple, with respective officers attending behind them: some of these I enquired into: at the first table was kept the office of Corruption. Seeing a solicitor extremely busy, and whispering every body that passed by, I kept my eye upon him very attentively, and saw him often going up to a person that had a pen in his hand, with a multiplication-table and an almanack before him, which, as I afterwards heard, was all the learning he was master of. The solicitor would often apply himself to his ear, and at the same time convey money into his hand, for which the other would give him out a piece of paper, or parchment, signed and sealed in form. The name of this dexterous and successful solicitor was Bribery.—At the next table was the office of Extortion: behind it sat a person in a bob-wig, counting over a great sum of money: he gave out little purses to several, who, after a short tour, brought him, in return, sacks full of the same kind of coin. I saw, at the same time, a person called Fraud, who sat behind the counter, with false scales, light weights, and scanty measures; by the skilful application of which instruments, ſhe had got together an immenſe heap of wealth: it would be endleſs to name the ſeveral officers, or deſcribe the votaries that attended in this temple: there were many old men, panting and breathleſs, repoſing their heads on bags of money; nay many of them actually dying, whoſe very pangs and convulſions (which rendered their purſes uſeleſs to them) only made them graſp them the faſter. There were ſome tearing with one hand all things, even to the garments and fleſh of many miſerable perſons who ſtood before them; and with the other hand throwing away what they had ſeized, to harlots, flatterers, and panders, that ſtood behind them. On a ſudden the whole aſſembly fell a trembling; and, upon enquiry, I found that the great room we were in was haunted with a ſpectre, that many times a day appeared to them, and terrified them to diſtraction. In the midſt of their terror and amazement, the apparition entered, which I immediately knew to be Poverty. Whether it were by my acquaintance with this phantom, which had rendered the ſight of her more familiar to me, or however it was, ſhe did not make ſo indigent or frightful a figure in my eye, as the god of this loathſome temple. The miſerable votaries of this place were, I found, of another mind: every one fancied himſelf threatened by the apparition as ſhe ſtalked about the room, and began to lock their coffers, and tie their bags, with the utmoſt fear and trembling. I muſt confeſs, I look upon the paſſion which I ſaw in this unhappy people, to be of the ſame nature with thoſe unaccountable antipathies which ſome perſons are born with, or rather as a kind of phrenzy, not unlike that which throws a man into terrors and agonies at the ſight of ſo uſeful and innocent a thing as water. The whole aſſembly was ſurprized, when, inſtead of paying my devotions to the deity whom they all adored, they ſaw me addreſs myſelf to the phantom. "Oh! Poverty! (ſaid I) my firſt petition to thee is, that thou wouldeſt never appear to me hereafter; but, if thou wilt not grant me this, that thou wouldeſt not bear a form more terrible than that in which thou appeareſt to me at preſent. Let not thy threats or menaces betray me to any thing that is ungrateful or unjuſt. Let me not ſhut my ears to the cries of the needy. Let me not forget the perſon that has deſerved well of me. Let me not, from any fear of Thee, deſert my friend, my principles, or my honour. If Wealth is to viſit me, and come with her uſual attendants, Vanity and Avarice, do thou, O Poverty! haſten to my reſcue; but bring along with Thee thy two ſiſters, in whoſe company thou art always chearful, Liberty and Innocence." *Tatler.*

§ 35. *The Stings of Poverty, Diſeaſe, and Violence, leſs pungent than thoſe of guilty Paſſions.*

Aſſemble all the evils which poverty, diſeaſe, or violence can inflict, and their ſtings will be found, by far, leſs pungent than thoſe which guilty paſſions dart into the heart. Amidſt the ordinary calamities of the world, the mind can exert its powers, and ſuggeſt relief: and the mind is properly the man; the ſufferer, and his ſufferings can be diſtinguiſhed. But thoſe diſorders of paſſion, by ſeizing directly on the mind, attack human nature in its ſtrong hold, and cut off its laſt reſource. They penetrate to the very ſeat of ſenſation; and convert all the powers of thought into inſtruments of torture. *Blair.*

§ 36. *On Gratitude.*

There is not a more pleasing exercise of the mind, than gratitude.

It is accompanied with such inward satisfaction, that the duty is sufficiently rewarded by the performance. It is not like the practice of many other virtues, difficult and painful, but attended with so much pleasure, that were there no positive command which enjoined it, nor any recompence laid up for it hereafter—a generous mind would indulge in it, for the natural gratification that accompanies it.

If gratitude is due from man to man—how much more from man to his Maker?—The Supreme Being does not only confer upon us those bounties which proceed more immediately from his hand, but even those benefits which are conveyed to us by others. Every blessing we enjoy, by what means soever it may be derived upon us, is the gift of Him who is the great Author of good, and Father of mercies.

If gratitude, when exerted towards one another, naturally produces a very pleasing sensation in the mind of a grateful man; it exalts the soul into rapture, when it is employed on this great object of gratitude, on this beneficent Being, who has given us every thing we already possess, and from whom we expect every thing we yet hope for.

Most of the works of the Pagan poets were either direct hymns of their deities, or tended indirectly to the celebration of their respective attributes and perfections. Those who are acquainted with the works of the Greek and Latin poets which are still extant, will, upon reflection, find this observation so true, that I shall not enlarge upon it. One would wonder that more of our Christian poets have not turned their thoughts this way, especially if we consider, that our idea of the Supreme Being, is not only infinitely more great and noble than could possibly enter into the heart of a heathen, but filled with every thing that can raise the imagination, and give an opportunity for the sublimest thoughts and conceptions.

Plutarch tells us of a heathen who was singing an hymn to Diana, in which he celebrated her for her delight in human sacrifices, and other instances of cruelty and revenge; upon which a poet who was present at this piece of devotion, and seems to have had a truer idea of the divine nature, told the votary, by way of reproof, that in recompence for his hymn, he heartily wished he might have a daughter of the same temper with the goddess he celebrated.—It was indeed impossible to write the praises of one of those false deities, according to the Pagan creed, without a mixture of impertinence and adsurdity.

The Jews, who before the time of Christianity were the only people who had the knowledge of the true God, have set the Christian world an example how they ought to employ this divine talent, of which I am speaking. As that nation produced men of great genius, without considering them as inspired writers, they have transmitted to us many hymns and divine odes, which excel those that are delivered down to us by the ancient Greeks and Romans, in the poetry as much as in the subject to which it is consecrated. This, I think, might be easily shewn, if there were occasion for it.

Spectator.

§ 37. *Bad company—meaning of the phrase—different classes of bad company—ill chosen company—*

company—what is meant by keeping bad company—the danger of it, from our aptneſs to imitate and catch the manners of others—from the great power and force of cuſtom—from our bad inclinations.

"Evil communication," ſays the text, "corrupts good manners." The aſſertion is general, and no doubt all people ſuffer from ſuch communication; but above all, the minds of youth will ſuffer; which are yet unformed, unprincipled, unfurniſhed; and ready to receive any impreſſion.

But before we conſider the danger of keeping bad company, let us firſt ſee the meaning of the phraſe.

In the phraſe of the world, good company means faſhionable people. Their ſtations in life, not their morals, are conſidered: and he, who aſſociates with ſuch, though they ſet him the example of breaking every commandment of the decalogue, is ſtill ſaid to keep good company.—I ſhould wiſh you to fix another meaning to the expreſſion; and to conſider vice in the ſame deteſtable light, in whatever company it is found; nay, to conſider all company in which it is found, be their ſtation what it will, as bad company.

The three following claſſes will perhaps include the greateſt part of thoſe, who deſerve this appellation.

In the firſt, I ſhould rank all who endeavour to deſtroy the principles of Chriſtianity—who jeſt upon Scripture—talk blaſphemy—and treat revelation with contempt.

A ſecond claſs of bad company are thoſe, who have a tendency to deſtroy in us the principles of common honeſty and integrity. Under this head we may rank gameſters of every denomination; and the low and infamous characters of every profeſſion.

A third claſs of bad company, and ſuch as are commonly moſt dangerous to youth, includes the long catalogue of men of pleaſure. In whatever way they follow the call of appetite, they have equally a tendency to corrupt the purity of the mind.

Beſides theſe three claſſes, whom we may call bad company, there are others who come under the denomination of ill-choſen company: trifling, inſipid characters of every kind; who follow no buſineſs—are led by no ideas of improvement—but ſpend their time in diſſipation and folly—whoſe higheſt praiſe it is, that they are only not vicious.—With none of theſe, a ſerious man would wiſh his ſon to keep company.

It may be aſked what is meant by keeping bad company? The world abounds with characters of this kind: they meet us in every place; and if we keep company at all, it is impoſſible to avoid keeping company with ſuch perſons.

It is true, if we were determined never to have any commerce with bad men, we muſt, as the apoſtle remarks, "altogether go out of the world." By keeping bad company, therefore, is not meant a caſual intercourſe with them, on occaſion of buſineſs, or as they accidentally fall in our way; but having an inclination to conſort with them—complying with that inclination—ſeeking their company, when we might avoid it—entering into their parties—and making them the companions of our choice. Mixing with them occaſionally, cannot be avoided.

The danger of keeping bad company, ariſes principally from our aptneſs to imitate and catch the manners and ſentiments of others—from

from the power of custom—from our own bad inclinations—and from the pains taken by the bad to corrupt us *.

In our earliest youth, the contagion of manners is observable. In the boy, yet incapable of having any thing instilled into him, we easily discover from his first actions, and rude attempts at language, the kind of persons with whom he has been brought up: we see the early spring of a civilized education, or the first wild shoots of rusticity.

As he enters farther into life, his behaviour, manners, and conversation, all take their cast from the company he keeps. Observe the peasant, and the man of education; the difference is striking. And yet God hath bestowed equal talents on each. The only difference is, they have been thrown into different scenes of life; and have had commerce with persons of different stations.

Nor are manners and behaviour more easily caught, than opinions, and principles. In childhood and youth, we naturally adopt the sentiments of those about us. And as we advance in life, how few of us think for ourselves? How many of us are satisfied with taking our opinions at second-hand?

The great power and force of custom forms another argument against keeping bad company. However seriously disposed we may be; and however shocked at the first approaches of vice; this shocking appearance goes off, upon an intimacy with it. Custom will soon render the most disgustful thing familiar. And this is indeed a kind provision of nature, to render labour, and toil, and danger, which are the lot of man, more easy to him. The raw soldier, who trembles at the first encounter, becomes a hardy veteran in a few campaigns. Habit renders danger familiar, and of course indifferent to him.

But habit, which is intended for our good, may, like other kind appointments of nature, be converted into a mischief. The well disposed youth, entering first into bad company, is shocked at what he hears, and what he sees. The good principles, which he had imbibed, ring in his ears an alarming lesson against the wickedness of his companions. But, alas! this sensibility is but of a day's continuance. The next jovial meeting makes the horrid picture of yesterday more easily endured. Virtue is soon thought a severe rule; the gospel, an inconvenient restraint: a few pangs of conscience now and then interrupt his pleasures; and whisper to him, that he once had better thoughts: but even these by degrees die away; and he who at first was shocked even at the appearance of vice, is formed by custom into a profligate leader of vicious pleasures—perhaps into an abandoned tempter to vice.—So carefully should we oppose the first approaches of sin! so vigilant should we be against so insidious an enemy!

Our own bad inclinations form another argument against bad company. We have so many passions and appetites to govern; so many bad propensities of different kinds to watch, that, amidst such a variety of enemies within, we ought at least to be on our guard against those without. The breast even of a good man is represented in scripture, and experienced in fact, to be in a state of warfare. His vicious inclinations are continually drawing him one way; while his virtue is making efforts another. And if the scriptures represent this as the case even of a good man, whose passions, it may be imagined, are become in some degree cool, and temperate, and

* See this subject treated more at large in an anonymous pamphlet, on the employment of time.

and who has made ſome progreſs in a virtuous courſe; what may we ſuppoſe to be the danger of a raw unexperienced youth, whoſe paſſions and appetites are violent and ſeducing, and whoſe mind is in a ſtill leſs confirmed ſtate? It is his part ſurely to keep out of the way of temptation; and to give his bad inclinations as little room as poſſible to acquire new ſtrength. *Gilpin.*

§ 38. *Ridicule one of the chief arts of corruption—bad company injures our characters, as well as manners—preſumption the forerunner of ruin—the advantages of good company equal to the diſadvantages of bad—cautions in forming intimacies.*

Theſe arguments againſt keeping bad company, will ſtill receive additional ſtrength, if we conſider farther, the great pains taken by the bad to corrupt others. It is a very true, but lamentable fact, in the hiſtory of human nature, that bad men take more pains to corrupt their own ſpecies, than virtuous men do to reform them. Hence thoſe ſpecious arts, that ſhow of friendſhip, that appearance of diſintereſtedneſs, with which the profligate ſeducer endeavours to lure the unwary youth; and at the ſame time, yielding to his inclinations, ſeems to follow rather than to lead him. Many are the arts of theſe corrupters; but their principal art is ridicule. By this they endeavour to laugh out of countenance all the better principles of their wavering proſelyte; and make him think contemptibly of thoſe, whom he formerly reſpected; by this they ſtifle the ingenuous bluſh, and finally deſtroy all ſenſe of ſhame. Their cauſe is below argument. They aim not therefore at reaſoning. Raillery is the weapon they employ; and who is there, that hath the ſteadineſs to hear perſons and things, whatever reverence he may have had for them, the ſubject of continual ridicule, without loſing that reverence by degrees?

Having thus conſidered what principally makes bad company dangerous, I ſhall juſt add, that even were your morals in no danger from ſuch intercourſe, your characters would infallibly ſuffer. The world will always judge of you by your companions: and nobody will ſuppoſe, that a youth of virtuous principles himſelf, can poſſibly form a connection with a profligate.

In reply to the danger ſuppoſed to ariſe from bad company, perhaps the youth may ſay, he is ſo firm in his own opinions, ſo ſteady in his principles, that he thinks himſelf ſecure; and need not reſtrain himſelf from the moſt unreſerved converſation.

Alas! this ſecurity is the very brink of the precipice: nor hath vice in her whole train a more dangerous enemy to you, than preſumption. Caution, ever awake to danger, is a guard againſt it. But ſecurity lays every guard aſleep. "Let him who thinketh he "ſtandeth," ſaith the apoſtle, "take heed, "leſt he fall." Even an apoſtle himſelf did fall, by thinking that he ſtood ſecure. "Though I ſhould die with thee," ſaid St. Peter to his maſter, "yet will I not deny thee." That very night, notwithſtanding this boaſted ſecurity, he repeated the crime three ſeveral times. And can we ſuppoſe, that preſumption, which occaſioned an apoſtle's fall, ſhall not ruin an unexperienced youth? The ſtory is recorded for our inſtruction; and ſhould be a ſtanding leſſon againſt preſuming upon our own ſtrength.

In concluſion, ſuch as the dangers are, which ariſe from bad company, ſuch are the advantages, which accrue from good. We imitate, and catch the manners and ſentiments

ments of good men, as we do of bad. Custom, which renders vice less a deformity, renders virtue more lovely. Good examples have a force beyond instruction, and warm us into emulation beyond precept; while the countenance and conversation of virtuous men encourage, and draw out into action every kindred disposition of our hearts.

Besides, as a sense of shame often prevents our doing a right thing in bad company; it operates in the same way in preventing our doing a wrong one in good. Our character becomes a pledge; and we cannot, without a kind of dishonour, draw back.

It is not possible, indeed, for a youth, yet unfurnished with knowledge (which fits him for good company) to chuse his companions as he pleases. A youth must have something peculiarly attractive, to qualify him for the acquaintance of men of established reputation. What he has to do, is, at all events, to avoid bad company; and to endeavour, by improving his mind and morals, to qualify himself for the best.

Happy is that youth, who, upon his entrance into the world, can chuse his company with discretion. There is often in vice, a gaiety, an unreserve, a freedom of manners, which are apt at sight to engage the unwary: while virtue, on the other hand, is often modest, reserved, diffident, backward, and easily disconcerted. That freedom of manners, however engaging, may cover a very corrupt heart: and this aukwardness, however unpleasing, may veil a thousand virtues. Suffer not your mind, therefore, to be easily either engaged, or disgusted at first sight. Form your intimacies with reserve: and if drawn unawares into an acquaintance you disapprove, immediately retreat. Open not your hearts to every profession of friendship. They, whose friendship is worth accepting, are, as you ought to be, reserved in offering it. Chuse your companions, not merely for the sake of a few outward accomplishments—for the idle pleasure of spending an agreeable hour; but mark their disposition to virtue or vice; and, as much as possible, chuse those for your companions, whom you see others respect: always remembering, that upon the choice of your company depends in a great measure the success of all you have learned; the hopes of your friends; your future characters in life; and, what you ought above all other things to value, the purity of your hearts. *Gilpin.*

§ 39. *On Honour.*

Every principle that is a motive to good actions ought to be encouraged, since men are of so different a make, that the same principle does not work equally upon all minds. What some men are prompted to by conscience, duty, or religion, which are only different names for the same thing, others are prompted to by honour.

The sense of honour is of so fine and delicate a nature, that it is only to be met with in minds which are naturally noble, or in such as have been cultivated by great examples, or a refined education. This essay therefore is chiefly designed for those, who by means of any of these advantages are, or ought to be, actuated by this glorious principle.

But as nothing is more pernicious than a principle of action, when it is misunderstood, I shall consider honour with respect to three sorts of men. First of all, with regard to those who have a right notion of it. Secondly, with regard to those who have a mistaken notion of it. And thirdly, with regard to those who treat it as chimerical, and turn it into ridicule.

In

In the firſt place, true honour, though it be a different principle from religion, is that which produces the ſame effects. The lines of action, though drawn from different parts, terminate in the ſame point. Religion embraces virtue as it is enjoined by the laws of God; honour, as it is graceful and ornamental to human nature. The religious man fears, the man of honour ſcorns, to do an ill action. The latter conſiders vice as ſomething that is beneath him; the other, as ſomething that is offenſive to the Divine Being: the one, as what is unbecoming; the other, as what is forbidden. Thus Seneca ſpeaks in the natural and genuine language of a man of honour, when he declares "that were there no God to ſee or puniſh vice, he would not commit it, becauſe it is of ſo mean, ſo baſe, and ſo vile a nature."

I ſhall conclude this head with the deſcription of honour in the part of young Juba:

> Honour's a ſacred tie, the law of kings,
> The noble mind's diſtinguiſhing perfection,
> That aids and ſtrengthens virtue when it
> meets her,
> And imitates her actions where ſhe is not;
> It ought not to be ſported with. Cato.

In the ſecond place, we are to conſider thoſe, who have miſtaken notions of honour. And theſe are ſuch as eſtabliſh any thing to themſelves for a point of honour, which is contrary either to the laws of God, or of their country; who think it more honourable to revenge, than to forgive an injury; who make no ſcruple of telling a lye, but would put any man to death that accuſes them of it; who are more careful to guard their reputation by their courage than by their virtue. True fortitude is indeed ſo becoming in human nature, that he who wants it ſcarce deſerves the name of a man; but we find ſeveral who ſo much abuſe this notion, that they place the whole idea of honour in a kind of brutal courage; by which means we have had many among us, who have called themſelves men of honour, that would have been a diſgrace to a gibbet. In a word, the man who ſacrifices any duty of a reaſonable creature to a prevailing mode or faſhion; who looks upon any thing as honourable that is diſpleaſing to his Maker, or deſtructive to ſociety; who thinks himſelf obliged by this principle to the practice of ſome virtues, and not of others, is by no means to be reckoned among true men of honour.

Timogenes was a lively inſtance of one actuated by falſe honour. Timogenes would ſmile at a man's jeſt who ridiculed his Maker, and at the ſame time run a man through the body that ſpoke ill of his friend. Timogenes would have ſcorned to have betrayed a ſecret that was intruſted with him, though the fate of his country depended upon the diſcovery of it. Timogenes took away the life of a young fellow in a duel, for having ſpoken ill of Belinda, a lady whom he himſelf had ſeduced in her youth, and betrayed into want and ignominy. To cloſe his character, Timogenes, after having ruined ſeveral poor tradeſmen's families who had truſted him, ſold his eſtate to ſatisfy his creditors; but, like a man of honour, diſpoſed of all the money he could make of it, in paying off his play debts, or, to ſpeak in his own language, his debts of honour.

In the third place, we are to conſider thoſe perſons, who treat this principle as chimerical, and turn it into ridicule. Men who are profeſſedly of no honour, are of a more profligate and abandoned nature than even thoſe who are actuated by falſe notions of it; as there is more hope of an heretic than of an atheiſt. Theſe ſons of infamy conſider honour, with old

old Syphax in the play before-mentioned, as a fine imaginary notion that leads astray young unexperienced men, and draws them into real mischiefs, while they are engaged in the pursuit of a shadow. These are generally persons who, in Shakespeare's phrase, "are worn and hackneyed in the ways of men;" whose imaginations are grown callous, and have lost all those delicate sentiments which are natural to minds that are innocent and undepraved. Such old battered miscreants ridicule every thing as romantic, that comes in competition with their present interest; and treat those persons as visionaries, who dare to stand up, in a corrupt age, for what has not its immediate reward joined to it. The talents, interest, or experience of such men, make them very often useful in all parties, and at all times. But whatever wealth and dignities they may arrive at, they ought to consider, that every one stands as a blot in the annals of his country, who arrives at the temple of honour by any other way than through that of virtue.

Guardian.

§ 40. *On Modesty.*

I know no two words that have been more abused by the different and wrong interpretations, which are put upon them, than these two, Modesty and Assurance. To say such a one is a modest man, sometimes indeed passes for a good character; but at present is very often used to signify a sheepish, awkward fellow, who has neither good-breeding, politeness, nor any knowledge of the world.

Again: A man of assurance, though at first it only denoted a person of a free and open carriage, is now very usually applied to a profligate wretch, who can break through all the rules of decency and morality without a blush.

I shall endeavour, therefore, in this essay, to restore these words to their true meaning, to prevent the idea of Modesty from being confounded with that of Sheepishness, and to hinder Impudence from passing for Assurance.

If I was put to define Modesty, I would call it, The reflection of an ingenuous mind, either when a man has committed an action for which he censures himself, or fancies that he is exposed to the censure of others.

For this reason, a man, truly modest, is as much so when he is alone as in company; and as subject to a blush in his closet as when the eyes of multitudes are upon him.

I do not remember to have met with any instance of modesty with which I am so well pleased, as that celebrated one of the young Prince, whose father, being a tributary king to the Romans, had several complaints laid against him before the senate, as a tyrant and oppressor of his subjects. The Prince went to Rome to defend his father; but coming into the senate, and hearing a multitude of crimes proved upon him, was so oppressed when it came to his turn to speak, that he was unable to utter a word. The story tells us, that the fathers were more moved at this instance of modesty and ingenuity, than they could have been by the most pathetic oration; and, in short, pardoned the guilty father for this early promise of virtue in the son.

I take Assurance to be, The faculty of possessing a man's self, or of saying and doing indifferent things without any uneasiness or emotion in the mind. That which generally gives a man assurance, is a moderate knowledge of the world; but above all, a mind fixed and determined in itself to do nothing against the rules of honour and decency. An open and assured behaviour is the natural consequence of such a resolution. A man thus armed, if his words or actions are at any time misinterpreted, retires within himself, and from a consciousness of his own integrity, assumes force enough to despise the little censures of ignorance or malice.

Every one ought to cherish and encourage in himself the modesty and assurance I have here mentioned.

A man without assurance is liable to be made uneasy by the folly or ill-nature of every one he converses with. A man without modesty is lost to all sense of honour and virtue.

It is more than probable, that the Prince above-mentioned possessed both those qualifications in a very eminent degree. Without assurance, he would never have undertaken to speak before the most august assembly in the world; without modesty, he would have pleaded the cause he had taken upon him, though it had appeared ever so scandalous.

From what has been said, it is plain that modesty and assurance are both amiable, and may very well meet in the same person. When they are thus mixed and blended together, they compose what we endeavour to express, when we say, a modest assurance; by which we understand, the just mean between bashfulness and impudence.

I shall conclude with observing, that as the same man may be both modest and assured, so it is also possible for the same person to be both impudent and bashful.

We have frequent instances of this odd kind of mixture in people of depraved minds and mean education; who, though they are not able to meet a man's eyes, or pronounce a sentence without confusion, can voluntarily commit the greatest villainies or most indecent actions.

Such a person seems to have made a resolution to do ill, even in spite of himself, and in defiance of all those checks and restraints his temper and complexion seem to have laid in his way.

Upon the whole, I would endeavour to establish this maxim, That the practice of virtue is the most proper method to give a man a becoming assurance in his words and actions. Guilt always seeks to shelter itself in one of the extremes; and is sometimes attended with both. *Spectator.*

§ 41. *The Choice of Hercules.*

When Hercules was in that part of his youth, in which it was natural for him to consider what course of life he ought to pursue, he one day retired into a desert, where the silence and solitude of the place very much favoured his meditations. As he was musing on his present condition, and very much perplexed in himself on the state of life he should chuse, he saw two women, of a larger stature than ordinary, approaching towards him. One of them had a very noble air, and graceful deportment; her beauty was natural and easy, her person clean and unspotted, her eyes cast towards the ground with an agreeable reserve, her motion and behaviour full of modesty, and her raiment as white as snow. The other had a great deal of health and floridness in her countenance, which she had helped with an artificial white and red; and she endeavoured to appear more graceful than ordinary in her mien, by a mixture of affectation in all her gestures. She had a wonderful confidence and assurance in her looks, and all the variety of colours in her dress, that she thought were the most proper to shew her complexion to advantage. She cast her eyes upon herself, then turned them on those that were present, to see how they liked her, and often looked on the figure she made in her own shadow. Upon her nearer approach to Hercules, she stepped before the other lady, who came forward with a regular, composed carriage, and running up to him, accosted him after the following manner.

"My dear Hercules," says she, "I find you are very much divided in your thoughts upon the way of life that you ought to chuse: be my friend, and follow me; I will lead you into the possession of pleasure, and out of the reach of pain, and remove you from all the noise and disquietude of business. The affairs of either war or peace shall have no power to disturb you. Your whole employment shall be to make your life easy, and to entertain every sense with its proper gratifications. Sumptuous tables, beds of roses, clouds of perfumes, concerts of music, crowds of beauties, are all in readiness to receive you. Come along with me into this region of delights, this world of pleasure, and bid farewel for ever to care, to pain, to business." Hercules hearing the lady talk after this manner, desired to know her name: to which she answered, "My friends, and those who are well acquainted with me, call me Happiness; but my enemies, and those who would injure my reputation, have given me the name of Pleasure."

By this time the other lady was come up, who addressed the young hero in a very different manner:—"Hercules," says she, "I offer myself to you, because I know you are descended from the Gods, and give proofs of that descent, by your love to virtue, and application to the studies proper for your age. This makes me hope you will gain, both for yourself and me, an immortal reputation. But before I invite you into my society and friendship, I will be open and sincere with you; and must lay this down as an established truth, that there is nothing truly valuable, which can be purchased without pains and labour. The Gods have set a price upon every real and noble pleasure. If you would gain the favour of the Deity, you must be at the pains of worshipping him; if the friendship of good men, you must study to oblige them; if you would be honoured by your country, you must take care to serve it: in short, if you would be eminent in war or peace, you must become master of all the qualifications that can make you so. These are the only terms and conditions upon which I can propose happiness."

The Goddess of Pleasure here broke in upon her discourse: "You see," said she, "Hercules, by her own confession, the way to her pleasures is long and difficult; whereas that which I propose is short and easy." "Alas!" said the other lady, whose visage glowed with passion, made up of scorn and pity, "what are the pleasures you propose? To eat before you are hungry, drink before you are athirst, sleep before you are tired; to gratify appetites before they are raised, and raise such appetites as nature never planted. You never heard the most delicious music, which is the praise of one's-self; nor saw the most beautiful object, which is the work of one's own hands. Your votaries pass away their youth in a dream of mistaken pleasures; while they are hoarding up anguish, torment, and remorse, for old age.

"As for me, I am the friend of Gods, and of good men; an agreeable companion to the artizan; an houshold guardian to the fathers of families; a patron and protector of servants; an associate in all true and generous friendships. The banquets of my votaries are never costly, but always delicious; for none eat or drink at them, who are not invited by hunger and thirst. Their slumbers are sound, and their wakings chearful. My young men have the pleasure of hearing themselves praised by those who are in years; and those who are in years, of being honoured by those who are young. In a word, my followers are favoured by the Gods, beloved by their acquaintance, esteemed by their country, and, after the close of their labours, honoured by posterity."

We know, by the life of this memorable hero, to which of these two ladies he gave up his heart; and, I believe, every one who reads this, will do him the justice to approve his choice. *Tatler.*

CATECHETICAL LECTURES.

§ 42. *Introduction to the Catechism.*

The Catechism begins with a recital of our baptismal vow, as a kind of preface to the whole. It then lays down the great christian principle of faith; and leaving all mysterious inquiries, in which this subject is involved, it passes on to the rules of practice. Having briefly recited these, it concludes with a simple, and a very intelligible explanation of baptism, and the Lord's Supper.

The chatechism then begins very properly, with a recital of our baptismal vow, as the best preface to that belief, and those rules of practice, in which that vow engaged us.—But before we examine the vow itself, two appendages of it require explanation—the use of sponsors—and the addition of a name.

With regard to the sponsor, the church probably imitates the appointment of the legal guardian, making the best provision it can for the pious education of orphans, and deserted children. The temporal and the spiritual guardian may equally betray their trust: both are culpable: both accountable: but surely the latter breaks the more sacred engagement.

As to promising and vowing in the name of another (which seems to carry so harsh a sound) the sponsor only engages for the child, as any one would engage for another, in a matter which is manifestly for his advantage: and on a supposition, that the child hereafter will see it to be so—that is, he promises, as he takes it for granted, the child itself would have promised, if it had been able.

With regard to the name, it is no part of the sacrament; nor pretends to scriptural authority. It rests merely on ancient usage. A custom had generally obtained, of giving a new name, upon adopting a new member into a family. We find it common among the Greeks, the Romans, and the Jews; nay, we read that even God himself, when he received Abram into covenant, giving an early sanction to this usage, changed his name to Abraham. In imitation of this common practice, the old christians gave baptismal names to their children, which were intended to point out their heavenly adoption, as their surnames distinguished their temporal alliance.

From considering the use of sponsors, and of the name in baptism, we proceed next to the vow itself, which is thus expressed, "My "godfathers did promise three things in my "name: 1st, That I should renounce the "devil, and all his works, the pomps and "vanities of this wicked world, and all the "sinful lusts of the flesh. 2dly, That I should "believe all the articles of the christian faith; "and 3dly, That I should keep God's holy "will, and commandments, and walk in the "same all the days of my life."

First then, we promise to "renounce the "devil, and all his works, the pomps and vanities of this wicked world, and all the sinful lusts of the flesh." "The devil, the "world, and the flesh," is a comprehensive mode of expressing every species of sin; however

ever distinguished; and from whatever source derived: all which we not only engage to renounce as far as we are able; but also to take pains in tracing the labyrinths of our own hearts; and in removing the glosses of self-deceit. Without this, all renunciation of sin is pretence.

Being thus injoined to renounce our gross, habitual sins, and those bad inclinations, which lead us into them; we are required next to "believe all the articles of the christian faith." This is a natural progression. When we are thoroughly convinced of the malignity of sin, we in course wish to avoid the ill consequences of it; and are prepared to give a fair hearing to the evidence of religion. There is a close connection between vice and infidelity. They mutually support each other. The same connection subsists between a well-disposed mind, and the truths of religion: and faith perhaps is not so involuntary an act, as many of our modern philosophers would persuade us.

After "believing the articles of the christian "faith," we are lastly injoined to "keep God's "holy will and commandments." Here too is the same natural progression. As the renunciation of sin prepares the way for faith, so does faith, lead directly to obedience. They seem related to each other, as the mean and the end. "The end of the commandment," saith the apostle, "is charity, out of a pure heart, "and good conscience, and faith, unfeigned." Faith (which is the act of believing upon rational evidence) is the great fountain, from which all christian virtues spring. No man will obey a law, till he hath informed himself whether it be properly authorized: or, in other words, till he believe in the jurisdiction that enacted it.—If our faith in Christ doth not lead us to obey him; it is what the scriptures call a dead faith, in opposition to a saving one.

To this inseparable connection between faith and obedience, St. Paul's doctrine may be objected, where he seems to lay the whole stress on faith, in opposition to works *.—But it is plain, that St. Paul's argument requires him to mean by faith, the whole system of the christian religion (which is indeed the meaning of the word in many other parts of scripture); and by works, which he sets in opposition to it, the moral law. So that in fact, the apostle's argument relates not to the present question; but tends only to establish the superiority of christianity. The moral law, argues the apostle, which claimed on the righteousness of works, makes no provision for the deficiencies of man. Christianity alone, by opening a door of mercy, gave him hopes of that salvation, which the other could not pretend to give.

Upon renouncing sin, believing the articles of the christian faith, and keeping God's holy commandments, as far as sinful man can keep them, we are intitled by promise to all the privileges of the gospel. We "become members "of Christ, children of God, and inheritors "of the kingdom of heaven." We are redeemed through the merits of Christ; pardoned through the mercies of God; and rewarded with a blessed immortality.

This account of our baptismal vow concludes with a question, leading us to acknowledge the necessity of observing this vow; and to declare our belief, that our only hope of keeping it rests upon the assistance of God.

Gilpin.

§ 43. *On the Creed—the Belief of God.*

The creed begins with a profession of our belief in "God the Father almighty, maker of heaven and earth."

* See Rom. iii. 28. and indeed great part of the epistle.

The

The being of a God is one of those truths, which scarce require proof. A proof seems rather an injury, as it supposes doubt. However, as young minds, though not sceptical, are uninformed, it may not be improper to select out of the variety of arguments, which evince this great truth, two or three of the most simple.

The existence of a Deity, we prove from the light of nature. For his attributes, at least in any perfection, we must look into scripture.

A few plain and simple arguments drawn from the creation of the world—the preservation of it—and the general consent of mankind, strike us with more conviction, than all the subtilties of metaphysical deduction.

We prove the being of a God first from the creation of the world.

The world must have been produced either by design, or by chance. No other mode of origin can be supposed. Let us see then with which of these characters it is impressed.

The characteristic of the works of design, is a relation of parts, in order to produce an end—The characteristic of the works of chance is just the reverse.—When we see stones, answering each other, laid in the form of a regular building, we immediately say, they were put together by design: but when we seen them thrown about in a disorderly heap, we say as confidently, they have been thrown so by chance.

Now, in the world, and all its appendages, there is plainly this appearance of design. One part relates to another; and the whole together produces an end. The sun, for instance, is connected with the earth, by warming it into a proper heat, for the production of its fruits; and furnishing it with rain and dew. The earth again is connected with all the vegetables which it produces, by providing them with proper soils, and juices for their nourishment. These again are connected with animals, by supplying them with food. And the whole together produces the great end of sustaining the lives of innumerable creatures.

Nor is design shewn only in the grand fabric of the world, and all its relative appendages: it is equally shewn in every part. It is seen in every animal, adapted in all its peculiarities to its proper mode of life. It is seen in every vegetable, furnished with parts exactly suited to its situation. In the least, as well as in the greatest of nature's productions, it is every where apparent. The little creeper upon the wall, extending its tenacious fibres, draws nourishment from the crannies of the stones; and flourishes where no other plant could live.

If then the world, and every part of it, are thus marked with the characters of design, there can be no difficulty in acknowledging the author of such design—of such amazing contrivance and variety, to be a being of infinite wisdom and power. We call a man ingenious, who makes even a common globe, with all the parts of the earth delineated upon it. What shall we say then of the author of the great original itself, in all its grandeur, and furnished with all its various inhabitants?

The argument drawn from the preservation of the world, is indeed rather the last argument advanced a step farther.

If chance could be supposed to produce a regular form, yet it is certainly beyond the highest degree of credulity, to suppose, it could continue this regularity for any time. But we find it has been continued: we find, that near 6000 years have made no change in the order and harmony of the world. The sun's action upon the earth hath ever been regular. The production of trees, plants, and herbs,

herbs, hath ever been uniform. Every ſeed produces now the ſame fruit it ever did. Every ſpecies of animal life is ſtill the ſame. Could chance continue this regular arrangement? Could any thing continue it, but the hand of an omnipotent God!

Laſtly, we ſee this great truth, the being of a God, witneſſed by the general conſent of mankind. This general conſent muſt ariſe either from tradition, or it muſt be the reſult of men's own reaſoning. Upon either ſuppoſition, it is an argument equally ſtrong. If the firſt ſuppoſition be allowed, it will be difficult to aſſign any ſource of this tradition, but God himſelf. If the ſecond, it can ſcarce be ſuppoſed that all mankind, in different parts of the world, ſhould agree in the belief of a thing, which never exiſted. For though doubts have ariſen concerning this general belief, yet it is now pretty well aſcertained, from the accounts of travellers, that no nation hath yet been diſcovered, among whom ſome traces of religious worſhip have not been found.

Be it ſo, ſays the objector; yet ſtill we find ſingle perſons, even in civilized countries, and ſome of them men of enlarged capacities, who have not only had their doubts on this ſubject; but have proclaimed aloud their diſbelief of a divine being.

We anſwer, that it is more than probable, no man's infidelity on this head was ever thoroughly ſettled. Bad men, rather endeavour to convince themſelves, than are really convinced.—But even on a ſuppoſition, that a few ſuch perſons could be found, what is their teſtimony againſt ſo great a majority, as the reſt of mankind? The light of the ſun is univerſally acknowledged, though it happens, that, now and then, a man may be born blind.

6

But ſince, it ſeems, there are difficulties in ſuppoſing a divine creator, and preſerver of the world, what ſyſtem of things does the atheiſt ſuppoſe attended with fewer? He ſees the world produced before him. He ſees it hath been created; and is preſerved. Some account of this matter muſt be given. If ours diſpleaſe him; let us have his.

The experiment hath been tried. We have had many atheiſtical creeds: none of which hath ſtood the teſt of being handed down with any degree of credit into future times.

The atheiſt's great argument indeed againſt a Deity, is levelled at the apparent injuſtice of his government. It was an objection of ancient date; and might have had its weight in heathen times: but it is one of the bleſſings, which attends chriſtianity, that it ſatisfies all our doubts on this head; and gives us a rational and eaſy ſolution of this poignant objection. What if we obſerve an inaccurate diſtribution of the things of this world? What if virtue be depreſſed, and vice triumphant? It is nothing, ſays the voice of religion, to him, who believes this life to be an inconſiderable part of his being; a point only in the expanſe of eternity: who believes he is ſent into this world, merely to prepare himſelf for a better. This world, he knows, is intended neither for reward, nor puniſhment. Happineſs unqueſtionably attends virtue even here, and miſery, vice: but it is not the happineſs of a ſplendid ſtation, but of a peaceful mind; nor is it the miſery of low circumſtances, but of a guilty conſcience. The things of this world are not, in their own nature, connected either with happineſs or miſery. Attended ſometimes by one, and ſometimes by the other, they are merely the means of trial. One man is tempted with riches, and another with poverty; but God intends

intends neither an elevated, nor a depressed situation as the ultimate completion of his will.

Besides, if worldly prosperity even was the indication of God's favour, yet good men may have failings and imprudencies enough about them to deserve misfortune; and bad men virtues, which may deserve success. Why should imprudence, though joined with virtue, partake of its reward? Or the generous purpose share in the punishment, though connected with vice?

Thus then we see the being of a God is the universal creed of nature But though nature could investigate the simple truth, she could not preserve it from error. Nature merely takes her notions from what she sees, and what she hears, and hath ever moulded her gods in the likeness of things in heaven, and things on earth. Hence every part of the creation, animate and inanimate, hath, by turns, been an object of worship. And even the most refined nations, we know, had gross conceptions on this head. The wisest of them indeed, by observing the wonders of creation, could clothe the Deity with wisdom and power: but they could go no farther. The virtues of their heroes afforded them the highest ideas of perfection: and with these they arrayed their gods; mixing also with their virtues, such vices, as are found in the characters of the best of men.

For just notions of the Deity, we must have recourse then to revelation alone. Revelation removes all these absurdities. It dispels the clouds of ignorance; and unveils the divine majesty, as far as it can be the object of human contemplation. The lax notions of libertinism, on one hand, which make the Deity an inobservant governor; and the gloomy ideas of superstition, on the other, which suppose him to be a dark malignant being, are equally exposed. Here we are informed of the omniscience and omnipresence of God. Here we learn, that his wisdom and power are equalled by his goodness; and that his mercy is over all his works. In short, we learn from revelation, that we are in the hands of a being, whose knowledge we cannot evade, and whose power we cannot resist; who is merciful and good to all his creatures; and will be ever ready to assist and reward those, who endeavour to conform themselves to his will: but whose justice, at the same time, accompanying his mercy, will punish the bold and careless sinner in proportion to his guilt. *Gilpin.*

§ 44. *On the Creed continued—the Belief of Jesus Christ.*

After professing our belief in God, the creed proceeds with a profession of our belief "in Jesus Christ, his son, our Lord."

A person celebrated as Jesus Christ was, we may suppose, would naturally find a place in the profane history of his times. It may not be amiss, therefore, to introduce the evidence we are about to collect, with the testimony of some of the more eminent of the heathen writers, who have mentioned him. They will at least inform us, that such a person lived at the time we assert; and that he was the author of a new religion.—I shall quote only Suetonius, Tacitus, and Pliny.

Suetonius *, tells us, that "the emperor Claudius drove all the Jews from Rome, who, at the instigation of one Christ, were continually making disturbances."

Tacitus †, speaking of the persecution of christians, tells us, "that the author of

* In vita Claud, Cæs. † Lib. 15.

that

that name was Christ, who was put to death by Pontius Pilate, in the reign of Tiberius."

Pliny's * testimony is more large. It is contained in a letter, written to the emperor Trajan, desiring his instructions with regard to christians. He blames their obstinacy in refusing to sacrifice to the Roman deities—but from their own confession can draw nothing, but that they assemble, on a certain day, before sun-rise—that they pay divine honours to Christ as a God—that they bind themselves by a sacrament not to steal, nor to commit adultery, nor to deceive—and that, after the performance of these rites, they join in one common meal. Nay, he examined, he says, two of them by torture: yet still he finds nothing obnoxious in their behaviour, except their absurd superstitions. He thinks, however, the matter should be inquired into: for christianity had brought religion into great disuse. The markets were crowded with victims; and scarce a purchaser came near them.

These writers afford us sufficient testimony, that Jesus Christ lived at the time we assert; and that he was the author of a new religion. They had opportunities of being well informed; could have no interest in falsifying; were no converts to the new sect; but talk of Christ, only as they would of any singular person, whom they had occasion to mention. Their testimony therefore is beyond cavil.

Let us now proceed a step farther, and examine the scripture evidence of Christ, which proves not only his existence; but that he is our Lord, or the Messiah—and not only that he was the author of a new religion; but that this religion is true.

* Lib. 10.

Upon examining
dence on this head,
laid upon miracles
which are direct app
to supernatural pow
these modes of evide
for us who live in re
who lived in the ea
from miracles seem
dressed to them; as
us. They were the
racles of the gospel
the evidence at secon
phecy is a mode of
through every age.
it in part; but to us
more unfolded; and
texture displayed.—I
order.

Among the eye-w
racles, were many lea
learned. The form
abilities to examine
to trace out fraud,
and did unquestiona
that circumspection
wonderful exhibition
the christian faith:
spectator was a com
fact; and many of
were such as could n
ture of the facts the
fraud.

It had a strange
mankind, that a cru
Saviour of the worl
pose, that any man,
tude of men, woul
without clear conv
worldly advantage l
lief; and the conv

world, and embraced a life of persecution.—Let us consider the single miracle of Christ's resurrection. Jesus had frequently mentioned it before his death; and the thing was so far in general credited, that the sepulchre was sealed, and an armed guard appointed to watch it. We may well suppose, therefore, that his favourers would naturally, upon this occasion, reason thus: "Jesus hath now put his pretensions upon a fair issue. He hath told us, he will arise from the dead on the third day:—here then let us suspend our judgment, and wait the result. Three days will determine whether he be an impostor, or the real Messiah."—It is very natural to suppose, that the favourers of Jesus would reason, after his death, in a manner like this: and it is beyond credibility, that any of them would have continued his disciples, had they found him falsifying in this point. But we know they did continue his disciples after this. We know also, that many proselytes, convinced by this very event, embraced the christian religion.—We have all the reason in the world therefore to believe, that they were fully satisfied. His miracles were to them a sufficient proof of his pretensions. All candid men would have acquiesced, as they did; and in their belief we have a very strong foundation for our own.

Again, with regard to prophecy, we observe, that the writers of the Old Testament seem, in various parts, to characterize some extraordinary person, who was in process of time to make his appearance in the world. The marks are peculiar, and can neither be mistaken nor misapplied. "He was to be born of a virgin—he was to turn the hearts of the disobedient to the wisdom of the just—though dignified with the characters of a prince, he was to be a man of sorrows, and acquainted with grief—though described to be without sin, he was to be numbered with transgressors——his hands and his feet were to be pierced—he was to be made an offering for sin—and was never to see corruption."—These prophecies were published many hundred years before the birth of Christ; and had been all along in the hands, not only of the Jews, but of all men of letters.—The Old Testament had been early translated into the Greek language; and received into the politest libraries of those times.

With these ideas, let us open the New Testament, and it is obvious that no picture can be more like its original, than these prophecies of Christ in one Testament, are to his history in the other. Here we see that extraordinary virgin-birth unravelled.—Here we see a life spent in turning the hearts of the disobedient to the wisdom of the just—Here we find the prince of his people, a man of sorrows, and acquainted with grief.——Here we see the Lord of righteousness numbered with transgressors—we see his hands and his feet pierced—we see him made an offering for sin—and we see realized that extraordinary idea of death without corruption.

It were an easy matter to carry this comparison through a more minute detail of circumstances: but I mean only to trace the outlines of this great resemblance. To compleat the picture would be a copious work.

Besides these predictions, which related immediately to the life and death of Christ; there were many others, which deserve notice. Among these the two great leading prophecies were those of the calling of the Gentiles, and of the dispersion of the Jews.

The calling of the Gentiles was one of the earliest prophecies of the Old Testament. The Jews were distinguished in appearance, as the favourite people of God; and they were sufficiently elated upon that distinction. But if they had attended closely to their prophets, they might have discovered, that all the prophecies, which described the happy state of the church, had evidently a more distant prospect, than to them. Those early promises, in particular, which were repeated to the patriarchs, were not merely confined to their posterity; but included "all the nations of the earth *."—And when the later prophets, as the great event approached, spoke a plainer, and a more intelligible language, the whole nation might have understood, as Simeon, and some of the wisest and most intelligible of them did understand, that "a light was sprung up to lighten the Gentiles."

The prophecy of the dispersion of the Jewish nation is also very antient, being attributed by Moses to the patriarch Jacob. "The sceptre shall not depart from Judah, until Shiloh come." Whatever may be the precise meaning of the word 'sceptre' in the original; and though it may not perhaps properly signify that idea of regal power, which it conveys to our ears; yet it certainly means some badge of authority, that implies a formed and settled government. And, as to the word 'Shiloh,' all commentators, jewish as well as christian, explain it to mean the Messiah—The sense therefore of the prophecy is plainly this—that the Jews should continue in the form of a society, till the time of the Messiah. Accordingly we find that, soon after Christ's death, the sceptre did depart from Judah; the Jews lost all form of a political society; and are a singular instance of a people, scattered over the whole earth, preserved to this day separate from all other people, and yet without a settlement any where.

Our Saviour's prophecy of the growth of his church, is likewise among the more remarkable predictions. He told his disciples, that "his religion was like a grain of mustard-seed, which was the least of all seeds; but when it grew up, it should become a great tree, and the fowls of the air should lodge in the branches of it." He told them also, that "the gates of hell should never prevail against it."

The Jewish religion was continually enforced by the idea of a jealous God, watching over it, and threatening judgments from heaven upon every transgression. The divine authority was stamped openly upon it. The people trembled, and worshipped.

When the impostor Mahomet set up for a reformer, he could not indeed enforce his religion by divine judgments; but he did it by temporal. He drew his sword, and held it to the breasts of his opposers; while he promised to the obedient a full gratification of their passions.

But in the christian religion, nothing of this kind appeared. No temporal judgments threatened on one hand: no sensual indulgences allured on the other. A few desponding ignorant mechanics, the disciples of a person crucified as a common malefactor, were all the parade, with which this religion was ushered into the world; and all the human assistance which it had to boast.——And yet this religion, which opposed the strongest prejudices, and was opposed by the greatest princes, made its way in a few years, from a remote corner, through the whole Roman empire.——Thus was our Saviour's prophecy, in opposition to all human calculation.

* See Gen. xii. 3. xviii. 8. xxii. 18. xxvi. 4.

tion, exactly fulfilled. The least of all seeds became a spreading tree; and a church was established, which could not be destroyed by all the powers of hell.

But although the church of Christ could not be destroyed, it was corrupted; and in a course of years fell from its genuine purity. This corrupt state of it—the delusions of popery—the efforts of reformation, and various other circumstances relating to it, are not unreasonably supposed to be held forth, in the prophetic parts of the New Testament.

But I forbear to dwell upon prophecies, which are not obvious enough to carry general conviction; though many of them have been well explained by those *, who are versed in the histories to which they allude. Future times will, in all probability, reflect a stronger light upon them. Some of the great prophecies, which we have just considered, shone but with a feeble ray, during the times they were fulfilling, though they now strike us in so forcible a manner. *Gilpin.*

* See Bishop Newton's Dissertations; and Bishop Hurd's sermons on prophecy.

§ 45. *The Creed continued—Conception and Birth of Christ, &c.*

We have now shewn upon what foundation we believe the second article of our creed; let us next consider the remaining articles—the history of Christ, as delivered in scripture, and the benefits which he procured for us—the assistance of the Holy Spirit—the remission of our sins—and everlasting life.

First, then, we believe that Christ was "conceived of the Holy Ghost, and born of the virgin Mary." The manner of this miraculous conception we inquire not into. It is a point not only beyond the limits of human inquiry; but to us at least a point very unimportant. We believe just the Scripture-account of it, and assure ourselves, that if it had concerned us, it would have been more plainly revealed.—One thing, however, we may observe on this head, that nothing is said in Scripture of paying divine honours to the virgin Mary. Those rites are totally of popish origin.

We farther believe, that Christ "suffered under Pontius Pilate, was crucified, dead, and buried; and that he descended into hell,"——that is, we declare our belief of the Scripture-account of the circumstances and the reality of Christ's death.

To make an action clear, it is necessary, first, to establish its date. This is usually done by ranging it under the magistrate who then presided, the time of whose government is always registered in some public record.—Thus we believe that Christ's death happened when Pontius Pilate was governor of Judea. We believe also, with regard to the manner of his death, that he was crucified; that he died as really as any mortal ever did; and that he was buried in the tomb of Joseph of Arimathea *.

The "descent into hell" is undoubtedly a more obscure expression than might be wished in a creed, and was not indeed added till many ages after the creed was first composed †. But as creeds are human compositions, we believe this, and every other difficulty, only as consistent with Scripture. Now the sense which seems most agreeable to Scrip-

* Isaiah foretold he should "make his grave with the rich." And St. Matthew tells us, that οψιας γενομενης, ηλθεν ανθρωπος πλουσιος. Matt. xxvii. 57. Isaiah liii. 9.

† See Bingham's Antiquities, vol. iii. c. 3.

ture, is, that his ſoul remained till his reſurrection in that place (whatever that place is) where the ſpirits of the bleſſed reſt: and the expreſſion ſeems to have been added, only that we may the more ſtrongly expreſs our belief of the reality of his death. This we do, when we expreſs our belief of the ſeparation of his ſoul and body. "He was buried,"—and "deſcended into hell." The firſt expreſſion relates to his body, which was laid in the grave; the ſecond to his ſoul, which paſſed into the place of departed ſpirits.

We farther believe, that "on the third day he roſe again from the dead." The reſurrection of Chriſt from the dead is a point of the utmoſt importance to chriſtians. On the certainty of Chriſt's reſurrection depend all hopes of our own. On this article, therefore, we ſhall be more large.

And, in the firſt place, what is there in it that need ſhock our reaſon? It was a wonderful event: but is not nature full of wonderful events? When we ſeriouſly weigh the matter, is it leſs ſtrange, that a grain of corn thrown into the ground ſhould die, and riſe again with new vegetation, than that a human body, in the ſame circumſtances, ſhould aſſume new life? The commonneſs of the former makes it familiar to us, but not in any degree leſs unaccountable. Are we at all more acquainted with the manner in which grain germinates, than with the manner in which a body is raiſed from the dead? And is it not obviouſly ſtriking, that the ſame power which can effect the one, may effect the other alſo?—But analogy, though it tend to convince, is no proof. Let us proceed then to matter of fact.

That the body was dead, and ſafely lodged in the tomb, and afterwards conveyed out of it, was agreed on, both by thoſe who oppoſed, and by thoſe who favoured the reſurrection. In the circumſtances of the latter fact, they differ widely.

The diſciples tell their ſtory—a very plain and ſimple one—that, ſcarce expecting the event, notwithſtanding their maſter had himſelf foretold it, they were ſurpriſed with an account that the body was gone—that they found afterwards, to their great aſtoniſhment, that their maſter was again alive—that they had been ſeveral times with him; and appealed for the truth of what they ſaid to great numbers, who, as well as themſelves, had ſeen him after his reſurrection.

The chief prieſts, on the other ſide, declared the whole to be a forgery; aſſerting, that the plain matter of fact was, the diſciples came by night, and ſtole the body away, while the ſoldiers ſlept.

Such a tale, unſupported by evidence, would be liſtened to in no court of juſtice. It has not even the air of probability. Can it be ſuppoſed, that the diſciples, who had fled with terror when they might have reſcued their maſter's life; would venture, in the face of an armed guard, to carry off his dead body?—Or is it more probable, that they found the whole guard aſleep; when we know, that the vigilance of centinels is ſecured by the ſtricteſt diſcipline?—Beſides, what advantage could ariſe from ſuch an attempt? If they miſcarried, it was certain ruin, both to them and their cauſe. If they ſucceeded, it is difficult to ſay what uſe they could make of their ſucceſs. Unleſs they could have produced their dead body alive, the ſecond error would be worſe than the firſt. Their maſter's prophecy of his own reſurrection was an unhappy circumſtance; yet ſtill it was wrapped in a veil of obſcurity. But

But if his disciples endeavoured to prove its completion, its was their business to look well to the event. A detection would be such a comment upon their master's text, as would never be forgotten.—When a cause depends on falshood, every body knows, the less it is moved the better.

This was the case of the other side. Obscurity there was wanted. If the chief priests had any proof, why did they not produce it? Why were not the disciples taken up, and examined upon the fact? They never absconded. Why were they not judicially tried? Why was not the trial made public? and why were not authentic memorials of the fraud handed down to posterity; as authentic memorials were of the fact, recorded at the very time, and place, where it happened? Christianity never wanted enemies to propagate its disparagement.—But nothing of this kind was done. No proof was attempted—except indeed the testimony of men asleep. The disciples were never questioned upon the fact; and the chief priests rested satisfied with spreading an inconsistent rumour among the people, impressed merely by their own authority.

Whatever records of heathen origin remain, evince the truth of the resurrection. One is very remarkable. Pontius Pilate sent the emperor Tiberius a relation of the death and resurrection of Christ; which were recorded at Rome, as usual, among other provincial matters. This intelligence made so great an impression, it seems, upon the emperor, that he referred it to the senate, whether Jesus Christ of Judea should not be taken into the number of the Roman gods?—Our belief of this fact is chiefly founded upon the testimony of Justin Martyr, and Tertullian, two learned heathens, in the age succeeding Christ, who became christians from this very evidence, among others, in favour of christianity. In their apologies *, still extant, one of which was made to the senate of Rome, the other to a Roman governor, they both appeal to these records of Pontius Pilate, as then generally known; which we cannot conceive such able apologists would have done, if no such records had ever existed †.

Having seen what was of old objected to the resurrection of Christ, it may be proper also to see the objections of modern disbelievers.

And, first, we have the stale objection, that nothing is more common among the propagators of every new religion, than to delude their ignorant proselytes with idle stories. What a variety of inconsistent tales did the votaries of heathenism believe! What absurdities are adopted into the Mahometan creed! To what strange facts do the vulgar papists give credit! And can we suppose better of the resurrection of Christ, than that it was

* Just. Mart. Apol. ad Anton. P.——Tertull. Apol. cap. 15.

† The acts of Pilate, as they are called, are often treated with contempt; for no reason, that I know. I never met with any thing against them of more authority than a sneer. Probable they certainly were; and a bare probability, when nothing opposes it, has its weight. But here the probability is strengthened by no small degree of positive evidence; which, if the reader wishes to see collected in one point of view, I refer him to the article of "Christ's suffering under Pontius Pilate," in Bishop Pearson's exposition of the Creed.

Among other authorities, that of the learned commentator on Eusebius, is worth remarking: "Fuere genuina Pilati acta; ad quæ provocabant primi christiani, tanquam ad certissima fidei monumenta."

one of those pious frauds, intended merely to impose upon the people, and advance the credit of the new sect?

This is just as easily said, as that his disciples stole him away, while the guard slept. Both are assertions without proof.

Others have objected Christ's partial discovery of himself, after his resurrection. If he had boldly shewn himself to the chief priests; or publickly to all the people; we might have had a more rational foundation for our belief. But as he had only for his witnesses, upon this occasion, a few of his chosen companions, the thing has certainly a more secret appearance than might be wished.

This insinuation is founded upon a passage in the acts of the apostles, in which it is said, that "God shewed him openly, not to all the people, but unto witnesses chosen before of God." The question is, what is meant by witnesses chosen before of God? Certainly nothing more than persons expresly, and by particular designation, intended to be the witnesses of this event. Others might see him if they pleased; but these were not the people, to whom God shewed him openly: this particular designation was confined to the "chosen witnesses."—And is there any thing more in this, than we see daily in all legal proceedings? Does not every body wish to have the fact, about which he is concerned, authenticated by indubitable records; or by living testimony, if it can be had? Do we not procure the hands of witnesses, appointed to this purpose, in all our deeds and writings?—Let us not, however, answer the objection by an arbitrary explanation of the text; but let us compare this explanation with the matter of fact.

On the morning of the resurrection, the apostles, who ran to the sepulchre to make themselves acquainted with what they had heard, received a message from their master, injoining them to meet him in Galilee. It does not appear, that this message was conveyed with any secrecy: it is rather probable it was not; and that the disciples told it to as many as they met. The women, it is expressly said, told it "to the eleven, and all the rest." Who the rest were, does not appear: but it is plain, from the sequel, that the thing was generally known; and that as many as chose either to satisfy their faith, or gratify their curiosity, repaired for that purpose to Galilee. And thus we find St. Peter making a distinction between the voluntary and the chosen witnesses—between those "who had companied with the apostles all the time that the Lord Jesus went in and out among them, from his baptism till his ascension," and those who "were ordained to be the witnesses of his resurrection *."

St. Paul goes farther, and in express words tells us, that Christ was seen † "after his resurrection of above five hundred brethren at once:" and it is probable, from the expression, "at once," that he was seen, at different times, by many more.

If then Christ thus appeared in Galilee to as many as chose to see him; or even if he appeared only to five hundred people, of whom St. Paul tells us the greatest part were still alive, when he wrote this epistle, there can surely be no reasonable cause of offence at his appearing, besides these, to a few of his chosen companions, who attended by express appointment, as persons designed to record the event.

In fact, if the same method be pursued in this inquiry, which is usual in all others, the

* Acts i. 21.

† 1 Cor. xv.

evidence

evidence of these chosen companions is all that is necessary. Here are twelve men produced (in general three or four men are thought sufficient) on whose evidence the fact depends. Are they competent witnesses? Have they those marks about them, which characterize men of integrity? Can they be challenged on any one ground of rational exception? If not, their evidence is as strictly legal, as full, and as satisfactory, as any reasonable man can require.——But in this great cause, we see the evidence is carried still farther. Here are five hundred persons waiting without, ready to add their testimony, if any one should require it, to what has already been more than legally proved. So that the argument even addresses itself to that absurd distinction, which we often find in the cavils of infidelity, between *rem certam*, and *rem certissimam*.

Upon the whole, then, we may affirm boldly, that this great event of the resurrection of Christ is founded upon evidence equal to the importance of it. If we expect still more, our answer is upon record: "If ye believe not Moses and the prophets," God's ordinary means of salvation, "neither will ye be persuaded, though one rose from the dead."—There must be bounds in all human evidence; and he who will believe nothing, unless he have every possible mode of proof, must be an infidel in almost every transaction of life. With such persons there is no reasoning. They who are not satisfied, because Christ did not appear in open parade at Jerusalem, would farther have asked, if he had appeared in the manner they expected, why did he not appear to every nation upon earth? Or, perhaps, why he did not shew himself to every individual?

To these objections may be added a scruple, taken from a passage of Scripture, in which it is said that "Christ should lie three days and three nights in the heart of the earth:" whereas, in fact, he only lay two nights, one whole day, and a part of two others.

But no figure in speech is more common than that of putting a part for the whole. In the Hebrew language perhaps this licence is more admissible, than in any other. A day and a night complete one whole day: and as our Saviour lay in the ground a part of every one of these three portions of time, he might be said, by an easy liberty of speech, to have lain the whole. *Gilpin.*

§ 46. *Creed continued.—Christ's Ascension.—Belief in the Holy Ghost.*

We believe farther, that Christ "ascended into heaven, and sitteth on the right-hand of God."

Christ's ascension into heaven rests on the same kind of proof, as his resurrection. Both of them are events, which the apostles were "ordained to witness." But though their testimony in this case, as well as in the resurrection, is certainly the most legal, and authentic proof, and fully sufficient for any reasonable man; yet this does not exclude the voluntary testimony of others. It is evident, that the apostles were not the sole eye-witnesses of this event: for when St. Peter called together the first assembly of the church to chuse a successor to Judas Iscariot, he tells them, they must necessarily chuse one, out of those men, who had been witnesses of all that Christ did, from his baptism "till his ascension:" and we find, there were in that meeting an hundred and twenty persons *, thus qualified.

Be it however as it will, if this article

* See Acts i. 15.

 should

should rest on a less formal proof, than the resurrection, it is of no great consequence: for if the resurrection be fully proved, nobody can well deny the ascension. If the testimony of the evangelists be allowed to prove the one; their word may be taken to establish the other.

With regard to "the right hand of God," it is a scriptural expression used merely in conformity to our gross conceptions; and is not intended to imply any distinction of parts, but merely the idea of pre-eminence.

We believe farther, that "Christ shall come to judge the quick and the dead."

This article contains the most serious truth, that ever was revealed to mankind. In part it was an article of the heathen creed. To unenlightened nature it seemed probable, that, as we had reason given us for a guide, we should hereafter be accountable for its abuse: and the poets, who were the prophets of early days, and durst deliver those truths under the veil of fable, which the philosopher kept more to himself, give us many traits of the popular belief on this subject *. But the gospel alone threw a full light upon this awful truth.

In examining this great article, the curiosity of human nature, ever delighting to explore unbeaten regions, hath often been tempted, beyond its limits, into fruitless inquiries; scrutinizing the time of this event; and settling, with vain precision, the circumstances of it. All curiosity of this kind is idle at least, if not presumptuous. When the Almighty hath thrown a veil over any part of his dispensation, it is the folly of man to endeavour to draw it aside.

* See particularly the 6th Book of Virgil's Æn.

Let us then leave all fruitless inquiries about this great event; and employ our thoughts chiefly upon such circumstances of it as most concern us.—Let us animate our hopes with the soothing reflection, that we have our sentence, in a manner, in our own power,—that the same gracious gospel, which directs our lives, shall direct the judgment we receive,—that the same gracious person shall be our judge, who died for our sins—and that his goodness, we are assured, will still operate towards us; and make the kindest allowances for all our infirmities.

But lest our hopes should be too buoyant, let us consider, on the other hand, what an awful detail against us will then appear. The subject of that grand enquiry will be all our transgressions of known duty—all our omissions of knowing better—our secret intentions—our indulged evil thoughts—the bad motives, which often accompany our most plausible actions—and, we are told, even our idle words.—"He that hath ears to hear, let him hear."—Then shall it be known, whether we have answered the great ends of life?—Whether we have made this world subservient to a better?—Whether we have prepared ourselves for a state of happiness in heaven, by endeavouring to communicate happiness to our fellow-creatures upon earth? Whether we have restrained our appetites, and passions; and reduced them within the bounds of reason and religion? Or, whether we have given ourselves up to pleasure, gain, or ambition; and formed such attachments to this world, as fit us for nothing else; and leave us no hopes either of gaining, or of enjoying a better? It will be happy for us, if on all these heads of inquiry, we can answer without dismay.— Worldly distinctions, we know, will then be of no avail. The proudest of them

them will be then confounded. "Naked came we into the world; and naked must we return." We can carry nothing beyond the grave, but our virtues, and our vices.

I shall conclude what hath been said on the last judgment with a collection of passages on this head from Scripture; where only our ideas of it can be obtained. And though most of these passages are figurative; yet as figures are intended to illustrate realities, and are indeed the only illustrations of which this subject is capable, we may take it for granted, that these figurative expressions are intended to convey a just idea of the truth.—With a view to make the more impression upon you, I shall place these passages in a regular series, though collected from various parts.

"The Lord himself shall descend from heaven with his holy angels—The trumpet shall sound; and all that are in the grave shall hear his voice, and come forth—Then shall he sit upon the throne of his glory; and all nations shall be gathered before him—the books shall be opened; and men shall be judged according to their works.—They who have sinned without law, shall perish, (that is, be judged) without law; and they who have sinned in the law, shall be judged by the law.—Unto whomsoever much is given, of him shall be much required.—Then shall he say to them on his right hand, Come, ye blessed, inherit the kingdom prepared for you. And to them on his left, Depart from me, ye cursed, into everlasting fire prepared for the devil and his angels.—Then shall the righteous shine forth in the presence of their Father; while the wicked shall go into everlasting punishment: there shall be wailing and gnashing of teeth.—What manner of persons ought we then to be in all holy conversation, and godliness? looking for, and hastening unto, the day of our Lord; when the heavens being on fire, shall be dissolved, and the elements shall melt with fervent heat.—Wherefore, beloved, seeing that we look for such things, let us be diligent, that we may be found of him in peace, without spot, and blameless; that each of us may receive that blessed sentence, "Well done, thou good and faithful servant: thou hast been faithful over a little, enter thou into the joy of thy Lord."

We believe, farther, in "the Holy Ghost;" that is, we believe every thing which the Scriptures tell us of the Holy Spirit of God.—We enquire not into the nature of its union with the Godhead. We take it for granted, that the Father, the Son, and the Holy Ghost, have some kind of union, and some kind of distinction; because both this union, and this distinction are plainly pointed out in Scripture; but how they exist we enquire not; concluding here, as in other points of difficulty, that if a clearer information had been necessary, it would have been afforded.

With regard to the operations of the Holy Spirit of God, (besides which, little more on this head is revealed) we believe, that it directed the apostles, and enabled them to propagate the gospel—and that it will assist all good men in the conscientious discharge of a pious life.

The Scripture doctrine, with regard to the assistance we receive from the Holy Spirit of God (which is the most essential part of this article) is briefly this:

Our best endeavours are insufficient. We are unprofitable servants, after all; and cannot please God, unless sanctified and assisted by his Holy Spirit. Hence the life of a good man hath been sometimes called a standing miracle;

racle; ſomething beyond the common courſe of nature. To attain any degree of goodneſs, we muſt be ſupernaturally aſſiſted.

At the ſame time, we are aſſured of this aſſiſtance, if we ſtrive to obtain it by fervent prayer, and a pious life. If we truſt in ourſelves, we ſhall fail. If we truſt in God, without doing all we can ourſelves, we ſhall fail likewiſe. And if we continue obſtinate in our perverſeneſs, we may at length totally incapacitate ourſelves from being the temples of the Holy Ghoſt,

And indeed what is there in all this, which common life does not daily illuſtrate? Is any thing more common, than for the intellect of one man to aſſiſt that of another? Is not the whole ſcheme of education an effuſion of knowledge and virtue not our own? Is it not evident too, that nothing of this kind can be communicated without application on the part of the learner? Are not the efforts of the teacher in a manner neceſſarily proportioned to this application? If the learner becomes languid in his purſuits, are not the endeavours of the teacher of courſe diſcouraged? And will they not at length wholly fail, if it be found in the end they anſwer no purpoſe?—In a manner analogous to this, the Holy Spirit of God co-operates with the endeavours of man. Our endeavours are neceſſary to obtain God's aſſiſtance: and the more earneſtly theſe endeavours are exerted, the meaſure of this grace will of courſe be greater.

But, on the other hand, if theſe endeavours languiſh, the aſſiſtance of Heaven will leſſen in proportion; and if we behave with obſtinate perverſeneſs, it will by degrees wholly fail. It will not always ſtrive with man; but will leave him a melancholy prey to his own vicious inclinations.

As to the manner, in which this ſpiritual aſſiſtance is conveyed, we make no inquiry. We can as little comprehend it, as we can the action of our ſouls upon our bodies. We are ſenſible, that our ſouls do act upon our bodies; and it is a belief equally conſonant to reaſon, that the divine influence may act upon our ſouls. The advocate for natural religion need not be reminded, that among the heathens a divine influence was a received opinion. The prieſts of every oracle were ſuppoſed to be inſpired by their gods; and the heroes of antiquity were univerſally believed to act under the influence of a ſupernatural aſſiſtance; by which it was conceived they performed actions beyond human power.—This ſhews, at leaſt, that there is nothing in this doctrine repugnant to reaſon. *Gilpin.*

§ 47. *Creed continued.—The Holy Catholic Church, &c.*

We believe, farther, in the "holy catholic church," and the "communion of ſaints."

"I believe in the holy catholic church," is certainly a very obſcure expreſſion to a proteſtant; as it is very capable of a popiſh conſtruction, implying our truſt in the infallibility of the church; whereas we attribute infallibility to no church upon earth. The moſt obvious ſenſe, therefore, in which it can be conſidered as a proteſtant article of our belief, is this, that we call no particular ſociety of chriſtians a holy catholic church; but believe, that all true and ſincere chriſtians, of whatever communion, or particular opinion, ſhall be the objects of God's mercy. The patriarchal covenant was confined to a few. The Jewiſh church ſtood alſo on a very narrow baſis. But the chriſtian church, we believe, is truly catholic: its gracious offers are made to all mankind;

mankind; and God through Christ will take out of every nation such as shall be saved."

The "communion of saints," is an expression equally obscure: and whatever might have been the original meaning of it, it certainly does not resolve itself into a very obvious one to us. If we say we mean by it, that good christians living together on earth, should exercise all offices of charity among themselves, no one will contradict the article; but many perhaps may ask, Why is it made an article of faith? It relates not so much to faith, as to practice: and the ten commandments might just as well be introduced as articles of our belief.

To this I can only suggest that it may have a place among the articles of our creed, as a test of our enlarged ideas of christianity, and as opposed to the narrow-mindedness of some christians, who harbour very uncharitable opinions against all who are not of their own church; and scruple not to shew their opinions by uncharitable actions. The papists particularly deny salvation to any but those of their own communion, and persecute those of other persuasions where they have the power.—In opposition to this, we profess our belief of the great christian law of charity. We believe we ought to think charitably of good christians of all denominations; and ought to practise a free and unrestrained communion of charitable offices towards them.

In this light the second part of the article depends upon the first. By the "holy catholic church," we mean all sincere christians, of whatever church, or peculiarity of opinion; and by "the communion of saints." A kind and charitable behaviour towards them.

Though it is probable this was not the original meaning of the article, yet as the reformers of the liturgy did not think it proper to make an alteration, we are led to seek such a sense as appears most consistent with scripture.—We are assured, that this article, as well as the "descent into hell," is not of the same antiquity as the rest of the creed *.

We profess our belief farther in the "forgiveness of sins."—The Scripture-doctrine of sin, and of the guilt, which arises from it, is this:

Man was originally created in a state of innocence, yet liable to fall. Had he persevered in his obedience, he might have enjoyed that happiness, which is the consequence of perfect virtue. But when this happy state was lost, his passions and appetites became disordered, and prone to evil. Since that time we have all been, more or less, involved in sin, and are all therefore, in the Scripture-language, "under the curse;" that is, we are naturally in a state of unpardoned guilt.

In this mournful exigence, what was to be done? In a state of nature, it is true, we might be sorry for our sins. Nature too might dictate repentance. But sorrow and repentance, though they may put us on our guard, for the future, can make no atonement for sins already committed. A resolution to run no more into debt may make us cautious; but can never discharge a debt already contracted †.

* See Bingham's Antiquities, vol. iv. chap. 3.

† Thus Mr. Jenyns expresses the same thing: "The punishment of vice is a debt due to justice, "which cannot be remitted without compensation: "repentance can be no compensation. It may "change a wicked man's dispositions, and prevent "his offending for the future; but can lay no "claim to pardon for what is past. If any one "by profligacy and extravagance contracts a debt, "repentance may make him wiser, and hinder "him from running into farther distresses, but "can never pay off his old bonds, for which he "must be ever accountable, unless they are discharged by himself, or some other in his stead."

View of the Intern. Evid. p. 112.

In this distress of nature, Jesus Christ came into the world. He threw a light upon the gloom that surrounded us.—He shewed us, that in this world we were lost—that the law of nature could not save us—that the tenor of that law was perfect obedience, with which we could not comply—but that God—thro' his mediation, offered us a method of regaining happiness—that he came to make that atonement for us, which we could not make for ourselves—and to redeem us from that guilt, which would otherwise overwhelm us—that faith and obedience were, on our parts, the conditions required in this gracious covenant—and that God promised us, on his, the pardon of our sins, and everlasting life—that we were first therefore to be made holy through the gospel of Christ, and then we might expect salvation through his death: "Us, who were dead in trespasses and sins, would he quicken. Christ would redeem us from the curse of the law. By grace we should be saved thro' faith; and that not of ourselves: it was the gift of God. Not of works, lest any man should boast." *Gilpin.*

§ 48. *Creed continued—Resurrection of the Body.*

We believe farther "in the resurrection of the body."—This article presumes our belief in the immortality of the soul.

What that principle of life is, which we lieved their souls were immortal from their own feelings, so impressed with an expectation of immortality—from observing the progressive state of the soul, capable, even after the body had attained its full strength, of still higher improvements both in knowledge, and in habits of virtue—from the analogy of all nature, dying and reviving in every part—from their situation here so apparently incomplete in itself; and from a variety of other topics, which the reason of man was able to suggest.—But though nature could obscurely suggest this great truth; yet Christianity alone threw a clear light upon it, and impressed it with a full degree of conviction upon our minds.

But the article before us proceeds a step farther. It not only implies the immortality of the soul; but asserts the resurrection of the body—Nor was this doctrine wholly new to nature. In its conceptions of a future life, we always find the soul in an imbodied state. It was airy indeed, and bloodless; but still it had the parts of a human body, and could perform all its operations.

In these particulars the Scripture does not gratify our curiosity. From various passages we are led to believe, that the body shall certainly rise again: but in what manner, or of what substance, we pretend not to examine. We learn "that it is sown in corruption, and raised in incorruption: that it is sown in dis-

taphyſical diſquiſitions of identity, or any other curious points in which this deep ſubject might engage us, all which, as they are founded upon uncertainty, muſt end in doubt, it is better to draw this doctrine, as well as all others, into practical uſe: and the uſe we ought to make of it is, to pay that regard to our bodies, which is due to them—not vainly to adorn—not luxuriouſly to pamper them; but to keep them as much as poſſible from the pollutions of the world; and to lay them down in the grave undefiled, there to be ſealed up in expectation of a bleſſed reſurrection.

Laſtly, we believe "in the life everlaſting:" in which article we expreſs our faith in the eternity of a future ſtate of rewards and puniſhments.

This article is nearly related to the laſt, and is involved in the ſame obſcurity. In what the reward of the virtuous will conſiſt, after death, our reaſon gives us no information. Conjecture indeed it will, in a matter which ſo nearly concerns us; and it hath conjectured in all ages: but information it hath none, except from the word of God; and even there, our limited capacities can receive it only in general and figurative expreſſions. We are told, "there will then reign fulneſs of joy, and pleaſures for evermore—that the righteous ſhall have an inheritance incorruptible, undefiled, that fadeth not away—where they ſhall ſhine forth, as the ſun, in the preſence of their father—where error, and ſin, and miſery ſhall be no more—where ſhall be aſſembled an innumerable company of angels, the general aſſembly of the church, the ſpirits of juſt men made perfect—that they ſhall neither hunger nor thirſt any more—that all tears ſhall be wiped from their eyes—that there ſhall be neither death, nor ſorrow, nor pain."

From theſe, and ſuch expreſſions as theſe, though we cannot collect the entire nature of a future ſtate of happineſs, yet we can eaſily gather a few circumſtances, which muſt of courſe attend it; as, that it will be very great—that it will laſt for ever—that it will be of a nature entirely different from the happineſs of this world—that, as in this world, our paſſions and appetites prevail; in the next, reaſon and virtue will have the ſuperiority—"hunger and thirſt, tears and ſorrow," we read, "will be no more"—that is, all uneaſy paſſions and appetites will then be annihilated—all vain fears will be then removed—all anxious and intruding cares—and we ſhall feel ourſelves compleat and perfect; and our happineſs, not dependent, as here, upon a thouſand precarious circumſtances, both within and without ourſelves, but conſiſtent, uniform, and ſtable.

On the other hand, we pretend not to inquire in what the puniſhment of the wicked conſiſts. In the Scripture we find many expreſſions, from which we gather, that it will be very great. It is there called, "an everlaſting fire, prepared for the devil and his angels—where the worm dieth not, and the fire is never quenched—where ſhall be weeping, and gnaſhing of teeth—where the wicked ſhall drink of the wrath of God, poured without mixture into the cup of his indignation—where they ſhall have no reſt, neither by day nor night."

Though it becomes us certainly to put our interpretations with the greateſt caution and humility upon ſuch paſſages as theſe; yet "the worm that never dieth," and "the fire that is never quenched," are ſtrong expreſſions, and hardly to be evaded by any refinements of verbal criticiſm. Let the deiſt bravely argue down his fears, by demonſtrating the abſurdity of conſuming a ſpirit in material fire. Let him fully explain the nature of future puniſhment; and convince us, that where it cannot reform, it must be unjust.—But let us, with more modesty, lay our hands humbly upon our breasts, confess our ignorance; revere the appointments of God, whatever they may be; and prepare to meet them with holy hope, and trembling joy, and awful submission to his righteous will.

To the unenlightened heathen the eternity of future punishments appeared no such unreasonable doctrine. Their state of the damned was of eternal duration. A vulture for ever tore those entrails, which were for ever renewed *.

Of one thing, however, we may be well assured (which may set us entirely at rest in all our enquiries on this deep subject), that every thing will, in the end, be right—that a just and merciful God must act agreably to justice and mercy—and that the first of these attributes will most assuredly be tempered with the latter.

From the doctrine of future rewards and punishments, the great and most convincing practical truth which arises, is, that we cannot exert too much pains in qualifying ourselves for the happiness of a future world. As this happiness will last for ever, how beneficial will be the exchange—this world, "which is but for a moment, for that everlasting weight of glory which fadeth not away!"

Vice, on the other hand, receives the greatest discouragement from this doctrine, as every sin we commit in this world may be considered as an addition to an everlasting account in the next. *Gilpin.*

§ 49. *On the Ten Commandments.*

Having considered the articles of our faith, we proceed to the rules of our practice. These, we know, are of such importance, that, let our faith be what it will, unless it influence our lives, it is of no value. At the same time, if it be what it ought to be, it will certainly have this influence.

On this head, the ten commandments are first placed before us; from which the composers of the catechism, as well as many other divines, have drawn a compleat system of christian duties. But this is perhaps rather too much †. Both Moses, in the law, and Christ in the gospel, seem to have enlarged greatly on morals: and each of them, especially the latter, to have added many practical rules, which do not obviously fall under any of the commandments.

But though we cannot call the decalogue a compleat rule of duty, we accept it with the utmost reverence, as the first great written

* ———Rostroque immanis vultur obunco
Immortale jecur tundens, fœcundaque pœnis
Viscera.————————————
Æn. vi. 596.

———Sedet, æternumque sedebit
Infelix Theseus.————————
Ib. 616.

† In the fourth volume of Bishop Warburton's commentary on Pope's works, in the second satire of Dr. Donne, are these lines:

Of whose strange crimes no cannonist can tell
In which commandment's large contents they dwell.

"The original," says the bishop, "is more humorous.

In which commandment's large receipt they dwell;

"as if the ten commandments were so wide, as "to stand ready to receive every thing, which "either the law of nature, or the gospel commands. A just ridicule on those practical commentators, as they are called, who include all "moral and religious duties within them."

law that ever God communicated to man. We consider it as an eternal monument, inscribed by the finger of God himself, with a few strong, indelible characters; not defining the minutiæ of morals, but injoining those great duties only, which have the most particular influence upon the happiness of society; and prohibiting those enormous crimes, which are the greatest sources of its distress.

The ten commandments are divided into two parts, from their being originally written upon two tables. From hence one table is supposed to contain our duty to God; the other our duty to man. But this seems to be an unauthorized division; and hath a tendency to a verbal mistake; as if some duties were owing to God; and others to man: whereas in fact we know that all duties are equally owing to God.—However, if we avoid this misconception, the division into our duty to God, and our duty to man, may be a convenient one.—The four first commandments are contained in the first table: the remaining six in the second.

At the head of them stands a prohibition to acknowledge more than one God.

The second commandment bears a near relation to the first. The former forbids polytheism; the latter idolatry: and with this belief, and practice, which generally accompanied each other, all the nations of the earth were tainted, when these commandments were given: especially those nations, by whom the Jews were surrounded.

The third commandment injoins reverence to God's name. This is a strong religious restraint in private life; and as a solemn oath is the strictest obligation among men, nothing can be of greater service to society, than to hold it in general respect.

The fourth commands the observance of the sabbath; as one of the best means of preserving a sense of God, and of religion in the minds of men.

The second table begins with injoining obedience to parents; a duty in a peculiar manner adapted to the Jewish state, before any regular government was erected. The temporal promise, which guards it, and which can relate only to the Jews, may either mean a promise of long life to each individual, who observed the precept: or, of stability to the whole nation upon the general observance of it: which is perhaps a better interpretation.

The five next commandments are prohibitions of the most capital crimes, which pollute the heart of man, and injure the peace of society.

The first of them forbids murder, which is the greatest injury that one man can do another; as of all crimes the damage in this is the most irreparable.

The seventh commandment forbids adultery. The black infidelity, and injury which accompany this crime; the confusion in families, which often succeeds it; and the general tendency it hath to destroy all the domestic happiness of society, stain it with a very high degree of guilt.

The security of our property is the object of the eighth commandment.

The security of our characters, is the object of the ninth.

The tenth restrains us not only from the actual commission of sin; but from those bad inclinations, which give it birth.

After the commandments follows a commentary upon them, intitled, "our duty to God," and "our duty to our neighbour;" the latter of which might more properly be intitled, "Our duty to our neighbour and ourselves."

ourselves."—These seem intended as an explanation of the commandments upon Christian principles; with the addition of other duties, which do not properly fall under any of them. On these we shall be more large.

The first part of our duty to God, is, "to "believe in him;" which is the foundation of all religion, and therefore offers itself first to our consideration. But this great point hath been already considered.

The next branch of our duty to God, is to fear him. The fear of God is impressed equally upon the righteous man, and the sinner. But the fear of the sinner consists only in the dread of punishment. It is the necessary consequence of guilt; and is not that fear, which we consider as a duty. The fear of God here meant, consists in that reverential awe, that constant apprehension of his presence, which secures us from offending him. —When we are before our superiors, we naturally feel a respect, which prevents our doing any thing indecent in their sight. Such (only in a higher degree) should be our reverence of God, in whose sight, we know, we always stand. If a sense of the divine presence hath such an influence over us, as to check the bad tendency of our thoughts, words, and actions; we may properly be said to be impressed with the fear of God.—If not, we neglect one of the best means of checking vice, which the whole circle of religious restraint affords.

Some people go a step farther; and say, that as every degree of light behaviour, though short of an indecency, is improper before our superiors; so is it likewise in the presence of Almighty God, who is so much superior to every thing that can be called great on earth.

But this is the language of superstition. Mirth, within the bounds of innocence, cannot be offensive to God. He is offended only with vice. Vice, in the lowest degree, is hateful to him: but a formal set behaviour can be necessary only to preserve human distinctions.

The next duty to God is that of love, which is founded upon his goodness to his creatures. Even this world, mixed as it is with evil, exhibits various marks of the goodness of the Deity. Most men indeed place their affections too much upon it, and rate it at too high a value: but in the opinion even of wise men, it deserves some estimation. The acquisition of knowledge, in all its branches; the intercourse of society; the contemplation of the wonderful works of God, and all the beauteous scenes of nature; nay, even the low inclinations of animal life, when indulged with sobriety and moderation, furnish various modes of pleasure and enjoyment.

Let this world however go for little. In contemplating a future life, the enjoyments of this are lost. It is in the contemplation of futurity, that the christian views the goodness of God in the fullest light. When he sees the Deity engaging himself by covenant to make our short abode here a preparation for our eternal happiness hereafter—when he is assured that this happiness is not only eternal, but of the purest and most perfect kind—when he sees God, as a father, opening all his stores of love and kindness, to bring back to himself a race of creatures fallen from their original perfection, and totally lost through their own folly, perverseness, and wickedness; then it is that the evils of life seem as atoms in the sun-beam; the divine nature appears overflowing with goodness to mankind, and calls

calls forth every exertion of our gratitude and love.

That the enjoyments of a future ſtate, in whatever thoſe enjoyments conſiſt, are the gift of God, is ſufficiently obvious: but with regard to the government of this world, there is often among men a ſort of infidelity, which aſcribes all events to their own prudence and induſtry. Things appear to run in a ſtated courſe; and the finger of God, which acts unſeen, is never ſuppoſed.

And, no doubt, our own induſtry and prudence have a great ſhare in procuring for us the bleſſings of life. God hath annexed them as the reward of ſuch exertions. But can we ſuppoſe, that ſuch exertions will be of any ſervice to us, unleſs the providence of God throw opportunities in our way? All the means of worldly happineſs are ſurely no other than the means of his government. Moſes ſaw among the Jews a kind of infidelity like this, when he forbad the people to ſay in their hearts, "My power, and the might of my hands hath gotten me this wealth," whereas, he adds, they ought to remember, "That it is the Lord who giveth power to get wealth."

Others again have objected to the goodneſs of God, his permiſſion of evil A good God, ſay they, would have prevented it; and have placed his creatures in a ſituation beyond the diſtreſſes of life.

With regard to man, there ſeems to be no great difficulty in this matter. It is enough, ſurely, that God has put the means of comfort in our power. In the natural world, he hath given us remedies againſt hunger, cold, and diſeaſe; and in the moral world, againſt the miſchief of ſin. Even death itſelf, the laſt great evil, he hath ſhewn us how we may change into the moſt conſummate bleſſing. A [illegible] ſeem eaſily to ſet things to rights on this head.

The miſery of the brute creation is indeed more unaccountable. But have we not the modeſty to ſuppoſe, that this difficulty may be owing to our ignorance? And that on the ſtrength of what we know of the wiſdom of God, we may venture to truſt him for thoſe parts which we cannot comprehend?

One truth, after all, is very apparent, that if we ſhould argue ourſelves into atheiſm, by the untractableneſs of theſe ſubjects, we ſhould be ſo far from getting rid of our difficulties, that, if we reaſon juſtly, ten thouſand greater would ariſe, either from conſidering the world under no ruler, or under one of our own imagining.

There remains one farther conſideration with regard to the love of God, and that is, the meaſure of it. We are told we ought to love him "with all our heart, with all our ſoul, and with all our ſtrength." Theſe are ſtrong expreſſions, and ſeem to imply a greater warmth of affection, than many people may perhaps find they can exert. The affections of ſome are naturally cool, and little excited by any objects. The guilty perſon, is he, whoſe affections are warm in every thing but religion.—The obvious meaning therefore of the expreſſion is, that whether our affections are cool or warm, we ſhould make God our chief good—that we ſhould ſet our affections more upon him, than upon any thing elſe—and that, for his ſake, and for the ſake of his laws, we ſhould be ready to reſign every thing we have, and even life itſelf. So that the words ſeem nearly of the ſame import with thoſe of the apoſtle, "Set your affections on things above, and not on things on the earth."

Gilpin.

§ 50. *Worſhip and Honour of God.*

Our next duty to God is, to worſhip him, to give him thanks, to put our whole truſt in him, and to call upon him.

Since the obſervance of the ſabbath is founded upon many wiſe and juſt reaſons, what have they to anſwer for, who not only neglect this inſtitution themſelves, but bring it by their example into contempt with others? I ſpeak not to thoſe who make it a day of common diverſion; who, laying aſide all decency, and breaking through all civil and religious regulations; ſpend it in the moſt licentious amuſements: ſuch people are paſt all reproof: but I ſpeak to thoſe, who in other things profeſs themſelves to be ſerious people; and, one might hope, would act right, when they were convinced what was ſo.

But our prayers, whether in public, or in private, are only an idle parade, unleſs we put our truſt in God.

By putting our truſt in God, is meant depending upon him, as our happineſs, and our refuge.

Human nature is always endeavouring either to remove pain; or, if eaſe be obtained, to acquire happineſs. And thoſe things are certainly the moſt eligible, which in theſe reſpects are the moſt effectual. The world, it is true, makes us flattering promiſes: but who can ſay that it will keep them? We conſiſt of two parts, a body, and a ſoul. Both of theſe want the means of happineſs, as well as the removal of evil. But the world cannot even afford them to the body. Its means of happineſs, to thoſe who depend upon them as ſuch, are, in a thouſand inſtances, unſatisfying. Even, at beſt, they will fail us in the end. While pain, diſeaſes, and death, ſhew us, that the world can afford no refuge againſt bodily diſtreſs. And if it cannot afford the means of happineſs, and of ſecurity, to the body, how much leſs can we ſuppoſe it able to afford them to the ſoul?

Nothing then, we ſee, in this world, is a ſufficient foundation for truſt: nor indeed can any thing be but Almighty God, who affords us the only means of happineſs, and is our only real refuge in diſtreſs. On him, the more we truſt, the greater we ſhall feel our ſecurity; and that man who has, on juſt religious motives, confirmed in himſelf this truſt, wants nothing elſe to ſecure his happineſs. The world may wear what aſpect it will: it is not on it that he depends. As far as prudence goes, he endeavours to avoid the evils of life; but when they fall to his ſhare (as ſooner or later we muſt all ſhare them) he reſigns himſelf into the hands of that God who made him, and who knows beſt how to diſpoſe of him. On him he thoroughly depends, and with him he has a conſtant intercourſe by prayer; truſting, that whatever happens is agreeable to that juſt government, which God has eſtabliſhed; and that, of conſequence, it muſt be beſt.

We are injoined next "to honour God's holy name."

The name of God is accompanied with ſuch ideas of greatneſs and reverence, that it ſhould never paſs our lips without ſuggeſting thoſe ideas. Indeed it ſhould never be mentioned, but with a kind of awful heſitation, and on the moſt ſolemn occaſions; either in ſerious diſcourſe, or, when we invoke God in prayer, or when we ſwear by his name.

In this laſt light we are here particularly injoined to honour the name of God. A ſolemn oath is an appeal to God himſelf; and is intitled to our utmoſt reſpect, were it only in a political light; as in all human concerns it it is the ſtrongeſt teſt of veracity; and has been approved as ſuch by the wiſdom of all nations.

Some religioniſts have diſapproved the uſe of oaths, under the idea of prophaneneſs. The language of the ſacred writers conveys a different idea. One of them ſays, "An oath for confirmation is an end of all ſtrife:" another, "I take God for record upon my ſoul:" and a third, "God is my witneſs."

To the uſe of oaths, others have objected, that they are nugatory. The good man will ſpeak the truth without an oath; and the bad man cannot be held by one. And this would be true, if mankind were divided into good and bad: but as they are generally of a mixed character, we may well ſuppoſe, that many would venture a ſimple falſehood, who would yet be ſtartled at the idea of perjury *.

As an oath therefore taken in a ſolemn manner, and on a proper occaſion, may be conſidered as one of the higheſt acts of religion; ſo perjury, or falſe ſwearing, is certainly one of the higheſt acts of impiety; and the greateſt diſhonour we can poſſibly ſhew to the name of God. It is, in effect, either denying our belief in a God, or his power to puniſh. Other crimes wiſh to eſcape the notice of Heaven; this is daring the Almighty to his face.

After perjury, the name of God is moſt diſhonoured by the horrid practice of curſing. Its effects in ſociety, it is true, are not ſo miſchievous as thoſe of perjury; nor is it ſo deliberate an act: but yet it conveys a ſtill more horrid idea. Indeed if there be one wicked practice more peculiarly diabolical, than another, it is this: for no employment can be conceived more ſuitable to infernal ſpirits, than that of ſpending their rage and impotence in curſes, and execrations. If this ſhocking vice were not ſo dreadfully familiar to our ears, it could not fail to ſtrike us with the utmoſt horror.

We next conſider common ſwearing; a ſin ſo univerſally practiſed, that one would imagine ſome great advantage, in the way either of pleaſure or profit, attended it. The wages of iniquity afford ſome temptation: but to commit ſin without any wages, is a ſtrange ſpecies of infatuation.—May we then aſk the common ſwearer, what the advantages are, which ariſe from this practice?

It will be difficult to point out one.—Perhaps it may be ſaid, that it adds ſtrength to an affirmation. But if a man commonly ſtrengthen his affirmations in this way, we may venture to aſſert, that the practice will tend rather to leſſen, than confirm his credit. It ſhews plainly what he himſelf thinks of his own veracity. We never prop a building, till it becomes ruinous.

Some forward youth may think, that an oath adds an air and ſpirit to his diſcourſe; that it is manly and important; and gives him conſequence. We may whiſper one ſecret in his ear, which he may be aſſured is a truth—Theſe airs of manlineſs give him conſequence with thoſe only, whoſe commendation is diſgrace; others he only convinces, at how early an age he wiſhes to be thought profligate.

Perhaps he may imagine, that an oath gives force and terror to his threatenings—In this he may be right; and the more horribly wicked he grows, the greater object of terror he may make himſelf. On this plan, the devil affords him a complete pattern for imitation.

* They who attend our courts of juſtice, often ſee inſtances among the common people of their aſſerting roundly what they will either refuſe to ſwear; or, when ſworn, will not aſſert.

Paltry

Paltry as these apologies are, I should suppose, the practice of common swearing has little more to say for itself.—Those however, who can argue in favour of this sin, I should fear, there is little chance to reclaim.—But it is probable, that the greater part of such as are addicted to it, act rather from habit, than principle. To deter such persons from indulging so pernicious a habit, and to shew them, that it is worth their while to be at some pains to conquer it, let us now see what arguments may be produced on the other side.

In the first place, common swearing leads to perjury. He who is addicted to swear on every trifling occasion, cannot but often, I had almost said unavoidably, give the sanction of an oath to an untruth. And though I should hope such perjury is not a sin of so heinous a nature, as what, in judicial matters, is called wilful and corrupt; yet it is certainly stained with a very great degree of guilt.

But secondly, common swearing is a large stride towards wilful and corrupt prejury, inasmuch as it makes a solemn oath to be received with less reverence. If nobody dared to take an oath, but on proper occasions, an oath would be received with respect; but when we are accustomed to hear swearing the common language of our streets, it is no wonder that people make light of oaths on every occasion; and that judicial, commercial, and official oaths, are all treated with so much indifference.

Thirdly, common swearing may be considered as an act of great irreverence to God; and as such, implying also a great indifference to religion. If it would disgrace a chief magistrate to suffer appeals on every trifling, or ludicrous occasion; we may at least think it as disrespectful to the Almighty.—If we lose our reverence for God, it is impossible we can retain it for his laws. You scarce remember a common swearer, who was in other respects an exact christian.

But, above all, we should be deterred from common swearing by the positive command of our Saviour, which is founded unquestionably upon the wickedness of the practice: "You have heard," saith Christ, "that it hath been said by them of old time, thou shalt not forswear thyself: but I say unto you, swear not at all; neither by heaven, for it is God's throne, neither by the earth, for it is his footstool: but let your communication" (that is, your ordinary conversation) "be yea, yea, nay, nay; for whatsoever is more than these cometh of evil."—St. James also, with great emphasis pressing his master's words, says, "Above all things, my brethren, swear not; neither by heaven, neither by the earth, neither by any other oath: but let your yea be yea, and your nay, nay, lest you fall into condemnation."

I shall just add, before I conclude this subject, that two things are to be avoided, which are very nearly allied to swearing.

The first is, the use of light exclamations, and invocations upon God, on every trivial occasion. We cannot have much reverence for God himself, when we treat his name in so familiar a manner; and may assure ourselves, that we are indulging a practice, which must weaken impressions, that ought to be preserved as strong as possible.

Secondly, such light expressions, and wanton phrases, as sound like swearing are to be avoided; and are often therefore indulged by silly people, for the sake of the sound; who think (if they think at all) that they add to their discourse the spirit of swearing without the

the guilt of it. Such people had better lay aside, together with swearing, every appearance of it. These appearances may both offend, and mislead others; and with regard to themselves, may end in realities. At least, they shew an inclination to swearing: and an inclination to vice indulged, is really vice. *Gilpin.*

§ 51. *Honour due to God's Word—what it is to serve God truly, &c.*

As we are injoined to honour God's holy name, so are we injoined also "to honour his holy word."

By God's holy word we mean, the Old Testament and the New.

The books of the Old Testament open with the earliest accounts of time, earlier than any human records reach; and yet, in many instances, they are strengthened by human records. The heathen mythology is often grounded upon remnants of the sacred story, and many of the Bible events are recorded, however imperfectly, in prophane history. The very face of nature bears witness to the deluge.

In the history of the patriarchs is exhibited a most beautiful picture of the simplicity of ancient manners; and of genuine nature unadorned indeed by science, but impressed strongly with a sense of religion. This gives an air of greatness and dignity to all the sentiments and actions of these exalted characters.

The patriarchal history is followed by the Jewish. Here we have the principal events of that peculiar nation, which lived under a theocracy, and was set apart to preserve and propagate * the knowledge of the true God through those ages of ignorance antecedent to Christ. Here too we find those types, and representations, which the apostle to the Hebrews calls the shadows of good things to come.

To those books, which contain the legislation and history of the Jews, succeed the prophetic writings. As the time of the promise drew still nearer, the notices of its approach became stronger. The kingdom of the Messiah, which was but obscurely shadowed by the ceremonies of the Jewish law, was marked in stronger lines by the prophets, and proclaimed in a more intelligible language. The office of the Messiah, his ministry, his life, his actions, his death, and his resurrection, are all very distinctly held out. It is true, the Jews, explaining the warm figures of the prophetic language too literally, and applying to a temporal dominion those expressions, which were intended only as descriptive of a spiritual, were offended at the meanness of Christ's appearance on earth; and would not own him for that Messiah, whom their prophets had foretold; though these very prophets, when they used a less figurative language, had described him, as he really was, a man of sorrows, and acquainted with grief.

To these books are added several others, poetical and moral, which administer much instruction, and matter of meditation to devout minds.

The New Testament contains first the simple history of Christ, as recorded in the four gospels. In this history also are delivered those excellent instructions, which our Saviour occasionally gave his disciples; the precepts and the example blended together.

To the gospels succeeds an account of the lives and actions of some of the principle apostles;

* See the subject very learnedly treated in one of the first Chapters of Jenkins's Reasonableness of Christianity.

apoſtles; together with the early ſtate of the chriſtian church.

The epiſtles of ſeveral of the apoſtles, particularly of St. Paul, to ſome of the new eſtabliſhed churches, make another part. Our Saviour had promiſed to endow his diſciples with power from on high to complete the great work of publiſhing the goſpel: and in the epiſtles that work is completed. The truths and doctrines of the chriſtian religion are here ſtill more unfolded, and inforced: as the great ſcheme of our redemption was now finiſhed by the death of Chriſt.

The ſacred volume is concluded with the revelations of St. John; which are ſuppoſed to contain a prophetic deſcription of the future ſtate of the church. Some of theſe prophecies, it is thought on very good grounds, are already fulfilled; and others, which now, as ſublime deſcriptions only, amuſe the imagination, will probably, in the future ages of the church, be the objects of the underſtanding alſo.

The laſt part of our duty to God is, "to ſerve him truly all the days of our life."

"To ſerve God truly all the days of our life," implies two things: firſt, the mode of this ſervice; and ſecondly, the term of it.

Firſt, we muſt ſerve God truly. We muſt not reſt ſatisfied with the outward action; but muſt take care that every action be founded on a proper motive. It is the motive alone that makes an action acceptable to God. The hypocrite "may faſt twice in the week, and give alms of all that he poſſeſſes:" nay, he may faſt the whole week, if he be able, and give all he has in alms; but if his faſts and his alms are intended as a matter of oſtentation only, neither the one, nor the other, is that true ſervice which God requires. God requires the heart: he requires that an earneſt deſire of acting agreeably to his will, ſhould be the general ſpring of our actions; and this will give even an indifferent action a value in his ſight.

As we are injoined to ſerve God truly, ſo are we injoined to ſerve him "all the days of our life." As far as human frailties will permit, we ſhould perſevere in a conſtant tenor of obedience. That lax behaviour, which inſtead of making a ſteady progreſs, is continually relapſing into former errors, and running the ſame round of ſinning and repenting, is rather the life of an irreſolute ſinner, than of a pious chriſtian. Human errors, and frailties, we know, God will not treat with too ſevere an eye; but he who, in the general tenor of his life, does not keep advancing towards chriſtian perfection; but ſuffers himſelf, at intervals, entirely to loſe ſight of his calling, cannot be really ſerious in his profeſſion: he is at a great diſtance from ſerving God truly all the days of his life; and has no ſcriptural ground to hope much from the mercy of God.

That man, whether placed in high eſtate, or low, has reached the ſummit of human happineſs, who is truly ſerious in the ſervice of his great Maſter. The things of this world may engage, but cannot engroſs, his attention; its ſorrows and its joys may affect, but cannot diſconcert him. No man, he knows, can faithfully ſerve two maſters. He hath hired himſelf to one—that great Maſter, whoſe commands he reveres, whoſe favour he ſeeks, whoſe diſpleaſure alone is the real object of his fears; and whoſe rewards alone are the real objects of his hope. Every thing elſe is trivial in his ſight. The world may ſooth; or it may threaten him: he perſeveres ſteadily in the ſervice of his God; and in that perſeverance perseverence feels his happiness every day the more established. *Gilpin.*

§ 52. *Duties owing to particular persons—duty of children to parents—respect and obedience—in what the former consists—in what the latter—succouring a parent—brotherly affection—obedience to law—founded on the advantages of society.*

From the two grand principles of "loving our neighbour as ourselves; and of doing to others, as we would have them do to us," which regulate our social intercourse in general, we proceed to those more confined duties, which arise from particular relations, connections, and stations in life.

Among these, we are first taught, as indeed the order of nature directs, to consider the great duty of children to parents.

The two points to be insisted on, are respect and obedience. Both these should naturally spring from love; to which parents have the highest claim. And indeed parents, in general, behave to their children, in a manner both to deserve and to obtain their love.

But if the kindness of the parent be not such as to work upon the affections of the child, yet still the parent has a title to respect and obedience, on the principle of duty; a principle, which the voice of nature dictates; which reason inculcates; which human laws, and human customs, all join to inforce; and which the word of God strictly commands.

The child will shew respect to his parent, by treating him, at all times, with deference. He will consult his parent's inclination, and shew a readiness, in a thousand nameless trifles, to conform himself to it. He will never peevishly contradict his parent; and when he offers a contrary opinion, he will offer it modestly. Respect will teach him also, not only to put the best colouring upon the infirmities of his parent; but even if those infirmities be great, it will soften and screen them, as much as possible, from the public eye.

Obedience goes a step further, and supposes a positive command. In things unlawful indeed, the parental authority cannot bind: but this is a case that rarely happens. The great danger is on the other side, that children, through obstinacy or sullenness, should refuse their parents' lawful commands; to the observance of all which, however inconvenient to themselves, they are tied by various motives; and above all, by the command of God, who in his sacred denunciations against sin, ranks disobedience to parents among the worst *.

They are farther bound, not only to obey the commands of their parents; but to obey them chearfully. He does but half his duty, who does it not from his heart.

There remains still a third part of filial duty, which peculiarly belongs to children, when grown up. This the catechism calls succouring or administering to the necessities of the parent; either in the way of managing his affairs, when he is less able to manage them himself; or in supplying his wants, should he need assistance in that way. And this the child should do, on the united principles of love, duty, and gratitude. The hypocritical Jew would sometimes evade this duty, by dedicating to sacred uses what should have been expended in assisting his parent. Our Saviour sharply rebukes this perversion of duty; and gives him to understand, that no

* Rom. i. 30.

pretence of serving God, can cover the neglect of assisting a parent. And if no pretence of serving God can do it, surely every other pretence must still be more unnatural.

Under this head also we may consider that attention, and love, which are due to other relations, especially that mutual affection which should subsist between brothers. The name of brother expresses the highest degree of tenderness; and is generally used in scripture, as a term of peculiar endearment, to call men to the practice of social virtue. It reminds them of every kindness, which man can shew to man. If then we ought to treat all mankind with the affection of brothers, in what light must they appear, who being really such, are ever at variance with each other; continually doing spiteful actions, and shewing, upon every occasion, not only a want of brotherly kindness, but even of common regard?

The next part of our duty is "to honour and obey the king, and all that are put in authority under him."

By the "king, and all that are put in authority under him," is meant the various parts of the government we live under, of which the king is the head: and the meaning of the precept is, that we ought to live in dutiful submission to legal authority.

Government and society are united. We cannot have one without the other; and we submit to the inconveniences, for the sake of the advantages.

The end of society is mutual safety and convenience. Without it, even safety could in no degree be obtained: the good would become a prey to the bad; nay, the very human species to the beasts of the field.

Still less could we obtain the conveniences of life; which cannot be had without the labour of many. If every man depended upon himself for what he enjoyed, how destitute would be the situation of human affairs!

But even safety and convenience are not the only fruits of society. Man, living merely by himself, would be an ignorant unpolished savage. It is the intercourse of society which cultivates the human mind. One man's knowledge and experience is built upon another's; and so the great edifice of science and polished life is reared.

To enjoy these advantages, therefore, men joined in society; and hence it became necessary, that government should be established. Magistrates were created; laws made; taxes submitted to; and every one, instead of righting himself (except in mere self-defence) is injoined to appeal to the laws he lives under, as the best security of his life and property. *Gilpin.*

§ 53. *Duty to our teachers and instructors—arising from the great importance of knowledge and religion—and the great necessity of gaining habits of attention, and of virtue, in our youth—analogy of youth and manhood to this world and the next.*

We are next injoined "to submit ourselves to all our governors, teachers, spiritual pastors, and masters." Here another species of government is pointed out. The laws of society are meant to govern our riper years: the instructions of our teachers, spiritual pastors, and masters, are meant to guide our youth.

By our "teachers, spiritual pastors, and masters," are meant all those who have the care of our education, and of our instruction in religion; whom we are to obey, and listen to, with humility and attention, as the means of our advancement in knowledge and religion.

religion. The inſtructions we receive from them are unqueſtionably ſubject to our own judgment in future life; for by his own judgment every man muſt ſtand or fall. But, during our youth, it is highly proper for us to pay a dutiful ſubmiſſion to their inſtructions, as we cannot yet be ſuppoſed to have formed any judgment of our own. At that early age it ſhould be our endeavour to acquire knowledge; and afterwards unprejudiced to form our opinions.

The duty which young people owe to their inſtructors, cannot be ſhewn better, than in the effect which the inſtructions they receive have upon them. They would do well, therefore, to conſider the advantages of an early attention to theſe two things, both of great importance, knowledge, and religion.

The great uſe of knowledge in all its various branches (to which the learned languages are generally conſidered as an introduction) is to free the mind from the prejudices of ignorance; and to give it juſter, and more enlarged conceptions, than are the mere growth of rude nature. By reading, you add the experience of others to your own. It is the improvement of the mind chiefly, that makes the difference between man and man; and gives one man a real ſuperiority over another.

Beſides, the mind muſt be employed. The lower orders of men have their attention much ingroſſed by thoſe employments in which the neceſſities of life engage them: and it is happy that they have. Labour ſtands in the room of education; and fills up thoſe vacancies of mind, which, in a ſtate of idleneſs, would be ingroſſed by vice. And if they, who have more leiſure, do not ſubſtitute ſomething in the room of this, their minds alſo will become the prey of vice; and the more ſo, as they have the means to indulge it more in their power. A vacant mind is exactly that houſe mentioned in the goſpel, which the devil found empty. In he entered; and taking with him ſeven other ſpirits more wicked than himſelf, they took poſſeſſion. It is an undoubted truth, that one vice indulged, introduces others; and that each ſucceeding vice becomes more depraved—If then the mind muſt be employed, what can fill up its vacuities more rationally than the acquiſition of knowledge? Let us therefore thank God for the opportunities he hath afforded us; and not turn into a curſe thoſe means of leiſure, which might become ſo great a bleſſing.

But however neceſſary to us knowledge may be, religion, we know, is infinitely more ſo. The one adorns a man, and gives him, it is true, ſuperiority, and rank in life: but the other is abſolutely eſſential to his happineſs.

In the midſt of youth, health, and abundance, the world is apt to appear a very gay and pleaſing ſcene; it engages our deſires; and in a degree ſatisfies them alſo. But it is wiſdom to conſider, that a time will come, when youth, health, and fortune, will all fail us; and if diſappointment and vexation do not ſour our taſte for pleaſure, at leaſt ſickneſs and infirmities will deſtroy it. In theſe gloomy ſeaſons, and above all, at the approach of death, what will become of us without religion? When this world fails, where ſhall we fly, if we expect no refuge in another? Without holy hope in God, and reſignation to his will, and truſt in him for deliverance, what is there that can ſecure us againſt the evils of life?

The great utility therefore of knowledge and religion being thus apparent, it is highly incumbent upon us to pay a ſtudious attention

tention to them in our youth. If we do not, it is more than probable that we ſhall never do it: that we ſhall grow old in ignorance, by neglecting the one; and old in vice by neleєting the other.

For improvement in knowledge, youth is certainly the fitteſt ſeaſon. The mind is then ready to receive any impreſſion. It is free from all that care and attention which, in riper age, the affairs of life bring with them. The memory too is then ſtronger and better able to acquire the rudiments of knowledge; and as the mind is then void of ideas, it is more ſuited to thoſe parts of learning which are converſant in words. Beſides, there is ſometimes in youth a modeſty and ductility, which in advanced years, if thoſe years eſpecially have been left a prey to ignorance, become ſelf-ſufficiency and prejudice; and theſe effectually bar up all the inlets to knowledge.—But, above all, unleſs habits of attention and application are early gained, we ſhall ſcarce acquire them afterwards.—The inconſiderate youth ſeldom reflects upon this; nor knows his loſs, till he knows alſo that it cannot be retrieved.

Nor is youth more the ſeaſon to acquire knowledge, than to form religious habits. It is a great point to get habit on the ſide of virtue. It will make every thing ſmooth and eaſy. The earlieſt principles are generally the moſt laſting; and thoſe of a religious caſt are ſeldom wholly loſt. Though the temptations of the world may, now and then, draw the well-principled youth aſide; yet his principles being continually at war with his practice, there is hope, that in the end the better part may overcome the worſe, and bring on a reformation. Whereas he, who has ſuffered habits of vice to get poſſeſſion of his youth, has little chance of being brought back to a ſenſe of religion. In a common courſe of things it can rarely happen. Some calamity muſt rouſe him. He muſt be awakened by a ſtorm, or ſleep for ever.—How much better is it then to make that eaſy to us, which we know is beſt! And to form thoſe habits now, which hereafter we ſhall wiſh we had formed!

There are, who would reſtrain youth from imbibing any religious principles, till they can judge for themſelves; leſt they ſhould imbibe prejudice for truth. But why ſhould not the ſame caution be uſed in ſcience alſo; and the minds of youth left void of all impreſſions? The experiment, I fear, in both caſes would be dangerous. If the mind were left uncultivated during ſo long a period, though nothing elſe ſhould find entrance, vice certainly would: and it would make the larger ſhoots, as the ſoil would be vacant. A boy had better receive knowledge and religion mixed with error, than none at all. For when the mind is ſet a thinking, it may depoſit its prejudices by degrees, and get right at laſt: but in a ſtate of ſtagnation it will infallibly become foul.

To conclude, our youth bears the ſame proportion to our more advanced life, as this world does to the next. In this life we muſt form and cultivate thoſe habits of virtue, which muſt qualify us for a better ſtate. If we neglect them here, and contract habits of an oppoſite kind, inſtead of gaining that exalted ſtate, which is promiſed to our improvement, we ſhall of courſe ſink into that ſtate, which is adapted to the habits we have formed.

Exactly thus is youth introductory to manhood; to which it is, properly ſpeaking, a ſtate of preparation. During this ſeaſon we muſt muft qualify ourfelves for the parts we are to act hereafter. In manhood we bear the fruit, which has in youth been planted. If we have fauntered away our youth, we muft expect to be ignorant men. If indolence and inattention have taken an early poffeffion of us, they will probably increafe as we advance in life; and make us a burden to ourfelves, and ufelefs to fociety. If again, we fuffer ourfelves to be mifled by vicious inclinations, they will daily get new ftrength, and end in diffolute lives. But if we cultivate our minds in our youth, attain habits of attention and induftry, of virtue and fobriety, we fhall find ourfelves well prepared to act our future parts in life; and what above all things ought to be our care, by gaining this command over ourfelves, we fhall be more able, as we get forward in the world, to refift every new temptation, as it arifes. *Gilpin.*

§ 54. *Behaviour to Superiors.*

We are next injoined "to order ourfelves lowly and reverently to all our betters."

By our betters are meant they who are in a fuperior ftation of life to our own; and by "ordering ourfelves lowly and reverently towards them," is meant paying them that refpect which is due to their ftation.

The word 'betters' indeed includes two kinds of perfons, to whom our refpect is due—thofe who have a natural claim to it: and thofe who have an acquired one; that is, a claim arifing from fome particular fituation in life.

Among the firft, are all our fuperior relations; not only parents, but all other relations who are in a line above us. All thefe have a natural claim to our refpect.—There is a refpect alfo due from youth to age; which is always becoming, and tends to keep youth within the bounds of modefty.

To others, refpect is due from thofe particular ftations which arife from fociety and government. Fear God, fays the text; and it adds, "honour the king."

It is due alfo from many other fituations in life. Employments, honours, and even wealth, will exact it; and all may juftly exact it, in a proper degree.

But it may here perhaps be enquired, why God fhould permit this latter diftinction among men? That fome fhould have more authority than others, we can eafily fee, is abfolutely neceffary in government; but among men, who are all born equal, why fhould the goods of life be diftributed in fo unequal a proportion?

To this inquiry, it may be anfwered, that, in the firft place, we fee nothing in this, but what is common in all the works of God. A gradation is every where obfervable. Beauty, ftrength, fwiftnefs, and other qualities, are varied through the creation in numberlefs degrees. In the fame manner likewife are varied the gifts of fortune, as they are called. Why therefore fhould one man's being richer than another furprize us more than his being ftronger than another, or more prudent?

Though we can but very inadequately trace the wifdom of God in his works, yet very wife reafons appear for this variety in the gifts of fortune. It feems neceffary both in a civil, and in a moral light.

In a civil light, it is the neceffary accompaniment of various employments; on which depend all the advantages of fociety. Like the ftones of a regular building, fome muft range higher, and fome lower; fome muft fupport, and others be fupported; fome will form the ftrength of the building, and others its

its ornament; but all unite in producing one regular and proportioned whole. If then different employments are neceſſary, of courſe different degrees of wealth, honour, and conſequence, muſt follow; a variety of diſtinctions and obligations; in ſhort, different ranks, and a ſubordination muſt take place.

Again, in a moral light, the diſproportion of wealth, and other worldly adjuncts, gives a range to the more extenſive exerciſe of virtue. Some virtues could but faintly exiſt upon the plan of an equality. If ſome did not abound, there were little room for temperance: if ſome did not ſuffer need, there were as little for patience. Other virtues again could hardly exiſt at all. Who could practice generoſity, where there was no object of it? Who humility, where all ambitious deſires were excluded?

Since then Providence, in ſcattering theſe various gifts, propoſes ultimately the good of man, it is our duty to acquieſce in this order, and "to behave ourſelves lowly and reverently" (not with ſervility, but with a decent reſpect) "to all our ſuperiors."

Before I conclude this ſubject, it may be proper to obſerve, in vindication of the ways of Providence, that we are not to ſuppoſe happineſs and miſery neceſſarily connected with riches and poverty. Each condition hath its particular ſources both of pleaſure and pain, unknown to the other. Thoſe in elevated ſtations have a thouſand latent pangs, of which their inferiors have no idea; while their inferiors again have as many pleaſures, which the others cannot taſte. I ſpeak only of ſuch modes of happineſs or miſery as ariſe immediately from different ſtations. Of miſery, indeed, from a variety of other cauſes, all men of every ſtation are equal heirs, either when God lays his hand upon us in ſickneſs, or misfortune; or when, by our own follies and vices, we become the miniſters of our own diſtreſs.

Who then would build his happineſs upon an elevated ſtation? Or who would envy the poſſeſſion of ſuch happineſs in another? We know not with what various diſtreſſes that ſtation, which is the object of our envy, may be attended.—Beſides, as we are accountable for all we poſſeſs, it may be happy for us that we poſſeſs ſo little. The means of happineſs, as far as ſtation can procure them, are commonly in our own power, if we are not wanting to ourſelves.

Let each of us then do his duty in that ſtation which Providence has aſſigned him; ever remembering, that the next world will ſoon deſtroy all earthly diſtinctions.—One diſtinction only will remain among the ſons of men at that time—the diſtinction between good and bad; and this diſtinction it is worth all our pains and all our ambition to acquire.

Gilpin.

§ 55. *Againſt wronging our neighbour by injurious words.*

We are next inſtructed "to hurt nobody by word or deed—to be true and juſt in all our dealings—to bear no malice nor hatred in our hearts—to keep our hands from picking and ſtealing—our tongues from evil ſpeaking, lying, and ſlandering."

The duties comprehended in theſe words are a little tranſpoſed. What ſhould claſs under one head is brought under another. "To hurt nobody by word or deed," is the general propoſition. The under parts ſhould follow: Firſt, "to keep the tongue from evil ſpeaking, lying, and ſlandering;" which is, "to hurt nobody by word." Secondly, "to be true and juſt in all our dealings;" and "to keep

keep our hands from picking and ſtealing;" which is, "to hurt nobody by deed." As to the injunction, "to bear no malice nor hatred in our hearts," it belongs properly to neither of theſe heads; but is a diſtinct one by itſelf. The duties being thus ſeparated, I ſhall proceed to explain them.

And, firſt, of injuring our neighbour by our "words." This may be done, we find, in three ways; by "evil-ſpeaking, by lying, and by ſlandering."

By "evil-ſpeaking," is meant ſpeaking ill of our neighbour; but upon a ſuppoſition, that this ill is the truth. In ſome circumſtances it is certainly right to ſpeak ill of our neighbour; as when we are called upon in a court of juſtice to give our evidence; or, when we can ſet any one right in his opinion of a perſon, in whom he is about to put an improper confidence. Nor can there be any harm in ſpeaking of a bad action, which has been determined in a court of juſtice, or is otherwiſe become notorious.

But on the other hand, it is highly diſallowable to ſpeak wantonly of the characters of others from common fame; becauſe, in a thouſand inſtances, we find that ſtories, which have no better foundation, are miſrepreſented. They are perhaps only half-told—they have been heard through the medium of malice or envy—ſome favourable circumſtance hath been omitted—ſome foreign circumſtance hath been added—ſome trifling circumſtance hath been exaggerated—the motive, the provocation, or perhaps the reparation hath been concealed—in ſhort, the repreſentation of the fact is, ſome way or other totally different from the fact itſelf.

But even, when we have the beſt evidence of a bad action, with all its circumſtances before us, we ſurely indulge a very ill-natured pleaſure in ſpreading the ſhame of an offending brother. We can do no good; and we may do harm: we may weaken his good reſolutions by expoſing him: we may harden him againſt the world. Perhaps it may be his firſt bad action. Perhaps nobody is privy to it but ourſelves. Let us give him at leaſt one trial. Let us not caſt the firſt ſtone. Which of our lives could ſtand ſo ſtrict a ſcrutiny? He only who is without ſin himſelf can have any excuſe for treating his brother with ſeverity.

Let us next conſider "lying;" which is an intention to deceive by falſehood in our words.—To warn us againſt lying, we ſhould do well to conſider the folly, the meanneſs, and the wickedneſs of it.

The folly of lying conſiſts in its defeating its own purpoſe. A habit of lying is generally in the end detected; and, after detection, the lyar, inſtead of deceiving, will not even be believed when he happens to ſpeak the truth. Nay, every ſingle lye is attended with ſuch a variety of circumſtances, which lead to a detection, that it is often diſcovered. The uſe generally made of a lye, is to cover a fault; but as the end is ſeldom anſwered, we only aggravate what we wiſh to conceal. In point even of prudence, an honeſt confeſſion would ſerve us better.

The meanneſs of lying ariſes from the cowardice which it implies. We dare not boldly and nobly ſpeak the truth; but have recourſe to low ſubterfuges, which always argue a ſordid and diſengenuous mind. Hence it is, that in the faſhionable world, the word lyar is always conſidered as a term of peculiar reproach.

The wickedneſs of lying conſiſts in its perverting one of the greateſt bleſſings of God, the uſe of ſpeech, in making that a miſchief to to mankind, which was intended for a benefit. Truth is the great bond of ſociety. Falſehood, of courſe, tends to its diſſolution. If one man may lye, why not another? And if there is no mutual truſt among men, there is an end of all intercourſe and dealing.

An equivocation is nearly related to a lye. It is an intention to deceive under words of a double meaning, or words which, literally ſpeaking, are true; and is equally criminal with the moſt downright breach of truth. When St. Peter aſked Sapphira (in the 5th chapter of the Acts) "whether her huſband had ſold the land for ſo much?" She anſwered, he had: and literally ſhe ſpoke the truth; for he had ſold it for that ſum, included in a larger. But having an intention to deceive, we find the apoſtle conſidered the equivocation as a lye.

In ſhort, it is the intention to deceive, which is criminal: the mode of deception, like the vehicle in which poiſon is conveyed, is of no conſequence. A nod, or ſign, may convey a lye as effectually as the moſt deceitful language.

Under the head of lying may be mentioned a breach of promiſe. While a reſolution remains in our own breaſts, it is ſubject to our own review: but when we make another perſon a party with us, an engagement is made; and every engagement, though only of the lighteſt kind, ſhould be punctually obſerved. If we have added to this engagement a ſolemn promiſe, the obligation is ſo much the ſtronger: and he who does not think himſelf bound by ſuch an obligation, has no pretenſions to the character of an honeſt man. A breach of promiſe is ſtill worſe than a lye. A lye is ſimply a breach of truth; but a breach of promiſe is a breach both of truth and truſt.

Forgetfulneſs is a weak excuſe: it only ſhews how little we are affected by ſo ſolemn an engagement. Should we forget to call for a ſum of money, of which we were in want, at an appointed time? Or do we think a ſolemn promiſe of leſs value than a ſum of money?

Having conſidered evil ſpeaking and lying, let us next conſider ſlandering. By ſlandering, we mean, injuring our neighbour's character by falſehood. Here we ſtill riſe higher in the ſcale of injurious words. Slandering our neighbour is the greateſt injury, which words can do him; and is, therefore, worſe than either evil-ſpeaking or lying. The miſchief of this ſin depends on the value of our characters. All men, unleſs they be paſt feeling, deſire naturally to be thought well of by their fellow-creatures: a good character is one of the principal means of being ſerviceable either to ourſelves or others; and among numbers, the very bread they eat depends upon it. What aggravated injury, therefore, do we bring upon every man, whoſe name we ſlander? And, what is ſtill worſe, the injury is irreparable. If you defraud a man; reſtore what you took, and the injury is repaired. But, if you ſlander him, it is not in your power to ſhut up all the ears, and all the mouths, to which your tale may have acceſs. The evil ſpreads, like the winged ſeeds of ſome noxious plants, which ſcatter miſchief on a breath of air, and diſperſe it on every ſide, and beyond prevention.

Before we conclude this ſubject, it may juſt be mentioned, that a ſlander may be ſpread, as a lye may be told, in various ways. We may do it by an inſinuation, as well as in a direct manner; we may ſpread it in a ſecret; or propagate it under the colour of friendſhip.

I may

I may add alſo, that it is a ſpecies of ſlander, and often a very malignant one, to leſſen the merits or exaggerate the failings of others; as it is likewiſe to omit defending a miſrepreſented character, or to let others bear the blame of our offences. *Gilpin.*

§ 56. *Againſt wronging our Neighbour by injurious Actions.*

Having thus conſidered injurious words, let us next conſider injurious actions. On this head we are injoined "to keep our hands from picking and ſtealing, and to be true and juſt in all our dealings."

As to theft, it is a crime of ſo odious and vile a nature, that one would imagine no perſon, who hath had the leaſt tincture of a virtuous education, even though driven to neceſſity, could be led into it.—I ſhall not, therefore, enter into a diſſuaſive from this crime; but go on with the explanation of the other part of the injunction, and ſee what it is to be true and juſt in all our dealings.

Juſtice is even ſtill more, if poſſible, the ſupport of ſociety, than truth: inaſmuch as a man may be more injurious by his actions, than by his words. It is for this reaſon, that the whole force of human law is bent to reſtrain injuſtice; and the happineſs of every ſociety will increaſe in proportion to this reſtraint.

We very much err, however, if we ſuppoſe, that every thing within the bounds of law is juſtice. The law was intended only for bad men; and it is impoſſible to make the meſhes of it ſo ſtrait, but that many very great enormities will eſcape. The well-meaning man, therefore, knowing that the law was not made for him, conſults a better guide—his own conſcience, informed by religion. And, indeed, the great difference between the good and the bad man conſiſts in this: the good man will do nothing, but what his conſcience will allow; the bad man will do any thing which the law cannot reach.

It would indeed, be endleſs to deſcribe the various ways, in which a man may be diſhoneſt within the limits of law. They are as various as our intercourſe with mankind. Some of the moſt obvious of them I ſhall curſorily mention.

In matters of commerce the knave has many opportunities. The different qualities of the ſame commodity—the different modes of adulteration—the ſpecious arts of vending—the frequent ignorance in purchaſing; and a variety of other circumſtances, open an endleſs field to the ingenuity of fraud. The honeſt fair dealer, in the mean time, has only one rule, which is, that all arts, however common in buſineſs, which are intended to deceive, are utterly unlawful. It may be added, upon this head, that if any one, conſcious of having been a tranſgreſſor, is deſirous of repairing his fault, reſtitution is by all means neceſſary: till that be done, he continues in a courſe of injuſtice.

Again, in matters of contract, a man has many opportunities of being diſhoneſt within the bounds of law. He may be ſtrict in obſerving the letter of an agreement, when the equitable meaning requires a laxer interpretation: or, he can take the laxer interpretation, when it ſerves his purpoſe; and at the loophole of ſome ambiguous expreſſion exclude the literal meaning, though it be undoubtedly the true one.

The ſame iniquity appears in with-holding from another his juſt right; or in putting him to expence in recovering it. The movements of the law are ſlow; and in many caſes cannot be otherwiſe; but he who takes the advantage of this to injure his neighbour, proves himself an undoubted knave.

It is a species of the same kind of injustice to withhold a debt, when we have ability to pay; or to run into debt, when we have not that ability. The former can proceed only from a bad disposition; the latter, from suffering our desires to exceed our station. Some are excused, on this head, as men of generous principles, which they cannot confine. But what is their generosity? They assist one man by injuring another. And what good arises to society from hence? Such persons cannot act on principle; and we need not hesitate to rank them with those, who run into debt to gratify their own selfish inclinations. One man desires the elegancies of life; another desires what he thinks an equal good, the reputation of generosity.

Oppression is another species of injustice; by which, in a thousand ways, under the cover of law, we may take the advantage of the superiority of our power, either to crush an inferior, or humble him to our designs.

Ingratitude is another. A loan, we know, claims a legal return. And is the obligation less, if, instead of a loan, you receive a kindness? The law, indeed, says nothing on this point of immorality, but an honest conscience will be very loud in the condemnation of it.

We may be unjust also in our resentment; by carrying it beyond what reason and religion prescribe.

But it would be endless to describe the various ways, in which injustice discovers itself. In truth, almost every omission of duty may be resolved into injustice.

The next precept is, "to bear no malice nor hatred in our hearts."

The malice and hatred of our hearts arise, in the first place, from injurious treatment; and surely no man, when he is injured, can at first help feeling that he is so. But Christianity requires, that we should subdue these feelings, as soon as possible; "and not suffer the sun to go down upon our wrath." Various are the passages of scripture, which inculcate the forgiveness of injuries. Indeed, no point is more laboured than this; and with reason, because no temper is more productive of evil, both to ourselves and others, than a malicious one. The sensations of a mind burning with revenge are beyond description; and as we are at these seasons very unable to judge coolly, and of course liable to carry our resentment too far, the consequence is, that, in our rage, we may do a thousand things, which can never be atoned for, and of which we may repent as long as we live.

Besides, one act draws on another; and retaliation keeps the quarrel alive. The gospel, therefore, ever gracious and kind to man, in all its precepts enjoins us to check all those violent emotions, and to leave our cause in the hands of God. "Vengeance is mine, I will repay, saith the Lord;" and he who, in opposition to this precept, takes vengeance into his own hands, and cherishes the malice and hatred of his heart, may assure himself that he has not yet learned to be a Christian. These precepts, perhaps, may not entirely agree with modern principles of honour: but let the man of honour see to that. The maxims of the world cannot change the truth of the gospel.

Nay, even in recovering our just right, or in pursuing a criminal to justice, we should take care that it be not done in the spirit of retaliation and revenge. If these be our motives,

tives, though we make the law our instrument, we are equally guilty.

But besides injurious treatment, the malice and hatred of our hearts have often another source, and that is envy: and thus in the litany; "envy, malice, and hatred," are all joined together with great propriety. The emotions of envy are generally cooler, and less violent, than those which arise from the resentment of injury; so that envy is seldom so mischievous in its effects as revenge: but with regard to ourselves, it is altogether as bad, and full as destructive of the spirit of christianity. What is the religion of that man, who instead of thanking Heaven for the blessings he receives, is fretting himself continually with a disagreeable comparison between himself and some other? He cannot enjoy what he has, because another has more wealth, a fairer fame, or perhaps more merit, than himself. He is miserable, because others are happy.

But to omit the wickedness of envy, how absurd and foolish is it, in a world where we must necessarily expect much real misery, to be perniciously inventive in producing it!

Besides, what ignorance! We see only the glaring outside of things. Under all that envied glare, many unseen distresses may lurk, from which our station may be free: for our merciful Creator seems to have bestowed happiness, as far as station is concerned, with great equality among all his creatures.

In conclusion, therefore, let it be the great object of our attention, and the subject of our prayers, to rid our minds of all this cursed intrusion of evil thoughts—whether they proceed from malice, or from an envious temper. Let all our malicious thoughts soften into charity and benevolence; and let us "forgive one another, as God, for Christ's sake, has forgiven us." As for our envious thoughts, as far as they relate to externals, let them subside in humility, acquiescence, and submission to the will of God. And when we are tempted to envy the good qualities of others, let us spurn so base a conception, and change it into a generous emulation—into an endeavour to raise ourselves to an equality with our rival, not to depress him to a level with us. *Gilpin.*

§ 57. *Duties to ourselves.*

Thus far the duties we have considered come most properly under the head of those which we owe to our neighbour; what follows, relates rather to ourselves. On this head, we are instructed "to keep our bodies in temperance, soberness, and chastity."

Though our souls should be our great concern, yet, as they are nearly connected with our bodies, and as the impurity of the one contaminates the other, a great degree of moral attention is, of course, due to our bodies also.

As our first station is in this world, to which our bodies particularly belong, they are formed with such appetites as are requisite to our commodious living in it; and the rule given us is, "to use the world so as not to abuse it." St. Paul, by a beautiful allusion, calls our bodies the "temples of the Holy Ghost;" by which he means to impress us with a strong idea of their dignity; and to deter us from debasing by low pleasures, what should be the seat of so much purity. To youth these cautions are above measure necessary, because their passions and appetites are strong; their reason and judgment weak. They are prone to pleasure, and void of reflection. How, therefore, these young adventurers in life may best steer their course, and

and uſe this ſinful world ſo as not to abuſe it, is a conſideration well worth their attention. Let us then ſee under what regulations their appetites ſhould be reſtrained.

By keeping our bodies in temperance is meant avoiding exceſs in eating, with regard both to the quantity and quality of our food. We ſhould neither eat more than our ſtomachs can well bear; nor be nice and delicate in our eating.

To preſerve the body in health is the end of eating; and they who regulate themſelves merely by this end, who eat without choice or diſtinction, paying no regard to the pleaſure of eating, obſerve perhaps the beſt rule of temperance. They go rather indeed beyond temperance, and may be called abſtemious. A man may be temperate, and yet allow himſelf a little more indulgence. Great care, however, is here neceſſary; and the more, as perhaps no preciſe rule can be affixed, after we have paſſed the firſt great limit, and let the palate looſe among variety *. Our own diſcretion muſt be our guide, which ſhould be conſtantly kept awake by conſidering the many bad conſequences which attend a breach of temperance.—Young men, in the full vigour of health, do not conſider theſe things; but as age comes on, and different maladies begin to appear, they may perhaps repent they did not a little earlier practiſe the rules of temperance.

In a moral and religious light, the conſequences of intemperance are ſtill worſe. To enjoy a comfortable meal, when it comes before us is allowable: but he who ſuffers his mind to dwell upon the pleaſures of eating, and makes them the employment of his thoughts, has at leaſt opened one ſource of mental corruption †.

After all, he who would moſt perfectly enjoy the pleaſures of the table, ſuch as they are, muſt look for them within the rules of temperance. The palate, accuſtomed to ſatiety, hath loſt its tone; and the greateſt ſenſualiſts have been brought to confeſs, that the coarſeſt fare, with an appetite kept in order by temperance, affords a more delicious repaſt, than the moſt luxurious meal without it.

As temperance relates chiefly to eating, ſoberneſs or ſobriety relates properly to drinking. And here the ſame obſervations recur. The ſtricteſt, and perhaps the beſt rule, is merely to ſatisfy the end of drinking. But if a little more indulgence be taken, it ought to be taken with the greateſt circumſpection.

With regard to youth indeed, I ſhould be inclined to great ſtrictneſs on this head. In eating, if they eat of proper and ſimple food, they cannot eaſily err. Their growing limbs, and ſtrong exerciſe, require larger ſupplies than full grown bodies, which muſt be kept in order by a more rigid temperance. But if more indulgence be allowed them in eating, leſs, ſurely, ſhould in drinking. With ſtrong liquors of every kind they have nothing to do; and if they ſhould totally abſtain on this head, it were ſo much the better. The languor

* ——— Nam variæ res,
Ut noceant homini, credas memor illius eſcæ,
Quæ ſimplex olim tibi ſederit. At ſimul aſſis
Miſcueris elixa, ſimul conchylia turdis
Dulcia ſe in bilem vertent, ſtomachoque tumultum
Lenta feret pituita.——— Hor.

† ———Corpus onuſtum
Heſternis vitiis, animum quoque prægravat una,
Atque affigit humo divinæ particulum auræ.
Hor. Sat.

which

which attends age *, requires perhaps, now and then, ſome aids ; but the ſpirits of youth want no recruits : a little reſt is ſufficient.

As to the bad conſequences derived from exceſſive drinking, beſides filling the blood with bloated and vicious humours, and debauching the purity of the mind, as in the caſe of intemperate eating, it is attended with this peculiar evil, the loſs of our ſenſes. Hence follow frequent inconveniences and mortifications. We expoſe our follies—we betray our ſecrets—we are often impoſed upon —we quarrel with our friends—we lay ourſelves open to our enemies ; and, in ſhort, make ourſelves the objects of contempt, and the topics of ridicule to all our acquaintance.—Nor is it only the act of intoxication which deprives us of our reaſon during the prevalence of it ; the habit of drunkenneſs ſoon beſots and impairs the underſtanding, and renders us at all times leſs fit for the offices of life.

We are next injoined " to keep our bodies in chaſtity." " Flee youthful luſts," ſays the apoſtle, " which war againſt the ſoul." And there is ſurely nothing which carries on a war againſt the ſoul more ſucceſsfully. Wherever we have a catalogue in ſcripture (and we have many ſuch catalogues) of thoſe ſins which in a peculiar manner debauch the mind, theſe youthful luſts have always, under ſome denomination, a place among them. ——To keep ourſelves free from all contagion of this kind, let us endeavour to preſerve a purity in our thoughts—our words—and our actions.

Firſt, let us preſerve a purity in our thoughts.

* ——————Ubi ve
Accedant anni, et tractari mollius ætas
Imbecilla volet. Hor. Sat.

Theſe dark receſſes, which the eye of the world cannot reach, are the receptacles of theſe youthful luſts. Here they find their firſt encouragement. The entrance of ſuch impure ideas perhaps we cannot always prevent. We may always however prevent cheriſhing them ; we may always prevent their making an impreſſion upon us : the devil may be caſt out as ſoon as diſcovered.

Let us always keep in mind, that even into theſe dark abodes the eye of Heaven can penetrate : that every thought of our hearts is open to that God, before whom we muſt one day ſtand ; and that however ſecretly we may indulge theſe impure ideas, at the great day of account they will certainly appear in an awful detail againſt us.

Let us remember again, that if our bodies be the temples of the Holy Ghoſt, our minds are the very ſanctuaries of thoſe temples : and if there be any weight in the apoſtle's argument againſt polluting our bodies, it urges with double force againſt polluting our minds.

But, above all other conſiderations, it behoves us moſt to keep our thoughts pure, becauſe they are the fountains from which our words and actions flow. " Out of the abundance of the heart the mouth ſpeaketh." Obſcene words and actions are only bad thoughts matured, and ſpring as naturally from them as the plant from its ſeed. It is the ſame vicious depravity carried a ſtep farther ; and only ſhews a more confirmed and a more miſchievous degree of guilt. While we keep our impurities in our thoughts, they debauch only ourſelves : bad enough, it is true. But when we proceed to words and actions, we let our impurities looſe : we ſpread the contagion, and become the corrupters of others.

Let it be our firſt care, therefore, to keep our

our thoughts pure. If we do this, our words and actions will be pure of course. And that we may be the better enabled to do it, let us use such helps as reason and religion prescribe. Let us avoid all company, and all books, that have a tendency to corrupt our minds; and every thing that can inflame our passions. He who allows himself in these things, holds a parley with vice; which will infallibly debauch him in the end, if he do not take the alarm in time, and break off such dalliance.

One thing ought to be our particular care, and that is, never to be unemployed. Ingenious amusements are of great use in filling up the vacuities of our time. Idle we should never be. A vacant mind is an invitation to vice. *Gilpin.*

§ 58. *On coveting and desiring other men's goods.*

We are forbidden, next, "to covet, or desire other men's goods."

There are two great paths of vice, into which bad men commonly strike; that of unlawful pleasure, and that of unlawful gain. —The path of unlawful pleasure we have just examined; and have seen the danger of obeying the headstrong impulse of our appetites. —We have considered also an immoderate love of gain, and have seen dishonesty and fraud in a variety of shapes. But we have yet viewed them only as they relate to society. We have viewed only the outward action. The rule before us, "We must not covet, nor desire other men's goods," comes a step nearer home, and considers the motive which governs the action.

Covetousness, or the love of money, is called in scripture "the root of all evil;" and it is called so for two reasons; because it makes us wicked, and because it makes us miserable.

First, it makes us wicked. When it once gets possession of the heart, it will let no good principle flourish near it. Most vices have their fits; and when the violence of the passion is spent, there is some interval of calm. The vicious appetite cannot always run riot. It is fatigued at least by its own impetuosity: and it is possible, that in this moment of tranquillity, a whisper from virtue may be heard. But in avarice, there is rarely intermission. It hangs like a dead weight upon the soul, always pulling it to earth. We might as well expect to see a plant grow upon a flint, as a virtue in the heart of a miser.

It makes us miserable as well as wicked. The cares and the fears of avarice are proverbial; and it must needs be, that he, who depends for happiness on what is liable to a thousand accidents, must of course feel as many distresses, and almost as many disappointments. The good man depends for happiness on something more permanent: and if his worldly affairs go ill, his great dependance is still left *. But as wealth is the god which the covetous man worships (for "covetousness," we are told, "is idolatry,") a disappointment here is a disappointment indeed. Be he ever so prosperous, his wealth cannot secure him against the evils of mortality; against that time, when he must give up all he values; when his bargains of advantage will be over, and nothing left but tears and despair.

But even a desiring frame of mind, though it be not carried to such a length, is always productive of misery. It cannot be otherwise.

* Sæviat, atque novos moveat fortuna tumultus;
Quantum hinc imminuet?——
HOR. Sat.

While we ſuffer ourſelves to be continually in queſt of what we have not, it is impoſſible that we ſhould be happy with what we have. In a word, to abridge our wants as much as poſſible, not to increaſe them, is the trueſt happineſs.

We are much miſtaken, however, if we think the man who hoards up his money is the only covetous man. The prodigal, though he differ in his end, may be as avaricious in his means *. The former denies himſelf every comfort; the latter graſps at every pleaſure. Both characters are equally bad in differents extremes. The miſer is more deteſtable in the eyes of the world, becauſe he enters into none of its joys; but it is a queſtion, which is more wretched in himſelf, or more pernicious to ſociety.

As covetouſneſs is eſteemed the vice of age, every appearance of it among young perſons ought particularly to be diſcouraged; becauſe if it gets ground at this early period, nobody can tell how far it may not afterwards proceed. And yet, on the other ſide, there may be great danger of encouraging the oppoſite extreme. As it is certainly right, under proper reſtrictions, both to ſave our money, and to ſpend it, it would be highly uſeful to fix the due bounds on each ſide. But nothing is more difficult than to raiſe theſe nice limits between extremes. Every man's caſe, in a thouſand circumſtances, differs from his neighbour's: and as no rule can be fixed for all, every man of courſe, in theſe diſquiſitions, muſt be left to his own conſcience. We are indeed very ready to give our opinions how others ought to act. We can adjuſt with great nicety what is proper for them to do; and point out their miſtakes with much preciſion; while nothing is neceſſary to us, but to act as properly as we can ourſelves; obſerving as juſt a mean as poſſible between prodigality and avarice; and applying, in all our difficulties, to the word of God, where theſe great landmarks of morality are the moſt accurately fixed.

* Alieni appetens, ſui profuſus. Sal. de Catal.

We have now taken a view of what is prohibited in our commerce with mankind: let us next ſee what is enjoined. (We are ſtill proceeding with thoſe duties which we owe to ourſelves). Inſtead of ſpending our fortune therefore in unlawful pleaſure, or increaſing it by unlawful gain; we are required "to learn, and labour truly (that is honeſtly) to get our own living, and to do our duty in that ſtate of life, unto which it ſhall pleaſe God to call us."—Theſe words will be ſufficiently explained by conſidering, firſt, that we all have ſome ſtation in life—ſome particular duties to diſcharge; and ſecondly, in what manner we ought to diſcharge them.

Firſt, that man was not born to be idle, may be inferred from the active ſpirit that appears in every part of nature. Every thing is alive; every thing contributes to the general good: even the very inanimate parts of the creation, plants, ſtones, metals, cannot be called totally inactive, but bear their part likewiſe in the general uſefulneſs. If then every part, even of inanimate nature, be thus employed, ſurely we cannot ſuppoſe it was the intention of the Almighty Father, that man, who is the moſt capable of employing himſelf properly, ſhould be the only creature without employment.

Again, that man was born for active life, is plain from the neceſſity of labour. If it had not been neceſſary, God would not originally have impoſed it. But without it, the body would become enervated, and the mind corrupted. Idleneſs, therefore, is juſtly eſteemed the origin both of diſeaſe and vice.

So that if labour and employment, either of body or mind, had no uſe, but what reſpected ourſelves, they would be highly proper: but they have farther uſe.

The neceſſity of them is plain, from the want that all men have of the aſſiſtance of others. If ſo, this aſſiſtance ſhould be mutual; every man ſhould contribute his part. We have already ſeen, that it is proper there ſhould be different ſtations in the world—that ſome ſhould be placed high in life, and others low. The loweſt, we know, cannot be exempt from labour; and the higheſt ought not: though their labour, according to their ſtation, will be of a different kind. Some, we ſee, "muſt labour (as the catechiſm phraſes it) to get their own living; and others ſhould do their duty in that ſtate of life, whatever that ſtate is, unto which it hath pleaſed God to call them." All are aſſiſted: all ſhould aſſiſt. God diſtributes, we read, various talents among men; to ſome he gives five talents, to others two, and to others one: but it is expected, we find, that notwithſtanding this inequality, each ſhould employ the talent that is given to the beſt advantage: and he who received five talents was under the ſame obligation of improving them, as he who had received only one; and would, if he had hid his talents in the earth, have been puniſhed, in proportion to the abuſe. Every man, even in the higheſt ſtation, may find a proper employment, both for his time and fortune, if he pleaſe: and he may aſſure himſelf that God, by placing him in that ſtation, never meant to exempt him from the common obligations of ſociety, and give him a licence to ſpend his life in eaſe and pleaſure. God meant aſſuredly, that he ſhould bear his part in the general commerce of life—that he ſhould conſider himſelf not as an individual, but as a member of the community; the intereſts of which he is under an obligation to ſupport with all his power;—and that his elevated ſtation gives him no other pre-eminence than that of being the more extenſively uſeful.

Having thus ſeen, that we have all ſome ſtation in life to ſupport—ſome particular duties to diſcharge; let us now ſee in what manner we ought to diſcharge them.

We have an eaſy rule given us in ſcripture on this head; that all our duties in life ſhould be performed "as to the Lord, and not unto man:" that is, we ſhould conſider our ſtations in life as truſts repoſed in us by our Maker; and as ſuch ſhould diſcharge the duties of them. What, though no worldly truſt be repoſed? What, though we are accountable to nobody upon earth? Can we therefore ſuppoſe ourſelves in reality leſs accountable? Can we ſuppoſe that God, for no reaſon that we can divine, has ſingled us out, and given us a large proportion of the things of this world (while others around us are in need) for no other purpoſe than to ſquander it away upon ourſelves? To God undoubtedly we are accountable for every bleſſing we enjoy. What mean, in ſcripture, the talents given, and the uſe aſſigned; but the conſcientious diſcharge of the duties of life, according to the advantages, with which they are attended?

It matters not whether theſe advantages be an inheritance, or an acquiſition: ſtill they are the gift of God. Agreeably to their rank in life, it is true, all men ſhould live: human diſtinctions require it; and in doing this properly, every one around will be benefited. Utility ſhould be conſidered in all our expences. Even the very amuſements of a man of fortune ſhould be founded in it.

In ſhort, it is the conſtant injunction of ſcripture,

ſcripture, in whatever ſtation we are placed, to conſider ourſelves as God's ſervants, and as acting immediately under his eye, not expecting our reward among men but from our great Maſter who is in heaven. This ſanctifies, in a manner, all our actions: it places the little difficulties of our ſtation in the light of God's appointments; and turns the moſt common duties of life into acts of religion. *Gilpin.*

§ 59. *On the Sacrament of Baptiſm.*

The ſacrament of baptiſm is next conſidered; in which, if we conſider the inward grace, we ſhall ſee how aptly the ſign repreſents it.—The inward grace, or thing ſignified, we are told, is "a death unto ſin, and a new birth unto righteouſneſs:" by which is meant that great renovation of nature, that purity of heart, which the chriſtian religion is intended to produce. And ſurely there cannot be a more ſignificant ſign of this than water, on account of its cleanſing nature. As water refreſhes the body, and purifies it from all contracted filth; it aptly repreſents that renovation of nature, which cleanſes the ſoul from the impurities of ſin. Water indeed, among the ancients, was more adapted to the thing ſignified, than it is at preſent among us. They uſed immerſion in baptiſing: ſo that the child being dipped into the water, and raiſed out again, baptiſm with them was more ſignificant of a new birth unto righteouſneſs. But though we, in theſe colder climates, think immerſion an unſafe practice; yet the original meaning is ſtill ſuppoſed.

It is next aſked, What is required of thoſe who are baptiſed? To this we anſwer, "Repentance, whereby they forſake ſin; and faith, whereby they ſtedfaſtly believe the promiſes of God, made to them in that ſacrament."

The primitive church was extremely ſtrict on this head. In thoſe times, before chriſtianity was eſtabliſhed, when adults offered themſelves to baptiſm, no one was admitted, till he had given a very ſatisfactory evidence of his repentance; and till, on good grounds, he could profeſs his faith in Chriſt: and it was afterwards expected from him, that he ſhould prove his faith and repentance, by a regular obedience during the future part of his life.

If faith and repentance are expected at baptiſm; it is a very natural queſtion, Why then are infants baptiſed, when, by reaſon of their tender age, they can give no evidence of either?

Whether infants ſhould be admitted to baptiſm, or whether that ſacrament ſhould be deferred till years of diſcretion; is a queſtion in the chriſtian church, which hath been agitated with ſome animoſity. Our church by no means looks upon baptiſm as neceſſary to the infant's ſalvation *. No man acquainted with the ſpirit of chriſtianity can conceive, that God will leave the ſalvation of ſo many innocent ſouls in the hands of others. But the practice is conſidered as founded upon the uſage of the earlieſt times: and the church obſerving, that circumciſion was the introductory rite to the Jewiſh covenant; and that baptiſm was intended to ſucceed circumciſion; it naturally ſuppoſes, that baptiſm ſhould be adminiſtered to infants, as circumciſion was. The church, however, in this caſe, hath pro-

* The catechiſm aſſerts the ſacraments to be only generally neceſſary to ſalvation, excepting particular caſes. Where the uſe of them is intentionally rejected, it is certainly criminal.—The Quakers indeed reject them on principle: but though we may wonder both at their logic and divinity, we ſhould be ſorry to include them in an anathema.

vided

vided ſponſors, who make a profeſſion of obedience in the child's name. But the nature and office of this proxy hath been already examined, under the head of our baptiſmal vow. *Gilpin.*

§ 60. *On the Sacrament of the Lord's Supper.*

The firſt queſtion is an enquiry into the original of the inſtitution: "Why was the ſacrament of the Lord's ſupper ordained?"

It was ordained, we are informed,—"for the continual remembrance of the ſacrifice of the death of Chriſt; and of the benefits which we receive thereby."

In examining a ſacrament in general, we have already ſeen, that both baptiſm, and the Lord's ſupper, were originally inſtituted as the "means of receiving the grace of God; and as pledges to aſſure us thereof."

But beſides theſe primary ends, they have each a ſecondary one; in repreſenting the two moſt important truths of religion; which gives them more force and influence. Baptiſm, we have ſeen, repreſents that renovation of our ſinful nature, which the goſpel was intended to introduce: and the peculiar end, which the Lord's ſupper had in view, was the ſacrifice of the death of Chriſt; with all the benefits which ariſe from it—the remiſſion of our ſins—and the reconciliation of the world to God. "This do," ſaid our Saviour (alluding to the paſſover, which the Lord's ſupper was deſigned to ſuperſede) not as hitherto, in memory of your deliverance from Egypt; but in memory of that greater deliverance, of which the other was only a type: "Do it in remembrance of me."

The outward part, or ſign of the Lord's ſupper, is "bread and wine"—the things ſignified are the "body and blood of Chriſt."—In examining the ſacrament of baptiſm, I endeavoured to ſhew, how very apt a ſymbol water is in that ceremony. Bread and wine alſo are ſymbols equally apt in repreſenting the body and blood of Chriſt: and in the uſe of theſe particular ſymbols, it is reaſonable to ſuppoſe, that our Saviour had an eye to the Jewiſh paſſover; in which it was a cuſtom to drink wine, and to eat bread. He might have inſtituted any other apt ſymbols for the ſame purpoſe; but it was his uſual practice, through the whole ſyſtem of his inſtitution, to make it, in every part, as familiar as poſſible: and for this reaſon he ſeems to have choſen ſuch ſymbols as were then in uſe; that he might give as little offence as poſſible in a matter of indifference.

As our Saviour, in the inſtitution of his ſupper, ordered both the bread and the wine to be received; it is certainly a great error in papiſts, to deny the cup to the laity. They ſay, indeed, that, as both fleſh and blood are united in the ſubſtance of the human body; ſo are they in the ſacramental bread; which, according to them, is changed, or, as they phraſe it, tranſubſtantiated into the real body of Chriſt. If they have no other reaſon, why do they adminiſter wine to the clergy? The clergy might participate equally of both in the bread.—But the plain truth is, they are deſirous, by this invention, to add an air of myſtery to the ſacrament, and a ſuperſtitious reverence to the prieſt, as if he, being endowed with ſome peculiar holineſs, might be allowed the uſe of both.

There is a difficulty in this part of the catechiſm, which ſhould not be paſſed over. We are told, that "the body and blood of Chriſt are verily and indeed taken, and received by the faithful in the Lord's ſupper." This expreſſion ſounds very like the popiſh doctrine,

doctrine, just mentioned, of transubstantiation. The true sense of the words undoubtedly is, that the faithful believer only, verily and indeed receives the benefit of the sacrament; but the expression must be allowed to be inaccurate, as it is capable of an interpretation so entirely opposite to that which the church of England hath always professed.—I would not willingly suppose, as some have done, that the compilers of the catechism meant to manage the affair of transubstantiation with the papists. It is one thing to shew a liberality of sentiment in matters of indifference; and another to speak timidly and ambiguously, where essentials are concerned.

It is next asked, What benefits we receive from the Lord's supper? To which it is answered, "The strengthening and refreshing of our souls by the body and blood of Christ, as our bodies are by the bread and wine." As our bodies are strengthened and refreshed, in a natural way, by bread and wine; so should our souls be, in a spiritual way, by a devout commemoration of the passion of Christ. By gratefully remembering what he suffered for us, we should be excited to a greater abhorrence of sin, which was the cause of his sufferings. Every time we partake of this sacrament, like faithful soldiers, we take a fresh oath to our leader; and should be animated anew, by his example, to persevere in the spiritual conflict in which, under him, we are engaged.

It is lastly asked, "What is required of them who come to the Lord's supper?" To which we answer, "That we should examine ourselves, whether we repent us truly of our former sins—stedfastly purposing to lead a new life—have a lively faith in God's mercy through Christ—with a thankful remembrance of his death; and to be in charity with all men."

That pious frame of mind is here, in very few words, pointed out, which a christian ought to cherish and cultivate in himself at all times; but especially, upon the performance of any solemn act of religion. Very little indeed is said in scripture, of any particular frame of mind, which should accompany the performance of this duty; but it may easily be inferred from the nature of the duty itself.

In the first place, "we should repent us truly of our former sins; stedfastly purposing to lead a new life." He who performs a religious exercise, without being earnest in this point; adds only a pharisaical hypocrisy to his other sins. Unless he seriously resolve to lead a good life, he had better be all of a piece; and not pretend, by receiving the sacrament, to a piety which he does not feel.

These "stedfast purposes of leading a new life," form a very becoming exercise to christians. The lives even of the best of men afford only a mortifying retrospect. Though they may have conquered some of their worst propensities; yet the triumphs of sin over them, at the various periods of their lives, will always be remembered with sorrow; and may always be remembered with advantage; keeping them on their guard for the future, and strengthening them more and more in all their good resolutions of obedience.—And when can these meditations arise more properly, than when we are performing a rite, instituted on purpose to commemorate the great atonement for sin?

To our repentance, and resolutions of obedience, we are required to add "a lively faith in God's mercy through Christ; with a thank-

ful

ful remembrance of his death." We ſhould impreſs ourſelves with the deepeſt ſenſe of humility—totally rejecting every idea of our own merit—hoping for God's favour only through the merits of our great Redeemer—and with hearts full of gratitude, truſting only to his all-ſufficient ſacrifice.

Laſtly, we are required, at the cebration of this great rite, to be "in charity with all men." It commemorates the greateſt inſtance of love that can be conceived; and ſhould therefore raiſe in us correſpondent affections. It ſhould excite in us that conſtant flow of benevolence, in which the ſpirit of religion conſiſts; and without which indeed we can have no religion at all. Love is the very diſtinguiſhing badge of chriſtianity: "By this," ſaid our great Maſter, "ſhall all men know that ye are my diſciples."

One ſpecies of charity ſhould, at this time, never be forgotten; and that is, the forgiveneſs of others. No acceptable gift can be offered at this altar, but in the ſpirit of reconciliation.—Hence it was, that the ancient chriſtians inſtituted, at the celebration of the Lord's ſupper, what they called love-feaſts. They thought, they could not give a better inſtance of their being in perfect charity with each other, than by joining all ranks together in one common meal.—By degrees, indeed, this well-meant cuſtom degenerated; and it may not be amiſs to obſerve here, that the paſſages * in which theſe enormities are rebuked, have been variouſly miſconſtrued; and have frightened many well meaning perſons from the ſacrament. Whereas what the apoſtle here ſays, hath no other relation to this rite, than as it was attended by a particular abuſe in receiving it; and as this is a mode of abuſe which doth not now exiſt, the apoſtle's reproof ſeems not to affect the chriſtians of this age.

What the primary, and what the ſecondary ends in the two ſacraments were, I have endeavoured to explain. But there might be others.

God might intend them as trials of our faith. The divine truths of the goſpel ſpeak for themſelves: but the performance of a poſitive duty reſts only on faith.

Theſe inſtitutions are alſo ſtrong arguments for the truth of chriſtianity. We trace the obſervance of them into the very earlieſt times of the goſpel. We can trace no other origin than what the ſcriptures give us. Theſe rites therefore greatly tend to corroborate the ſcriptures.

God alſo, who knows what is in man, might condeſcend ſo far to his weakneſs, as to give him theſe external badges of religion, to keep the ſpirit of it more alive. And it is indeed probable, that nothing has contributed more than theſe ceremonies to preſerve a ſenſe of religion among mankind. It is a melancholy proof of this, that no contentions in the chriſtian church have been more violent, nor carried on with more acrimony, and unchriſtian zeal, than the contentions about baptiſm and the Lord's ſupper; as if the very eſſence of religion conſiſted in this or that mode of obſerving theſe rites.—But this is the abuſe of them.

Let us be better taught: let us receive theſe ſacraments, for the gracious purpoſes for which our Lord injoined them, with gratitude, and with reverence. But let us not lay a greater ſtreſs upon them than our Lord intended. Heaven, we doubt not, may be gained, when there have been the means of receiving neither the one ſacrament nor the other. But unleſs our affections are right, and

* See 1 Cor. xi.

and our lives anſwerable to them, we can never pleaſe God, though we perform the externals of religion with ever ſo much exactneſs. We may err in our notions about the ſacraments: the world has long been divided on theſe ſubjects; and a gracious God, it may be hoped, will pardon our errors. But in matters of practice we have no apology for error. The great lines of our duty are drawn ſo ſtrong, that a deviation here is not error, but guilt.

Let us then, to conclude from the whole, make it our principal care to purify our hearts in the ſight of God. Let us beſeech him to increaſe the influence of his Holy Spirit within us, that our faith may be of that kind "which worketh by love;" that all our affections, and from them our actions, may flow in a ſteady courſe of obedience; that each day may correct the laſt by a ſincere repentance of our miſtakes in life; and that we may continue gradually to approach nearer the idea of chriſtian perfection. Let us do this, diſclaiming, after all, any merits of our own; and not truſting in outward obſervances; but truſting in the merits of Chriſt to make up our deficiencies; and we need not fear our acceptance with God. *Gilpin.*

§ 61. *Of the Scriptures, as the Rule of Life.*

As you advance in years and underſtanding, I hope you will be able to examine for yourſelf the evidences of the Chriſtian religion; and that you will be convinced, on rational grounds, of its divine authority. At preſent, ſuch enquiries would demand more ſtudy, and greater powers of reaſoning, than your age admits of. It is your part, therefore, till you are capable of underſtanding the proofs, to believe your parents and teachers, that the holy Scriptures are writings inſpired by God, containing a true hiſtory of facts, in which we are deeply concerned—a true recital of the laws given by God to Moſes, and of the precepts of our bleſſed Lord and Saviour, delivered from his own mouth to his diſciples, and repeated and enlarged upon in the edifying epiſtles of his apoſtles—who were men choſen from amongſt thoſe who had the advantage of converſing with our Lord, to bear witneſs of his miracles and reſurrection—and who, after his aſcenſion, were aſſiſted and inſpired by the Holy Ghoſt. This ſacred volume muſt be the rule of your life. In it you will find all truths neceſſary to be believed; and plain and eaſy directions for the practice of every duty. Your Bible, then, muſt be your chief ſtudy and delight: but, as it contains many various kinds of writing—ſome parts obſcure and difficult of interpretation, others plain and intelligible to the meaneſt capacity—I would chiefly recommend to your frequent peruſal ſuch parts of the ſacred writings as are moſt adapted to your underſtanding, and moſt neceſſary for your inſtruction. Our Saviour's precepts were ſpoken to the common people amongſt the Jews; and were therefore given in a manner eaſy to be underſtood, and equally ſtriking and inſtructive to the learned and unlearned: for the moſt ignorant may comprehend them, whilſt the wiſeſt muſt be charmed and awed by the beautiful and majeſtic ſimplicity with which they are expreſſed. Of the ſame kind are the Ten Commandments, delivered by God to Moſes; which, as they were deſigned for univerſal laws, are worded in the moſt conciſe and ſimple manner, yet with a majeſty which commands our utmoſt reverence.

I think you will receive great pleaſure, as well as improvement, from the hiſtorical books of the Old Teſtament—provided you read

read them as an history, in a regular course, and keep the thread of it in your mind as you go on. I know of none, true or fictitious, that is equally wonderful, interesting, and affecting; or that is told in so short and simple a manner as this, which is, of all histories, the most authentic.

I shall give you some brief directions, concerning the method and course I wish you to pursue, in reading the Holy Scriptures. May you be enabled to make the best use of this most precious gift of God—this sacred treasure of knowledge!—May you read the Bible, not as a task, nor as the dull employment of that day only, in which you are forbidden more lively entertainments—but with a sincere and ardent desire of instruction: with that love and delight in God's word, which the holy Psalmist so pathetically felt and described, and which is the natural consequence of loving God and virtue! Though I speak this of the Bible in general, I would not be understood to mean, that every part of the volume is equally interesting. I have already said that it consists of various matter, and various kinds of books, which must be read with different views and sentiments. The having some general notion of what you are to expect from each book, may possibly help you to understand them, and will heighten your relish of them. I shall treat you as if you were perfectly new to the whole; for so I wish you to consider yourself; because the time and manner in which children usually read the Bible, are very ill calculated to make them really acquainted with it; and too many people, who have read it thus, without understanding it, in their youth, satisfy themselves that they know enough of it, and never afterwards study it with attention, when they come to a maturer age.

If the feelings of your heart, whilst you read, correspond with those of mine, whilst I write, I shall not be without the advantage of your partial affection, to give weight to my advice; for, believe me, my heart and eyes overflow with tenderness, when I tell you how warm and earnest my prayers are for your happiness here and hereafter.

Mrs. Chapone.

§ 62. *Of Genesis.*

I now proceed to give you some short sketches of the matter contained in the different books of the Bible, and of the course in which they ought to be read.

The first book, Genesis, contains the most grand, and, to us, the most interesting events, that ever happened in the universe:—The creation of the world, and of man:—The deplorable fall of man, from his first state of excellence and bliss, to the distressed condition in which we see all his descendants continue:—The sentence of death pronounced on Adam, and on all his race—with the reviving promise of that deliverance which has since been wrought for us by our blessed Saviour:—The account of the early state of the world:—Of the universal deluge:—The division of mankind into different nations and languages:—The story of Abraham, the founder of the Jewish people; whose unshaken faith and obedience, under the severest trial human nature could sustain, obtained such favour in the sight of God, that he vouchsafed to style him his friend, and promised to make of his posterity a great nation, and that in his seed—that is, in one of his descendants—all the kingdoms of the earth should be blessed. This, you will easily see, refers to the Messiah, who was to be the blessing and deliverance of all nations.—It is amazing that the Jews,

Jews, possessing this prophecy, among many others, should have been so blinded by prejudice, as to have expected, from this great personage, only a temporal deliverance of their own nation from the subjection to which they were reduced under the Romans: It is equally amazing, that some Christians should, even now, confine the blessed effects of his appearance upon earth, to this or that particular sect or profession, when he is so clearly and emphatically described as the Saviour of the whole world.—The story of Abraham's proceeding to sacrifice his only son, at the command of God, is affecting in the highest degree; and sets forth a pattern of unlimited resignation, that every one ought to imitate, in those trials of obedience under temptation, or of acquiescence under afflicting dispensations, which fall to their lot. Of this we may be assured, that our trials will be always proportioned to the powers afforded us: if we have not Abraham's strength of mind, neither shall we be called upon to lift the bloody knife against the bosom of an only child; but if the almighty arm should be lifted up against him, we must be ready to resign him, and all we hold dear, to the divine will.—This action of Abraham has been censured by some, who do not attend to the distinction between obedience to a special command, and the detestably cruel sacrifices of the Heathens, who sometimes voluntarily, and without any divine injunctions, offered up their own children, under the notion of appeasing the anger of their gods. An absolute command from God himself—as in the case of Abraham—entirely alters the moral nature of the action; since he, and he only, has a perfect right over the lives of his creatures, and may appoint whom he will, either angel or man, to be his instrument of destruction. That it was really the voice of God which pronounced the command, and not a delusion, might be made certain to Abraham's mind, by means we do not comprehend, but which we know to be within the power of him who made our souls as well as bodies, and who can controul and direct every faculty of the human mind: and we may be assured, that if he was pleased to reveal himself so miraculously, he would not leave a possibility of doubting whether it was a real or an imaginary revelation. Thus the sacrifice of Abraham appears to be clear of all superstition: and remains the noblest instance of religious faith and submission that was ever given by a mere man: we cannot wonder that the blessings bestowed on him for it should have been extended to his posterity.—This book proceeds with the history of Isaac, which becomes very interesting to us, from the touching scene I have mentioned—and still more so, if we consider him as the type of our Saviour. It recounts his marriage with Rebecca—the birth and history of his two sons, Jacob, the father of the twelve tribes, and Esau, the father of the Edomites, or Idumeans—the exquisitely affecting story of Joseph and his brethren—and of his transplanting the Israelites into Egypt, who there multiplied to a great nation.

Mrs. Chapone.

§ 63. *Of Exodus.*

In Exodus, you read of a series of wonders, wrought by the Almighty to rescue the oppressed Israelites from the cruel tyranny of the Egyptians, who, having first received them as guests, by degrees reduced them to a state of slavery. By the most peculiar mercies and exertions in their favour, God prepared his chosen people to receive, with reverent and obedient hearts, the solemn restitution of those primitive laws, which probably he had re-

† vealed

vealed to Adam and his immediate descendants, or which, at least, he had made known by the dictates of conscience; but which time, and the degeneracy of mankind, had much obscured. This important revelation was made to them in the Wilderness of Sinah; there, assembled before the burning mountain, surrounded "with blackness, and darkness, and tempest," they heard the awful voice of God pronounce the eternal law, impressing it on their hearts with circumstances of terror, but without those encouragements, and those excellent promises, which were afterwards offered to mankind by Jesus Christ. Thus were the great laws of morality restored to the Jews, and through them transmitted to other nations; and by that means a great restraint was opposed to the torrent of vice and impiety, which began to prevail over the world.

To those moral precepts, which are of perpetual and universal obligation, were superadded, by the ministration of Moses, many peculiar institutions, wisely adapted to different ends—either to fix the memory of those past deliverances, which were figurative of a future and far greater salvation—to place inviolable barriers between the Jews and the idolatrous nations by whom they were surrounded—or, to be the civil law by which the community was to be governed.

To conduct this series of events, and to establish these laws with his people, God raised up that great prophet Moses, whose faith and piety enabled him to undertake and execute the most arduous enterprizes; and to pursue, with unabated zeal, the welfare of his countrymen. Even in the hour of death, this generous ardour still prevailed: his last moments were employed in fervent prayers for their prosperity, and in rapturous gratitude for the glimpse vouchsafed him of a Saviour, far greater than himself, whom God would one day raise up to his people.

Thus did Moses, by the excellency of his faith, obtain a glorious pre-eminence among the saints and prophets in heaven; while, on earth, he will be ever revered as the first of those benefactors to mankind, whose labours for the public good have endeared their memory to all ages. *Mrs. Chapone.*

§ 64. *Of Leviticus, Numbers, and Deuteronomy.*

The next book is Leviticus, which contains little besides the laws for the peculiar ritual observance of the Jews, and therefore affords no great instruction to us now: you may pass it over entirely—and, for the same reason, you may omit the first eight chapters of Numbers. The rest of Numbers is chiefly a continuation of the history, with some ritual laws.

In Deuteronomy, Moses makes a recapitulation of the foregoing history, with zealous exhortations to the people, faithfully to worship and obey that God, who had worked such amazing wonders for them: he promises them the noblest temporal blessings, if they prove obedient; and adds the most awful and striking denunciations against them, if they rebel, or forsake the true God. I have before observed, that the sanctions of the Mosaic law were temporal rewards and punishments: those of the New Testament are eternal; these last, as they are so infinitely more forcible than the first, were reserved for the last, best gift to mankind—and were revealed by the Messiah, in the fullest and clearest manner. Moses, in this book, directs the method in which the Israelites were to deal with the seven nations, whom they were appointed to punish for their profligacy and idolatry, and whose land they were to possess, when they had driven out the old

old inhabitants. He gives them excellent laws, civil as well as religious, which were ever after the ſtanding municipal laws of that people.—This book concludes with Moſes's ſong and death. *Mrs. Chapone.*

§ 65. *Of Joſhua.*

The book of Joſhua contains the conqueſts of the Iſraelites over the ſeven nations, and their eſtabliſhment in the promiſed land.—Their treatment of theſe conquered nations muſt appear to you very cruel and unjuſt, if you conſider it as their own act, unauthoriſed by a poſitive command: but they had the moſt abſolute injunctions, not to ſpare theſe corrupt people—"to make no covenant with them, nor ſhew mercy to them, but utterly to deſtroy them:"—and the reaſon is given,—"leſt they ſhould turn away the Iſraelites from following the Lord, that they might ſerve other gods." The children of Iſrael are to be conſidered as inſtruments, in the hand of the Lord, to puniſh thoſe, whoſe idolatry and wickedneſs had deſervedly brought deſtruction on them: this example, therefore, cannot be pleaded in behalf of cruelty, or bring any imputation on the character of the Jews. With regard to other cities, which did not belong to theſe ſeven nations, they were directed to deal with them according to the common law of arms at that time. If the city ſubmitted, it became tributary, and the people were ſpared; if it reſiſted, the men were to be ſlain, but the women and children ſaved. Yet, though the crime of cruelty cannot be juſtly laid to their charge on this occaſion, you will obſerve, in the courſe of their hiſtory, many things recorded of them, very different from what you would expect from the choſen people of God, if you ſuppoſed them ſelected on account of their own merit: their national character was by no means amiable; and we are repeatedly told, that they were not choſen for their ſuperior righteouſneſs—"for they were a ſtiff-necked people, and provoked the Lord with their rebellions from the day they left Egypt."—"You have been rebellious againſt the Lord," ſays Moſes, "from the day that I knew you."—And he vehemently exhorts them, not to flatter themſelves that their ſucceſs was, in any degree, owing to their own merits. They were appointed to be the ſcourge of other nations, whoſe crimes rendered them fit objects of divine chaſtiſement. For the ſake of righteous Abraham, their founder, and perhaps for many other wiſe reaſons, undiſcovered to us, they were ſelected from a world over-run with idolatry, to preſerve upon earth the pure worſhip of the one only God, and to be honoured with the birth of the Meſſiah amongſt them. For this end they were precluded, by divine command, from mixing with any other people, and defended by a great number of peculiar rites and obſervances, from falling into the corrupt worſhip practiſed by their neighbours. *Ibid.*

§ 66. *Of Judges, Samuel, and Kings.*

The book of Judges, in which you will find the affecting ſtories of Sampſon and Jephtha, carries on the hiſtory from the Death of Joſhua, about two hundred and fifty years; but the facts are not told in the times in which they happened, which makes ſome confuſion; and it will be neceſſary to conſult the marginal dates and notes, as well as the index, in order to get any clear idea of the ſucceſſion of events during that period.

The hiſtory then proceeds regularly through the two books of Samuel, and thoſe of Kings; nothing can be more intereſting and entertaining than the reigns of Saul, David, and Solomon:

lomon: but, after the death of Solomon, when ten tribes revolted from his ſon Rehoboam, and became a ſeparate kingdom, you will find ſome difficulty in underſtanding diſtinctly the hiſtories of the two kingdoms of Iſrael and Judah, which are blended together; and by the likeneſs of the names, and other particulars, will be apt to confound your mind, without great attention to the different threads thus carried on together: the index here will be of great uſe to you. The ſecond book of Kings concludes with the Babyloniſh captivity, 588 years before Chriſt—till which time the kingdom of Judah had deſcended uninterruptedly in the line of David.

Mrs. Chapone.

§ 67. *Of Chronicles, Ezra, Nehemiah, and Eſther.*

The firſt book of Chronicles begins with a genealogy from Adam, through all the tribes of Iſrael and Judah; and the remainder is the ſame hiſtory which is contained in the books of Kings, with little or no variation, till the ſeparation of the ten tribes. From that period, it proceeds with the hiſtory of the kingdom of Judah alone, and gives therefore a more regular and clear account of the affairs of Judah than the book of Kings. You may paſs over the firſt book of Chronicles, and the nine firſt chapters of the ſecond book; but, by all means, read the remaining chapters, as they will give you more clear and diſtinct ideas of the hiſtory of Judah, than that you read in the ſecond book of Kings. The ſecond of Chronicles ends, like the ſecond of Kings, with the Babyloniſh captivity.

You muſt purſue the hiſtory in the book of Ezra, which gives an account of the return of ſome of the Jews on the edict of Cyrus, and of the rebuilding the Lord's temple.

Nehemiah carries on the hiſtory for about twelve years, when he himſelf was governor of Jeruſalem, with authority to rebuild the walls, &c.

The ſtory of Eſther is prior in time to that of Ezra and Nehemiah; as you will ſee by the marginal dates; however, as it happened during the ſeventy years captivity, and is a kind of epiſode, it may be read in its own place.

This is the laſt of the canonical books that is properly hiſtorical; and I would therefore adviſe, that you paſs over what follows, till you have continued the hiſtory through the apocryphal books.

Ibid.

§ 68. *Of Job.*

The ſtory of Job is probably very ancient, though that is a point upon which learned men have differed: it is dated, however, 1520 years before Chriſt: I believe it is uncertain by whom it was written: many parts of it are obſcure; but it is well worth ſtudying, for the extreme beauty of the poetry, and for the noble and ſublime devotion it contains. The ſubject of the diſpute between Job and his pretended friends ſeems to be, whether the Providence of God diſtributes the rewards and puniſhments of this life in exact proportion to the merit or demerit of each individual. His antagoniſts ſuppoſe that it does; and therefore infer, from Job's uncommon calamities, that, notwithſtanding his apparent righteouſneſs, he was in reality a grievous ſinner. They aggravate his ſuppoſed guilt, by the imputation of hypocriſy, and call upon him to confeſs it, and to acknowledge the juſtice of his puniſhment. Job aſſerts his own innocence and virtue in the moſt pathetic manner, yet does not preſume to accuſe the Supreme Being of injuſtice. Elihu attempts to arbitrate the matter, by alledging the impoffibility that fo frail and ignorant a creature as man fhould comprehend the ways of the Almighty; and therefore condemns the unjuft and cruel inference the three friends had drawn from the fufferings of Job. He alfo blames Job for the prefumption of acquitting himfelf of all iniquity, fince the beft of men are not pure in the fight of God—but all have fomething to repent of; and he advifes him to make this ufe of his afflictions. At laft, by a bold figure of poetry, the Supreme Being himfelf is introduced, fpeaking from the whirlwind, and filencing them all by the moft fublime difplay of his own power, magnificence, and wifdom, and of the comparative littlenefs and ignorance of man.—This indeed is the only conclufion of the argument, which could be drawn at a time when life and immortality were not yet brought to light. A future retribution is the only fatisfactory folution of the difficulty arifing from the fufferings of good people in this life.

Mrs. Chapone.

§ 69. *Of the Pfalms.*

Next follow the Pfalms, with which you cannot be too converfant. If you have any tafte, either for poetry or devotion, they will be your delight, and will afford you a continual feaft. The bible tranflation is far better than that ufed in the common-prayer book, and will often give you the fenfe, when the other is obfcure. In this, as well as in all other parts of the fcripture, you muft be careful always to confult the margin, which gives you the corrections made fince the laft tranflation, and it is generally preferable to the words of the text. I would wifh you to felect fome of the Pfalms that pleafe you beft, and get them by heart: or, at leaft, make yourfelf mafter of the fentiments contained in them. Dr. Delany's Life of David will fhew you the occafions on which feveral of them were compofed, which add much to their beauty and propriety; and by comparing them with the events of David's life, you will greatly enhance your pleafure in them. Never did the fpirit of true piety breathe more ftrongly than in thefe divine fongs: which, being added to a rich vein of poetry, makes them more captivating to my heart and imagination, than any thing I ever read. You will confider how great difadvantages any poem muft fuftain from being rendered literally into profe, and then imagine how beautiful thefe muft be in the original. May you be enabled, by reading them frequently, to transfufe into your own breaft that holy flame which infpired the writer!—to delight in the Lord, and in his laws, like the Pfalmift—to rejoice in him always, and to think " one day in his courts better than a thoufand!"—But may you efcape the heart-piercing forrow of fuch repentance as that of David—by avoiding fin, which humbled this unhappy king to the duft—and which coft him fuch bitter anguifh, as it is impoffible to read of without being moved! Not all the pleafures of the moft profperous finners would counterbalance the hundredth part of thofe fenfations defcribed in his penitential Pfalms—and which muft be the portion of every man, who has fallen from a religious ftate into fuch crimes, when once he recovers a fenfe of religion and virtue, and is brought to a real hatred of fin. However available fuch repentance may be to the fafety and happinefs of the foul after death, it is a ftate of fuch exquifite fuffering here, that one cannot be enough furprized at the folly of thofe, who indulge fin, with the hope of living to make their peace with God by repentance. Happy are they who preſerve their innocence unſullied by any great or wilful crimes, and who have only the common failings of humanity to repent of; theſe are ſufficiently mortifying to a heart deeply ſmitten with the love of virtue, and with the deſire of perfection.—There are many very ſtriking prophecies of the Meſſiah in theſe divine ſongs, particularly in Pſalm xxii.—ſuch may be found ſcattered up and down almoſt throughout the Old Teſtament. To bear teſtimony to *him*, is the great and ultimate end for which the ſpirit of prophecy was beſtowed on the ſacred writers;—but this will appear more plainly to you, when you enter on the ſtudy of prophecy, which you are now much too young to undertake.

Mrs. Chapone.

§ 70. *Of the Proverbs, Eccleſiaſtes, Solomon's Song, the Prophecies, and Apocrypha.*

The Proverbs and Eccleſiaſtes are rich ſtores of wiſdom, from which I wiſh you to adopt ſuch maxims as may be of infinite uſe both to your temporal and eternal intereſt. But detached ſentences are a kind of reading not proper to be continued long at a time; a few of them, well choſen and digeſted, will do you much more ſervice, than to read half a dozen chapters together. In this reſpect, they are directly oppoſite to the hiſtorical books, which, if not read in continuation, can hardly be underſtood, or retained to any purpoſe.

The Song of Solomon is a fine poem—but its myſtical reference to religion lies too deep for a common underſtanding: if you read it, therefore, it will be rather as matter of curioſity than of edification.

Next follow the Prophecies; which though highly deſerving the greateſt attention and ſtudy, I think you had better omit for ſome years, and then read them with a good expoſition, as they are much too difficult for you to underſtand without aſſiſtance. Dr. Newton on the prophecies will help you much, whenever you undertake this ſtudy—which you ſhould by all means do, when your underſtanding is ripe enough; becauſe one of the main proofs of our religion reſts on the teſtimony of the prophecies; and they are very frequently quoted, and referred to, in the New Teſtament; beſides, the ſublimity of the language and ſentiments, through all the diſadvantages of antiquity and tranſlation, muſt, in very many paſſages, ſtrike every perſon of taſte; and the excellent moral and religious precepts found in them muſt be uſeful to all.

Though I have ſpoken of theſe books in the order in which they ſtand, I repeat, that they are not to be read in that order—but that the thread of the hiſtory is to be purſued, from Nehemiah to the firſt book of the Maccabees, in the Apocrypha; taking care to obſerve the chronology regularly, by referring to the index, which ſupplies the deficiencies of this hiſtory from Joſephus's Antiquities of the Jews. The firſt of Maccabees carries on the ſtory till within 195 years of our Lord's circumciſion: the ſecond book is the ſame narrative, written by a different hand, and does not bring the hiſtory ſo forward as the firſt; ſo that it may be entirely omitted, unleſs you have the curioſity to read ſome particulars of the heroic conſtancy of the Jews, under the tortures inflicted by their heathen conquerors, with a few other things not mentioned in the firſt book.

You muſt then connect the hiſtory by the help of the index, which will give you brief heads of the changes that happened in the ſtate of the Jews, from this time till the birth of the Meſſiah.

The other books of the Apocrypha, though not admitted as of ſacred authority, have many things well worth your attention: particularly the admirable book called Eccleſiaſticus, and the book of Wiſdom. But, in the courſe of reading which I adviſe, theſe muſt be omitted till after you have gone through the Goſpels and Acts, that you may not loſe the hiſtorical thread. *Mrs. Chapone.*

§ 71. *Of the New Teſtament, which is conſtantly to be referred to, as the Rule and Direction of our moral Conduct.*

We come now to that part of ſcripture, which is the moſt important of all, and which you muſt make your conſtant ſtudy, not only till you are thoroughly acquainted with it, but all your life long; becauſe, how often ſoever repeated, it is impoſſible to read the life and death of our bleſſed Saviour, without renewing and increaſing in our hearts that love and reverence, and gratitude towards him, which is ſo juſtly due for all he did and ſuffered for us! Every word that fell from his lips is more precious than all the treaſures of the earth; for his "are the words of eternal life!" They muſt therefore be laid up in your heart, and conſtantly referred to, on all occaſions, as the rule and direction of all your actions; particularly thoſe very comprehenſive moral precepts he has graciouſly left with us, which can never fail to direct us aright, if fairly and honeſtly applied: ſuch as, "whatſoever ye would that men ſhould do unto you, even ſo do unto them."—There is no occaſion, great or ſmall, on which you may not ſafely apply this rule for the direction of your conduct: and, whilſt your heart honeſtly adheres to it, you can never be guilty of any ſort of injuſtice or unkindneſs. The two great commandments, which contain the ſummary of our duty to God and man, are no leſs eaſily retained, and made a ſtandard by which to judge our own hearts—"To love the lord our God, with all our hearts, with all our minds, with all our ſtrength; and our neighbour (or fellow-creature) as ourſelves." "Love worketh no ill to his neighbour." Therefore if you have true benevolence, you will never do any thing injurious to individuals, or to ſociety. Now, all crimes whatever are (in their remoter conſequences at leaſt, if not immediately and apparently) injurious to the ſociety in which we live. It is impoſſible to love God without deſiring to pleaſe him, and, as far as we are able, to reſemble him; therefore the love of God muſt lead to every virtue in the higheſt degree; and, we may be ſure, we do not truly love him, if we content ourſelves with avoiding flagrant ſins, and do not ſtrive, in good earneſt, to reach the greateſt degree of perfection we are capable of. Thus do theſe few words direct us to the higheſt Chriſtian virtue. Indeed, the whole tenor of the Goſpel is to offer us every help, direction, and motive, that can enable us to attain that degree of perfection on which depends our eternal good. *Ibid.*

§ 72. *Of the Example ſet by our Saviour, and his Character.*

What an example is ſet before us in our bleſſed Maſter! How is his whole life, from earlieſt youth, dedicated to the purſuit of true wiſdom, and to the practice of the moſt exalted virtue! When you ſee him, at twelve years of age, in the temple amongſt the doctors, hearing them, and aſking them queſtions on the ſubject of religion, and aſtonishing them all with his understanding and answers—you will say, perhaps, —— "Well "might the Son of God, even at those years, "be far wiser than the aged; but, can a "mortal child emulate such heavenly wisdom? "Can such a pattern be proposed to my imi-"tation?"—Yes, certainly;—remember that he has bequeathed to you his heavenly wisdom, as far as concerns your own good. He has left you such declarations of his will, and of the consequences of your actions, as you are, even now, fully able to understand, if you will but attend to them. If, then, you will imitate his zeal for knowledge, if you will delight in gaining information and improvement; you may even now become "wise unto salvation."—Unmoved by the praise he acquired amongst these learned men, you see him meekly return to the subjection of a child, under those who appeared to be his parents, though he was in reality their Lord: you see him return to live with them, to work for them, and to be the joy and solace of their lives; till the time came, when he was to enter on that scene of public action, for which his heavenly Father had sent him from his own right hand, to take upon him the form of a poor carpenter's son. What a lesson of humility is this, and of obedience to parents!—When, having received the glorious testimony from heaven, of his being the beloved Son of the Most High, he enters on his public ministry, what an example does he give us, of the most extensive and constant benevolence!—how are all his hours spent in doing good to the souls and bodies of men!—not the meanest sinner is below his notice:—to reclaim and save them, he condescends to converse familiarly with the most corrupt, as well as the most abject. All his miracles are wrought to benefit mankind: not one to punish and afflict them. Instead of using the almighty power, which accompanied him, to the purpose of exalting himself, and treading down his enemies, he makes no other use of it than to heal and to save.

When you come to read of his sufferings and death, the ignominy and reproach, the sorrow of mind, and torment of body, which he submitted to—when you consider that it was all for our sakes—"that by his stripes we are healed"—and by his death we are raised from destruction to everlasting life—what can I say, that can add any thing to the sensations you must then feel?—No power of language can make the scene more touching than it appears in the plain and simple narrations of the evangelists. The heart that is unmoved by it, can be scarcely human;—but the emotions of tenderness and compunction, which almost every one feels in reading this account, will be of no avail, unless applied to the true end—unless it inspires you with a sincere and warm affection towards your blessed Lord—with a firm resolution to obey his commands;—to be his faithful disciple—and ever to renounce and abhor those sins, which brought mankind under divine condemnation, and from which we have been redeemed at so dear a rate. Remember that the title of Christian, or follower of Christ, implies a more than ordinary degree of holiness and goodness. As our motives to virtue are stronger than those which are afforded to the rest of mankind, our guilt will be proportionably greater, if we depart from it.

Our Saviour appears to have had three great purposes, in descending from his glory, and dwelling amongst men. The first, to teach them true virtue, both by his example and precepts. The second, to give them the most forcible

forcible motives to the practice of it, by "bringing life and immortality to light;" by shewing them the certainty of a resurrection and judgment, and the absolute necessity of obedience to God's laws. The third, to sacrifice himself for us, to obtain, by his death, the remission of our sins, upon our repentance and reformation, and the power of bestowing on his sincere followers the inestimable gift of immortal happiness. *Mrs. Chapone.*

§ 73. *A comparative View of the Blessed and Cursed at the Last Day, and the Inference to be drawn from it.*

What a tremendous scene of the last day does the gospel place before our eyes!—of that day, when you and every one of us shall awake from the grave, and behold the Son of God, on his glorious tribunal, attended by millions of celestial beings, of whose superior excellence we can now form no adequate idea—when, in presence of all mankind, of those holy angels, and of the great Judge himself, you must give an account of your past life, and hear your final doom, from which there can be no appeal, and which must determine your fate to all eternity; then think—if for a moment you can bear the thought—what will be the desolation, shame, and anguish, of those wretched souls, who shall hear these dreadful words;—— "Depart from me, ye cursed, into everlasting fire, prepared for the devil and his angels."—Oh!—I cannot support even the idea of your becoming one of those undone, lost creatures!—I trust in God's mercy, that you will make a better use of that knowledge of his will, which he has vouchsafed you, and of those amiable dispositions he has given you. Let us therefore turn from this horrid, this insupportable view—and rather endeavour to imagine, as far as is possible, what will be the sensations of your soul, if you shall hear our Heavenly Judge address you in these transporting words—" Come, thou blessed of my Father, inherit the kingdom prepared for you, from the foundation of the world."—Think, what it must be, to become an object of the esteem and applause—not only of all mankind assembled together—but of all the host of heaven, of our blessed Lord himself—nay, of his and our Almighty Father:—to find your frail flesh changed, in a moment, into a glorious celestial body, endowed with perfect beauty, health, and agility:—to find your soul cleansed from all its faults, and infirmities; exalted to the purest and noblest affections; overflowing with divine love and rapturous gratitude!—to have your understanding enlightened and refined; your heart enlarged and purified; and every power and disposition of mind and body adapted to the highest relish of virtue and happiness!—Thus accomplished, to be admitted into the society of amiable and happy beings, all united in the most perfect peace and friendship, all breathing nothing but love to God, and to each other;—with them to dwell in scenes more delightful than the richest imagination can paint—free from every pain and care, and from all possibility of change or satiety:—but, above all, to enjoy the more immediate presence of God himself—to be able to comprehend and admire his adorable perfections in a high degree, though still far short of their infinity—to be conscious of his love and favour, and to rejoice in the light of his countenance!—But here all imagination fails:—we can form no idea of that bliss, which may be communicated to us by such a near approach to the Source of all beauty and all good:—we must content ourselves with believing,

 "that

" that it is what mortal eye hath not ſeen, nor ear heard, neither hath it entered into the heart of man to conceive." The crown of all our joys will be, to know that we are ſecure of poſſeſſing them for ever—what a tranſporting idea!

Can you reflect on all theſe things, and not feel the moſt earneſt longings after immortality?—Do not all other views and deſires ſeem mean and trifling, when compared with this?—And does not your inmoſt heart reſolve, that this ſhall be the chief and conſtant object of its wiſhes and purſuit, through the whole courſe of your life?—If you are not inſenſible to that deſire of happineſs which ſeems woven into our nature, you cannot ſurely be unmoved by the proſpect of ſuch a tranſcendant degree of it; and that continued to all eternity—perhaps continually increaſing. You cannot but dread the forfeiture of ſuch an inheritance, as the moſt inſupportable evil!—Remember then—remember the conditions on which alone it can be obtained. God will not give to vice, to careleſſneſs, or ſloth, the prize he has propoſed to virtue. You have every help that can animate your endeavours:—You have written laws to direct you—the example of Chriſt and his diſciples to encourage you—the moſt awakening motives to engage you—and you have beſides, the comfortable promiſe of conſtant aſſiſtance from the Holy Spirit, if you diligently and ſincerely pray for it.—O! let not all this mercy be loſt upon you—but give your attention to this your only important concern, and accept, with profound gratitude, the ineſtimable advantages that are thus affectionately offered you.

Though the four Goſpels are each of them a narration of the life, ſayings, and death of Chriſt; yet as they are not exactly alike, but ſome circumſtances and ſayings, omitted in one, are recorded in another, you muſt make yourſelf perfectly maſter of them all.

The Acts of the holy Apoſtles, endowed with the Holy Ghoſt, and authorized by their divine Maſter, come next in order to be read.—Nothing can be more intereſting and edifying, than the hiſtory of their actions—of the piety, zeal, and courage, with which they preached the glad tidings of ſalvation; and of the various exertions, of the wonderful powers conferred on them by the Holy Spirit, for the confirmation of their miſſion.

Mrs. Chapone.

§ 74. *Character of St. Paul.*

The Character of St. Paul, and his miraculous converſion, demand your particular attention: moſt of the apoſtles were men of low birth and education; but St. Paul was a Roman citizen; that is, he poſſeſſed the privileges annexed to the freedom of the city of Rome, which was conſidered as a high diſtinction, in thoſe countries that had been conquered by the Romans. He was educated amongſt the moſt learned ſect of the Jews, and by one of their principal doctors. He was a man of extraordinary eloquence, as appears not only in his writings, but in ſeveral ſpeeches in his own defence, pronounced before governors and courts of juſtice, when he was called to account for the doctrines he taught.—He ſeems to have been of an uncommonly warm temper, and zealous in whatever religion he profeſſed: this zeal, before his converſion, ſhewed itſelf in the moſt unjuſtifiable actions, by furiouſly perſecuting the innocent Chriſtians: but, tho' his actions were bad, we may be ſure his intentions were good; otherwiſe we ſhould not have ſeen a miracle employed to convince him of his miſtake, and to bring him into the right way. This

This example may assure us of the mercy of God towards mistaken consciences, and ought to inspire us with the most enlarged charity and good-will towards those whose erroneous principles mislead their conduct: instead of resentment and hatred against their persons, we ought only to feel an active wish of assisting them to find the truth; since we know not whether, if convinced, they might not prove, like St. Paul, chosen vessels to promote the honour of God, and of true religion. It is not now my intention to enter with you into any of the arguments for the truth of Christianity; otherwise it would be impossible wholly to pass over that, which arises from this remarkable conversion, and which has been so admirably illustrated by a noble writer, whose tract on this subject is in every body's hands. *Mrs. Chapone.*

§ 75. *Of the Epistles.*

Next follow the Epistles, which make a very important part of the New Testament; and you cannot be too much employed in reading them. They contain the most excellent precepts and admonitions; and are of particular use in explaining more at large several doctrines of Christianity, which we could not so fully comprehend without them. There are, indeed, in the Epistles of St. Paul, many passages hard to be understood: such, in particular, are the first eleven chapters to the Romans; the greater part of his Epistles to the Corinthians and Galatians; and several chapters of that to the Hebrews. Instead of perplexing yourself with these more obscure passages of scripture, I would wish you to employ your attention chiefly on those that are plain; and to judge of the doctrines taught in the other parts, by comparing them with what you find in these. It is through the neglect of this rule, that many have been led to draw the most absurd doctrines from the holy scriptures.—Let me particularly recommend to your careful perusal the xii. xiii. xiv. and xv. chapters of the Epistle to the Romans. In the xiv. chapter St. Paul has in view the difference between the Jewish and Gentile (or Heathen) converts, at that time: the former were disposed to look with horror on the latter, for their impiety, in not paying the same regard to the distinctions of days and meats that they did; and the latter, on the contrary, were inclined to look with contempt on the former, for their weakness and superstition. Excellent is the advice which the Apostle gives to both parties: he exhorts the Jewish converts not to judge, and the Gentiles not to despise; remembering, that the kingdom of Heaven is not meat and drink, but righteousness and peace, and joy in the Holy Ghost.—Endeavour to conform yourself to this advice; to acquire a temper of universal candour and benevolence; and learn neither to despise nor condemn any persons on account of their particular modes of faith and worship; remembering always, that goodness is confined to no party—that there are wise and worthy men among all the sects of Christians—and that, to his own master, every one must stand or fall.

I will enter no farther into the several points discussed by St. Paul in his various epistles—most of them too intricate for your understanding at present, and many of them beyond my abilities to state clearly. I will only again recommend to you, to read those passages frequently, which, with so much fervour and energy, excite you to the practice of the most exalted piety and benevolence. If the effusions of a heart, warmed with the tenderest affection for the whole human race—if precept, warning, encouragement, example, urged by an eloquence which ſuch affection only could inſpire, are capable of influencing your mind—you cannot fail to find, in ſuch parts of his epiſtles as are adapted to your underſtanding, the ſtrongeſt perſuaſives to every virtue that can adorn and improve your nature.

Mrs. Chapone.

§ 76. *The Epiſtle of St. James.*

The epiſtle of St. James is entirely practical, and exceedingly fine; you cannot ſtudy it too much. It ſeems particularly deſigned to guard Chriſtians againſt miſunderſtanding ſome things in St. Paul's writings, which have been fatally perverted to the encouragement of a dependance on faith alone, without good works. But the more rational commentators will tell you, that, by the works of the law, which the apoſtle aſſerts to be incapable of juſtifying us, he means, not the works of moral righteouſneſs, but the ceremonial works of the Moſaic law; on which the Jews laid the greateſt ſtreſs, as neceſſary to ſalvation. But St. James tells us, that, "if "any man among us ſeem to be religious, "and bridleth not his tongue, but deceiveth "his own heart, that man's religion is vain;" —and that "pure religion, and undefiled "before God and the Father, is this, to viſit "the fatherleſs and widow in their affliction, "and to keep himſelf unſpotted from the "world." Faith in Chriſt, if it produce not theſe effects, he declareth is dead, or of no power.

Ibid.

§ 77. *Epiſtles of St. Peter, and the firſt of St. John.*

The Epiſtles of St. Peter are alſo full of the beſt inſtructions and admonitions, concerning the relative duties of life; amongſt which, are ſet forth the duties of women in general, and of wives in particular. Some part of his ſecond Epiſtle is prophetical; warning the church of falſe teachers, and falſe doctrines, which ſhould undermine morality, and diſgrace the cauſe of Chriſtianity.

The firſt of St. John is written in a highly figurative ſtyle, which makes it, in ſome parts, hard to be underſtood; but the ſpirit of divine love, which it ſo fervently expreſſes, renders it highly edifying and delightful.—That love of God and of man, which this beloved apoſtle ſo pathetically recommends, is in truth the eſſence of religion, as our Saviour himſelf informs us.

Ibid.

§ 78. *Of the Revelations.*

The book of the Revelations contains a prophetical account of moſt of the great events relating to the Chriſtian church, which were to happen from the time of the writer, St. John, to the end of the world. Many learned men have taken a great deal of pains to explain it; and they have done this, in many inſtances, very ſucceſsfully: but I think it is yet too ſoon for you to ſtudy this part of ſcripture; ſome years hence, perhaps, there may be no objection to your attempting it, and taking into your hands the beſt expoſitions, to aſſiſt you in reading ſuch of the moſt difficult parts of the New Teſtament, as you cannot now be ſuppoſed to underſtand.—May Heaven direct you in ſtudying this ſacred volume, and render it the means of making you wiſe unto ſalvation!—May you love and reverence, as it deſerves, this bleſſed and invaluable book, which contains the beſt rule of life, the cleareſt declaration of the will and laws of the Deity, the reviving aſſurance of favour to true penitents, and the unſpeakably joyful tidings of eternal life and happineſs to all the truly virtuous, through Jesus Christ the Saviour and Deliverer of the world! *Mrs. Chapone.*

§ 79. *A Morning Prayer for a young Student at School, or for the common Use of a School.*

Father of All! we return thee most humble and hearty thanks for thy protection of us in the night season, and for the refreshment of our souls and bodies, in the sweet repose of sleep. Accept also our unfeigned gratitude for all thy mercies during the helpless age of infancy.

Continue, we beseech thee, to guard us under the shadow of thy wing. Our age is tender, and our nature frail; and, without the influence of thy grace, we shall surely fall.

Let that influence descend into our hearts, and teach us to love thee and truth above all things. O guard us from temptations to deceit, and grant that we may abhor a lye, both as a sin and as a disgrace.

Inspire us with an abhorrence of the loathsomeness of vice, and the pollutions of sensual pleasure. Grant, at the same time, that we may early feel the delight of conscious purity, and wash our hands in innocency, from the united motives of inclination and of duty.

Give us, O thou parent of all knowledge, a love of learning, and a taste for the pure and sublime pleasures of the understanding. Improve our memory, quicken our apprehension, and grant that we may lay up such a store of learning, as may fit us for the station to which it shall please thee to call us, and enable us to make great advances in virtue and religion, and shine as lights in the world, by the influence of a good example.

Give us grace to be diligent in our studies, and that whatever we read we may strongly mark, and inwardly digest it.

Bless our parents, guardians, and instructors; and grant that we may make them the best return in our power, for giving us opportunities of improvement, and for all their care and attention to our welfare. They ask no return, but that we should make use of those opportunities, and co-operate with their endeavours—O grant that we may not disappoint their anxious expectations.

Assist us mercifully, O Lord, that we may immediately engage in the studies and duties of the day, and go through them chearfully, diligently, and successfully.

Accept our endeavours, and pardon our defects, through the merits of our blessed Saviour, Jesus Christ our Lord. Amen.

§ 80. *An Evening Prayer.*

O Almighty God! again we approach thy mercy-seat, to offer unto thee our thanks and praises for the blessings and protection afforded us this day; and humbly to implore thy pardon for our manifold transgressions.

Grant that the words of various instruction which we have heard or read this day, may be so inwardly grafted in our hearts and memories, as to bring forth the fruits of learning and virtue.

Grant that as we recline on our pillows, we may call to mind the transactions of the day, condemn those things of which our conscience accuses us, and make and keep resolutions of amendment.

Grant that thy holy angels may watch over us this night, and guard us from temptation, excluding all improper thoughts, and filling our breasts with the purest sentiments of piety. Like as the hart panteth for the water-brook, so let our souls thirst for thee, O Lord, and for whatever is excellent and beautiful in learning and behaviour.

Correct, by the sweet influence of Christian charity, the irregularities of our temper; and restrain every tendency to ingratitude, and to ill-usage of our parents, teachers, pastors, and masters. Teach us to know the value of a good education, and to be thankful to those who labour in the improvement of our minds and morals. Give us grace to be reverent to our superiors, gentle to our equals or inferiors, and benevolent to all mankind. Elevate and enlarge our sentiments, and let all our conduct be regulated by right reason, attended with Christian charity, and that peculiar generosity of mind, which becomes a liberal scholar and a sincere Christian.

O Lord, bestow upon us whatever may be good for us, even though we should omit to pray for it; and avert whatever is hurtful, though in the blindness of our hearts we should desire it.

Into thy hands we resign ourselves, as we retire to rest; hoping by thy mercy, to rise again with renewed spirits, to go through the business of the morrow, and to prepare ourselves for this life, and for a blessed immortality; which we ardently hope to attain, through the merits and intercession of thy Son, our Saviour, Jesus Christ our Lord. Amen.

§ 81. THE LORD'S PRAYER.

Our Father, which art in heaven; Hallowed be thy name. Thy kingdom come. Thy will be done in earth, as it is in heaven. Give us this day our daily bread. And forgive us our trespasses, as we forgive them that trespass against us. And lead us not into temptation; but deliver us from evil: For thine is the kingdom, and the power, and the glory, for ever and ever. Amen.

END OF THE FIRST BOOK.

THE
PROSE EPITOME;
OR,
ELEGANT EXTRACTS ABRIDGED, &c.

BOOK II. CLASSICAL AND HISTORICAL.

§ 1. *Beneficial Effects of a Taste for the* Belles Lettres.

BELLES Lettres and criticiſm chiefly conſider Man as a being endowed with thoſe powers of taſte and imagination, which were intended to embelliſh his mind, and to ſupply him with rational and uſeful entertainment. They open a field of inveſtigation peculiar to themſelves. All that relates to beauty, harmony, grandeur, and elegance; all that can ſoothe the mind, gratify the fancy, or move the affections, belongs to their province. They preſent human nature under a different aſpect from that which it aſſumes when viewed by other ſciences. They bring to light various ſprings of action, which, without their aid, might have paſſed unobſerved; and which, though of a delicate nature, frequently exert a powerful influence on ſeveral departments of human life.

Such ſtudies have alſo this peculiar advantage, that they exerciſe our reaſon without fatiguing it. They lead to enquiries acute, but not painful; profound, but not dry nor abſtruſe. They ſtrew flowers in the path of ſcience; and, while they keep the mind bent, in ſome degree, and active, they relieve it at the ſame time from that more toilſome labour to which it muſt ſubmit in the acquiſition of neceſſary erudition, or the inveſtigation of abſtract truth. *Blair.*

§ 2. *Beneficial Effects of the Cultivation of* Taste.

The cultivation of taſte is further recommended by the happy effects which it naturally tends to produce on human life. The moſt buſy man, in the moſt active ſphere, cannot be always occupied by buſineſs. Men of ſerious profeſſions cannot always be on the ſtretch of ſerious thought. Neither can the moſt gay and flouriſhing ſituations of fortune afford any man the power of filling all his hours with pleaſure. Life muſt always languiſh in the hands of the idle. It will frequently languiſh even in the hands of the buſy, if they have not ſome employment ſubſidiary to that which forms their main purſuit. How then ſhall theſe vacant ſpaces, thoſe unemployed intervals, which, more or leſs, occur in the life of every one, be filled up? How can we contrive to diſpoſe of them in any way that ſhall be more agreeable in itſelf,

or

or more consonant to the dignity of the human mind, than in the entertainments of taste, and the study of polite literature? He who is so happy as to have acquired a relish for these, has always at hand an innocent and irreproachable amusement for his leisure hours, to save him from the danger of many a pernicious passion. He is not in hazard of being a burden to himself: He is not obliged to fly to low company, or to court the riot of loose pleasures, in order to cure the tediousness of existence.

Providence seems plainly to have pointed out this useful purpose, to which the pleasures of taste may be applied, by interposing them in a middle station between the pleasures of sense, and those of pure intellect. We were not designed to grovel always among objects so low as the former; nor are we capable of dwelling constantly in so high a region as the latter. The pleasures of taste refresh the mind after the toils of the intellect, and the labours of abstract study; and they gradually raise it above the attachments of sense, and prepare it for the enjoyments of virtue.

So consonant is this to experience, that, in the education of youth, no object has in every age appeared more important to wise men than to tincture them early with a relish for the entertainments of taste. The transition is commonly made with ease from these to the discharge of the higher and more important duties of life. Good hopes may be entertained of those whose minds have this liberal and elegant turn. It is favourable to many virtues. Whereas to be entirely devoid of relish for eloquence, poetry, or any of the fine arts, is justly construed to be an unpromising symptom of youth; and raises suspicions of their being prone to low gratifications, or destined to drudge in the more vulgar and illiberal pursuits of life. *Blair.*

§ 3. *Improvement of* Taste *connected with Improvement in* Virtue.

There are indeed few good dispositions of any kind with which the improvement of taste is not more or less connected. A cultivated taste increases sensibility to all the tender and humane passions, by giving them frequent exercise; while it tends to weaken the more violent and fierce emotions.

> —— Ingenuas didicisse fideliter artes
> Emollit mores, nec sinit esse feros *.

The elevated sentiments and high examples which poetry, eloquence, and history are often bringing under our view, naturally tend to nourish in our minds public spirit, the love of glory, contempt of external fortune, and the admiration of what is truly illustrious and great.

I will not go so far as to say, that the improvement of taste and virtue is the same; or that they may always be expected to co-exist in an equal degree. More powerful correctives than taste can apply, are necessary for reforming the corrupt propensities which too frequently prevail among mankind. Elegant speculations are sometimes found to float on the surface of the mind, while bad passions possess the interior regions of the heart. At the same time this cannot but be admitted, that the exercise of taste is, in its native tendency, moral and purifying. From reading the most admired productions of genius, whether in poetry or prose, almost every one rises

* These polish'd arts have humaniz'd mankind,
Soften'd the rude, and calm'd the boist'rous mind.

with

with ſome good impreſſions left on his mind; and though theſe may not always be durable, they are at leaſt to be ranked among the means of diſpoſing the heart to virtue. One thing is certain, and I ſhall hereafter have occaſion to illuſtrate it more fully, that, without poſſeſſing the virtuous affections in a ſtrong degree, no man can attain eminence in the ſublime parts of eloquence. He muſt feel what a good man feels, if he expects greatly to move or to intereſt mankind. They are the ardent ſentiments of honour, virtue, magnanimity, and public ſpirit, that only can kindle that fire of genius, and call up into the mind thoſe high ideas, which attract the admiration of ages; and if this ſpirit be neceſſary to produce the moſt diſtinguiſhed efforts of eloquence, it muſt be neceſſary alſo to our reliſhing them with proper taſte and feeling.

Blair.

§ 4. *On* Style.

It is not eaſy to give a preciſe idea of what is meant by Style. The beſt definition I can give of it is, the peculiar manner in which a man expreſſes his conceptions, by means of Language. It is different from mere Language or words. The words which an author employs, may be proper and faultleſs; and his Style may, nevertheleſs, have great faults; it may be dry, or ſtiff, or feeble, or affected. Style has always ſome reference to an author's manner of thinking. It is a picture of the ideas which riſe in his mind, and of the manner in which they riſe there; and hence, when we are examining an author's compoſition, it is, in many caſes, extremely difficult to ſeparate the Style from the ſentiment. No wonder theſe two ſhould be ſo intimately connected, as Style is nothing elſe, than that ſort of expreſſion which our thoughts moſt readily aſſume. Hence, different countries have been noted for peculiarities of Style, ſuited to their different temper and genius. The eaſtern nations animated their Style with the moſt ſtrong and hyperbolical figures. The Athenians, a poliſhed and acute people, formed a Style, accurate, clear, and neat. The Aſiatics, gay and looſe in their manners, affected a Style florid and diffuſe. The like ſort of characteriſtical differences are commonly remarked in the Style of the French, the Engliſh, and the Spaniards. In giving the general characters of Style, it is uſual to talk of a nervous, a feeble, or a ſpirited Style; which are plainly the characters of a writer's manner of thinking, as well as of expreſſing himſelf: ſo difficult it is to ſeparate theſe two things from one another. Of the general characters of Style, I am afterwards to diſcourſe; but it will be neceſſary to begin with examining the more ſimple qualities of it; from the aſſemblage of which its more complex denominations, in a great meaſure, reſult.

All the qualities of a good Style may be ranged under two heads, Perſpicuity and Ornament. For all that can poſſibly be required of Language is, to convey our ideas clearly to the minds of others, and, at the ſame time, in ſuch a dreſs, as, by pleaſing and intereſting them, ſhall moſt effectually ſtrengthen the impreſſions which we ſeek to make. When both theſe ends are anſwered, we certainly accompliſh every purpoſe for which we uſe Writing and Diſcourſe.

Ibid.

§ 5. *On* Perspicuity.

Perſpicuity, it will be readily admitted, is the fundamental quality of Style*; a quality ſo

* "Nobis prima ſit virtus, perſpicuitas, propria verba, rectus ordo, non in longum dilata concluſio; nihil neque deſit, neque ſuperfluat."
Quinctil. lib. viii.

so essential in every kind of writing, that for the want of it nothing can atone. Without this, the richest ornaments of Style only glimmer through the dark; and puzzle, instead of pleasing, the reader. This, therefore, must be our first object, to make our meaning clearly and fully understood, and understood without the least difficulty. "Oratio," says Quinctilian, "debet negligenter quoque audientibus esse aperta; ut in animum audientis, sicut sol in oculos, etiamsi in eum non intendatur, occurrat. Quare, non solum ut intelligere possit, sed ne omnino possit non intelligere, curandum *." If we are obliged to follow a writer with much care, to pause, and to read over his sentences a second time, in order to comprehend them fully, he will never please us long. Mankind are too indolent to relish so much labour. They may pretend to admire the author's depth after they have discovered his meaning; but they will seldom be inclined to take up his work a second time.

Authors sometimes plead the difficulty of their subject as an excuse for the want of Perspicuity. But the excuse can rarely, if ever, be admitted. For whatever a man conceives clearly, that it is in his power, if he will be at the trouble, to put into distinct propositions, or to express clearly to others: and upon no subject ought any man to write, where he cannot think clearly. His ideas, indeed, may, very excusably, be on some subjects incomplete or inadequate; but still, as far as they go, they ought to be clear; and, wherever this is the case, Perspicuity in expressing them is always attainable. The obscurity which reigns so much among many metaphysical writers, is, for the most part, owing to the indistinctness of their own conceptions. They see the object but in a confused light; and, of course, can never exhibit it in a clear one to others.

Perspicuity in writing, is not to be considered as merely a sort of negative virtue, or freedom from defect. It has higher merit: it is a degree of positive beauty. We are pleased with an author, we consider him as deserving praise, who frees us from all fatigue of searching for his meaning; who carries us through his subject without any embarrassment or confusion? whose style flows always like a limpid stream, where we see to the very bottom. *Blair.*

§ 6. *On* Purity *and* Propriety.

Purity and Propriety of Language, are often used indiscriminately for each other; and, indeed, they are very nearly allied. A distinction however obtains between them. Purity, is the use of such words, and such constructions, as belong to the idiom of the Language which we speak; in opposition to words and phrases that are imported from other Languages, or that are obsolete or new-coined, or used without proper authority. Propriety is the selection of such words in the Language, as the best and most established usage has appropriated to those ideas which we intend to express by them. It implies the correct and happy application of them, according to that usage, in opposition to vulga-

* "Discourse ought always to be obvious, even to the most careless and negligent hearer; so that the sense shall strike his mind, as the light of the sun does our eyes, though they are not directed upwards to it. We must study, not only that every hearer may understand us, but that it shall be impossible for him not to understand us."

risins, or low expressions; and to words and phrases, which would be less significant of the ideas that we mean to convey. Style may be pure, that is, it may all be strictly English, without Scotticisms or Gallicisms, or ungrammatical, irregular expressions of any kind, and may, nevertheless, be deficient in propriety. The words may be ill-chosen; not adapted to the subject, nor fully expressive of the author's sense. He has taken all his words and phrases from the general mass of English Language; but he has made his selection among these words unhappily. Whereas Style cannot be proper without being also pure; and where both Purity and Propriety meet, besides making Style perspicuous, they also render it graceful. There is no standard, either of Purity or of Propriety, but the practatice of the best writers and speakers in the country.

When I mentioned obsolete or new-coined words as incongruous with Purity of Style, it will be easily understood, that some exceptions are to be made. On certain occasions, they may have grace. Poetry admits of greater latitude than prose, with respect to coining, or, at least, new-compounding words; yet, even here, this liberty should be used with a sparing hand. In prose, such innovations are more hazardous, and have a worse effect. They are apt to give Style an affected and conceited air; and should never be ventured upon except by such, whose established reputation gives them some degree of dictatorial power over Language.

The introduction of foreign and learned words, unless where necessity requires them, should always be avoided. Barren Languages may need such assistances; but ours is not one of these. Dean Swift, one of our most correct writers, valued himself much on using no words but such as were of native growth: and his language may, indeed, be considered as a standard of the strictest Purity and Propriety in the choice of words. At present, we seem to be departing from this standard. A multitude of Latin words have, of late, been poured in upon us. On some occasions, they give an appearance of elevation and dignity to Style. But often, also, they render it stiff and forced: and, in general, a plain native Style, as it is more intelligible to all readers, so, by a proper management of words, it may be made equally strong and expressive with this Latinized English.

Blair.

§ 7. *On* Precision.

The exact import of Precision may be drawn from the etymology of the word. It comes from "precidere," to cut off: it imports retrenching all superfluities, and pruning the expression so as to exhibit neither more nor less than an exact copy of his idea who uses it. I observed before, that it is often difficult to separate the qualities of Style from the qualities of Thought; and it is found so in this instance. For, in order to write with Precision, though this be properly a quality of Style, one must possess a very considerable degree of distinctness and accuracy in his manner of thinking.

The words, which a man uses to express his ideas, may be faulty in three respects: They may either not express that idea which the author intends, but some other which only resembles, or is a-kin to it; or, they may express that idea, but not quite fully and completely; or, they may express it, together with something more than he intends. Precision stands opposed to all these three faults; but chiefly to the last. In an author's writing with

with propriety, his being free from the two former faults seems implied. The words which he uses are proper; that is, they express that idea which he intends, and they express it fully; but to be precise, signifies, that they express that idea, and no more. There is nothing in his words which introduces any foreign idea, any superfluous, unseasonable accessory, so as to mix it confusedly with the principal object, and thereby to render our conception of that object loose and indistinct. This requires a writer to have, himself, a very clear apprehension of the object he means to present to us; to have laid fast hold of it in his mind; and never to waver in any one view he takes of it; a perfection to which, indeed, few writers attain. *Blair.*

§ 8. *On the Use and Importance of* Precision.

The use and importance of Precision may be deduced from the nature of the human mind. It never can view, clearly and distinctly, above one object at a time. If it must look at two or three together, especially objects among which there is resemblance or connection, it finds itself confused and embarrassed. It cannot clearly perceive in what they agree, and in what they differ. Thus, were any object, suppose some animal, to be presented to me, of whose structure I wanted to form a distinct notion, I would desire all its trappings to be taken off, I would require it to be brought before me by itself, and to stand alone, that there might be nothing to distract my attention. The same is the case with words. If, when you would inform me of your meaning, you also tell me more than what conveys it; if you join foreign circumstances to the principal object; if, by unnecessarily varying the expression, you shift the point of view, and make me see sometimes the object itself, and sometimes another thing that is connected with it; you thereby oblige me to look on several objects at once, and I lose sight of the principal. You load the animal you are shewing me with so many trappings and collars, and bring so many of the same species before me, somewhat resembling, and yet somewhat differing, that I see none of them clearly.

This forms what is called a Loose Style: and is the proper opposite to Precision. It generally arises from using a superfluity of words. Feeble writers employ a multitude of words, to make themselves understood, as they think, more distinctly; and they only confound the reader. They are sensible of not having caught the precise expression, to convey what they would signify: they do not, indeed, conceive their own meaning very precisely themselves; and, therefore, help it out, as they can, by this and the other word, which may, as they suppose, supply the defect, and bring you somewhat nearer to their idea: they are always going about it, and about it, but never just hit the thing. The image, as they set it before you, is always seen double; and no double image is distinct. When an author tells me of his hero's *courage* in the day of battle, the expression is precise, and I understand it fully. But if, from the desire of multiplying words, he will needs praise his *courage* and *fortitude*; at the moment he joins these words together, my idea begins to waver. He means to express one quality more strongly; but he is, in truth, expressing two. *Courage* resists danger; *fortitude* supports pain. The occasion of exerting each of these qualities is different; and being led to think of both together, when only one of them should be in my view, my view is rendered unsteady,

unsteady, and my conception of the object indistinct.

From what I have said, it appears that an author may, in a qualified sense, be perspicuous, while yet he is far from being precise. He uses proper words, and proper arrangement: he gives you the idea as clear as he conceives it himself; and so far he is perspicuous: but the ideas are not very clear in his own mind: they are loose and general; and, therefore, cannot be expressed with Precision. All subjects do not equally require Precision. It is sufficient, on many occasions, that we have a general view of the meaning. The subject, perhaps, is of the known and familiar kind; and we are in no hazard of mistaking the sense of the author, though every word which he uses be not precise and exact.

Blair.

§ 9. *The Causes of a Loose* Style.

The great source of a Loose Style, in opposition to Precision, is the injudicious use of those words termed Synonymous. They are called Synonymous, because they agree in expressing one principal idea: but, for the most part, if not always, they express it with some diversity in the circumstances. They are varied by some accessory idea which every word introduces, and which forms the distinction between them. Hardly, in any Language, are there two words that convey precisely the same idea; a person thoroughly conversant in the propriety of the Language, will always be able to observe something that distinguishes them. As they are like different shades of the same colour, an accurate writer can employ them to great advantage, by using them so as to heighten and finish the picture which he gives us. He supplies by one what was wanting in the other, to the force, or to the lustre of the image which he means to exhibit. But in order to this end, he must be extremely attentive to the choice which he makes of them. For the bulk of writers are very apt to confound them with each other: and to employ them carelessly, merely for the sake of filling up a period, or of rounding and diversifying the Language, as if the signification were exactly the same, while, in truth, it is not. Hence a certain mist, and indistinctness, is unwarily thrown over Style. *Ibid.*

§ 10. *On the general Characters of* Style.

That different subjects require to be treated of in different sorts of Style, is a position so obvious, that I shall not stay to illustrate it. Every one sees that Treatises of Philosophy, for instance, ought not to be composed in the same Style with Orations. Every one sees also that different parts of the same composition require a variation in the Style and manner. In a sermon, for instance, or any harangue, the application, or peroration admits of more ornament, and requires more warmth, than the didactic part. But what I mean at present to remark is, that, amidst this variety, we still expect to find, in the compositions of any one man, some degree of uniformity or consistency with himself in manner; we expect to find some predominant character of Style impressed on all his writings, which shall be suited to, and shall mark, his particular genius and turn of mind. The orations in Livy differ much in Style, as they ought to do, from the rest of his history. The same is the case with those in Tacitus. Yet both in Livy's orations, and in those of Tacitus, we are able clearly to trace the distinguishing manner of each historian: the magnificent fulness of the one, and the sententious conciseness of the other. The "Lettres Persanes,"

Perſanes," and " L'Eſprit de Loix," are the works of the ſame author. They required very different compoſition ſurely, and accordingly they differ widely; yet ſtill we ſee the ſame hand. Wherever there is real and native genius, it gives a determination to one kind of Style rather than another. Where nothing of this appears; where there is no marked nor peculiar character in the compoſitions of any author, we are apt to infer, not without reaſon, that he is a vulgar and trivial author, who writes from imitation, and not from the impulſe of original genius. As the moſt celebrated painters are known by their hand, ſo the beſt and moſt original writers are known and diſtinguiſhed, throughout all their works, by their Style and peculiar manner. This will be found to hold almoſt without exception. *Blair.*

§ 11. *On the Auſtere, the Florid, and the Middle* STYLE.

The ancient Critics attended to theſe general characters of Style, which we are now to conſider. Dionyſius of Halicarnaſſus divides them into three kinds; and calls them the Auſtere, the Florid, and the Middle. By the Auſtere, he means a Style diſtinguiſhed for ſtrength and firmneſs, with a neglect of ſmoothneſs and ornament; for examples of which he gives Pindar and Æſchylus among the Poets, and Thucydides among the Proſe writers. By the Florid, he means, as the name indicates, a Style ornamented, flowing, and ſweet; reſting more upon numbers and grace, than ſtrength; he inſtances Heſiod, Sappho, Anacreon, Euripides, and principally Iſocrates. The Middle kind is the juſt mean between theſe, and comprehends the beauties of both; in which claſs he places Homer and Sophocles among the Poets; in Proſe, Herodotus, Demoſthenes, Plato, and (what ſeems ſtrange) Ariſtotle. This muſt be a very wide claſs indeed, which comprehends Plato and Ariſtotle under one article as to Style *. Cicero and Quinctilian make alſo a threefold diviſion of Style, though with reſpect to different qualities of it; in which they are followed by moſt of the modern writers in Rhetoric; the *Simplex, Tenue*, or *Subtile*; the *Grave*, or *Vehemens*; and the *Medium*, or *temperatum genus dicendi*. But theſe diviſions, and the illuſtrations they give of them, are ſo looſe and general, that they cannot advance us much in our ideas of Style. I ſhall endeavour to be a little more particular in what I have to ſay on this ſubject. *Ibid.*

§ 12. *On the Conciſe* STYLE.

One of the firſt and moſt obvious diſtinctions of the different kinds of Style, is what ariſes from an author's ſpreading out his thoughts more or leſs. This diſtinction forms what are called the Diffuſe and the Conciſe Styles. A conciſe writer compreſſes his thought into the feweſt poſſible words; he ſeeks to employ none but ſuch as are moſt expreſſive; he lops off, as redundant, every expreſſion which does not add ſomething material to the ſenſe. Ornament he does not reject; he may be lively and figured; but his ornament is intended for the ſake of force rather than grace. He never gives you the ſame thought twice. He places it in the light which appears to him the moſt ſtriking; but if you do not apprehend it well in that light, you need not expect to find it in any other. His ſentences are arranged with compactneſs and ſtrength, rather than with cadence and harmony. The utmoſt

* De Compoſitione Verborum, Cap. 25.

precision

precision is studied in them; and they are commonly designed to suggest more to the reader's imagination than they directly express. *Blair.*

§ 13. *On the Diffuse* Style.

A diffuse writer unfolds his thought fully. He places it in a variety of lights, and gives the reader every possible assistance for understanding it completely. He is not very careful to express it at first in its full strength, because he is to repeat the impression; and what he wants in strength, he proposes to supply by copiousness. Writers of this character generally love magnificence and amplification. Their periods naturally run out into some length, and having room for ornament of every kind, they admit it freely.

Each of these manners has its peculiar advantages; and each becomes faulty, when carried to the extreme. The extreme of conciseness becomes abrupt and obscure; it is apt also to lead into a Style too pointed, and bordering on the epigrammatic. The extreme of diffuseness becomes weak and languid, and tires the reader. However, to one or other of these two manners a writer may lean, according as his genius prompts him: and, under the general character of a concise, or of a more open and diffuse Style, may possess much beauty in his composition.

For illustrations of these general characters farther, are Tacitus the historian, and the President Montesquieu in "L'Esprit de Loix." Aristotle too holds an eminent rank among didactic writers for his brevity. Perhaps no writer in the world was ever so frugal of his words as Aristotle; but this frugality of expression frequently darkens his meaning. Of a beautiful and magnificent diffuseness, Cicero is, beyond doubt, the most illustrious instance that can be given. Addison, also, and Sir William Temple, come in some degree under this class. *Ibid.*

§ 14. *On the Nervous and the Feeble* Style.

The Nervous and the Feeble, are generally held to be characters of Style, of the same import with the Concise and the Diffuse. They do indeed very often coincide. Diffuse writers have, for the most part, some degree of feebleness; and nervous writers will generally be inclined to a concise expression. This, however, does not always hold: and there are instances of writers, who, in the midst of a full and ample Style, have maintained a great degree of strength. Livy is an example; and in the English language, Dr. Barrow. Barrow's Style has many faults. It is unequal, incorrect, and redundant; but withal, for force and expressiveness uncommonly distinguished. On every subject, he multiplies words with an overflowing copi-

writing, so carelessly exerted, that he has no firm hold of the conception which he would communicate to us; the marks of all this will clearly appear in his Style. Several unmeaning words and loose epithets will be found; his expressions will be vague and general; his arrangement indistinct and feeble; we shall conceive somewhat of his meaning, but our conception will be faint. Whereas a nervous writer, whether he employs an extended or a concise Style, gives us always a strong impression of his meaning; his mind is full of his subject, and his words are all expressive: every phrase and every figure which he uses, tends to render the picture, which he would set before us, more lively and complete.

Blair.

§ 15. *On Harshness of* Style.

As every good quality in Style has an extreme, when pursued to which it becomes faulty, this holds of the Nervous Style as well as others. Too great a study of strength, to the neglect of the other qualities of Style, is found to betray writers into a harsh manner. Harshness arises from unusual words, from forced inversions in the construction of a sentence, and too much neglect of smoothness and ease. This is reckoned the fault of some of our earliest classics in the English Language; such as Sir Walter Raleigh, Sir Francis Bacon, Hooker, Chillingworth, Milton in his prose works, Harrington, Cudworth, and other writers of considerable note in the days of Queen Elizabeth, James I. and Charles I. These writers had nerves and strength in a high degree, and are to this day eminent for that quality in Style. But the language in their hands was exceedingly different from what it is now, and was indeed entirely formed upon the idiom and construction of the Latin, in the arrangement of sentences Hooker, for instance, begins the Preface to his celebrated work of Ecclesiastical Polity with the following sentence: "Though for no other cause, "yet for this, that posterity may know we "have not loosely, through silence, permitted "things to pass away as in dream, there "shall be, for men's information, extant this "much, concerning the present state of the "church of God established amongst us, and "their careful endeavours which would have "upheld the same." Such a sentence now sounds harsh in our ears. Yet some advantages certainly attended this sort of Style; and whether we have gained, or lost, upon the whole, by departing from it, may bear a question. By the freedom of arrangement, which it permitted, it rendered the language susceptible of more strength, of more variety of collocation, and more harmony of period. But however this be, such a Style is now obsolete; and no modern writer could adopt it without the censure of harshness and affectation. The present form which the Language has assumed, has, in some measure, sacrificed the study of strength to that of perspicuity and ease. Our arrangement of words has become less forcible, perhaps, but more plain and natural: and this is now understood to be the genius of our Language.

Ibid.

§ 16. *On the Dry* Style.

The dry manner excludes all ornament of every kind, content with being understood, it has not the least aim to please either the fancy or the ear. This is tolerable only in pure didactic writing; and even there to make us bear it, great weight and solidity of matter is requisite; and entire perspicuity of language. Ariſtotle is the complete example of a Dry Style. Never, perhaps, was there any author who adhered ſo rigidly to the ſtrictneſs of a didactic manner, throughout all his writings, and conveyed ſo much inſtruction, without the leaſt approach to ornament. With the moſt profound genius, and extenſive views, he writes like a pure intelligence, who addreſſes himſelf ſolely to the underſtanding, without making any uſe of the channel of the imagination. But this is a manner which deſerves not to be imitated. For, although the goodneſs of the matter may compenſate the dryneſs or harſhneſs of the Style, yet is that dryneſs a conſiderable defect; as it fatigues attention, and conveys our ſentiments, with diſadvantage, to the reader or hearer. *Blair.*

§ 17. *On the Plain* Style.

A Plain Style riſes one degree above a dry one. A writer of this character employs very little ornament of any kind, and reſts almoſt entirely upon his ſenſe. But, if he is at no pains to engage us by the employment of figures, muſical arrangement, or any other art of writing, he ſtudies, however, to avoid diſguſting us, like a dry and a harſh writer. Beſides Perſpicuity, he purſues Propriety, Purity, and Preciſion, in his language; which form one degree, and no inconſiderable one, of beauty. Livelineſs too, and force, may be conſiſtent with a very Plain Style: and therefore, ſuch an author, if his ſentiments be good, may be abundantly agreeable. The difference between a dry and plain writer, is, that the former is incapable of ornament, and ſeems not to know what it is; the latter ſeeks not after it. He gives us his meaning, in good language, diſtinct and pure; any further ornament he gives himſelf no trouble about; either, becauſe he thinks it unneceſſary to his ſubject; or, becauſe his genius does not lead him to delight in it; or, becauſe it leads him to deſpiſe it *.

This laſt was the caſe with Dean Swift, who may be placed at the head of thoſe that have employed the Plain Style. Few writers have diſcovered more capacity. He treats every ſubject which he handles, whether ſerious or ludicrous, in a maſterly manner. He knew, almoſt beyond any man, the Purity, the Extent, the Preciſion of the Engliſh Language; and, therefore, to ſuch as wiſh to attain a pure and correct Style, he is one of the moſt uſeful models. But we muſt not look for much ornament and grace in his Language. His haughty and moroſe genius made him deſpiſe any embelliſhment of this kind, as beneath his dignity. He delivers his ſentiments in a plain, downright, poſitive manner, like one who is ſure he is in the right; and is very indifferent whether you be pleaſed or not. His ſentences are commonly negligently arranged; diſtinctly enough as to the ſenſe, but without any regard to ſmoothneſs of ſound, often without much regard to compactneſs or elegance. If a metaphor, or any other figure, chanced to render his ſatire more poignant, he would, perhaps, vouchſafe to adopt it, when it came in his way; but if it tended only to embelliſh and illuſtrate, he would rather throw it aſide. Hence, in his

* On this head, of the General Characters of Style, particularly the Plain and the Simple, and the characters of thoſe Engliſh authors who are claſſed under them, in this, and the following Lectures (xix) ſeveral ideas have been taken from a manuſcript treatiſe on rhetoric, part of which was ſhewn to me, many years ago, by the learned and ingenious Author, Dr. Adam Smith, and which, it is hoped, will be given by him to the Public.

ferious pieces, his ftyle often borders upon the dry and unpleafing; in his humorous ones, the plainnefs of his manner fets off his wit to the higheft advantage. There is no froth nor affectation in it; it feems native and unftudied; and while he hardly appears to fmile himfelf, he makes his reader laugh heartily. To a writer of fuch a genius as Dean Swift, the Plain Style was moft admirably fitted. Among our philofophical writers, Mr. Locke comes under this clafs; perfpicuous and pure, but almoft without any ornament whatever. In works which admit, or require, ever fo much ornament, there are parts where the plain manner ought to predominate. But we muft remember, that when this is the character which a writer affects throughout his whole compofition, great weight of matter, and great force of fentiment, are required, in order to keep up the reader's attention, and prevent him from becoming tired of the author. *Blair.*

§ 18. *On the Neat* STYLE.

What is called a Neat Style comes next in order; and here we are got into the region of ornament; but that ornament not of the higheft or moft fparkling kind. A writer of this character fhews, that he does not defpife the beauty of language. It is an object of his attention. But his attention is fhewn in the choice of his words, and in a graceful collocation of them; rather than in any high efforts of imagination, or eloquence. His fentences are always clean, and free from the incumbrance of fuperfluous words; of a moderate length; rather inclining to brevity, than a fwelling ftructure; clofing with propriety; without any tails, or adjections dragging after the proper clofe. His cadence is varied; but not of the ftudied mufical kind. His figures, if he ufes any, are fhort and correct; rather than bold and glowing. Such a Style as this may be attained by a writer who has no great powers of fancy or genius, by induftry merely, and careful attention to the rules of writing; and it is a Style always agreeable. It imprints a character of moderate elevation on our compofition, and carries a decent degree of ornament, which is not unfuitable to any fubject whatever. A familiar letter, or a law paper, on the drieft fubject, may be written with neatnefs; and a fermon, or a philofophical treatife, in a Neat Style, will be read with pleafure. *Ibid.*

§ 19. *On an Elegant* STYLE.

An Elegant Style is a character, expreffing a higher degree of ornament than a neat one; and, indeed, is the term ufually applied to Style, when poffeffing all the virtues of ornament, without any of its exceffes or defects. From what has been formerly delivered, it will eafily be underftood, that complete Elegance implies great perfpicuity and propriety; purity in the choice of words, and care and dexterity in their harmonious and happy arrangement. It implies farther, the grace and beauty of imagination fpread over Style, as far as the fubject admits it; and all the illuftration which figurative language adds, when properly employed. In a word, an elegant writer is one who pleafes the fancy and the ear, while he informs the underftanding; and who gives us his ideas clothed with all the beauty of expreffion, but not overcharged with any of its mifplaced finery. In this clafs, therefore, we place only the firft rate writers in the language; fuch as Addifon, Dryden, Pope, Temple, Bolingbroke, Atterbury, and a few more; writers who differ widely from one another in many of the attributes

attributes of Style, but whom we now claſs together, under the denomination of Elegant, as, in the ſcale of Ornament, poſſeſſing nearly the ſame place. *Blair.*

§ 20. *On the Florid* STYLE.

When the ornaments, applied to Style, are too rich and gaudy in proportion to the ſubject; when they return upon us too faſt, and ſtrike us either with a dazzling luſtre, or a falſe brilliancy, this forms what is called a Florid Style; a term commonly uſed to ſignify the exceſs of ornament. In a young compoſer this is very pardonable. Perhaps, it is even a promiſing ſymptom, in young people, that their Style ſhould incline to the Florid and Luxuriant: "Volo ſe efferat in "adoleſcente fæcunditas," ſays Quinctilian, "multum inde decoquent anni, multum ratio "limabit, aliquid velut uſu ipſo deteretur; ſit "modo unde excidi poſſit quid et exculpi.— "Audeat hæc ætas plura, et inveniat et in"ventis gaudeat; ſint licet illa non ſatis in"terim ſicca et ſevera. Facile remedium eſt "ubertatis: ſterilia nullo labore vincuntur *." But, although the Florid Style may be allowed to youth, in their firſt eſſays, it muſt not receive the ſame indulgence from writers of maturer years. It is to be expected, that judgment, as it ripens, ſhould chaſten imagination, and reject, as juvenile, all ſuch ornaments as are redundant, unſuitable to the ſubject, or not conducive to illuſtrate it. Nothing can be more contemptible than that tinſel ſplendour of language, which ſome writers perpetually affect. It were well, if this could be aſcribed to the real overflowing of a rich imagination. We ſhould then have ſomething to amuſe us, at leaſt, if we found little to inſtruct us. But the worſt is, that with thoſe frothy writers, it is a luxuriancy of words, not of fancy. We ſee a laboured attempt to riſe to a ſplendour of compoſition, of which they have formed to themſelves ſome looſe idea; but having no ſtrength of genius for attaining it, they endeavour to ſupply the defect by poetical words, by cold exclamations, by common-place figures, and every thing that has the appearance of pomp and magnificence. It has eſcaped theſe writers, that ſobriety in ornament, is one great ſecret for rendering it pleaſing; and that without a foundation of good ſenſe and ſolid thought, the moſt Florid Style is but a childiſh impoſition on the Public. The Public, however, are but too apt to be ſo impoſed on; at leaſt, the mob of readers; who are very ready to be caught, at firſt, with whatever is dazzling and gaudy.

I cannot help thinking, that it reflects more honour on the religious turn, and good diſpoſitions of the preſent age, than on the public taſte, that Mr. Hervey's Meditations have had ſo great a currency. The pious and benevolent heart, which is always diſplayed in them, and the lively fancy which, on ſome occaſions, appears, juſtly merited applauſe: but the perpetual glitter of expreſſion, the ſwoln imagery, and ſtrained deſcription which abound in them, are ornaments of a falſe kind. I would, therefore, adviſe ſtudents of

* "In youth, I wiſh to ſee luxuriancy of fancy "appear. Much of it will be diminiſhed by years; "much will be corrected by ripening judgment; "ſome of it, by the mere practice of compoſition, "will be worn away. Let there be only ſufficient "matter, at firſt, that can bear ſome pruning and "lopping off. At this time of life, let genius be "bold and inventive, and pride itſelf in its efforts, "though theſe ſhould not, as yet, be correct. "Luxuriancy can eaſily be cured; but for barrenneſs there is no remedy."

of oratory, to imitate Mr. Harvey's piety, rather than his Style; and, in all compositions of a serious kind, to turn their attention, as Mr. Pope says, "from sounds to "things, from fancy to the heart." Admonitions of this kind I have already had occasion to give, and may hereafter repeat them; as I conceive nothing more incumbent on me, in this course of Lectures, than to take every opportunity of cautioning my readers against the affected and frivolous use of ornament; and, instead of that slight and superficial taste in writing, which I apprehend to be at present too fashionable, to introduce, as far as my endeavours can avail, a taste for more solid thought, and more manly simplicity in Style. *Blair.*

§ 21. *On the different Kinds of* Simplicity.

The first is, Simplicity of Composition, as opposed to too great a variety of parts. Horace's precept refers to this:

Denique sit quod vis simplex duntaxat et unum*.

This is the simplicity of plan in a tragedy, as distinguished from double plots, and crowded incidents; the Simplicity of the Iliad, or Æneid, in opposition to the digressions of Lucan, and the scattered tales of Ariosto; the Simplicity of Grecian architecture, in opposition to the irregular variety of the Gothic. In this sense, Simplicity is the same with Unity.

The second sense is, Simplicity of Thought, as opposed to refinement. Simple thoughts are what arise naturally; what the occasion or the subject suggest unsought; and what, when once suggested, are easily apprehended by all. Refinement in writing, expresses a less natural and obvious train of thought, and which it required a peculiar turn of genius to pursue; within certain bounds very beautiful; but when carried too far, approaching to intricacy, and hurting us by the appearance of being *recherché*, or far sought. Thus, we would naturally say, that Mr. Parnell is a poet of far greater simplicity, in his turn of thought, than Mr. Cowley: Cicero's thoughts on moral subjects are natural; Seneca's too refined and laboured. In these two senses of Simplicity, when it is opposed either to variety of parts, or to refinement of thought, it has no proper relation to Style.

There is a third sense of Simplicity, in which it has respect to Style; and stands opposed to too much ornament, or pomp of language; as when we say, Mr. Locke is a simple, Mr. Hervey a florid, writer; and it is in this sense, that the "*simplex*," the "*tenue*," or "*subtile genus dicendi*," is understood by Cicero and Quinctilian. The simple style, in this sense, coincides with the plain or the neat style, which I before mentioned; and, therefore, requires no farther illustration.

But there is a fourth sense of Simplicity, also respecting Style; but not respecting the degree of ornament employed, so much as the easy and natural manner in which our language expresses our thoughts. This is quite different from the former sense of the word just now mentioned, in which Simplicity was equivalent to Plainness: whereas, in this sense, it is compatible with the highest ornament. Homer, for instance, possesses this Simplicity

* "Then learn the wand'ring humour to controul,
"And keep one equal tenour through the whole." Francis.

Simplicity in the greateſt perfection; and yet no writer has more ornament and beauty. This Simplicity, which is what we are now to conſider, ſtands oppoſed, not to ornament, but to affectation of ornament, or appearance of labour about our Style; and it is a diſtinguiſhing excellency in writing. *Blair.*

§ 22. SIMPLICITY *appears eaſy.*

A writer of Simplicity expreſſes himſelf in ſuch a manner, that every one thinks he could have written in the ſame way; Horace deſcribes it,

> ——— ut ſibi quivis
> Speret idem, ſudet multum, fruſtraque laboret
> Auſus idem *.

There are no marks of art in his expreſſion; it ſeems the very language of nature; you ſee, in the Style, not the writer and his labour, but the man, in his own natural character. He may be rich in his expreſſion; he may be full of figures, and of fancy; but theſe flow from him without effort; and he appears to write in this manner, not becauſe he has ſtudied it, but becauſe it is the manner of expreſſion moſt natural to him. A certain degree of negligence, alſo, is not inconſiſtent with this character of ſtyle, and even not ungraceful in it; for too minute an attention to words is foreign to it: " Habeat ille," ſays

" rantis †." This is the great advantage of Simplicity of Style, that, like ſimplicity of manners, it ſhows us a man's ſentiments and turn of mind laid open without diſguiſe. More ſtudied and artificial manners of writing, however beautiful, have always this diſadvantage, that they exhibit an author in form, like a man at court, where the ſplendour of dreſs, and the ceremonial of behaviour, conceal thoſe peculiarities which diſtinguiſh one man from another. But reading an author of Simplicity, is like converſing with a perſon of diſtinction at home, and with eaſe, where we find natural manners, and a marked character. *Ibid.*

§ 23. *On Naïveté.*

The higheſt degree of this Simplicity, is expreſſed by a French term to which we have none that fully anſwers in our language, *Naïveté.* It is not eaſy to give a preciſe idea of the import of this word. It always expreſſes a diſcovery of character. I believe the beſt account of it is given by a French critic, M. Marmontel, who explains it thus: That ſort of amiable ingenuity, or undiſguiſed openneſs, which ſeems to give us ſome degree of ſuperiority over the perſon who ſhews it; a certain infantine Simplicity, which we love in our hearts, but which diſplays ſome features of the character that we think we could have art enough to

This, however, is to be underſtood, as deſcriptive of a particular ſpecies only of Simplicity. *Blair.*

§ 24. *Ancients eminent for Simplicity.*

With reſpect to Simplicity, in general, we may remark, that the ancient original writers are always the moſt eminent for it. This happens from a plain reaſon, that they wrote from the dictates of natural genius, and were not formed upon the labours and writings of others, which is always in hazard of producing affectation. Hence, among the Greek writers, we have more models of a beautiful Simplicity than among the Roman. Homer, Heſiod, Anacreon, Theocritus, Herodotus, and Xenophon, are all diſtinguiſhed for it. Among the Romans, alſo, we have ſome writers of this character; particularly Terence, Lucretius, Phædrus, and Julius Cæſar. The following paſſage of Terence's Andria, is a beautiful inſtance of Simplicity of manner in deſcription:

——— Funus interim
Procedit; ſequimur; ad ſepulchrum venimus;
In ignem impoſita eſt; fletur; interea hæc ſoror
Quam dixi, ad flammam acceſſit imprudentiùs
Satis cum periculo. Ibi tum exanimatus Pamphilus
Benè diſſimulatum amorem, & celatum indicat;
Occurrit præceps, mulierum ab igne retrahit,
Mea Glycerium, inquit, quid agis? Cur te is perditum?
Tum illa, ut conſuetum facilè amorem cerneres,
Rejecit ſe in eum, flens quam familiariter *.
Act. I. Sc. I.

All the words here are remarkably happy and elegant: and convey a moſt lively picture of the ſcene deſcribed: while, at the ſame time, the Style appears wholly artleſs and unlaboured. Let us next conſider ſome Engliſh writers, who come under this claſs. *Ibid.*

§ 25. *Simplicity the Characteriſtic of* Tillotson's *Style.*

Simplicity is the great beauty of Archbiſhop Tillotſon's manner. Tillotſon has long been admired as an eloquent writer, and a model for preaching. But his eloquence, if we can call it ſuch, has been often miſunderſtood. For if we include in the idea of eloquence, vehemence and ſtrength, pictureſque deſcription, glowing figures, or correct arrangement of ſentences, in all theſe parts of oratory the Archbiſhop is exceedingly deficient. His Style is always pure, indeed, and perſpicuous, but careleſs and remiſs, too often feeble and languid; little beauty in the conſtruction of his ſentences, which are frequently ſuffered to drag unharmoniouſly; ſeldom any attempt towards ſtrength or ſublimity. But, notwithſtanding theſe defects, ſuch a conſtant vein of good ſenſe and piety runs through his works, ſuch an earneſt and ſerious manner, and ſo much uſeful inſtruction.

* "Meanwhile the funeral proceeds; we follow;
"Come to the ſepulchre: the body's plac'd
"Upon the pile; lamented; whereupon
"This ſiſter I was ſpeaking of, all wild,
"Ran to the flames with peril of her life.
"There! there! the frighted Pamphilus betrays
"His well-diſſembled and long-hidden love;
"Runs up, and takes her round the waiſt, and cries,
"Oh! my Glycerium! what is it you do?
"Why, why endeavour to deſtroy yourſelf?
"Then ſhe, in ſuch a manner that you thence
"Might eaſily perceive their long, long love,
"Threw herſelf back into his arms, and wept.
"Oh! how familiarly!" Colman.

tion, conveyed in a Style ſo pure, natural, and unaffected, as will juſtly recommend him to high regard, as long as the Engliſh language remains; not, indeed, as a model of the higheſt eloquence, but as a ſimple and amiable writer, whoſe manner is ſtrongly expreſſive of great goodneſs and worth. I obſerved before, that Simplicity of manner may be conſiſtent with ſome degree of negligence in Style; and it is only the beauty of that Simplicity which makes the negligence of ſuch writers ſeem graceful. But, as appears in the Archbiſhop, negligence may ſometimes be carried ſo far as to impair the beauty of Simplicity, and make it border on a flat and languid manner. *Blair.*

§ 26. *Simplicity of Sir* William Temple*'s Style.*

Sir William Temple is another remarkable writer in the Style of Simplicity. In point of ornament and correctneſs, he riſes a degree above Tillotſon; though, for correctneſs, he is not in the higheſt rank. All is eaſy and flowing in him; he is exceedingly harmonious; ſmoothneſs, and what may be called amænity, are the diſtinguiſhing characters of his manner; relaxing, ſometimes, as ſuch a manner will naturally do, into a prolix and remiſs Style. No writer whatever has ſtamped upon his Style a more lively impreſſion of his own character. In reading his works, we ſeem engaged in converſation with him; we become thoroughly acquainted with him, not merely as an author, but as a man; and contract a friendſhip for him. He may be claſſed as ſtanding in the middle, between a negligent Simplicity, and the higheſt degree of Ornament which this character of Style admits. *Ibid.*

§ 27. *Simplicity of Mr.* Addison*'s Style.*

Of the latter of theſe, the higheſt, moſt correct, and ornamented degree of the ſimple manner, Mr. Addiſon is beyond doubt, in the Engliſh language, the moſt perfect example: and therefore, though not without ſome faults, he is, on the whole, the ſafeſt model for imitation, and the freeſt from conſiderable defects, which the language affords. Perſpicuous and pure he is in the higheſt degree; his preciſion, indeed, not very great; yet nearly as great as the ſubjects which he treats of require: the conſtruction of his ſentences eaſy, agreeable, and commonly very muſical; carrying a character of ſmoothneſs, more than of ſtrength. In figurative language he is rich, particularly in ſimilies and metaphors; which are ſo employed, as to render his Style ſplendid without being gaudy. There is not the leaſt affectation in his manner; we ſee no marks of labour; nothing forced or conſtrained; but great elegance joined with great eaſe and ſimplicity. He is, in particular, diſtinguiſhed by a character of modeſty and of politeneſs, which appears in all his writings. No author has a more popular and inſinuating manner; and the great regard which he every where ſhews for virtue and religion, recommends him highly. If he fails in any thing, it is in want of ſtrength and preciſion, which renders his manner, though perfectly ſuited to ſuch eſſays as he writes in the Spectator, not altogether a proper model for any of the higher and more elaborate kinds of compoſition. Though the public have ever done much juſtice to his merit, yet the nature of his merit has not always been ſeen in its true light: for, though his poetry be elegant, he certainly bears a higher rank among the proſe writers, than he is intitled to among the poets; and, in prose, his humour is of a much higher and more original strain than his philosophy. The character of Sir Roger de Coverley discovers more genius than the critique on Milton. *Blair.*

§ 28. *Simplicity of Style never wearies.*

Such authors as those, whose characters I have been giving, one never tires of reading. There is nothing in their manner that strains or fatigues our thoughts: we are pleased, without being dazzled by their lustre. So powerful is the charm of Simplicity in an author of real genius, that it atones for many defects, and reconciles us to many a careless expression. Hence, in all the most excellent authors, both in prose and verse, the simple and natural manner may be always remarked; although, other beauties being predominant, this form not their peculiar and distinguishing character. Thus Milton is simple in the midst of all his grandeur; and Demosthenes in the midst of all his vehemence. To grave and solemn writings, Simplicity of manner adds the more venerable air. Accordingly, this has often been remarked as the prevailing character throughout all the sacred Scriptures: and indeed no other character of Style was so much suited to the dignity of inspiration. *Ibid.*

§ 29. *Lord* Shaftsbury *deficient in Simplicity of Style.*

Of authors who, notwithstanding many excellencies, have rendered their Style much less beautiful by want of Simplicity, I cannot give a more remarkable example than Lord Shaftsbury. This is an author on whom I have made observations several times before; and shall now take leave of him, with giving his general character under this head. Considerable merit, doubtless, he has. His works might be read with profit for the moral philosophy which they contain, had he not filled them with so many oblique and invidious insinuations against the Christian Religion; thrown out, too, with so much spleen and satire, as do no honour to his memory, either as an author or a man. His language has many beauties. It is firm and supported in an uncommon degree: it is rich and musical. No English author, as I formerly shewed, has attended so much to the regular construction of his sentences, both with respect to propriety, and with respect to cadence. All this gives so much elegance and pomp to his language, that there is no wonder it should have been sometimes highly admired. It is greatly hurt, however, by perpetual stiffness and affectation. This is its capital fault. His lordship can express nothing with Simplicity. He seems to have considered it as vulgar, and beneath the dignity of a man of quality, to speak like other men. Hence he is ever in buskins; full of circumlocutions and artificial elegance. In every sentence, we see the marks of labour and art; nothing of that ease which expresses a sentiment coming natural and warm from the heart. Of figures and ornament of every kind, he is exceedingly fond; sometimes happy in them; but his fondness for them is too visible; and having once laid hold of some metaphor or allusion that pleased him, he knows not how to part with it. What is most wonderful, he was a professed admirer of Simplicity; is always extolling it in the ancients, and censuring the moderns for the want of it; though he departs from it himself as far as any one modern whatever. Lord Shaftsbury possessed delicacy and refinement of taste, to a degree that we may call excessive and sickly; but he had

had little warmth of passion; few strong or vigorous feelings; and the coldness of his character led him to that artificial and stately manner which appears in his writings. He was fonder of nothing than of wit and raillery; but he is far from being happy in it. He attempts it often, but always awkwardly; he is stiff, even in his pleasantry; and laughs in form, like an author, and not like a man *.

From the account which I have given of Lord Shaftsbury's manner, it may easily be imagined, that he would mislead many who blindly admired him. Nothing is more dangerous to the tribe of imitators, than an author, who with many imposing beauties, has also some very considerable blemishes. This is fully exemplified in Mr. Blackwall of Aberdeen, the author of the Life of Homer, the Letters on Mythology, and the Court of Augustus; a writer of considerable learning, and of ingenuity also; but infected with an extravagant love of an artificial Style, and of that parade of language which distinguishes the Shaftsburean manner.

Having now said so much to recommend Simplicity, or the easy and natural manner of writing, and having pointed out the defects of an opposite manner; in order to prevent mistakes on this subject, it is necessary for me to observe, that it is very possible for an author to write simply, and yet not beautifully. One may be free from affectation, and not have merit. The beautiful Simplicity supposes an author to possess real genius; to write with solidity, purity, and liveliness of imagination. In this case, the simplicity or unaffectedness of his manner, is the crowning ornament; it heightens every other beauty; it is the dress of nature, without which all beauties are imperfect. But if mere unaffectedness were sufficient to constitute the beauty of Style, weak, trifling, and dull writers might often lay claim to this beauty. And accordingly we frequently meet with pretended critics, who extol the dullest writers on account of what they call the "Chaste Simplicity of their manner;" which, in truth, is no other than the absence of every ornament, through the mere want of genius and imagination. We must distinguish, therefore, between that Simplicity which accompanies true genius, and which is perfectly compatible with every proper ornament of Style; and that which is no other than a careless and slovenly manner. Indeed the distinction is easily made from the effect produced. The one never fails to interest the reader; the other is insipid and tiresome. *Blair.*

* It may, perhaps, be not unworthy of being mentioned, that the first edition of his Enquiry into Virtue was published, surreptitiously I believe, in a separate form, in the year 1699; and is sometimes to be met with: by comparing which with the corrected edition of the same treatise, as it now stands among his works, we see one of the most curious and useful examples, that I know, of what is called *Limæ Labor*; the art of polishing language, breaking long sentences, and working up an imperfect draught into a highly-finished performance.

§ 30. *On the Vehement* STYLE.

I proceed to mention one other manner or character of Style, different from any that I have yet spoken of; which may be distinguished by the name of the Vehement. This always implies strength; and is not, by any means, inconsistent with Simplicity: but, in its predominant character, is distinguishable from either the strong or the simple manner. It has a peculiar ardour; it is a glowing Style; the language of a man, whose imagination

nation and passions are heated, and strongly affected by what he writes; who is therefore negligent of lesser graces, but pours himself forth with the rapidity and fulness of a torrent. It belongs to the higher kinds of oratory; and indeed is rather expected from a man who is speaking, than from one who is writing in his closet. The orations of Demosthenes furnish the full and perfect example of this species of Style. *Blair.*

§ 31. *Lord* Bolingbroke *excelled in the Vehement Style.*

Among English writers, the one who has most of this character, though mixed, indeed, with several defects, is Lord Bolingbroke. Bolingbroke was formed by nature to be a factious leader; the demagogue of a popular assembly. Accordingly, the Style that runs through all his political writings, is that of one declaiming with heat, rather than writing with deliberation. He abounds in rhetorical figures; and pours himself forth with great impetuosity. He is copious to a fault; places the same thought before us in many different views; but generally with life and ardour. He is bold, rather than correct; a torrent that flows strong, but often muddy. His sentences are varied as to length and shortness; inclining, however, most to long periods, sometimes including parentheses, and frequently crowding and heaping a multitude of things upon one another, as naturally happens in the warmth of speaking. In the choice of his words, there is great felicity and precision. In exact construction of sentences, he is much inferior to Lord Shaftsbury; but greatly superior to him in life and ease. Upon the whole, his merit, as a writer, would have been very considerable, if his matter had equalled his Style. But whilst we find many things to commend in the latter, in the former, as I before remarked, we can hardly find any thing to commend. In his reasonings, for the most part, he is flimsy and false; in his political writings, factious: in what he calls his philosophical ones, irreligious and sophistical in the highest degree. *Ibid.*

§ 32. *Directions for forming a* Style.

It will be more to the purpose, that I conclude these dissertations upon Style with a few directions concerning the proper method of attaining a good Style in general; leaving the particular character of that Style to be either formed by the subject on which we write, or prompted by the bent of genius.

The first direction which I give for this purpose, is, to study clear ideas on the subject concerning which we are to write or speak. This is a direction which may at first appear to have small relation to Style. Its relation to it, however, is extremely close. The foundation of all good Style, is good sense, accompanied with a lively imagination. The Style and thoughts of a writer are so intimately connected, that, as I have several times hinted, it is frequently hard to distinguish them. Wherever the impressions of things upon our minds are faint and indistinct, or perplexed and confused, our Style in treating of such things will infallibly be so too. Whereas, what we conceive clearly and feel strongly, we will naturally express with clearness and with strength. This, then, we may be assured, is a capital rule as to Style, to think closely of the subject, till we have attained a full and distinct view of the matter which we are to clothe in words, till we become warm and interested in it; then, and not till then, shall we find expression begin to flow. Generally speaking, the best and most proper expressions,

expressions, are those which a clear view of the subject suggests, without much labour or enquiry after them. This is Quinctilian's observation, Lib. viii. c. 1. "Plerumque optima verba rebus cohærent, et cernuntur "suo lumine. At nos quærimus illa, tan"quam lateant seque subducant. Ita nun"quam putamus verba esse circa id de quo "dicendum est; sed ex aliis locis petimus, "et inventis vim afferimus *." *Blair.*

§ 33. *Practice necessary for forming a* Style.

In the second place, in order to form a good Style, the frequent practice of composing is indispensably necessary. Many rules concerning Style I have delivered; but no rules will answer the end without exercise and habit. At the same time, it is not every sort of composing that will improve Style. This is so far from being the case, that by frequent careless and hasty composition, we shall acquire certainly a very bad Style; we shall have more trouble afterwards in unlearning faults, and correcting negligences, than if we had not been accustomed to composition at all. In the beginning, therefore, we ought to write slowly, and with much care. Let the facility and speed of writing, be the fruit of longer practice. "Moram et solicitudinem," says Quinctilian with the greatest reason, L. x. c. 3. "initiis impero. Nam primum hoc "constituendum ac obtinendum est, ut quam "optimè scribamus: celeritatem dabit con"suetudo. Paulatim res faciliùs se ostendent, "verba respondebunt, compositio proseque"tur. Cuncta denique et in familia benè "instituta in officio erunt. Summa hæc est "rei: citò scribendo non fit ut benè scriba"tur; benè scribendo, fit ut citò *." *Ibid.*

§ 34. *Too anxious a Care about* Words *to be avoided.*

We must observe, however, that there may be an extreme in too great and anxious a care about Words. We must not retard the course of thought, nor cool the heat of imagination, by pausing too long on every word we employ. There is, on certain occasions, a glow of composition which should be kept up, if we hope to express ourselves happily, though at the expence of allowing some inadvertencies to pass. A more severe examination of these must be left to be the work of correction. For if the practice of composition be useful, the laborious work of correcting is no less so; it is indeed absolutely necessary to our reaping any benefit from the habit of

* "The most proper words for the most part "adhere to the thoughts which are to be expressed "by them, and may be discovered as by their own "light. But we hunt after them, as if they were "hidden, and only to be found in a corner. Hence, "instead of conceiving the words to lie near the "subject, we go in quest of them to some other "quarter, and endeavour to give force to the ex"pressions we have found out."

* "I enjoin that such as are beginning the "practice of composition, write slowly, and with "anxious deliberation. Their great object at first "should be, to write as well as possible; practice "will enable them to write speedily. By degrees "matter will offer itself still more readily; words "will be at hand; composition will flow; every "thing, as in the arrangement of a well-ordered "family, will present itself in its proper place. "The sum of the whole is this: by hasty com"position, we shall never acquire the art of com"posing well; by writing well we shall come to "write speedily."

composition. What we have written should be laid by for some little time, till the ardour of composition be past, till the fondness for the expressions we have used be worn off, and the expressions themselves be forgotten; and then reviewing our work with a cool and critical eye, as if it were the performance of another, we shall discern many imperfections which at first escaped us. Then is the season for pruning redundancies; for weighing the arrangement of sentences; for attending to the juncture and connecting particles; and bringing Style into a regular, correct, and supported form. This "*Limæ Labor*" must be submitted to by all who would communicate their thoughts with proper advantage to others; and some practice in it will soon sharpen their eye to the most necessary objects of attention, and render it a much more easy and practicable work than might at first be imagined. *Blair.*

§ 35. *An Acquaintance with the best Authors necessary to the Formation of a* STYLE.

In the third place, with respect to the assistance that is to be gained from the writings of others, it is obvious that we ought to render ourselves well acquainted with the Style of the best authors. This is requisite, both in order to form a just taste in Style, and to supply us with a full stock of words on every subject. In reading authors with a view to Style, attention should be given to the peculiarities of their different manners; and in this and former Lectures I have endeavoured to suggest several things that may be useful in this view. I know no exercise that will be found more useful for acquiring a proper Style, than to translate some passage from an eminent English author, into our own words. What I mean is, to take, for instance, some page of one of Mr. Addison's Spectators, and read it carefully over two or three times, till we have got a firm hold of the thoughts contained in it; then to lay aside the book; to attempt to write out the passage from memory, in the best way we can; and having done so, next to open the book, and compare what we have written with the Style of the author. Such an exercise will, by comparison, shew us where the defects of our Style lie; will lead us to the proper attentions for rectifying them; and, among the different ways in which the same thought may be expressed, will make us perceive that which is the most beautiful. *Ibid.*

§ 36. *A servile Imitation to be avoided.*

In the fourth place, I must caution, at the same time, against a servile imitation of any one author whatever. This is always dangerous. It hampers genius; it is likely to produce a stiff manner; and those who are given to close imitation, generally imitate an author's faults as well as his beauties. No man will ever become a good writer, or speaker, who has not some degree of confidence to follow his own genius. We ought to beware, in particular, of adopting any author's noted phrases, or transcribing passages from him. Such a habit will prove fatal to all genuine composition. Infinitely better it is to have something that is our own, though of moderate beauty, than to affect to shine in borrowed ornaments, which will, at last, betray the utter poverty of our genius. On these heads of composing, correcting, reading, and imitating, I advise every student of oratory to consult what Quinctilian has delivered in the Tenth Book of his Institutions, where he will find a variety of excellent observations and directions, that well deserve attention. *Ibid.*

§ 37. STYLE *must be adapted to the Subject.*

In the fifth place, it is an obvious but material rule, with respect to Style, that we always study to adapt it to the subject, and also to the capacity of our hearers, if we are to speak in public. Nothing merits the name of eloquent or beautiful, which is not suited to the occasion, and to the persons to whom it is addressed. It is to the last degree awkward and absurd, to attempt a poetical florid Style, on occasions when it should be our business only to argue and reason; or to speak with elaborate pomp of expression, before persons who comprehend nothing of it, and who can only stare at our unseasonable magnificence. These are defects not so much in point of Style, as, what is much worse, in point of common sense. When we begin to write, or speak, we ought previously to fix in our minds a clear conception of the end to be aimed at; to keep this steadily in our view, and to suit our Style to it. If we do not sacrifice to this great object every ill-timed ornament that may occur to our fancy, we are unpardonable; and, though children and fools may admire, men of sense will laugh at us and our Style. *Blair.*

§ 38. *Attention to* STYLE *must not detract from Attention to* THOUGHT.

In the last place, I cannot conclude the subject without this admonition, that, in any case, and on any occasion, attention to Style must not engross us so much, as to detract from a higher degree of attention to the Thoughts. "Curam verborum," says the great Roman Critic, "rerum volo esse solicitudinem *." A direction the more necessary, as the present taste of the age, in writing, seems to lean more to Style than to Thought. It is much easier to dress up trivial and common sentiments with some beauty of expression, than to afford a fund of vigorous, ingenious, and useful thoughts. The latter requires true genius; the former may be attained by industry, with the help of very superficial parts. Hence we find so many writers frivolously rich in Style, but wretchedly poor in sentiment. The public ear is now so much accustomed to a correct and ornamented Style, that no writer can, with safety, neglect the study of it. But he is a contemptible one, who does not look to something beyond it; who does not lay the chief stress upon his matter, and employ such ornaments of Style to recommend it, as are manly, not foppish. "Majore animo," says the writer whom I have so often quoted, "aggre-
"dienda est eloquentia; quæ si toto corpore
"valet, ungues polire et capillum componere,
"non existimabit ad curam suam pertinere.
"Ornatus et virilis et fortis et sanctus sit;
"nec effeminatam levitatem et fuco emen-
"titum colorem amet; sanguine et viribus
"niteat †." *Ibid.*

* "To your expression be attentive; but about "your matter be solicitous."

† "A higher spirit ought to animate those who "study eloquence. They ought to consult the "health and soundness of the whole body, rather "than bend their attention to such trifling objects "as paring the nails and dressing the hair. Let "ornament be manly and chaste, without effeminate gaiety, or artificial colouring, let it shine "with the glow of health and strength."

§ 39. *Of the Rise of Poetry among the* Romans.

The Romans, in the infancy of their ſtate, were entirely rude and unpoliſhed. They came from ſhepherds; they were increaſed from the refuſe of the nations around them; and their manners agreed with their original. As they lived wholly on tilling their ground at home, or on plunder from their neighbours, war was their buſineſs, and agriculture the chief art they followed. Long after this, when they had ſpread their conqueſts over a great part of Italy, and began to make a conſiderable figure in the world,—even their great men retained a roughneſs, which they raiſed into a virtue, by calling it Roman Spirit; and which might often much better have been called Roman Barbarity. It ſeems to me, that there was more of auſterity than juſtice, and more of inſolence than courage, in ſome of their moſt celebrated actions. However that be, this is certain, that they were at firſt a nation of ſoldiers and huſbandmen: roughneſs was long an applauded character among them; and a ſort of ruſticity reigned, even in their ſenate-houſe.

In a nation originally of ſuch a temper as this, taken up almoſt always in extending their territories, very often in ſettling the balance of power among themſelves, and not unfrequently in both theſe at the ſame time, it was long before the politer arts made any appearance; and very long before they took root or flouriſhed to any degree. Poetry was the firſt that did ſo; but ſuch a poetry, as one might expect among a warlike, buſied, unpoliſhed people.

Not to enquire about the ſongs of triumph, mentioned even in Romulus's time, there was certainly ſomething of poetry among them in the next reign under Numa: a prince, who pretended to converſe with the Muſes, as well as with Egeria; and who might poſſibly himſelf have made the verſes which the Salian prieſts ſung in his time. Pythagoras, either in the ſame reign, or if you pleaſe ſome time after, gave the Romans a tincture of poetry as well as of philoſophy; for Cicero aſſures us, that the Pythagoreans made great uſe of poetry and muſic: and probably they, like our old Druids, delivered moſt of their precepts in verſe. Indeed the chief employment of poetry, in that and the following ages, among the Romans, was of a religious kind. Their very prayers, and perhaps their whole liturgy, was poetical. They had alſo a ſort of prophetic or ſacred writers, who ſeem to have wrote generally in verſe; and were ſo numerous, that there were above two thouſand of their volumes remaining even to Auguſtus's time. They had a kind of plays too, in theſe early times, derived from what they had ſeen of the Tuſcan actors, when ſent for to Rome to expiate a plague that raged in the city. Theſe ſeem to have been either like our dumb-ſhews, or elſe a kind of extempore farces; a thing to this day a good deal in uſe all over Italy, and in Tuſcany. In a more particular manner add to theſe, that extempore kind of jeſting dialogues begun at their harveſt and vintage feaſts; and carried on ſo rudely and abuſively afterwards, as to occaſion a very ſevere law to reſtrain their licentiouſneſs—and thoſe lovers of poetry and good eating, who ſeem to have attended the tables of the richer ſort, much like the old provincial poets, or our own Britiſh bards, and ſang there, to ſome inſtrument of muſic, the atchievements of their anceſtors, and the noble deeds of thoſe who

who had gone before them, to inflame others to follow their great examples.

The names of almost all these poets sleep in peace with all their works; and, if we may take the word of the other Roman writers of a better age, it is no great loss to us. One of their best poets represents them as very obscure and very contemptible; one of their best historians avoids quoting them, as too barbarous for politer ears; and one of their most judicious emperors ordered the greatest part of their writings to be burnt, that the world might be troubled with them no longer.

All these poets therefore may very well be dropt in the account: there being nothing remaining of their works; and probably no merit to be found in them, if they had remained. And so we may date the beginning of the Roman poetry from Livius Andronicus, the first of their poets of whom any thing does remain to us; and from whom the Romans themselves seem to have dated the beginning of their poetry, even in the Augustan age.

The first kind of poetry that was followed with any success among the Romans, was that for the stage. They were a very religious people; and stage plays in those times made no inconsiderable part in their public devotions; it is hence, perhaps, that the greatest number of their oldest poets, of whom we have any remains, and indeed almost all of them, are dramatic poets. *Spence.*

§ 40. *Of* Livius, Nævius, *and* Ennius.

The foremost in this list, were Livius, Nævius, and Ennius. Livius's first play (and it was the first written play that ever appeared at Rome, whence perhaps Horace calls him Livius Scriptor) was acted in the 514th year from the building of the city. He seems to have got whatever reputation he had, rather as their first, than as a good writer; for Cicero, who admired these old poets more than they were afterwards admired, is forced to give up Livius; and says, that his pieces did not deserve a second reading. He was for some time the sole writer for the stage; till Nævius rose to rival him, and probably far exceeded his master. Nævius ventured too on an epic, or rather an historical poem, on the first Carthaginian war. Ennius followed his steps in this, as well as in the dramatic way; and seems to have excelled him as much as he had excelled Livius; so much at least, that Lucretius says of him, "That he was the first of their poets who deserved a lasting crown from the Muses." These three poets were actors as well as poets; and seem all of them to have wrote whatever was wanted for the stage, rather than to have consulted their own turn or genius. Each of them published, sometimes tragedies, sometimes comedies, and sometimes a kind of dramatic satires; such satires, I suppose, as had been occasioned by the extempore poetry that had been in fashion the century before them. All the most celebrated dramatic writers of antiquity excel only in one kind. There is no tragedy of Terence, or Menander; and no comedy of Actius, or Euripedes. But these first dramatic poets, among the Romans, attempted every thing indifferently; just as the present fancy, or the demand of the people, led them.

The quiet the Romans enjoyed after the second Punic war, when they had humbled their great rival Carthage; and their carrying on their conquests afterwards, without any great difficulties, into Greece,—gave them leisure and opportunities for making very great improvements in their poetry. Their dramatic

dramatic writers began to act with more steadiness and judgment; they followed one point of view; they had the benefit of the excellent patterns the Greek writers had set them; and formed themselves on those models. *Spence.*

§ 41. *Of* Plautus.

Plautus was the first that consulted his own genius, and confined himself to that species of dramatic writing, for which he was the best fitted by nature. Indeed his comedy (like the old comedy at Athens) is of a ruder kind, and far enough from the polish that was afterwards given it among the Romans. His jests are often rough, and his wit coarse; but there is a strength and spirit in him, that make one read him with pleasure, at least he is much to be commended for being the first that considered what he was most capable of excelling in, and not endeavouring to shine in too many different ways at once. Cæcilius followed his example in this particular; but improved their comedy so much beyond him, that he is named by Cicero, as perhaps the best of all the comic writers they ever had. This high character of him was not for his language, which is given up by Cicero himself as faulty and incorrect; but either for the dignity of his characters, or the strength and weight of his sentiments. *Ibid.*

§ 42. *Of* Terence.

Terence made his first appearance when Cæcilius was in high reputation. It is said, that when he offered his first play to the Ediles, they sent him with it to Cæcilius for his judgment of the piece. Cæcilius was at supper when he came to him; and as Terence was drest very meanly, he was placed on a little stool, and desired to read away: but upon his having read a very few lines only, Cæcilius altered his behaviour, and placed him next himself at the table. They all admired him as a rising genius; and the applause he received from the public, answered the compliments they had made him in private. His Eunuchus, in particular, was acted twice in one day; and he was paid more for that piece than ever had been given before for a comedy: and yet, by the way, it was not much above thirty pounds. We may see by that, and the rest of his plays which remain to us, to what a degree of exactness and elegance the Roman Comedy was arrived in his time. There is a beautiful simplicity, which reigns through all his works. There is no searching after wit, and no ostentation of ornament in him. All his speakers seem to say just what they should say, and no more. The story is always going on; and goes on just as it ought. This whole age, long before Terence and long after, is rather remarkable for strength than beauty in writing. Were we to compare it with the following age, the compositions of this would appear to those of the Augustan, as the Doric order in building if compared with the Corinthian; but Terence's work is to those of the Augustan age, as the Ionic is to the Corinthian order: it is not so ornamented, or so rich; but nothing can be more exact and pleasing. The Roman language itself, in his hands, seems to be improved beyond what one could ever expect; and to be advanced almost a hundred years forwarder than the times he lived in. There are some who look upon this as one of the strangest phænomena in the learned world: but it is a phænomenon which may be well enough explained from Cicero. He says, "that in several families the Roman language was spoken in perfection, even in those

those times;" and instances particularly in the families of the Lælii and the Scipio's. Every one knows that Terence was extremely intimate in both these families: and as the language of his pieces is that of familiar conversation, he had indeed little more to do, than to write as they talked at their tables. Perhaps, too, he was obliged to Scipio and Lælius, for more than their bare conversations. That is not at all impossible; and indeed the Romans themselves seem generally to have imagined that he was assisted by them in the writing part too. If it was really so, that will account still better for the elegance of the language in his plays: because Terence himself was born out of Italy; and though he was brought thither very young, he received the first part of his education in a family, where they might not speak with so much correctness as Lælius and Scipio had been used to from their very infancy. Thus much for the language of Terence's plays: as for the rest, it seems, from what he says himself, that his most usual method was to take his plans chiefly, and his characters wholly, from the Greek comic poets. Those who say that he translated all the comedies of Menander, certainly carry the matter too far. They were probably more than Terence ever wrote. Indeed this would be more likely to be true of Afranius than Terence; though, I suppose, it would scarce hold, were we to take both of them together. *Spence.*

§ 43. *Of* Afranius.

We have a very great loss in the works of Afranius: for he was regarded, even in the Augustan Age, as the most exact imitator of Menander. He owns himself, that he had no restraint in copying him; or any other of the Greek comic writers, wherever they set him a good example. Afranius's stories and persons were Roman, as Terence's were Grecian. This was looked upon as so material a point in those days, that it made two different species of comedy. Those on a Greek story were called, Palliatæ; and those on a Roman, Togatæ. Terence excelled all the Roman poets in the former, and Afranius in the latter. *Ibid.*

§ 44. *Of* Pacuvius *and* Actius.

About the same time that comedy was improved so considerably, Pacuvius and Actius (one a cotemporary of Terence, and the other of Afranius) carried tragedy as far towards perfection as it ever arrived in Roman hands. The step from Ennius to Pacuvius was a very great one; so great, that he was reckoned, in Cicero's time, the best of all their tragic poets. Pacuvius, as well as Terence, enjoyed the acquaintance and friendship of Lælius and Scipio: but he did not profit so much by it, as to the improvement of his language. Indeed his style was not to be the common conversation style, as Terence's was; and all the stiffenings given to it, might take just as much from its elegance as they added to its dignity. What is remarkable in him, is, that he was almost as eminent for painting as he was for poetry. He made the decorations for his own plays; and Pliny speaks of some paintings by him, in a temple of Hercules, as the most celebrated work of their kind, done by any Roman of condition after Fabius Pictor. Actius began to publish when Pacuvius was leaving off: his language was not so fine, nor his verses so well-turned, even as those of his predecessor. There is a remarkable story of him in an old critic, which, as it may give some light into their different manners of writing, may be worth relating. Pacuvius, in his old age, retired to Tarentum, to enjoy the soft air and mild winters of that place. As Actius was obliged, on some affairs, to make a journey into Asia, he took Tarentum in his way, and staid there some days with Pacuvius. It was in this visit that he read his tragedy of Atreus to him, and desired his opinion of it. Old Pacuvius, after hearing it out, told him very honestly, that the poetry was sonorous and majestic, but that it seemed to him too stiff and harsh. Actius replied, that he was himself very sensible of that fault in his writings; but that he was not at all sorry for it: "for," says he, "I have always been of opinion, that it is the same with writers as with fruits; among which, those that are most soft and palatable, decay the soonest; whereas those of a rough taste last the longer, and have the finer relish, when once they come to be mellowed by time."—Whether this style ever came to be thus mellowed, I very much doubt; however that was, it is a point that seems generally allowed, that he and Pacuvius were the two best tragic poets the Romans ever had.

Spence.

§ 45. *Of the Rise of Satire: Of* Lucilius, Lucretius, *and* Catullus.

All this while, that is, for above one hundred years, the stage, as you see, was almost solely in possession of the Roman poets. It was now time for the other kinds of poetry to have their turn; however, the first that sprung up and flourished to any degree, was still a cyon from the same root. What I mean, is Satire; the produce of the old comedy. This kind of poetry had been attempted in a different manner by some of the former writers, and in particular by Ennius: but it was so altered and so improved by Lucilius, that he was called the inventor of it. This was a kind of poetry wholly of the Roman growth; and the only one they had that was so; and even as to this, Lucilius improved a good deal by the side lights he borrowed from the old comedy at Athens. Not long after, Lucretius brought their poetry acquainted with philosophy: and Catullus began to shew the Romans something of the excellence of the Greek lyric poets. Lucretius discovers a great deal of spirit wherever his subject will give him leave; and the first moment he steps a little aside from it, in all his digressions, he is fuller of life and fire, and appears to have been of a more poetical turn, than Virgil himself; which is partly acknowledged in the fine compliment the latter seems to pay him in his Georgics. His subject often obliges him to go on heavily for an hundred lines together: but wherever he breaks out, he breaks out like lightning from a dark cloud; all at once, with force and brightness. His character, in this, agrees with what is said of him: that a philtre he took had given him a frenzy, and that he wrote in his lucid intervals. He and Catullus wrote, when letters in general began to flourish at Rome much more than ever they had done. Catullus was too wise to rival him; and was the most admired of all his cotemporaries, in all the different ways of writing he attempted. His odes perhaps are the least valuable part of his works. The strokes of satire in his epigrams are very severe; and the descriptions in his Idylliums, very full and picturesque. He paints strongly; but all his paintings have more of force than elegance, and put one more in mind of Homer than Virgil.

With these I shall chuse to close the first age of the Roman poetry: an age more remarkable

able for ſtrength than for refinement in writing. I have dwelt longer on it perhaps than I ought; but the order and ſucceſſion of theſe poets wanted much to be ſettled: and I was obliged to ſay ſomething of each of them, becauſe I may have recourſe to each on ſome occaſion or another, in ſhewing you my collection. All that remains to us of the poetical works of this age, are the miſcellaneous poems of Catullus; the philoſophical poem of Lucretius; ſix comedies by Terence; and twenty by Plautus. Of all the reſt, there is nothing left us, except ſuch paſſages from their works as happened to be quoted by the ancient writers, and particularly by Cicero and the old critics. *Spence.*

§ 46. *Of the Criticiſms of* Cicero, Horace, and Quinctilian *on the above Writers.*

The beſt way to ſettle the characters and merits of theſe poets of the firſt age, where ſo little of their own works remains, is by conſidering what is ſaid of them by the other Roman writers, who were well acquainted with their works. The beſt of the Roman critics we can conſult now, and perhaps the beſt they ever had, are Cicero, Horace, and Quinctilian. If we compare their ſentiments of theſe poets together, we ſhall find a diſagreement in them; but a diſagreement which I think may be accounted for, without any great difficulty. Cicero (as he lived before the Roman poetry was brought to perfection, and poſſibly as no very good judge of poetry himſelf) ſeems to think more highly of them than the others. He gives up Livius indeed; but then he makes it up in commending Nævius. All the other comic poets he quotes often with reſpect; and as to the tragic, he carries it ſo far as to ſeem ſtrongly inclined to oppoſe old Ennius to Æſchilus, Pacuvius to Sophocles, and Actius to Euripides.—This high notion of the old poets was probably the general faſhion in his time; and it continued afterwards (eſpecially among the more elderly ſort of people) in the Auguſtan age; and indeed much longer. Horace, in his epiſtle to Auguſtus, combats it as a vulgar error in his time; and perhaps it was an error from which that prince himſelf was not wholly free. However that be, Horace, on this occaſion, enters into the queſtion very fully, and with a good deal of warmth. The character he gives of the old dramatic poets (which indeed includes all the poets I have been ſpeaking of, except Lucilius, Lucretius, and Catullus) is perhaps rather too ſevere. He ſays, "That their language was in a great degree ſuperannuated, even in his time; that they are often negligent and incorrect; and that there is generally a ſtiffneſs in their compoſitions: that people indeed might pardon theſe things in them, as the fault of the times they lived in; but that it was provoking they ſhould think of commending them for thoſe very faults." In another piece of his, which turns pretty much on the ſame ſubject, he gives Lucilius's character much in the ſame manner. He owns, "that he had a good deal of wit; but then it is rather of the farce kind, than true genteel wit. He is a rapid writer, and has a great many good things in him; but is often very ſuperfluous and incorrect; his language is daſhed affectedly with Greek; and his verſes are hard and unharmonious."—Quinctilian ſteers the middle way between both. Cicero perhaps was a little miſled by his nearneſs to their times; and Horace by his ſubject, which was profeſſedly to ſpeak againſt the old writers. Quinctilian, therefore, does not

not commend them so generally as Cicero, nor speak against them so strongly as Horace; and is perhaps more to be depended upon, in this case, than either of them. He compares the works of Ennius to some sacred grove, in which the old oaks look rather venerable than pleasing. He commends Pacuvius and Actius, for the strength of their language and the force of their sentiments; but says, "they wanted that polish which was set on the Roman poetry afterwards." He speaks of Plautus and Cæcilius, as applauded writers; of Terence as a most elegant, and of Afranius, as an excellent one; but they all, says he, fall infinitely short of the grace and beauty which is to be found in the Attic writers of comedy, and which is perhaps peculiar to the dialect they wrote in. To conclude: According to him, Lucilius is too much cried up by many, and too much run down by Horace; Lucretius is more to be read for his matter than for his style; and Catullus is remarkable in the satirical part of his works, but scarce so in the rest of his lyric poetry. *Spence.*

§ 47. *Of the flourishing State of Poetry among the* Romans.

The first age was only as the dawning of the Roman poetry, in comparison of the clear full light that opened all at once afterwards, under Augustus Cæsar. The state, which had been so long tending towards a monarchy, was quite settled down to that form by this prince. When he had no longer any dangerous opponents, he grew mild, or at least concealed the cruelty of his temper. He gave peace and quiet to the people that were fallen into his hands; and looked kindly on the improvement of all the arts and elegancies of life among them. He had a minister, too, under him, who (though a very bad writer himself) knew how to encourage the best; and who admitted the best poets, in particular, into a very great share of friendship and intimacy with him. Virgil was one of the foremost in this list; who, at his first setting out, grew soon their most applauded writer for genteel pastorals: then gave them the most beautiful and most correct poem that ever was wrote in the Roman language, in his rules of agriculture (so beautiful, that some of the ancients seem to accuse Virgil of having studied beauty too much in that piece); and last of all, undertook a political poem, in support of the new establishment. I have thought this to be the intent of the Æneid, ever since I first read Bossu; and the more one considers it, the more I think one is confirmed in that opinion. Virgil is said to have begun this poem the very year that Augustus was freed from his great rival Anthony: the government of the Roman empire was to be wholly in him: and though he chose to be called their father, he was, in every thing but the name, their king. This monarchical form of government must naturally be apt to displease the people. Virgil seems to have laid the plan of his poem to reconcile them to it. He takes advantage of their religious turn; and of some old prophecies that must have been very flattering to the Roman people, as promising them the empire of the whole world: he weaves this in with the most probable account of their origin, that of their being descended from the Trojans. To be a little more particular: Virgil, in his Æneid, shews that Æneas was called into their country by the express order of the Gods; that he was made king of it, by the will of heaven, and by all the human rights that could be; that there was an uninterrupted

terrupted ſucceſſion of kings from him to Romulus; that his heirs were to reign there for ever; and that the Romans, under them, were to obtain the monarchy of the world. It appears from Virgil, and the other Roman writers, that Julius Cæſar was of the royal race, and that Auguſtus was his ſole heir. The natural reſult of all this is, that the promiſes made to the Roman people, in and through this race, terminating in Auguſtus, the Romans, if they would obey the Gods, and be maſters of the world, were to yield obedience to the new eſtabliſhment under that prince. As odd a ſcheme as this may ſeem now, it is ſcarce ſo odd as that of ſome people among us, who perſuaded themſelves, that an abſolute obedience was owing to our kings, on their ſuppoſed deſcent from ſome unknown patriarch: and yet that had its effect with many, about a century ago; and ſeems not to have quite loſt all its influence, even in our remembrance. However that be, I think it appears plain enough, that the two great points aimed at by Virgil in his Æneid, were to maintain their old religious tenets, and to ſupport the new form of government in the family of the Cæſars. That poem therefore may very well be conſidered as a religious and political work; or rather (as the vulgar religion with them was ſcarce any thing more than an engine of ſtate) it may fairly enough be conſidered as a work merely political. If this was the caſe, Virgil was not ſo highly encouraged by Auguſtus and Mæcenas for nothing. To ſpeak a little more plainly: He wrote in the ſervice of the new uſurpation on the ſtate: and all that can be offered in vindication of him, in this light, is, that the uſurper he wrote for, was grown a tame one; and that the temper and bent of their conſtitution, at that time, was ſuch, that the reins of government muſt have fallen into the hands of ſome one perſon or another; and might probably, on any new revolution, have fallen into the hands of ſome one leſs mild and indulgent than Auguſtus was, at the time when Virgil wrote this poem in his ſervice. But whatever may be ſaid of his reaſons for writing it, the poem itſelf has been highly applauded in all ages, from its firſt appearance to this day; and though left unfiniſhed by its author, has been always reckoned as much ſuperior to all the other epic poems among the Romans, as Homer's is among the Greeks. *Spence.*

§ 48. *Obſervations on the* Æneid, *and the Author's Genius.*

It preſerves more to us of the religion of the Romans, than all the other Latin poets (excepting only Ovid) put together: and gives us the forms and appearances of their deities, as ſtrongly as if we had ſo many pictures of them preſerved to us, done by ſome of the beſt hands in the Auguſtan age. It is remarkable, that he is commended by ſome of the ancients themſelves, for the ſtrength of his imagination as to this particular, though in general that is not his character, ſo much as exactneſs. He was certainly the moſt correct poet even of his time; in which all falſe thoughts and idle ornaments in writing were diſcouraged: and it is as certain, that there is but little of invention in his Æneid; much leſs, I believe, than is generally imagined. Almoſt all the little facts in it are built on hiſtory; and even as to the particular lines, no one perhaps ever borrowed more from the poets that preceded him, than he did. He goes ſo far back as to old Ennius; and often inſerts whole verſes from him, and ſome other of their

their earlieſt writers. The obſoleteneſs of their ſtyle, did not hinder him much in this: for he was a particular lover of their old language; and no doubt inſerted many more antiquated words in his poem, than we can diſcover at preſent. Judgment is his diſtinguiſhing character: and his great excellence conſiſted in chuſing and ranging things aright. Whatever he borrowed he had the ſkill of making his own, by weaving it ſo well into his work, that it looks all of a piece; even thoſe parts of his poems, where this may be moſt practiſed, reſembling a fine piece of Moſaic, in which all the parts, though of ſuch different marbles, unite together; and the various ſhades and colours are ſo artfully diſpoſed as to melt off inſenſibly into one another.

One of the greateſt beauties in Virgil's private character was, his modeſty and good-nature. He was apt to think humbly of himſelf, and handſomely of others: and was ready to ſhew his love of merit, even where it might ſeem to claſh with his own. He was the firſt who recommended Horace to Mæcenas.

Spence.

§ 49. *Of* Horace.

Horace was the fitteſt man in the world for a court where wit was ſo particularly encouraged. No man ſeems to have had more, and all of the genteeleſt ſort; or to have been better acquainted with mankind. His gaiety, and even his debauchery, made him ſtill the more agreeable to Mæcenas: ſo that it is no wonder that his acquaintance with that miniſter grew up to ſo high a degree of friendſhip, as is very uncommon between a firſt miniſter and a poet; and which had poſſibly ſuch an effect on the latter, as one ſhall ſcarce ever hear of between any two friends, the moſt on a level: for there is ſome room to conjecture, that he haſtened himſelf out of this world to accompany his great friend in the next. Horace has been moſt generally celebrated for his lyric poems; in which he far excelled all the Roman poets, and perhaps was no unworthy rival of ſeveral of the Greek: which ſeems to have been the height of his ambition. His next point of merit, as it has been uſually reckoned, was his refining ſatire; and bringing it from the coarſeneſs and harſhneſs of Lucilius to that genteel, eaſy manner, which he, and perhaps nobody but he and one perſon more in all the ages ſince, has ever poſſeſſed. I do not remember that any one of the ancients ſays any thing of his epiſtles: and this has made me ſometimes imagine, that his epiſtles and ſatires might originally have paſſed under one and the ſame name; perhaps that of Sermones. They are generally written in a ſtyle approaching to that of converſation; and are ſo much alike, that ſeveral of the ſatires might juſt as well be called epiſtles, as ſeveral of his epiſtles have the ſpirit of ſatire in them. This latter part of his works, by whatever name you pleaſe to call them (whether ſatires and epiſtles, or diſcourſes in verſe on moral and familiar ſubjects) is what, I muſt own, I love much better even than the lyric part of his works. It is in theſe that he ſhews that talent for criticiſm, in which he ſo very much excelled; eſpecially in his long epiſtle to Auguſtus: and that other to the Piſo's, commonly called his Art of Poetry. They abound in ſtrokes which ſhew his great knowledge of mankind, and in that pleaſing way he had of teaching philoſophy, of laughing away vice, and inſinuating virtue into the minds of his readers. They may ſerve as much as almoſt any writings can, to make men wiſer and better: for he has the moſt agreeable

agreeable way of preaching that ever was. He was in general, an honeft, good man himfelf; at leaft he does not feem to have had any one ill-natured vice about him. Other poets we admire; but there is not any of the ancient poets that I could wifh to have been acquainted with, fo much as Horace. One cannot be very converfant with his writings, without having a friendfhip for the man; and longing to have juft fuch another as he was for one's friend. *Spence.*

§ 50. *Of* Tibullus, Propertius, *and* Ovid.

In that happy age, and in the fame court flourifhed Tibullus. He enjoyed the acquaintance of Horace, who mentions him in a kind and friendly manner, both in his Odes and in his Epiftles. Tibullus is evidently the moft exact and moft beautiful writer of love-verfes among the Romans, and was efteemed fo by their beft judges: though there were fome, it feems, even in their better ages of writing and judging, who preferred Propertius to him. Tibullus's talent feems to have been only for elegiac verfe: at leaft his compliment on Meffala (which is his only poem out of it) fhews, I think, too plainly, that he was neither defigned for heroic verfe, nor panegyric. Elegance is as much his diftinguifhing character, among the elegiac writers of this age, as it is Terence's among the comic writers of the former: and if his fubject will never let him be fublime, his judgment at leaft always keeps him from being faulty. His rival and cotemporary, Propertius, feems to have fet himfelf too many different models, to copy either of them fo well as he might otherwife have done. In one place, he calls himfelf the Roman Callimachus; in another, he talks of rivalling Philetas: and he is faid to have ftudied Mimnermus, and fome other of the Greek lyric writers, with the fame view. You may fee by this, and the practice of all their poets in general, that it was the conftant method of the Romans (whenever they endeavoured to excel) to fet fome great Greek pattern or other before them. Propertius, perhaps, might have fucceeded better, had he fixed on any one of thefe; and not endeavoured to improve by all of them indifferently.—Ovid makes up the triumvirate of the elegiac writers of this age; and is more loofe and incorrect than either of the other. As Propertius followed too many mafters, Ovid endeavoured to fhine in too many different kinds of writing at the fame time. Befides he had a redundant genius; and almoft always chofe rather to indulge, than to give any reftraint to it. If one was to give any opinion of the different merits of his feveral works, one fhould not perhaps be much befide the truth, in faying, that he excels moft in his Fafti; then perhaps in his love-verfes; next in his heroic epiftles; and laftly, in his Metamorphofes. As for the verfes he wrote after his misfortunes, he has quite loft his fpirit in them; and though you may difcover fome difference in his manner, after his banifhment came to fit a little lighter on him, his genius never fhines out fairly after that fatal ftroke. His very love of being witty had forfaken him; though before it feems to have grown upon him, when it was leaft becoming, toward his old age: for his Metamorphofes (which was the laft poem he wrote at Rome, and which indeed was not quite finifhed when he was fent into banifhment) has more inftances of falfe wit in it, it, than perhaps all his former writings put together. One of the things I have heard him most cried up for, in that piece, is his transitions from one story to another. The ancients thought differently of this point; and Quinctilian, where he is speaking of them, endeavours rather to excuse than to commend him on that head. We have a considerable loss in the latter half of his Fasti; and in his Medea, which is much commended. Dramatic poetry seems not to have flourished, in proportion to the other sorts of poetry, in the Augustan age. We scarce hear any thing of the comic poets of that time; and if tragedy had been much cultivated then, the Roman writers would certainly produce some names from it, to oppose to the Greeks, without going so far back as to those of Actius and Pacuvius. Indeed their own critics, in speaking of the dramatic writings of this age, boast rather of single pieces, than of authors: and the two particular tragedies, which they talk of in the highest strain, are the Medea of Ovid, and Varius's Thyestes. However, if it was not the age for plays, it was certainly the age in which almost all the other kinds of poetry were in their greatest excellence at Rome. *Spence.*

§ 51. *Of* PHÆDRUS.

Under this period of the best writing, I should be inclined to insert Phædrus. For though he published after the good manner of writing was in general on the decline, he flourished and formed his style under Augustus: and his book, though it did not appear till the reign of Tiberius, deserves, on all accounts, to be reckoned among the works of the Augustan age. Fabulæ Æsopeæ, was probably the title which he gave his fables. He professedly follows Æsop in them: and declares, that he keeps to his manner, even where the subject is of his own invention. By this it appears, that Æsop's way of telling stories was very short and plain; for the distinguishing beauty of Phædrus's fables is, their conciseness and simplicity. The taste was so much fallen, at the time when he published them, that both these were objected to him as faults. He used those critics as they deserved. He tells a long, tedious story to those who objected against the conciseness of his style; and answers some others, who condemned the plainness of it, with a run of bombast verses, that have a great many noisy elevated words in them, without any sense at the bottom. *Ibid.*

§ 52. *Of* MANILIUS.

Manilius can scarce be allowed a place in this list of the Augustan poets; his poetry is inferior to a great many of the Latin poets, who have wrote in these lower ages, so long since Latin has ceased to be a living language. There is at least, I believe, no instance, in any one poet of the flourishing ages, of such language, or such versification, as we meet with in Manilius; and there is not any one ancient writer that speaks one word of any such poet about those times, I doubt not, there were bad poets enough in the Augustan age; but I question whether Manilius may deserve the honour of being reckoned even among the bad poets of that time. What must be said, then, to the many passages in the poem, which relate to the times in which the author lived, and which all have a regard to the Augustan age? If the whole be not a modern forgery, I do not see how one can deny his being of that age: and if it be be a modern forgery, it is very lucky that it should agree so exactly, in so many little particulars, with the ancient globe of the heavens, in the Farnese palace. Allowing Manilius's poem to pass for what it pretends to be, there is nothing remains to us of the poetical works of this Augustan age, besides what I have mentioned: except the garden poem of Columella; the little hunting piece of Gratius; and, perhaps, an elegy or two of Gallus.

Spence.

§ 53. *Of the Poets whose Works have not come down to us.*

These are but small remains for an age in which poetry was so well cultivated and followed by very great numbers, taking the good and the bad together. It is probable, most of the best have come down to us. As for the others, we only hear of the elegies of Capella and Montanus; that Proculus imitated Callimachus; and Rufus, Pindar: that Fontanus wrote a sort of Piscatory eclogues; and Macer, a poem on the nature of birds, beasts, and plants. That the same Macer, and Rabirinus, and Marsus, and Ponticus, and Pedo Albinovanus, and several others, were epic writers in that time (which, by the way, seems to have signified little more, than that they wrote in hexameter verse): that Fundanius was the best comic poet then, and Melissus no bad one: that Varius was the most esteemed for epic poetry, before the Æneid appeared; and one of the most esteemed for tragedy always: that Pollio (besides his other excellencies at the bar, in the camp, and in affairs of state) is much commended for tragedy; and Varius, either for tragedy or epic poetry; for it does not quite appear which of the two he wrote. These last are great names; but there remain some of still higher dignity, who were, or at least desired to be thought, poets in that time. In the former part of Augustus's reign, his first minister for home affairs, Mæcenas; and in the latter part, his Grandson Germanicus, were of this number. Germanicus in particular translated Aratus; and there are some (I do not well know on what grounds) who pretend to have met with a considerable part of his translation. The emperor himself seems to have been both a good critic, and a good author. He wrote chiefly in prose; but some things in verse too; and particularly good part of a tragedy, called Ajax.

It is no wonder, under such encouragements, and so great examples, that poetry should arise to a higher pitch than it had ever done among the Romans. They had been gradually improving it for above two centuries; and in Augustus found a prince, whose own inclinations, the temper of whose reign, and whose very politics, led him to nurse all the arts; and poetry, in a more particular manner. The wonder is, when they had got so far toward perfection, that they should fall as it were all at once; and from their greatest purity and simplicity, should degenerate so immediately into a lower and more affected manner of writing, than had been ever known among them.

Ibid.

§ 54. *Of the Fall of Poetry among the Romans.*

There are some who assert, that the great age of the Roman eloquence I have been speaking of, began to decline a little even in the latter part of Augustus's reign. It certainly fell very much under Tiberius; and grew every day weaker and weaker, till it was wholly changed under Caligula. Hence therefore we may date the third age, or the fall

fall of the Roman poetry. Auguſtus, whatever his natural temper was, put on at leaſt a mildneſs, that gave a calm to the ſtate during his time: the ſucceeding emperors flung off the maſk; and not only were, but openly appeared to be, rather monſters than men. We need not go to their hiſtorians for proofs of their prodigious vileneſs: it is enough to mention the bare names of Tiberius, Caligula, Nero. Under ſuch heads, every thing that was good run to ruin. All diſcipline in war, all domeſtic virtues, the very love of liberty, and all the taſte for ſound eloquence and good poetry, ſunk gradually; and faded away, as they had flouriſhed, together. Inſtead of the ſenſible, chaſte, and manly way of writing, that had been in uſe in the former age, there now roſe up a deſire of writing ſmartly, and an affectation of ſhining in every thing they ſaid. A certain prettineſs, and glitter, and luxuriance of ornaments, was what diſtinguiſhed their moſt applauded writers in proſe; and their poetry was quite loſt in high flights and obſcurity. Seneca, the favourite proſe writer of thoſe times; and Petronius Arbiter, ſo great a favourite with many of our own; afford too many proofs of this. As to the proſe in Nero's time; and as to the poets, it is enough to ſay, that they had then Lucan and Perſius, inſtead of Virgil and Horace. *Spence.*

§ 55. *Of* Lucan.

Perſius and Lucan, who were the moſt celebrated poets under the reign of Nero, may very well ſerve for examples of the faults I juſt mentioned, one of the ſwelling, and the other of the obſcure ſtyle, then in faſhion. Lucan's manner in general runs too much into fuſtian and bombaſt. His muſe has a kind of dropſy, and looks like the ſoldier deſcribed in his own Pharſalia, who in paſſing the deſert ſands of Africa, was bit by a ſerpent, and ſwelled to ſuch an immoderate ſize, "that he was loſt (as he expreſſes it) in the tumours of his own body." Some critics have been in too great haſte to make Quinctilian ſay ſome good things of Lucan, which he never meant to do. What this poet has been always for, and what he will ever deſerve to be admired for, are the ſeveral philoſophical paſſages that abound in his works; and his generous ſentiments, particularly on the love of liberty and the contempt of death. In his calm hours, he is very wiſe; but he is often in his rants, and never more ſo than when he is got into a battle, or a ſtorm at ſea: but it is remarkable, that even on thoſe occaſions, it is not ſo much a violence of rage, as a madneſs of affectation, that appears moſt ſtrongly in him. To give a few inſtances of it, out of many: In the very beginning of Lucan's ſtorm, when Cæſar ventured to croſs the ſea in ſo ſmall a veſſel; "the fixt ſtars themſelves ſeem to be put in motion." Then "the waves riſe over the mountains, and carry away the tops of them." Their next ſtep is to heaven; where they catch the rain "in the clouds:" I ſuppoſe, to increaſe their force. The ſea opens in ſeveral places, and leaves its bottom dry land. All the foundations of the univerſe are ſhaken; and nature is afraid of a ſecond chaos. His little ſkiff, in the mean time, ſometimes cuts along the clouds with her ſails; and ſometimes ſeems in danger of being ſtranded on the ſands at the bottom of the ſea; and muſt inevitably have been loſt, had not the ſtorm (by good fortune) been ſo ſtrong from every quarter, that ſhe did not know on which ſide to bulge firſt.

When the two armies are going to join battle

battle in the plains of Pharſalia, we are told, that all the ſoldiers were incapable of any fear for themſelves, becauſe they were wholly taken up with their concern for the danger which threatened Pompey and the commonwealth. On this great occaſion, the hills about them, according to his account, ſeem to be more afraid than the men; for ſome of the mountains looked as if they would thruſt their heads into the clouds; and others, as if they wanted to hide themſelves under the valleys at their feet. And theſe diſturbances in nature were univerſal: for that day, every ſingle Roman, in whatever part of the world he was, felt a ſtrange gloom ſpread all over his mind, on a ſudden; and was ready to cry, though he did not know why or wherefore. *Spence.*

§ 56. *Of* PERSIUS.

Perſius is ſaid to have been Lucan's ſchool-fellow under Cornutus; and like him, was bred up more a philoſopher than a poet. He has the character of a good man; but ſcarce deſerves that of a good writer, in any other than the moral ſenſe of the word: for his writings are very virtuous, but not very poetical. His great fault is obſcurity. Several have endeavoured to excuſe or palliate this fault in him, from the danger of the times he lived in; and the neceſſity a ſatiriſt then lay under, of writing ſo, for his own ſecurity. This may hold as to ſome paſſages in him; but to ſay the truth, he ſeems to have a tendency and love to obſcurity in himſelf: for it is not only to be found where he may ſpeak of the emperor, or the ſtate; but in the general courſe of his ſatires. So that, in my conſcience, I muſt give him up for an obſcure writer; as I ſhould Lucan for a tumid and ſwelling one.

Such was the Roman poetry under Nero. The three emperors after him were made in an hurry, and had ſhort tumultuous reigns. Then the Flavian family came in. Veſpaſian, the firſt emperor of that line, endeavoured to recover ſomething of the good taſte that had formerly flouriſhed in Rome; his ſon Titus, the delight of mankind, in his ſhort reign, encouraged poetry by his example, as well as by his liberalities: and even Domitian loved to be thought a patron of the muſes. After him, there was a ſucceſſion of good emperors, from Nerva to the Antonines. And this extraordinary good fortune (for indeed, if one conſiders the general run of the Roman emperors, it would have been ſuch, to have had any two good ones only together) gave a new ſpirit to the arts, that had long been in ſo languiſhing a condition, and made poetry revive, and raiſe up its head again, once more among them. Not that there were very good poets even now; but they were better, at leaſt, than they had been under the reign of Nero. *Ibid.*

§ 57. *Of* SILIUS, STATIUS, *and* VALERIUS FLACCUS.

This period produced three epic poets, whoſe works remain to us; Silius, Statius, and Valerius Flaccus. Silius, as if he had been frightened at the high flight of Lucan, keeps almoſt always on the ground, and ſcarce once attempts to ſoar throughout his whole work. It is plain, however, though it is low; and if he has but little of the ſpirit of poetry, he is free at leaſt from the affectation, and obſcurity, and bombaſt, which prevailed ſo much among his immediate predeceſſors. Silius was honoured with the conſulate; and lived to ſee his ſon in the ſame high office. He was a great lover and collector of pictures and ſtatues; ſome of which he worſhipped;

 eſpecially

especially one he had of Virgil. He used to offer sacrifices too at his tomb near Naples. It is a pity that he could not get more of his spirit in his writings: for he had scarce enough to make his offerings acceptable to the genius of that great poet.—Statius had more of spirit, with a less share of prudence: for his Thebaid is certainly ill conducted, and scarcely well written. By the little we have of his Achilleid, that would probably have been a much better poem, at least as to the writing part, had he lived to finish it. As it is, his description of Achilles's behaviour at the feast which Lycomedes makes for the Grecian ambassadors, and some other parts of it, read more pleasingly to me than any part of the Thebaid. I cannot help thinking, that the passage quoted so often from Juvenal, as an encomium on Statius, was meant as a satire on him. Martial seems to strike at him too, under the borrowed name of Sabellus. As he did not finish his Achilleid, he may deserve more reputation perhaps as a miscellaneous than as an epic writer; for though the odes and other copies of verses in his Sylvæ are not without their faults, they are not so faulty as his Thebaid. The chief faults of Statius, in his Sylvæ and Thebaid, are said to have proceeded from very different causes: the former, from their having been written incorrectly and in a great deal of haste; and the other, from its being over corrected and hard. Perhaps his greatest fault of all, or rather the greatest sign of his bad judgment, is his admiring Lucan so extravagantly as he does. It is remarkable, that poetry run more lineally in Statius's family, than perhaps in any other. He received it from his father; who had been an eminent poet in his time, and lived to see his son obtain the laurel-crown at the Alban games; as he had formerly done himself.—Valerius Flaccus wrote a little before Statius. He died young, and left his poem unfinished. We have but seven books of his Argonautics, and part of the eighth, in which the Argonauts are left on the sea, in their return homewards. Several of the modern critics, who have been some way or other concerned in publishing Flaccus's works, make no scruple of placing him next to Virgil, of all the Roman epic poets; and I own I am a good deal inclined to be seriously of their opinion; for he seems to me to have more fire than Silius, and to be more correct than Statius: and as for Lucan, I cannot help looking upon him as quite out of the question. He imitates Virgil's language much better than Silius, or even Statius; and his plan, or rather his story, is certainly less embarrassed and confused than the Thebaid. Some of the ancients themselves speak of Flaccus with a great deal of respect; and particularly Quinctilian; who says nothing at all of Silius or Statius; unless the latter is to be included in that general expression of 'several others,' whom he leaves to be celebrated by posterity.

As to the dramatic writers of this time, we have not any one comedy, and only ten tragedies, all published under the name of Lucius Annæus Seneca. They are probably the work of different hands; and might be a collection of favourite plays, put together by some bad grammarian; for either the Roman tragedies of this age were very indifferent, or these are not their best. They have been attributed to authors as far distant as the reigns of Augustus and Trajan. It is true, the person who is so positive that one of them in particular must be of the Augustan age, says this of a piece that he seems resolved to cry up at all rates; and I believe one should do

no

no injury to any one of them, in ſuppoſing them all to have been written in this third age, under the decline of the Roman poetry.

Of all the other poets under this period, there are none whoſe works remain to us, except Martial and Juvenal. The former flouriſhed under Domitian; and the latter under Nerva, Trajan, and Adrian. *Spence.*

§ 58. *Of* Martial.

Martial is a dealer only in a little kind of writing; for Epigram is certainly (what it is called by Dryden) the loweſt ſtep of poetry. He is at the very bottom of the hill; but he diverts himſelf there, in gathering flowers and playing with inſects, prettily enough. If Martial made a new-year's gift, he was ſure to ſend a diſtich with it: if a friend died, he made a few verſes to put on his tomb-ſtone: if a ſtatue was ſet up, they came to him for an inſcription. Theſe were the common offices of his muſe. If he ſtruck a fault in life, he marked it down in a few lines; and if he had a mind to pleaſe a friend, or to get the favour of the great, his ſtyle was turned to panegyric; and theſe were his higheſt employments. He was, however, a good writer in his way; and there are inſtances even of his writing wth ſome dignity on higher occaſions. *Ibid.*

§ 59. *Of* Juvenal.

Juvenal began to write after all I have mentioned; and, I do not know by what good fortune, writes with a greater ſpirit of poetry than any of them. He has ſcarce any thing of the gentility of Horace: yet he is not without humour, and exceeds all the ſatiriſts in ſeverity. To ſay the truth, he flaſhes too much like an angry executioner; but the depravity of the times, and the vices then in faſhion, may often excuſe ſome degree of rage in him. It is ſaid he did not write till he was elderly; and after he had been too much uſed to declaiming. However, his ſatires have a great deal of ſpirit in them; and ſhew a ſtrong hatred of vice, with ſome very fine and high ſentiments of virtue. They are indeed ſo animated, that I do not know any poem of this age, which one can read with near ſo much pleaſure as his ſatires.

Juvenal may very well be called the laſt of the Roman poets. After his time, poetry continued decaying more and more, quite down to the time of Conſtantine; when all the arts were ſo far loſt and extinguiſhed among the Romans, that from that time they themſelves may very well be called by the name they uſed to give to all the world, except the Greeks; for the Romans then had ſcarce any thing to diſtinguiſh them from the Barbarians.

There are, therefore, but three ages of the Roman poetry, that can carry any weight with them in an enquiry of this nature. The firſt age, from the firſt Punic war to the time of Auguſtus, is more remarkable for ſtrength, than any great degree of beauty in writing. The ſecond age, or the Auguſtan, is the time when they wrote with a due mixture of beauty and ſtrength. And the third, from the beginning of Nero's reign to the end of Adrian's, when they endeavoured after beauty more than ſtrength: when they loſt much of their vigour, and run too much into affectation. Their poetry, in its youth, was ſtrong and nervous; in its middle age, it was manly and polite; in its latter days, it grew tawdry and feeble; and endeavoured to hide the decays of its former beauty and ſtrength, in falſe ornaments of dreſs, and a borrowed fluſh on the face; which did not ſo much render it

 pleaſing,

pleasing, as it shewed that its natural complexion was faded and lost. *Spence.*

§ 60. *Of the Introduction, Improvement, and Fall of the Arts at Rome.*

The city of Rome, as well as its inhabitants, was in the beginning rude and unadorned. Those old rough soldiers looked on the effects of the politer arts as things fit only for an effeminate people; as too apt to soften and unnerve men; and to take from that martial temper and ferocity, which they encouraged so much and so universally in the infancy of their state. Their houses were (what the name they gave them signified) only a covering for them, and a defence against bad weather. These sheds of theirs were more like the caves of wild beasts, than the habitations of men; and were rather flung together as chance led them, than formed into regular streets and openings: their walls were half mud, and their roofs, pieces of wood stuck together; nay, even this was an after-improvement; for in Romulus's time, their houses were only covered with straw. If they had any thing that was finer than ordinary, that was chiefly taken up in setting off the temples of their gods; and when these began to be furnished with statues (for they had none till long after Numa's time) they were probably more fit to give terror than delight; and seemed rather formed so as to be horrible enough to strike an awe into those who worshipped them, than handsome enough to invite any one to look upon them for pleasure. Their design, I suppose, was answerable to the materials they were made of; and if their gods were of earthen ware, they were reckoned better than ordinary; for many of them were chopt out of wood. One of the chief ornaments in those times, both of the temples and private houses, consisted in their ancient trophies: which were trunks of trees cleared of their branches, and so formed into a rough kind of posts. These were loaded with the arms they had taken in war; and you may easily conceive what sort of ornaments these posts must make, when half decayed by time, and hung about with old rusty arms, besmeared with the blood of their enemies. Rome was not then that beautiful Rome, whose very ruins at this day are sought after with so much pleasure: it was a town, which carried an air of terror in its appearance; and which made people shudder, whenever they first entered within its gates. *Ibid.*

§ 61. *On the Decline of the Arts, Eloquence, and Poetry, upon the Death of Augustus.*

On the death of Augustus, though the arts, and the taste for them, did not suffer so great a change, as appeared immediately in the taste of eloquence and poetry, yet they must have suffered a good deal. There is a secret union, a certain kind of sympathy between all the polite arts, which makes them languish and flourish together. The same circumstances are either kind or unfriendly to all of them. The favour of Augustus, and the tranquillity of his reign, was as a gentle dew from heaven, in a favourable season, that made them bud forth and flourish; and the sour reign of Tiberius, was as a sudden frost that checked their growth, and at last killed all their beauties. The vanity, and tyranny, and disturbances of the times that followed, gave the finishing stroke to sculpture as well as eloquence, and to painting as well as poetry. The Greek artists at Rome were not so soon or so much infected by the bad taste of the

the court, as the Roman writers were; but it reached them too, though by flower and more imperceptible degrees. Indeed what elſe could be expected from ſuch a run of monſters as Tiberius, Caligula, and Nero? For theſe were the emperors under whoſe reigns the arts began to languiſh; and they ſuffered ſo much from their baleful influence, that the Roman writers ſoon after them ſpeak of all the arts as being brought to a very low ebb. They talk of their being extremely fallen in general; and as to painting, in particular, they repreſent it as in a moſt feeble and dying condition. The ſeries of ſo many good emperors, which happened after Domitian, gave ſome ſpirit again to the arts; but ſoon after the Antonines, they all declined apace, and, by the time of the thirty tyrants, were quite fallen, ſo as never to riſe again under any future Roman emperor.

You may ſee by theſe two accounts I have given you of the Roman poetry, and of the other arts, that the great periods of their riſe, their flouriſhing, and their decline, agree very well; and, as it were, tally with one another. Their ſtyle was prepared, and a vaſt collection of fine works laid in, under the firſt period, or in the times of the republic: In the ſecond, or the Auguſtan age, their writers and artiſts were both in their higheſt perfection; and in the third, from Tiberius to the Antonines, they both began to languiſh; and then revived a little; and at laſt ſunk totally together.

In comparing the deſcriptions of their poets with the works of art, I ſhould therefore chuſe to omit all the Roman poets after the Antonines. Among them all, there is perhaps no one whoſe omiſſion need be regretted, except that of Claudian; and even as to him it may be conſidered, that he wrote when the true knowledge of the arts was no more; and when the true taſte of poetry was ſtrangely corrupted and loſt; even if we were to judge of it by his own writings only, which are extremely better than any of the poets long before and long after him. It is therefore much better to confine one's ſelf to the three great ages, than to run ſo far out of one's way for a ſingle poet or two; whoſe authorities, after all, muſt be very diſputable, and indeed ſcarce of any weight. *Spence.*

§ 62. *On the Great Hiſtorical Ages.*

Every age has produced heroes and politicians; all nations have experienced revolutions; and all hiſtories are nearly alike, to thoſe who ſeek only to furniſh their memories with facts; but whoſoever thinks, or, what is ſtill more rare, whoſoever has taſte, will find but four ages in the hiſtory of the world. Theſe four happy ages are thoſe in which the arts were carried to perfection; and which, by ſerving as the æra of the greatneſs of the human mind, are examples for poſterity.

The firſt of theſe ages to which true glory is annexed, is that of Philip and Alexander, or that of a Pericles, a Demoſthenes, an Ariſtotle, a Plato, an Apelles, a Phidias, and a Praxiteles; and this honour has been confined within the limits of ancient Greece; the reſt of the known world was then in a ſtate of barbariſm.

The ſecond age is that of Cæſar and Auguſtus, diſtinguiſhed likewiſe by the names of Lucretius, Cicero, Titus, Livius, Virgil, Horace, Ovid, Varro, and Vitruvius.

The third is that which followed the taking of Conſtantinople by Mahomet II. Then a family of private citizens was ſeen to do that which the kings of Europe ought to have undertaken. The Medicis invited to Florence the Learned, who had been driven out of Greece by the Turks.—This was the age of Italy's glory. The polite arts had already recovered a new life in that country; the Italians honoured them with the title of Virtu, as the first Greeks had distinguished them by the name of Wisdom. Every thing tended towards perfection; a Michael Angelo, a Raphael, a Titian, a Tasso, and an Ariosto, flourished. The art of engraving was invented; elegant architecture appeared again, as admirable as in the most triumphant ages of Rome; and the Gothic barbarism, which had disfigured Europe in every kind of production, was driven from Italy, to make way for good taste.

The arts, always transplanted from Greece to Italy, found themselves in a favourable soil, where they instantly produced fruit. France, England, Germany, and Spain, aimed in their turns to gather these fruits; but either they could not live in those climates, or else they degenerated very fast.

Francis I. encouraged learned men, but such as were merely learned men: he had architects; but he had no Michael Angelo, nor Palladio: he endeavoured in vain to establish schools for painting; the Italian masters whom he invited to France, raised no pupils there. Some epigrams, and a few loose tales, made the whole of our poetry. Rabelais was the only prose writer in vogue in the time of

fection of all the four: enriched by the discoveries of the three former ones, it has done greater things in certain kinds than those three together. All the arts, indeed, were not carried farther than under the Medicis, Augustus, and Alexander; but human reason in general was more improved. In this age we first became acquainted with sound philosophy. It may truly be said, that from the last years of Cardinal Richelieu's administration till those which followed the death of Lewis XIV. there has happened such a general revolution in our arts, our genius, our manners, and even in our government, as will serve as an immortal mark to the true glory of our country. This happy influence has not been confined to France; it has communicated itself to England, where it has stirred up an emulation which that ingenious and deeply-learned nation stood in need of at that time; it has introduced taste into Germany, and the sciences into Russia; it has even re-animated Italy, which was languishing; and Europe is indebted for its politeness and spirit of society, to the court of Lewis XIV.

Before this time, the Italians called all the people on this side the Alps by the name of Barbarians. It must be owned that the French, in some degree, deserved this reproachful epithet. Our forefathers joined the romantic gallantry of the Moors with the Gothic rudeness. They had hardly any of the

and the Mediterranean ſea, were without ſhips; and who, though fond of luxury to an exceſs, were hardly provided with the moſt common manufactures.

The Jews, the Genoeſe, the Venetians, the Portugueſe, the Flemiſh, the Dutch, and the Engliſh, carried on, in their turns, the trade of France, which was ignorant even of the firſt principles of commerce. Lewis XIII. at his acceſſion to the crown, had not a ſingle ſhip; the city of Paris contained not quite four hundred thouſand men, and had not above four fine public edifices; the other cities of the kingdom reſembled thoſe pitiful villages which we ſee on the other ſide of the Loire. The nobility, who were all ſtationed in the country, in dungeons ſurrounded with deep ditches, oppreſſed the peaſant who cultivated the land. The high roads were almoſt impaſſable; the towns were deſtitute of police; and the government had hardly any credit among foreign nations.

We muſt acknowledge, that, ever ſince the decline of the Carlovingian family, France had languiſhed more or leſs in this infirm ſtate, merely for want of the benefit of a good adminiſtration.

For a ſtate to be powerful, the people muſt either enjoy a liberty founded on the laws, or the royal authority muſt be fixed beyond all oppoſition. In France, the people were ſlaves till the reign of Philip Auguſtus; the noblemen were tyrants till Lewis XI.; and the kings, always employed in maintaining their authority againſt their vaſſals, had neither leiſure to think about the happineſs of their ſubjects, nor the power of making them happy.

Lewis XI. did a great deal for the regal power, but nothing for the happineſs or glory of the nation. Francis I. gave birth to trade, navigation, and all the arts; but he was too tion during his time, ſo that they all periſhed with him. Henry the Great was on the point of raiſing France from the calamities and barbariſms in which ſhe had been plunged by thirty years of diſcord, when he was aſſaſſinated in his capital, in the midſt of a people whom he had begun to make happy. The Cardinal de Richelieu, buſied in humbling the houſe of Auſtria, the Calviniſts, and the Grandees, did not enjoy a power ſufficiently undiſturbed to reform the nation; but he had at leaſt the honour of beginning this happy work.

Thus, for the ſpace of 900 years, our genius had been almoſt always reſtrained under a Gothic government, in the midſt of diviſions and civil wars; deſtitute of any laws or fixed cuſtoms; changing every ſecond century a language which ſtill continued rude and unformed. The nobles were without diſcipline, and ſtrangers to every thing but war and idleneſs: the clergy lived in diſorder and ignorance; and the common people without induſtry, and ſtupified in their wretchedneſs.

The French had no ſhare either in the great diſcoveries, or admirable inventions of other nations: they have no title to the diſcoveries of printing, gunpowder, glaſſes, teleſcopes, the ſector, compaſs, the air-pump, or the true ſyſtem of the univerſe: they were making tournaments, while the Portugueſe and Spaniards were diſcovering and conquering new countries from the eaſt to the weſt of the known world. Charles V. had already ſcattered the treaſures of Mexico over Europe, before the ſubjects of Francis I. had diſcovered the uncultivated country of Canada; but, by the little which the French did in the beginning of the ſixteenth century, we may ſee what they are capable of when properly conducted. *Voltaire.*

§ 63. *On the Constitution of* England.

In every government there are three ſorts of power: the legiſlative; the executive, in reſpect to things dependent on the law of nations; and the executive, in regard to things that depend on the civil law.

By virtue of the firſt, the prince or magiſtrate enacts temporary or perpetual laws, and amends or abrogates thoſe that have been already enacted. By the ſecond, he makes peace or war, ſends or receives embaſſies, he eſtabliſhes the public ſecurity, and provides againſt invaſions. By the third, he puniſhes criminals, or determines the diſputes that ariſe between individuals. The latter we ſhall call the judiciary power, and the other ſimply the executive power of the ſtate.

The political liberty of the ſubject is a tranquillity of mind, ariſing from the opinion each perſon has of his ſafety. In order to have this liberty, it is requiſite the government be ſo conſtituted as one man need not to be afraid of another.

When the legiſlative and executive powers are united in the ſame perſon, or in the ſame body of magiſtrates, there can be no liberty; becauſe apprehenſions may ariſe, leſt the ſame monarch or ſenate ſhould enact tyrannical laws, to execute them in a tyrannical manner.

Again, there is no liberty, if the power of judging be not ſeparated from the legiſlative and executive powers. Were it joined with the legiſlative, the life and liberty of the ſubject would be expoſed to arbitrary controul; for the judge would be then the legiſlator. Were it joined to the executive power, the judge might behave with all the violence of an oppreſſor.

There would be an end of every thing, were the ſame man, or the ſame body, whether of the nobles, or of the people, to exerciſe thoſe three powers, that of enacting laws, that of executing the public reſolutions, and that of judging the crimes or differences of individuals.

Moſt kingdoms of Europe enjoy a moderate government, becauſe the prince, who is inveſted with the two firſt powers, leaves the third to his ſubjects. In Turky, where theſe three powers are united in the Sultan's perſon, the ſubjects groan under the weight of a moſt frightful oppreſſion.

In the republics of Italy, where theſe three powers are united, there is leſs liberty than in our monarchies. Hence their government is obliged to have recourſe to as violent methods for its ſupport, as even that of the Turks; witneſs the ſtate inquiſitors at Venice, and the lion's mouth, into which every informer may at all hours throw his written accuſations.

What a ſituation muſt the poor ſubject be in under thoſe republics! The ſame body of magiſtrates are poſſeſſed, as executors of the law, of the whole power they have given themſelves in quality of legiſlators. They may plunder the ſtate by their general determinations; and, as they have likewiſe the judiciary power in their hands, every private citizen may be ruined by their particular deciſions.

The whole power is here united in one body; and though there is no external pomp that indicates a deſpotic ſway, yet the people feel the effects of it every moment.

Hence it is that many of the princes of Europe, whoſe aim has been levelled at arbitrary power, have conſtantly ſet out with uniting in their own perſons all the branches of magiſtracy, and all the great offices of ſtate.

I allow, indeed, that the mere hereditary ariſtocracy of the Italian republics does not anſwer exactly to the deſpotic power of the eaſtern princes. The number of magiſtrates ſometimes ſoftens the power of the magiſ-

tracy.

tracy; the whole body of the nobles do not always concur in the ſame deſigns; and different tribunals are erected, that temper each other. Thus, at Venice, the legiſlative power is in the Council, the executive in the Pregadi, and the judiciary in the Quarantia. But the miſchief is, that theſe different tribunals are compoſed of magiſtrates all belonging to the ſame body, which conſtitutes almoſt one and the ſame power.

The judiciary power ought not to be given to a ſtanding ſenate; it ſhould be exerciſed by perſons taken from the body of the people (as at Athens) at certain times of the year, and purſuant to a form and manner preſcribed by law, in order to erect a tribunal that ſhould laſt only as long as neceſſity requires.

By this means the power of judging, a power ſo terrible to mankind, not being annexed to any particular ſtate or profeſſion, becomes, as it were, inviſible. People have not then the judges continually preſent to their view; they fear the office, but not the magiſtrate.

In accuſations of a deep or criminal nature, it is proper the perſon accuſed ſhould have the privilege of chuſing in ſome meaſure his judges, in concurrence with the law; or at leaſt he ſhould have a right to except againſt ſo great a number, that the remaining part may be deemed his own choice.

The other two powers may be given rather to magiſtrates or permanent bodies, becauſe they are not exerciſed on any private ſubject; one being no more than the general will of the ſtate, and the other the execution of that general will.

But though the tribunals ought not to be fixed, yet the judgments ought, and to ſuch a degree as to be always conformable to the exact letter of the law. Were they to be the private opinion of the judge, people would then live in ſociety without knowing exactly the obligations it lays them under.

The judges ought likewiſe to be in the ſame ſtation as the accuſed, or in other words, his peers, to the end that he may not imagine he is fallen into the hands of perſons inclined to treat him with rigour.

If the legiſlature leaves the executive power in poſſeſſion of a right to impriſon thoſe ſubjects who can give ſecurity for their good behaviour, there is an end of liberty; unleſs they are taken up, in order to anſwer without delay to a capital crime: in this caſe they are really free, being ſubject only to the power of the law.

But ſhould the legiſlature think itſelf in danger by ſome ſecret conſpiracy againſt the ſtate, or by a correſpondence with a foreign enemy, it might authoriſe the executive power, for a ſhort and limited time, to impriſon ſuſpected perſons, who in that caſe would loſe their liberty only for a while, to preſerve it for ever.

And this is the only reaſonable method that can be ſubſtituted to the tyrannical magiſtracy of the Ephori, and to the ſtate inquiſitors of Venice, who are alſo deſpotical.

As in a free ſtate, every man who is ſuppoſed a free agent, ought to be his own governor; ſo the legiſlative power ſhould reſide in the whole body of the people. But ſince this is impoſſible in large ſtates, and in ſmall ones is ſubject to many inconveniences, it is fit the people ſhould act by their repreſentatives, what they cannot act by themſelves.

The inhabitants of a particular town are much better acquainted with its wants and intereſts, than with thoſe of other places; and are better judges of the capacity of their neighbours, than of that of the reſt of their countrymen. The members therefore of the legiſlature ſhould not be choſen from the general body of the nation; but it is proper, that in every conſiderable place, a repreſentative ſhould be elected by the inhabitants.

The great advantage of repreſentatives is their being capable of diſcuſſing affairs. For this the people collectively are extremely unfit, which is one of the greateſt inconveniences of a democracy.

It is not at all neceſſary that the repreſentatives, who have received a general inſtruction from their electors, ſhould wait to be particularly inſtructed in every affair, as is practiſed in the diets of Germany. True it is, that by this way of proceeding, the ſpeeches of the deputies might with greater propriety be called the voice of the nation; but on the other hand, this would throw them into infinite delays, would give each deputy a power of controlling the aſſembly; and on the moſt urgent and preſſing occaſions, the ſprings of the nation might be ſtopped by a ſingle caprice.

When the deputies, as Mr. Sidney well obſerves, repreſent a body of people, as in Holland, they ought to be accountable to their conſtituents: but it is a different thing in England, where they are deputed by boroughs.

All the inhabitants of the ſeveral diſtricts ought to have a right of voting at the election of a repreſentative, except ſuch as are in ſo mean a ſituation, as to be deemed to have no will of their own.

One great fault there was in moſt of the ancient republics; that the people had a right to active reſolutions, ſuch as require ſome execution; a thing of which they are abſolutely incapable. They ought to have no hand in the government, but for the chuſing of repreſentatives, which is within their reach. For though few can tell the exact degree of men's capacities, yet there are none but are capable of knowing in general, whether the perſon they chuſe is better qualified than moſt of his neighbours.

Neither ought the repreſentative body to be choſen for active reſolutions, for which it is not ſo fit; but for the enacting of laws, or to ſee whether the laws already enacted be duly executed; a thing they are very capable of, and which none indeed but themſelves can properly perform.

In a ſtate, there are always perſons diſtinguiſhed by their birth, riches, or honours; but were they to be confounded with the common people, and to have only the weight of a ſingle vote like the reſt, the common liberty would be their ſlavery, and they would have no intereſt in ſupporting it, as moſt of the popular reſolutions would be againſt them. The ſhare they have, therefore, in the legiſlature, ought to be proportioned to the other advantages they have in the ſtate; which happens only when they form a body that has a right to put a ſtop to the enterprizes of the people, as the people have a right to put a ſtop to theirs.

The legiſlative power is therefore committed to the body of the nobles, and to the body choſen to repreſent the people, which have each their aſſemblies and deliberations apart, each their ſeparate views and intereſts.

Of the three powers above-mentioned, the judiciary is in ſome meaſure next to nothing. There remains therefore only two; and as thoſe have need of a regulating power to temper them, the part of the legiſlative body compoſed of the nobility is extremely proper for this very purpoſe.

The body of the nobility ought to be hereditary.

ditary. In the first place, it is so in its own nature: and in the next, there must be a considerable interest to preserve its privileges; privileges that in themselves are obnoxious to popular envy, and of course, in a free state, are always in danger.

But as an hereditary power might be tempted to pursue its own particular interests, and forget those of the people; it is proper that, where they may reap a singular advantage from being corrupted, as in the laws relating to the supplies, they should have no other share in the legislation, than the power of rejecting, and not that of resolving.

By the power of resolving, I mean the right of ordaining by their own authority, or of amending what has been ordained by others. By the power of rejecting, I would be understood to mean the right of annulling a resolution taken by another, which was the power of the tribunes at Rome. And though the person possessed of the privilege of rejecting may likewise have the right of approving, yet this approbation passes for no more than a declaration that he intends to make no use of his privilege of rejecting, and is derived from that very privilege.

The executive power ought to be in the hands of a monarch; because this branch of government, which has always need of expedition, is better administered by one than by many: whereas, whatever depends on the legislative power, is oftentimes better regulated by many than by a single person.

But if there was no monarch, and the executive power was committed to a certain number of persons selected from the legislative body, there would be an end then of liberty; by reason the two powers would be united, as the same persons would actually sometimes have, and would moreover be always able to have, a share in both.

Were the legislative body to be a considerable time without meeting, this would likewise put an end to liberty. For one of these two things would naturally follow; either that there would be no longer any legislative resolutions, and then the state would fall into anarchy; or that these resolutions would be taken by the executive power, which would render it absolute.

It would be needless for the legislative body to continue always assembled. This would be troublesome to the representatives, and moreover would cut out too much work for the executive power, so as to take off its attention from executing, and oblige it to think only of defending its own prerogatives, and the right it has to execute.

Again, were the legislative body to be always assembled, it might happen to be kept up only by filling the places of the deceased members with new representatives; and in that case, if the legislative body was once corrupted, the evil would be past all remedy. When different legislative bodies succeed one another, the people, who have a bad opinion of that which is actually sitting, may reasonably entertain some hopes of the next; but were it to be always the same body, the people upon seeing it once corrupted, would no longer expect any good from its laws; and of course they would either become desperate, or fall into a state of indolence.

The legislative body should not assemble of itself. For a body is supposed to have no will but when it is assembled: and besides, were it not to assemble unanimously, it would be impossible to determine which was really the legislative body, the part assembled, or the other. And if it had a right to prorogue itself, it might happen never to be prorogued; which would be extremely dangerous in case it should ever attempt to encroach on the executive power. Besides, there are seasons, some of which are more proper than others, for assembling the legislative body: it is fit therefore that the executive power should regulate the time of convening as well as the duration of those assemblies, according to the circumstances and exigencies of state known to itself.

Were the executive power not to have a right of putting a stop to the incroachments of the legislative body, the latter would become despotic; for as it might arrogate to itself what authority it pleased, it would soon destroy all the other powers.

But it is not proper, on the other hand, that the legislative power should have a right to stop the executive. For as the executive has its natural limits, it is useless to confine it; besides, the executive power is generally employed in momentary operations. The power, therefore, of the Roman tribunes was faulty, as it put a stop not only to the legislation, but likewise to the execution itself; which was attended with infinite mischiefs.

But if the legislative power, in a free government, ought to have no right to stop the executive, it has a right, and ought to have the means of examining in what manner its laws have been executed; an advantage which this government has over that of Crete and Sparta, where the Cosmi and the Ephori ave no account of their administration.

But whatever may be the issue of that examination, the legislative body ought not to have a power of judging the person, nor of course the conduct, of him who is intrusted with the executive power. His person should be sacred, because, as it is necessary for the good of the state to prevent the legislative body from rendering themselves arbitrary, the moment he is accused or tried, there is an end of liberty.

In this case the state would be no longer a monarchy, but a kind of republican, though not a free government. But as the person intrusted with the executive power cannot abuse it without bad counsellors, and such as hate the laws as ministers, though the laws favour them as subjects; these men may be examined and punished. An advantage which this government has over that of Gnidus, where the law allowed of no such thing as calling the Amymones * to an account, even after their administration †; and therefore the people could never obtain any satisfaction for the injuries done them.

Though, in general, the judiciary power ought not to be united with any part of the legislative, yet this is liable to three exceptions, founded on the particular interest of the party accused.

The great are always obnoxious to popular envy; and were they to be judged by the people, they might be in danger from their judges, and would moreover be deprived of the privilege which the meanest subject is possessed of, in a free state, of being tried by their peers. The nobility, for this reason, ought not to be cited before the ordinary courts of judicature, but before that part of

* These were magistrates chosen annually by the people. See Stephen of Byzantium.

† It was lawful to accuse the Roman magistrates after the expiration of their several offices. See Dionys. Halicarn. l. 9. the affair of Genutius the tribune.

the

the legiſlature which is compoſed of their own body.

It is poſſible that the law, which is clear-ſighted in one ſenſe, and blind in another, might in ſome caſes be too ſevere. But as we have already obſerved, the national judges are no more than the mouth that pronounces the words of the law, mere paſſive beings, incapable of moderating either its force or rigour. That part, therefore, of the legiſlative body, which we have juſt now obſerved to be a neceſſary tribunal on another occaſion, is alſo a neceſſary tribunal in this; it belongs to its ſupreme authority to moderate the law in favour of the law itſelf, by mitigating the ſentence.

It might alſo happen, that a ſubject intruſted with the adminiſtration of public affairs, might infringe the rights of the people, and be guilty of crimes which the ordinary magiſtrates either could not, or would not puniſh. But in general the legiſlative power cannot judge; and much leſs can it be a judge in this particular caſe, where it repreſents the party concerned, which is the people. It can only therefore impeach: but before what court ſhall it bring its impeachment? Muſt it go and abaſe itſelf before the ordinary tribunals, which are its inferiors, and being compoſed moreover of men who are choſen from the people as well as itſelf, will naturally be ſwayed by the authority of ſo powerful an accuſer? No: in order to preſerve the dignity of the people, and the ſecurity of the ſubject, the legiſlative part which repreſents the people muſt bring in its charge before the legiſlative part which repreſents the nobility, who have neither the ſame intereſts nor the ſame paſſions.

Here is an advantage which this government has over moſt of the ancient republics, where there was this abuſe, that the people were at the ſame time both judge and accuſer.

The executive power, purſuant to what has been already ſaid, ought to have a ſhare in the legiſlature by the power of rejecting, otherwiſe it would ſoon be ſtripped of its prerogative. But ſhould the legiſlative power uſurp a ſhare of the executive, the latter would be equally undone.

If the prince were to have a ſhare in the legiſlature by the power of reſolving, liberty would be loſt. But as it is neceſſary he ſhould have a ſhare in the legiſlature, for the ſupport of his own prerogative, this ſhare muſt conſiſt in the power of rejecting.

The change of government at Rome was owing to this, that neither the ſenate, who had one part of the executive power, nor the magiſtrates, who were entruſted with the other, had the right of rejecting, which was entirely lodged in the people.

Here then is the fundamental conſtitution of the government we are treating of. The legiſlative body being compoſed of two parts, one checks the other by the mutual privilege of rejecting: they are both checked by the executive power, as the executive is by the legiſlative.

Theſe three powers ſhould naturally form a ſtate of repoſe or inaction. But as there is a neceſſity for movement in the courſe of human affairs, they are forced to move, but ſtill to move in concert.

As the executive power has no other part in the legiſlative than the privilege of rejecting, it can have no ſhare in the public debates. It is not even neceſſary that it ſhould propoſe, becauſe, as it may always diſapprove of the reſolutions that ſhall be taken, it may likewiſe likewife reject the decifions on thofe propofals which were made againft its will.

In fome ancient commonwealths, where public debates were carried on by the people in a body, it was natural for the executive power to propofe and debate with the people, otherwife their refolutions muft have been attended with a ftrange confufion.

Were the executive power to ordain the raifing of public money, otherwife than by giving its confent, liberty would be at an end; becaufe it would become legiflative in the moft important point of legiflation.

If the legiflative power was to fettle the fubfidies, not from year to year, but for ever, it would run the rifk of lofing its liberty, becaufe the executive power would no longer be dependent; and when once it was poffeffed of fuch a perpetual right, it would be a matter of indifference, whether it held it of itfelf, or of another. The fame may be faid, if it fhould fix, not from year to year, but for ever, the fea and land forces with which it is to intruft the executive power.

To prevent the executive power from being able to oppress, it is requifite that the armies with which it is intrufted fhould confift of the people, and have the fame fpirit as the people; as was the cafe at Rome till the time of Marius. To obtain this end, there are only two ways; either that the perfons employed in the army fhould have fufficient property to anfwer for their conduct to their fellow-fubjects, and be enlifted only for a year, as was cuftomary at Rome: or if there fhould be a ftanding army, compofed chiefly of the moft defpicable part of the nation, the legiflative power fhould have a right to difband them as foon as it pleafed; the foldiers fhould live in common with the reft of the people; and no feparate camp, barracks, or fortrefs, fhould be fuffered.

When once an army is eftablifhed, it ought not to depend immediately on the legiflative, but on the executive power; and this from the very nature of the thing; its bufinefs confifting more in acting than in deliberation.

From a manner of thinking that prevails amongft mankind, they fet a higher value upon courage than timoroufnefs, on activity than prudence, on ftrength than counfel. Hence the army will ever defpife a fenate, and refpect their own officers. They will naturally flight the orders fent them by a body of men, whom they look upon as cowards, and therefore unworthy to command them. So that as foon as the army depends on the legiflative body, the government becomes a military one; and if the contrary has ever happened, it has been owing to fome extraordinary circumftances. It is becaufe the army has always kept divided; it is becaufe it was compofed of feveral bodies, that depended each on their particular province: it is becaufe the capital towns were ftrong places, defended by their natural fituation, and not garrifoned with regular troops. Holland, for inftance, is ftill fafer than Venice: fhe might drown or ftarve the revolted troops; for as they are not quartered in towns capable of furnifhing them with neceffary fubfiftence, this fubfiftence is of courfe precarious.

Whoever fhall read the admirable treatife of Tacitus on the manners of the Germans, will find that it is from them the Englifh have borrowed the idea of their political government. This beautiful fyftem was invented firft in the woods.

As

As all human things have an end, the ſtate we are ſpeaking of will loſe its liberty, it will periſh. Have not Rome, Sparta, and Carthage periſhed? It will periſh when the legiſlative power ſhall be more corrupted than the executive.

It is not my buſineſs to examine whether the Engliſh actually enjoy this liberty, or not. It is ſufficient for my purpoſe to obſerve, that it is eſtabliſhed by their laws; and I enquire no further.

Neither do I pretend by this to undervalue other governments, nor to ſay that this extreme political liberty ought to give uneaſineſs to thoſe who have only a moderate ſhare of it. How ſhould I have any ſuch deſign, I, who think that even the exceſs of reaſon is not always deſirable, and that mankind generally find their account better in mediums than in extremes?

Harrington, in his Oceana, has alſo inquired into the higheſt point of liberty to which the conſtitution of a ſtate may be carried. But of him indeed it may be ſaid, that for want of knowing the nature of real liberty, he buſied himſelf in purſuit of an imaginary one; and that he built a Chalcedon, though he had a Byzantium before his eyes.

Monteſquieu.

§ 64. *Of* Columbus, *and the Diſcovery of* America.

It is to the diſcoveries of the Portugueſe in the old world, that we are indebted for the new; if we may call the conqueſt of America an obligation, which proved ſo fatal to its inhabitants, and at times to the conquerors themſelves.

This was doubtleſs the moſt important event that ever happened on our globe, one half of which had been hitherto ſtrangers to the other. Whatever had been eſteemed moſt great or noble before, ſeemed abſorbed in this kind of new creation. We ſtill mention with reſpectful admiration, the names of the Argonauts, who did not perform the hundredth part of what was done by the ſailors under Gama and Albuquerque. How many Altars would have been raiſed by the ancients to a Greek, who had diſcovered America! and yet Bartholomew and Chriſtopher Columbus were not thus rewarded.

Columbus, ſtruck with the wonderful expeditions of the Portugueſe, imagined that ſomething greater might be done; and from a bare inſpection of the map of our world, concluded that there muſt be another, which might be found by ſailing always weſt. He had courage equal to his genius, or indeed ſuperior, ſeeing he had to ſtruggle with the prejudices of his contemporaries, and the repulſes of ſeveral princes to whom he tendered his ſervices. Genoa, which was his native country, treated his ſchemes as viſionary, and by that means loſt the only opportunity that could have offered of aggrandizing her power. Henry VII. king of England, who was too greedy of money to hazard any on this noble attempt, would not liſten to the propoſals made by Columbus's brother; and Columbus himſelf was rejected by John II. of Portugal, whoſe attention was wholly employed upon the coaſt of Africa. He had no proſpect of ſucceſs in applying to the French, whoſe marine lay totally neglected, and their affairs more confuſed than ever, during the minority of Charles VIII. The emperor Maximilian had neither ports for ſhipping, money to fit out a fleet, nor ſufficient courage to engage in a ſcheme of this nature. The Venetians, indeed, might have undertaken it; but whether the natural averſion of the Genoeſe to these people would not suffer Columbus to apply to the rivals of his country, or that the Venetians had no idea of any thing more important than the trade they carried on from Alexandria and in the Levant, Columbus at length fixed all his hopes on the court of Spain.

Ferdinand, king of Arragon, and Isabella, queen of Castile, had by their marriage united all Spain under one dominion, excepting only the kingdom of Grenada, which was still in the possession of the Moors; but which Ferdinand soon after took from them. The union of these two princes had prepared the way for the greatness of Spain; which was afterwards begun by Columbus; he was, however, obliged to undergo eight years of incessant application, before Isabella's court would consent to accept of the inestimable benefit this great man offered it. The bane of all great projects is the want of money. The Spanish court was poor; and the prior, Perez, and two merchants, named Pinzono, were obliged to advance seventeen thousand ducats towards fitting out the armament. Columbus procured a patent from the court, and at length set sail from the port of Palos in Andalusia, with three ships, on August 23, in the year 1492.

It was not above a month after his departure from the Canary islands, where he had come to an anchor to get refreshment, when Columbus discovered the first island in America; and during this short run, he suffered more from the murmurings and discontent of the people of his fleet, than he had done even from the refusals of the princes he had applied to. This island, which he discovered, and named St. Salvador, lies about a thousand leagues from the Canaries; presently after, he likewise discovered the Lucayan islands, together with those of Cuba and Hispaniola, now called St. Domingo.

Ferdinand and Isabella were in the utmost surprise to see him return, at the end of nine months, with some of the American natives of Hispaniola, several rarities from that country, and a quantity of gold, with which he presented their Majesties.

The king and queen made him sit down in their presence, covered like a grandee of Spain, and created him high admiral and viceroy of the new world. Columbus was now every where looked upon as an extraordinary person sent from heaven. Every one was vying who should be foremost in assisting him in his undertakings, and embarking under his command. He soon set sail again with a fleet of seventeen ships. He now made the discovery of several other new islands, particularly the Caribbees and Jamaica. Doubt had been changed into admiration on his first voyage; in this, admiration was turned into envy.

He was admiral and viceroy, and to these titles might have been added that of the benefactor of Ferdinand and Isabella. Nevertheless he was brought home prisoner to Spain, by judges who had been purposely sent out on board to observe his conduct. As soon as it was known that Columbus was arrived, the people ran in shoals to meet him, as the guardian genius of Spain. Columbus was brought from the ship, and appeared on shore chained hands and feet.

He had been thus treated by the orders of Fonseca, bishop of Burgos, the intendant of the expedition, whose ingratitude was as great as the other's services. Isabella was ashamed of what she saw, and did all in her power to make Columbus amends for the injuries done to him: however he was not suffered to depart for four years, either because they feared that

that he would ſeize upon what he had diſcovered for himſelf, or that they were willing to have time to obſerve his behaviour. At length he was ſent on another voyage to the new world; and now it was that he diſcovered the continent, at ſix degrees diſtance from the equator, and ſaw that part of the coaſt on which Carthagena has been ſince built.

At the time that Columbus firſt promiſed a new hemiſphere, it was inſiſted upon that no ſuch hemiſphere could exiſt; and after he had made the actual diſcovery of it, it was pretended that it had been known long before. I ſhall not mention one Martin Behem, of Nuremberg, who, it is ſaid, went from that city to the Straits of Magellan in 1460, with a patent from the Dutcheſs of Burgundy, who, as ſhe was not alive at that time, could not iſſue patents. Nor ſhall I take notice of the pretended charts of this Martin Behem, which are ſtill ſhewn; nor of the evident contradictions which diſcredit this ſtory: but, in ſhort, it was not pretended that Martin Behem had peopled America; the honour was given to the Carthaginians, and a book of Ariſtotle was quoted on the occaſion, which he never wrote. Some found out a conformity between ſome words in the Caribbee and Hebrew languages, and did not fail to follow ſo fine an opening. Others were poſitive that the children of Noah, after ſettling in Siberia, paſſed from thence over to Canada on the ice; and that their deſcendants, afterwards born in Canada, had gone and peopled Peru. According to others again the Chineſe and Japaneſe ſent colonies into America, and carried over lions with them for their diverſion, though there are no lions either in China or Japan. In this manner have many learned men argued upon the diſcoveries made by men of genius. If it ſhould be aſked, how men firſt came upon the continent of America? is it not eaſily anſwered, that they were placed there by the ſame Power who cauſes trees and graſs to grow?

The reply which Columbus made to ſome of thoſe who envied him the high reputation he had gained, is ſtill famous. Theſe people pretended that nothing could be more eaſy than the diſcoveries he had made; upon which he propoſed to them to ſet an egg upright on one of its ends; but when they had tried in vain to do it, he broke one end of the egg, and ſet it upright with eaſe. They told him any one could do that: How comes it then, replied Columbus, that not one among you thought of it?—This ſtory is related of Brunelleſchi, who improved architecture at Florence many years before Columbus was born. Moſt bon mots are only the repetition of things that have been ſaid before.

The aſhes of Columbus cannot be affected by the reputation he gained while living, in having doubled for us the works of the creation. But mankind delight to do juſtice to the illuſtrious dead, either from a vain hope that they enhance thereby the merit of the living, or that they are naturally fond of truth. Americo Veſpucci, whom we call Americus Veſpuſius, a merchant of Florence, had the honour of giving his name to this new half of the globe, in which he did not poſſeſs one acre of land, and pretended to be the firſt who diſcovered the continent. But ſuppoſing it true that he was the firſt diſcoverer, the glory was certainly due to him, who had the penetration and courage to undertake and perform the firſt voyage. Honour, as Newton ſays in his diſpute with Leibnitz, is due only to the firſt inventor; thoſe that follow after are only his ſcholars. Columbus had

had made three voyages, as admiral and viceroy, five years before Americus Veſpuſius had made one as a geographer, under the command of admiral Ojeda; but this latter writing to his friends at Florence, that he had diſcovered a new world, they believed him on his word; and the citizens of Florence decreed, that a grand illumination ſhould be made before the door of his houſe every three years, on the feaſt of All Saints. And yet could this man be ſaid to deſerve any honours, for happening to be on board a fleet that, in 1489, ſailed along the coaſt of Brazil, when Columbus had, five years before, pointed out the way to the reſt of the world?

There has lately appeared at Florence a life of this Americus Veſpuſius, which ſeems to be written with very little regard to truth, and without any concluſive reaſoning. Several French authors are there complained of, who have done juſtice to Columbus's merit; but the writer ſhould not have fallen upon the French authors, but on the Spaniſh, who were the firſt that did this juſtice. This writer ſays, that "he will confound the vanity "of the French nation, who have always "attacked with impunity the honour and ſuc-"ceſs of the Italian nation." What vanity can there be in ſaying that it was a Genoeſe who firſt diſcovered America? or how is the honour of the Italian nation injured in owning, that it was to an Italian, born in Genoa, that we are indebted for the new world? I purpoſely remark this want of equity, good-breeding, and good-ſenſe, as we have too many examples of it; and I muſt ſay, that the good French writers have in general been the leaſt guilty of this inſufferable fault; and one great reaſon of their being ſo univerſally read throughout Europe, is their doing juſtice to all nations.

The inhabitants of theſe iſlands, and of the continent were a new race of men. They were all without beards, and were as much aſtoniſhed at the faces of the Spaniards, as they were at their ſhips and artillery: they at firſt looked upon theſe new viſitors as monſters or gods, who had come out of the ſky or the ſea. Theſe voyages, and thoſe of the Portugueſe, had now taught us how inconſiderable a ſpot of the globe our Europe was, and what an aſtoniſhing variety reigns in the world. Indoſtan was known to be inhabited by a race of men whoſe complexions were yellow. In Africa and Aſia, at ſome diſtance from the equator, there had been found ſeveral kinds of black men; and after travellers had penetrated into America as far as the line, they met with a race of people who were tolerably white. The natives of Brazil are of the colour of bronze. The Chineſe ſtill appear to differ entirely from the reſt of mankind, in the make of their eyes and noſes. But what is ſtill to be remarked is, that into whatſoever regions theſe various races are tranſplanted, their complexions never change, unleſs they mingle with the natives of the country. The mucous membrane of the negroes, which is known to be of a black colour, is a manifeſt proof that there is a differential principle in each ſpecies of men, as well as plants.

Dependant upon this principle, nature has formed the different degrees of genius, and the characters of nations, which are ſeldom known to change. Hence the negroes are ſlaves to other men, and are purchaſed on the coaſt of Africa, like beaſts, for a ſum of money; and the vaſt multitudes of negroes tranſplanted into our American colonies, ſerve as ſlaves under a very inconſiderable number of Europeans. Experience has likewiſe taught us how great a ſuperiority the Europeans have over the Americans, who are every where eaſily overcome, and have not dared to attempt a revolution, though a thouſand to one ſuperior in numbers.

This part of America was alſo remarkable on account of its animals and plants, which are not to be found in the other three parts of the world, and which are of ſo great uſe to us. Horſes, corn of all kinds, and iron, were not wanting in Mexico and Peru; and among the many valuable commodities unknown to the old world, cochineal was the principal, and was brought us from this country. Its uſe in dying has now made us forget the ſcarlet, which for time immemorial had been the only thing known for giving a fine red colour.

The importation of cochineal was ſoon ſucceeded by that of indigo, cacao, vanille, and thoſe woods which ſerve for ornament and medicinal purpoſes, particularly the quinquina, or jeſuits bark, which is the only ſpecific againſt intermitting fevers. Nature has placed this remedy in the mountains of Peru, whilſt ſhe had diſperſed the diſeaſe it cured through all the reſt of the world. This new continent likewiſe furniſhed pearls, coloured ſtones, and diamonds.

It is certain that America at preſent furniſhes the meaneſt citizen of Europe with his conveniencies and pleaſures. The gold and ſilver mines, at their firſt diſcovery, were of ſervice only to the kings of Spain and the merchants; the reſt of the world was impoveriſhed by them, for the great multitudes who did not follow buſineſs, found themſelves poſſeſſed of a very ſmall quantity of ſpecie, in compariſon with the immenſe ſums accumulated by thoſe, who had the advantage of the firſt diſcoveries. But by degrees, the great quantity of gold and ſilver which was ſent from America, was diſperſed throughout all Europe, and by paſſing into a number of hands, the diſtribution is become more equal. The price of commodities is likewiſe increaſed in Europe, in proportion to the increaſe of ſpecie.

To comprehend how the treaſures of America paſſed from the poſſeſſion of the Spaniards into that of other nations, it will be ſufficient to conſider theſe two things: the uſe which Charles V. and Philip II. made of their money; and the manner in which other nations acquired a ſhare in the wealth of Peru.

The emperor Charles V. who was always travelling, and always at war, neceſſarily diſperſed a great quantity of that ſpecie which he received from Mexico and Peru, through Germany and Italy. When he ſent his ſon Philip over to England, to marry queen Mary, and take upon him the title of King of England, that prince depoſited in the tower of London twenty-ſeven large cheſts of ſilver in bars, and an hundred horſe-loads of gold and ſilver coin. The troubles in Flanders, and the intrigues of the league in France, coſt this Philip, according to his own confeſſion, above three thouſand millions of livres of our money.

The manner in which the gold and ſilver of Peru is diſtributed amongſt all the people of Europe, and from thence is ſent to the Eaſt-Indies, is a ſurpriſing, though well-known circumſtance. By a ſtrict law enacted by Ferdinand and Iſabella, and afterwards confirmed by Charles V. and all the kings of Spain, all other nations were not only excluded the entrance into any of the ports in Spaniſh America, but likewiſe from having the leaſt ſhare, directly or indirectly, in the trade of that part of the world. One would have imagined, that this law would have enabled the Spaniards to ſubdue all Europe; and yet

Spain ſubſiſts only by the continual violation of this very law. It can hardly furniſh exports for America to the value of four millions; wheareas the reſt of Europe ſometimes ſend over merchandize to the amount of near fifty millions. This prodigious trade of the nations at enmity or in alliance with Spain, is carried on by the Spaniards themſelves, who are always faithful in their dealings with individuals, and always cheating their king. The Spaniards gave no ſecurity to foreign merchants for the performance of their contracts; a mutual credit, without which there never could have been any commerce, ſupplies the place of other obligations.

The manner in which the Spaniards for a long time conſigned the gold and ſilver to foreigners, which was brought home by their galleons, was ſtill more ſurpriſing. The Spaniard, who at Cadiz, is properly factor for the foreigner, delivered the bullion he received to the care of certain bravoes, called Meteors: theſe, armed with piſtols at their belt, and a long ſword carried the bullion in parcels properly marked, to the ramparts, and flung them over to other meteors, who waited below, and carried them to the boats which were to receive them, and theſe boats carried them on board the ſhips in the road. Theſe meteors and the factors, together with the commiſſaries and the guards, who never diſturbed them, had each a ſtated fee, and the foreign merchant was never cheated. The king, who received a duty upon this money at the arrival of the galleons, was likewiſe a gainer; ſo that, properly ſpeaking, the law only was cheated; a law which would be abſolutely uſeleſs if not eluded, and which nevertheleſs, cannot yet be abrogated, becauſe old prejudices are always the moſt difficult to be overcome amongſt men.

The greateſt inſtance of the violation of this law, and of the fidelity of the Spaniards, was in the year 1684, when war was declared between France and Spain. His catholic majeſty endeavoured to ſeize upon the effects of all the French in his kingdom; but he in vain iſſued edicts and admonitions, inquiries and excommunications; not a ſingle Spaniſh factor would betray his French correſpondent. This fidelity, which does ſo much honour to the Spaniſh nation, plainly ſhews, that men only willingly obey thoſe laws, which they themſelves have made for the good of ſociety, and that thoſe which are the mere effects of a ſovereign's will, always meet with oppoſition.

As the diſcovery of America was at firſt the ſource of much good to the Spaniards, it afterwards occaſioned them many and conſiderable evils. One has been, the depriving that kingdom of its ſubjects, by the great numbers neceſſarily required to people the colonies: another was, the infecting the world with a diſeaſe, which was before known only in the new world, and particularly in the iſland of Hiſpaniola. Several of the companions of Chriſtopher Columbus returned home infected with this contagion, which afterwards ſpread over Europe. It is certain, that this poiſon, which taints the ſprings of life, was peculiar to America, as the plague and the ſmall-pox were diſeaſes originally endemial to the ſouthern parts of Numidia. We are not to believe, that the eating of human fleſh, practiſed by ſome of the American ſavages, occaſioned this diſorder. There were no cannibals on the iſland of Hiſpaniola, where it was moſt frequent and inveterate; neither are we to ſuppoſe with ſome, that it proceeded from too great an exceſs of ſenſual pleaſures. Nature had never puniſhed exceſſes of this kind with ſuch diſorders in the world;

and even to this day, we find that a momentary indulgence, which has been paſſed for eight or ten years, may bring this cruel and ſhameful ſcourge upon the chaſteſt union.

The great Columbus, after having built ſeveral houſes on theſe iſlands, and diſcovered the continent, returned to Spain, where he enjoyed a reputation unſullied by rapine or cruelty, and died at Valladolid in 1506. But the governors of Cuba and Hiſpaniola, who ſucceeded him, being perſuaded that theſe provinces furniſhed gold, reſolved to make the diſcovery at the price of the lives of the inhabitants. In ſhort, whether they thought the natives had conceived an implacable hatred to them; or that they were apprehenſive of their ſuperior numbers; or that the rage of ſlaughter, when once begun, knows no bounds, they in the ſpace of a few years entirely depopulated Hiſpaniola and Cuba, the former of which contained three millions of inhabitants, and the latter above ſix-hundred thouſand.

Bartholomew de la Caſas, biſhop of Chiapa, who was an eye-witneſs to theſe deſolations, relates, that they hunted down the natives with dogs. Theſe wretched ſavages, almoſt naked and without arms, were purſued like wild beaſts in the foreſts, devoured alive by dogs, ſhot to death, or ſurpriſed and burnt in their habitations.

He farther declares, from ocular teſtimony, that they frequently cauſed a number of theſe miſerable wretches to be ſummoned by a prieſt to come in, and ſubmit to the Chriſtian religion, and to the king of Spain; and that after this ceremony, which was only an additional act of injuſtice, they put them to death without the leaſt remorſe.—I believe that De la Caſas has exaggerated in many parts of his relation; but, allowing him to have ſaid ten times more than is truth, there remains enough to make us ſhudder with horror.

It may ſeem ſurpriſing, that this maſſacre of a whole race of men could have been carried on in the ſight, and under the adminiſtration of ſeveral religious of the order of St. Jerome; for we know that Cardinal Ximenes, who was prime miniſter of Caſtile before the time of Charles V. ſent over four monks of this order, in quality of preſidents of the royal council of the iſland. Doubtleſs they were not able to reſiſt the torrent; and the hatred of the natives to their new maſters, being with juſt reaſon become implacable, rendered their deſtruction unhappily neceſſary. *Voltaire.*

§ 65. *The Influence of the Progreſs of Science on the Manners and Characters of Men.*

The progreſs of ſcience, and the cultivation of literature, had conſiderable effect in changing the manners of the European nations, and introducing that civility and refinement by which they are now diſtinguiſhed. At the time when their empire was overturned, the Romans, though they had loſt that correct taſte which has rendered the productions of their anceſtors the ſtandards of excellence, and models for imitation to ſucceeding ages, ſtill preſerved their love of letters, and cultivated the arts with great ardour. But rude Barbarians were ſo far from being ſtruck with any admiration of theſe unknown accompliſhments, that they deſpiſed them. They were not arrived at that ſtate of ſociety, in which thoſe faculties of the human mind, that have beauty and elegance for their objects, begin to unfold themſelves. They were ſtrangers to all thoſe wants and deſires which are the parents of ingenious invention; and as they did not comprehend either the merit or utility of the Roman arts, they destroyed the monuments of them, with industry not inferior to that with which their posterity have since studied to preserve, or to recover them. The convulsions occasioned by their settlement in the empire; the frequent as well as violent revolutions in every kingdom which they established; together with the interior defects in the form of government which they introduced, banished security and leisure; prevented the growth of taste or the culture of science; and kept Europe, during several centuries, in a state of ignorance. But as soon as liberty and independance began to be felt by every part of the community, and communicated some taste of the advantages arising from commerce, from public order, and from personal security, the human mind became conscious of powers which it did not formerly perceive, and fond of occupations or pursuits of which it was formerly incapable. Towards the beginning of the twelfth century, we discern the first symptons of its awakening from that lethargy in which it had long been sunk, and observe it turning with curiosity and attention towards new objects.

The first literary efforts, however, of the European nations, in the middle ages, were extremely ill-directed. Among nations, as well as individuals, the powers of imagination attain some degree of vigour before the intellectual faculties are much exercised in speculative or abstract disquisition. Men are poets before they are philosophers. They feel with sensibility, and describe with force, when they have made but little progress in investigation or reasoning. The age of Homer and of Hesiod long preceeded that of Thales, or of Socrates. But unhappily for literature, our ancestors, deviating from this course which nature points out, plunged at once into the depths of abstruse and metaphysical enquiry. They had been converted to the Christian faith soon after they settled in their new conquests: but they did not receive it pure. The presumption of men had added to the simple and instructive doctrines of Christianity, the theories of a vain philosophy, that attempted to penetrate into mysteries, and to decide questions which the limited faculties of the human mind are unable to comprehend, or to resolve. These over-curious speculations were incorporated with the system of religion, and came to be considered as the most essential part of it. As soon, then, as curiosity prompted men to inquire and to reason, these were the subjects which first presented themselves, and engaged their attention. The scholastic theology, with its infinite train of bold disquisitions, and subtile distinctions concerning points which are not the object of human reason, was the first production of the spirit of enquiry after it began to resume some degree of activity and vigour in Europe.

It was not this circumstance alone that gave such a wrong turn to the minds of men, when they began again to exercise talents which they had so long neglected. Most of the persons who attempted to revive literature in the twelfth and thirteenth centuries, had received instruction, or derived their principles of science from the Greeks in the eastern empire, or from the Arabians in Spain and Africa. Both these people, acute and inquisitive to excess, corrupted those sciences which they cultivated. The former rendered theology a system of speculative refinement, or of endless controversy. The latter communicated to philosophy a spirit of metaphysical and frivolous subtlety. Missed by these guides,

guides, the persons who first applied to science were involved in a maze of intricate inquiries. Instead of allowing their fancy to take its natural range, and to produce such works of invention as might have improved their taste, and refined their sentiments; instead of cultivating those arts which embellish human life, and render it comfortable; they were fettered by authority; they were led astray by example, and wasted the whole force of their genius in speculations as unavailing as they were difficult.

But fruitless and ill-directed as these speculations were, their novelty roused, and their boldness interested, the human mind. The ardour with which men pursued these uninviting studies was astonishing. Genuine philosophy was never cultivated, in any enlightened age, with greater zeal. Schools, upon the model of those instituted by Charlemagne were opened in every cathedral, and almost in every monastery of note. Colleges and universities were erected, and formed into communities, or corporations, governed by their own laws, and invested with separate and extensive jurisdiction over their own members. A regular course of studies was planned. Privileges of great value were conferred on masters and scholars. Academical titles and honours of various kinds were invented, as a recompence for both. Nor was it in the schools alone that superiority in science led to reputation and authority; it became the object of respect in life, and advanced such as acquired it to a rank of no inconsiderable eminence. Allured by all these advantages, an incredible number of students resorted to these new seats of learning, and crowded with eagerness into that new path which was open to fame and distinction.

But how considerable soever these first efforts may appear, there was one circumstance which prevented the effects of them from being as extensive as they ought to have been. All the languages in Europe, during the period under review*, were barbarous, They were destitute of elegance, of force, and even of perspicuity. No attempt had been hitherto made to improve or to polish them. The Latin tongue was consecrated by the church to religion. Custom, with authority scarce less sacred, had appropriated it to literature. All the sciences cultivated in the twelfth and thirteenth centuries were taught in Latin. All the books with respect to them, were written in that language. To have treated of any important subject in a modern language, would have been deemed a degradation of it. This confined science within a very narrow circle. The learned alone were admitted into the temple of knowledge; the gate was shut against all others, who were allowed to remain involved in their former darkness and ignorance.

But though science was thus prevented, during several ages, from diffusing itself through society, and its influence was circumscribed, the progress of it may be mentioned, nevertheless, among the great causes which contributed to introduce a change of manners into Europe. That ardent, though ill-judged, spirit of inquiry, which I have described, occasioned a fermentation of mind, which put ingenuity and invention in motion, and gave them vigour. It led men to a new employment of their faculties, which they found to be agreeable, as well as interesting. It accustomed them to exercises and occupations which tended to soften their manners, and to

* From the subversion of the Roman empire to the beginning of the sixteenth century.

give

give them some relish for those gentle virtues which are peculiar to nations among whom science hath been cultivated with success.

Robertson.

§ 66. *On the Respect paid by the* Lacedæmonians *and* Athenians *to old Age.*

It happened at Athens, during a public representation of some play exhibited in honour of the commonwealth, that an old gentleman came too late for a place suitable to his age and quality. Many of the young gentlemen, who observed the difficulty and confusion he was in, made signs to him that they would accommodate him if he came where they sat: the good man bustled through the croud accordingly; but when he came to the seats to which he was invited, the jest was, to sit close and expose him, as he stood out of countenance, to the whole audience. The frolic went round all the Athenian benches. But on those occasions, there were also particular places assigned for foreigners: when the good man skulked towards the boxes appointed for the Lacedæmonians, that honest people, more virtuous than polite, rose up all to a man, and, with the greatest respect, received him among them. The Athenians, being suddenly touched with a sense of the Spartan virtue, and their own degeneracy, gave a thunder of applause; and the old man cried out, "The Athenians understand what "is good, but the Lacedæmonians practise "it."

Spectator.

§ 67. *On* Pætus *and* Arria.

In the reign of Claudius, the Roman emperor, Arria, the wife of Cæcinna Pætus, was an illustrious pattern of magnanimity and conjugal affection.

It happened that her husband and her son were both at the same time attacked with a dangerous illness. The son died. He was a youth endowed with every quality of mind and person which could endear him to his parents. His mother's heart was torn with all the anguish of grief; yet she resolved to conceal the distressing event from her husband. She prepared and conducted his funeral so privately, that Pætus did not know of his death. Whenever she came into her husband's bed-chamber, she pretended her son was better; and, as often as he inquired after his health, would answer, that he had rested well, or had eaten with an appetite. When she found that she could no longer restrain her grief, but her tears were gushing out, she would leave the room, and, having given vent to her passion, return again with dry eyes and a serene countenance, as if she had left her sorrow behind her at the door of the chamber.

Camillus Scribonianus, the governor of Dalmatia, having taken up arms against Claudius, Pætus joined himself to his party, and was soon after taken prisoner, and brought to Rome. When the guards were going to put him on board the ship, Arria besought them that she might be permitted to go with him. "Certainly," said she, "you "cannot refuse a man of consular dignity, as "he is, a few attendants to wait upon him; "but, if you will take me, I alone will "perform their office." This favour however, was refused; upon which she hired a small fishing vessel, and boldly ventured to follow the ship.

Returning to Rome, Arria met the wife of Scribonianus in the emperor's palace, who pressing her to discover all that she knew of the insurrection,—"What!" said she, "shall "I

" I regard thy advice, who saw thy husband " murdered in thy very arms, and yet survivest him?"

Pætus being condemned to die, Arria formed a deliberate resolution to share his fate, and made no secret of her intention. Thrasea, who married her daughter, attempting to dissuade her from her purpose, among other arguments which he used, said to her, " Would you then, if my life were to be " taken from me, advise your daughter to " die with me?" " Most certainly I would," she replied, " if she had lived as long, and in " as much harmony with you, as I have lived " with Pætus."

Persisting in her determination, she found means to provide herself with a dagger: and one day, when she observed a more than usual gloom on the countenance of Pætus, and perceived that death by the hand of the executioner appeared to him more terrible than in the field of glory—perhaps, too, sensible that it was chiefly for her sake that he wished to live—she drew the dagger from her side, and stabbed herself before his eyes. Then instantly plucking the weapon from her breast, she presented it to her husband, saying, " My Pætus, it is not painful *." *Pliny.*

§ 68. Abdolonymus *raised to the Government of* Sidon.

The city of Sidon having surrendered to Alexander, he ordered Hephæstion to bestow the crown on him whom the Sidonians should think most worthy of that honour. Hephæstion being at that time resident with two young men of distinction, offered them the kingdom; but they refused it, telling him that it was contrary to the laws of their country, to admit any one to that honour, who was not of the royal family. He then, having expressed his admiration of their disinterested spirit, desired them to name one of the royal race, who might remember that he received the crown through their hands. Overlooking many who would have been ambitious of this high honour, they made choice of Abdolonymus, whose singular merit had rendered him conspicuous even in the vale of obscurity. Though remotely related to the royal family, a series of misfortunes had reduced him to the necessity of cultivating a garden, for a small stipend, in the suburbs of the city.

While Abdolonymus was busily employed in weeding his garden, the two friends of Hephæstion, bearing in their hands the ensigns of royalty, approached him, and saluted him king, informing him that Alexander had appointed him to that office; and requiring him immediately to exchange his rustic garb, and utensils of husbandry, for the regal robe and sceptre. At the same time, they urged him, when he should be seated on the throne, and have a nation in his power, not to forget the humble condition from which he had been raised.

All this, at the first, appeared to Abdolonymus as an illusion of the fancy, or an insult offered to his poverty. He requested them not to trouble him farther with their impertinent jests, and to find some other way of amusing themselves, which might leave him in the peaceable enjoyment of his obscure habitation.—At length, however, they convinced him that they

* In the Tatler, N° 72, a fancy piece is drawn, founded on the principal fact in this story, but wholly fictitious in the circumstances of the tale. The author, mistaking Cæcinna Pætus for Thrasea Pætus, has accused even Nero unjustly: charging him with an action which certainly belonged to Claudius. See Pliny's Epistles, Book iii. Ep. 16. Dion. Cassius, Lib. lx. and Tacitus, Lib. xvi. § 35.

they were ſerious in their propoſal, and prevailed upon him to accept the regal office, and accompany them to the palace.

No ſooner was he in poſſeſſion of the government, than pride and envy created him enemies, who wiſpered their murmurs in every place, till at laſt they reached the ear of Alexander; who, commanding the new-elected prince to be ſent for, required of him, with what temper of mind he had borne his poverty. "Would to Heaven," replied Abdolonymus, "that I may be able to bear "my crown with equal moderation: for "when I poſſeſſed little, I wanted nothing: "theſe hands ſupplied me with whatever I "deſired." From this anſwer, Alexander formed ſo high an idea of his wiſdom, that he confirmed the choice which had been made, and annexed a neighbouring province to the government of Sidon. *Quintus Curtius.*

§ 69. *The Reſignation of the Emperor* CHARLES V.

Charles reſolved to reſign his kingdoms to his ſon, with a ſolemnity ſuitable to the importance of the tranſaction; and to perform this laſt act of ſovereignty with ſuch formal pomp, as might leave an indelible impreſſion on the minds, not only of his ſubjects, but of his ſucceſſor. With this view, he called Philip out of England, where the peeviſh temper of his queen, which increaſed with her deſpair of having iſſue, rendered him extremely unhappy; and the jealouſy of the Engliſh left him no hopes of obtaining the direction of their affairs. Having aſſembled the ſtates of the Low Countries, at Bruſſels, on the twenty-fifth of October, one thouſand five hundred and fifty-five, Charles ſeated himſelf, for the laſt time, in the chair of ſtate; on one ſide of which was placed his ſon, and on the other his ſiſter, the queen of Hungary, regent of the Netherlands; with a ſplendid retinue of the grandees of Spain, and princes of the empire, ſtanding behind him. The preſident of the council of Flanders, by his command, explained, in a few words, his intention in calling this extraordinary meeting of the ſtates. He then read the inſtrument of reſignation by which Charles ſurrendered to his ſon Philip all his territories, juriſdiction, and authority in the Low Countries; abſolving his ſubjects there from their oath of allegiance to him, which he required them to transfer to Philip, his lawful heir, and to ſerve him with the ſame loyalty and zeal which they had manifeſted, during ſo long a courſe of years, in ſupport of his government.

Charles then roſe from his ſeat, and leaning on the ſhoulder of the prince of Orange, becauſe he was unable to ſtand without ſupport, he addreſſed himſelf to the audience, and from a paper which he held in his hand, in order to aſſiſt his memory, he recounted with dignity, but without oſtentation, all the great things which he had undertaken and performed ſince the commencement of his adminiſtration. He obſerved, that, from the ſeventeenth year of his age, he had dedicated all his thoughts and attention to public objects; reſerving no portion of his time for the indulgence of his eaſe, and very little for the enjoyment of private pleaſure: that, either in a pacific or hoſtile manner, he had viſited Germany nine times, Spain ſix times, France four times, Italy ſeven times, the Low Countries ten times, England twice, Africa as often, and had made eleven voyages by ſea: that, while his health permitted him to diſcharge his duty, and the vigour of his conſtitution was equal, in any degree, to the arduous office of governing ſuch extenſive dominions, he had never ſhunned

ſhunned labour, nor repined under fatigue: that now, when his health was broken, and his vigour exhauſted by the rage of an incurable diſtemper, his growing infirmities admoniſhed him to retire; nor was he ſo fond of reigning, as to retain the ſceptre in an impotent hand, which was no longer able to protect his ſubjects, or to render them happy: that, inſtead of a ſovereign worn out with diſeaſes, and ſcarcely half alive, he gave them one in the prime of life, accuſtomed already to govern, and who added to the vigour of youth, all the attention and ſagacity of maturer years: that if, during the courſe of a long adminiſtration, he had committed any material error in government; or if, under the preſſure of ſo many and great affairs, and amidſt the attention which he had been obliged to give to them, he had either neglected, or injured any of his ſubjects, he now implored their forgiveneſs: that for his part, he ſhould ever retain a grateful ſenſe of their fidelity and attachment, and would carry the remembrance of it along with him to the place of his retreat, as his ſweeteſt conſolation, as well as the beſt reward for all his ſervices; and, in his laſt prayers to Almighty God, would pour forth his ardent wiſhes for their welfare.

Then, turning towards Philip, who fell on his knees, and kiſſed his father's hand, "If," ſays he, "I had left you by my death, this "rich inheritance, to which I have made "ſuch large additions, ſome regard would "have been juſtly due to my memory on "that account: but now, when I voluntarily "reſign to you what I might ſtill have "retained, I may well expect the warmeſt "expreſſions of thanks on your part. With "theſe, however, I diſpenſe; and ſhall conſider "your concern for the welfare of your ſubjects, and your love of them, as the beſt and "moſt acceptable teſtimony of your gratitude "to me. It is in your power, by a wiſe and "virtuous adminiſtration, to juſtify the extraordinary proof which I this day give of my "paternal affection; and to demonſtrate, that "you are worthy of the confidence which I "repoſe in you. Preſerve an inviolable regard "for religion; maintain the Catholic faith in "its purity; let the laws of your country be "ſacred in your eyes; encroach not on the "rights and privileges of your people: and, "if the time ſhall ever come, when you ſhall "wiſh to enjoy the tranquillity of private life, "may you have a ſon endowed with ſuch "qualities, that you can reſign your ſceptre "to him with as much ſatisfaction as I "give up mine to you!"

As ſoon as Charles had finiſhed this long addreſs to his ſubjects, and to their new ſovereign, he ſunk into the chair, exhauſted, and ready to faint with the fatigue of ſuch an extraordinary effort. During his diſcourſe, the whole audience melted into tears; ſome, from admiration of his magnanimity; others, ſoftened by the expreſſions of tenderneſs towards his ſon, and of love to his people; and all were affected with the deepeſt ſorrow, at loſing a ſovereign, who had diſtinguiſhed the Netherlands, his native country, with particular marks of his regard and attachment.

A few weeks afterwards, Charles, in an aſſembly no leſs ſplendid, and with a ceremonial equally pompous, reſigned to his ſon the crowns of Spain, with all the territories depending on them, both in the Old and in the New World. Of all theſe vaſt poſſeſſions he reſerved nothing to himſelf, but an annual penſion of a hundred thouſand crowns, to defray the charges of his family, and to afford him a ſmall ſum for acts of beneficence and charity.

The place he had chosen for his retreat, was the monastery of St. Justus, in the province of Estramadura. It was seated in a vale of no great extent, watered by a small brook, and surrounded by rising grounds, covered with lofty trees. From the nature of the soil, as well as the temperature of the climate, it was esteemed the most healthful and delicious situation in Spain. Some months before his resignation, he had sent an architect thither, to add a new apartment to the monastery, for his accommodation; but he gave strict orders, that the style of the building should be such as suited his present situation rather than his former dignity. It consisted only of six rooms; four of them in the form of friars' cells, with naked walls; the other two, each twenty feet square, were hung with brown cloth, and furnished in the most simple manner. They were all on a level with the ground; with a door on one side, into a garden, of which Charles himself had given the plan, and which he had filled with various plants, intending to cultivate them with his own hands. On the other side, they communicated with the chapel of the monastery, in which he was to perform his devotions. Into this humble retreat, hardly sufficient for the comfortable accommodation of a private gentleman, did Charles enter, with twelve domestics only. He buried there, in solitude and silence, his grandeur, his ambition, together with all those vast projects which, during half a century, had alarmed and agitated Europe, filling every kingdom in it, by turns, with the terror of his arms, and the dread of being subjected to his power. *Robertson.*

§ 70. *A remarkable Instance of filial Duty.*

The prætor had given up to the triumvir a woman of some rank, condemned, for a capital crime, to be executed in the prison. He who had charge of the execution, in consideration of her birth, did not immediately put her to death. He even ventured to let her daughter have access to her in prison; carefully searching her, however, as she went in, lest she should carry with her any sustenance; concluding, that in a few days the mother must of course perish for want, and that the severity of putting a woman of family to a violent death, by the hand of the executioner, might thus be avoided. Some days passing in this manner, the triumvir began to wonder that the daugher still came to visit her mother, and could by no means comprehend, how the latter should live so long. Watching, therefore, carefully, what passed in the interview between them, he found, to his great astonishment, that the life of the mother had been, all this while, supported by the milk of the daughter, who came to the prison every day, to give her mother her breasts to suck. The strange contrivance between them was represented to the judges, and procured a pardon for the mother. Nor was it thought sufficient to give to so dutiful a daughter the forfeited life of her condemned mother, but they were both maintained afterwards by a pension settled on them for life. And the ground upon which the prison stood was consecrated, and a temple to filial piety built upon it.

What will not filial duty contrive, or what hazards will it not run, if it will put a daughter upon venturing, at the peril of her own life, to maintain her imprisoned and condemned mother in so unusual a manner! For what was ever heard of more strange, than a mother sucking the breasts of her own daughter? It might even seem so unnatural as to render it doubtful whether it might not be, in some

ſome ſort, wrong, if it were not that duty to parents is the firſt law of nature.

Val. Max. Plin.

§ 71 *The Continence of* Scipio Africanus.

The ſoldiers, after the taking of New Carthage, brought before Scipio a young lady of ſuch diſtinguiſhed beauty, that ſhe attracted the eyes of all wherever ſhe went. Scipio, by enquiring concerning her country and parents, among other things learned, that ſhe was betrothed to Allucius, prince of the Celtiberians. He immediately ordered her parents and bridegroom to be ſent for. In the mean time he was informed, that the young prince was ſo exceſſively enamoured of his bride, that he could not ſurvive the loſs of her. For this reaſon, as ſoon as he appeared, and before he ſpoke to her parents, he took great care to talk with him. "As you and I are "both young," ſaid he, "we can converſe "together with greater freedom. When your "bride, who had fallen into the hands of my "ſoldiers, was brought before me, I was in"formed that you loved her paſſionately; "and, in truth, her perfect beauty left me no "room to doubt of it. If I were at liberty "to indulge a youthful paſſion, I mean ho"nourable and lawful wedlock, and were "not ſolely engroſſed by the affairs of "my republic, I might have hoped to have "been pardoned my exceſſive love for ſo "charming a miſtreſs. But as I am ſituated, "and have it in my power, with pleaſure I "promote your happineſs. Your future "ſpouſe has met with as civil and modeſt "treatment from me, as if ſhe had been "amongſt her own parents, who are ſoon to "be yours too. I have kept her pure, in "order to have it in my power to make you "a preſent worthy of you and of me. The "only return I aſk of you for this favour is, "that you will be a friend to the Roman "people; and that if you believe me to be "a man of worth, as the ſtates of Spain for"merly experienced my father and uncle to "be, you may know there are many in Rome "who reſemble us; and that there are not a "people in the univerſe, whom you ought leſs "to deſire to be an enemy, or more a friend, "to you or yours." The youth, covered with bluſhes, and full of joy, embraced Scipio's hands, praying the immortal gods to reward him, as he himſelf was not capable to do it in the degree he himſelf deſired, or he deſerved. Then the parents and relations of the virgin were called. They had brought a great ſum of money to ranſom her. But ſeeing her reſtored without it, they began to beg Scipio to accept that ſum as a preſent; proteſting they would acknowledge it as a favour, as much as they did the reſtoring the virgin without injury offered to her. Scipio, unable to reſiſt their importunate ſolicitations, told them, he accepted it; and ordering it to be laid at his feet, thus addreſſed Allucius: "To the portion you are to receive from "your father-in-law, I add this, and beg you "would accept it as a nuptial preſent." So he deſired him to take up the gold, and keep it for himſelf. Tranſported with joy at the preſents and honours conferred on him, he returned home, and expatiated to his countrymen on the merits of Scipio. "There is "come amongſt us," ſaid he, "a young hero, "like the gods, who conquers all things, as "well by generoſity and beneficence, as by "arms." For this reaſon, having raiſed troops among his own ſubjects, he returned a few days after to Scipio with a body of 1400 horſe.

Livy.

§ 72. *The private Life of* ÆMILIUS SCIPIO.

The taking of Numantia, which terminated a war that difgraced the Roman name, completed Scipio's military exploits. But, in order to have a more perfect idea of his merit and character, it feems that, after having feen him at the head of armies, in the tumult of battles, and in the pomp of triumphs, it will not be loft labour to confider him in the repofe of a private life, in the midft of his friends, family, and houfehold. The truly great man ought to be fo in all things. The magiftrate, general, and prince, may conftrain themfelves, whilft they are in a manner exhibiting themfelves as fpectacles to the public, and appear quite different from what they really are. But reduced to themfelves, and without the witneffes who force them to wear the mafk, all their luftre, like the pomp of the theatre, often abandons them, and leaves little more to be feen in them than meannefs and narrownefs of mind.

Scipio did not depart from himfelf in any refpect. He was not like certain paintings, that are to be feen only at a diftance: he could not but gain by a nearer view. The excellent education which he had had, through the care of his father Paulus Æmilius, who had provided him with the moft learned mafters of thofe times, as well in polite learning as the fciences; and the inftructions he had received from Polybius, enabled him to fill up the vacant hours he had from public affairs profitably, and to fupport the leifure of a private life, with pleafure and dignity. This is the glorious teftimony given of him by an hiftorian: "Nobody knew better how to "mingle leifure and action, nor to ufe the "intervals of reft from public bufinefs with "more elegance and tafte. Divided between "arms and books, between the military "labours of the camp, and the peaceful oc-"cupations of the clofet, he either exercifed "his body in the dangers and fatigues of "war, or his mind in the ftudy of the "fciences *."

The firft Scipio Africanus ufed to fay, That he was never lefs idle, than when at leifure, nor lefs alone, than when alone. A fine faying, cries Cicero, and well worthy of that great man. And it fhews that, even when inactive, he was always employed; and that when alone, he knew how to converfe with himfelf. A very extraordinary difpofition in perfons accuftomed to motion and agitation, whom leifure and folitude, when they are reduced to them, plunge into a difguft for every thing, and fill with melancholy; fo that they are difpleafed in every thing with themfelves, and fink under the heavy burden of having nothing to do. This faying of the firft Scipio feems to me to fuit the fecond ftill better, who having the advantage of the other by being educated in a tafte for polite learning and the fciences, found in that a great refource againft the inconvenience of which we have been fpeaking. Befides which, having ufually Polybius and Panætius with him, even in the field, it is eafy to judge that his houfe was open, in times of peace, to all the learned. Every body knows, that the comedies of Terence, the moft accomplifhed work of that kind Rome ever produced, for natural elegance and beauties, are afcribed to him and Lælius, of whom we fhall foon fpeak. It was publicly enough reported, that they affifted that poet in the compofition of his pieces; and Terence himfelf makes it an

* Velleius Paterculus.

honour

honour to him in the prologue to the Adelphi. I ſhall undoubtedly not adviſe any body, and leaſt of all perſons of Scipio's rank, to write comedies. But on this occaſion, let us only conſider taſte in general for letters. Is there a more ingenious, a more affecting pleaſure, and one more worthy of a wiſe and virtuous man, I might perhaps add, or one more neceſſary to a military perſon, than that which reſults from reading works of wit, and from the converſation of the learned? Providence thought fit, according to the obſervation of a Pagan, that he ſhould be above thoſe trivial pleaſures, to which perſons without letters, knowledge, curioſity, and taſte for reading, are obliged to give themſelves up.

Another kind of pleaſure, ſtill more ſenſible, more warm, more natural, and more implanted in the heart of man, conſtituted the greateſt felicity of Scipio's life; this was that of friendſhip; a pleaſure ſeldom known by great perſons or princes, becauſe, generally loving only themſelves, they do not deſerve to have friends. However, this is the moſt grateful tie of human ſociety; ſo that the poet Ennius ſays with great reaſon, that to live without friends is not to live. Scipio had undoubtedly a great number of them, and thoſe very illuſtrious: but I ſhall ſpeak here only of Lælius, whoſe probity and prudence acquired him the ſurname of the Wiſe.

Never, perhaps, were two friends better ſuited to each other than thoſe great men. They were almoſt of the ſame age, and had the ſame inclination, benevolence of mind, taſte for learning of all kinds, principles of government, and zeal for the public good. Scipio, no doubt, took place in point of military glory; but Lælius did not want merit of that kind; and Cicero tells us, that he ſignalized himſelf very much in the war with Viriathus. As to the talents of the mind, the ſuperiority, in reſpect of eloquence, ſeems to have been given to Lælius; though Cicero does not agree that it was due to him, and ſays, that Lælius's ſtyle ſavoured more of the ancient manner, and had ſomething leſs agreeable in it than that of Scipio.

Let us hear Lælius himſelf (that is, the words Cicero puts into his mouth) upon the ſtrict union which ſubſiſted between Scipio and him. "As for me," ſays Lælius, "of all the gifts of nature or fortune, "there are none, I think, comparable to the "happineſs of having Scipio for my friend. "I found in our friendſhip a perfect con-"formity of ſentiments in reſpect to public "affairs; an inexhauſtible fund of counſels "and ſupports in private life; with a tran-"quillity and delight not to be expreſſed. I "never gave Scipio the leaſt offence, to my "knowledge, nor ever heard a word eſcape "him that did not pleaſe me. We had but "one houſe, and one table at our common "expence, the frugality of which was equally "the taſte of both. In war, in travelling, "in the country, we were always together. "I do not mention our ſtudies, and the at-"tention of us both always to learn ſome-"thing; this was the employment of all our "leiſure hours, removed from the ſight and "commerce of the world."

Is there any thing comparable to a friendſhip like that which Lælius has juſt deſcribed? What a conſolation is it to have a ſecond ſelf, to whom we have nothing ſecret, and in whoſe heart we may pour out our own with perfect effuſion! Could we taſte proſperity ſo ſenſibly, if we had no one to ſhare in our joy with us? And what a relief is it in adverſity, and the accidents of life, to have a friend ſtill more affected with them than ourſelves! What highly exalts the value of the friendſhip we ſpeak of, was its not being founded at all upon intereſt, but ſolely upon eſteem for each other's virtues. "What "occaſion," ſays Lælius, "could Scipio "have of me? Undoubtedly none; nor I "of him. But my attachment to him was "the effect of my high eſteem and admira- "tion of his virtues; and his to me aroſe "from the favourable idea of my character "and manners. This friendſhip increaſed "afterwards upon both ſides, by habit and com- "merce. We both, indeed, derived great ad- "vantages from it; but thoſe were not our "view, when we began to love each other."

I cannot place the famous embaſſy of Scipio Africanus into the Eaſt and Egypt, better than here; we ſhall ſee the ſame taſte of ſimplicity and modeſty, as we have juſt been repreſenting in his private life, ſhine out in it. It was a maxim with the Romans, frequently to ſend ambaſſadors to their allies, to take cognizance of their affairs, and to accommodate their differences. It was with this view that three illuſtrious perſons, P. Scipio Africanus, Sp. Mummius, and L. Metellus, were ſent into Egypt, where Ptolemy Phyſcon then reigned, the moſt cruel tyrant mentioned in hiſtory. They had orders to go from thence to Syria, which the indolence, and afterwards the captivity of Demetrius Nicanor amongſt the Parthians, made a prey to troubles, factions, and revolts. They were next to viſit Aſia Minor, and Greece; to inſpect into the affairs of thoſe countries; to inquire in what manner the treaties made with the Romans were obſerved; and to remedy, as far as poſſible, all the diſorders that ſhould come to their knowledge. They acquitted themſelves with ſo much equity, wiſdom, and ability, and did ſuch great ſervices to thoſe to whom they were ſent, in re-eſtabliſhing order amongſt them, and in accommodating their differences, that, when they returned to Rome, ambaſſadors arrived there from all the parts in which they had been, to thank the ſenate for having ſent perſons of ſuch great merit to them, whoſe wiſdom and goodneſs they could not ſufficiently commend.

The firſt place to which they went, according to their inſtructions, was Alexandria. The king received them with great magnificence. As for them, they affected it ſo little, that at their entry, Scipio, who was the richeſt and moſt powerful perſon of Rome, had only one friend, the philoſopher Panætius, with him, and five domeſtics. His victories, ſays an ancient writer, and not his attendants, were conſidered; and his perſonal virtues and qualities were eſteemed in him, and not the glitter of gold and ſilver.

Though, during their whole ſtay in Egypt, the king cauſed their table to be covered with the moſt exquiſite proviſions of every kind, they never touched any but the moſt ſimple and common, deſpiſing all the reſt, which only ſerve to ſoften the mind and enervate the body.—But, on ſuch occaſions, ought not the ambaſſadors of ſo powerful a ſtate as Rome to have ſuſtained its reputation of majeſty in a foreign nation, by appearing in public with a numerous train and magnificent equipages? This was not the taſte of the Romans, that is, of the people that, among all the nations of the earth, thought the moſt juſtly of true greatneſs and ſolid glory. *Rollin.*

END OF THE SECOND BOOK.

THE PROSE EPITOME; OR, ELEGANT EXTRACTS ABRIDGED, &c.

BOOK III. ORATIONS, CHARACTERS, &c.

§ 1. HAMLET *to the Players.*

SPEAK the ſpeech, I pray you, as I pronounced it to you, trippingly on the tongue. But if you mouth it, as many of our players do, I had as lieve the town crier had ſpoke my lines. And do not ſaw the air too much with your hand; but uſe all gently: for in the very torrent, tempeſt, and, as I may ſay, whirlwind of your paſſion, you muſt acquire and beget a temperance that may give it ſmoothneſs. Oh! it offends me to the ſoul, to hear a robuſtous periwig-pated fellow tear a paſſion to tatters, to very rags, to ſplit the ears of the groundlings; who (for the moſt part) are capable of nothing, but inexplicable dumb ſhews and noiſe. Pray you, avoid it.

Be not too tame neither; but let your own diſcretion be your tutor. Suit the action to the word, the word to the action; with this ſpecial obſervance, that you o'erſtep not the modeſty of nature; for any thing ſo overdone, is from the purpoſe of playing; whoſe end is—to hold, as 'twere, the mirror up to nature; to ſhew Virtue her own feature, Scorn her own image, and the very age and body of the time his form and preſſure. Now, this overdone, or come tardy off, though it make the unſkilful laugh, cannot but make the judicious grieve; the cenſure of one of which muſt, in your allowance, o'erweigh a whole theatre of others. Oh! there be players that I have ſeen play, and heard others praiſe, and that highly, that, neither having the accent of Chriſtian, nor the gait of Chriſtian, Pagan, nor man, have ſo ſtrutted and bellowed, that I have thought ſome of nature's journeymen had made them, and not made them well; they imitated humanity ſo abominably.

And let thoſe that play your clowns, ſpeak no more than is ſet down for them: for there be of them that will themſelves laugh, to ſet on ſome quantity of barren ſpectators to laugh too; though, in the mean time, ſome neceſſary queſtion of the play be then to be conſidered:—that's villainous, and ſhews a moſt pitiful ambition in the fool that uſes it.

Shakeſpeare.

§ 2. *The Character of* MARIUS.

The birth of Marius was obſcure, though ſome call it equeſtrian, and his education

wholly

wholly in camps; where he learnt the first rudiments of war, under the greatest master of that age, the younger Scipio, who destroyed Carthage; till by long service, distinguished valour, and a peculiar hardiness and patience of discipline, he advanced himself gradually through all the steps of military honour, with the reputation of a brave and complete soldier. The obscurity of his extraction, which depressed him with the nobility, made him the greater favourite of the people; who, on all occasions of danger, thought him the only man fit to be trusted with their lives and fortunes; or to have the command of a difficult and desperate war: and in truth, he twice delivered them from the most desperate, with which they had ever been threatened by a foreign enemy. Scipio, from the observation of his martial talents, while he had yet but an inferior command in the army, gave a kind of prophetic testimony of his future glory; for being asked by some of his officers, who were supping with him at Numantia, what general the republic would have, in case of any accident to himself? That man, replied he, pointing to Marius at the bottom of the table. In the field he was cautious and provident; and while he was watching the most favourable opportunities of action, affected to take all his measures from augurs and diviners; nor ever gave battle, till by pretended omens and divine admonitions he had inspired his soldiers with a confidence of victory; so that his enemies dreaded him as something more than mortal; and both friends and foes believed him to act always by a peculiar impulse and direction from the gods. His merit however was wholly military, void of every accomplishment of learning, which he openly affected to despise; so that Arpinum had the singular felicity to produce the most glorious contemner, as well as the most illustrious improver, of the arts and eloquence of Rome *. He made no figure, therefore, in the gown, nor had any other way of sustaining his authority in the city, than by cherishing the natural jealousy between the senate and the people; that by this declared enmity to the one he might always be at the head of the other; whose favour he managed, not with any view to the public good, for he had nothing in him of the statesman or the patriot, but to the advancement of his private interest and glory. In short, he was crafty, cruel, covetous, and perfidious; of a temper and talents greatly serviceable abroad, but turbulent and dangerous at home; an implacable enemy to the nobles, ever seeking occasions to mortify them, and ready to sacrifice the republic, which he had saved, to his ambition and revenge. After a life spent in the perpetual toils of foreign or domestic wars, he died at last in his bed, in a good old age, and in his seventh consulship; an honour that no Roman before him ever attained. *Middleton.*

§ 3. Romulus *to the People of Rome, after building the City.*

If all the strength of cities lay in the height of their ramparts, or the depth of their ditches, we should have great reason to be in fear for that which we have now built. But are there in reality any walls too high to be scaled by a valiant enemy? and of what use are ramparts in intestine divisions? They may serve for a defence against sudden incursions from abroad; but it is by courage and prudence chiefly, that the invasions of foreign enemies are repelled; and by unanimity, so-

* Arpinum was also the native city of Cicero.

briety,

briety, and juftice, that domeftic feditions are prevented. Cities fortified by the ftrongeft bulwarks have been often feen to yield to force from without, or to tumults from within. An exact military difcipline, and a fteady obfervance of civil polity, are the fureft barriers againft thefe evils.

But there is ftill another point of great importance to be confidered. The profperity of fome rifing colonies, and the fpeedy ruin of others, have in a great meafure been owing to their form of government. Were there but one manner of ruling ftates and cities that could make them happy, the choice would not be difficult; but I have learnt, that of the various forms of government among the Greeks and Barbarians, there are three which are highly extolled by thofe who have experienced them; and yet, that no one of thefe is in all refpects perfect, but each of them has fome innate and incurable defect. Chufe you, then, in what manner this city fhall be governed. Shall it be by one man? fhall it be by a felect number of the wifeft among us? or fhall the legiflative power be in the people? As for me, I fhall fubmit to whatever form of adminiftration you fhall pleafe to eftablifh. As I think myfelf not unworthy to command, fo neither am I unwilling to obey. Your having chofen me to be the leader of this colony, and your calling the city after my name, are honours fufficient to content me; honours of which, living or dead, I never can be deprived. *Hooke.*

§ 4. *The Character of* SYLLA.

Sylla died after he had laid down the dictatorfhip, and reftored liberty to the republic, and, with an uncommon greatnefs of mind, lived many months as a private fenator, and with perfect fecurity, in that city where he had exercifed the moft bloody tyranny: but nothing was thought to be greater in his character, than that, during the three years in which the Marians were mafters of Italy, he neither diffembled his refolution of purfuing them by arms, nor neglected the war which he had upon his hands; but thought it his duty, firft to chaftife a foreign enemy, before he took his revenge upon citizens. His family was noble and patrician, which yet, through the indolency of his anceftors, had made no figure in the republic for many generations, and was almoft funk into obfcurity, till he produced it again into light, by afpiring to the honours of the ftate. He was a lover and patron of polite letters, having been carefully inftituted himfelf in all the learning of Greece and Rome; but from a peculiar gaiety of temper, and fondnefs for the company of mimics and players, was drawn, when young, into a life of luxury and pleafure; fo that when he was fent quæftor to Marius, in the Jugurthine war, Marius complained, that in fo rough and defperate a fervice chance had given him fo foft and delicate a quæftor. But, whether roufed by the example, or ftung by the reproach of his general, he behaved himfelf in that charge with the greateft vigour and courage, fuffering no man to outdo him in any part of military duty or labour, making himfelf equal and familiar even to the loweft of the foldiers, and obliging them by all his good offices and his money; fo that he foon acquired the favour of his army, with the character of a brave and fkilful commander; and lived to drive Marius himfelf, banifhed and profcribed, into that very province where he had been contemned by him at firft as his quæftor. He had a wonderful faculty of concealing his paffions and purpoſes; and was ſo different from himſelf in different circumſtances, that he ſeemed as it were to be two men in one: no man was ever more mild and moderate before victory; none more bloody and cruel after it. In war, he practiſed the ſame art that he had ſeen ſo ſucceſsful to Marius, of raiſing a kind of enthuſiaſm and contempt of danger in his army, by the forgery of auſpices and divine admonitions; for which end, he carried always about with him a little ſtatue of Apollo, taken from the temple of Delphi; and whenever he had reſolved to give battle, uſed to embrace it in ſight of the ſoldiers, and beg the ſpeedy confirmation of its promiſes to him. From an uninterrupted courſe of ſucceſs and proſperity, he aſſumed a ſurname, unknown before to the Romans, of Felix, or the Fortunate; and would have been fortunate indeed, ſays Velleius, if his life had ended with his victories. Pliny calls it a wicked title, drawn from the blood and oppreſſion of his country; for which poſterity would think him more unfortunate, even than thoſe whom he had put to death. He had one felicity, however, peculiar to himſelf, of being the only man in hiſtory, in whom the odium of the moſt barbarous cruelties was extinguiſhed by the glory of his great acts. Cicero, though he had a good opinion of his cauſe, yet deteſted the inhumanity of his victory, and never ſpeaks of him with reſpect, nor of his government but as a proper tyranny; calling him, "a maſter of three moſt peſ-"tilent vices, luxury, avarice, cruelty." He was the firſt of his family whoſe dead body was burnt: for, having ordered Marius's remains to be taken out of his grave, and thrown into the river Anio, he was apprehenſive of the ſame inſult upon his own, if left to the uſual way of burial. A little before his death, he made his own epitaph, the ſum of which was, "that no man had "ever gone beyond him, in doing good to "his friends, or hurt to his enemies."

Middleton.

§ 5. HANNIBAL *to* SCIPIO AFRICANUS *at their Interview preceding the Battle of Zama.*

Since fate has ſo ordained it, that I, who began the war, and who have been ſo often on the point of ending it by a compleat conqueſt, ſhould now come of my own motion to aſk a peace; I am glad that it is of you, Scipio, I have the fortune to aſk it. Nor will this be among the leaſt of your glories, that Hannibal, victorious over ſo many Roman generals, ſubmitted at laſt to you.

I could wiſh, that our fathers and we had confined our ambition within the limits which nature ſeems to have preſcribed to it; the ſhores of Africa, and the ſhores of Italy. The gods did not give us that mind. On both ſides we have been ſo eager after foreign poſſeſſions, as to put our own to the hazard of war. Rome and Carthage have had, each in her turn, the enemy at her gates. But ſince errors paſt may be more eaſily blamed than corrected, let it now be the work of you and me to put an end, if poſſible, to the obſtinate contention. For my own part, my years, and the experience I have had of the inſtability of fortune, inclines me to leave nothing to her determination, which reaſon can decide. But much I fear, Scipio, that your youth, your want of the like experience, your uninterrupted ſucceſs, may render you averſe from the thoughts of peace. He whom fortune has never failed, rarely reflects upon her inconſtancy. Yet, without recurring to former examples,

amples, my own may perhaps ſuffice to teach you moderation. I am that ſame Hannibal, who, after my victory at Cannæ, became maſter of the greateſt part of your country, and deliberated with myſelf what fate I ſhould decree to Italy and Rome. And now—ſee the change! Here, in Africa, I am come to treat with a Roman, for my own preſervation and my country's. Such are the ſports of fortune. Is ſhe then to be truſted becauſe ſhe ſmiles? An advantageous peace is preferable to the hope of victory. The one is in your own power, the other at the pleaſure of the gods. Should you prove victorious, it would add little to your own glory, or the glory of your country; if vanquiſhed, you loſe in one hour all the honour and reputation you have been ſo many years acquiring. But what is my aim in all this?—that you ſhould content yourſelf with our ceſſion of Spain, Sicily, Sardinia, and all the iſlands between Italy and Africa. A peace on theſe conditions will, in my opinion, not only ſecure the future tranquillity of Carthage, but be ſufficiently glorious for you, and for the Roman name. And do not tell me, that ſome of our citizens dealt fraudulently with you in the late treaty—it is I, Hannibal, that now aſk a peace: I aſk it, becauſe I think it expedient for my country; and, thinking it expedient, I will inviolably maintain it. *Hooke.*

§ 6. Scipio's *Anſwer.*

I knew very well, Hannibal, that it was the hope of your return which emboldened the Carthaginians to break the truce with us, and to lay aſide all thoughts of a peace, when it was juſt upon the point of being concluded; and your preſent propoſal is a proof of it. You retrench from their conceſſions every thing but what we are, and have been long, poſſeſſed of. But as it is your care that your fellow-citizens ſhould have the obligations to you of being eaſed from a great part of their burden, ſo it ought to be mine that they draw no advantage from their perfidiouſneſs. Nobody is more ſenſible than I am of the weakneſs of man, and the power of fortune, and that whatever we enterprize is ſubject to a thouſand chances. If, before the Romans paſſed into Africa, you had of your own accord quitted Italy, and made the offers you now make, I believe they would not have been rejected. But as you have been forced out of Italy, and we are maſters here of the open country, the ſituation of things is much altered. And, what is chiefly to be conſidered, the Carthaginians, by the late treaty which we entered into at their requeſt, were, over and above what you offer, to have reſtored to us our priſoners without ranſom, delivered up their ſhips of war, paid us five thouſand talents, and to have given hoſtages for the performance of all. The ſenate accepted theſe conditions, but Carthage failed on her part; Carthage deceived us. What then is to be done? Are the Carthaginians to be releaſed from the moſt important articles of the treaty, as a reward of their breach of faith? No, certainly. If, to the conditions before agreed upon, you had added ſome new articles to our advantage, there would have been matter of reference to the Roman people; but when, inſtead of adding, you retrench, there is no room for deliberation. The Carthaginians therefore muſt ſubmit to us at diſcretion, or muſt vanquiſh us in battle. *Ibid.*

§ 7. *The Character of* Pompey.

Pompey had early acquired the ſurname of the Great, by that ſort of merit which, from the

the conftitution of the republic, neceffarily made him great; a fame and fuccefs in war, fuperior to what Rome had ever known in the moft celebrated of her generals. He had triumphed, at three feveral times, over the three different parts of the known world, Europe, Afia, Africa; and by his victories had almoft doubled the extent, as well as the revenues, of the Roman dominion; for, as he declared to the people on his return from the Mithridatic war, he had found the leffer Afia the boundary, but left it the middle of their empire. He was about fix years older than Cæfar; and while Cæfar, immerfed in pleafures, oppreffed with debts, and fufpected by all honeft men, was hardly able to fhew his head, Pompey was flourifhing in the height of power and glory; and, by the confent of all parties, placed at the head of the republic. This was the poft that his ambition feemed to aim at, to be the firft man in Rome; the leader, not the tyrant of his country; for he more than once had it in his power to have made himfelf the mafter of it without any rifk, if his virtue, or his phlegm at leaft, had not reftrained him: but he lived in a perpetual expectation of receiving from the gift of the people, what he did not care to feize by force; and, by fomenting the diforders of the city, hoped to drive them to the neceffity of creating him dictator. It is an obfervation of all the hiftorians, that while Cæfar made no difference of power, whether it was conferred or ufurped, whether over thofe who loved, or thofe who feared him; Pompey feemed to value none but what was offered; nor to have any defire to govern, but with the good-will of the governed. What leifure he found from his wars, he employed in the ftudy of polite letters, and efpecially of eloquence, in which he would have acquired great fame, if his genius had not drawn him to the more dazzling glory of arms; yet he pleaded feveral caufes with applaufe, in the defence of his friends and clients; and fome of them in conjunction with Cicero. His language was copious and elevated; his fentiments juft; his voice fweet; his action noble, and full of dignity. But his talents were better formed for arms than the gown; for though in both he obferved the fame difcipline, a perpetual modefty, temperance, and gravity of outward behaviour; yet in the licence of camps the example was more rare and ftriking. His perfon was extremely graceful, and imprinting refpect; yet with an air of referved haughtinefs, which became the general better than the citizen. His parts were plaufible, rather than great; fpecious, rather than penetrating; and his views of politics but narrow; for his chief inftrument of governing was diffimulation; yet he had not always the art to conceal his real fentiments. As he was a better foldier than a ftatefman, fo what he gained in the camp he ufually loft in the city; and though adored when abroad, was often affronted and mortified at home, till the imprudent oppofition of the fenate drove him to that alliance with Craffus and Cæfar, which proved fatal both to himfelf and the republic. He took in thefe two, not as the partners, but the minifters rather of his power; that by giving them fome fhare with him, he might make his own authority uncontrollable: he had no reafon to apprehend that they could ever prove his rivals; fince neither of them had any credit or character of that kind which alone could raife them above the laws; a fuperior fame and experience in war, with the militia of the empire at their devotion: all this was purely his own; till, by cherifhing Cæfar, and throwing into his hands the only thing

thing which he wanted, arms, and military command, he made him at last too strong for himself, and never began to fear him till it was too late. Cicero warmly dissuaded both his union and his breach with Cæsar; and after the rupture, as warmly still, the thought of giving him battle: if any of these counsels had been followed, Pompey had preserved his life and honour, and the republic its liberty. But he was urged to his fate by a natural superstition, and attention to those vain auguries, with which he was flattered by all the Haruspices: he had seen the same temper in Marius and Sylla, and observed the happy effects of it: but they assumed it only out of policy, he out of principle: they used it to animate their soldiers, when they had found a probable opportunity of fighting: but he, against all prudence and probability, was encouraged by it to fight to his own ruin. He saw his mistakes at last, when it was out of his power to correct them; and in his wretched flight from Pharsalia, was forced to confess, that he had trusted too much to his hopes; and that Cicero had judged better, and seen farther into things than he. The resolution of seeking refuge in Egypt finished the sad catastrophe of this great man: the father of the reigning prince had been highly obliged to him for his protection at Rome, and restoration to his kingdom: and the son had sent a considerable fleet to his assistance in the present war: but in this ruin of his fortunes, what gratitude was there to be expected from a court governed by eunuchs and mercenary Greeks? all whose politics turned, not on the honour of the king, but the establishment of their own power; which was likely to be eclipsed by the admission of Pompey. How happy had it been for him to have died in that sickness, when all Italy was putting up vows and prayers for his safety! or, if he had fallen by the chance of war, on the plains of Pharsalia, in the defence of his country's liberty, he had died still glorious, though unfortunate; but, as if he had been reserved for an example of the instability of human greatness, he, who a few days before commanded kings and consuls, and all the noblest of Rome, was sentenced to die by a council of slaves; murdered by a base deserter; cast out naked and headless on the Egyptian strand; and when the whole earth, as Velleius says, had scarce been sufficient for his victories, could not find a spot upon it at last for a grave. His body was burnt on the shore by one of his freedmen, with the planks of an old fishing-boat; and his ashes, being conveyed to Rome, were deposited privately, by his wife Cornelia, in a vault by his Alban villa. The Egyptians however raised a monument to him on the place, and adorned it with figures of brass, which being defaced afterwards by time, and buried almost in sand and rubbish, was sought out, and restored by the emperor Hadrian.

Middleton.

§ 8. *Submission; Complaint; Intreating—The Speech of* SENECA, *the Philosopher, to* NERO, *complaining of the Envy of his Enemies, and requesting the Emperor to reduce him back to his former narrow Circumstances, that he might no longer be an Object of their Malignity.*

May it please the imperial majesty of Cæsar favourably to accept the humble submissions and grateful acknowledgments of the weak though faithful guide of his youth.

It is now a great many years since I first had the honour of attending your imperial majesty as preceptor. And your bounty has rewarded my labours with such affluence, as has

has drawn upon me, what I had reaſon to expect, the envy of many of thoſe perſons, who are always ready to preſcribe to their prince where to beſtow, and where to withhold his favours. It is well known, that your illuſtrious anceſtor, Auguſtus, beſtowed on his deſerving favourites, Agrippa and Mæcenas, honours and emoluments, ſuitable to the dignity of the benefactor, and to the ſervices of the receivers: nor has his conduct been blamed. My employment about your imperial majeſty has, indeed, been purely domeſtic: I have neither headed your armies, nor aſſiſted at your councils. But you know, Sir, (though there are ſome who do not ſeem to attend to it) that a prince may be ſerved in different ways, ſome more, others leſs conſpicuous; and that the latter may be to him as valuable as the former.

"But what!" ſay my enemies, "ſhall a "private perſon, of equeſtrian rank, and a "provincial by birth, be advanced to an "equality with the patricians? Shall an upſtart, of no name nor family, rank with "thoſe who can, by the ſtatues which make "the ornament of their palaces, reckon backward a line of anceſtors, long enough to "tire out the faſti *? Shall a philoſopher "who has written for others precepts of moderation, and contempt of all that is external, himſelf live in affluence and luxury? "Shall he purchaſe eſtates, and lay out money at intereſt? Shall he build palaces, "plant gardens, and adorn a country at his "own expence, and for his own pleaſure?"

Cæſar has given royally, as became imperial magnificence. Seneca has received what his prince beſtowed; nor did he ever aſk: he is only guilty of—not refuſing. Cæſar's rank places him above the reach of invidious malignity. Seneca is not, nor can be, high enough to deſpiſe the envious. As the overloaded ſoldier, or traveller, would be glad to be relieved of his burden, ſo I, in this laſt ſtage of the journey of life, now that I find myſelf unequal to the lighteſt cares, beg, that Cæſar would kindly eaſe me of the trouble of my unwieldy wealth. I beſeech him to reſtore to the imperial treaſury, from whence it came, what is to me ſuperfluous and cumbrous. The time and the attention, which I am now obliged to beſtow upon my villa and my gardens, I ſhall be glad to apply to the regulation of my mind. Cæſar is in the flower of life; long may he be equal to the toils of government! His goodneſs will grant to his worn-out ſervant leave to retire. It will not be derogatory from Cæſar's greatneſs to have it ſaid, that he beſtowed favours on ſome, who, ſo far from being intoxicated with them, ſhewed—that they could be happy, when (at their own requeſt) diveſted of them.

Corn. Tacit.

§ 9. *Speech of* Charidemus, *an* Athenian *Exile at the Court of* Darius, *on being aſked his Opinion of the warlike Preparations making by that Prince againſt* Alexander.

Perhaps your Majeſty may not bear the truth from the mouth of a Grecian, and an exile: and if I do not declare it now, I never will, perhaps I may never have another opportunity.—Your Majeſty's numerous army, drawn from various nations, and which unpeoples the eaſt, may ſeem formidable to the neighbouring countries. The gold, the purple, and the ſplendor of arms, which ſtrike the

* The faſti, or calendars, or, if you pleaſe, almanacs, of the ancients, had, as our almanacs, tables of kings, conſuls, &c.

the eyes of beholders, make a ſhow which ſurpaſſes the imagination of all who have not ſeen it. The Macedonian army, with which your Majeſty's forces are going to contend, is, on the contrary, grim, and horrid of aſpect, and clad in iron. The irreſiſtible phalanx is a body of men who, in the field of battle, fear no onſet, being practiſed to hold together, man to man, ſhield to ſhield, and ſpear to ſpear; ſo that a brazen wall might as ſoon be broke through. In advancing, in wheeling to right or left, in attacking, in every exerciſe of arms, they act as one man. They anſwer the ſlighteſt ſign from the commander, as if his ſoul animated the whole army. Every ſoldier has a knowledge of war ſufficient for a general. And this diſcipline, by which the Macedonian army is become ſo formidable, was firſt eſtabliſhed, and has been all along kept up, by a fixed contempt of what your Majeſty's troops are ſo vain of, I mean gold and ſilver. The bare earth ſerves them for beds. Whatever will ſatisfy nature, is their luxury. Their repoſe is always ſhorter than the night. Your Majeſty may, therefore, judge, whether the Theſſalian, Acarnanian, and Ætolian cavalry, and the Macedonian phalanx—an army that has, in ſpite of all oppoſition, over-run half the world—are to be repelled by a multitude (however numerous) armed with ſlings, and ſtakes hardened at the points by fire. To be upon equal terms with Alexander, your Majeſty ought to have an army compoſed of the ſame ſort of troops: and they are no where to be had, but in the ſame countries which produced thoſe conquerors of the world.—It is therefore my opinion, that, if your Majeſty were to apply the gold and ſilver, which now ſo ſuperfluouſly adorns your men, to the purpoſe of hiring an army from Greece, to contend with Greeks, you might have ſome chance for ſucceſs; otherwiſe I ſee no reaſon to expect any thing elſe, than that your army ſhould be defeated, as all the others have been who have encountered the irreſiſtible Macedonians.

Q. Curtius.

§ 10. *The Character of* JULIUS CÆSAR.

Cæſar was endowed with every great and noble quality, that could exalt human nature, and give a man the aſcendant in ſociety: formed to excel in peace, as well as war; provident in council; fearleſs in action; and executing what he had reſolved with an amazing celerity: generous beyond meaſure to his friends; placable to his enemies; and for parts, learning, eloquence, ſcarce inferior to any man. His orations were admired for two qualities, which are ſeldom found together, ſtrength and elegance; Cicero ranks him among the greateſt orators that Rome ever bred; and Quinctilian ſays, that he ſpoke with the ſame force with which he fought; and if he had devoted himſelf to the bar, would have been the only man capable of rivalling Cicero. Nor was he a maſter only of the politer arts; but converſant alſo with the moſt abſtruſe and critical parts of learning; and, among other works which he publiſhed, addreſſed two books to Cicero, on the analogy of language, or the art of ſpeaking and writing correctly. He was a moſt liberal patron of wit and learning, whereſoever they were found; and out of his love of thoſe talents, would readily pardon thoſe who had employed them againſt himſelf: rightly judging, that by making ſuch men his friends, he ſhould draw praiſes from the ſame fountain from which he had been aſperſed. His capital paſſions were ambition, and love of pleaſure; which he indulged in their turns to the greateſt exceſs: yet the firſt was always predominant; to which he could eaſily ſacrifice all

all the charms of the second, and draw pleasure even from toils and dangers, when they ministered to his glory. For he thought Tyranny, as Cicero says, the greatest of goddesses; and had frequently in his mouth a verse of Euripedes, which expressed the image of his soul, that if right and justice were ever to be violated, they were to be violated for the sake of reigning. This was the chief end and purpose of his life; the scheme that he had formed from his early youth; so that, as Cato truly declared of him, he came with sobriety and meditation to the subversion of the republic. He used to say, that there were two things necessary, to acquire and to support power — soldiers and money; which yet depended mutually upon each other: with money therefore he provided soldiers, and with soldiers extorted money; and was, of all men, the most rapacious in plundering both friends and foes; sparing neither prince, nor state, nor temple, nor even private persons, who were known to possess any share of treasure. His great abilities would necessarily have made him one of the first citizens of Rome; but, disdaining the condition of a subject, he could never rest till he made himself a monarch. In acting this last part, his usual prudence seemed to fail him; as if the height to which he was mounted, had turned his head, and made him giddy: for, by a vain ostentation of his power, he destroyed the stability of it: and as men shorten life by living too fast, so by an intemperance of reigning, he brought his reign to a violent end. *Middleton.*

§ 11. CALISTHENES'*s Reproof of* CLEON'*s Flattery to* ALEXANDER, *on whom he had proposed to confer Divinity by Vote.*

If the king were present, Cleon, there would be no need of my answering to what you have just proposed: he would himself reprove you for endeavouring to draw him into an imitation of foreign absurdities, and for bringing envy upon him by such unmanly flattery. As he is absent, I take upon me to tell you, in his name, that no praise is lasting, but what is rational; and that you do what you can to lessen his glory, instead of adding to it. Heroes have never, among us, been deified till after their death; and, whatever may be your way of thinking, Cleon, for my part, I wish the king may not, for many years to come, obtain that honour.

You have mentioned, as precedents of what you propose, Hercules and Bacchus. Do you imagine, Cleon, that they were deified over a cup of wine? and are you and I qualified to make gods? Is the king, our sovereign, to receive his divinity from you and me, who are his subjects? First try your power, whether you can make a king. It is, surely, easier to make a king than a god; to give an earthly dominion, than a throne in heaven. I only wish that the gods may have heard, without offence, the arrogant proposal you have made of adding one to their number; and that they may still be so propitious to us, as to grant the continuance of that success to our affairs with which they have hitherto favoured us. For my part, I am not ashamed of my country; nor do I approve of our adopting the rites of foreign nations, or learning from them how we ought to reverence our kings. To receive laws or rules of conduct from them, what is it but to confess ourselves inferior to them? *Q. Curtius.*

§ 12. *The Character of* CATO.

If we consider the character of Cato without prejudice, he was certainly a great and worthy man; a friend to truth, virtue, liberty; yet, falsely measuring all duty by the abſurd rigour of the ſtoical rule, he was generally diſappointed of the end which he ſought by it, the happineſs both of his private and public life. In his private conduct he was ſevere, morofe, inexorable; baniſhing all the ſofter affections, as natural enemies to juſtice, and as ſuggeſting falſe motives of acting, from favour, clemency, and compaſſion: in public affairs he was the ſame; had but one rule of policy, to adhere to what was right, without regard to time or circumſtances, or even to a force that could control him; for, inſtead of managing the power of the great, ſo as to mitigate the ill, or extract any good from it, he was urging it always to acts of violence by a perpetual defiance; ſo that, with the beſt intentions in the world, he often did great harm to the republic. This was his general behaviour; yet from ſome particular facts, it appears that his ſtrength of mind was not always impregnable, but had its weak places of pride, ambition, and party zeal; which, when managed and flattered to a certain point, would betray him ſometimes into meaſures contrary to his ordinary rule of right and truth. The laſt act of his life was agreeable to his nature and philoſophy: when he could no longer be what he had been; or when the ills of life overbalanced the good, which, by the principles of his ſect, was a juſt cauſe for dying; he put an end to his life with a ſpirit and reſolution which would make one imagine, that he was glad to have found an occaſion of dying in his proper character. On the whole, his life was rather admirable than amiable; fit to be praiſed, rather than imitated. *Middleton.*

§ 13. Brutus's *Speech in Vindication of* Cæsar's *Murder.*

Romans, countrymen, and lovers!—Hear me, for my cauſe; and be ſilent, that you may hear. Believe me, for mine honour; and have reſpect to mine honour, that you may believe. Cenſure me, in your wiſdom; and awake your ſenſes, that you may the better judge.

If there be any in this aſſembly, any dear friend of Cæſar's, to him I ſay, that Brutus's love to Cæſar was no leſs than his. If, then, that friend demand why Brutus roſe againſt Cæſar? this is my anſwer—Not that I loved Cæſar leſs, but that I loved Rome more. Had you rather Cæſar were, and die all ſlaves; than that Cæſar were dead, to live all freemen? As Cæſar loved me, I weep for him; as he was fortunate, I rejoice at it; as he was valiant, I honour him; but, as he was ambitious, I ſlew him. There are tears for his love, joy for his fortune, honour for his valour, and death for his ambition. Who's here ſo baſe, that would be a bond-man?—If any, ſpeak; for him have I offended. Who's here ſo rude, that would not be a Roman?—If any, ſpeak; for him have I offended. Who's here ſo vile, that will not love his country?—If any, ſpeak; for him have I offended. I pauſe for a reply.——

None?—Then none have I offended. I have done no more to Cæſar, than you ſhould do to Brutus. The queſtion of his death is inrolled in the capitol: his glory not extenuated, wherein he was worthy; nor his offences inforced, for which he ſuffered death.

Here comes his body, mourned by Mark Antony; who, though he had no hand in his death, ſhall receive the benefit of his dying, a place in the common-wealth; as, which of you ſhall not? With this I depart —That, as I ſlew my beſt lover for the good of Rome, I have the ſame dagger for myſelf, when

when it shall please my country to need my death. *Shakespeare.*

§ 14. *A Comparison of* CÆSAR *with* CATO.

As to their extraction, years, and eloquence, they were pretty nigh equal. Both of them had the same greatness of mind, both the same degree of glory, but in different ways: Cæsar was celebrated for his great bounty and generosity; Cato for his unsullied integrity: the former became renowned by his humanity and compassion; an austere severity heightened the dignity of the latter. Cæsar acquired glory by a liberal, compassionate, and forgiving temper; as did Cato, by never bestowing any thing. In the one, the miserable found a sanctuary; in the other, the guilty met with a certain destruction. Cæsar was admired for an easy yielding temper; Cato for his immoveable firmness. Cæsar, in a word, had formed himself for a laborious active life; was intent upon promoting the interest of his friends, to the neglect of his own; and refused to grant nothing that was worth accepting: what he desired for himself, was to have sovereign command, to be at the head of armies, and engaged in new wars, in order to display his military talents. As for Cato, his only study was moderation, regular conduct, and, above all rigorous severity: he did not vie with the rich in riches, nor in faction with the factious; but, taking a nobler aim, he contended in bravery with the brave, in modesty with the modest, in integrity with the upright; and was more desirous to be virtuous, than appear so: so that the less he courted fame, the more it followed him. *Sallust, by Mr. Rose.*

§ 15. CAIUS MARIUS *to the* ROMANS, *shewing the Absurdity of their hesitating to confer on him the Rank of General, merely on Account of his Extraction.*

It is but too common, my countrymen, to observe a material difference between the behaviour of those who stand candidates for places of power and trust, before and after their obtaining them. They solicit them in one manner, and execute them in another. They set out with a great appearance of activity, humility, and moderation; and they quickly fall into sloth, pride, and avarice.—It is, undoubtedly, no easy matter to discharge, to the general satisfaction, the duty of supreme commander, in troublesome times. I am, I hope, duly sensible of the importance of the office I propose to take upon me for the service of my country. To carry on, with effect, an expensive war, and yet be frugal of the public money; to oblige those to serve, whom it may be delicate to offend; to conduct, at the same time, a complicated variety of operations; to concert measures at home, answerable to the state of things abroad; and to gain every valuable end, in spite of opposition from the envious, the factious, and the disaffected—to do all this, my countrymen, is more difficult than is generally thought.

But, besides the disadvantages which are common to me with all others in eminent stations, my case is, in this respect, peculiarly hard—that whereas a commander of Patrician rank, if he is guilty of a neglect or breach of duty, has his great connections, the antiquity of his family, the important services of his ancestors, and the multitudes he has, by power, engaged in his interest, to screen him from condign punishment, my whole safety depends upon myself: which renders it the more indispensably necessary for me to take care that my conduct be clear and unexceptionable. Besides, I am well aware, my countrymen, that

that the eye of the public is upon me; and that, though the impartial, who prefer the real advantage of the commonwealth to all other confiderations, favour my pretenfions, the Patricians want nothing fo much as an occafion againft me. It is, therefore, my fixed refolution, to ufe my beft endeavours, that you be not difappointed in me, and that their indirect defigns againft me may be defeated.

I have, from my youth, been familiar with toils and with dangers. I was faithful to your intereft, my countrymen, when I ferved you for no reward, but that of honour. It is not my defign to betray you, now that you have conferred upon me a place of profit. You have committed to my conduct the war againft Jugurtha. The Patricians are offended at this. But where would be the wifdom of giving fuch a command to one of their honourable body? a perfon of illuftrious birth, of ancient family, of innumerable ftatues, but —of no experience! What fervice would his long line of dead anceftors, or his multitude of motionlefs ftatues, do his country in the day of battle? What could fuch a general do, but, in his trepidation and inexperience, have recourfe to fome inferior commander, for direction in difficulties to which he was not himfelf equal? Thus your Patrician general would, in fact, have a general over him; fo that the acting commander would ftill be a Plebeian. So true is this, my countrymen, that I have myfelf, known thofe who have been chofen confuls, begin then to read the hiftory of their own country, of which, till that time, they were totally ignorant; that is, they firft obtained the employment, and then bethought themfelves of the qualifications neceffary for the proper difcharge of it.

I fubmit to your judgment, Romans, on which fide the advantage lies, when a comparifon is made between Patrician haughtinefs and Plebeian experience. The very actions, which they have only read, I have partly feen, and partly myfelf atchieved. What they know by reading, I know by action. They are pleafed to flight my mean birth; I defpife their mean characters. Want of birth and fortune is the objection againft me; want of perfonal worth, againft them. But are not all men of the fame fpecies? What can make a difference between one man and another, but the endowments of the mind? For my part, I fhall always look upon the braveft man as the nobleft man. Suppofe it were enquired of the fathers of fuch Patricians as Albinus and Beftia, whether, if they had their choice, they would defire fons of their character, or of mine; what would they anfwer but that they fhould wifh the worthieft to be their fons? If the Patricians have reafon to defpife me, let them likewife defpife their anceftors; whofe nobility was the fruit of their virtue. Do they envy the honours beftowed upon me? Let them envy, likewife, my labours, my abftinence, and the dangers I have undergone for my country, by which I have acquired them. But thofe worthlefs men lead fuch a life of inactivity, as if they defpifed any honours you can beftow, whilft they afpire to honours as if they had deferved them by the moft induftrious virtue. They lay claim to the rewards of activity, for their having enjoyed the pleafures of luxury; yet none can be more lavifh than they are in praife of their anceftors: and they imagine they honour themfelves by celebrating their forefathers; whereas they do the very contrary: for, as much as their anceftors were diftinguifhed tinguished for their virtues, so much are they disgraced by their vices. The glory of ancestors casts a light, indeed, upon their posterity; but it only serves to shew what the descendants are. It alike exhibits to public view their degeneracy and their worth. I own, I cannot boast of the deeds of my forefathers; but I hope I may answer the cavils of the Patricians, by standing up in defence of what I have myself done.

Observe now, my countrymen, the injustice of the Patricians. They arrogate to themselves honours, on account of the exploits done by their forefathers; whilst they will not allow me the due praise, for performing the very same sort of actions in my own person, He has no statues, they cry, of his family. He can trace no venerable line of ancestors.—What then? Is it matter of more praise to disgrace one's illustrious ancestors, than to become illustrious by one's own good behaviour? What if I can shew no statues of my family! I can shew the standards, the armour, and the trappings, which I have myself taken from the vanquished: I can shew the scars of those wounds which I have received by facing the enemies of my country. These are my statues. These are the honours I boast of. Not left me by inheritance, as theirs: but earned by toil, by abstinence, by valour; amidst clouds of dust, and seas of blood: scenes of action, where those effeminate Patricians, who endeavour by indirect means to depreciate me in your esteem, have never dared to shew their faces. *Sallust.*

§ 16. *The Character of* CATILINE.

Lucius Catiline was descended of an illustrious family: he was a man of great vigour, both of body and mind, but of a disposition extremely profligate and depraved. From his youth he took pleasure in civil wars, massacres, depredations, and intestine broils; and in these he employed his younger days. His body was formed for enduring cold, hunger, and want of rest, to a degree indeed incredible: his spirit was daring, subtle, and changeable: he was expert in all the arts of simulation and dissimulation; covetous of what belonged to others, lavish of his own; violent in his passions; he had eloquence enough, but a small share of wisdom. His boundless soul was constantly engaged in extravagant and romantic projects, too high to be attempted.

After Sylla's usurpation, he was fired with a violent desire of seizing the government; and, provided he could but carry his point, he was not at all solicitous by what means. His spirit, naturally violent, was daily more and more hurried on to the execution of his design, by his poverty, and the consciousness of his crimes; both which evils he had heightened by the practices above-mentioned. He was encouraged to it by the wickedness of the state, thoroughly debauched by luxury and avarice; vices equally fatal, though of contrary natures. *Sallust, by Mr. Rose.*

§ 17. *Speech of* TITUS QUINCTIUS *to the* ROMANS, *when the* ÆQUI *and* VOLSCI, *taking Advantage of their intestine Commotions, ravaged their Country to the Gates of* ROME.

Though I am not conscious, O Romans, of any crime by me committed, it is yet with the utmost shame and confusion that I appear in your assembly. You have seen it—posterity will know it!—in the fourth consulship

ſhip of Titus Quinctius, the Æqui and Volſci (ſcarce a match for the Hernici alone) came in arms to the very gates of Rome, and went away again unchaſtiſed! The courſe of our manners, indeed, and the ſtate of our affairs, have long been ſuch, that I had no reaſon to preſage much good; but, could I have imagined that ſo great an ignominy would have befallen me this year, I would, by baniſhment or death (if all other means had failed) have avoided the ſtation I am now in. What! might Rome then have been taken, if thoſe men who were at our gates had not wanted courage for the attempt?—Rome taken, whilſt I was conſul!—Of honours I had ſufficient—of life enough—more than enough—I ſhould have died in my third conſulate.

But who are they that our daſtardly enemies thus deſpiſe?—the conſuls, or you, Romans? If we are in fault, depoſe us, or puniſh us yet more ſeverely. If you are to blame—may neither gods nor men puniſh your faults! only may you repent! No, Romans, the confidence of our enemies is not owing to their courage, or to their belief of your cowardice: they have been too often vanquiſhed, not to know both themſelves and you. Diſcord, diſcord, is the ruin of this city! The eternal diſputes between the ſenate and the people are the ſole cauſe of our misfortunes. While we will ſet no bounds to our dominion, nor you to your liberty; while you impatiently endure Patrician magiſtrates, and we Plebeian; our enemies take heart, grow elated, and preſumptuous. In the name of the immortal gods, what is it, Romans, you would have? You deſired Tribunes; for the ſake of peace, we granted them. You were eager to have Decemvirs; we conſented to their creation. You grew weary of theſe Decemvirs; we obliged them to abdicate. Your hatred purſued them when reduced to private men; and we ſuffered you to put to death, or baniſh, Patricians of the firſt rank in the republic. You inſiſted upon the reſtoration of the Tribuneſhip; we yielded: we quietly ſaw Conſuls of your own faction elected. You have the protection of your Tribunes, and the privilege of appeal: the Patricians are ſubjected to the decrees of the Commons. Under pretence of equal and impartial laws, you have invaded our rights; and we have ſuffered it, and we ſtill ſuffer it. When ſhall we ſeen an end of diſcord? When ſhall we have one intereſt, and one common country? Victorious and triumphant, you ſhew leſs temper than we under defeat. When you are to contend with us, you can ſeize the Aventine hill, you can poſſeſs yourſelves of the Mons Sacer.

The enemy is at our gates, the Æſquiline is near being taken, and nobody ſtirs to hinder it. But againſt us you are valiant, againſt us you can arm with diligence. Come on then, beſiege the ſenate-houſe, make a camp of the forum, fill the jails with our chief nobles; and, when you have atchieved theſe glorious exploits, then, at laſt, ſally out at the Æſquiline gate, with the ſame fierce ſpirits againſt the enemy. Does your reſolution fail you for this? Go then, and behold from our walls your lands ravaged, your houſes plundered and in flames, the whole country laid waſte with fire and ſword. Have you any thing here to repair theſe damages? Will the Tribunes make up your loſſes to you? They'll give you words as many as you pleaſe; bring impeachments in abundance againſt the prime men in the ſtate; heap laws upon laws: aſſemblies you ſhall have without end: but will any of you return the richer from thoſe aſſemblies? Extinguiſh, O Romans, theſe fatal diviſions; generouſly break this curſed enchantment,

enchantment, which keeps you buried in a ſcandalous inaction. Open your eyes, and conſider the management of thoſe ambitious men, who, to make themſelves powerful in their party, ſtudy nothing but how they may foment diviſions in the commonwealth.—If you can but ſummon up your former courage, if you will now march out of Rome with your conſuls, there is no puniſhment you can inflict which I will not ſubmit to, if I do not in a few days drive thoſe pillagers out of our territory. This terror of war, with which you ſeem ſo grievouſly ſtruck, ſhall quickly be removed from Rome to their own cities.

Hooke.

§ 18. Micipsa *to* Jugurtha.

You know, Jugurtha, that I received you under my protection in your early youth, when left a helpleſs and hopeleſs orphan. I advanced you to high honours in my kingdom, in the full aſſurance that you would prove grateful for my kindneſs to you; and that, if I came to have children of my own, you would ſtudy to repay to them what you owed to me. Hitherto I have had no reaſon to repent of my favours to you. For, to omit all former inſtances of your extraordinary merit, your late behaviour in the Numantian war has reflected upon me, and my kingdom, a new and diſtinguiſhed glory. You have, by your valour, rendered the Roman commonwealth, which before was well affected to our intereſt, much more friendly. In Spain, you have raiſed the honour of my name and crown. And you have ſurmounted what is juſtly reckoned one of the greateſt difficulties; having, by your merit, ſilenced envy. My diſſolution ſeems now to be faſt approaching. I therefore beſeech and conjure you, my dear Jugurtha! by this right hand, by the remembrance of my paſt kindneſs to you; by the honour of my kingdom; and by the majeſty of the gods; be kind to my two ſons, whom my favour to you has made your brothers; and do not think of forming a connection with any ſtranger, to the prejudice of your relations. It is not by arms, nor by treaſures, that a kingdom is ſecured, but by well affected ſubjects and allies. And it is by faithful and important ſervices, that friendſhip (which neither gold will purchaſe, nor arms extort) is ſecured. But what friendſhip is more perfect, than that which ought to obtain between brothers? What fidelity can be expected among ſtrangers, if it is wanting among relations? The kingdom I leave you is in good condition, if you govern it properly; if otherwiſe, it is weak. For by agreement a ſmall ſtate increaſes: by diviſion a great one falls into ruin. It will lie upon you, Jugurtha, who are come to riper years than your brothers, to provide that no miſconduct produce any bad effect. And, if any difference ſhould ariſe between you and your brothers (which may the gods avert!) the public will charge you, however innocent you may be, as the aggreſſor, becauſe your years and abilities give you the ſuperiority. But I firmly perſuade myſelf, that you will treat them with kindneſs, and that they will honour and eſteem you, as your diſtinguiſhed virtue deſerves.

Salluſt.

§ 19. *The Character of* Hannibal.

Hannibal being ſent to Spain, on his arrival there attracted the eyes of the whole army. The veterans believed Hamilcar was revived and reſtored to them: they ſaw the ſame vigorous countenance, the ſame piercing eye, the ſame complexion and features. But in a ſhort time his behaviour occaſioned this reſemblance

ſemblance of his father to contribute the leaſt towards his gaining their favour. And, in truth, never was there a genius more happily formed for two things, moſt manifeſtly contrary to each other—to obey and to command. This made it difficult to determine, whether the general or ſoldiers loved him moſt. Where any enterprize required vigour, and valour in the performance, Aſdrubal always choſe him to command at the executing it; nor were the troops ever more confident of ſucceſs, or more intrepid, than when he was at their head. None ever ſhewed greater bravery in undertaking hazardous attempts, or more preſence of mind and conduct in the execution of them. No hardſhip could fatigue his body, or daunt his courage: he could equally bear cold and heat. The neceſſary refection of nature, not the pleaſure of his palate, he ſolely regarded in his meals. He made no diſtinction of day and night in his watching, or taking reſt; and appropriated no time to ſleep, but what remained after he had completed his duty: he never ſought for a ſoft or retired place of repoſe; but was often ſeen lying on the bare ground, wrapt in a ſoldier's cloak, amongſt the centinels and guards. He did not diſtinguiſh himſelf from his companions by the magnificence of his dreſs, but by the quality of his horſe and arms. At the ſame time, he was by far the beſt foot and horſe ſoldier in the army; ever the foremoſt in a charge, and the laſt who left the field after the battle was begun. Theſe ſhining qualities were however balanced by great vices; inhuman cruelty; more than Carthaginian treachery; no reſpect for truth or honour, no fear of the gods, no regard for the ſanctity of oaths, no ſenſe of religion. With a diſpoſition thus chequered with virtues and vices, he ſerved three years under Aſdrubal, without neglecting to pry into, or perform any thing, that could contribute to make him hereafter a complete general. *Livy.*

§ 20. *The* SCYTHIAN *Ambaſſadors to* ALEXANDER, *on his making Preparations to attack their Country.*

If your perſon were as gigantic as your deſires, the world would not contain you. Your right hand would touch the eaſt, and your left the weſt at the ſame time: you graſp at more than you are equal to. From Europe you reach Aſia; from Aſia you lay hold on Europe. And if you ſhould conquer all mankind, you ſeem diſpoſed to wage war with woods and ſnows, with rivers and wild beaſts, and to attempt to ſubdue nature. But, have you conſidered the uſual courſe of things? have you reflected, that great trees are many years in growing to their height, and are cut down in an hour? It is fooliſh to think of the fruit only, without conſidering the height you have to climb to come at it. Take care leſt, while you ſtrive to reach the top, you fall to the ground with the branches you have laid hold on.

Beſides, what have you to do with the Scythians, or the Scythians with you? We have never invaded Macedon; why ſhould you attack Scythia? You pretend to be the puniſher of robbers; and are yourſelf the general robber of mankind. You have taken Lydia; you have ſeized Syria; you are maſter of Perſia; you have ſubdued the Bactrians, and attacked India: all this will not ſatisfy you, unleſs you lay your greedy and inſatiable hands upon our flocks and our herds. How imprudent is your conduct! you graſp at riches, the poſſeſſion of which only increaſes your avarice. You increaſe your hunger, by what ſhould produce ſatiety; ſo that the

 more

more you have, the more you desire. But have you forgot how long the conquest of the Bactrians detained you? while you were subduing them the Sogdians revolted. Your victories serve to no other purpose than to find you employment by producing new wars; for the business of every conquest is twofold, to win, and to preserve: and though you may be the greatest of warriors, you must expect that the nations you conquer will endeavour to shake off the yoke as fast as possible: for what people chuse to be under foreign dominion?

If you will cross the Tanais, you may travel over Scythia, and observe how extensive a territory we inhabit. But to conquer us is quite another business; you will find us at one time, too nimble for your pursuit; and at another time, when you think we are fled far enough from you, you will have us surprise you in your camp: for the Scythians attack with no less vigour than they fly. It will therefore be your wisdom to keep with strict attention what you have gained: catching at more, you may lose what you have. We have a proverbial saying in Scythia, That Fortune has no feet, and is furnished only with hands to distribute her capricious favours, and with fins to elude the grasp of those to whom she has been bountiful.—You give yourself out to be a god, the son of Jupiter Ammon: it suits the character of a god to bestow favours on mortals, not to deprive them of what they have. But if you are no god, reflect on the precarious condition of humanity. You will thus shew more wisdom, than by dwelling on those subjects which have puffed up your pride, and made you forget yourself.

You see how little you are likely to gain by attempting the conquest of Scythia. On the other hand, you may, if you please, have in us a valuable alliance. We command the borders of both Europe and Asia. There is nothing between us and Bactria but the river Tanais; and our territory extends to Thrace, which, as we have heard, borders on Macedon. If you decline attacking us in a hostile manner, you may have our friendship. Nations which have never been at war are on an equal footing; but it is in vain that confidence is reposed in a conquered people: there can be no sincere friendship between the oppressors and the oppressed; even in peace, the latter think themselves entitled to the rights of war against the former. We will, if you think good, enter into a treaty with you, according to our manner, which is not by signing, sealing, and taking the gods to witness, as is the Grecian custom; but by doing actual services. The Scythians are not used to promise, but perform without promising. And they think an appeal to the gods superfluous; for that those who have no regard for the esteem of men will not hesitate to offend the gods by perjury.—You may therefore consider with yourself, whether you had better have a people of such a character, and so situated as to have it in their power either to serve you or to annoy you, according as you treat them, for allies or for enemies. *Q. Curtius.*

§ 21. Junius Brutus *over the dead Body of* Lucretia, *who had stabbed herself in consequence of the Rape of* Tarquin.

Yes, noble lady, I swear by this blood which was once so pure, and which nothing but royal villainy could have polluted, that I will pursue Lucius Tarquinius the Proud, his wicked wife, and their children, with fire and sword: nor will I suffer any of that family, or of any other whatsoever, to be king

king in Rome.—Ye gods, I call you to witness this my oath!

There, Romans, turn your eyes to that sad spectacle! — the daughter of Lucretius, Collatinus's wife—she died by her own hand! See there a noble lady, whom the lust of a Tarquin reduced to the necessity of being her own executioner, to attest her innocence. Hospitably entertained by her as a kinsman of her husband, Sextus, the perfidious guest, became her brutal ravisher. The chaste, the generous Lucretia could not survive the insult. Glorious woman! but once only treated as a slave, she thought life no longer to be endured. Lucretia, a woman, disdained a life that depended on a tyrant's will; and shall we, shall men, with such an example before our eyes, and after five-and-twenty years of ignominious servitude, shall we, through a fear of dying, defer one single instant to assert our liberty? No, Romans; now is the time; the favourable moment we have so long waited for is come. Tarquin is not at Rome: the Patricians are at the head of the enterprize: the city is abundantly provided with men, arms, and all things necessary. There is nothing wanting to secure the success, if our own courage does not fail us. And shall those warriors who have ever been so brave when foreign enemies were to be subdued, or when conquests were to be made to gratify the ambition and avarice of Tarquin, be then only cowards, when they are to deliver themselves from slavery?

Some of you are perhaps intimidated by the army which Tarquin now commands: the soldiers, you imagine, will take the part of their general. Banish such a groundless fear: the love of liberty is natural to all men. Your fellow citizens in the camp feel the weight of oppression with as quick a sense as you that are in Rome; they will as eagerly seize the occasion of throwing off the yoke. But let us grant there may be some among them who, through baseness of spirit, or a bad education, will be disposed to favour the tyrant: the number of these can be but small, and we have means sufficient in our hands to reduce them to reason. They have left us hostages more dear to them than life; their wives, their children, their fathers, their mothers, are here in the city. Courage, Romans, the gods are for us; those gods, whose temples and altars the impious Tarquin has profaned by sacrifices and libations made with polluted hands, polluted with blood, and with numberless unexpiated crimes committed against his subjects.

Ye gods, who protected our forefathers! ye genii, who watch for the preservation and glory of Rome! do you inspire us with courage and unanimity in this glorious cause, and we will to our last breath defend your worship from all profanation. *Livy.*

§ 22. *Speech* of ADHERBAL *to the* ROMAN SENATE, *imploring their Assistance against* JUGURTHA.

Fathers!

It is known to you that king Micipsa, my father, on his death-bed, left in charge to Jugurtha, his adopted son, conjunctly with my unfortunate brother Hiempsal and myself, the children of his own body, the administration of the kingdom of Numidia, directing us to consider the senate and people of Rome as proprietors of it. He charged us to use our best endeavours to be serviceable to the Roman commonwealth, in peace and war; assuring us, that your protection would prove to us us a defence againſt all enemies, and would be inſtead of armies, fortifications, and treaſures.

While my brother and I were thinking of nothing but how to regulate ourſelves according to the directions of our deceaſed father, Jugurtha—the moſt infamous of mankind! breaking through all ties of gratitude and common humanity, and trampling on the authority of the Roman commonwealth—procured the murder of my unfortunate brother, and has driven me from my throne and native country, though he knows I inherit, from my grandfather Maſſiniſſa, and my father Micipſa, the friendſhip and alliance of the Romans.

For a prince to be reduced, by villainy, to my diſtreſsful circumſtances, is calamity enough; but my misfortunes are heightened by the conſideration, that I find myſelf obliged to ſolicit your aſſiſtance, Fathers, for the ſervices done you by my anceſtors, not for any I have been able to render you in my own perſon. Jugurtha has put it out of my power to deſerve any thing at your hands, and has forced me to be burdenſome before I could be uſeful to you. And yet, if I had no plea but my undeſerved miſery, who, from a powerful prince, the deſcendant of a race of illuſtrious monarchs, find myſelf, without any fault of my own, deſtitute of every ſupport, and reduced to the neceſſity of begging foreign aſſiſtance againſt an enemy who has ſeized my throne and kingdom; if my unequalled diſtreſſes were all I had to plead, it would become the greatneſs of the Roman commonwealth, the arbitreſs of the world, to protect the injured, and to check the triumph of daring wickedneſs over helpleſs innocence. But, to provoke your vengeance to the utmoſt, Jugurtha has driven me from the very dominions which the ſenate and people of Rome gave to my anceſtors, and from which my grandfather and my father, under your umbrage, expelled Syphax and the Carthaginians. Thus, Fathers, your kindneſs to our family is defeated; and Jugurtha, in injuring me, throws contempt on you.

O wretched prince! O cruel reverſe of fortune! O father Micipſa! is this the conſequence of your generoſity, that he whom your goodneſs raiſed to an equality with your own children, ſhould be the murderer of your children? Muſt then the royal houſe of Numidia always be a ſcene of havock and blood? While Carthage remained, we ſuffered, as was to be expected, all ſorts of hardſhips from their hoſtile attacks; our enemy near; our only powerful ally, the Roman commonwealth, at a diſtance; while we were ſo circumſtanced, we were always in arms, and in action. When that ſcourge of Africa was no more, we congratulated ourſelves on the proſpect of eſtabliſhed peace. But inſtead of peace, behold the kingdom of Numidia drenched with royal blood, and the only ſurviving ſon of its late king flying from an adopted murderer, and ſeeking that ſafety in foreign parts, which he cannot command in his own kingdom.

Whither—O whither ſhall I fly! If I return to the royal palace of my anceſtors, my father's throne is ſeized by the murderer of my brother. What can I there expect, but that Jugurtha ſhould haſten to imbrue in my blood thoſe hands which are now reeking with my brother's? If I were to fly for refuge, or for aſſiſtance to any other courts, from what prince can I hope for protection, if the Roman commonwealth gives me up? From my own family or friends I have no expectations. My royal father is no more: he is beyond the reach of violence, and out of hearing of the complaints of his unhappy son. Were my brother alive, our mutual sympathy would be some alleviation: but he is hurried out of life in his early youth, by the very hand which should have been the last to injure any of the royal family of Numidia. The bloody Jugurtha has butchered all whom he suspected to be in my interest. Some have been destroyed by the lingering torment of the cross; others have been given a prey to wild beasts, and their anguish made the sport of men more cruel than wild beasts. If there be any yet alive, they are shut up in dungeons, there to drag out a life more intolerable than death itself.

Look down, illustrious senators of Rome! from that height of power to which you are raised, on the unexampled distresses of a prince, who is, by the cruelty of a wicked intruder, become an outcast from all mankind. Let not the crafty insinuations of him who returns murder for adoption, prejudice your judgment. Do not listen to the wretch who has butchered the son and relations of a king, who gave him power to sit on the same throne with his own sons.—I have been informed that he labours by his emissaries to prevent your determining any thing against him in his absence, pretending that I magnify my distress, and might for him have staid in peace in my own kingdom. But, if ever the time comes when the due vengeance from above shall overtake him, he will then dissemble as I do. Then he who now, hardened in wickedness, triumphs over those whom his violence has laid low, will in his turn feel distress, and suffer for his impious ingratitude to my father, and his bloodthirsty cruelty to my brother.

O murdered, butchered brother! O dearest to my heart—now gone for ever from my sight!—But why should I lament his death? He is indeed deprived of the blessed light of heaven, of life, and kingdom, at once, by the very person who ought to have been the first to hazard his own life in defence of any one of Micipsa's family? But as things are, my brother is not so much deprived of these comforts, as delivered from terror, from flight, from exile, and the endless train of miseries which render life to me a burden. He lies full low, gored with wounds, and festering in his own blood; but he lies in peace: he feels none of the miseries which rend my soul with agony and distraction, whilst I am set up a spectacle to all mankind of the uncertainty of human affairs. So far from having it in my power to revenge his death, I am not master of the means of securing my own life: so far from being in a condition to defend my kingdom from the violence of the usurper, I am obliged to apply for foreign protection for my own person.

Fathers! Senators of Rome! the arbiters of the world!—to you I fly for refuge from the murderous fury of Jugurtha.—By your affection for your children, by your love for your country, by your own virtues, by the majesty of the Roman commonwealth, by all that is sacred, and all that is dear to you—deliver a wretched prince from undeserved, unprovoked injury, and save the kingdom of Numidia, which is your own property, from being the prey of violence, usurpation, and cruelty. *Sallust.*

§ 23. *Speech of* CANULEIUS, *a Roman Tribune, to the Consuls; in which he demands that the Plebeians may be admitted into the Consulship, and that the Law prohibiting*

hibiting Patricians and Plebeians from intermarrying may be repealed.

What an infult upon us is this! If we are not fo rich as the patricians, are we not citizens of Rome as well as they? inhabitants of the fame country? members of the fame community? The nations bordering upon Rome, and even ftrangers more remote, are admitted not only to marriages with us, but to what is of much greater importance, the freedom of the city. Are we, becaufe we are commoners, to be worfe treated than ftrangers?—And, when we demand that the people may be free to beftow their offices and dignities on whom they pleafe, do we afk any thing unreafonable or new? do we claim more than their original inherent right? What occafion then for all this uproar, as if the univerfe were falling to ruin!—They were juft going to lay violent hands upon me in the fenate-houfe.

What! muft this empire then be unavoidably overturned? muft Rome of neceffity fink at once, if a plebeian, worthy of the office, fhould be raifed to the confulfhip? The patricians, I am perfuaded, if they could, would deprive you of the common light. It certainly offends them that you breathe, that you fpeak, that you have the fhapes of men. Nay, but to make a commoner a conful, would be, fay they, a moft enormous thing. Numa Pompilius, however, without being fo much as a Roman citizen, was made king of Rome: the elder Tarquin, by birth not even an Italian, was neverthelefs placed upon the throne: Servius Tullius, the Son of a captive woman (nobody knows who his father was) obtained the kingdom as the reward of his wifdom and virtue. In thofe days, no man in whom virtue fhone confpicuous was rejected, or defpifed, on account of his race and defcent. And did the ftate profper lefs for that? were not thefe ftrangers the very beft of all our kings? And, fuppofing now that a plebeian fhould have their talents and merit, muft not he be fuffered to govern us?

But, "we find that, upon the abolition "of the regal power, no commoner was "chofen to the confulate." And what of that? Before Numa's time there were no pontiffs in Rome. Before Servius Tullius's days there was no Cenfus, no divifion of the people into claffes and centuries. Who ever heard of confuls before the expulfion of Tarquin the Proud? Dictators, we all know, are of modern invention; and fo are the offices of tribunes, ædiles, quæftors. Within thefe ten years we have made decemvirs, and we have unmade them. Is nothing to be done but what has been done before? That very law forbidding marriages of patricians with plebeians, is not that a new thing? was there any fuch law before the decemvirs enacted it? and a moft fhameful one it is in a free eftate. Such marriages, it feems, will taint the pure blood of the nobility! why, if they think fo, let them take care to match their fifters and daughters with men of their own fort. No plebeian will do violence to the daughter of a patrician; thofe are exploits for our prime nobles. There is no need to fear, that we fhall force any body into a contract of marriage. But, to make an exprefs law to prohibit marriages of patricians with plebeians, what is this but to fhew the utmoft contempt of us, and to declare one part of the community to be impure and unclean?

They talk to us of the confufion there will be in families, if this ftatute fhould be repealed. I wonder they do not make a law againft a com-a commoner's living near a nobleman, or going the ſame road that he is going, or being preſent at the ſame feaſt, or appearing in the ſame market-place: they might as well pretend, that theſe things make confuſion in families, as that intermarriages will do it. Does not every one know, that the child will be ranked according to the quality of his father, let him be a patrician or a plebeian? In ſhort, it is manifeſt enough, that we have nothing in view but to be treated as men and citizens; nor can they who oppoſe our demand, have any motive to do it, but the love of domineering. I would fain know of you, conſuls and patricians, is the ſovereign power in the people of Rome, or in you? I hope you will allow, that the people can, at their pleaſure, either make a law or repeal one. And will you then, as ſoon as any law is propoſed to them, pretend to liſt them immediately for the war, and hinder them from giving their ſuffrages, by leading them into the field?

Hear me, conſuls: whether the news of the war you talk of be true, or whether it be only a falſe rumour, ſpread abroad for nothing but a colour to ſend the people out of the city, I declare, as tribune, that this people, who have already ſo often ſpilt their blood in our country's cauſe, are again ready to arm for its defence and its glory, if they may be reſtored to their natural rights, and you will no longer treat us like ſtrangers in our own country: but if you account us unworthy of your alliance by intermarriages; if you will not ſuffer the entrance to the chief offices in the ſtate to be open to all perſons of merit indifferently, but will confine your choice of magiſtrates to the ſenate alone—talk of wars as much as ever you pleaſe; paint, in your ordinary diſcourſes, the league and power of our enemies ten times more dreadful than you do now—I declare that this people, whom you ſo much deſpiſe, and to whom you are nevertheleſs indebted for all your victories, ſhall never more inliſt themſelves; not a man of them ſhall take arms; not a man of them ſhall expoſe his life for imperious lords, with whom he can neither ſhare the dignities of the ſtate, nor in private life have any alliance by marriage.

Hooke.

§ 24. *Character of* WILLIAM *the Conqueror.*

Few princes have been more fortunate than this great monarch, or were better entitled to proſperity and grandeur for the abilities and vigour of mind which he diſplayed in all his conduct. His ſpirit was bold and enterpriſing, yet guided by prudence. His ambition, which was exorbitant, and lay little under the reſtraints of juſtice, and ſtill leſs under thoſe of humanity, ever ſubmitted to the dictates of reaſon and ſound policy. Born in an age when the minds of men were intractable and unacquainted with ſubmiſſion, he was yet able to direct them to his purpoſes; and, partly from the aſcendant of his vehement diſpoſition, partly from art and diſſimulation, to eſtabliſh an unlimited monarchy. Though not inſenſible to generoſity, he was hardened againſt compaſſion, and ſeemed equally oſtentatious and ambitious of eclat in his clemency and his ſeverity. The maxims of his adminiſtration were ſevere; but might have been uſeful, had they been ſolely employed in preſerving order in an eſtabliſhed government: they were ill calculated for ſoftening the rigours which under the moſt gentle management are inſeparable from conqueſt. His attempt againſt England was the laſt enterprize of the kind, which, during the courſe of ſeven hundred years, had fully ſucceeded in in Europe; and the greatneſs of his genius broke through thoſe limits, which firſt the feudal inſtitutions, then the refined policy of princes, have fixed on the ſeveral ſtates of Chriſtendom. Though he rendered himſelf infinitely odious to his Engliſh ſubjects, he tranſmitted his power to his poſterity, and the throne is ſtill filled by his deſcendants; a proof that the foundation which he laid was firm and ſolid, and that amongſt all his violences, while he ſeemed only to gratify the preſent paſſion, he had ſtill an eye towards futurity. Died Sept. 9, 1087, aged 63*. *Hume.*

§ 25. *Another Character of* WILLIAM *the Conqueror.*

From the tranſactions of William's reign, he appears to have been a prince of great courage, capacity, and ambition; politic, cruel, vindictive, and rapacious; ſtern and haughty in his deportment, reſerved and jealous in his diſpoſition. He was fond of glory; and, though parſimonious in his houſehold, delighted much in oſtentation. Though ſudden and impetuous in his enterprizes, he was cool, deliberate, and indefatigable, in times of danger and difficulty. His aſpect was nobly ſevere and imperious, his ſtature tall and portly; his conſtitution robuſt, and the compoſition of his bones and muſcles ſtrong: there was hardly a man of that age, who could bend his bow, or handle his arms. *Smollett.*

§ 26. *Another Character of* WILLIAM *the Conqueror.*

The character of this prince has ſeldom been ſet in its true light; ſome eminent writers having been dazzled ſo much by the more ſhining parts of it, that they have hardly ſeen his faults; while others, out of a ſtrong deteſtation of tyranny, have been unwilling to allow him the praiſe he deſerves.

* Smollett ſays, 61.

He may with juſtice be ranked among the greateſt generals any age has produced. There was united in him activity, vigilance, intrepidity, caution, great force of judgment, and never-failing preſence of mind. He was ſtrict in his diſcipline, and kept his ſoldiers in perfect obedience; yet preſerved their affection. Having been from his very childhood continually in war, and at the head of armies, he joined to all the capacity that genius could give, all the knowledge and ſkill that experience could teach, and was a perfect maſter of the military art, as it was practiſed in the times wherein he lived. His conſtitution enabled him to endure any hardſhips, and very few were equal to him in perſonal ſtrength, which was an excellence of more importance than it is now, from the manner of fighting then in uſe. It is ſaid of him, that none except himſelf could bend his bow. His courage was heroic, and he poſſeſſed it not only in the field, but (which is more uncommon) in the cabinet, attempting great things with means that to other men appeared totally unequal to ſuch undertakings, and ſteadily proſecuting what he had boldly reſolved; being never diſturbed or diſheartened by difficulties, in the courſe of his enterprizes; but having that noble vigour of mind, which, inſtead of bending to oppoſition, riſes againſt it, and ſeems to have a power of controlling and commanding Fortune herſelf.

Nor was he leſs ſuperior to pleaſure than to fear: no luxury ſoftened him, no riot diſordered, no ſloth relaxed. It helped not a little to maintain the high reſpect his ſubjects had for him, that the majeſty of his character was never let down by any incontinence or indecent

cent excess. His temperance and his chastity were constant guards, that secured his mind from all weakness, supported its dignity, and kept it always as it were on the throne. Through his whole life he had no partner of his bed but his queen; a most extraordinary virtue in one who had lived, even from his earliest youth, amidst all the licence of camps, the allurements of a court, and the seductions of sovereign power! Had he kept his oaths to his people as well as he did his marriage vow, he would have been the best of kings; but he indulged other passions of a worse nature, and infinitely more detrimental to the public than those he restrained. A lust of power, which no regard to justice could limit, the most unrelenting cruelty, and the most insatiable avarice, possessed his soul. It is true, indeed, that among many acts of extreme inhumanity, some shining instances of great clemency may be produced, that were either effects of his policy, which taught him this method of acquiring friends, or of his magnanimity, which made him slight a weak and subdued enemy, such as was Edgar Atheling, in whom he found neither spirit nor talents able to contend with him for the crown. But where he had no advantage nor pride in forgiving, his nature discovered itself to be utterly void of all sense of compassion; and some barbarities which he committed exceeded the bounds that even tyrants and conquerors prescribe to themselves.

Most of our ancient historians give him the character of a very religious prince; but his religion was after the fashion of those times, belief without examination, and devotion without piety. It was a religion that prompted him to endow monasteries, and at the same time allowed him to pillage kingdoms; that threw him on his knees before a relic or cross, but suffered him unrestrained to trample upon the liberties and rights of mankind.

As to his wisdom in government, of which some modern writers have spoken very highly, he was indeed so far wise that, through a long unquiet reign, he knew how to support oppression by terror, and employ the properest means for the carrying on a very iniquitous and violent administration. But that which alone deserves the name of wisdom in the character of a king, the maintaining of authority by the exercise of those virtues which make the happiness of his people, was what, with all his abilities, he does not appear to have possessed. Nor did he excel in those soothing and popular arts, which sometimes change the complexion of a tyranny, and give it a fallacious appearance of freedom. His government was harsh and despotic, violating even the principles of that constitution which he himself had established. Yet so far he performed the duty of a sovereign, that he took care to maintain a good police in his realm; curbing licentiousness with a strong hand, which, in the tumultuous state of his government, was a great and difficult work. How well he performed it we may learn even from the testimony of a contemporary Saxon historian, who says, that during his reign a man might have travelled in perfect security all over the kingdom with his bosom full of gold, nor durst any kill another in revenge of the greatest offences, nor offer violence to the chastity of a woman. But it was a poor compensation, that the highways were safe, when the courts of justice were dens of thieves, and when almost every man in authority, or in office, used his power to oppress and pillage the people. The king himself did not only tolerate, but encourage, support, and even share these extortions. Though the greatness of the ancient landed estate of the crown, and the feudal profits to which he legally was entitled, rendered him one of the richest monarchs in Europe, he was not content with all that opulence, but by authorizing the sheriffs, who collected his revenues in the several counties, to practise the most grievous vexations and abuses, for the raising of them higher, by a perpetual auction of the crown lands, so that none of his tenants could be secure of possession, if any other would come and offer more; by various iniquities in the court of exchequer, which was entirely Norman; by forfeitures wrongfully taken; and, lastly, by arbitrary and illegal taxations, he drew into his treasury much too great a proportion of the wealth of his kingdom.

It must however be owned, that if his avarice was insatiably and unjustly rapacious, it was not meanly parsimonious, nor of that sordid kind which brings on a prince dishonour and contempt. He supported the dignity of his crown with a decent magnificence; and though he never was lavish, he sometimes was liberal, more especially to his soldiers and to the church. But looking on money as a necessary means of maintaining and increasing power, he desired to accumulate as much as he could, rather, perhaps, from an ambitious than a covetous nature; at least his avarice was subservient to his ambition, and he laid up wealth in his coffers, as he did arms in his magazines, to be drawn out, when any proper occasion required it, for the defence and enlargement of his dominions.

Upon the whole, he had many great qualities, but few virtues; and if those actions that most particularly distinguish the man or the king are impartially considered, we shall find that in his character there is much to admire, but still more to abhor. *Lyttelton.*

§ 27. *The Character of* William Rufus.

The memory of this monarch is transmitted to us with little advantage by the churchmen, whom he had offended; and though we may suspect in general that their account of his vices is somewhat exaggerated, his conduct affords little reason for contradicting the character which they have assigned him, or for attributing to him any very estimable qualities: he seems to have been a violent and tyrannical prince; a perfidious, encroaching, and dangerous neighbour; an unkind and ungenerous relation. He was equally prodigal and rapacious in the management of the treasury; and, if he possessed abilities, he lay so much under the government of impetuous passions, that he made little use of them in his administration; and he indulged intirely the domineering policy which suited his temper, and which, if supported, as it was in him, with courage and vigour, proves often more successful in disorderly times, than the deepest foresight and most refined artifice. The monuments which remain of this prince in England are, the Tower, Westminster-Hall, and London Bridge, which he built. Died August 2, 1100, aged 40. *Hume.*

§ 28. *Another Character of* William Rufus.

Thus fell William *, surnamed Rufus, from his red hair and florid complexion, after he had lived four-and-forty years, and reigned

* By the hand of Tyrrel, a French gentleman, remarkable for his address in archery, attending him in the recreation of hunting, as William had dismounted after a chace. Tyrrel, impatient to shew his dexterity, let fly at a stag which suddenly started before him; the arrow glancing from a tree, struck the king in his breast, and instantly slew him.

near thirteen; during which time he oppressed his people in every form of tyranny and insult. He was equally void of learning, principle, and honour; haughty, passionate, and ungrateful; a scoffer at religion, a scourge to the clergy; vain-glorious, talkative, rapacious, lavish, and dissolute; and an inveterate enemy to the English, though he owed his crown to their valour and fidelity, when the Norman lords intended to expel him from the throne. In return for this instance of their loyalty, he took *all* opportunities to fleece and enslave them; and at one time imprisoned fifty of the best families in the kingdom, on pretence of killing his deer; so that they were compelled to purchase their liberty at the expence of their wealth, though not before they had undergone the *fiery ordeal*. He lived in a scandalous commerce with prostitutes, professing his contempt for marriage; and, having no legitimate issue, the crown devolved to his brother Henry, who was so intent upon the succession, that he paid very little regard to the funeral of the deceased king. *Smollett.*

§ 29. *Character of* HENRY I.

This prince was one of the most accomplished that has filled the English throne; and possessed all the qualities both of body and mind, natural and acquired, which could fit him for the high station to which he attained: his person was manly; his countenance engaging; his eyes clear, serene, and penetrating. The affability of his address encouraged those who might be overawed by the sense of his dignity or his wisdom; and though he often indulged his facetious humour, he knew how to temper it with discretion, and ever kept at a distance from all indecent familiarities with his courtiers. His superior eloquence and judgment would have given him an ascendant, even if he had been born in a private station; and his personal bravery would have procured him respect, even though it had been less supported by art and policy. By his great progress in literature he acquired the name of *Beau Clerc*, or the Scholar; but his application to sedentary pursuits abated nothing of the activity and vigilance of his government: and though the learning of that age was better fitted to corrupt than improve the understanding; his natural good sense preserved itself untainted both from the pedantry and superstition which were then so prevalent among men of letters. His temper was very susceptible of the sentiments as well of friendship as resentment; and his ambition, though high, might be esteemed moderate, had not his conduct towards his brother shewed, that he was too much disposed to sacrifice to it all the maxims of justice and equity. Died December 1, 1135, aged 67, having reigned 35 years. *Hume.*

§ 30. *Another Character of* HENRY I.

Henry was of a middle stature and robust make, with dark brown hair, and blue serene eyes. He was facetious, fluent, and affable to his favourites. His capacity, naturally good, was improved and cultivated in such a manner, that he acquired the name of *Beau Clerc* by his learning. He was cool, cautious, politic, and penetrating; his courage was unquestioned, and his fortitude invincible. He was vindictive, cruel, and implacable, inexorable to offenders, rigid and severe in the execution of justice; and, though temperate in his diet, a voluptuary in his amours, which produced a numerous family of illegitimate issue. His Norman deſcent and connections with the continent inſpired him with a contempt for the Engliſh, whom he oppreſſed in the moſt tyrannical manner. *Smollett.*

§ 31. *Character of* Stephen.

England ſuffered great miſeries during the reign of this prince: but his perſonal character, allowing for the temerity and injuſtice of his uſurpation, appears not liable to any great exception; and he ſeems to have been well qualified, had he ſucceeded by a juſt title, to have promoted the happineſs and proſperity of his ſubjects. He was poſſeſſed of induſtry, activity, and courage, to a great degree; was not deficient in ability, had the talent of gaining men's affections; and, notwithſtanding his precarious ſituation, never indulged himſelf in the exerciſe of any cruelty or revenge. His advancement to the throne procured him neither tranquillity nor happineſs. Died 1154. *Hume.*

§ 32. *Another Character of* Stephen.

Stephen was a prince of great courage, fortitude, and activity, and might have reigned with the approbation of his people, had he not been harraſſed by the efforts of a powerful competitor, which obliged him to take ſuch meaſures for his ſafety as were inconſiſtent with the dictates of honour, which indeed his ambition prompted him to forego, in his firſt endeavours to aſcend the throne. His neceſſities afterwards compelled him to infringe the charter of privileges he granted at his acceſſion; and he was inſtigated by his jealouſy and reſentment to commit the moſt flagrant outrages againſt gratitude and ſound policy. His vices, as a king, ſeem to have been the effect of troubles in which he was involved; for, as a man, he was brave, open, and liberal; and, during the ſhort calm that ſucceeded the tempeſt of his reign, he made a progreſs through his kingdom, publiſhed an edict to reſtrain all rapine and violence, and diſbanded the foreign mercenaries who had preyed ſo long on his people. *Smollett.*

§ 33. *Character of* Henry II.

Thus died, in the 58th year of his age, and thirty-fifth of his reign, the greateſt prince of his time for wiſdom, virtue, and ability, and the moſt powerful in extent of dominion, of all thoſe that had ever filled the throne of England. His character, both in public and private life, is almoſt without a blemiſh; and he ſeems to have poſſeſſed every accompliſhment, both of body and mind, which makes a man eſtimable or amiable. He was of a middle ſtature, ſtrong, and well proportioned; his countenance was lively and engaging; his converſation affable, and entertaining; his elocution eaſy, perſuaſive, and ever at command. He loved peace, but poſſeſſed both conduct and bravery in war; was provident without timidity; ſevere in the execution of juſtice without rigour; and temperate without auſterity. He preſerved health, and kept himſelf from corpulency, to which he was ſomewhat inclined, by an abſtemious diet, and by frequent exerciſe, particularly by hunting. When he could enjoy leiſure, he recreated himſelf in learned converſation, or in reading; and he cultivated his natural talents by ſtudy, above any prince of his time. His affections, as well as his enmities, were warm and durable; and his long experience of ingratitude and infidelity of men never deſtroyed the natural ſenſibility of his temper, which diſpoſed him to friendſhip and ſociety. His character has been tranſmitted to us by by many writers who were his contemporaries; and it resembles extremely, in its most remarkable strokes, that of his maternal grandfather, Henry I. excepting only that ambition, which was a ruling passion in both, found not in the first Henry such unexceptionable means of exerting itself, and pushed that prince into measures which were both criminal in themselves, and were the cause of further crimes, from which his grandson's conduct was happily exempted. Died 1189. *Hume.*

§ 34. *Another Character of* Henry II.

Thus died Henry in the fifty-seventh year of his age (Hume says 58) and thirty-fifth of his reign, in the course of which he had, on sundry occasions, displayed all the abilities of a politician, all the sagacity of a legislator, and all the magnanimity of a hero. He lived revered above all the princes of his time; and his death was deeply lamented by his subjects, whose happiness seems to have been the chief aim of all his endeavours. He not only enacted wholesome laws, but saw them executed with great punctuality. He was generous, even to admiration, with regard to those who committed offences against his own person; but he never forgave the injuries that were offered to his people, for atrocious crimes were punished severely without respect of persons. He was of a middle stature, and the most exact proportion; his countenance was round, fair, and ruddy; his blue eyes were mild and engaging, except in a transport of passion, when they sparkled like lightning, to the terror of the beholders. He was broad-chested, strong, muscular, and inclined to be corpulent, though he prevented the bad effects of this disposition by hard exercise and continual fatigue; he was temperate in his meals, even to a degree of abstinence, and seldom or ever sat down, except at supper; he was eloquent, agreeable, and facetious; remarkably courteous and polite; compassionate to all in distress; so charitable, that he constantly allotted one tenth of his houshold provisions to the poor, and in time of dearth he maintained ten thousand indigent persons, from the beginning of spring till the end of autumn. His talents, naturally good, he had cultivated with great assiduity, and delighted in the conversation of learned men, to whom he was a generous benefactor. His memory was so surprisingly tenacious, that he never forgot a face nor a circumstance that was worth remembering. Though superior to his contemporaries in strength, riches, true courage, and military skill; he never engaged in war without reluctance, and was so averse to bloodshed, that he expressed an uncommon grief at the loss of every private soldier: yet he was not exempt from human frailties; his passions, naturally violent, often hurried him to excess; he was prone to anger, transported with the lust of power, and particularly accused of incontinence, not only in the affair of Rosamond, whom he is said to have concealed in a labyrinth at Woodstock, from the jealous enquiry of his wife, but also in a supposed commerce with the French princess Adalais, who was bred in England as the future wife of his son Richard. This infamous breach of honour and hospitality, if he was actually guilty, is the foulest stain upon his character; though the fact is doubtful, and we hope the charge untrue. *Smollett.*

§ 35. *Character of* Richard I.

The most shining part of this prince's character was his military talents; no man ever in in that romantic age carried courage and intrepidity to a greater height; and this quality gained him the appellation of the *lion-hearted, cœur de lion.* He passionately loved glory; and as his conduct in the field was not inferior to his valour, he seems to have possessed every talent necessary for acquiring it: his resentments also were high, his pride unconquerable, and his subjects, as well as his neighbours, had therefore reason to apprehend, from the continuance of his reign, a perpetual scene of blood and violence. Of an impetuous and vehement spirit, he was distinguished by all the good as well as the bad qualities which are incident to that character. He was open, frank, generous, sincere, and brave; he was revengeful, domineering, ambitious, haughty, and cruel, and was thus better calculated to dazzle men by the splendour of his enterprizes, than either to promote their happiness, or his own grandeur by a sound and well-regulated policy. As military talents make great impression on the people, he seems to have been much beloved by his English subjects; and he is remarked to have been the first prince of the Norman line who bore a sincere affection and regard for them. He passed, however, only four months of his reign in that kingdom: the crusade employed him near three years: he was detained about four months in captivity; the rest of his reign was spent either in war, or preparations for war against France: and he was so pleased with the fame which he had acquired in the East, that he seemed determined, notwithstanding all his past misfortunes, to have further exhausted his kingdom, and to have exposed himself to new hazards, by conducting another expedition against the infidels. Died April 6, 1199, aged 42. Reigned ten years. *Hume.*

§ 36. *Another Character of* Richard I.

This renowned prince was tall, strong, straight, and well-proportioned. His arms were remarkably long, his eyes blue, and full of vivacity; his hair was of a yellowish colour; his countenance fair and comely, and his air majestic. He was endowed with good natural understanding; his penetration was uncommon; he possessed a fund of manly eloquence; his conversation was spirited, and he was admired for his talents of repartee; as for his courage and ability in war, both Europe and Asia resound with his praise. The Saracens stilled their children with the terror of his name; and Saladine, who was an accomplished prince, admired his valour to such a degree of enthusiasm, that immediately after Richard had defeated him on the plains of Joppa, he sent him a couple of fine Arabian horses, in token of his esteem; a polite compliment, which Richard returned with magnificent presents. These are the shining parts of his character, which, however, cannot dazzle the judicious observer so much, but that he may perceive a number of blemishes, which no historian has been able to efface from the memory of this celebrated monarch. His ingratitude and want of filial affection are unpardonable. He was proud, haughty, ambitious, choleric, cruel, vindictive, and debauched; nothing could equal his rapaciousness but his profusion, and, indeed, the one was the effect of the other; he was a tyrant to his wife, as well as to his people, who groaned under his taxations to such a degree, that even the glory of his victories did not exempt him from their execrations; in a word, he has been aptly compared to a lion, a species of animals which he resembled not only in courage, but likewise in ferocity. *Smollett.*

§ 37. *Character* of John.

The character of this prince is nothing but a complication of vices, equally mean and odious, ruinous to himself, and destructive to his people: cowardice, inactivity, folly, levity, licentiousness, ingratitude, treachery, tyranny, and cruelty; all these qualities too evidently appear in the several incidents of his life, to give us room to suspect, that the disagreeable picture has been anywise overcharged by the prejudice of the ancient historians. It is hard to say, whether his conduct to his father, his brother, his nephew, or his subjects, was most culpable; or whether his crimes in these respects were not even exceeded by the baseness which appeared in his transactions with the king of France, the pope, and the barons. His dominions, when they devolved to him by the death of his brother, were more extensive than have ever since his time been ruled by any English monarch. But he first lost, by his misconduct, the flourishing provinces in France; the ancient patrimony of his family. He subjected his kingdom to a shameful vassalage, under the see of Rome; he saw the prerogatives of his crown diminished by law, and still more reduced by faction; and he died at last when in danger of being totally expelled by a foreign power, and of either ending his life miserably in a prison, or seeking shelter as a fugitive from the pursuit of his enemies.

The prejudices against this prince were so violent, that he was believed to have sent an embassy to the emperor of Morocco, and to have offered to change his religion and become Mahometan, in order to purchase the protection of that monarch; but, though that story is told us on plausible authority, it is in itself utterly improbable, except that there is nothing so incredible as may not become likely from the folly and wickedness of John. Died 1216. *Hume.*

§ 38. *Another Character of* John.

John was in his person taller than the middle size, of a good shape and agreeable countenance; with respect to his disposition, it is strongly delineated in the transactions of his reign. If his understanding was contemptible, his heart was the object of detestation; we find him slothful, shallow, proud, imperious, cowardly, libidinous, and inconstant, abject in adversity, and overbearing in success; contemned and hated by his subjects, over whom he tyrannized to the utmost of his power; abhorred by the clergy, whom he oppressed with exactions; and despised by all the neighbouring princes of Europe: though he might have passed through life without incurring such a load of odium and contempt, had not his reign been perplexed by the turbulence of his barons, the rapaciousness of the pope, and the ambition of such a monarch as Philip Augustus; his character could never have afforded one quality that would have exempted him from the disgust and scorn of his people: nevertheless, it must be owned, that his reign is not altogether barren of laudable transactions. He regulated the form of the government in the city of London, and several other places in the kingdom. He was the first who coined sterling money.

Smollett.

§ 39. *Character of* Henry III.

The most obvious circumstance of Henry the Third's character, is his incapacity for government, which rendered him as much a prisoner in in the hands of his own miniſters and favourites, and as little at his own diſpoſal, as when detained a captive in the hands of his enemies. From this ſource, rather than from inſincerity and treachery, aroſe his negligence in obſerving his promiſes; and he was too eaſily induced, for the ſake of preſent convenience, to ſacrifice the laſting advantages ariſing from the truſt and confidence of his people. Hence were derived his profuſion to favourites, his attachment to ſtrangers, the variableneſs of his conduct, his haſty reſentments, and his ſudden forgiveneſs and return of affection. Inſtead of reducing the dangerous power of his nobles, by obliging them to obſerve the laws towards their inferiors, and ſetting them the ſalutary example in his own government, he was ſeduced to imitate their conduct, and to make his arbitrary will, or rather that of his miniſters, the rule of his actions.

Inſtead of accommodating himſelf by a ſtrict frugality, to the embarraſſed ſituation in which his revenue had been left, by the military expedition of his uncle, the diſſipations of his father, and the uſurpations of the barons; he was tempted to levy money by irregular exactions, which, without enriching himſelf, impoveriſhed, or at leaſt diſguſted, his people. Of all men, nature ſeemed leaſt to have fitted him for being a tyrant; yet are there inſtances of oppreſſion in his reign, which, though derived from the precedents left him by his predeceſſors, had been carefully guarded againſt by the great charter; and are inconſiſtent with all rules of good government: and, on the whole, we may ſay, that greater abilities, with his good diſpoſitions, would have prevented him from falling into his faults; or, with worſe diſpoſitions, would have enabled him to maintain and defend them. Died November 16, 1272, aged 64. Reigned 56 years. *Hume.*

§ 40. *Another Character of* Henry III.

Henry was of a middle ſize and robuſt make, and his countenance had a peculiar caſt from his left eye-lid, which hung down ſo far as to cover part of his eye. The particulars of his character may be gathered from the detail of his conduct. He was certainly a prince of very mean talents; irreſolute, inconſtant, and capricious; proud, inſolent, and arbitrary; arrogant in proſperity, and abject in adverſity; profuſe, rapacious, and choleric, though deſtitute of liberality, œconomy, and courage; yet his continence was praiſeworthy, as well as his averſion to cruelty; for he contented himſelf with puniſhing the rebels in their effects, when he might have glutted his revenge with their blood. He was prodigal even to exceſs, and therefore always in neceſſity. Notwithſtanding the great ſums he levied from his ſubjects, and though his occaſions were never ſo preſſing, he could not help ſquandering away his money upon worthleſs favourites, without conſidering the difficulty he always found in obtaining ſupplies from parliament. *Smollett.*

§ 41. *Character of* Edward I.

The enterprizes finiſhed by this prince, and the projects which he formed, and brought very near to a concluſion, were more prudent and more regularly conducted, and more advantageous to the ſolid intereſts of this kingdom, than thoſe which were undertaken in any reign either of his anceſtors or ſucceſſors. He reſtored authority to the government, diſordered by the weakneſs of his father; he maintained the laws againſt all the efforts of his turbulent barons; he fully annexed

annexed to the crown the principality of Wales, he took the wiſeſt and moſt effectual meaſures for reducing Scotland to a like condition; and though the equity of this latter enterprize may reaſonably be queſtioned, the circumſtances of the two kingdoms promiſed ſuch ſucceſs, and the advantage was ſo viſible, of uniting the whole iſland under one head, that thoſe who give great indulgence to reaſons of ſtate in the meaſures of princes, will not be apt to regard this part of his conduct with much ſeverity.

But Edward, however exceptionable his character may appear on the head of juſtice, is the model of a politic and warlike king. He poſſeſſed induſtry, penetration, courage, vigour, and enterprize. He was frugal in all expences that were not neceſſary; he knew how to open the public treaſures on proper occaſions; he puniſhed criminals with ſeverity; he was gracious and affable to his ſervants and courtiers; and being of a majeſtic figure, expert at all bodily exerciſe, and in the main well proportioned in his limbs, notwithſtanding the great length of his legs, he was as well qualified to captivate the populace by his exterior appearance, as to gain the approbation of men of ſenſe by his more ſolid virtues. Died July 7, 1307, aged 69. Reigned 35 years, *Hume.*

§ 42. *Another Character of* Edward I.

He was a prince of a very dignified appearance, tall in ſtature; regular and comely in his features; with keen piercing eyes, and of an aſpect that commanded reverence and eſteem. His conſtitution was robuſt; his ſtrength and dexterity perhaps unequalled in his kingdom: and his ſhape was unblemiſhed in all other reſpects, but that of his legs, which are ſaid to have been too long in proportion to his body; whence he derived the epithet of *Long Shanks.* In the qualities of his head, he equalled the greateſt monarchs who have ſat on the Engliſh throne. He was cool, penetrating, ſagacious, and circumſpect. The remoteſt corners of the earth ſounded with the fame of his courage; and all over Europe he was conſidered as the flower of chivalry. Nor was he leſs conſummate in his legiſlative capacity, than eminent for his proweſs. He may be ſtyled the Engliſh Juſtinian: for, beſides the excellent ſtatutes that were enacted in his reign, he new-modelled the adminiſtration of juſtice, ſo as to render it more ſure and ſummary; he fixed proper bounds to the courts of juriſdiction; ſettled a new and eaſy method of collecting the revenue, and eſtabliſhed wiſe and effectual methods of preſerving peace and order among his ſubjects. Yet, with all theſe good qualities, he cheriſhed a dangerous ambition, to which he did not ſcruple to ſacrifice the good of his country: witneſs his ruinous war with Scotland, which drained the kingdom of men and money, and gave riſe to that rancorous enmity which proved ſo prejudicial to both nations. Though he is celebrated for his chaſtity and regular deportment, there is not, in the whole courſe of his reign, one inſtance of his liberality and munificence. He had great abilities, but no genius; and was an accompliſhed warrior, without the leaſt ſpark of heroiſm.

Smollett.

§ 43. *Character of* Edward II.

It is not eaſy to imagine a man more innocent or inoffenſive than this unhappy king; nor a prince leſs fitted for governing that fierce and turbulent people ſubjected to his authority. He was obliged to devolve on others the weight of government, which he had neither ability

ability nor inclination to bear; the same indolence and want of penetration led him to make choice of ministers and favourites, which were not always best qualified for the trust committed to them. The seditious grandees, pleased with his weakness, and complaining of it, under pretence of attacking his ministers, insulted his person, and invaded his authority; and the impatient populace, ignorant of the source of their grievances, threw all the blame upon the king, and increased the public disorders by their faction and insolence. It was in vain to look for protection from the laws, whose voice, always feeble in those times, was not heard in the din of arms: what could not defend the king, was less able to give shelter to any one of his people; the whole machine of government was torn in pieces, with fury and violence; and men, instead of complaining against the manners of the age, and the form of their constitution, which required the most steady and the most skilful hand to conduct them, imputed all errors to his person who had the misfortune to be intrusted with the reins of empire. Murdered 21 September, 1327. *Hume.*

§ 44. *Another Character of* EDWARD II.

Thus perished Edward II. after having atoned by his sufferings for all the errors of his conduct. He is said to have resembled his father in the accomplishments of his person, as well as in his countenance: but in other respects he seems only to have inherited the defects of his character; for he was cruel and illiberal, without his valour or capacity. He had levity, indolence, and irresolution, in common with other weak princes; but the distinguishing foible of his character was that unaccountable passion for the reigning favourites, to which he sacrificed every other consideration of policy and convenience, and at last fell a miserable victim. *Smollett.*

§ 45. *Character of* EDWARD III.

The English are apt to consider with peculiar fondness the history of Edward the Third, and to esteem his reign, as it was one of the longest, the most glorious also, which occurs in the annals of the nation. The ascendant which they began to have over France, their rival and national enemy, makes them cast their eyes on this period with great complacency, and sanctifies every measure which Edward embraced for that end. But the domestic government is really more admirable than his foreign victories; and England enjoyed, by his prudence and vigour of administration, a longer interval of domestic peace and tranquillity, than she had been blest with in any former period, or than she experienced for many years after. He gained the affections of the great, and curbed their licentiousness: he made them feel his power, without their daring, or even being inclined to murmur at it; his affable and obliging behaviour, his munificence and generosity, made them submit with pleasure to his dominion; his valour and conduct made them successful in most of their enterprizes; and their unquiet spirits, directed against a public enemy, had no leisure to breed disturbances, to which they were naturally so much inclined, and which the form of the government seemed so much to authorize. This was the chief benefit which resulted from Edward's victories and conquests. His foreign wars were, in other respects, neither founded in justice, nor directed to any very salutary purpose. His attempt against the king of Scotland, a minor, and a brother-in-law, and the revival of his grandfather's claim of superiority over that kingdom,

kingdom, were both unreasonable and ungenerous: and he allowed himself to be too soon seduced by the glaring prospects of French conquest, from the acquisition of a point which was practicable, and which might really, if attained, have been of lasting utility to his country and to his successors. But the glory of a conqueror is so dazzling to the vulgar, and the animosity of nations so extreme, that the fruitless desolation of so fine a part of Europe as France is totally disregarded by us, and never considered as a blemish in the character or conduct of this prince: and indeed, from the unfortunate state of human nature, it will commonly happen that a sovereign of great genius, such as Edward, who usually finds every thing easy in the domestic government, will turn himself towards military enterprizes, where alone he meets opposition, and where he has full exercise for his industry and capacity. Died 21st of June, aged 65, in the 51st year of his reign. *Hume.*

§ 46. *Another Character of* Edward III.

Edward's constitution had been impaired by the fatigues of his youth: so that he began to feel the infirmities of old age, before they approach the common course of nature: and now he was seized with a malignant fever, attended with eruptions, that soon put a period to his life. When his distemper became so violent, that no hope of his recovery remained, all his attendants forsook him as a bankrupt no longer able to requite their services. The ungrateful Alice, waiting until she perceived him in the agonies of death, was so inhuman as to strip him of his rings and jewels, and leave him without one domestic to close his eyes, and do the last offices to his breathless corse. In this deplorable condition, bereft of comfort and assistance, the mighty Edward lay expiring; when a priest, not quite so savage as the rest of his domestics, approached his bed; and, finding him still breathing, began to administer some comfort to his soul. Edward had not yet lost all perception, when he found himself thus abandoned and forlorn, in the last moments of his life. He was just able to express a deep sense of sorrow and contrition for the errors of his conduct, and died pronouncing the name of Jesus.

Such was the piteous and obscure end of Edward the Third, undoubtedly one of the greatest princes that ever swayed the sceptre of England; whether we respect him as a warrior, a lawgiver, a monarch, or a man. He possessed all the romantic spirit of Alexander; the penetration, the fortitude, the polished manners of Julius; the liberality, the munificence, the wisdom of Augustus Cæsar. He was tall, majestic, finely shaped, with a piercing eye, and aquiline visage. He excelled all his contemporaries in feats of arms, and personal address. He was courteous, affable, and eloquent; of a free deportment, and agreeable conversation; and had the art of commanding the affection of his subjects, without seeming to solicit popularity. The love of glory was certainly the predominant passion of Edward, to the gratification of which he did not scruple to sacrifice the feelings of humanity, the lives of his subjects, and the interests of his country. And nothing could have induced or enabled his people to bear the load of taxes with which they were encumbered in his reign, but the love and admiration of his person, the fame of his victories, and the excellent laws and regulations which the parliament enacted with his advice and concurrence. *Smollett.*

§ 47.

§ 47. *Character of* Richard II.

All the writers who have tranſmitted to us the hiſtory of Richard, compoſed their works during the reign of the Lancaſtrian princes; and candour requires that we ſhould not give entire credit to the reproaches which have been thrown upon his memory. But after making all proper abatements, he ſtill appears to have been a weak prince, and unfit for government; leſs for want of natural parts and capacity, than of ſolid judgment and good education. He was violent in his temper, profuſe in his expences, fond of idle ſhow and magnificence, devoted to favourites, and addicted to pleaſure; paſſions, all of them, the moſt inconſiſtent with a prudent œconomy, and conſequently dangerous in a limited and mixed government. Had he poſſeſſed the talents of gaining, and, ſtill more, of overawing his great barons, he might have eſcaped all the misfortunes of his reign, and been allowed to carry much further his oppreſſions over his people, if he really was guilty of any, without their daring to rebel, or even murmur, againſt him. But when the grandees were tempted, by his want of prudence and rigour, to reſiſt his authority, and execute the moſt violent enterprizes upon him, he was naturally led to ſeek for an opportunity of retaliation; juſtice was neglected; the lives of the chief nobility ſacrificed; and all theſe evils ſeem to have proceeded more from a ſettled deſign of eſtabliſhing arbitrary power, than from the inſolence of victory, and the neceſſities of the king's ſituation. The manners, indeed, of the age, were the chief ſources of ſuch violence; laws, which were feebly executed in peaceable times, loſt all their authority in public convulſions. Both parties were alike guilty; or, if any difference may be remarked between them, we ſhall find the authority of the crown, being more legal, was commonly carried, when it prevailed, to leſs deſperate extremities than thoſe of ariſtocracy *. *Hume.*

§ 48. *Another Character of* Richard II.

Such was the laſt concluſion of Richard II. a weak, vain, frivolous, inconſtant prince; without weight to balance the ſcales of government, without diſcernment to chooſe a good miniſtry; without virtue to oppoſe the meaſures, or advice, of evil counſellors, even where they happened to claſh with his own principles and opinion. He was a dupe to flattery, a ſlave to oſtentation, and not more apt to give up his reaſon to the ſuggeſtion of ſycophants, and vicious miniſters, than to ſacrifice thoſe miniſters to his ſafety. He was idle, profuſe, and profligate; and, though brave by ſtarts, naturally puſillanimous, and irreſolute. His pride and reſentment prompted him to cruelty and breach of faith; while his neceſſities obliged him to fleece his people, and degrade the dignity of his character and ſituation. Though we find none of his charities on record, all his hiſtorians agree, that he excelled all his predeceſſors in ſtate hoſpitality, and fed a thouſand every day from his kitchen. *Smollett.*

§ 49. *Another Character of* Richard II.

Richard of Bourdeaux (ſo called from the place of his birth) was remarkably beautiful, and handſome in his perſon; and doth not ſeem to be naturally defective, either in courage or underſtanding. For on ſome occaſions,

* He was ſtarved to death in priſon, or murdered, after having been dethroned, A. D. 1399. in the year of his age 34: of his reign 23.

ſions, particularly in the dangerous inſurrections of the crown, he acted with a degree of ſpirit and prudence ſuperior to his years. But his education was miſerably neglected; or, rather, he was intentionally corrupted and debauched by three ambitious uncles, who, being deſirous of retaining the management of his affairs, encouraged him to ſpend his time in the company of diſſolute young people of both ſexes, in a continual courſe of feaſting and diſſipation. By this means, he contracted a taſte for pomp and pleaſure, and a diſlike to buſineſs. The greateſt foible in the character of this unhappy prince was an exceſſive fondneſs for, and unbounded liberality to his favourites, which enraged his uncles, particularly the duke of Glouceſter, and diſguſted ſuch of the nobility as did not partake of his bounty. He was an affectionate huſband, a generous maſter, and a faithful friend; and if he had received a proper education, might have proved a great and good king. *Henry.*

§ 50. *Character of* Henry IV.

The great popularity which Henry enjoyed before he attained the crown, and which had ſo much aided him in the acquiſition of it, was entirely loſt, many years before the end of his reign, and he governed the people more by terror than affection, more by his own policy than their ſenſe of duty and allegiance. When men came to reflect in cold blood on the crimes which led him to the throne; and the rebellion againſt his prince; the depoſition of a lawful king, guilty ſometimes of oppreſſion, but more frequently of imprudences; the excluſion of the true heir; the murder of his ſovereign and near relation; theſe were ſuch enormities, as drew on him the hatred of his ſubjects, ſanctified all the rebellions againſt him, and made the executions, though not remarkably ſevere, which he found neceſſary for the maintenance of his authority, appear cruel as well as iniquitous to his people. Yet, without pretending to apologize for theſe crimes, which muſt ever be held in deteſtation, it may be remarked, that he was inſenſibly led into this blameable conduct, by a train of incidents, which few men poſſeſs virtue enough to withſtand. The injuſtice with which his predeceſſor had treated him, in firſt condemning him to baniſhment, and then deſpoiling him of his patrimony, made him naturally think of revenge, and of recovering his loſt rights; the headſtrong zeal of the people hurried him into the throne, the care of his own ſecurity, as well as his ambition, made him an uſurper; and the ſteps have always been ſo few between the priſons of princes and their graves, that we need not wonder that Richard's fate was no exception to the general rule. All theſe conſiderations made the king's ſituation, if he retained any ſenſe of virtue, very much to be lamented; and the inquietudes, with which he poſſeſſed his envied greatneſs, and the remorſes by which, it is ſaid, he was continually haunted, rendered him an object of our pity, even when ſeated upon the throne. But it muſt be owned, that his prudence, vigilance, and foreſight in maintaining his power, were admirable; his command of temper remarkable; his courage, both military and political, without blemiſh: and he poſſeſſed many qualities, which fitted him for his high ſtation, and which rendered his uſurpation of it, though pernicious in after-times, rather ſalutary during his own reign, to the Engliſh nation. *Hume.*

Died 1413. Aged 43.

§ 51.

§ 51. *Another Character of* Henry IV.

Henry IV. was of a middle stature, well proportioned, and perfect in all the exercises of arms and chivalry; his countenance was severe, rather than serene, and his disposition sour, sullen, and reserved: he possessed a great share of courage, fortitude, and penetration; was naturally imperious, though he bridled his temper with a great deal of caution; superstitious though without the least tincture of virtue and true religion; and meanly parsimonious, though justly censured for want of œconomy, and ill-judged profusion. He was tame from caution, humble from fear, cruel from policy, and rapacious from indigence. He rose to the throne by perfidy and treason; and established his authority in the blood of his subjects, and died a penitent for his sins, because he could no longer enjoy the fruit of his transgressions.

Smollett.

§ 52. *Character of* Henry V.

This prince possessed many eminent virtues; and, if we give indulgence to ambition in a monarch, or rank it, as the vulgar do, among his virtues, they were unstained by any considerable blemish; his abilities appeared equally in the cabinet and in the field: the boldness of his enterprizes was no less remarkable than his personal valour in conducting them. He had the talent of attaching his friends by affability, and gaining his enemies by address and clemency.

The English, dazzled by the lustre of his character, still more by that of his victories, were reconciled to the defects of his title. The French almost forgot he was an enemy; and his care of maintaining justice in his civil administration, and preserving discipline in his armies, made some amends to both nations for the calamities inseparable from those wars in which his short reign was almost occupied. That he could forgive the Earl of Marche, who had a better right to the throne than himself, is a sure proof of his magnanimity; and that the earl relied so on his friendship, is no less a proof of his established character for candour and sincerity.

There remain, in history, few instances of such mutual trust; and still fewer, where neither found reason to repent it.

The exterior figure of this great prince, as well as his deportment, was engaging. His stature was somewhat above the middle size; his countenance beautiful, his limbs genteel and slender, but full of vigour; and he excelled in all warlike and manly exercises.

Hume.

Died 31st August, 1422: in the year of his age 34; of his reign, the 10th.

§ 53. *Another Character of* Henry V.

Henry was tall and slender, with a long neck, and engaging aspect, and limbs of the most elegant turn. He excelled all the youth of that age, in agility, and the exercise of arms; was hardy, patient, laborious, and more capable of enduring cold, hunger, and fatigue, than any individual in his army. His valour was such as no danger could startle, and no difficulty oppose; nor was his policy inferior to his courage.

He managed the dissensions among his enemies with such address, as spoke him consummate in the arts of the cabinet. He fomented their jealousy, and converted their mutual resentment to his own advantage.

Henry possessed a self-taught genius, that blazed out at once, without the aid of instruction and experience; and a fund of natural sagacity,

sagacity, that made ample amends for all these defects. He was chaste, temperate, moderate and devout, scrupulously just in his administration, and severely exact in the discipline of his army; upon which he knew his glory and success, in a great measure, depended. In a word, it must be owned, he was without an equal in the arts of war, policy, and government. But we cannot be so far dazzled with his great qualities, as to overlook the defects in his character. His pride and imperious temper lost him the hearts of the French nobility, and frequently fell out into outrage and abuse; as at the siege of Melun, when he treated the Marechal l'Isle d'Adam with the utmost indignity, although that nobleman had given him no other offence, than that of coming into his presence in plain decent apparel.

Smollett.

§ 54. Hume's *Account of* Henry VI. *(for there is no regular Character of this Prince given by this Historian) is expressed in the following Manner.*

In this manner finished the reign of Henry VI. who, while yet in his cradle, had been proclaimed king both of France and England, and who began his life with the most splendid prospects which any prince in Europe had ever enjoyed. The revolution was unhappy for his people, as it was the source of civil wars; but was almost entirely indifferent to Henry himself, who was utterly incapable of exercising his authority, and who, provided he met perpetually with good usage, was equally easy; as he was equally enslaved, in the hands of his enemies and of his friends. His weakness, and his disputed title, were the chief causes of his public misfortunes: but whether his queen and his ministers were not guilty of some great abuses of power, it is not easy for us, at this distance of time, to determine. There remain no proofs on record of any considerable violation of the laws, except in the death of the duke of Gloucester, which was a private crime, formed no precedent, and was but too much of a piece with the usual ferocity and cruelty of the times.

§ 55. Smollett's *Account of the Death of* Henry VI. *with some Strictures of Character, is as follows.*

This insurrection * in all probability hastened the death of the unfortunate Henry, who was found dead in the Tower, in which he had been confined since the restoration of Edward. The greater part of historians have alledged that he was assassinated by the duke of Gloucester, who was a prince of the most brutal disposition; while some moderns, from an affectation of singularity, affirm that Henry died of grief and vexation. This, no doubt, might have been the case; and it must be owned, that nothing appears in history, from which either Edward or Richard could be convicted of having contrived or perpetrated his murder: but, at the same time, we must observe some concurring circumstances that amount to strong presumption against the reigning monarch. Henry was of a hale constitution, but just turned of fifty, naturally insensible of affliction, and hackneyed in the vicissitudes of fortune, so that one would not expect he should have died of age and infirmity, or that his life would have been affected by grief arising from his last disaster. His sudden death was suspicious, as well as the conjuncture at which he died, immediately after the suppression of a rebellion, which seemed to declare that

* Revolt of the bastard of Falconbridge.

that Edward would never be quiet, while the head of the houſe of Lancaſter remained alive: and laſtly, the ſuſpicion is confirmed by the characters of the reigning king and his brother Richard, who were bloody, barbarous, and unrelenting. Very different was the diſpoſition of the ill-fated Henry, who, without any princely virtue or qualification, was totally free from cruelty or revenge: on the contrary, he could not, without reluctance, conſent to the puniſhment of thoſe malefactors who were ſacrificed to the public ſafety; and frequently ſuſtained indignities of the groſſeſt nature, without diſcovering the leaſt mark of reſentment. He was chaſte, pious, compaſſionate, and charitable; and ſo inoffenſive, that the biſhop, who was his confeſſor for ten years, declares, that in all that time he had never committed any ſin that required penance or rebuke. In a word, he would have adorned a cloiſter, though he diſgraced a crown; and was rather reſpectable for thoſe vices he wanted, than for thoſe virtues he poſſeſſed. He founded the colleges of Eaton and Windſor, and King's College, in Cambridge, for the reception of thoſe ſcholars who had begun their ſtudies at Eaton.

On the morning that ſucceeded his death, his body was expoſed at St. Paul's church, in order to prevent unfavourable conjectures, and, next day, ſent by water to the abbey of Chertſey, where he was interred; but it was afterwards removed, by order of Richard III. to Windſor, and there buried with great funeral ſolemnity.

§ 56. *Character of* Edward IV.

Edward IV. was a prince more ſplendid and ſhewy, than either prudent or virtuous; brave, though cruel; addicted to pleaſure, though capable of activity in great emergencies; and leſs fitted to prevent ills by wiſe precautions, than to remedy them after they took place, by his vigour and enterprize.

Hume.

§ 57. *Another Character of* Edward IV.

He was a prince of the moſt elegant perſon and inſinuating addreſs; endowed with the utmoſt fortitude and intrepidity; poſſeſſed of uncommon ſagacity and penetration; but, like all his anceſtors, was brutally cruel and vindictive, perfidious, lewd, perjured, and rapacious; without one liberal thought, without one ſentiment of humanity. *Smollett.*

§ 58. *Another Character of* Edward IV.

When Edward aſcended the throne, he was one of the handſomeſt men in England, and perhaps in Europe. His noble mien, his free and eaſy way, his affable carriage, won the hearts of all at firſt ſight. Theſe qualities gained him eſteem and affection, which ſtood him in great ſtead in ſeveral circumſtances of his life. For ſome time he was exceeding liberal; but at length he grew covetous, not ſo much from his natural temper, as out of a neceſſity to bear the immediate expences which his pleaſures ran him into.

Though he had a great deal of wit, and a ſound judgment, he committed, however, ſeveral overſights. But the crimes Edward is moſt juſtly charged with, are his cruelty, perjury, and incontinence. The firſt appears in the great number of princes and lords he put to death, on the ſcaffold, after he had taken them in battle. If there ever was reaſon to ſhew mercy in caſe of rebellion, it was at that fatal time, when it was almoſt impoſſible to ſtand neuter, and ſo difficult to chuſe the

the justest side between the two houses that were contending for the crown.

And yet we do not see that Edward had any regard to that consideration. As for Edward's incontinence, one may say, that his whole life was one continued scene of excess that way; he had abundance of mistresses, but especially three, of whom he said, that one was the merriest, the other the wittiest, and the other the holiest in the world, since she would not stir from the church but when he sent for her.—What is most astonishing in the life of this prince is his good fortune, which seemed to be prodigious.

He was raised to the throne, after the loss of two battles, one by the duke his father, the other by the Earl of Warwick, who was devoted to the house of York. The head of the father was still upon the walls of York, when the son was proclaimed in London.

Edward escaped, as it were, by miracle, out of his confinement at Middleham. He was restored to the throne, or at least received into London, at his return from Holland, before he had overcome, and whilst his fortune yet depended upon the issue of a battle which the Earl of Warwick was ready to give him. In a word, he was ever victorious in all the battles wherein he fought in person. Edward died the 9th of April, in the 42d year of his age, after a reign of twenty-two years and one month. *Rapin.*

§ 59. Edward V.

Immediately after the death of the fourth Edward, his son was proclaimed king of England, by the name of Edward V. though that young prince was but just turned of twelve years of age, never received the crown, nor exercised any function of royalty; so that the interval between the death of his father, and the usurpation of his uncle, the Duke of Gloucester, afterwards Richard III. was properly an interregnum, during which the uncle took his measures for wresting the crown from his nephew.

§ 60. *Character of* Richard III.

Those historians who favour Richard, for even *He* has met partizans among later writers, maintain that he was well qualified for government, had he legally obtained it; and that he committed no crimes but such as were necessary to procure him possession of the crown: but this is a very poor apology, when it is confessed, that he was ready to commit the most horrid crimes which appeared necessary for that purpose; and it is certain that all his courage and capacity, qualities in which he really seems not to have been deficient, would never have made compensation to the people, for the danger of the precedent, and for the contagious example of vice and murder, exalted upon the throne. This prince was of small stature, hump-backed, and had a very harsh disagreeable visage; so that his body was in every particular no less deformed than his mind. *Hume.*

§ 61. *Another Character of* Richard III.

Such was the end * of Richard III. the most cruel, unrelenting tyrant that ever sat on the throne of England. He seems to have been an utter stranger to the softer emotions of the human heart, and entirely destitute of every social enjoyment. His ruling passion was ambition; for the gratification of which he trampled upon every law, both human and divine; but this thirst of dominion was unattended with the least work of generosity, or any

* Slain at the battle of Bosworth.

desire of rendering himself agreeable to his fellow-creatures: it was the ambition of a savage, not of a prince; for he was a solitary king, altogether detached from the rest of mankind, and incapable of that satisfaction which results from private friendship and disinterested society. We must acknowledge, however, that after his accession to the throne, his administration in general was conducted by the rules of justice; that he enacted salutary laws, and established wise regulations; and that, if his reign had been protracted, he might have proved an excellent king to the English nation. He was dark, silent, and reserved, and so much master of dissimulation, that it was almost impossible to dive into his real sentiments, when he wanted to conceal his designs. His stature was small, his aspect cloudy, severe, and forbidding: one of his arms was withered, and one shoulder higher than another, from which circumstance of deformity he acquired the epithet of Crook-backed. *Smollett.*

§ 62. *Character of* HENRY VII.

The reign of Henry VII. was in the main fortunate for his people at home, and honourable abroad. He put an end to the civil wars with which the nation had been so long harrassed; he maintained peace and order to the state; he depressed the former exorbitant power of the nobility; and, together with the friendship of some foreign princes, he acquired the consideration and regard of all.

He loved peace, without fearing war; though agitated with criminal suspicions of his servants and ministers, he discovered no timidity, either in the conduct of his affairs, or in the day of battle; and, though often severe in his punishments, he was commonly less actuated by revenge than by the maxims of policy.

The services which he rendered his people were derived from his views of private interest, rather than the motives of public spirit; and where he deviated from selfish regards, it was unknown to himself, and ever from malignant prejudices, or the mean projects of avarice; not from the sallies of passion, or allurements of pleasure; still less from the benign motives of friendship and generosity.

His capacity was excellent, but somewhat contracted by the narrowness of his heart; he possessed insinuation and address, but never employed these talents except some great point of interest was to be gained; and while he neglected to conciliate the affections of his people, he often felt the danger of resting his authority on their fear and reverence alone. He was always extremely attentive to his affairs; but possessed not the faculty of seeing far into futurity; and was more expert at promoting a remedy for his mistakes, than judicious in avoiding them. Avarice was on the whole his ruling passion; and he remained an instance almost singular, of a man placed in a high station, and possessed of talents for great affairs, in whom that passion predominated above ambition. Even among private persons, avarice is nothing but a species of ambition, and is chiefly incited by the prospect of that regard, distinction, and consideration, which attends on riches.

Died April 12th, 1509, aged 52, having reigned 23 years. *Hume.*

§ 63. *Another Character of* HENRY VII.

Henry was tall, straight, and well-shaped, though slender; of a grave aspect, and saturnine complexion; austere in his dress, and reserved in conversation, except when he had a favourite a favourite point to carry; and then he would fawn, flatter, and practise all the arts of insinuation. He inherited a natural fund of sagacity, which was improved by study and experience; nor was he deficient in personal bravery and political courage. He was cool, close, cunning, dark, distrustful, and designing; and of all the princes who had sat on the English throne, the most sordid, selfish, and ignorant. He possessed, in a peculiar manner, the art of turning all his domestic troubles, and all his foreign disputes, to his own advantage; hence he acquired the appellation of the English Solomon; and all the powers of the continent courted his alliance, on account of his wealth, wisdom, and uninterrupted prosperity.

The nobility he excluded entirely from the administration of public affairs, and employed clergymen and lawyers, who, as they had no interest in the nation, and depended entirely upon his favour, were more obsequious to his will, and ready to concur in all his arbitrary measures. At the same time it must be owned, he was a wise legislator; chaste, temperate, and assiduous in the exercise of religious duties; decent in his deportment, and exact in the administration of justice, when his private interest was not concerned; though he frequently used religion and justice as cloaks for perfidy and oppression. His soul was continually actuated by two ruling passions, equally base and unkingly, namely, the fear of losing his crown, and the desire of amassing riches: and these motives influenced his whole conduct. Nevertheless, his apprehension and avarice redounded, on the whole, to the advantage of the nation. The first induced him to depress the nobility, and abolish the feudal tenures, which rendered them equally formidable to the prince and people; and his avarice prompted him to encourage industry and trade, because it improved his customs, and enriched his subjects, whom he could afterwards pillage at discretion.

Smollett.

§ 64. *Character of* Henry VIII.

It is difficult to give a just summary of this prince's qualities; he was so different from himself in different parts of his reign, that, as is well remarked by Lord Herbert, his history is his best character and description. The absolute and uncontrouled authority which he maintained at home, and the regard he obtained among foreign nations, are circumstances which entitle him to the appellation of a great prince; while his tyranny and cruelty seem to exclude him from the character of a good one.

He possessed, indeed, great vigour of mind, which qualified him for exercising dominion over men; courage, intrepidity, vigilance, inflexibility; and though these qualities lay not always under the guidance of a regular and solid judgment, they were accompanied with good parts, and an extensive capacity; and every one dreaded a contest with a man who was never known to yield, or to forgive; and who, in every controversy, was determined to ruin himself, or his antagonist.

A catalogue of his vices would comprehend many of the worst qualities incident to human nature. Violence, cruelty, profusion, rapacity, injustice, obstinacy, arrogance, bigotry, presumption, caprice; but neither was he subject to all these vices in the most extreme degree, nor was he at intervals altogether devoid of virtues. He was sincere, open, gallant, liberal, and capable at least of a temporary friendship and attachment. In this respect he was unfortunate, that the incidents of his times ſerved to diſplay his faults in their full light; the treatment he met with from the court of Rome provoked him to violence; the danger of a revolt from his ſuperſtitious ſubjects ſeemed to require the moſt extreme ſeverity. But it muſt at the ſame time be acknowledged, that his ſituation tended to throw an additional luſtre on what was great and magnanimous in his character.

The emulation between the emperor and the French King rendered his alliance, notwithſtanding his impolitic conduct, of great importance to Europe. The extenſive powers of his prerogative, and the ſubmiſſion, not to ſay ſlaviſh diſpoſition of his parliament, made it more eaſy for him to aſſume and maintain that entire dominion, by which his reign is ſo much diſtinguiſhed in Engliſh hiſtory.

It may ſeem a little extraordinary, that notwithſtanding his cruelty, his extortion, his violence, his arbitrary adminiſtration, this prince not only acquired the regard of his ſubjects, but never was the object of their hatred; he ſeems even, in ſome degree, to have poſſeſſed their love and affection. His exterior qualities were advantageous, and fit to captivate the multitude; his magnificence, and perſonal bravery, rendered him illuſtrious to vulgar eyes; and it may be ſaid with truth, that the Engliſh in that age were ſo thoroughly ſubdued, that, like eaſtern ſlaves, they were inclined to admire even thoſe acts of violence and tyranny, which were exerciſed over themſelves, and at their own expence.

Died January 28th, 1547, anno ætatis 57, regni 37. *Hume.*

§ 65. *Another Character of* Henry VIII.

Henry VIII. before he became corpulent, was a prince of a goodly perſonage, and commanding aſpect, rather imperious than dignified. He excelled in all the exerciſes of youth, and poſſeſſed a good underſtanding, which was not much improved by the nature of his education. Inſtead of learning that philoſophy which opens the mind, and extends the qualities of the heart, he was confined to the ſtudy of gloomy and ſcholaſtic diſquiſitions, which ſerved to cramp his ideas, and pervert the faculty of reaſon, qualifying him for the diſputant of a cloiſter, rather than the lawgiver of a people. In the firſt years of his reign, his pride and vanity ſeemed to domineer over all his other paſſions; though from the beginning he was impetuous, headſtrong, impatient of contradiction and advice. He was raſh, arrogant, prodigal, vain-glorious, pedantic, and ſuperſtitious. He delighted in pomp and pageantry, the baubles of a weak mind. His paſſions, ſoothed by adulation, rejected all reſtraint; and as he was an utter ſtranger to the finer feelings of the ſoul, he gratified them at the expence of juſtice and humanity, without remorſe or compunction.

He wreſted the ſupremacy from the biſhop of Rome, partly on conſcientious motives, and partly from reaſons of ſtate and conveniency. He ſuppreſſed the monaſteries, in order to ſupply his extravagance with their ſpoils; but he would not have made thoſe acquiſitions, had they not been productive of advantage to his nobility, and agreeable to the nation in general. He was frequently at war; but the greateſt conqueſt he obtained was over his own parliament and people.—Religious diſputes had divided them into two factions. As he had it in his power to make either ſcale preponderate, each courted his favour with the moſt obſequious ſubmiſſion, and, in trimming the balance, he kept them both in ſubjection. In accuſtoming them to theſe abject compliances, they degenerated into

into ſlaves, and he from their proſtitution acquired the moſt deſpotic authority. He became rapacious, arbitrary, froward, fretful, and ſo cruel that he ſeemed to delight in the blood of his ſubjects.

He never ſeemed to betray the leaſt ſymptoms of tenderneſs in his diſpoſition; and, as we already obſerved, his kindneſs to Cranmer was an inconſiſtence in his character. He ſeemed to live in defiance of cenſure, whether eccleſiaſtical or ſecular; he died in apprehenſion of futurity; and was buried at Windſor, with idle proceſſions and childiſh pageantry, which in thoſe days paſſed for real taſte and magnificence. *Smollett.*

§ 66. *Character of* Edward VI.

Thus died Edward VI. in the ſixteenth year of his age. He was counted the wonder of his time; he was not only learned in the tongues and the liberal ſciences, but he knew well the ſtate of his kingdom. He kept a table-book, in which he had written the characters of all the eminent men of the nation: he ſtudied fortification, and underſtood the mint well. He knew the harbours in all his dominions, with the depth of the water, and way of coming into them. He underſtood foreign affairs ſo well, that the ambaſſadors who were ſent into England, publiſhed very extraordinary things of him, in all the courts of Europe. He had great quickneſs of apprehenſion; but, being diſtruſtful of his memory, he took notes of every thing he heard (that was conſiderable) in Greek characters, that thoſe about him might not underſtand what he writ, which he afterwards copied out fair in the journal that he kept. His virtues were wonderful: when he was made to believe that his uncle was guilty of conſpiring the death of the other counſellors, he upon that abandoned him.

Barnaby Fitz Patrick was his favourite; and when he ſent him to travel, he writ oft to him to keep good company, to avoid exceſs and luxury; and to improve himſelf in thoſe things that might render him capable of employment at his return. He was afterwards made Lord of Upper Oſſory in Ireland, by Queen Elizabeth, and did anſwer the hopes this excellent king had of him. He was very merciful in his nature, which appeared in his unwillingneſs to ſign the warrant for burning the maid of Kent. He took great care to have his debts well paid, reckoning that a prince who breaks his faith, and loſes his credit, has thrown up that which he can never recover, and made himſelf liable to perpetual diſtruſt, and extreme contempt. He took ſpecial care of the petitions that were given him by poor and oppreſt people. But his great zeal for religion crowned all the reſt—it was not an angry heat about it that actuated him, but it was a true tenderneſs of conſcience, founded on the love of God and his neighbour. Theſe extraordinary qualities, ſet off with great ſweetneſs and affability, made him univerſally beloved by his people. *Burnet.*

§ 67. *Another Character of* Edward VI.

All the Engliſh hiſtorians dwell with pleaſure on the excellencies of this young prince, whom the flattering promiſes of hope, joined to many real virtues, had made an object of the moſt tender affections of the public. He poſſeſſed mildneſs of diſpoſition, application to ſtudy and buſineſs, a capacity to learn and judge, and an attachment to equity and juſtice. He ſeems only to have contracted, from his education, and from the age in which

which he lived, too much of a narrow prepossession in matters of religion, which made him incline somewhat to bigotry and persecution. But as the bigotry of Protestants, less governed by priests, lies under more restraints than that of Catholics, the effects of this malignant quality were the less to be apprehended, if a longer life had been granted to young Edward. *Hume.*

§ 68. *Another Character of* Edward VI.

Edward is celebrated by historians for the beauty of his person, the sweetness of his disposition, and the extent of his knowledge. By that time he had attained his sixteenth year, he understood the Greek, Latin, French, Italian, and Spanish languages; he was versed in the sciences of logic, music, natural philosophy, and master of all theological disputes; insomuch that the famous Cardanus, in his return from Scotland, visiting the English court, was astonished at the progress he had made in learning; and afterwards extolled him in his works as a prodigy of nature. Notwithstanding these encomiums, he seems to have had an ingredient of bigotry in his disposition, that would have rendered him very troublesome to those of tender consciences, who might have happened to differ with him in religious principles; nor can we reconcile either to his boasted humanity or penetration, his consenting to the death of his uncle, who had served him faithfully; unless we suppose he wanted resolution to withstand the importunities of his ministers, and was deficient in that vigour of mind, which often exists independent of learning and culture.

Smollett.

§ 69. *Character of* Mary.

It is not necessary to employ many words in drawing the character of this princess. She possessed few qualities either estimable or amiable, and her person was as little engaging as her behaviour and address. Obstinacy, bigotry, violence, cruelty, malignity, revenge, and tyranny; every circumstance of her character took a tincture from her bad temper and narrow understanding. And amidst that complication of vices which entered into her composition, we shall scarcely find any virtue but sincerity; a quality which she seems to have maintained throughout her whole life, except in the beginning of her reign, when the necessity of her affairs obliged her to make some promises to the Protestants, which she certainly never intended to perform. But in these cases a weak bigoted woman, under the government of priests, easily finds casuistry sufficient to justify to herself the violation of an engagement. She appears, as well as her father, to have been susceptible of some attachment of friendship; and that without caprice and inconstancy, which were so remarkable in the conduct of that monarch. To which we may add, that in many circumstances of her life, she gave indications of resolution and vigour of mind; a quality which seems to have been inherent in her family.

Died Nov. 7, A.D. 1558. *Hume.*

§ 70. *Another Character of* Mary.

We have already observed, that the characteristics of Mary were bigotry and revenge; we shall only add, that she was proud, imperious, froward, avaricious, and wholly destitute of every agreeable qualification.

Smollett.

§ 71. *Character of* Elizabeth.

Elizabeth had a great deal of wit, and was

was naturally of a sound and solid judgment. This was visible by her whole management, from one end of her reign to the other. Nothing shews her capacity more, than her address in surmounting all the difficulties and troubles created by her enemies, especially when it is considered who these enemies were; persons the most powerful, the most artful, the most subtile, and the least scrupulous in Europe. The following are the maxims which she laid down for the rule and measures of her whole conduct, and from which she never swerved: "To make herself beloved "by her people: To be frugal of her trea-"sure: To keep up dissension amongst her "neighbours."

Her enemies pretend that her abilities consisted wholly in overstrained dissimulation, and a profound hypocrisy. In a word, they say she was a perfect comedian. For my part, I don't deny that she made great use of dissimulation, as well with regard to the courts of France and Spain, as to the queen of Scotland and the Scots. I am also persuaded that, being as much concerned to gain the love and esteem of her subjects, she affected to speak frequently, and with exaggeration, of her tender affection for them. And that she had a mind to make it believed that she did some things from an excessive love to her people, which she was led to more by her own interest.

Avarice is another failing which her own friends reproach her with. I will not deny that she was too parsimonious, and upon some occasions stuck too close to the maxims she had laid down, not to be at any expence but what was absolutely necessary. However in general I maintain, that if her circumstances did not require her to be covetous, at least they required that she should not part with her money but with great caution, both in order to preserve the affection of her people, and to keep herself always in a condition to withstand her enemies.

She is accused also of not being so chaste, as she affected to appear. Nay, some pretend that there are now in England, the descendants of a daughter she had by the Earl of Leicester; but as hitherto nobody has undertaken to produce any proofs of this accusation, one may safely reckon it among the slanders which they endeavoured to stain her reputation with, both in her life-time and after her decease.

It is not so easy to justify her concerning the death of the queen of Scots. Here it must be owned she sacrificed equity, justice, and it may be her own conscience, to her safety. If Mary was guilty of the murder of her husband, as there is ground to believe, it was not Elizabeth's business to punish her for it. And truly it was not for that she took away her life; but she made use of that pretence to detain her in prison, under the deceitful colour of making her innocence appear. On this occasion her dissimulation was blameworthy. This first piece of injustice, drew her in afterwards to use a world of artful devices to get a pretence to render Mary's imprisonment perpetual. From hence arose in the end, the necessity of putting her to death on the scaffold. This doubtless is Elizabeth's great blemish, which manifestly proves to what degree she carried the fear of losing a crown. The continual fear and uneasiness she was under on that account, is what characterises her reign, because it was the main spring of almost all her actions. The best thing that can be said in Elizabeth's behalf is, that the queen of Scots and her friends had brought matters to such a pass, that one of the two queens must perish, and it was natural that the weakest should fall. I don't believe any body ever questioned her being a true Protestant. But, as it was her interest to be so, some have taken occasion to doubt whether the zeal she expressed for her religion, was the effect of her persuasion or policy. All that can be said is, that she happened sometimes to prefer her temporal concerns, before those of religion. To sum up in two words what may serve to form Elizabeth's character, I shall add she was a good and illustrious queen, with many virtues and noble qualities, and few faults. But what ought above all things to make her memory precious is, that she caused the English to enjoy a state of felicity unknown to their ancestors, under most part of the kings, her predecessors.

Died March 24, 1603, aged 70, having reigned 44 years, 4 months, and 8 days.

Rapin.

§ 72. *Another Character of* ELIZABETH.

There are few great personages in history who have been more exposed to the calumny of enemies, and the adulation of friends, than queen Elizabeth; and yet there is scarce any whose reputation has been more certainly determined, by the unanimous consent of posterity. The unusual length of her administration, and the strong features of her character, were able to overcome all prejudices; and obliging her detractors to abate much of their invectives, and her admirers somewhat their panegyricks, have at last, in spite of political factions, and, what is more, of religious animosities, produced an uniform judgment with regard to her conduct. Her vigour, her constancy, her magnanimity, her penetration, and vigilance, are allowed to merit the highest praise, and appear not to have been surpassed by any person who ever filled a throne. A conduct less vigorous, less imperious; more sincere, more indulgent to her people, would have been requisite to form a perfect character. By the force of her mind, she controuled all her more active and stronger qualities, and prevented them from running into excess. Her heroism was exempt from all temerity, her frugality from avarice, her friendship from partiality, her active spirit from turbulency and a vain ambition. She guarded not herself with equal care, or equal success from lesser infirmities; the rivalship of beauty, the desire of admiration, the jealousy of love, and the sallies of anger.

Her singular talents for government were founded equally on her temper and on her capacity. Endowed with a great command of herself, she obtained an uncontrouled ascendant over her people; and while she merited all their esteem by her real virtues, she also engaged their affection by her pretended ones. Few sovereigns of England succeeded to the throne in more difficult circumstances; and none ever conducted the government with such uniform success and felicity. Though unacquainted with the practice of toleration, the true secret for managing religious factions, she preserved her people, by her superior prudence, from those confusions in which theological controversy had involved all the neighbouring nations: and though her enemies were the most powerful princes in Europe, the most active, the most enterprizing, the least scrupulous, she was able by her vigour to make deep impressions on their state; her own greatness mean while untouched and unimpaired.

The wise ministers and brave warriors, who flourished during her reign, share the praise

praiſe of her ſucceſs; but inſtead of leſſening the applauſe due to her, they make great addition to it. They owed all of them their advancement to her choice, they were ſupported by her conſtancy; and with all their ability they were never able to acquire any undue aſcendant over her. In her family, in her court, in her kingdom, ſhe remained equally miſtreſs. The force of the tender paſſions was great over her, but the force of her mind was ſtill ſuperior; and the combat which her victory viſibly coſt her, ſerves only to diſplay the firmneſs of her reſolution, and the loftineſs of her ambitious ſentiments.

The fame of this princeſs, though it has ſurmounted the prejudices both of faction and bigotry, yet lies ſtill expoſed to another prejudice which is more durable, becauſe more natural, and which, according to the different views in which we ſurvey her, is capable either of exalting beyond meaſure, or diminiſhing the luſtre of her character. This prejudice is founded in conſideration of her ſex. When we contemplate her as a woman, we are apt to be ſtruck with the higheſt admiration of her great qualities and extenſive capacity; but we are apt alſo to require ſome more ſoftneſs of diſpoſition, ſome greater lenity of temper, ſome of thoſe amiable weakneſſes by which her ſex is diſtinguiſhed. But the true method of eſtimating her merit is, to lay aſide all thoſe conſiderations, and conſider her merely as a rational being, placed in authority, and entruſted with the government of mankind. We may find it difficult to reconcile our fancy to her as a wife, or a miſtreſs; but her qualities as a ſovereign, though with ſome conſiderable exceptions, are the object of undiſputed applauſe and approbation.

* * * * *
* * * * *

thus left unfiniſhed by *Hume.*

§ 73. *Another Character of* ELIZABETH.

Elizabeth, in her perſon, was maſculine, tall, ſtraight, and ſtrong-limbed, with an high round forehead, brown eyes, fair complexion, fine white teeth, and yellow hair; ſhe danced with great agility; her voice was ſtrong and ſhrill; ſhe underſtood muſic, and played upon ſeveral inſtruments. She poſſeſſed an excellent memory, and underſtood the dead and living languages, and made good proficiency in the ſciences, and was well read in hiſtory. Her converſation was ſprightly and agreeable; her judgment ſolid, her apprehenſion acute, her application indefatigable, and her courage invincible. She was the great bulwark of the Proteſtant religion; ſhe was highly commendable for her general regard to the impartial adminiſtration of juſtice; and even for her rigid œconomy, which ſaved the public money, and evinced that love for her people which ſhe ſo warmly profeſſed. Yet ſhe deviated from juſtice in ſome inſtances when her intereſt and paſſions were concerned; and, notwithſtanding all her great qualities, we cannot deny ſhe was vain, proud, imperious, and in ſome caſes cruel: her predominant paſſion was jealouſy and avarice; though ſhe was alſo ſubject to ſuch violent guſts of anger as overwhelmed all regard to the dignity of her ſtation, and even hurried her beyond the common bounds of decency. She was wiſe and ſteady in her principles of government, and above all princes fortunate in a miniſtry.

Smollett.

§ 74. *Character of* JAMES I.

James was of a middle ſtature, of a fine complexion, and a ſoft ſkin; his perſon plump, but not corpulent, his eyes large and rolling, his beard thin, his tongue too big for his mouth, his countenance diſagreeable, his air awkward, and his gait remarkably ungraceful, from a weakness in his knees that prevented his walking without assistance; he was tolerably temperate in his diet, but drank of little else than rich and strong wines. His character, from the variety of grotesque qualities that compose it, is not easy to be delineated. The virtues he possessed were so loaded with a greater proportion of their neighbouring vices, that they exhibit no lights, to set off the dark shades; his principles of generosity were tainted by such a childish profusion, that they left him without means of paying his just obligations, and subjected him to the necessity of attempting irregular, illegal, and unjust methods of acquiring money. His friendship, not to give it the name of vice, was directed by so puerile a fancy, and so absurd a caprice, that the objects of it were contemptible, and its consequences attended with such an unmerited profusion of favours, that it was perhaps the most exceptionable quality of any he possessed. His distinctions were formed on principles of selfishness; he valued no person for any endowments that could not be made subservient to his pleasures or his interest; and thus he rarely advanced any man of real worth and preferment. His familiar conversation, both in writing and in speaking, was stuffed with vulgar and indecent phrases. Though proud and arrogant in his temper, and full of the importance of his station, he descended to buffoonery, and suffered his favourites to address him in the most disrespectful terms of gross familiarity.

Himself affected a sententious wit, but rose no higher in those attempts than to quaint, and often stale conceits. His education had been a more learned one than is commonly bestowed on princes; this, from the conceit it gave him, turned out a very disadvantageous circumstance, by contracting his opinions to his own narrow views; his pretences to a consummate knowledge in divinity, politics, and the art of governing, expose him to a high degree of ridicule; his conduct shewing him more than commonly deficient in all these points. His romantic idea of the natural rights of princes, caused him publicly to avow pretensions that impressed into the minds of the people an incurable jealousy; this, with an affectation of a profound skill in the art of dissembling, or kingcraft, as he termed it, rendered him the object of fear and distrust; when at the same time he was himself the only dupe to an impertinent useless hypocrisy.

If the laws and constitution of England received no prejudice from his government, it was owing to his want of ability to effect a change suitable to the purpose of an arbitrary sway. Stained with these vices, and sullied with these weaknesses, if he is even exempt from our hatred, the exemption must arise from motives of contempt. Despicable as he appears through his own Britannic government, his behaviour when king of Scotland was in many points unexceptionable; but, intoxicated with the power he received over a people whose privileges were but feebly established, and who had been long subjected to civil and ecclesiastical tyranny, he at once flung off that moderation that hid his deformities from the common eye. It is alledged that the corruption he met with in the court of England, and the time-serving genius of the English noblemen, were the great means that debauched him from his circumspect conduct. Among the forwardest of the worthless tribe was Cecil, afterwards Earl of Salisbury, who told him on his coming to the crown, that he should find his English subjects like asses, on whom

whom he might lay any burden, and ſhould need neither bit nor bridle, but their aſſes ears. Died March 27, A.D. 1625. Aged 59.

Macaulay.

§ 75. *Another Character of* JAMES.

James was in his ſtature of the middle ſize, inclining to corpulency; his forehead was high, his beard ſcanty, and his aſpect mean; his eyes, which were weak and languid, he rolled about inceſſantly, as if in queſt of novelty; his tongue was ſo large, that in ſpeaking or drinking, he beſlabbered the by-ſtanders; his knees were ſo weak as to bend under the weight of his body; his addreſs was awkward, and his appearance ſlovenly. There was nothing dignified either in the compoſition of his mind or perſon. We have in the courſe of his reign exhibited repeated inſtances of his ridiculous vanity, prejudices, profuſion, folly, and littleneſs of ſoul. All that we can add in his favour is, that he was averſe to cruelty and injuſtice; very little addicted to exceſs, temperate in his meals, kind to his ſervants, and even deſirous of acquiring the love of his ſubjects, by granting that as a favour, which they claimed as a privilege. His reign, though ignoble to himſelf, was happy to his people. They were enriched by commerce, which no war interrupted. They felt no ſevere impoſitions; and the commons made conſiderable progreſs in aſcertaining the liberties of the nation. *Smollett.*

§ 76. *Another Character of* JAMES.

No prince, ſo little enterprizing and ſo inoffenſive, was ever ſo much expoſed to the oppoſite extremes of calumny and flattery, of ſatire and panegyric. And the factions which began in his time, being ſtill continued, have made his character be as much diſputed to this day, as is commonly that of princes who are our contemporaries. Many virtues, however, it muſt be owned, he was poſſeſſed of; but not one of them pure, or free from the contagion of the neighbouring vices. His generoſity bordered on profuſion, his learning on pedantry, his pacific diſpoſition on puſillanimity, his wiſdom on cunning, his friendſhip on light fancy, and boyiſh fondneſs. While he imagined that he was only maintaining his own authority, he may perhaps be ſuſpected in ſome of his actions, and ſtill more of his pretenſions, to have encroached on the liberties of his people. While he endeavoured, by an exact neutrality, to acquire the good will of all his neighbours, he was able to preſerve fully the eſteem and regard of none. His capacity was conſiderable, but fitter to diſcourſe on general maxims than to conduct any intricate buſineſs.

His intentions were juſt, but more adapted to the conduct of private life, than to the government of kingdoms. Awkward in his perſon, and ungainly in his manners, he was ill qualified to command reſpect; partial and undiſcerning in his affections, he was little fitted to acquire general love. Of a feeble temper more than of a frugal judgment; expoſed to our ridicule from his vanity, but exempt from our hatred by his freedom from pride and arrogance. And upon the whole it may be pronounced of his character, that all his qualities were ſullied with weakneſs, and embelliſhed by humanity. Political courage he was certainly devoid of; and from thence chiefly is derived the ſtrong prejudice which prevails againſt his perſonal bravery: an inference, however, which muſt be owned, from general experience, to be extremely fallacious. *Hume.*

§ 77. *Another Character of* James.

The principal thing which is made to ſerve for matter for king James's panegyric, is the conſtant peace he cauſed his ſubjects to enjoy. This cannot be ſaid to be the effect of chance, ſince it clearly appears, it was his ſole, or at leaſt his chief aim in the whole courſe of his adminiſtration. Nothing, ſay his friends, is more worthy a great king than ſuch a deſign. But the ſame deſign loſes all its merit, if the prince diſcovers by his conduct, that he preſerves peace only out of fear, careleſſneſs, exceſſive love of eaſe and repoſe; and king James's whole behaviour ſhews he acted from theſe motives, though he coloured it with the pretence of his affection for the people.

His liberality, which ſome praiſe him for, is exclaimed againſt by others as prodigality. Theſe laſt pretend he gave without meaſure and diſcretion, without any regard to his own wants, or the merit of thoſe whom he heaped his favours upon.

As to his manners, writers are no leſs divided: ſome will have him to be looked on as a very wiſe and virtuous prince; whilſt others ſpeak of him as a prince of a diſſolute life, given to drinking, and a great ſwearer in common converſation, eſpecially when in a paſſion. He is likewiſe taxed with diſſolving the Earl of Eſſex's marriage, the pardoning the Earl and Counteſs of Somerſet, the death of Sir Walter Raleigh, and the confidence wherewith in full parliament he called God to witneſs, that he never had any thoughts of giving the Papiſts a toleration, which he could not affirm but by means of ſome mental reſervation.

But whatever may be ſaid for or againſt James's perſon, it is certain England never flouriſhed leſs than in his reign; the Engliſh ſaw themſelves expoſed to the inſults and jeſts of other nations, and all the world in general threw the blame on the king. *Rapin.*

§ 78. *Character of* Charles I.

Such was the unworthy and unexampled fate of Charles I. king of England, who fell a ſacrifice to the moſt atrocious inſolence of treaſon, in the forty-ninth year of his age, and in the twenty-fourth of his reign. He was a prince of a middling ſtature, robuſt, and well proportioned. His hair was of a dark colour, his forehead high, his complexion pale, his viſage long, and his aſpect melancholy. He excelled in riding, and other manly exerciſes; he inherited a good underſtanding from nature, and had cultivated it with great aſſiduity. His perception was clear and acute, his judgment ſolid and deciſive; he poſſeſſed a refined taſte for the liberal arts, and was a munificent patron to thoſe who excelled in painting, ſculpture, muſic, and architecture. In his private morals he was altogether unblemiſhed and exemplary. He was merciful, modeſt, chaſte, temperate, religious, perſonally brave, and we may join the noble hiſtorian in ſaying, "He was the "worthieſt gentleman, the beſt maſter, the "beſt friend, the beſt huſband, the beſt fa-"ther, and the beſt chriſtian of the age in "which he lived." He had the misfortune to be bred up in high notions of the prerogative, which he thought his honour and his duty obliged him to maintain. He lived at a time when the ſpirit of the people became too mighty for thoſe reſtraints which the regal power derived from the conſtitution; and when the tide of fanaticiſm began to overbear the religion of his country, to which he was conſcientiouſly devoted. He ſuffered himſelf to be guided by counſellors, who were not only

only inferior to himſelf in knowledge and judgment, but generally proud, partial, and inflexible; and from an exceſs of conjugal affection that bordered upon weakneſs, he paid too much deference to the advice and deſires of his conſort, who was ſuperſtitiouſly attached to the errors of popery, and importuned him inceſſantly in favour of the Roman Catholics.

Such were the ſources of all that miſgovernment which was imputed to him during the firſt fifteen years of his reign. From the beginning of the civil war to his fatal cataſtrophe, his conduct ſeems to have been unexceptionable. His infirmities and imperfections have been candidly owned in the courſe of this narration. He was not very liberal to his dependants; his converſation was not eaſy, nor his addreſs pleaſing; yet the probity of his heart, and the innocence of his manners, won the affection of all who attended his perſon, not even excepting thoſe who had the charge of his confinement. In a word, he certainly deſerved the epithet of a virtuous prince, though he wanted ſome of thoſe ſhining qualities which conſtitute the character of a great monarch. Beheaded January 30, 1648-9. *Smollett.*

§ 79. *Another Character of* Charles I.

The character of this prince, as that of moſt men, if not of all men, was mixed, but his virtues predominated extremely above his vices; or, more properly ſpeaking, his imperfections: for ſcarce any of his faults aroſe to that pitch, as to merit the appellation of vices. To conſider him in the moſt favourable light, it may be affirmed, that his dignity was exempted from pride, his humanity from weakneſs, his bravery from raſhneſs, his temperance from auſterity, and his frugality from avarice: all theſe virtues in him maintained their proper bounds, and merited unreſerved praiſe. To ſpeak the moſt harſhly of him, we may affirm, that many of his good qualities were attended with ſome latent frailty, which, though ſeemingly inconſiderable, was able, when ſeconded by the extreme malevolence of his fortune, to diſappoint them of all their influence. His beneficent diſpoſition was clouded by a manner not gracious, his virtue was tinctured with ſuperſtition, his good ſenſe was disfigured by a deference to perſons of a capacity much inferior to his own, and his moderate temper exempted him not from haſty and precipitate reſolutions. He deſerves the epithet of a good, rather than of a great man; and was more fitted to rule in a regular eſtabliſhed government, than either to give way to the encroachments of a popular aſſembly, or finally to ſubdue their pretenſions. He wanted ſuppleneſs and dexterity ſufficient for the firſt meaſure; he was not endowed with vigour requiſite for the ſecond. Had he been born an abſolute prince, his humanity and good ſenſe had rendered his reign happy, and his memory precious. Had the limitations on the prerogative been in his time quite fixed and certain, his integrity had made him regard as ſacred the boundaries of the conſtitution. Unhappily his fate threw him into a period, when the precedents of many former reigns ſavoured ſtrongly of arbitrary power, and the genius of the people ran violently towards liberty. And if his political prudence was not ſufficient to extricate him from ſo perilous a ſituation, he may be excuſed; ſince, even after the event, when it is commonly eaſy to correct all errors, one is at a loſs to determine what conduct in his circumſtances

cumstances would have maintained the authority of the crown, and preserved the peace of the nation. Exposed without revenue, without arms, to the assault of furious, implacable, and bigoted factions; it was never permitted him, but with the most fatal consequences, to commit the smallest mistake; a condition too rigorous to be imposed on the greatest human capacity.

Some historians have rashly questioned the good faith of this prince: but, for this reproach, the most malignant scrutiny of his conduct, which in every circumstance is now thoroughly known, affords not any reasonable foundation. On the contrary, if we consider the extreme difficulties to which he was so frequently reduced, and compare the sincerity of his professions and declarations, we shall avow, that probity and honour ought justly to be numbered among his most shining qualities. In every treaty, those concessions which he thought in conscience he could not maintain, he never would by any motive or persuasion be induced to make.

And though some violations of the petition of right may be imputed to him; those are more to be ascribed to the necessity of his situation, and to the lofty ideas of royal prerogative which he had imbibed, than to any failure of the integrity of his principles. This prince was of a comely presence; of a sweet and melancholy aspect; his face was regular, handsome, and well complexioned; his body strong, healthy, and justly proportioned; and being of middle stature, he was capable of enduring the greatest fatigues. He excelled in horsemanship and other exercises; and he possessed all the exterior, as well as many of the essential qualities, which form an accomplished prince. *Hume.*

§ 80. *Another Character of* Charles I.

In the character of Charles, as represented by his panegyrists, we find the qualities of temperance, chastity, regularity, piety, equity, humanity, dignity, condescension, and equanimity; some have gone so far as to allow him integrity, and many writers, who condemn his political principles, give him the title of a moral man. In the comparison of this representation with Charles's conduct, accurately and justly described, it is discernible that vices of the worst tendency, when shaded by a plausible and formal carriage, when concordant to the interests of a faction, and the prejudices of the vulgar, assume the appearances of, and are imposed on the credulous world as, virtues of the first rank.

Passion for power was Charles's predominant vice; idolatry to his regal prerogatives, his governing principle. The interests of the crown, legitimated every measure, and sanctified in his eye the widest deviation from moral rule.

Neither gratitude, clemency, humanity, equity, nor generosity, have place in the fair part of Charles's character; of the virtues of temperance, fortitude, and personal bravery, he was undeniably possessed. His manners partook of dissipation, and his conversation of the indecency of a court. His chastity has been called in question, by an author of the highest repute; and were it allowed, it was tainted by an excess of uxoriousness, which gave it the properties and the consequences of vice. The want of integrity is manifest in every part of his conduct; which, whether the corruption of his judgment or heart, lost him fair opportunities of reinstatement in the throne, and was the vice for which above all others he paid the tribute of of his life. His intellectual powers were naturally good, and so improved by a continual exercise, that, though in the beginning of his reign he spoke with difficulty and hesitation, towards the close of his life he discovered in his writings purity of language and dignity of style; in his debates elocution, and quickness of perception. The high opinion he entertained of regal dignity, occasioned him to observe a stateliness and imperiousness in his manner; which, to the rational and intelligent, was unamiable and offensive; by the weak and formal it was mistaken for dignity.

In the exercise of horsemanship he excelled; had a good taste, and even skill, in several of the polite arts; but though a proficient in some branches of literature, was no encourager of useful learning, and only patronized adepts in jargon of the divine right, and utility of kings and bishops. His understanding in this point was so depraved by the prejudices of his education, the flattery of priests, and the affections of his heart, that he would never endure conversation which tended to inculcate the principles of equal right in men; and notwithstanding that the particularity of his situation enforced his attention to doctrines of this kind, he went out of the world with the same fond prejudices with which he had been fostered in his nursery, and cajoled in the zenith of his power.

Charles was of a middle stature, his body strong, healthy, and justly proportioned; and his aspect melancholy, yet not unpleasing. His surviving issue, were three sons and three daughters. He was executed in the 49th year of his age, and buried, by the appointment of the parliament, at Windsor, decently, yet without pomp.

Macaulay.

§ 81. *Character of* Oliver Cromwell*.

Oliver Cromwell was of a robust make and constitution, his aspect manly though clownish. His education extended no farther than a superficial knowledge of the Latin tongue, but he inherited great talents from nature; though they were such as he could not have exerted to advantage at any juncture than that of a civil war, inflamed by religious contests. His character was formed from an amazing conjuncture of enthusiasm, hypocrisy, and ambition. He was possessed of courage and resolution, that overlooked all dangers, and saw no difficulties. He dived into the characters of mankind with wonderful sagacity, whilst he concealed his own purposes, under the impenetrable shield of dissimulation.

He reconciled the most atrocious crimes to the most rigid notions of religious obligations. From the severest exercise of devotion, he relaxed into the most ridiculous and idle buffoonry: yet he preserved the dignity and distance of his character, in the midst of the coarsest familiarity. He was cruel and tyrannic from policy; just and temperate from inclination; perplexed and despicable in his discourse; clear and consummate in his designs; ridiculous in his reveries; respectable in his conduct; in a word, the strangest compound of villainy and virtue, baseness and magnanimity, absurdity and good sense, that we find on record in the annals of mankind †.

Noble.

§ 82.

* From Noble's Memoirs of the Protectoral house of Cromwell.

† Cromwell died more than five millions in debt; though the parliament had left him in the treasury above five hundred thousand pounds, and in

§ 82. *Character of* CHARLES II.

If we ſurvey the character of Charles the Second in the different lights which it will admit of, it will appear very various, and give riſe to different and even oppoſite ſentiments. When conſidered as a companion, he appears the moſt amiable and engaging of men; and indeed, in this view, his deportment muſt be allowed altogether unexceptionable. His love of raillery was ſo tempered with good-breeding, that it was never offenſive. His propenſity to ſatire was ſo checked with diſcretion, that his friends never dreaded their becoming the object of it. His wit, to uſe the expreſſion of one who knew him well, and who was himſelf an exquiſite judge *, could not be ſaid ſo much to be very refined or elevated, qualities apt to beget jealouſy and apprehenſion in company, as to be a plain, gaining, well-bred, recommending kind of wit. And though perhaps he talked more than ſtrict rules of behaviour might permit, men were ſo pleaſed with the affable communicative deportment of the monarch, that they always went away contented both with him and with themſelves. This indeed is the moſt ſhining part of the king's character, and he ſeems to have been ſenſible of it; for he was fond of dropping the formalities of ſtate, and of relapſing every moment into the companion.

in ſtores to the value of ſeven hundred thouſand pounds.

Richard, the ſon of Cromwell, was proclaimed protector in his room; but Richard, being of a very different diſpoſition to his father, reſigned his authority the 22d of April 1659; and ſoon after ſigned his abdication in form, and retired to live ſeveral years after his reſignation, at firſt on the Continent, and afterwards upon his paternal fortune at home.

* Marquis of Halifax.

In the duties of private life, his conduct, though not free from exception, was in the main laudable. He was an eaſy generous lover, a civil obliging huſband, a friendly brother, an indulgent father, and a good-natured maſter. The voluntary friendſhips, however, which this prince contracted, nay, even his ſenſe of gratitude, were feeble; and he never attached himſelf to any of his miniſters or courtiers with a very ſincere affection. He believed them to have no other motive for ſerving him but ſelf-intereſt, and he was ſtill ready, in his turn, to ſacrifice them to preſent eaſe and convenience.

With a detail on his private character we muſt ſet bounds to our panegyric on Charles. The other parts of his conduct may admit of ſome apology, but can deſerve ſmall applauſe. He was indeed ſo much fitted for private life, preferably to public, that he even poſſeſſed order, frugality, œconomy in the former; was profuſe, thoughtleſs, negligent in the latter. When we conſider him as a ſovereign, his character, though not altogether void of virtues, was in the main dangerous to his people, and diſhonourable to himſelf. Negligent of the intereſts of the nation, careleſs of its glory, averſe to its religion, jealous of its liberty, laviſh of its treaſure, and ſparing only of its blood; he expoſed it by his meaſures (though he appeared ever but in ſport) to the danger of a furious civil war, and even to the ruin and ignominy of a foreign conteſt. Yet may all theſe enormities, if fairly and candidly examined, be imputed, in a great meaſure, to the indolence of his temper: a fault, which, however unfortunate in a monarch, it is impoſſible for us to regard with great ſeverity.

It has been remarked of this king, that he never ſaid a fooliſh thing, nor ever did a wiſe one: a cenſure, which, though too far carried.

carried, ſeems to have ſome foundation in his character and deportment. Died Feb. 6, 1685, aged 54. *Hume.*

§ 83. *Another Character of* Charles II.

Charles II. was in his perſon tall and ſwarthy, and his countenance marked with ſtrong, harſh lineaments. His penetration was keen, his judgment clear, his underſtanding extenſive, his converſation lively and entertaining, and he poſſeſſed the talent of wit and ridicule. He was eaſy of acceſs, polite, and affable; had he been limited to a private ſtation, he would have paſſed for the moſt agreeable and beſt-natured man of the age in which he lived. His greateſt enemies allow him to have been a civil huſband, an obliging lover, an affectionate father, and an indulgent maſter; even as a prince, he manifeſted an averſion to cruelty and injuſtice. Yet theſe good qualities were more than overbalanced by his weakneſs and defects. He was a ſcoffer at religion, and a libertine in his morals; careleſs, indolent, profuſe, abandoned to effeminate pleaſure, incapable of any noble enterprize, a ſtranger to any manly friendſhip and gratitude, deaf to the voice of honour, blind to the allurements of glory, and in a word, wholly deſtitute of every active virtue. Being himſelf unprincipled, he believed mankind were falſe, perfidious, and intereſted; and therefore practiſed diſſimulation for his own convenience. He was ſtrongly attached to the French manners, government, and monarch; he was diſſatisfied with his own limited prerogative. The majority of his own ſubjects he deſpiſed or hated, as hypocrites, fanatics, and republicans; who had perſecuted his father and himſelf, and ſought the deſtruction of the monarchy. In theſe ſentiments, he could not be ſuppoſed to purſue the intereſt of the nation; on the contrary, he ſeemed to think that his own ſafety was incompatible with the honour and advantage of his people. *Smollett.*

§ 84. *Another Character of* Charles II.

Thus lived and died king Charles the Second. He was the greateſt inſtance in hiſtory of the various revolutions of which any one man ſeemed capable. He was bred up the firſt twelve years of his life, with the ſplendour that became the heir of ſo great a crown. After that, he paſſed through eighteen years in great inequalities, unhappy in the war, in the loſs of his father, and of the crown of England.—While he was abroad at Paris, Colen, or Bruſſels, he never ſeemed to lay any thing to heart. He purſued all his diverſions, and irregular pleaſures, in a free career; and ſeemed to be as ſerene under the loſs of a crown, as the greateſt philoſopher could have been. Nor did he willingly hearken to any of thoſe projects, with which, he complained often, his chancellor perſecuted him. That in which he ſeemed moſt concerned was, to find money for ſupporting his expence. And it was often ſaid, that if Cromwell would have compounded the matter, and have given him a good round penſion, he might have been induced to reſign his title to him. During his exile, he delivered himſelf ſo entirely to his pleaſures, that he became incapable of application. He ſpent little of his time in reading and ſtudy; and yet leſs in thinking. And in the ſtate his affairs were then in, he accuſtomed himſelf to ſay to every perſon, and upon all occaſions, that which he thought would pleaſe moſt: ſo that words or promiſes went very eaſily from him. And he had ſo ill an opinion of mankind, that he thought the great art of living and governing

verning was, to manage all things, and all persons, with a depth of craft and dissimulation. He desired to become absolute, and to overturn both our religion and laws; yet he would neither run the risque, nor give himself the trouble, which so great a design required. He had an appearance of gentleness in his outward deportment; but he seemed to have no bowels nor tenderness in his nature; and in the end of his life he became cruel.

Burnet.

§ 85. *Another Character of* Charles II.

The character of Charles the Second, like the transactions of his reign, has assumed various appearances, in proportion to the passions and prejudices of different writers. To affirm that he was a great and good king, would be as unjust as to alledge that he was destitute of all virtue, and a bloody and inhuman tyrant. The indolence of his disposition, and the dissipation occasioned by his pleasures, as they were at first the source of his misfortunes, became afterwards the safety of the nation. Had he joined the ambition of power, and the perseverance and attention of his brother, to his own insinuating and engaging address, he might have secured his reputation with writers, by enslaving them with the nation.

In his person he was tall and well made. His complexion was dark, the lines of his face strong and harsh, when singly traced: but when his features were comprehended in one view, they appeared dignified and even pleasing. In the motions of his person he was easy, graceful, and firm. His constitution was strong, and communicated an active vigour to all his limbs. Though a lover of ease of mind, he was fond of bodily exercise. He rose early, he walked much, he mixed with the meanest of his subjects, and joined in their conversation, without diminishing his own dignity, or raising their presumption. He was acquainted with many persons in the lower stations of life. He captivated them with sprightly terms of humour, and with a kind of good-natured wit, which rendered them pleased with themselves. His guards only attended him on public occasions. He took the air frequently in company with a single friend; and though crowds followed him, it was more from a wish to attract his notice, than from an idle curiosity. When evident designs against his life were daily exhibited before the courts of justice, he changed not his manner of appearing in public. It was soon after the Rye-house plot was discovered, he is said to have been severe on his brother's character, when he exhibited a striking feature of his own. The duke returning from hunting with his guards, found the king one day in Hyde Park. He expressed his surprise how his majesty could venture his person alone at such a perilous time. "James," (replied the king,) "take you "care of yourself, and I am safe. No man "in England will kill ME, to make YOU "king."

When he was opposed with most violence in parliament, he continued the most popular man in the kingdom. His good-breeding as a gentleman, overcame the opinion conceived of his faults as a king. His affability, his easy address, his attention to the very prejudices of his people, rendered him independent of all the arts of his enemies to inflame the vulgar. He is said with reason to have died opportunely for his country. Had his life extended to the number of years which the strength of his constitution seemed to promise, the nation would have lost all memory of their liberties.

liberties. Had his fate placed Charles the Second in these latter times; when influence supplies the place of obvious power; when the crown has ceased to be distressed through the channel of its necessities; when the representatives of the people, in granting supplies for the public service, provide for themselves; his want of ambition would have precluded the jealousy, and his popular qualities secured the utmost admiration of his subjects. His gallantry itself would be construed into spirit, in an age where decency is only an improvement on vice. *Macpherson.*

§ 86. *Character of* James II.

In many respects it must be owned, that he was a virtuous man, as well as a good monarch. He was frugal of the public money; he encouraged commerce with great attention; he applied himself to naval affairs with success; he supported the fleet as the glory and protection of England. He was also zealous for the honour of his country; he was capable of supporting its interest with a degree of dignity in the scale of Europe. In his private life he was almost irreproachable; he was an indulgent parent, a tender husband, a generous and steady friend; in his deportment he was affable, though stately; he bestowed favours with peculiar grace; he prevented solicitation by the suddenness of his dispesal of places; though scarce any prince was ever so generally deserted, few ever had so many private friends; those who injured him most were the first to implore his forgiveness, and even after they had raised another prince to the throne, they respected his person, and were anxious for his safety. To these virtues he added a steadiness of counsels, a perseverance in his plans, and courage in his enterprizes. He was honourable and fair in all his dealings; he was unjust to men in their principles, but never with regard to their property. Though few monarchs ever offended a people more, he yielded to none in his love of his subjects; he even affirmed, that he quitted England to prevent the horrors of a civil war, as much as from fear of a restraint upon his person from the prince of Orange. His great virtue was a strict adherence to facts and truth in all he wrote and said, though some parts of his conduct had rendered his sincerity in his political profession suspected by his enemies. Abdicated his throne 1689. *Ibid.*

§ 87. *Another Character of* James II.

The enemies of James did not fail to make the most of the advantages they had gained by their subtle manœuvres; some said, that the king's flight was the effect of a disturbed conscience, labouring under the load of secret guilt; and those whose censures were more moderate, asserted, that his incurable bigotry had led him even to sacrifice his crown to the interests of his priests; and that he chose rather to depend on the precarious support of a French force to subdue the refractory spirit of his people, than to abide the issue of events which threatened such legal limitations as should effectually prevent any further abuse of power.

The whole tenor of the king's past conduct undoubtedly gave a countenance to insinuations which were in themselves sufficiently plausible to answer all the purposes for which they were industriously circulated; but when the following circumstances are taken into consideration, namely, that timidity is natural to the human mind, when oppressed with an uninterrupted series of misfortunes; that the king's life was put entirely into the hands of a rival, whose ambitious views were alto-

gether

gether incompatible even with the ſhadow of regal power in his perſon; that the means taken to increaſe the apprehenſions which reflections of this nature muſt neceſſarily occaſion, were of the moſt mortifying kind; it muſt be acknowledged, that if the principles of heroic virtue might have produced conduct in ſome exalted individuals, yet that the generality of mankind would, in James's ſituation, have ſought ſhelter in the profeſſed generoſity of a truſted friend, from perſonal inſult, perſonal danger, and from all the harraſſing ſuſpenſe under which the mind of this imprudent and unfortunate monarch had long laboured.

The oppoſition of James's religious principles to thoſe of his ſubjects, his unpopular connections with the court of France; but, above all, the permanent eſtabliſhment of a rival family on the throne of England, has formed in his favour ſuch an union of prejudice and intereſt, as to deſtroy in the minds of poſterity, all that ſympathy which, on ſimilar occaſions, and in ſimilar misfortunes, has ſo wonderfully operated in favour of other princes; and whilſt we pay the tribute of unavailing tears over the memory of Charles the Firſt; whilſt, with the Church of England, we venerate him as a martyr to the power and office of prelates; whilſt we ſee, with regret, that he was ſtripped of his dignity and life at the very time when the chaſtening hand of affliction had, in a great meaſure, corrected the errors of a faulty education; the irreſiſtible power of truth muſt oblige us to confeſs, that the adherence to religious principle, which coſt the father his life, deprived the ſon of his dominions; that the enormous abuſes of power with which both ſovereigns are accuſed, owed their origin to the ſame ſource; the errors ariſing from a bad education, aggravated and extended by the impious flattery of deſigning prieſts; we ſhall alſo be obliged to confeſs, that the parliament itſelf, by an unprecedented ſervility, helped to confirm James in the exalted idea he had entertained of the royal office, and that the doctrines of an abſolute and unconditional ſubmiſſion on the part of ſubjects, which, in the reign of his father, was, in a great meaſure, confined to the precepts of a Laud, a Sibthorpe, and a Maynwaring, were now taught as the avowed doctrines of the Church of England, were acknowledged by the two Univerſities, and implicitly avowed by a large majority of the nation; ſo great, indeed, was the change in the temper, manners, and opinions of the people, from the commencement of the reign of Charles the Firſt to the commencement of the reign of his ſon James, that at this ſhameful period the people gloried in having laid all their privileges at the foot of the throne, and execrated every generous principle of freedom, as ariſing from a ſpirit totally incompatible with the peace of ſociety, and altogether repugnant to the doctrines of Chriſtianity.

This was the ſituation of affairs at the acceſſion of the unfortunate James; and had he been equally unprincipled as his brother, the deceaſed king; had he profeſſed himſelf a Proteſtant, whilſt he was in his heart a Papiſt; had he not regarded it as his duty to uſe his omnipotent power for the reſtoring to ſome parts of its ancient dignity a Church which he regarded as the only true Church of Chriſt; or had he, inſtead of attacking the prerogative of the prelacy, ſuffered them to ſhare the regal deſpotiſm which they had fixed on the baſis of conſcience, the moſt flagrant abuſes of civil power would never have been called in judgment againſt him, and parliament

liament themſelves would have lent their conſtitutional authority to have riveted the chains of the empire in ſuch a manner as ſhould have put it out of the power of the moſt determined votaries of freedom to have re-eſtabliſhed the government on its ancient foundation. From this immediate evil England owes its deliverance to the bigoted ſincerity of James; a circumſtance which ought, in ſome meaſure, to conciliate our affections to the memory of the ſufferer, and induce us to treat thoſe errors with lenity, which have led to the enjoyment of privileges which can never be entirely loſt, but by a general corruption of principle and depravity of manners.

It was ſaid by the witty duke of Buckingham, "that Charles the Second might do "well if he would, and that James would do "well if he could;" an obſervation which ſays little for the underſtanding of James, but a great deal for his heart; and, with all the blemiſhes with which his public character is ſtained, he was not deficient in ſeveral qualities neceſſary to compoſe a good ſovereign. His induſtry and buſineſs were exemplary, he was frugal of the public money, he cheriſhed and extended the maritime power of the empire, and his encouragement of trade was attended with ſuch ſucceſs, that, according to the obſervation of the impartial hiſtorian Ralph, as the frugality of his adminiſtration helped to increaſe the number of malcontents, ſo his extreme attention to trade was not leſs alarming to the whole body of the Dutch, than his reſolution not to ruſh into a war with France was mortifying to their ſtadtholder.

In domeſtic life, the character of James, though not irreproachable, was comparatively good. It is true, he was in a great meaſure tainted with that licentiouſneſs of manners, which at this time pervaded the whole ſociety, and which reigned triumphant within the circle of the court; but he was never carried into any exceſſes which trenched deeply on the duties of ſocial life; and if the qualities of his heart were only to be judged by his different conduct in the different characters of huſband, father, maſter, and friend, he might be pronounced a man of very amiable diſpoſition. But thoſe who know not how to forgive injuries, and can never pardon the errors, the infirmities, the vices, or even the virtues of their fellow-creatures, when in any reſpect they affect perſonal intereſt or inclination, will aim againſt them the ſenſibility of every humane mind, and can never expect from others that juſtice and commiſeration which themſelves have never exerciſed: but whilſt we execrate that rancorous cruelty with which James, in the ſhort hour of triumph, perſecuted all thoſe who endeavoured to thwart his ambitious hopes, it is but juſtice to obſerve, that the rank vices of pride, malice, and revenge, which blacken his conduct, whilſt he figured in the ſtation of preſumptive heir to the crown, and afterwards in the character of ſovereign, on the ſucceſsful quelling of the Monmouth rebellion, were thoroughly corrected by the chaſtiſing hand of affliction: that the whole period of his life, from his return to Ireland to the day of his death, was ſpent in the exerciſe of the firſt Chriſtian virtues, patience, fortitude, humility, and reſignation. Bretonneau, his biographer, records, that he always ſpoke with an extreme moderation of the individuals who had acted the moſt ſucceſsfully in his diſfavour; that he reproved thoſe who mentioned their conduct with ſeverity; that he read, even with a ſtoical apathy, the bittereſt writings

writings which were published against him; that he regarded the loss of empire as a necessary correction of the misdemeanors of his life, and even rebuked those who expressed any concern for the issue of events, which he respected as ordinations of the divine will.

According to the same biographer, James was exact in his devotion, moderate even to abstinence in his life; full of sentiments of the highest contrition for past offences; and, according to the discipline of the Romish church, was very severe in the austerities which he inflicted on his person. As this prince justly regarded himself as a martyr to the Catholic faith, as his warmest friends were all of this persuasion, as his conversation in his retirement at St. Germains was entirely, in a great measure, confined to priests and devotees, it is natural that this superstition should increase with the increase of religious sentiment; and as he had made use of his power and authority, whilst in England, to enlarge the number of proselytes in popery, so, in a private station, he laboured incessantly, by prayer, exhortation, and example, to confirm the piety of his Popish adherents, and to effect a reformation in those who still continued firm to the doctrines of the church of England. He visited the monks of La Trappe once a year, the severest order of religionists in France; and his conformity to the discipline of the convent was so strict and exact, that he impressed those devotees with sentiments of admiration at his piety, humility, and constancy.

Thus having spent twelve years with a higher degree of peace and tranquillity than he had ever experienced in the most triumphant part of his life, he was seized with a palsy in September 1701, and after having languished fifteen days, died in the sixty-eighth year of his age, having filled up the interval between his first seizure and final exit with the whole train of religious exercises enjoined on similar occasions by the church of Rome, with solemn and repeated professions of his faith, and earnest exhortation to his two children, the youngest of whom was born in the second year of his exile, to keep stedfast to the religion in which they had been educated. These precepts and commands have acted with a force superior to all the temptations of a crown, and have been adhered to with a firmness which obliges an historian to acknowledge the superiority which James's descendants, in the nice points of honour and conscience, have gained over the character of Henry the Fourth, who, at the period when he was looked up to as the great hero of the Protestant cause, made no scruple to accept a crown on the disgraceful terms of abjuring the principles of the Reformation, and embracing the principles of a religion, which, from his early infancy, he had been taught to regard as idolatrous and profane.

The dominion of error over the minds of the generality of mankind is irresistible. James, to the last hour of his life, continued as great a bigot to his political as his religious errors: he could not help considering the strength and power of the crown as a circumstance necessary to the preservation and happiness of the people; and in a letter of advice which he wrote to his son, whilst he conjures him to pay a religious observance to all the duties of a good sovereign, he cautions him against suffering any entrenchment on the royal prerogative. Among several heads, containing

containing excellent inſtructions on the art of reigning happily and juſtly, he warns the young prince never to diſquiet his ſubjects in their property or their religion; and, what is remarkable, to his laſt breath he perſiſted in aſſerting, that he never attempted to ſubvert the laws, or procure more than a toleration and equality of privilege to his Catholic ſubjects. As there is great reaſon to believe this aſſertion to be true, it ſhews, that the deluſion was incurable under which the king laboured, by the truſt he had put in the knaviſh doctrines of lawyers and prieſts; and that neither himſelf, nor his Proteſtant abettors, could fathom the conſequences of that enlarged toleration which he endeavoured to eſtabliſh. *Macaulay.*

§ 88. *Character of* William III.

William III. was in his perſon of the middle ſtature, a thin body, and delicate conſtitution, ſubject to an aſthma and continual cough from his infancy. He had an aquiline noſe, ſparkling eyes, a large forehead, and a grave ſolemn aſpect. He was very ſparing of ſpeech; his converſation was dry, and his manner diſguſting, except in battle, when his deportment was free, ſpirited, and animating. In courage, fortitude, and equanimity, he rivalled the moſt eminent warriors of antiquity; and his natural ſagacity made amends for the defects of his education, which had not been properly ſuperintended. He was religious, temperate, generally juſt and ſincere, a ſtranger to violent tranſports of paſſion, and might have paſſed for one of the beſt princes of the age in which he lived, had he never aſcended the throne of Great Britain. But the diſtinguiſhing criterion of his character was ambition; to this he ſacrificed the punctilios of honour and decorum, in depoſing his own father-in-law and uncle; and this he gratified at the expence of the nation that raiſed him to ſovereign authority. He aſpired to the honour of acting as umpire in all the conteſts of Europe; and the ſecond object of his attention was, the proſperity of that country to which he owed his birth and extraction. Whether he really thought the intereſts of the Continent and Great Britain were inſeparable, or ſought only to drag England into the confederacy as a convenient ally; certain it is, he involved theſe kingdoms in foreign connections, which, in all probability, will be productive of their ruin. In order to eſtabliſh this favourite point, he ſcrupled not to employ all the engines of corruption, by which means the morals of the nation were totally debauched. He procured a parliamentary ſanction for a ſtanding army, which now ſeems to be interwoven in the conſtitution. He introduced the pernicious practice of borrowing upon remote funds; an expedient that neceſſarily hatched a brood of uſurers, brokers, and ſtock-jobbers, to prey upon the vitals of their country. He entailed upon the nation a growing debt, and a ſyſtem of politics big with miſery, deſpair, and deſtruction. To ſum up his character in a few words, William was a fataliſt in religion, indefatigable in war, enterpriſing in politics, dead to all the warm and generous emotions of the human heart, a cold relation, an indifferent huſband, a diſagreeable man, an ungracious prince, and an imperious ſovereign.

Died March 8th, 1701, aged 52, having reigned 13 years. *Smollett.*

§ 89. *Another Character of* William III.

William the Third, king of Great Britain and Ireland, was in his perſon of middle ſize, ill-

ill-shaped in his limbs, somewhat round in his shoulders, light brown in the colour of his hair, and in his complexion. The lines of his face were hard, and his nose was aquiline; but a good and penetrating eye threw a kind of light on his countenance, which tempered its severity, and rendered his harsh features, in some measure, agreeable. Though his constitution was weak, delicate, and infirm, he loved the manly exercises of the field; and often indulged himself in the pleasures, and even sometimes in the excesses, of the table. In his private character he was frequently harsh, passionate, and severe, with regard to trifles; but when the subject rose equal to his mind, and in the tumult of battle, he was dignified, cool, and serene. Though he was apt to form bad impressions, which were not easily removed, he was neither vindictive in his disposition, nor obstinate in his resentment. Neglected in his education, and, perhaps, destitute by nature of an elegance of mind, he had no taste for literature, none for the sciences, none for the beautiful arts. He paid no attention to music, he understood no poetry; he disregarded learning; he encouraged no men of letters, no painters, no artists of any kind. In fortification and the mathematics he had a considerable degree of knowledge. Though unsuccessful in the field, he understood military operations by land; but he neither possessed nor pretended to any skill in maritime affairs.

In the distributions of favours he was cold and injudicious. In the punishment of crimes, often too easy, and sometimes too severe. He was parsimonious where he should have been liberal; where he ought to be sparing, frequently profuse. In his temper he was silent and reserved, in his address ungraceful; and though not destitute of dissimulation, and qualified for intrigue, less apt to conceal his passions than his designs: these defects, rather than vices of the mind, combining with an indifference about humouring mankind through their ruling passions, rendered him extremely unfit for gaining the affections of the English nation. His reign, therefore, was crowded with mortifications of various kinds; the discontented parties among his subjects found no difficulty in estranging the minds of the people from a prince possessed of few talents to make him popular. He was trusted, perhaps, less than he deserved, by the most obsequious of his parliaments; but it seems, upon the whole, apparent, that the nation adhered to his government more from a fear of the return of his predecessor, than from any attachment to his own person, or respect for his right to the throne.

Macpherson.

§ 90. *Character of* Mary, *Queen Consort of* William III.

Mary was in her person tall and well proportioned, with an oval visage, lively eyes, agreeable features, a mild aspect, and an air of dignity. Her apprehension was clear, her memory tenacious, and her judgment solid. She was a zealous Protestant, scrupulously exact in all the duties of devotion, of an even temper, of a calm and mild conversation; she was ruffled by no passion, and seems to have been a stranger to the emotions of natural affection, for she ascended the throne from which her father had been deposed, and treated her sister as an alien to her blood. In a word, Mary seems to have imbibed the cold disposition and apathy of her husband, and to have centered all her ambition in deserving the epithet of an humble and obedient wife.

Smollett.

Died 28th December, 1694, aged 33.

§ 91. *Character of* ANNE.

The queen continued to dose in a lethargic insensibility, with very short intervals, till the first day of August in the morning, when she expired, in the fiftieth year of her age, and in the thirteenth of her reign. Anne Stuart, queen of Great Britain, was in her person of the middle size, well proportioned; her hair was of dark brown colour, her complexion ruddy, her features were regular, her countenance was rather round than oval, and her aspect more comely than majestic: her voice was clear and melodious, and her presence engaging; her capacity was naturally good, but not much cultivated by learning; nor did she exhibit any marks of extraordinary genius, or personal ambition: she was certainly deficient in that vigour of mind by which a prince ought to preserve her independence, and avoid the snares and fetters of sycophants and favourites; but, whatever her weakness in this particular might have been, the virtues of her heart were never called in question; she was a pattern of conjugal affection and fidelity, a tender mother, a warm friend, an indulgent mistress, a munificent patron, a mild and merciful princess; during whose reign no blood was shed for treason. She was zealously attached to the Church of England, from conviction rather than from prepossession; unaffectedly pious, just, charitable, and compassionate. She felt a mother's fondness for her people, by whom she was universally beloved with a warmth of affection which even the prejudice of party could not abate. In a word, if she was not the greatest, she was certainly one of the best and most unblemished sovereigns that ever sat upon the throne of England, and well deserved the expressive, though simple epithet of, the "good queen Anne." *Smollett.*

She died in 1714.

§ 92. *Another Character of* ANNE.

Thus died Anne Stuart, queen of Great Britain, and one of the best and greatest monarchs that ever filled that throne. What was most remarkable, was a clear harmonious voice, always admired in her graceful delivery of her speeches to parliament, insomuch that it used to be a common saying in the mouth of every one, "that her very speech was music." Good-nature, the true characteristic of the Stuarts, predominated in her temper, which was a compound of benevolence, generosity, indolence, and timidity, but not without a due sensibility of any slight which she thought was offered to her person or her dignity; to these all her actions, both as a monarch and as a woman, may be ascribed; these were the sources both of her virtues and her failings; her greatest blessing upon earth was that entire union of affections and inclinations between her and her royal consort; which made them a perfect pattern of conjugal love. She was a fond and tender mother, an easy and indulgent mistress, and a most gracious sovereign; but she had more than once reason to repent her giving up her heart, and trusting her secrets without reserve to her favourites. She retained to the last the principle of that true religion which she had imbibed early; being devout without affectation, and charitable without ostentation. She had a great reverence for clergymen eminent for learning and good lives, and was particularly beneficent to the poorer sort of them, of which she left an evidence which bears her name, and will perpetuate both that and her bounty to all ſucceeding generations.

Chamberlaine.

§ 93. *Another Character of* Anne.

Thus died Anne Stuart, queen of Great Britain and Ireland, in the fiftieth year of her age, and thirteenth of her reign. In her perſon ſhe was of a middle ſtature, and, before ſhe bore children, well made. Her hair was dark, her complexion ſanguine, her features ſtrong, but not irregular, her whole countenance more dignified than agreeable. In the accompliſhments of the mind, as a woman, ſhe was not deficient; ſhe underſtood muſic; ſhe loved painting; ſhe had even ſome taſte for works of genius; ſhe was always generous, ſometimes liberal, but never profuſe. Like the reſt of the family, ſhe was good-natured to a degree of weakneſs; indolent in her diſpoſition, timid by nature, devoted to the company of her favourites, eaſily led. She poſſeſſed all the virtues of her father, except political courage; ſhe was ſubject to all his weakneſſes, except enthuſiaſm in religion; ſhe was jealous of her authority, and ſullenly irreconcilable towards thoſe who treated either herſelf or prerogative with diſreſpect; but, like him alſo, ſhe was much better qualified to diſcharge the duties of a private life than to act the part of a ſovereign. As a friend, a mother, a wife, ſhe deſerved every praiſe. Her conduct as a daughter could ſcarcely be exceeded by a virtue much ſuperior to all theſe. Upon the whole, though her reign was crowded with great events, ſhe cannot, with any juſtice, be called a great princeſs. Subject to terror, beyond the conſtitutional timidity of her ſex, ſhe was altogether incapable of deciſive counſels, and nothing but her irreſiſtible popularity could have ſupported her authority amidſt the ferment of thoſe diſtracted times. *Macpherſon.*

§ 94. *The Character of* Mary *Queen of* Scots.

To all the charms of beauty, and the utmoſt elegance of external form, Mary added thoſe accompliſhments which render their impreſſion irreſiſtible. Polite, affable, inſinuating, ſprightly, and capable of ſpeaking and of writing with equal eaſe and dignity. Sudden, however, and violent in all her attachments; becauſe her heart was warm and unſuſpicious. Impatient of contradiction, becauſe ſhe had been accuſtomed from her infancy to be treated as a queen. No ſtranger, on ſome occaſions, to diſſimulation; which, in that perfidious court where ſhe received her education, was reckoned among the neceſſary arts of government, Not inſenſible to flattery, or unconſcious of that pleaſure, with which almoſt every woman beholds the influence of her own beauty. Formed with the qualities that we love, not with the talents that we admire; ſhe was an agreeable woman rather than an illuſtrious queen. The vivacity of her ſpirit, not ſufficiently tempered with ſound judgment, and the warmth of her heart, which was not at all times under the reſtraint of diſcretion, betrayed her both into errors and into crimes. To ſay that ſhe was always unfortunate, will not account for that long and almoſt uninterrupted ſucceſſion of calamities which befel her; we muſt likewiſe add, that ſhe was often imprudent. Her paſſion for Darnly was raſh, youthful, and exceſſive. And though the ſudden tranſition to the oppoſite extreme was the natural effect of her ill-requited love, and of his ingratitude, inſolence, and brutality; yet neither theſe, nor Bothwell's artful addreſs and important ſervices,

ſervices, can juſtify her attachments to that nobleman. Even the manners of the age, licentious as they were, are no apology for this unhappy paſſion; nor can they induce us to look on that tragical and infamous ſcene, which followed upon it, with leſs abhorrence. Humanity will draw a veil over this part of her character, which it cannot approve, and may, perhaps, prompt ſome to impute her actions to her ſituation, more than to her diſpoſition; and to lament the unhappineſs of the former, rather than accuſe the perverſeneſs of the latter. Mary's ſufferings exceed, both in degree and in duration, thoſe tragical diſtreſſes which fancy has feigned to excite ſorrow and commiſeration; and while we ſurvey them, we are apt altogether to forget her frailties, we think of her faults with leſs indignation, and approve of our tears, as if they were ſhed for a perſon who had attained much nearer to pure virtue.

With regard to the queen's perſon, a circumſtance not to be omitted in writing the hiſtory of a female reign, all contemporary authors agree in aſcribing to Mary the utmoſt beauty of countenance and elegance of ſhape of which the human form is capable. Her hair was black, though, according to the faſhion of that age, ſhe frequently wore borrowed locks, and of different colours. Her eyes were a dark grey, her complexion was exquiſitely fine, and her hands and arms remarkably delicate, both as to ſhape and colour. Her ſtature was of a height that roſe to the majeſtic. She danced, ſhe walked, and rode with equal grace. Her taſte for muſic was juſt, and ſhe both ſung and played upon the lute with uncommon ſkill. Towards the end of her life ſhe began to grow fat; and her long confinement, and the coldneſs of the houſes in which ſhe was impriſoned, brought on a rheumatiſm which deprived her of the uſe of her limbs. No man, ſays Brantome, ever beheld her perſon without admiration and love, or will read her hiſtory without ſorrow.

Robertſon.

END OF THE THIRD BOOK.

THE
PROSE EPITOME;
OR,
ELEGANT EXTRACTS ABRIDGED, &c.

BOOK IV. NARRATIVES, DIALOGUES, &c.

With other HUMOROUS, FACETIOUS, and ENTERTAINING PIECES;

And with SPECIMENS of NATURAL HISTORY.

§ 1. *The Story of* LE FEVRE.

IT was ſome time in the ſummer of that year in which Dendermond was taken by the allies,—which was about ſeven years before my father came into the country,—and about as many after the time that my uncle Toby and Trim had privately decamped from my father's houſe in town, in order to lay ſome of the fineſt ſieges to ſome of the fineſt fortified cities in Europe—When my uncle Toby was one evening getting his ſupper, with Trim ſitting behind him at a ſmall ſideboard;—The landlord of a little inn in the village came into the parlour with an empty phial in his hand to beg a glaſs or two of ſack; 'tis for a poor gentleman,—I think, of the army, ſaid the landlord, who has been taken ill at my houſe four days ago, and has never held up his head ſince, or had a deſire to taſte any thing 'till juſt now, that he has a fancy for a glaſs of ſack and a thin toaſt.—*I think*, ſays he, taking his hand from his forehead, *it would comfort me*.——

——If I could neither beg, borrow, nor buy ſuch a thing,—added the landlord,—I would almoſt ſteal it for the poor gentleman, he is ſo ill.——I hope in God he will ſtill mend, continued he—we are all of us concerned for him.

Thou art a good-natured ſoul, I will anſwer for thee, cried my uncle Toby; and thou ſhalt drink the poor gentleman's health in a glaſs of ſack thyſelf,—and take a couple of bottles, with my ſervice, and tell him he is heartily welcome to them, and to a dozen more, if they will do him good.

Though I am perſuaded, ſaid my uncle Toby, as the landlord ſhut the door, he is a very compaſſionate fellow—Trim,—yet I cannot help entertaining an high opinion of his gueſt too; there muſt be ſomething more than common

common in him, that in so short a time should win so much upon the affections of his host; ——And of his whole family, added the corporal, for they are all concerned for him. ——Step after him, said my uncle Toby,—do Trim,—and ask if he knows his name.

——I have quite forgot it, truly, said the landlord, coming back into the parlour with the corporal,—but I can ask his son again: ——Has he a son with him then? said my uncle Toby.——A boy, replied the landlord, of about eleven or twelve years of age;—but the poor creature has tasted almost as little as his father; he does nothing but mourn and lament for him night and day;—he has not stirred from the bed-side these two days.

My uncle Toby laid down his knife and fork, and thrust his plate from before him, as the landlord gave him the account; and Trim, without being ordered, took away without saying one word, and in a few minutes after brought him his pipe and tobacco.

——Stay in the room a little, says my uncle Toby.——

Trim!—said my uncle Toby, after he had lighted his pipe, and smoked about a dozen whiffs—Trim came in front of his master, and made his bow;—my uncle Toby smoked on, and said no more.——Corporal! said my uncle Toby—the corporal made his bow.——My uncle Toby proceeded no farther, but finished his pipe.

Trim! said my uncle Toby, I have a project in my head, as it is a bad night, of wrapping myself up warm in my roquelaure, and paying a visit to this poor gentleman.—Your honour's roquelaure, replied the corporal, has not once been had on, since the night before your honour received your wound, when we mounted guard in the trenches before the gate of St. Nicholas;—and besides, it is so cold and rainy a night, that what with the roquelaure, and what with the weather, 'twill be enough to give your honour your death, and bring on your honour's torment in your groin. —I fear so, replied my uncle Toby; but I am not at rest in my mind, Trim, since the account the landlord has given me.—I wish I had not known so much of this affair,—added my uncle Toby,—or that I had known more of it: How shall we manage it?—Leave it, an't please your honour, to me, quoth the corporal; —I'll take my hat and stick, and go to the house and reconnoitre, and act accordingly; and I will bring your honour a full account in an hour.—Thou shalt go, Trim, said my uncle Toby, and here's a shilling for thee to drink with his servant—I shall get it all out of him, said the corporal, shutting the door.

My uncle Toby filled his second pipe; and had it not been that he now and then wandered from the point, with considering whether it was not full as well to have the curtain of the tennaile a straight line, as a crooked one,—he might be said to have thought of nothing else but poor Le Fevre and his boy the whole time he smoked it.

It was not till my uncle Toby had knocked the ashes out of his third pipe, that corporal Trim returned from the inn, and gave him the following account.

I despaired at first, said the corporal, of being able to bring back your honour any kind of intelligence concerning the poor sick lieutenant—Is he in the army then? said my uncle Toby—He is, said the corporal—And in what regiment? said my uncle Toby—I'll tell your honour, replied the corporal, every thing straight forwards, as I learnt it.—Then, Trim, I'll fill another pipe, said my uncle Toby, and not interrupt thee till thou hast done; so sit down at thy ease, Trim, in the

the window-ſeat, and begin thy ſtory again. The corporal made his old bow, which generally ſpoke, as plain as a bow could ſpeak it—" Your honour is good :" —And having done that, he ſat down, as he was ordered,—and began the ſtory to my uncle Toby over again in pretty near the ſame words.

I deſpaired at firſt, ſaid the corporal, of being able to bring back any intelligence to your honour about the lieutenant and his ſon; for when I aſked where his ſervant was, from whom I made myſelf ſure of knowing every thing which was proper to be aſked—That's a right diſtinction, Trim, ſaid my uncle Toby —I was anſwered, an' pleaſe your honour, that he had no ſervant with him;—that he had come to the inn with hired horſes, which, upon finding himſelf unable to proceed, (to join, I ſuppoſe, the regiment) he had diſmiſſed the morning after he came.—If I get better, my dear, ſaid he, as he gave his purſe to his ſon to pay the man,—we can hire horſes from hence.—But alas! the poor gentleman will never get from hence, ſaid the landlady to me, —for I heard the death-watch all night long; —and when he dies, the youth, his ſon, will certainly die with him; for he is broken-hearted already.

I was hearing this account, continued the corporal, when the youth came into the kitchen, to order the thin toaſt the landlord ſpoke of;—but I will do it for my father myſelf, ſaid the youth.—Pray let me ſave you the trouble, young gentleman, ſaid I, taking up a fork for the purpoſe, and offering him my chair to ſit down upon by the fire, whilſt I did it.—I believe, ſir, ſaid he, very modeſtly, I can pleaſe him beſt myſelf.—I am ſure, ſaid I, his honour will not like the toaſt the worſe for being toaſted by an old ſoldier. — The youth took hold of my hand, and inſtantly burſt into tears. — Poor youth! ſaid my uncle Toby,—he has been bred up from an infant in the army, and the name of a ſoldier, Trim, ſounded in his ears like the name of a friend; I wiſh I had him here.

——I never, in the longeſt march, ſaid the corporal, had ſo great a mind to my dinner, as I had to cry with him for company:—What could be the matter with me, an' pleaſe your honour? Nothing in the world, Trim, ſaid my uncle Toby, blowing his noſe,—but that thou art a good-natured fellow.

When I gave him the toaſt, continued the corporal, I thought it was proper to tell him I was Captain Shandy's ſervant, and that your honour (though a ſtranger) was extremely concerned for his father;—and that if there was any thing in your houſe or cellar—(and thou might'ſt have added my purſe too, ſaid my uncle Toby) he was heartily welcome to it: —he made a very low bow, (which was meant to your honour) but no anſwer,—for his heart was full—ſo he went up ſtairs with the toaſt; —I warrant you, my dear, ſaid I, as I opened the kitchen-door, your father will be well again.—Mr. Yorick's curate was ſmoking a pipe by the kitchen fire—but ſaid not a word good or bad to comfort the youth.——I thought it was wrong, added the corporal——I think ſo too, ſaid my uncle Toby.

When the lieutenant had taken his glaſs of ſack and toaſt, he felt himſelf a little revived, and ſent down into the kitchen, to let me know, that in about ten minutes he ſhould be glad if I would ſtep up ſtairs.—I believe, ſaid the landlord, he is going to ſay his prayers,—for there was a book laid upon the chair by his bed-ſide; and as I ſhut the door I ſaw his ſon take up a cuſhion.—

I thought, ſaid the curate, that you gentlemen of the army, Mr. Trim, never ſaid your prayers

prayers at all.——I heard the poor gentleman ſay his prayers laſt night, ſaid the landlady, very devoutly, and with my own ears, or I could not have believed it.—Are you ſure of it? replied the curate:——A ſoldier, an' pleaſe your reverence, ſaid I, prays as often (of his own accord) as a parſon;—and when he's fighting for his king, and for his own life, and for his honour too, he has the moſt reaſon to pray to God of any one in the whole world. —'Twas well ſaid of thee, Trim, ſaid my uncle Toby.—But when a ſoldier, ſaid I, an' pleaſe your reverence, has been ſtanding for twelve hours together in the trenches, up to his knees in cold water,—or engaged, ſaid I, for months together in long and dangerous marches;—harraſſed, perhaps, in his rear to-day;—harraſſing others to-morrow:—detached here;—countermanded there;—reſting this night upon his arms;—beat up in his ſhirt the next;—benumbed in his joints;—perhaps without ſtraw in his tent to kneel on;—he muſt ſay his prayers how and when he can.—I believe, ſaid I,—for I was piqued, quoth the corporal, for the reputation of the army,—I believe, an't pleaſe your reverence, ſaid I, that when a ſoldier gets time to pray,—he prays as heartily as a parſon—though not with all his fuſs and hypocriſy.——Thou ſhould'ſt not have ſaid that, Trim, ſaid my uncle Toby,—for God only knows who is a hypocrite, and who is not:—At the great and general review of us all, corporal, at the day of judgment, (and not till then)—it will be ſeen who has done their duties in this world,—and who has not; and we ſhall be advanced, Trim, accordingly.—I hope we ſhall, ſaid Trim.——It is in the Scripture, ſaid my uncle Toby; and I will ſhew it thee to-morrow:—In the mean time, we may depend upon it, Trim, for our comfort, ſaid my uncle Toby, that God Almighty is ſo good and juſt a governor of the world, that if we have but done our duties in it,—it will never be enquired into, whether we have done them in a red coat or a black one:—I hope not, ſaid the corporal.—But go on, Trim, ſaid my uncle Toby, with thy ſtory.

When I went up, continued the corporal, into the lieutenant's room, which I did not do till the expiration of the ten minutes,—he was lying in his bed with his head raiſed upon his hand, with his elbow upon the pillow, and a clean white cambric handkerchief beſide it:—The youth was juſt ſtooping down to take up the cuſhion, upon which I ſuppoſe he had been kneeling—the book was laid upon the bed,—and as he roſe, in taking up the cuſhion with one hand, he reached out his other to take it away at the ſame time.——Let it remain there, my dear, ſaid the lieutenant.

He did not offer to ſpeak to me, till I had walked up cloſe to his bed-ſide:—If you are Captain Shandy's ſervant, ſaid he, you muſt preſent my thanks to your maſter, with my little boy's thanks along with them, for his courteſy to me,—if he was of Leven's—ſaid the lieutenant.—I told him your honour was.——Then, ſaid he, I ſerved three compaigns with him in Flanders, and remember him—but 'tis moſt likely, as I had not the honour of any acquaintance with him, that he knows nothing of me.—You will tell him, however, that the perſon his good-nature has laid under obligations to him, is one Le Fevre, a lieutenant in Angus's——but he knows me not,—ſaid he, a ſecond time, muſing;—poſſibly he may my ſtory—added he—pray tell the captain, I was the enſign at Breda, whoſe wife was moſt unfortunately killed with a muſket-ſhot, as ſhe lay in my arms in my tent.——I remember the ſtory, an't pleaſe your honour, ſaid

ſaid I, very well.——Do you ſo, ſaid he, wiping his eyes with his handkerchief,—then well may I.—In ſaying this, he drew a little ring out of his boſom, which ſeemed tied with a black ribband about his neck, and kiſſed it twice.——Here, Billy, ſaid he,—the boy flew acroſs the room to the bed-ſide, and falling down upon his knee, took the ring in his hand, and kiſſed it too,—then kiſſed his father, and ſat down upon the bed and wept.

I wiſh, ſaid my uncle Toby, with a deep ſigh,——I wiſh, Trim, I was aſleep.

Your honour, replied the corporal, is too much concerned;—ſhall I pour your honour out a glaſs of ſack to your pipe?——Do, Trim, ſaid my uncle Toby.

I remember, ſaid my uncle Toby, ſighing again, the ſtory of the enſign and his wife, with a circumſtance his modeſty omitted;—and particularly well that he, as well as ſhe, upon ſome account or other, (I forget what) was univerſally pitied by the whole regiment;—but finiſh the ſtory thou art upon:——'Tis finiſhed already, ſaid the corporal,—for I could ſtay no longer,—ſo wiſhed his honour a good night; young Le Fevre roſe from off the bed, and ſaw me to the bottom of the ſtairs; and as we went down together, told me, they had come from Ireland, and were on their route to join their regiment in Flanders—But alas! ſaid the corporal,—the lieutenant's laſt day's march is over.——Then what is to become of his poor boy? cried my uncle Toby.

It was to my uncle Toby's eternal honour,—though I tell it only for the ſake of thoſe, who, when cooped in betwixt a natural and a poſitive law, know not for their ſouls which way in the world to turn themſelves——That notwithſtanding my uncle Toby was warmly engaged at that time in carrying on the ſiege of Dendermond, parallel with the allies, who preſſed theirs on ſo vigorouſly that they ſcarce allowed him time to get his dinner——that nevertheleſs he gave up Dendermond, though he had already made a lodgment upon the counterſcarp; and bent his whole thoughts towards the private diſtreſſes at the inn; and, except that he ordered the garden-gate to be bolted up, by which he might be ſaid to have turned the ſiege of Dendermond into a blockade—he left Dendermond to itſelf,—to be relieved or not by the French king, as the French king thought good; and only conſidered how he himſelf ſhould relieve the poor lieutenant and his ſon.

—— That kind Being, who is a friend to the friendleſs, ſhall recompenſe thee for this.

Thou haſt left this matter ſhort, ſaid my uncle Toby to the corporal, as he was putting him to bed,—and I will tell thee in what, Trim.—In the firſt place, when thou madeſt an offer of my ſervices to Le Fevre,—as ſickneſs and travelling are both expenſive, and thou knoweſt he was but a poor lieutenant, with a ſon to ſubſiſt as well as himſelf, out of his pay,—that thou didſt not make an offer to him of my purſe; becauſe, had he ſtood in need, thou knoweſt, Trim, he had been as welcome to it as myſelf.——Your honour knows, ſaid the corporal, I had no orders;——True, quoth my uncle Toby,——thou didſt very right, Trim, as a ſoldier,—but certainly very wrong as a man.

In the ſecond place, for which, indeed, thou haſt the ſame excuſe, continued my uncle Toby,——when thou offeredſt him whatever was in my houſe,——thou ſhouldſt have offered him my houſe too:——A ſick brother officer ſhould have the beſt quarters, Trim; and if we had him with us,—we could tend and

and look to him:——thou art an excellent nurse thyself, Trim,——and what with thy care of him, and the old woman's, and his boy's, and mine together, we might recruit him again at once, and set him upon his legs.—

——In a fortnight or three weeks, added my uncle Toby, smiling,—he might march. —He will never march, an' please your honour, in the world, said the corporal:——He will march, said my uncle Toby, rising up from the side of the bed, with one shoe off:— An' please your honour, said the corporal, he will never march but to his grave:—He shall march, cried my uncle Toby, marching the foot which had a shoe on, though without advancing an inch,—he shall march to his regiment.—He cannot stand it, said the corporal. —He shall be supported, said my uncle Toby. —He'll drop at last, said the corporal, and what will become of his boy?—He shall not drop, said my uncle Toby, firmly.—A-well-o'day,—do what we can for him, said Trim, maintaining his point, the poor soul will die: ——He shall not die, by G—, cried my uncle Toby.

——The *accusing spirit*, which flew up to heaven's chancery with the oath, blushed as he gave it in—and the *recording angel*, as he wrote it down, dropp'd a tear upon the word, and blotted it out for ever.

——My uncle Toby went to his bureau,— put his purse into his breeches pocket, and having ordered the corporal to go early in the morning for a physician,—he went to bed and fell asleep.

The sun looked bright the morning after, to every eye in the village but Le Fevre's and his afflicted son's; the hand of death pressed heavy upon his eye-lids,—and hardly could the wheel at the cistern turn round its circle,— when my uncle Toby, who had rose up an hour before his wonted time, entered the lieutenant's room, and without preface or apology sat himself down upon the chair, by the bed-side, and independently of all modes and customs opened the curtain in the manner an old friend and brother officer would have done it, and asked him how he did,—how he had rested in the night,—what was his complaint,—where was his pain,—and what he could do to help him?——and without giving him time to answer any one of the enquiries, went on and told him of the little plan which he had been concerting with the corporal the night before for him.—

——You shall go home directly, Le Fevre, said my uncle Toby, to my house, and we'll send for a doctor to see what's the matter,— and we'll have an apothecary,—and the corporal shall be your nurse;—and I'll be your servant, Le Fevre.

There was a frankness in my uncle Toby, —not the effect of familiarity,—but the cause of it,—which let you at once into his soul, and shewed you the goodness of his nature; to this, there was something in his looks, and voice, and manner, superadded, which eternally beckoned to the unfortunate to come and take shelter under him; so that before my uncle Toby had half finished the kind offers he was making to the father, had the son insensibly pressed up close to his knees, and had taken hold of the breast of his coat, and was pulling it towards him.——The blood and spirits of Le Fevre, which were waxing cold and slow within him, and were retreating to their last citadel, the heart,—rallied back, the film forsook his eyes for a moment,—he looked up wishfully in my uncle Toby's face, —then cast a look upon his boy,—and that ligament, fine as it was,—was never broken.

Nature inſtantly ebb'd again,——the film returned to its place,——the pulſe flutter'd—ſtopp'd—went on—throbb'd—ſtopp'd again—mov'd—ſtopp'd—ſhall I go on?——No.

Sterne.

§ 2. Yorick's *Death.*

A few hours before Yorick breathed his laſt, Eugenius ſtept in, with an intent to take his laſt ſight and laſt farewell of him. Upon his drawing Yorick's curtain, and and aſking how he felt himſelf, Yorick looking up in his face, took hold of his hand,——and, after thanking him for the many tokens of his friendſhip to him, for which, he ſaid, if it was their fate to meet hereafter, he would thank him again and again; he told him, he was within a few hours of giving his enemies the ſlip for ever.—I hope not, anſwered Eugenius, with tears trickling down his cheeks, and with the tendereſt tone that ever man ſpoke,—I hope not, Yorick, ſaid he,——Yorick replied, with a look up, and a gentle ſqueeze of Eugenius's hand,—and that was all,—but it cut Eugenius to his heart.—Come, come, Yorick, quoth Eugenius, wiping his eyes, and ſummoning up the man within him,—my dear lad, be comforted,—let not all thy ſpirits and fortitude forſake thee at this criſis when thou moſt wanteſt them;—who knows what reſources are in ſtore, and what the power of God may yet do for thee?—Yorick laid his hand upon his heart, and gently ſhook his head; for my part, continued Eugenius, crying bitterly as he uttered the words,—I declare, I know not, Yorick, how to part with thee; and would gladly flatter my hopes, added Eugenius, chearing up his voice, that there is ſtill enough of thee left to make a biſhop,—and that I may live to ſee it.——I beſeech thee, Eugenius, quoth Yorick, taking off his night-cap as well as he could with his left hand,——his right being ſtill graſped cloſe in that of Eugenius,——I beſeech thee to take a view of my head.——I ſee nothing that ails it, replied Eugenius. Then, alas! my friend, ſaid Yorick; let me tell you, that it is ſo bruiſed and miſ-ſhapened with the blows which have been ſo unhandſomely given me in the dark, that I might ſay with Sancho Panca, that ſhould I recover, and "mitres thereupon be ſuffered to rain down "from heaven as thick as hail, not one of "them would fit it."——Yorick's laſt breath was hanging upon his trembling lips, ready to depart as he uttered this;—yet ſtill it was uttered with ſomething of a Cervantic tone;—and as he ſpoke it, Eugenius could perceive a ſtream of lambent fire lighted up for a moment in his eyes;——faint picture of thoſe flaſhes of his ſpirit, which (as Shakeſpeare ſaid of his anceſtor) were wont to ſet the table in a roar!

Eugenius was convinced from this, that the heart of his friend was broke; he ſqueezed his hand,——and then walked ſoftly out of the room, weeping as he walked. Yorick followed Eugenius with his eyes to the door,——he then cloſed them——and never opened them more.

He lies buried in a corner of his church-yard, under a plain marble ſlab, which his friend Eugenius, by leave of his executors, laid upon his grave, with no more than theſe three words of inſcription, ſerving both for his epitaph and elegy——

Alas, poor YORICK!

Ten

Ten times a day has Yorick's ghost the consolation to hear his monumental inscription read over with such a variety of plaintive tones, as denote a general pity and esteem for him;——a foot-way crossing the church-yard close by his grave,—not a passenger goes by, without stopping to cast a look upon it,—— and sighing as he walks on,

Alas, poor YORICK!

Sterne.

§ 3. *The Story of* ALCANDER *and* SEPTIMIUS. *Taken from a Byzantine Historian.*

Athens, long after the decline of the Roman empire, still continued the seat of learning, politeness, and wisdom. Theodoric the Ostrogoth repaired the schools which barbarity was suffering to fall into decay, and continued those pensions to men of learning which avaricious governors had monopolized.

In this city, and about this period, Alcander and Septimius were fellow-students together: the one the most subtle reasoner of all the Lyceum, the other the most eloquent speaker in the academic grove. Mutual admiration soon begot a friendship. Their fortunes were nearly equal, and they were natives of the two most celebrated cities in the world; for Alcander was of Athens, Septimius came from Rome.

In this state of harmony they lived for some time together; when Alcander, after passing the first part of his youth in the indolence of philosophy, thought at length of entering into the busy world; and, as a step previous to this, placed his affections on Hypatia, a lady of exquisite beauty. The day of their intended nuptials was fixed; the previous ceremonies were performed; and nothing now remained but her being conducted in triumph to the apartment of the intended bridegroom.

Alcander's exultation in his own happiness, or being unable to enjoy any satisfaction without making his friend Septimius a partner, prevailed upon him to introduce Hypatia to his fellow-student; which he did with all the gaiety of a man who found himself equally happy in friendship and love. But this was an interview fatal to the future peace of both; for Septimius no sooner saw her, but he was smitten with an involuntary passion; and, though he used every effort to suppress desires at once so imprudent and unjust, the emotions of his mind in a short time became so strong, that they brought on a fever, which the physicians judged incurable.

During this illness, Alcander watched him with all the anxiety of fondness, and brought his mistress to join in those amiable offices of friendship. The sagacity of the physicians, by these means, soon discovered that the cause of their patient's disorder was love: and Alcander being apprized of their discovery, at length extorted a confession from the reluctant dying lover.

It would but delay the narrative to describe the conflict between love and friendship in the breast of Alcander on this occasion; it is enough to say, that the Athenians were at that time arrived at such refinement in morals, that every virtue was carried to excess. In short, forgetful of his own felicity, he gave up his intended bride, in all her charms, to the young Roman. They were married privately by his connivance, and this unlooked-for change of fortune wrought as unexpected a change in the constitution of the now happy Septimius: in a few days he was perfectly recovered, and set out with his fair partner for Rome. Here, by an exertion of those talents which he was so eminently possessed of, Septimius in a few years arrived at the highest dignities of the state, and was constituted the city-judge, or prætor.

In the mean time Alcander not only felt the pain of being separated from his friend and his mistress, but a prosecution was also commenced against him by the relations of Hypatia, for having basely given up his bride, as was suggested, for money. His innocence of the crime laid to his charge, and even his eloquence in his own defence, were not able to withstand the influence of a powerful party. He was cast, and condemned to pay an enormous fine. However, being unable to raise so large a sum at the time appointed, his possessions were confiscated, he himself was stripped of the habit of freedom, exposed as a slave in the market-place, and sold to the highest bidder.

A merchant of Thrace becoming his purchaser, Alcander, with some other companions of distress, was carried into that region of desolation and sterility. His stated employment was to follow the herds of an imperious master, and his success in hunting was all that was allowed him to supply his precarious subsistence. Every morning awaked him to a renewal of famine or toil, and every change of season served but to aggravate his unsheltered distress. After some years of bondage, however, an opportunity of escaping offered; he embraced it with ardour; so that travelling by night, and lodging in caverns by day, to shorten a long story, he at last arrived in Rome. The same day on which Alcander arrived, Septimius sat administering justice in the forum, whither our wanderer came, expecting to be instantly known, and publicly acknowledged by his former friend. Here he stood the whole day amongst the crowd, watching the eyes of the judge, and expecting to be taken notice of; but he was so much altered by a long succession of hardships, that he continued unnoted among the the rest; and, in the evening, when he was going up to the prætor's chair, he was brutally repulsed by the attending lictors. The attention of the poor is generally driven from one ungrateful object to another; for night coming on, he now found himself under a necessity of seeking a place to lie in, and yet knew not where to apply. All emaciated, and in rags as he was, none of the citizens would harbour so much wretchedness; and sleeping in the streets might be attended with interruption or danger: in short, he was obliged to take up his lodging in one of the tombs without the city, the usual retreat of guilt, poverty, and despair. In this mansion of horror, laying his head upon an inverted urn, he forgot his miseries for a while in sleep; and found on his flinty couch, more ease than beds of down can supply to the guilty.

As he continued here, about midnight two robbers came to make this their retreat; but happening to disagree about the division of their plunder, one of them stabbed the other to the heart, and left him weltering in blood at the entrance. In these circumstances he was found next morning dead at the mouth of the vault. This naturally inducing a farther enquiry, an alarm was spread; the cave was examined; and Alcander being found, was immediately apprehended, and accused of robbery and murder. The circumstances against him were strong, and the wretchedness of his appearance confirmed suspicion. Misfortune and he were now so long acquainted, that he at last became regardless of life. He detested a world where he had found only ingratitude,

gratitude, falsehood, and cruelty; he was determined to make no defence; and thus, lowering with resolution, he was dragged, bound with cords, before the tribunal of Septimius. As the proofs were positive against him, and he offered nothing in his own vindication, the judge was proceeding to doom him to a most cruel and ignominious death, when the attention of the multitude was soon divided by another object. The robber, who had been really guilty, was apprehended selling his plunder, and, struck with a panic, had confessed his crime. He was brought bound to the same tribunal, and acquitted every other person of any partnership in his guilt. Alcander's innocence therefore appeared, but the sullen rashness of his conduct remained a wonder to the surrounding multitude; but their astonishment was still farther encreased, when they saw their judge start from his tribunal to embrace the supposed criminal: Septimius recollected his friend and former benefactor, and hung upon his neck with tears of pity and of joy. Need the sequel be related? Alcander was acquitted: shared the friendship and honours of the principal citizens of Rome; lived afterwards in happiness and ease; and left it to be engraved on his tomb, That no circumstances are so desperate, which Providence may not relieve.

§ 4. *The Monk.*

A poor Monk of the order of St. Francis came into the room to beg something for his convent. The moment I cast my eyes upon him, I was pre-determined not to give him a single sous, and accordingly I put my purse into my pocket—buttoned it up—set myself a little more upon my centre, and advanced up gravely to him: there was something, I fear, forbidding in my look: I have his figure this moment before my eyes, and think there was that in it which deserved better.

The Monk, as I judge from the break in his tonsure, a few scattered white hairs upon his temples being all that remained of it, might be about seventy——but from his eyes, and that sort of fire which was in them, which seemed more tempered by courtesy than years, could be no more than sixty——truth might lie between——He was certainly sixty five; and the general air of his countenance, notwithstanding something seemed to have been planting wrinkles in it before their time, agreed to the account.

It was one of those heads which Guido has often painted—mild—pale—penetrating, free from all common-place ideas of fat contented ignorance looking downwards upon the earth—it look'd forwards; but look'd as if it look'd at something beyond this world. How one of his order came by it, Heaven above, who let it fall upon a monk's shoulders, best knows; but it would have suited a Bramin, and had I met it upon the plains of Indostan, I had reverenced it.

The rest of his outline may be given in a few strokes; one might put it into the hands of any one to design, for 'twas neither elegant nor otherwise, but as character and expression made it so: it was a thin, spare form, something above the common size, if it lost not the distinction by a bend forwards in the figure—but it was the attitude of entreaty; and as it now stands present to my imagination, it gain'd more than it lost by it.

When he had entered the room three paces, he stood still; and laying his left hand upon his breast (a slender white staff with which he journeyed being in his right)—when I had got close up to him, he introduced himself with the little story of the wants of his convent,

vent, and the poverty of his order——and did it with so simple a grace—and such an air of deprecation was there in the whole cast of his look and figure—I was bewitched not to have been struck with it——

—A better reason was, I had pre-determined not to give him a single sous.

—'Tis very true, said I, replying to a cast upwards with his eyes, with which he had concluded his address—'tis very true—and Heaven be their resource who have no other but the charity of the world, the stock of which, I fear, is no way sufficient for the many great claims which are hourly made upon it.

As I pronounced the words "great claims," he gave a slight glance with his eye downwards upon the sleeve of his tunic—I felt the full force of the appeal—I acknowledge it, said I—a coarse habit, and that but once in three years, with meagre diet—are no great matters: and the true point of pity is, as they can be earn'd in the world with so little industry, that your order should wish to procure them by pressing upon a fund which is the property of the lame, the blind, the aged, and the infirm: the captive, who lies down counting over and over again the days of his affliction, languishes also for his share of it; and had you been of the order of Mercy, instead of the order of St. Francis, poor as I am, continued I, pointing at my portmanteau, full cheerfully should it have been opened to you for the ransom of the unfortunate. The Monk ma[illegible] me a bow—but of all others, resumed I, the unfortunate of our own country, surely, have the first rights; and I have left thousands in distress upon our own shore——The Monk gave a cordial wave with his head—as much as to say, No doubt, there is misery enough in every corner of the world, as well as within our convent——But we distinguish, said I, laying my hand upon the sleeve of his tunic, in return for his appeal—we distinguish, my good father! betwixt those who wish only to eat the bread of their own labour—and those who eat the bread of other people's, and have no other plan in life, but to get through it in sloth and ignorance, for the love of God.

The poor Franciscan made no reply: a hectic of a moment pass'd across his cheek, but could not tarry—Nature seemed to have had done with her resentments in him; he shewed none—but letting his staff fall within his arm, he pressed both his hands with resignation upon his breast, and retired.

My heart smote me the moment he shut the door——Psha! said I, with an air of carelessness, three several times——but it would not do; every ungracious syllable I had uttered crowded back into my imagination; I reflected I had no right over the poor Franciscan, but to deny him; and that the punishment of that was enough to the disappointed, without the addition of unkind language—I considered his grey hairs—his courteous figure seemed to re-enter, and gently ask me, what injury he had done me? and why I could use him thus?—I would have given twenty livres for an advocate—I have behaved very ill, said I within myself; but I have only just set out upon my travels; and shall learn better manners as I get along. *Sterne.*

§ 5. *Sir Bertrand. A Fragment.*

——— Sir Bertrand turned his steed towards the woulds, hoping to cross these dreary moors before the curfew. But ere he had proceeded half his journey, he was bewildered by the different tracks; and not being able, as far as the eye could reach, to espy any object

But

but the brown heath surrounding him, he was at length quite uncertain which way he should direct his course. Night overtook him in this situation. It was one of those nights when the moon gives a faint glimmering of light through the thick black clouds of a lowering sky. Now and then she suddenly emerged in full splendour from her veil, and then instantly retired behind it; having just served to give the forlorn Sir Bertrand a wide extended prospect over the desolate waste. Hope and native courage awhile urged him to push forwards, but at length the increasing darkness and fatigue of body and mind overcame him; he dreaded moving from the ground he stood on, for fear of unknown pits and bogs, and alighting from his horse in despair, he threw himself on the ground. He had not long continued in that posture, when the sullen toll of a distant bell struck his ears—he started up, and turning towards the sound, discerned a dim twinkling light. Instantly he seized his horse's bridle, and with cautious steps advanced towards it. After a painful march, he was stopped by a moated ditch, surrounding the place from whence the light proceeded; and by a momentary glimpse of moon-light he had a full view of a large antique mansion, with turrets at the corners, and an ample porch in the centre. The injuries of time were strongly marked on every thing about it. The roof in various places was fallen in, the battlements were half demolished, and the windows broken and dismantled. A draw-bridge, with a ruinous gate-way at each end, led to the court before the building—He entered, and instantly the light, which proceeded from a window in one of the turrets, glided along and vanished; at the same moment the moon sunk beneath a black cloud, and the night was darker than ever. All was silent—Sir Bertrand fastened his steed under a shed, and approaching the house, traversed its whole front with light and slow footsteps—All was still as death—He looked in at the lower windows, but could not distinguish a single object through the impenetrable gloom. After a short parley with himself, he entered the porch, and seizing a massy iron knocker at the gate, lifted it up, and hesitating, at length struck a loud stroke—the noise resounded through the whole mansion with hollow echoes. All was still again—he repeated the strokes more boldly and louder—another interval of silence ensued—A third time he knocked, and a third time all was still. He then fell back to some distance, that he might discern whether any light could be seen in the whole front—It again appeared in the same place, and quickly glided away, as before—at the same instant a deep sullen toll sounded from the turret. Sir Bertrand's heart made a fearful stop—he was a while motionless; then terror impelled him to make some hasty steps towards his steed—but shame stopt his flight; and urged by honour, and a resistless desire of finishing the adventure, he returned to the porch; and working up his soul to a full steadiness of resolution, he drew forth his sword with one hand, and with the other lifted up the latch of the gate. The heavy door creaking upon its hinges reluctantly yielded to his hand—he applied his shoulder to it, and forced it open—he quitted it, and stept forward—the door instantly shut with a thundering clap. Sir Bertrand's blood was chilled—he turned back to find the door, and it was long ere his trembling hands could seize it—but his utmost strength could not open it again. After several ineffectual attempts, he looked behind him, and beheld, across a hall, upon a large stair-case, a pale bluish flame, which caſt a diſmal gleam of light around. He again ſummoned forth his courage, and advanced towards it—it retired. He came to the foot of the ſtairs, and after a moment's deliberation aſcended. He went ſlowly up, the flame retiring before him, till he came to a wide gallery.—The flame proceeded along it, and he followed in ſilent horror, treading lightly, for the echoes of his footſteps ſtartled him. It led him to the foot of another ſtair-caſe, and then vaniſhed—At the ſame inſtant another toll ſounded from the turret—Sir Bertrand felt it ſtrike upon his heart. He was now in total darkneſs, and, with his arms extended, began to aſcend the ſecond ſtair-caſe. A dead cold hand met his left hand, and firmly graſped it, drawing him forcibly forwards—he endeavoured to diſengage himſelf, but could not—he made a furious blow with his ſword, and inſtantly a loud ſhriek pierced his ears, and the dead hand was left powerleſs with his—He dropt it, and ruſhed forwards with a deſperate valour. The ſtairs were narrow and winding, and interrupted by frequent breaches, and looſe fragments of ſtone. The ſtair-caſe grew narrower and narrower, and at length terminated in a low iron grate. Sir Bertrand puſhed it open—it led to an intricate winding paſſage, juſt large enough to admit a perſon upon his hands and knees. A faint glimmering of light ſerved to ſhew the nature of the place—Sir Bertrand entered—A deep hollow groan reſounded from a diſtance through the vault—He went forwards, and proceeding beyond the firſt turning, he diſcerned the ſame blue flame which had before conducted him—He followed it. The vault, at length, ſuddenly opened into a lofty gallery, in the midſt of which a figure appeared, completely armed, thruſting forwards the bloody ſtump of an arm, with a terrible frown and menacing geſture, and brandiſhing a ſword in his hand. Sir Bertrand undauntedly ſprung forwards; and aiming a fierce blow at the figure, it inſtantly vaniſhed, letting fall a maſſy iron key. The flame now reſted upon a pair of ample folding doors at the end of the gallery. Sir Bertrand went up to it, and applied the key to a brazen lock—with difficulty he turned the bolt—inſtantly the doors flew open, and diſcovered a large apartment, at the end of which was a coffin reſted upon a bier, with a taper burning on each ſide of it. Along the room, on both ſides, were gigantic ſtatues of black marble, attired in the Mooriſh habit, and holding enormous ſabres in their right hands. Each of them reared his arm, and advanced one leg forwards, as the knight entered; at the ſame moment the lid of the coffin flew open, and the bell tolled. The flame ſtill glided forwards, and Sir Bertrand reſolutely followed, till he arrived within ſix paces of the coffin. Suddenly a lady in a ſhroud and black veil roſe up in it, and ſtretched out her arms towards him—at the ſame time the ſtatues claſhed their ſabres and advanced. Sir Bertrand flew to the lady, and claſped her in his arms—ſhe threw up her veil, and kiſſed his lips; and inſtantly the whole building ſhook as with an earthquake, and fell aſunder with a horrible craſh. Sir Bertrand was thrown into a ſudden trance, and on recovering found himſelf ſeated on a velvet ſofa, in the moſt magnificent room he had ever ſeen, lighted with innumerable tapers, in luſtres of pure cryſtal. A ſumptuous banquet was ſet in the middle. The doors opening to ſoft muſic, a lady of incomparable beauty, attired with amazing ſplendour, entered, ſurrounded by a troop of gay nymphs more fair than the Graces—She advanced to the knight, and falling on her knees,

knees, thanked him as her deliverer. The nymphs placed a garland of laurel upon his head, and the lady led him by the hand to the banquet, and sat beside him. The nymphs placed themselves at the table, and a numerous train of servants entering, served up the feast? delicious music playing all the time. Sir Bertrand could not speak for astonishment —he could only return their honours by courteous looks and gestures. After the banquet was finished, all retired but the lady, who leading back the knight to the sofa, addressed him in these words: — —

— — — — — —

— — — — — —

Aikin's Miscel.

§ 6. *On Human Grandeur.*

An alehouse keeper near Islington, who had long lived at the sign of the French King, upon the commencement of the last war pulled down his old sign, and put up that of the Queen of Hungary. Under the influence of her red face and golden sceptre, he continued to sell ale, till she was no longer the favourite of his customers; he changed her, therefore, some time ago, for the King of Prussia, who may probably be changed, in turn, for the next great man that shall be set up for vulgar admiration.

In this manner the great are dealt out, one after the other, to the gazing crowd. When we have sufficiently wondered at one of them, he is taken in, and another exhibited in his room, who seldom holds his station long: for the mob are ever pleased with variety.

I must own I have such an indifferent opinion of the vulgar, that I am ever led to suspect that merit which raises their shout: at least I am certain to find those great, and sometimes good men, who find satisfaction in such acclamations, made worse by it; and history has too frequently taught me, that the head which has grown this day giddy with the roar of the million, has the very next been fixed upon a pole.

As Alexander VI. was entering a little town in the neighbourhood of Rome, which had been just evacuated by the enemy, he perceived the townsmen busy in the market-place in pulling down from a gibbet a figure which had been designed to represent himself. There were some also knocking down a neighbouring statue of one of the Orsini family, with whom he was at war, in order to put Alexander's effigy in its place. It is possible a man who knew less of the world would have condemned the adulation of those bare-faced flatterers; but Alexander seemed pleased at their zeal, and turning to Borgia, his son, said with a smile, "Vides, mi fili, quam leve discrimen, patibulum inter et statuam." "You see, my son, the small difference between a gibbet and a statue." If the great could be taught any lesson, this might serve to teach them upon how weak a foundation their glory stands: for, as popular applause is excited by what seems like merit, it as quickly condemns what has only the appearance of guilt.

Popular glory is a perfect coquet: her lovers must toil, feel every inquietude, indulge every caprice; and, perhaps, at last, be jilted for their pains. True glory, on the other hand, resembles a woman of sense; her admirers must play no tricks; they feel no great anxiety, for they are sure, in the end, of being rewarded in proportion to their merit. When Swift used to appear in public, he generally had the mob shouting at his train. "Pox take these fools," he would say, "how much joy might all this bawling give my lord-mayor?"

We

We have seen those virtues which have, while living, retired from the public eye, generally transmitted to posterity, as the truest objects of admiration and praise. Perhaps the character of the late duke of Marlborough may one day be set up, even above that of his more talked-of predecessor; since an assemblage of all the mild and amiable virtues are far superior to those vulgarly called the great ones. I must be pardoned for this short tribute to the memory of a man, who, while living, would as much detest to receive any thing that wore the appearance of flattery, as I should to offer it.

I know not how to turn so trite a subject out of the beaten road of common-place, except by illustrating it, rather by the assistance of my memory than judgment; and, instead, of making reflections, by telling a story.

A Chinese, who had long studied the works of Confucius, who knew the characters of fourteen thousand words, and could read a great part of every book that came in his way, once took it into his head to travel into Europe, and observe the customs of a people which he thought not very much inferior even to his own countrymen. Upon his arrival at Amsterdam, his passion for letters naturally led him to a bookseller's shop; and, as he could speak a little Dutch, he civilly asked the bookseller for the works of the immortal Xixofou. The bookseller assured him he had never heard the book mentioned before. "Alas!" cries our traveller, "to what purpose, then, has "he fasted to death, to gain a renown which "has never travelled beyond the precincts of "China!"

There is scarce a village in Europe, and not one university, that is not thus furnished with its little great men. The head of a petty corporation, who opposes the designs of a prince, who would tyrannically force his subjects to save their best cloaths for Sundays; the puny pedant, who finds one undiscovered quality in the polype, or describes an unheeded process in the skeleton of a mole; and whose mind, like his microscope, perceives nature only in detail: the rhymer, who makes smooth verses, and paints to our imagination, when he should only speak to our hearts; all equally fancy themselves walking forward to immortality, and desire the crowd behind them to look on. The crowd takes them at their word. Patriot, philosopher, and poet, are shouted in their train. "Where was "there ever so much merit seen? no times so "important as our own! ages, yet unborn, "shall gaze with wonder and applause!" To such music the important pigmy moves forward, bustling and swelling, and aptly compared to a puddle in a storm.

I have lived to see generals who once had crowds hallooing after them where-ever they went, who were bepraised by news-papers and magazines, those echoes of the voice of the vulgar, and yet they have long sunk into merited obscurity, with scarce even an epitaph left to flatter. A few years ago the herring-fishery employed all Grub-street; it was the topic in every coffee-house, and the burden of every ballad. We were to drag up oceans of gold from the bottom of the sea; we were to supply all Europe with herrings upon our own terms. At present, we hear no more of all this. We have fished up very little gold that I can learn; nor do we furnish the world with herrings, as was expected. Let us wait but a few years longer, and we shall find all our expectations an herring-fishery.

Goldsmith.

§ 7.

§ 7. *The Hill of Science. A Viſion.*

In that ſeaſon of the year when the ſerenity of the ſky, the various fruits which cover the ground, the diſcoloured foliage of the trees, and all the ſweet, but fading graces of inſpiring autumn, open the mind to benevolence, and diſpoſe it for contemplation, I was wandering in a beautiful and romantic country, till curioſity began to give way to wearineſs; and I ſat me down on the fragment of a rock overgrown with moſs, where the ruſtling of the falling leaves, the daſhing of waters, and the hum of the diſtant city, ſoothed my mind into the moſt perfect tranquillity, and ſleep inſenſibly ſtole upon me, as I was indulging the agreeable reveries which the objects around me naturally inſpired.

I immediately found myſelf in a vaſt extended plain, in the middle of which aroſe a mountain higher than I had before any conception of. It was covered with a multitude of people, chiefly youth; many of whom preſſed forwards with the livelieſt expreſſion of ardour in their countenance, though the way was in many places ſteep and difficult. I obſerved, that thoſe who had but juſt begun to climb the hill thought themſelves not far from the top; but as they proceeded, new hills were continually riſing to their view, and the ſummit of the higheſt they could before diſcern ſeemed but the foot of another, till the mountain at length appeared to loſe itſelf in the clouds. As I was gazing on theſe things with aſtoniſhment, my good genius ſuddenly appeared: The mountain before thee, ſaid he, is the Hill of Science. On the top is the temple of Truth, whoſe head is above the clouds, and a veil of pure light covers her face. Obſerve the progreſs of her votaries; be ſilent and attentive.

I ſaw that the only regular approach to the mountain was by a gate, called the gate of Languages. It was kept by a woman of a penſive and thoughtful appearance, whoſe lips were continually moving, as though ſhe repeated ſomething to herſelf. Her name was Memory. On entering this firſt encloſure, I was ſtunned with a confuſed murmur of jarring voices, and diſſonant ſounds; which increaſed upon me to ſuch a degree, that I was utterly confounded, and could compare the noiſe to nothing but the confuſion of tongues at Babel. The road was alſo rough and ſtony; and rendered more difficult by heaps of rubbiſh continually tumbled down from the higher parts of the mountain; and broken ruins of ancient buildings, which the travellers were obliged to climb over at every ſtep; inſomuch that many, diſguſted with ſo rough a beginning, turned back, and attempted the mountain no more: while others, having conquered this difficulty, had no ſpirits to aſcend further, and ſitting down on ſome fragment of the rubbiſh, harangued the multitude below with the greateſt marks of importance and ſelf-complacency.

About half way up the hill, I obſerved on each ſide the path a thick foreſt covered with continual fogs, and cut out into labyrinths, croſs alleys, and ſerpentine walks, entangled with thorns and briars. This was called the wood of Error: and I heard the voices of many who were toſt up and down in it, calling to one another, and endeavouring in vain to extricate themſelves. The trees in many places ſhot their boughs over the path, and a thick miſt often reſted on it; yet never ſo much but that it was diſcernible by the light which beamed from the countenance of Truth.

In the pleaſanteſt part of the mountain were placed the bowers of the Muſes, whoſe office

office it was to cheer the ſpirits of the travellers, and encourage their fainting ſteps with ſongs from their divine harps. Not far from hence were the fields of Fiction, filled with a variety of wild flowers ſpringing up in the greateſt luxuriance, of richer ſcents and brighter colours than I had obſerved in any other climate. And near them was the dark walk of Allegory, ſo artificially ſhaded, that the light at noon-day was never ſtronger than that of a bright moon-ſhine. This gave it a pleaſing romantic air for thoſe who delighted in contemplation. The paths and alleys were perplexed with intricate windings, and were all terminated with the ſtatue of a Grace, a Virtue, or a Muſe.

After I had obſerved theſe things, I turned my eye towards the multitudes who were climbing the ſteep aſcent, and obſerved amongſt them a youth of a lively look, a piercing eye, and ſomething fiery and irregular in all his motions. His name was Genius. He darted like an eagle up the mountain, and left his companions gazing after him with envy and admiration: but his progreſs was unequal, and interrupted by a thouſand caprices. When Pleaſure warbled in the valley he mingled in her train. When Pride beckoned towards the precipice he ventured to the tottering edge. He delighted in devious and untried paths; and made ſo many excurſions from the road, that his feebler companions often out-ſtripped him. I obſerved that the Muſes beheld him with partiality; but truth often frowned, and turned aſide her face. While Genius was thus waſting his ſtrength in eccentric flights, I ſaw a perſon of a very different appearance, named Application. He crept along with a ſlow and unremitting pace, his eyes fixed on the top of the mountain, patiently removing every ſtone that obſtructed his way, till he ſaw moſt of thoſe below him who had at firſt derided his ſlow and toilſome progreſs. Indeed there were few who aſcended the hill with equal and uninterrupted ſteadineſs; for, beſide the difficulties of the way, they were continually ſolicited to turn aſide by a numerous crowd of Appetites, Paſſions, and Pleaſures, whoſe importunity, when they had once complied with, they became leſs and leſs able to reſiſt; and though they often returned to the path, the aſperities of the road were more ſeverely felt, the hill appeared more ſteep and rugged, the fruits which were wholeſome and refreſhing ſeemed harſh and ill-taſted, their ſight grew dim, and their feet tript at every little obſtruction.

I ſaw, with ſome ſurpriſe, that the Muſes, whoſe buſineſs was to cheer and encourage thoſe who were toiling up the aſcent, would often ſing in the bowers of Pleaſure, and accompany thoſe who were enticed away at the call of the Paſſions; they accompanied them, however, but a little way, and always forſook them when they loſt ſight of the hill. The tyrants then doubled their chains upon the unhappy captives, and led them away, without reſiſtance, to the cells of Ignorance, or the manſions of Miſery. Amongſt the innumerable ſeducers, who were endeavouring to draw away the votaries of Truth from the path of Science, there was one, ſo little formidable in her appearance, and ſo gentle and languid in her attempts, that I ſhould ſcarcely have taken notice of her, but for the numbers ſhe had imperceptibly loaded with her chains. Indolence (for ſo ſhe was called) far from proceeding to open hoſtilities, did not attempt to turn their feet out of the path, but contented herſelf with retarding their progreſs; and the purpoſe ſhe could not force them to abandon, ſhe perſuaded them to delay. Her touch had a power a power like that of the torpedo, which withered the ſtrength of thoſe who came within its influence. Her unhappy captives ſtill turned their faces towards the temple, and always hoped to arrive there; but the ground ſeemed to ſlide from beneath their feet, and they found themſelves at the bottom, before they ſuſpected they had changed their place. The placid ſerenity, which at firſt appeared in their countenance, changed by degrees into a melancholy languor, which was tinged with deeper and deeper gloom, as they glided down the ſtream of Inſignificance; a dark and ſluggiſh water which is curled by no breeze, and enlivened by no murmur, till it falls into a dead ſea, where ſtartled paſſengers are awakened by the ſhock, and the next moment buried in the gulph of Oblivion.

Of all the unhappy deſerters from the paths of Science, none ſeemed leſs able to return than the followers of Indolence. The captives of Appetite and Paſſion could often ſeize the moment when their tyrants were languid or aſleep to eſcape from their enchantment; but the dominion of Indolence was conſtant and unremitted, and ſeldom reſiſted, till reſiſtance was in vain.

After contemplating theſe things, I turned my eyes towards the top of the mountain, where the air was always pure and exhilarating, the path ſhaded with laurels and other evergreens, and the effulgence which beamed from the face of the goddeſs ſeemed to ſhed a glory round her votaries. Happy, ſaid I, are they who are permitted to aſcend the mountain!—but while I was pronouncing this exclamation with uncommon ardour, I ſaw ſtanding beſide me a form of diviner features and a more benign radiance. Happier, ſaid ſhe, are thoſe whom Virtue conducts to the manſions of Content! What, ſaid I, does Virtue then reſide in the vale? I am found, ſaid ſhe, in the vale, and I illuminate the mountain: I cheer the cottager at his toil, and inſpire the ſage at his meditation. I mingle in the crowd of cities, and bleſs the hermit in his cell. I have a temple in every heart that owns my influence; and to him that wiſhes for me I am already preſent. Science may raiſe you to eminence, but I alone can guide you to felicity! While the goddeſs was thus ſpeaking, I ſtretched out my arms towards her with a vehemence which broke my ſlumbers. The chill dews were falling around me, and the ſhades of evening ſtretched over the landſcape. I haſtened homeward, and reſigned the night to ſilence and meditation. *Aikin's Miſcel.*

§ 8. *The Canal and the Brook. A Reverie.*

A delightfully pleaſant evening ſucceeding a ſultry ſummer-day, invited me to take a ſolitary walk; and, leaving the duſt of the highway, I fell into a path which led along a pleaſant little valley watered by a ſmall meandring brook. The meadow ground on its banks had been lately mown, and the new graſs was ſpringing up with a lively verdure. The brook was hid in ſeveral places by the ſhrubs that grew on each ſide, and intermingled their branches. The ſides of the valley were roughened by ſmall irregular thickets; and the whole ſcene had an air of ſolitude and retirement, uncommon in the neighbourhood of a populous town. The Duke of Bridgewater's canal croſſed the valley, high raiſed on a mound of earth, which preſerved a level with the elevated ground on each ſide. An arched road was carried under it, beneath which the brook that ran along the valley was conveyed by a ſubterraneous paſſage. I threw myſelf upon a green bank, ſhaded by a leafy thicket,

thicket, and resting my head upon my hand, after a welcome indolence had overcome my senses, I saw, with the eyes of fancy, the following scene.

The firm-built side of the aqueduct suddenly opened, and a gigantic form issued forth, which I soon discovered to be the Genius of the Canal. He was clad in a close garment of russet hue. A mural crown, indented with battlements, surrounded his brow. His naked feet were discoloured with clay. On his left shoulder he bore a huge pick-axe; and in his right hand he held certain instruments, used in surveying and levelling. His looks were thoughtful, and his features harsh. The breach through which he proceeded instantly closed, and with a heavy tread he advanced into the valley. As he approached the brook, the Deity of the Stream arose to meet him. He was habited in a light green mantle, and the clear drops fell from his dark hair, which was encircled with a wreath of water-lily, interwoven with sweet-scented flag: an angling rod supported his steps. The Genius of the Canal eyed him with a contemptuous look, and in a hoarse voice thus began:

" Hence, ignoble rill! with thy scanty " tribute to thy lord the Mersey; nor thus " waste thy almost-exhausted urn in lingering " windings along the vale. Feeble as thine " aid is, it will not be unacceptable to that " master stream himself; for, as I lately " crossed his channel, I perceived his sands " loaded with stranded vessels. I saw, and " pitied him, for undertaking a task to which " he is unequal. But thou, whose languid " current is obscured by weeds, and inter- " rupted by misshapen pebbles; who losest " thyself in endless mazes, remote from any " sound but thy own idle gurgling; how " canst thou support an existence so con- " temptible and useless? For me, the noblest " child of Art, who hold my unremitting " course from hill to hill, over vales and " rivers; who pierce the solid rock for my " passage, and connect unknown lands with " distant seas; wherever I appear I am view- " ed with astonishment, and exulting Com- " merce hails my waves. Behold my chan- " nel thronged with capacious vessels for the " conveyance of merchandize, and splendid " barges for the use and pleasure of travel- " lers; my banks crowned with airy bridges " and huge warehouses, and echoing with " the busy sounds of industry! Pay then the " homage due from Sloth and Obscurity to " Grandeur and Utility."

" I readily acknowledge," replied the Deity of the Brook, in a modest accent, " the " superior magnificence and more extensive " utility of which you so proudly boast; yet, " in my humble walk, I am not void of a " praise less shining, but not less solid than " yours. The nymph of this peaceful valley, " rendered more fertile and beautiful by my " stream; the neighbouring sylvan deities, to " whose pleasure I contribute; will pay a " grateful testimony to my merit. The " windings of my course, which you so much " blame, serve to diffuse over a greater extent " of ground the refreshment of my waters; " and the lovers of nature and the Muses, " who are fond of straying on my banks, are " better pleased that the line of beauty marks " my way, than if, like yours, it were di- " rected in a straight, unvaried line. They " prize the irregular wildness with which " I am decked, as the charms of beauteous " simplicity. What you call the weeds " which darken and obscure my waves, afford " to the botanist a pleasing speculation of the " works of nature; and the poet and painter think

" think the lustre of my stream greatly improved by glittering through them. The " pebbles which diversify my bottom, and " make these ripplings in my current, are " pleasing objects to the eye of taste; and " my simple murmurs are more melodious to " the learned ear than all the rude noises of " your banks, or even the music that resounds " from your stately barges. If the unfeeling sons of Wealth and Commerce judge of " me by the mere standard of usefulness, I " may claim no undistinguished rank. While " your waters, confined in deep channels, or " lifted above the valleys, roll on, a useless " burden to the fields, and only subservient to " the drudgery of bearing temporary merchandizes, my stream will bestow unvarying fertility on the meadows, during the summers " of future ages. Yet I scorn to submit my " honours to the decision of those whose hearts " are shut up to taste and sentiment: let me " appeal to nobler judges. The philosopher " and poet, by whose labours the human " mind is elevated and refined, and opened to " pleasures beyond the conception of vulgar " souls, will acknowledge that the elegant " deities who preside over simple and natural " beauty have inspired them with their charming and instructive ideas. The sweetest and " most majestic bard that ever sung has taken " a pride in owning his affection to woods " and streams; and, while the stupendous monuments of Roman grandeur, the columns " which pierced the skies, and the aqueducts " which poured their waves over mountains " and vallies, are sunk in oblivion, the gently-winding Mincius still retains his tranquil " honours. And when thy glories, proud " Genius! are lost and forgotten; when the " flood of commerce, which now supplies thy " urn, is turned into a another course, and " has left thy channel dry and desolate; the " softly-flowing Avon shall still murmur in " song, and his banks receive the homage of " all who are beloved by Phœbus and the " Muses." *Aikin's Miscell.*

§ 9. *The Story of a disabled Soldier.*

No observation is more common, and at the same time more true, than, That one half of the world are ignorant how the other half lives. The misfortunes of the great are held up to engage our attention; are enlarged upon in tones of declamation; and the world is called upon to gaze at the noble sufferers: the great, under the pressure of calamity, are conscious of several others sympathizing with their distress; and have, at once, the comfort of admiration and pity.

There is nothing magnanimous in bearing misfortunes with fortitude, when the whole world is looking on: men in such circumstances will act bravely, even from motives of vanity; but he who, in the vale of obscurity, can brave adversity; who, without friends to encourage, acquaintances to pity, or even without hope to alleviate his misfortunes, can behave with tranquillity and indifference, is truly great: whether peasant or courtier, he deserves admiration, and should be held up for our imitation and respect.

While the slightest inconveniences of the great are magnified into calamities; while tragedy mouths out their sufferings in all the strains of eloquence; the miseries of the poor are entirely disregarded; and yet some of the lower ranks of people undergo more real hardships in one day than those of a more exalted station suffer in their whole lives. It is inconceivable what difficulties the meanest of

our

our common ſailors and ſoldiers endure without murmuring or regret; without paſſionately declaiming againſt Providence, or calling their fellows to be gazers on their intrepidity. Every day is to them a day of miſery, and yet they entertain their hard fate without repining.

With what indignation do I hear an Ovid, a Cicero, or a Rabutin, complain of their miſfortunes and hardſhips, whoſe greateſt calamity was that of being unable to viſit a certain ſpot of earth, to which they had fooliſhly attatched an idea of happineſs! Their diſtreſſes were pleaſures, compared to what many of the adventuring poor every day endure without murmuring. They ate, drank, and ſlept; they had ſlaves to attend them; and were ſure of ſubſiſtence for life: while many of their fellow-creatures are obliged to wander without a friend to comfort or aſſiſt them, and even without ſhelter from the ſeverity of the ſeaſon.

I have been led into theſe reflections from accidentally meeting, ſome days ago, a poor fellow, whom I knew when a boy, dreſſed in a ſailor's jacket, and begging at one of the outlets of the town with a wooden leg. I knew him to have been honeſt and induſtrious when in the country, and was curious to learn what had reduced him to his preſent ſituation. Wherefore, after having given him what I thought proper, I deſired to know the hiſtory of his life and misfortunes, and the manner in which he was reduced to his preſent diſtreſs. The diſabled ſoldier, for ſuch he was, though dreſſed in a ſailor's habit, ſcratching his head, and leaning on his crutch, put himſelf into an attitude to comply with my requeſt, and gave me his hiſtory as follows:

"As for my misfortunes, maſter, I can't "pretend to have gone through any more "than other folks; for, except the loſs of "my limb, and my being obliged to beg, I "don't know any reaſon, thank Heaven, that "I have to complain: there is Bill Tibbs, "of our regiment, he has loſt both his legs, "and an eye to boot; but, thank Heaven, it "is not ſo bad with me yet.

"I was born in Shropſhire; my father "was a labourer, and died when I was five "years old; ſo that I was put upon the pa"riſh. As he had been a wandering ſort of "a man, the pariſhioners were not able to "tell to what pariſh I belonged, or where I "was born, ſo they ſent me to another pariſh, "and that pariſh ſent me to a third. I "thought in my heart, they kept ſending me "about ſo long, that they would not let me "be born in any pariſh at all; but at laſt, "however, they fixed me. I had ſome diſ"poſition to be a ſcholar, and was reſolved, "at leaſt, to know my letters; but the maſ"ter of the workhouſe put me to buſineſs as "ſoon as I was able to handle a mallet; and "here I lived an eaſy kind of life for five "years. I only wrought ten hours in the "day, and had my meat and drink provided "for my labour. It is true, I was not ſuf"fered to ſtir out of the houſe, for fear, as "they ſaid, I ſhould run away; but what of "that, I had the liberty of the whole houſe, "and the yard before the door, and that was "enough for me. I was then bound out to "a farmer, where I was up both early and "late; but I ate and drank well, and liked "my buſineſs well enough, till he died, when "I was obliged to provide for myſelf; ſo I "was reſolved to go ſeek my fortune.

"In this manner I went from town to "town, worked when I could get employ"ment,

" ment, and ſtarved when I could get none: " when happening one day to go through a " field belonging to a juſtice of peace, I ſpy'd " a hare croſſing the path juſt before me; " and I believe the devil put it in my head to " fling my ſtick at it:—well, what will you " have on't? I killed the hare, and was " bringing it away, when the juſtice himſelf " met me; he called me a poacher and a " villain; and, collaring me, deſired I would " give an account of myſelf. I fell upon my " knees, begged his worſhip's pardon, and " began to give a full account of all that I " knew of my breed, feed, and generation; " but, though I gave a very true account, the " juſtice ſaid I could give no account; ſo I " was indicted at ſeſſions, found guilty of " being poor, and ſent up to London to New- " gate, in order to be tranſported as a vaga- " bond.

" People may ſay this and that of being " in jail, but, for my part, I found Newgate " as agreeable a place as ever I was in in all " my life. I had my belly-full to eat and " drink, and did no work at all. This kind " of life was too good to laſt for ever; ſo I " was taken out of priſon, after five months, " put on board a ſhip, and ſent off, with two " hundred more, to the plantations. We " had but an indifferent paſſage, for being all " confined in the hold, more than a hundred " of our people died for want of ſweet air; " and thoſe that remained were ſickly enough, " God knows. When we came a-ſhore, we " were ſold to the planters, and I was bound " for ſeven years more. As I was no ſcho- " lar, for I did not know my letters, I was " obliged to work among the negroes; and " I ſerved out my time, as in duty bound to " do.

" When my time was expired, I worked " my paſſage home, and glad I was to ſee " Old England again, becauſe I loved my " country. I was afraid, however, that I " ſhould be indicted for a vagabond once " more, ſo I did not much care to go down " into the country, but kept about the town, " and did little jobs when I could get them.

" I was very happy in this manner for " ſome time, till one evening, coming home " from work, two men knocked me down, " and then deſired me to ſtand. They be- " longed to a preſs-gang: I was carried " before the juſtice, and, as I could give no " account of myſelf, I had my choice left, " whether to go on board a man of war, or " liſt for a ſoldier: I choſe the latter; and, " in this poſt of a gentleman, I ſerved two " campaigns in Flanders, was at the battles " of Val and Fontenoy, and received but one " wound, through the breaſt here; but the " doctor of our regiment ſoon made me well " again.

" When the peace came on I was diſ- " charged; and, as I could not work, be- " cauſe my wound was ſometimes trouble- " ſome, I liſted for a landman in the Eaſt " India company's ſervice. I have fought " the French in ſix pitched battles; and I " verily believe that, if I could read or " write, our captain would have made me " a corporal. But it was not my good for- " tune to have any promotion, for I ſoon " fell ſick, and ſo got leave to return home " again with forty pounds in my pocket. " This was at the beginning of the preſen " war, and I hoped to be ſet on ſhore, and " to have the pleaſure of ſpending my mo- " ney; but the government wanted men, " and ſo I was preſſed for a ſailor before " ever I could ſet foot on ſhore.

" The boatſwain found me, as he ſaid, an

"obstinate fellow: he swore he knew that I "understood my business well, but that I "shammed Abraham, to be idle; but, God "knows, I knew nothing of sea-business, "and he beat me, without considering what "he was about. I had still, however, my "forty pounds, and that was some comfort "to me under every beating; and the mo-"ney I might have had to this day, but that "our ship was taken by the French, and so "I lost all.

"Our crew was carried into Brest, and "many of them died, because they were not "used to live in a jail; but, for my part, it "was nothing to me, for I was seasoned. "One night, as I was asleep on the bed of "boards, with a warm blanket about me, for "I always loved to lie well, I was awakened "by the boatswain, who had a dark lanthorn "in his hand: 'Jack,' says he to me, 'will "you knock out the French centry's brains?' 'I don't care,' says I, striving to keep my-"self awake, 'if I lend a hand.' 'Then "follow me,' says he, 'and I hope we shall "do business.' So up I got, and tied my "blanket, which was all the cloaths I had, "about my middle, and went with him to "fight the Frenchmen. I hate the French, "because they are all slaves, and wear wooden "shoes.

"Though we had no arms, one English-"man is able to beat five French at any "time; so we went down to the door, "where both the centries were posted, and, "rushing upon them, seized their arms in a "moment, and knocked them down. From "thence nine of us ran together to the quay, "and seizing the first boat we met, got out "of the harbour, and put to sea. We had "not been here three days before we were "taken up by the Dorset privateer, who were "glad of so many good hands, and we con-"sented to run our chance. However, we "had not as much luck as we expected. In "three days we fell in with the Pompadour "privateer, of forty guns, while we had but "twenty-three; so to it we went, yard-arm "and yard-arm. The fight lasted for three "hours, and I verily believe we should have "taken the Frenchman, had we but had "some more men left behind; but, unfortu-"nately, we lost all our men just as we were "going to get the victory.

"I was once more in the power of the "French, and I believe it would have gone "hard with me had I been brought back to "Brest; but, by good fortune, we were re-"taken by the Viper. I had almost forgot "to tell you that, in that engagement, I was "wounded in two places; I lost four fingers "off the left hand, and my leg was shot off. "If I had had the good fortune to have lost "my leg and use of my hand on board a "king's ship, and not a-board a privateer, I "should have been entitled to cloathing and "maintenance during the rest of my life! "but that was not my chance: one man is "born with a silver spoon in his mouth, and "another with a wooden ladle. However, "blessed be God, I enjoy good health, and "will for ever love liberty and Old Eng-"land. Liberty, property, and Old England "for ever, huzza!"

Thus saying, he limped off, leaving me in admiration at his intrepidity and content; nor could I avoid acknowledging, that an habitual acquaintance with misery serves better than philosophy to teach us to despise it. *Goldsmith.*

§ 10. *A Dialogue between* ULYSSES *and* CIRCE, *in* CIRCE'*s Island.*

Circe. You will go then, Ulysses; but why will you go? I desire you to speak the thoughts

thoughts of your heart. Speak without reserve.—What carries you from me?

Ulysses. Pardon, goddess, the weakness of human nature. My heart will sigh for my country. It is a tenderness which all my attachment to you cannot overcome.

Circe. This is not all. I perceive you are afraid to declare your whole mind: but what do you fear? my terrors are gone. The proudest goddess on earth, when she has favoured a mortal as I have favoured you, has laid her divinity and power at his feet.

Ulysses. It may be so, while there still remains in her heart the fondness of love, or in her mind the fear of shame. But you, Circe, are above those vulgar sensations.

Circe. I understand your caution, it belongs to your character; and, therefore, to take all diffidence from you, I swear by Styx, I will do no harm to you or your friends for any thing which you say, though it should offend me ever so much, but will send you away with all marks of my friendship. Tell me now, truly, what pleasures you hope to enjoy in the barren island of Ithaca, which can compensate for those you leave in this paradise, exempt from all cares, and overflowing with all delights?

Ulysses. The pleasures of virtue; the supreme happiness of doing good. Here I do nothing: my mind is in a palsy; its faculties are benumbed. I long to return into action again, that I may employ those talents and virtues which I have cultivated from the earliest days of my youth. Toils and cares fright not me: they are the exercise of my soul; they keep it in health and in vigour. Give me again the fields of Troy, rather than those vacant groves: there I could reap the bright harvest of glory; here I am hid from the eyes of mankind, and begin to appear contemptible in my own. The image of my former self haunts and seems to upbraid me wherever I go: I meet it under the gloom of every shade; it even intrudes itself into your presence, and chides me from your arms. O goddess! unless you have power to lay that troublesome spirit, unless you can make me forget myself, I cannot be happy here, I shall every day be more wretched.

Circe. May not a wise and good man, who has spent all his youth in active life and honourable danger, when he begins to decline, have leave to retire, and enjoy the rest of his days in quiet and pleasure?

Ulysses. No retreat can be honourable to a wise and good man, but in company with the Muses; I am deprived of that sacred society here. The Muses will not inhabit the abodes of voluptuousness and sensual pleasure. How can I study, how can I think, while so many beasts (and the worst beasts I know are men turned into beasts) are howling, or roaring, or grunting about me?

Circe. There is something in this; but this is not all: you suppress the strongest reason that draws you to Ithaca. There is another image, besides that of your former self, which appears to you in all parts of this island, which follows your walks, which interposes itself between you and me, and chides you from my arms: it is Penelope, Ulysses; I know it is.—Do not pretend to deny it: you sigh for her in my bosom itself.—And yet she is not an immortal.—She is not, as I am, endowed with the gift of unfading youth: several years have past since her's has been faded. I think, without vanity, that she was never so handsome as I. But what is she now?

Ulysses. You have told me yourself, in a former conversation, when I enquired of you about her, that ſhe is true to my bed, and as fond of me now, after twenty years abſence, as when I left her to go to Troy. I left her in the bloom of her youth and her beauty. How much muſt her conſtancy have been tried ſince that time! how meritorious is her fidelity! Shall I reward her with falſhood? ſhall I forget her who cannot forget me; who has nothing ſo dear to her as my remembrance?

Circe. Her love is preſerved by the continual hope of your ſpeedy return. Take that hope from her: let your companions return, and let her know that you have fixed your abode here with me; that you have fixed it for ever: let her know that ſhe is free to diſpoſe of her heart and her hand as ſhe pleaſes. Send my picture to her; bid her compare it with her own face.—If all this does not cure her of the remains of her paſſion, if you do not hear of her marrying Eurymachus in a twelvemonth, I underſtand nothing of womankind.

Ulyſſes. O cruel goddeſs! why will you force me to tell you thoſe truths I wiſh to conceal? If by ſuch unjuſt, ſuch barbarous uſage, I could loſe her heart, it would break mine. How ſhould I endure the torment of thinking that I had wronged ſuch a wife? what could make me amends for her not being mine, for her being another's? Do not frown, Circe: I own, (ſince you will have mind. She bid me go to the ſiege of Troy, though the parting with me was worſe than death to herſelf: ſhe bid me expoſe myſelf there to all perils among the foremoſt heroes of Greece, though her poor heart trembled to think of the leaſt I ſhould meet, and would have given all its own blood to ſave a drop of mine. Then there was ſuch a conformity in all our inclinations! when Minerva taught me the leſſons of wiſdom, ſhe loved to be preſent; ſhe heard, ſhe retained the moral inſtructions, the ſublime truths of nature, ſhe gave them back to me, ſoftened and ſweetened with the peculiar graces of her own mind. When we unbent our thoughts with the charms of poetry, when we read together the poems of Orpheus, Muſæus, and Linus, with what taſte did ſhe mark every excellence in them! My feelings were dull, compared to her's. She ſeemed herſelf to be the Muſe who had inſpired thoſe verſes, and had tuned their lyres to infuſe into the hearts of mankind the love of wiſdom and virtue, and the fear of the gods. How beneficent was ſhe, how good to my people! what care did ſhe take to inſtruct them in the finer and more elegant arts; to relieve the neceſſities of the ſick and the aged; to ſuperintend the education of children; to do my ſubjects every good office of kind interceſſion; to lay before me their wants; to aſſiſt their petitions; to mediate for thoſe who were objects of mercy: to

to ſtay. The daughter of the Sun is not ſo mean-ſpirited as to ſolicit a mortal to ſhare her happineſs with her. It is a happineſs which I find you cannot enjoy. I pity you and deſpiſe you. That which you ſeem to value ſo much I have no notion of. All you have ſaid ſeems to me a jargon of ſentiments fitter for a ſilly woman than for a great man. Go, read, and ſpin too, if you pleaſe, with your wife. I forbid you to remain another day in my iſland. You ſhall have a fair wind to carry you from it. After that, may every ſtorm that Neptune can raiſe purſue and overwhelm you! Be gone, I ſay; quit my ſight.

Ulyſſes. Great Goddeſs, I obey—but remember your oath.——

§ II. *Scene between Colonel* RIVERS *and Sir* HARRY; *in which the Colonel, from Principles of Honour, refuſes to give his Daughter to Sir* HARRY.

Sir *Har.* Colonel, your moſt obedient: I am come upon the old buſineſs; for, unleſs I am allowed to entertain hopes of Miſs Rivers, I ſhall be the moſt miſerable of all human beings.

Riv. Sir Harry, I have already told you by letter, and I now tell you perſonally, I cannot liſten to your propoſals.

Sir *Har.* No, Sir!

Riv. No, Sir: I have promiſed my daughter to Mr. Sidney. Do you know that, Sir?

Sir *Har.* I do: but what then? Engagements of this kind, you know——

Riv. So then, you do know I have promiſed her to Mr. Sidney?

Sir *Har.* I do—But I alſo know that matters are not finally ſettled between Mr. Sidney and you; and I moreover know, that his fortune is by no means equal to mine; therefore——

Riv. Sir Harry, let me aſk you one queſtion before you make your conſequence.

Sir *Har.* A thouſand, if you pleaſe, Sir.

Riv. Why then, Sir, let me aſk you, what you have ever obſerved in me, or my conduct, that you deſire me ſo familiarly to break my word? I thought, Sir, you conſidered me as a man of honour?

Sir *Har.* And ſo I do, Sir—a man of the niceſt honour.

Riv. And yet, Sir, you aſk me to violate the ſanctity of my word; and tell me directly, that it is my intereſt to be a raſcal!

Sir *Har.* I really don't underſtand you, Colonel; I thought, when I was talking to you, I was talking to a man who knew the world; and as you have not yet ſigned——

Riv. Why, this is mending matters with a witneſs! And ſo you think, becauſe I am not legally bound, I am under no neceſſity of keeping my word? Sir Harry, laws were never made for men of honour: they want no bond but the rectitude of their own ſentiments; and laws are of no uſe but to bind the villains of ſociety.

Sir *Har.* Well! but, my dear Colonel, if you have no regard for me, ſhew ſome little regard for your daughter.

Riv. I ſhew the greateſt regard for my daughter, by giving her to a man of honour; and I muſt not be inſulted with any farther repetition of your propoſals.

Sir *Har.* Inſult you, Colonel! Is the offer of my alliance an inſult? Is my readineſs to make what ſettlements you think proper——

Riv. Sir Harry, I ſhould conſider the offer of a kingdom an inſult, if it were to be purchaſed by the violation of my word. Beſides,

ſides, though my daughter ſhall never go a beggar to the arms of her huſband, I would rather ſee her happy than rich; and if ſhe has enough to provide handſomely for a young family, and ſomething to ſpare for the exigencies of a worthy friend, I ſhall think her as affluent as if ſhe were miſtreſs of Mexico.

Sir *Har.* Well, Colonel, I have done; but I believe——

Riv. Well, Sir Harry, and as our conference is done, we will, if you pleaſe, retire to the ladies. I ſhall be always glad of your acquaintance, though I cannot receive you as a ſon-in-law; for a union of intereſt I look upon as a union of diſhonour, and conſider a marriage for money at beſt but a legal proſtitution.

§ 12. *On Vulgarity.*

A vulgar, ordinary way of thinking, acting, or ſpeaking, implies a low education, and a habit of low company. Young people contract it at ſchool, or among ſervants, with whom they are too often uſed to converſe; but, after they frequent good company, they muſt want attention and obſervation very much, if they do not lay it quite aſide; and indeed, if they do not, good company will be very apt to lay them aſide. The various kinds of vulgariſms are infinite; I cannot pretend, to point them out to you; but I will give ſome ſamples, by which you may gueſs at the reſt.

A vulgar man is captious and jealous; eager and impetuous about trifles: he ſuſpects himſelf to be ſlighted; thinks every thing that is ſaid meant at him; if the company happens to laugh, he is perſuaded they laugh at him; he grows angry and teſty, ſays ſomething very impertinent, and draws himſelf into a ſcrape, by ſhewing what he calls a proper ſpirit, and aſſerting himſelf. A man of faſhion does not ſuppoſe himſelf to be either the ſole or principal object of the thoughts, looks, or words of the company; and never ſuſpects that he is either ſlighted or laughed at, unleſs he is conſcious that he deſerves it. And if (which very ſeldom happens) the company is abſurd or ill-bred enough to do either, he does not care two-pence, unleſs the inſult be ſo groſs and plain as to require ſatisfaction of another kind. As he is above trifles, he is never vehement and eager about them; and wherever they are concerned, rather acquieſces than wrangles. A vulgar man's converſation always ſavours ſtrongly of the lowneſs of his education and company: it turns chiefly upon his domeſtic affairs, his ſervants, the excellent order he keeps in his own family, and the little anecdotes of the neighbourhood; all which he relates with emphaſis, as intereſting matters.—He is a man-goſſip.

Vulgariſm in language is the next, and diſtinguiſhing characteriſtic of bad company, and a bad education. A man of faſhion avoids nothing with more care than this. Proverbial expreſſions and trite ſayings are the flowers of the rhetoric of a vulgar man. Would he ſay, that men differ in their taſtes; he both ſupports and adorns that opinion, by the good old ſaying, as he reſpectfully calls it, that "what is one man's meat is another "man's poiſon." If any body attempts being *ſmart*, as he calls it, upon him; he gives them *tit for tat*, aye, that he does. He has always ſome favourite word for the time being; which, for the ſake of uſing often, he commonly abuſes. Such as, *vaſtly* angry, *vaſtly* kind, *vaſtly* handſome, and *vaſtly* ugly. Even his pronunciation of proper words

words carries the mark of the beast along with it. He calls the earth *yearth*; he is *obleiged*, not *obliged* to you. He goes *to wards*, and not *towards* ſuch a place. He ſometimes affects hard words, by way of ornament, which he always mangles. A man of faſhion never has recourſe to proverbs and vulgar aphoriſms; uſes neither favourite words nor hard words; but takes great care to ſpeak very correctly and grammatically, and to pronounce properly; that is, according to the uſage of the beſt companies.

An awkward addreſs, ungraceful attitudes and actions, and a certain left-handedneſs (if I may uſe that word) loudly proclaim low education and low company; for it is impoſſible to ſuppoſe, that a man can have frequented good company, without having catched ſomething, at leaſt, of their air and motions. A new-raiſed man is diſtinguiſhed in a regiment by his awkwardneſs; but he muſt be impenetrably dull, if, in a month or two's time, he cannot perform at leaſt the common manual exerciſe, and look like a ſoldier. The very accoutrements of a man of faſhion are grievous incumbrances to a vulgar man. He is at a loſs what to do with his hat, when it is not upon his head; his cane (if unfortunately he wears one) is at perpetual war with every cup of tea or coffee he drinks; deſtroys them firſt, and then accompanies them in their fall. His ſword is formidable only to his own legs, which would poſſibly carry him faſt enough out of the way of any ſword but his own. His cloaths fit him ſo ill, and conſtrain him ſo much, that he ſeems rather their priſoner than their proprietor. He preſents himſelf in company like a criminal in a court of juſtice; his very air condemns him; and people of faſhion will no more connect themſelves with the one, than people of character will with the other. This repulſe drives and ſinks him into low company; a gulph from whence no man, after a certain age, ever emerged.

Lord Cheſterfield.

§ 13. *On Good-breeding.*

A friend of yours and mine has very juſtly defined good-breeding to be, "the reſult of much good ſenſe, ſome good-nature, and a little ſelf-denial for the ſake of others, and with a view to obtain the ſame indulgence from them." Taking this for granted (as I think it cannot be diſputed) it is aſtoniſhing to me, that any body, who has good ſenſe and good-nature, can eſſentially fail in good-breeding. As to the modes of it, indeed, they vary according to perſons, places, and circumſtances; and are only to be acquired by obſervation and experience; but the ſubſtance of it is every where and eternally the ſame. Good manners are, to particular ſocieties, what good morals are to ſociety in general, their cement and their ſecurity. And as laws are enacted to enforce good morals, or at leaſt to prevent the ill effects of bad ones; ſo there are certain rules of civility, univerſally implied and received, to enforce good manners, and puniſh bad ones. And, indeed, there ſeems to me to be leſs difference both between the crimes and puniſhments, than at firſt one would imagine. The immoral man, who invades another's property, is juſtly hanged for it; and the ill-bred man who, by his ill-manners, invades and diſturbs the quiet and comforts of private life, is by common conſent as juſtly baniſhed ſociety. Mutual complaiſances, attentions, and ſacrifices of little conveniencies, are as natural an implied compact between civilized people, as protection

protection and obedience are between kings and subjects; whoever, in either case, violates that compact, justly forfeits all advantages arising from it. For my own part, I really think, that, next to the consciousness of doing a good action, that of doing a civil one is the most pleasing: and the epithet which I should covet the most, next to that of Aristides, would be that of well-bred. Thus much for good-breeding in general; I will now consider some of the various modes and degrees of it.

Very few, scarcely any, are wanting in the respect which they should shew to those whom they acknowledge to be infinitely their superiors; such as crowned heads, princes, and public persons of distinguished and eminent posts. It is the manner of shewing that respect which is different. The man of fashion, and of the world, expresses it in its fullest extent; but naturally, easily, and without concern; whereas a man, who is not used to keep good company, expresses it awkwardly; one sees that he is not used to it, and that it costs him a great deal: but I never saw the worst-bred man living guilty of lolling, whistling, scratching his head, and such-like indecencies, in companies that he respected. In such companies, therefore, the only point to be attended to is, to shew that respect which every body means to shew, in an easy, unembarrassed, and graceful manner. This is what observation and experience must teach you.

In mixed companies, whoever is admitted to make part of them, is, for the time at least, supposed to be upon a footing of equality with the rest; and, consequently, as there is no one principal object of awe and respect, people are apt to take a greater latitude in their behaviour, and to be less upon their guard; and so they may, provided it be within certain bounds, which are upon no occasion to be transgressed. But, upon these occasions, though no one is entitled to distinguished marks of respect, every one claims, and very justly, every mark of civility and good-breeding. Ease is allowed, but carelessness and negligence are strictly forbidden. If a man accosts you, and talks to you ever so dully or frivolously; it is worse than rudeness, it is brutality, to shew him, by a manifest inattention to what he says, that you think him a fool or a blockhead, and not worth hearing. It is much more so with regard to women; who, of whatever rank they are, are entitled, in consideration of their sex, not only to an attentive, but an officious good-breeding from men. Their little wants, likings, dislikes, preferences, antipathies, and fancies, must be officiously attended to, and, if possible, guessed at and anticipated, by a well-bred man. You must never usurp to yourself those conveniencies and gratifications which are of common right; such as the best places, the best dishes, &c. but on the contrary, always decline them yourself, and offer them to others; who, in their turns, will offer them to you: so that, upon the whole, you will, in your turn, enjoy your share of the common right. It would be endless for me to enumerate all the particular instances in which a well-bred man shews his good-breeding in good company; and it would be injurious to you to suppose that your own good sense will not point them out to you; and then your own good-nature will recommend, and your self-interest enforce the practice.

There is a third sort of good-breeding, in which people are the most apt to fail, from a very mistaken notion that they cannot fail at all.

all. I mean, with regard to one's most familiar friends and acquaintances, or those who really are our inferiors; and there, undoubtedly, a greater degree of ease is not only allowed, but proper, and contributes much to the comforts of a private, social life. But ease and freedom have their bounds, which must by no means be violated. A certain degree of negligence and carelessness becomes injurious and insulting, from the real or supposed inferiority of the persons; and that delightful liberty of conversation among a few friends, is soon destroyed, as liberty often has been, by being carried to licentiousness. But example explains things best, and I will put a pretty strong case: — Suppose you and me alone together; I believe you will allow that I have as good a right to unlimited freedom in your company, as either you or I can possibly have in any other; and I am apt to believe too, that you would indulge me in that freedom, as far as any body would. But, notwithstanding this, do you imagine that I should think there was no bounds to that freedom? I assure you, I should not think so; and I take myself to be as much tied down by a certain degree of good manners to you, as by other degrees of them to other people. The most familiar and intimate habitudes, connections, and friendships, require a degree of good-breeding, both to preserve and cement them. The best of us have our bad sides; and it is as imprudent as it is ill-bred, to exhibit them. I shall not use ceremony with you; it would be misplaced between us: but I shall certainly observe that degree of good-breeding with you, which is, in the first place, decent, and which, I am sure, is absolutely necessary to make us like one another's company long. *Lord Chesterfield.*

§ 14. *A Dialogue betwixt* MERCURY, *an English Duellist, and a North-American Savage.*

Duellist. Mercury, Charon's boat is on the other side of the water; allow me, before it returns, to have some conversation with the North-American Savage, whom you brought hither at the same time as you conducted me to the shades. I never saw one of that species before, and am curious to know what the animal is. He looks very grim.—Pray, Sir, what is your name? I understand you speak English.

Savage. Yes, I learned it in my childhood, having been bred up for some years in the town of New-York: but before I was a man I returned to my countrymen, the valiant Mohawks; and being cheated by one of yours in the sale of some rum, I never cared to have any thing to do with them afterwards. Yet I took up the hatchet for them with the rest of my tribe in the war against France, and was killed while I was out upon a scalping party. But I died very well satisfied: for my friends were victorious, and before I was shot I had scalped seven men and five women and children. In a former war I had done still greater exploits. My name is The Bloody Bear: it was given me to express my fierceness and valour

Duellist. Bloody Bear, I respect you, and am much your humble servant. My name is Tom Pushwell, very well known at Arthur's. I am a gentleman by my birth, and by profession a gamester, and man of honour. I have killed men in fair fighting, in honourable single combat, but do not understand cutting the throats of women and children.

Savage. Sir, that is our way of making war. Every nation has its own customs.

But by the grimneſs of your countenance, and that hole in your breaſt, I preſume you were killed, as I was myſelf, in ſome ſcalping party. How happened it that your enemy did not take off your ſcalp?

Duelliſt. Sir, I was killed in a duel. A friend of mine had lent me ſome money; after two or three years, being in great want himſelf, he aſked me to pay him; I thought his demand an affront to my honour, and ſent him a challenge. We met in Hyde-Park; the fellow could not fence: I was the adroiteſt ſwordſman in England. I gave him three or four wounds; but at laſt he ran upon me with ſuch impetuoſity, that he put me out of my play, and I could not prevent him from whipping me through the lungs. I died the next day, as a man of honour ſhould, without any ſniveling ſigns of repentance: and he will follow me ſoon; for his ſurgeon has declared his wounds to be mortal. It is ſaid that his wife is dead of her fright, and that his family of ſeven children will be undone by his death. So I am well revenged; and that is a comfort. For my part, I had no wife—I always hated marriage: my whore will take good care of herſelf, and my children are provided for at the Foundling Hoſpital.

Savage. Mercury, I won't go in a boat with that fellow. He has murdered his countryman; he has murdered his friend: I ſay, I won't go in a boat with that fellow. I will ſwim over the river: I can ſwim like a duck.

Mercury. Swim over the Styx! it muſt not be done; it is againſt the laws of Pluto's empire. You muſt go in the boat, and be quiet.

Savage. Do not tell me of laws: I am a Savage: I value no laws. Talk of laws to the Engliſhman: there are laws in his country, and yet you ſee he did not regard them. For they could never allow him to kill his fellow-ſubject in time of peace, becauſe he aſked him to pay a debt. I know that the Engliſh are a barbarous nation; but they cannot be ſo brutal as to make ſuch things lawful.

Mercury. You reaſon well againſt him. But how comes it that you are ſo offended with murder: you who have maſſacred women in their ſleep, and children in their cradles.

Savage. I killed none but my enemies: I never killed my own countrymen: I never killed my friend. Here, take my blanket, and let it come over in the boat; but ſee that the murderer does not ſit upon it, or touch it; if he does I will burn it in the fire I ſee yonder. Farewell.—I am reſolved to ſwim over the water.

Mercury. By this touch of my wand I take all thy ſtrength from thee.—Swim now if thou canſt.

Savage. This is a very potent enchanter. ——Reſtore me my ſtrength, and I will obey thee.

Mercury. I reſtore it; but be orderly, and do as I bid you, otherwiſe worſe will befal you.

Duelliſt. Mercury, leave him to me. I will tutor him for you. Sirrah, Savage, doſt thou pretend to be aſhamed of my company? Doſt thou know that I have kept the beſt company in England?

Savage. I know thou art a ſcoundrel.—Not pay thy debts! kill thy friend, who lent thee money, for aſking thee for it! Get out of my ſight. I will drive thee into Styx.

Mercury. Stop—I command thee. No violence.—Talk to him calmly.

Savage.

Savage. I muſt obey thee.—Well, Sir, let me know what merit you had to introduce you into good company. What could you do?

Duelliſt. Sir, I gamed, as I told you.—Beſides, I kept a good table.—I eat as well as any man in England or France.

Savage. Eat! Did you ever eat the chine of a Frenchman, or his leg, or his ſhoulder? there is fine eating! I have eat twenty.—My table was always well ſerved. My wife was the beſt cook for dreſſing of man's fleſh in all North America. You will not pretend to compare your eating with mine.

Duelliſt. I danced very finely.

Savage. I will dance with thee for thy ears.—I can dance all day long. I can dance the war-dance with more ſpirit and vigour than any man of my nation: let us ſee thee begin it. How thou ſtandeſt like a poſt! Has Mercury ſtruck thee with his enfeebling rod? or art thou aſhamed to let us ſee how awkward thou art? If he would permit me, I would teach thee to dance in a way that thou haſt not yet learnt. I would make thee caper and leap like a buck. But what elſe canſt thou do, thou bragging raſcal?

Duelliſt. Oh, heavens! muſt I bear this? what can I do with this fellow? I have neither ſword nor piſtol; and his ſhade ſeems to be twice as ſtrong as mine.

Mercury. You muſt anſwer his queſtions. It was your own deſire to have a converſation with him. He is not well-bred; but he will tell you ſome truths which you muſt hear in this place. It would have been well for you if you had heard them above. He aſked you what you could do beſides eating and dancing.

Duelliſt. I ſung very agreeably.

Savage. Let me hear you ſing your death-ſong, or the war-hoop. I challenge you to ſing.—The fellow is mute.—Mercury, this is a liar.—He tells us nothing but lies. Let me pull out his tongue.

Duelliſt. The lie given me!—and, alas! I dare not reſent it. Oh, what a diſgrace to the family of the Puſhwells! this indeed is damnation.

Mercury. Here, Charon, take theſe two ſavages to your care. How far the barbariſm of the Mohawk will excuſe his horrid acts, I leave Minos to judge; but the Engliſhman, what excuſe can he plead? The cuſtom of duelling? A bad excuſe at the beſt! but in his caſe cannot avail. The ſpirit that made him draw his ſword in this combat againſt his friend is not that of honour; it is the ſpirit of the furies, of Alecto herſelf. To her he muſt go, for ſhe hath long dwelt in his merciless boſom.

Savage. If he is to be puniſhed, turn him over to me. I underſtand the art of tormenting. Sirrah, I begin with this kick on your breech. Get you into the boat, or I'll give you another. I am impatient to have you condemned.

Duelliſt. Oh, my honour, my honour, to what infamy art thou fallen!

Dialogues of the Dead.

§ 15. *The Art of Pleaſing.*

The deſire of being pleaſed is univerſal: the deſire of pleaſing ſhould be ſo too. It is included in that great and fundamental principle of morality, of doing to others what one wiſhes they ſhould do to us. There are indeed ſome moral duties of a much higher nature, but none of a more amiable; and I do not heſitate to place it at the head of the minor virtues.

The manner of conferring favours or benefits is, as to pleaſing, almoſt as important as the matter itſelf. Take care, then, never to throw away the obligations, which perhaps you may have it in your power to confer upon others, by an air of inſolent protection, or by a cold and comfortleſs manner, which ſtifles them in their birth. Humanity inclines, religion requires, and our moral duties oblige us, as far as we are able, to relieve the diſtreſſes and miſeries of our fellow-creatures: but this is not all; for a true heart-felt benevolence and tenderneſs will prompt us to contribute what we can to their eaſe, their amuſement, and their pleaſure, as far as innocently we may. Let us then not only ſcatter benefits, but even ſtrew flowers for our fellow-travellers, in the rugged ways of this wretched world.

There are ſome, and but too many in this country particularly, who, without the leaſt viſible taint of ill-nature and malevolence, ſeem to be totally indifferent, and do not ſhew the leaſt deſire to pleaſe; as, on the other hand, they never deſignedly offend. Whether this proceeds from a lazy, negligent, and liſtleſs diſpoſition, from a gloomy and melancholic nature, from ill health, low ſpirits, or from a ſecret and ſullen pride, ariſing from the conſciouſneſs of their boaſted liberty and independency, is hard to determine, conſidering the various movements of the human heart, and the wonderful errors of the human head. But, be the cauſe what it will, that neutrality, which is the effect of it, makes theſe people, as neutralities do, deſpicable, and mere blanks in ſociety. They would ſurely be rouſed from their indifference, if they would ſeriouſly conſider the infinite utility of pleaſing.

The perſon who manifeſts a conſtant deſire to pleaſe, places his, perhaps, ſmall ſtock of merit at great intereſt. What vaſt returns, then, muſt real merit, when thus adorned, neceſſarily bring in! A prudent uſurer would with tranſport place his laſt ſhilling at ſuch intereſt, and upon ſo ſolid a ſecurity.

The man who is amiable, will make almoſt as many friends as he does acquaintances. I mean in the current acceptation of the word, but not ſuch ſentimental friends, as Pylades or Oreſtes, Nyſus and Euryalus, &c. but he will make people in general wiſh him well, and inclined to ſerve him in any thing not inconſiſtent with their own intereſt.

Civility is the eſſential article towards pleaſing, and is the reſult of good-nature and of good-ſenſe; but good-breeding is the decoration, the luſtre of civility, and only to be acquired by a minute attention to, and experience of, good company. A good-natured ploughman or fox-hunter, may be intentionally as civil as the politeſt courtier; but their manner often degrades and vilifies the matter; whereas, in good-breeding, the manner always adorns and dignifies the matter to ſuch a degree, that I have often known it give currency to baſe coin.

Civility is often attended by a ceremoniouſneſs, which good-breeding corrects, but will not quite aboliſh. A certain degree of ceremony is a neceſſary out-work of manners, as well as of religion: it keeps the forward and petulant at a proper diſtance, and is a very ſmall reſtraint to the ſenſible, and to the well-bred part of the world. *Cheſterfield.*

§ 16. *Humorous Scene at an Inn between* Boniface *and* Aimwell.

Bon. This way, this way, Sir.
Aim. You're my landlord, I ſuppoſe?
Bon. Yes, Sir, I'm old Will Boniface: pretty

pretty well known upon this road, as the saying is.

Aim. O, Mr. Boniface, your ſervant.

Bon. O, Sir, what will your honour pleaſe to drink, as the ſaying is?

Aim. I have heard your town of Litchfield much famed for ale; I think I'll taſte that.

Bon. Sir, I have now in my cellar ten tun of the beſt ale in Staffordſhire: 'tis ſmooth as oil, ſweet as milk, clear as amber, and ſtrong as brandy; and will be juſt fourteen years old the fifth day of next March, old ſtyle.

Aim. You're very exact, I find, in the age of your ale.

Bon. As punctual, Sir, as I am in the age of my children: I'll ſhew you ſuch ale!—Here, Tapſter, broach number 1706, as the ſaying is.—Sir, you ſhall taſte my anno domini.—I have lived in Litchfield, man and boy, above eight-and-fifty years, and, I believe, have not conſumed eight-and-fifty ounces of meat.

Aim. At a meal, you mean, if one may gueſs by your bulk.

Bon. Not in my life, Sir; I have fed purely upon ale: I have eat my ale, drank my ale, and I always ſleep upon my ale.

Enter Tapſter *with a Tankard.*

Now, Sir, you ſhall ſee——Your worſhip's health: [*Drinks*]—Ha! delicious, delicious!—Fancy it Burgundy, only fancy it—and 'tis worth ten ſhillings a quart.

Aim. [*Drinks*] 'Tis confounded ſtrong.

Bon. Strong! it muſt be ſo, or how would we be ſtrong that drink it?

Aim. And have you liv'd ſo long upon this ale, landlord?

Bon. Eight-and-fifty years, upon my credit, Sir: but it killed my wife, poor woman! as the ſaying is.

Aim. How came that to paſs?

Bon. I don't know how, Sir—She would not let the ale take its natural courſe, Sir: ſhe was for qualifying it every now and then with a dram, as the ſaying is; and an honeſt gentleman that came this way from Ireland, made her a preſent of a dozen bottles of uſquebaugh—But the poor woman was never well after—but, however, I was obliged to the gentleman, you know.

Aim. Why, was it the uſquebaugh that killed her?

Bon. My lady Bountiful ſaid ſo—She, good lady did what could be done: ſhe cured her of three tympanies: but the fourth carried her off: but ſhe's happy, and I'm contented, as the ſaying is.

Aim. Who's that lady Bountiful you mentioned?

Bon. Ods my life, Sir, We'll drink her health: [*Drinks.*]—My lady Bountiful is one of the beſt of women. Her laſt huſband, Sir Charles Bountiful, left her worth a thouſand pounds a year; and, I believe, ſhe lays out one-half on't in charitable uſes for the good of her neighbours.

Aim. Has the lady any children?

Bon. Yes, Sir, ſhe has a daughter by Sir Charles; the fineſt woman in all our county, and the greateſt fortune. She has a ſon too, by her firſt huſband, 'ſquire Sullen, who married a fine lady from London t'other day: if you pleaſe, Sir, we'll drink his health. [*Drinks.*]

Aim. What ſort of a man is he?

Bon. Why, Sir, the man's well enough: ſays little, thinks leſs, and does nothing at all, faith: but he's a man of great eſtate, and values nobody.

Aim.

Aim. A sportsman, I suppose?

Bon. Yes, he's a man of pleasure; he plays at whist, and smokes his pipe eight-and-forty hours together sometimes.

Aim. A fine sportsman, truly!—and married you say?

Bon. Ay; and to a curious woman, Sir. —But he's my landlord, and so a man you know, would not—— Sir, my humble service to you. [*Drinks.*] — Tho' I value not a farthing what he can do to me: I pay him his rent at quarter-day; I have a good running trade; I have but one daughter, and I can give her——but no matter for that.

Aim. You're very happy, Mr. Boniface: pray, what other company have you in town?

Bon. A power of fine ladies; and then we have the French officers.

Aim. O, that's right, you have a good many of those gentlemen: pray, how do you like their company?

Bon. So well, as the saying is, that I could wish we had as many more of 'em. They're full of money, and pay double for every thing they have. They know, Sir, that we pay good round taxes for the taking of 'em; and so they are willing to reimburse us a little: one of 'em lodges in my house. [*Bell rings.*] I beg your worship's pardon—I'll wait on you in half a minute.

§ 17. *A Dialogue between* M. Apicius *and* Darteneuf.

Darteneuf. Alas! poor Apicius.—I pity thee much, for not having lived in my age and my country. How many good dishes have I eat in England, that were unknown at Rome in thy days!

Apicius. Keep your pity for yourself.—How many good dishes have I eat in Rome, the knowledge of which has been lost in these latter degenerate days! the fat paps of a sow, the livers of scari, the brains of phenicopters, and the tripotanum, which consisted of three sorts of fish for which you have no names, the lupus marinus, the myxo, and the murænus.

Darteneuf. I thought the muræna had been our lamprey. We have excellent ones in the Severn.

Apicius. No:—the muræna was a salt-water fish, and kept in ponds into which the sea was admitted.

Darteneuf. Why then I dare say our lampreys are better. Did you ever eat any of them potted or stewed?

Apicius. I was never in Britain. Your country then was too barbarous for me to go thither. I should have been afraid that the Britons would have eat me.

Darteneuf. I am sorry for you, very sorry: for if you never were in Britain, you never eat the best oysters in the whole world.

Apicius. Pardon me, Sir, your Sandwich oysters were brought to Rome in my time.

Darteneuf. They could not be fresh: they were good for nothing there:—You should have come to Sandwich to eat them: it is a shame for you that you did not.—An epicure talk of danger when he is in search of a dainty! did not Leander swim over the Hellespont to get to his mistress? and what is a wench to a barrel of excellent oysters?

Apicius. Nay—I am sure you cannot blame me for any want of alertness in seeking fine fishes. I sailed to the coast of Afric, from Minturnæ in Campania, only to taste of one species, which I heard was larger there than it was on our coast, and finding that I had received a false information, I returned again without deigning to land.

Darteneuf. There was some sense in that; but

but why did you not alſo make a voyage to Sandwich? Had you taſted thoſe oyſters in their perfection you would never have come back: you would have eat till you burſt.

Apicius. I wiſh I had:—It would have been better than poiſoning myſelf, as I did, becauſe, when I came to make up my accounts, I found I had not much above the poor ſum of fourſcore thouſand pounds left, which would not afford me a table to keep me from ſtarving.

Darteneuf. A ſum of fourſcore thouſand pounds not keep you from ſtarving! would I had had it! I ſhould not have ſpent it in twenty years, though I had kept the beſt table in London, ſuppoſing I had made no other expence.

Apicius. Alas, poor man! this ſhews that you Engliſh have no idea of the luxury that reigned in our tables. Before I died, I had ſpent in my kitchen 807,291 *l.* 13 *s.* 4 *d.*

Darteneuf. I do not believe a word of it: there is an error in the account.

Apicius. Why, the eſtabliſhment of Lucullus for his ſuppers in the Apollo, I mean for every ſupper he eat in the room which he called by that name, was 5000 drachms, which is in your money 1614 *l.* 11 *s.* 8 *d.*

Darteneuf. Would I had ſupped with him there! But is there no blunder in theſe calculations?

Apicius. Aſk your learned men that.—I count as they tell me.—But perhaps you may think that theſe feaſts were only made by great men, like Lucullus, who had plundered all Aſia to help him in his houſe-keeping. What will you ſay, when I tell you that the player Æſopus had one diſh that coſt him 6000 ſeſtertia, that is, 4843 *l.* 10 *s.* Engliſh.

Darteneuf. What will I ſay! why that I pity poor Cibber and Booth; and that, if I had known this when I was alive, I ſhould have hang'd myſelf for vexation that I did not live in thoſe days.

Apicius. Well you might, well you might.—You do not know what eating is. You never could know it. Nothing leſs than the wealth of the Roman empire is ſufficient to enable a man to keep a good table. Our players were richer by far than your princes.

Darteneuf. Oh that I had but lived in the bleſſed reign of Caligula, or of Vitellius, or of Heliogabalus, and had been admitted to the honour of dining with their ſlaves!

Apicius. Aye, there you touch me.—I am miſerable that I died before their good times. They carried the glories of their table much farther than the beſt eaters of the age that I lived in. Vitellius ſpent in eating and drinking, within one year, what would amount in your money to above ſeven millions two hundred thouſand pounds. He told me ſo himſelf in a converſation I had with him not long ago. And the others you mentioned did not fall ſhort of his royal magnificence.

Darteneuf. Theſe indeed were great princes. But what affects me moſt is the diſh of that player, that d——d fellow Æſopus. I cannot bear to think of his having lived ſo much better than I. Pray, of what ingredients might the diſh he paid ſo much for conſiſt?

Apicius. Chiefly of ſinging birds. It was that which ſo greatly enhanced the price.

Darteneuf. Of ſinging birds! choak him!—I never eat but one, which I ſtole from a lady of my acquaintance, and all London was in an uproar about it, as if I had ſtolen and roaſted a child. But, upon recollection, I begin to doubt whether I have ſo much reaſon to envy Æſopus; for the ſinging bird which I eat was no better in its taſte

taſte than a fat lark or a thruſh; it was not ſo good as a wheatear or becafigue; and therefore I ſuſpect that all the luxury you have bragged of was nothing but vanity and fooliſh expence. It was like that of the ſon of Æſopus, who diſſolved pearls in vinegar, and drunk them at ſupper. I will be d——d, if a haunch of veniſon, and my favourite ham-pye, were not much better diſhes than any at the table of Vitellius himſelf. I do not find that you had ever any good ſoups; without which no man of taſte can poſſibly dine. The rabbits in Italy are not fit to eat, and what is better than the wing of one of our Engliſh wild rabbits? I have been told that you had no turkies. The mutton in Italy is very ill-flavoured; and as for your boars roaſted whole, I deſpiſe them; they were only fit to be ſerved up to the mob at a corporation feaſt, or election dinner. A ſmall barbecued hog is worth a hundred of them; and a good collar of Shrewſbury brawn is a much better diſh.

Apicius. If you had ſome kinds of meat that we wanted, yet our cookery muſt have been greatly ſuperior to yours. Our cooks were ſo excellent, that they could give to hog's fleſh the taſte of all other meats.

Darteneuf. I ſhould not have liked their d——d imitations. You might as eaſily have impoſed on a good connoiſſeur the copy of a fine picture for the original. Our cooks, on the contrary, give to all other meats a rich flavour of bacon, without deſtroying that which makes the diſtinction of one from another. I have not the leaſt doubt that our eſſence of hams is a much better ſauce than any that ever was uſed by the ancients. We have a hundred ragouts, the compoſition of which exceeds all deſcription. Had yours been as good, you could not have lolled, as you did, upon couches, while you were eating; they would have made you ſit up and attend to your buſineſs. Then you had a cuſtom of hearing things read to you while you were at ſupper. This ſhews you were not ſo well entertained as we are with our meat. For my own part, when I was at table, I could mind nothing elſe: I neither heard, ſaw, nor ſpoke: I only ſmelt and taſted. But the worſt of all is, that you had no wine fit to be named with good claret, or Burgundy, or Champagne, or old hock, or Tokay. You boaſted much of your Falernum; but I have taſted the Lachrymæ Chriſti, and other wines that grow upon the ſame coaſt, not one of which would I drink above a glaſs or two of if you would give me the kingdom of Naples. You boiled your wines, and mixed water with them, which ſhews that in themſelves they were not fit to drink.

Apicius. I am afraid you beat us in wines, not to mention your cyder, perry, and beer, of all which I have heard great fame from ſome Engliſh with whom I have talked; and their report has been confirmed by the teſtimony of their neighbours who have travelled into England. Wonderful things have been alſo ſaid to me of a liquor called punch.

Darteneuf. Aye — to have died without taſting that is unhappy indeed! There is rum-punch and arrack-punch; it is hard to ſay which is beſt: but Jupiter would have given his nectar for either of them, upon my word and honour.

Apicius. The thought of it puts me into a fever with thirſt. From whence do you get your arrack and your rum?

Darteneuf. Why, from the Eaſt and Weſt Indies, which you knew nothing of. That is enough to decide the diſpute. Your trade to the Eaſt Indies was very far ſhort of what we we carry on, and the West Indies were not discovered. What a new world of good things for eating and drinking has Columbus opened to us! Think of that, and despair.

Apicius. I cannot indeed but lament my ill fate, that America was not found before I was born. It tortures me when I hear of chocolate, pine-apples, and twenty other fine meats or fine fruits produced there, which I have never tasted. What an advantage it is to you, that all your sweet-meats, tarts, cakes, and other delicacies of that nature, are sweetened with sugar instead of honey, which we were obliged to make use of for want of that plant! but what grieves me most is, that I never eat a turtle; they tell me that it is absolutely the best of all foods.

Darteneuf. Yes, I have heard the Americans say so:—but I never eat any; for, in my time, they were not brought over to England.

Apicius. Never eat any turtle! how didst thou dare to accuse me of not going to Sandwich to eat oysters, and didst not thyself take a trip to America to riot on turtles? but know, wretched man, that I am informed they are now as plentiful in England as sturgeon. There are turtle boats that go regularly to London and Bristol from the West-Indies. I have just seen a fat Alderman, who died in London last week of a surfeit he got at a turtle feast in that city.

Darteneuf. What does he say? Does he tell you that turtle is better than venison?

Apicius. He says there was a haunch of venison untouched, while every mouth was employed on the turtle; that he ate till he fell asleep in his chair? and, that the food was so wholesome he should not have died, if he had not unluckily caught cold in his sleep, which stopped his perspiration, and hurt his digestion.

Darteneuf. Alas! how imperfect is human felicity! I lived in an age when the pleasure of eating was thought to be carried to its highest perfection in England and France; and yet a turtle feast is a novelty to me! Would it be impossible, do you think, to obtain leave from Pluto of going back for one day, just to taste of that food? I would promise to kill myself by the quantity I would eat before the next morning.

Apicius. You have forgot, Sir, that you have no body: that which you had has been rotten a great while ago; and you can never return to the earth with another, unless Pythagoras carries you thither to animate that of a hog. But comfort yourself, that, as you have ate dainties which I never tasted, so the next generation will eat some unknown to the present. New discoveries will be made, and new delicacies brought from other parts of the world. We must both be philosophers. We must be thankful for the good things we have had, and not grudge others better, if they fall to their share. Consider that, after all, we could but have eat as much as our stomachs would hold, and that we did every day of our lives.—But see, who comes hither? I think it is Mercury.

Mercury. Gentlemen, I must tell you that I have stood near you invisible, and heard your discourse; a privilege which we deities use when we please. Attend therefore to a discovery which I shall make to you, relating to the subject upon which you were talking. I know two men, one of whom lived in ancient, and the other in modern times, that had more pleasure in eating than either of you ever had in your lives.

Apicius. One of these, I presume, was a Sybarite,

Sybarite, and the other a French gentleman settled in the West Indies.

Mercury. No; one was a Spartan soldier, and the other an English farmer.—I see you both look astonished; but what I tell you is truth. The soldier never ate his black broth till the exercises, to which by their discipline the Spartan troops were obliged, had got him such an appetite, that he could have gnawed a bone like a dog. The farmer was out at the tail of his plough, or some other wholesome labour, from morning till night; and when he came home his wife dressed him a piece of good beef, or a fine barn door fowl and a pudding, for his dinner, which he ate much more ravenously, and consequently with a great deal more relish and pleasure, than you did your tripotanum or your ham-pye. Your stomachs were always so overcharged, that I question if ever you felt real hunger, or eat one meal in twenty years without forcing your appetites, which makes all things insipid. I tell you therefore again, that the soldier and the farmer had much more of the joy of eating than you.

Darteneuf. This is more mortifying than not to have shared a turtle feast. I fear indeed we have been in quite a wrong system, and never had any true notions of pleasure.

Apicius. It is a sad thing not to know what good living is before one is dead. I wish, Mercury, you had taught me your art of cookery in my life-time, or held your tongue about it here.

Dialogues of the Dead.

§ 18. *Scene between* IAGO *and* CASSIO, *in which* CASSIO *regrets his Folly in getting drunk.*

Iago. What! are you hurt, Lieutenant?

Cas. Past all surgery.

Iago. Marry, Heav'n forbid!

Cas. Reputation, reputation, reputation! Oh I have lost my reputation! I have lost the immortal part of myself, and what remains is bestial. My reputation! Iago, my reputation——

Iago. As I am an honest man, I thought you had received some bodily wound: there is more sense in that, than in reputation. Reputation is an idle and most false imposition: oft got without merit, and lost without deserving. What, man! —there are ways to recover the general again. Sue to him, and he's your's.

Cas. I will rather sue to be despis'd, ——— Drunk! and squabble! swagger! swear! and discourse fustian with one's own shadow! O thou invincible spirit of wine! if thou hast no name to be known by, let us call thee Devil.

Iago. What was he that you followed with your sword? what had he done to you?

Cas. I know not.

Iago. Is't possible?

Cas. I remember a mass of things, but nothing distinctly; a quarrel, but nothing wherefore. Oh, that men should put an enemy in their mouths to steal away their brains! that we should with joy, pleasance, revel, and applause, transform ourselves into beasts!

Iago. Why, but you are now well enough: how came you thus recovered?

Cas. It has pleased the devil Drunkenness to give place to the devil Wrath; one imperfectness shews me another, to make me frankly despise myself.

Iago. Come, you are too severe a moraler. As the time, the place, and the condition of this

this country ſtands, I could heartily wiſh this had not befallen; but ſince it is as it is, mend it for your own good.

Caſ. I will aſk him for my place again—he ſhall tell me I am a drunkard!——Had I as many mouths as Hydra, ſuch an anſwer would ſtop them all. To be now a ſenſible man, by and by a fool, and preſently a beaſt!——Every inordinate cup is unbleſs'd, and the ingredient is a devil.

Iago. Come, come, good wine is a good familiar creature, if it be well uſed; exclaim no more againſt it. And, good Lieutenant, I think you think I love you.

Caſ. I have well approv'd it, Sir.—I drunk!

Iago. You, or any man living, may be drunk at ſome time, man. I tell you what you ſhall do. Our general's wife is now the general. Confeſs yourſelf freely to her: importune her help, to put you in your place again. She is of ſo free, ſo kind, ſo apt, ſo bleſſed a diſpoſition, ſhe holds it a vice in her goodneſs not to do more than ſhe is requeſted. This broken joint between you and her huſband, entreat her to ſplinter; and, my fortunes againſt any lay worth naming, this crack of your love ſhall grow ſtronger than it was before.

Caſ. You adviſe me well.

Iago. I proteſt, in the ſincerity of love and honeſt kindneſs.

Caſ. I think it freely; and, betimes in the morning, I will beſeech the virtuous Deſdemona to undertake for me.

Iago. You are in the right. Good night, Lieutenant: I muſt to the watch.

Caſ. Good night, honeſt Iago.

Shakeſpeare.

§ 19. *A Dialogue between* MERCURY and *a modern fine Lady.*

Mrs. Modiſh. Indeed, Mr. Mercury, I cannot have the pleaſure of waiting upon you now. I am engaged, abſolutely engaged.

Mercury. I know you have an amiable affectionate huſband, and ſeveral fine children: but you need not be told, that neither conjugal attachments, maternal affections, nor even the care of a kingdom's welfare or a nation's glory, can excuſe a perſon who has received a ſummons to the realms of death. If the grim meſſenger was not as peremptory as unwelcome, Charon would not get a paſſenger (except now and then an hypochondriacal Engliſhman) once in a century. You muſt be content to leave your huſband and family, and paſs the Styx.

Mrs. Modiſh. I did not mean to inſiſt on any engagement with my huſband and children; I never thought myſelf engaged to them. I had no engagements but ſuch as were common to women of my rank. Look on my chimney-piece, and you will ſee I was engaged to the play on Mondays, balls on Tueſdays, the opera on Saturdays, and to card aſſemblies the reſt of the week, for two months to come; and it would be the rudeſt thing in the world not to keep my appointments. If you will ſtay for me till the ſummer ſeaſon, I will wait on you with all my heart. Perhaps the Elyſian fields may be leſs deteſtable than the country in our world. Pray, have you a fine Vauxhall and Ranelagh? I think I ſhould not diſlike drinking the Lethe waters, when you have a full ſeaſon.

Mercury. Surely you could not like to drink the waters of oblivion, who have made pleaſure

pleaſure the buſineſs, end, and aim of your life! It is good to drown cares: but who would waſh away the remembrance of a life of gaiety and pleaſure?

Mrs. Modiſh. Diverſion was indeed the buſineſs of my life; but as to pleaſure, I have enjoyed none ſince the novelty of my amuſements was gone off. Can one be pleaſed with ſeeing the ſame thing over and over again? Late hours and fatigue gave me the vapours, ſpoiled the natural chearfulneſs of my temper, and even in youth wore away my youthful vivacity.

Mercury. If this way of life did not give you pleaſure, why did you continue in it? I ſuppoſe you did not think it was very meritorious?

Mrs. Modiſh. I was too much engaged to think at all: ſo far indeed my manner of life was agreeable enough. My friends always told me diverſions were neceſſary, and my doctor aſſured me diſſipation was good for my ſpirits; my huſband inſiſted that it was not; and you know that one loves to oblige one's friends, comply with one's doctor, and contradict one's huſband; and beſides, I was ambitious to be thought *du bon ton* *.

Mercury. Bon ton! what's that, Madam? Pray define it.

Mrs. Modiſh. Oh, Sir, excuſe me; it is one of the privileges of the *bon ton* never to define or be defined. It is the child and the parent of jargon. It is—I can never tell you what it is; but I will try to tell you what it is not. In converſation it is not wit; in manners it is not politeneſs; in behaviour it is not addreſs; but it is a little like them all. It can only belong to people of a certain rank, who live in a certain manner, with certain perſons who have not certain virtues, and who have certain vices, and who inhabit a certain part of the town. Like a place by courteſy, it gets an higher rank than the perſon can claim, but which thoſe who have a legal title to precedency dare not diſpute, for fear of being thought not to underſtand the rules of politeneſs. Now, Sir, I have told you as much as I know of it, though I have admired and aimed at it all my life.

Mercury. Then, Madam, you have waſted your time, faded your beauty, and deſtroyed your health, for the laudable purpoſes of contradicting your huſband, and being this ſomething and this nothing called the *bon ton?*

Mrs. Modiſh. What would you have had me do?

Mercury. I will follow your mode of inſtructing: I will tell you what I would not have had you do. I would not have had you ſacrifice your time, your reaſon, and your duties to faſhion and folly. I would not have had you neglect your huſband's happineſs, and your children's education.

Mrs. Modiſh. As to my daughters' education I ſpared no expence: they had a dancing-maſter, muſic-maſter, and drawing-maſter, and a French governeſs to teach them behaviour and the French language.

Mercury. So their religion, ſentiments, and manners, were to be learnt from a dancing-maſter, muſic-maſter, and a chambermaid! perhaps they might prepare them to catch the *bon ton.* Your daughters muſt have been ſo educated as to fit them to be wives without conjugal affection, and mothers without

* *Du bon ton* is a cant phraſe in the modern French language, for the faſhionable air of converſation and manners.

without maternal care. I am ſorry for the ſort of life they are commencing, and for that which you have juſt concluded. Minos is a ſour old gentleman, without the leaſt ſmattering of the *bon ton*; and I am in a fright for you. The beſt thing I can adviſe you is, to do in this world as you did in the other, keep happineſs in your view, but never take the road that leads to it. Remain on this ſide Styx; wander about without end or aim; look into the Elyſian fields, but never attempt to enter into them, leſt Minos ſhould puſh you into Tartarus: for duties neglected may bring on a ſentence not much leſs ſevere than crimes committed.

Dialogues of the Dead.

§ 20. *Scene between the Jews* SHYLOCK *and* TUBAL; *in which the latter alternately torments and pleaſes the former, by giving him an Account of the Extravagance of his Daughter* JESSICA, *and the Misfortunes of* ANTONIO.

Shy. How now, Tubal? What news from Genoa? haſt thou heard of my daughter?

Tub. I often came where I did hear of her, but cannot find her.

Shy. Why there, there, there! a diamond gone that coſt me two thouſand ducats in Francfort! The curſe never fell upon our nation till now; I never felt it till now. Two thouſand ducats in that, and other precious, precious jewels! I would my daughter were dead at my foot, and the jewels in her ear! O would ſhe were hears'd at my foot, and the ducats in her coffin! No news of them; and I know not what ſpent in the ſearch: loſs upon loſs! the thief gone with ſo much, and ſo much to find the thief; and no ſatisfaction, no revenge; no ill luck ſtirring but what lights on my ſhoulders; no ſighs, but o' my breathing; no tears, but o' my ſhedding!

Tub. Yes, other men have ill luck too; Antonio, as I heard in Genoa——

Shy. What, what, what? ill luck, ill luck?

Tub. Hath an argoſie caſt away, coming from Tripolis.

Shy. Thank God! thank God! is it true? is it true?

Tub. I ſpoke with ſome of the ſailors that eſcaped the wreck.

Shy. I thank thee, good Tubal; good news, good news!

Tub. Your daughter ſpent in Genoa, as I heard, in one night, fourſcore ducats.

Shy. Thou ſtick'ſt a dagger in me; I ſhall never ſee my gold again: fourſcore ducats at a ſitting! fourſcore ducats!

Tub. There came divers of Antonio's creditors in my company to Venice, that ſwear he cannot but break.

Shy. I am glad of it: I'll plague him, I'll torture him: I am glad of it.

Tub. One of them ſhewed me a ring that he had of your daughter for a monkey.

Shy. Out upon her! thou tortureſt me, Tubal! it was my ruby, I had it of Leah when I was a batchelor; I would not have given it for a wilderneſs of monkies.

Tub. But Antonio is certainly undone.

Shy. Nay, that's true, that's very true: go fee me an officer, beſpeak him a fortnight before. I will have the heart of him, if he forfeit; for were he out of Venice, I can make what merchandize I will. Go, go, Tubal, and meet me at our ſynagogue; go, good Tubal; at our ſynagogue, Tubal.

Shakeſpeare.

§ 21.

§ 21. *Humorous Scene between Prince* Henry *and* Falstaff, *in which the Prince detects* Falstaff's *monstrous Lies.*

P. Henry. Welcome, Jack!—Where hast thou been?

Fal. A plague of all cowards, I say, and a vengeance too, marry and amen! Give me a cup of sack, boy:—ere I lead this life long, I'll sew nether socks and mend them, and foot them too. A plague of all cowards! give me a cup of sack, rogue. Is there no virtue extant? [*He drinks.*]—You rogue, here's lime in this sack too. There is nothing but roguery to be found in villainous man; yet a coward is worse than a cup of sack with lime in it. A villainous coward!—Go thy ways, old Jack; die when thou wilt, if manhood, good manhood, be not forgot upon the face of the earth, then am I a shotten herring. There live not three good men unhang'd in England, and one of them is fat, and grows old, Heaven help the while! A bad world! I say—A plague of all cowards! I say still.

P. Henry. How now Woolsack! what mutter you?

Fal. A king's son! If I do not beat thee out of thy kingdom with a dagger of lath, and drive all thy subjects afore thee like a flock of wild geese, I'll never wear hair on my face more! You Prince of Wales!

P. Henry. Why, what's the matter?

Fal. Are you not a coward? answer me that.

P. Henry. Ye fat paunch, an' ye call me coward, I'll stab thee.

Fal. I call thee coward! I'll see thee hang'd ere I'll call thee coward; but I would give a thousand pound I could run as fast as thou canst. Your straight enough in the shoulders; you care not who sees your back. Call you that backing of friends? a plague upon such backing! give me them that will face me—give me a cup of sack: I am a rogue if I drank to-day.

P. Henry. O villain! thy lips are scarce wip'd since thou drank'st last.

Fal. All's one for that. [*He drinks.*] A plague of all cowards! still, say I.

P. Henry. What's the matter?

Fal. What's the matter! here be four of us have ta'en a thousand pound this morning.

P. Henry. Where is it, Jack? where is it?

Fal. Where is it! taken from us, it is: a hundred upon four of us.

P. Henry. What! a hundred, man?

Fal. I am a rogue if I were not at half-sword with a dozen of them two hours together. I have escaped by miracle. I am eight times thrust through the doublet, four through the hose, my buckler cut through and through, my sword hack'd like a hand-saw, *ecce signum!* I never dealt better since I was a man: all would not do. A plague of all cowards!

P. Henry. What, fought you with them all?

Fal. All! I know not what ye call all; but if I fought not with fifty of them, I am a bunch of radish; if there were not two or three and fifty upon poor old Jack, then I am no two-legg'd creature.

P. Henry. Pray Heav'n you have not murder'd some of them!

Fal. Nay, that's past praying for. I have pepper'd two of them; two, I am sure, I have paid; two rogues in buckram suits. I tell

I tell thee what, Hal, if I tell thee a lie, ſpit in my face, call me horſe. Thou knoweſt my old ward: here I lay, and thus I bore my point: four rogues in buckram let drive at me.

P. Henry. What, four! thou ſaidſt but two even now.

Fal. Four, Hal, I told thee four.—— Theſe four came all a-front, and mainly thruſt at me: I made no more ado, but took all their ſeven points in my target, thus.

P. Henry. Seven! why they were but four even now.

Fal. In buckram?

P. Henry. Ay, four, in buckram ſuits.

Fal. Seven by theſe hilts, or I am a villain elſe. Doſt thou hear me, Hal?

P. Henry. Ay, and mark thee too, Jack.

Fal. Do ſo, for it is worth the liſtening to. Theſe nine in buckram, that I told thee of—

P. Henry. So, two more already.

Fal. Their points being broken, began to give me ground; but I followed me cloſe, came in foot and hand, and, with a thought—ſeven of the eleven I paid.

P. Henry. O monſtrous! eleven buckram men grown out of two.

Fal. But as the devil would have it, three miſbegotten knaves, in Kendal-green, came at my back, and let drive at me; (for it was ſo dark, Hal, that thou couldſt not ſee thy hand.)

P. Henry. Theſe lies are like the father that begets them, groſs as a mountain, open, palpable. Why, thou clay-brained guts, thou knotty-pated fool, thou obſcene greaſy tallow-catch—

Fal. What, art thou mad? art thou mad? is not the truth the truth?

P. Henry. Why, how couldſt thou know theſe men in Kendal-green, when it was ſo dark thou couldſt not ſee thy hand? Come, tell us your reaſon: what ſay'ſt thou to this? Come, your reaſon, Jack, your reaſon.

Fal. What upon compulſion!—No: were I at the ſtrappado, or all the racks in the world, I would not tell you on compulſion! Give you a reaſon on compulſion! If reaſons were as plenty as blackberries, I would give no man a reaſon upon compulſion.

P. Henry. I'll be no longer guilty of this ſin. This ſanguine coward, this bed-preſſer, this horſe-back-breaker, this huge hill of fleſh—

Fal. Away, you ſtarveling, you elf-ſkin, you dry'd neat's tongue, you ſtock-fiſh! O, for breath to utter! what is like thee? you taylor's yard, you ſheath, you bow-caſe, you vile ſtanding tuck—

P. Henry. Well, breath a while, and then to't again; and when thou haſt tir'd thyſelf in baſe compariſons, hear me ſpeak but this: —Poins and I ſaw you four ſet on four; you bound them, and were maſters of their wealth: mark now, how a plain tale ſhall put you down. Then did we two ſet on you four, and with a word out-fac'd you from your prize, and have it; yea, and can ſhew it you here in the houſe. And, Falſtaff, you carry'd your guts away as nimbly, with as quick dexterity, and roar'd for mercy, and ſtill ran and roar'd, as ever I heard bull-calf. What a ſlave art thou, to hack thy ſword as thou haſt done, and then ſay it was in fight! What trick, what device, what ſtarting-hole canſt thou now find out, to hide thee from this open and apparent ſhame?

Fal. Ha! ha! ha!—D'ye think I did not know you?—By the Lord, I knew you as well as he that made you. Why, hear ye, my maſter, was it for me to kill the heir-apparent?

apparent? should I turn upon the true prince? why, thou knowest I am as valiant as Hercules; but beware instinct; the lion will not touch the true prince; instinct is a great matter. I was a coward on instinct, I grant you: and I shall think the better of myself and thee during my life; I for a valiant lion, and thou for a true prince. But I am glad you have the money. Let us clap to the doors; watch to-night, pray to-morrow. What, shall we be merry? shall we have a play extempore?

P. Henry. Content!—and the argument shall be, thy running away.

Fal. Ah!—no more of that, Hal, if thou lovest me. *Shakespeare.*

§ 21. *Scene in which* MOODY *gives* MANLY *an Account of the Journey to* LONDON.

Manly. Honest John!—

Moody. Measter Manly! I am glad I ha' sun ye.—Well, and how d'ye do, Measter?

Manly. I am glad to see you in London. I hope all the good family are well.

Moody. Thanks be prais'd, your honour, they are all in pretty good heart; thot' we have had a power of crosses upo' the road.

Manly. What has been the matter, John?

Moody. Why, we came up in such a hurry, you mun think, that our tackle was not so tight as it should be.

Manly. Come, tell us all—Pray, how do they travel?

Moody. Why, i'the awld coach, Measter; and 'cause my Lady loves to do things handsome, to be sure, she would have a couple of cart-horses clapt to the four old geldings, that neighbours might see she went up to London in her coach and six; and so Giles Joulter, the ploughman, rides postillion.

Manly. And when do you expect them here, John?

Moody. Why, we were in hopes to ha' come yesterday, an' it had no' been that th' awld weazle-belly horse tired: and then we were so cruelly loaden, that the two fore-wheels came crash dawn at once, in Waggon-rut-lane, and there we lost four hours 'fore we could set things to rights again.

Manly. So they bring all their baggage with the coach, then?

Moody. Ay, ay, and good store on't there is—Why, my lady's gear alone were as much as filled four portmantel trunks, besides the great deal box that heavy Ralph and the monkey sit upon behind.

Manly. Ha, ha, ha!—And pray, how many are there within the coach?

Moody. Why there's my lady and his worship, and the younk 'squoire, and Miss Jenny, and the fat lap-dog, and my lady's maid Mrs. Handy, and Doll Tripe the cook, that's all—only Doll puked a little with riding backward; so they hoisted her into the coach-box, and then her stomach was easy.

Manly. Ha, ha, ha!

Moody. Then you mun think, Measter, there was some stowage for the belly, as well as th' back too; children are apt to be famish'd upo' the road; so we had such cargoes of plumb-cake, and baskets of tongues and biscuits, and cheese, and cold boil'd beef—and then, in case of sickness, bottles of cherry brandy, plague-water, sack, tent, and strong beer so plenty, as made th' awld coach crack again. Mercy upon them! and send them all well to town, I say.

Manly. Ay, and well out on't again, John.

Moody.

Moody. Meaſter! you're a wiſe mon; and, for that matter, ſo am I—Whoam's whoam, I ſay: I am ſure we ha' got but little good e'er ſin' we turn'd our backs on't. Nothing but miſchief! ſome devil's trick or other plagued us aw th' day lung. Crack, goes one thing! bawnce, goes another! Woa! ſays Roger—Then, ſowſe! we are all ſet faſt in a ſlough. Whaw! cries Miſs: Scream! go the maids; and bawl juſt as thof they were ſtuck. And ſo, mercy on us! this was the trade from morning to night.

Manly. Ha, ha, ha!

Moody. But I mun hie me whoam; the coach will be coming every hour naw.

Manly. Well, honeſt John——

Moody. Dear Meaſter Manly! the goodneſs of goodneſs bleſs and preſerve you!

§ 22. *Cruelty to Animals.*

Montaigne thinks it ſome reflection upon human nature itſelf, that few people take delight in ſeeing beaſts careſs or play together, but almoſt every one is pleaſed to ſee them lacerate and worry one another. I am ſorry this temper is become almoſt a diſtinguiſhing character of our own nation, from the obſervation which is made by foreigners of our beloved paſtimes, bear-baiting, cock-fighting, and the like. We ſhould find it hard to vindicate the deſtroying of any thing that has life, merely out of wantonneſs: yet in this principle our children are bred up; and one of the firſt pleaſures we allow them, is the licence of inflicting pain upon poor animals: almoſt as ſoon as we are ſenſible what life is ourſelves, we make it our ſport to take it from other creatures. I cannot but believe a very good uſe might be made of the fancy which children have for birds and inſects. Mr. Locke takes notice of a mother who permitted them to her children, but rewarded or puniſhed them as they treated them well or ill. This was no other than entering them betimes into a daily exerciſe of humanity, and improving their very diverſion to a virtue.

I fancy, too, ſome advantage might be taken of the common notion, that 'tis ominous or unlucky to deſtroy ſome ſorts of birds, as ſwallows and martins. This opinion might poſſibly ariſe from the confidence theſe birds ſeem to put in us by building under our roofs; ſo that this is a kind of violation of the laws of hoſpitality to murder them. As for Robin red-breaſts in particular, it is not improbable they owe their ſecurity to the old ballad of "The children in the wood." However it be, I don't know, I ſay, why this prejudice, well improved, and carried as far as it would go, might not be made to conduce to the preſervation of many innocent creatures, which are now expoſed to all the wantonneſs of an ignorant barbarity.

There are other animals that have the miſfortune, for no manner of reaſon, to be treated as common enemies, wherever found. The conceit that a cat has nine lives has coſt at leaſt nine lives in ten of the whole race of them: ſcarce a boy in the ſtreets but has in this point outdone Hercules himſelf, who was famous for killing a monſter that had but three lives. Whether the unaccountable animoſity againſt this uſeful domeſtic may be any cauſe of the general perſecution of owls (who are a ſort of feathered cats) or whether it be only an unreaſonable pique the moderns have taken to a ſerious countenance, I ſhall not determine: though I am inclined to believe the former; ſince I observe the sole reason alledged for the destruction of frogs is because they are like toads. Yet, amidst all the misfortunes of these unfriended creatures, 'tis some happiness that we have not yet taken a fancy to eat them: for should our countrymen refine upon the French never so little, 'tis not to be conceived to what unheard-of torment, owls, cats, and frogs may be yet reserved.

When we grow up to men, we have another succession of sanguinary sports; in particular, hunting. I dare not attack a diversion which has such authority and custom to support it; but must have leave to be of opinion, that the agitation of that exercise, with the example and number of the chasers, not a little contributes to resist those checks, which compassion would naturally suggest in behalf of the animal pursued. Nor shall I say, with Monsieur Fleury, that this sport is a remain of the Gothic barbarity; but I must animadvert upon a certain custom yet in use with us, and barbarous enough to be derived from the Goths, or even the Scythians: I mean that savage compliment our huntsmen pass upon ladies of quality, who are present at the death of a stag, when they put the knife in their hands to cut the throat of a helpless, trembling, and weeping creature.

Questuque cruentus,
Atque imploranti similis.——

But if our sports are destructive, our gluttony is more so, and in a more inhuman manner. Lobsters roasted alive, pigs whipped to death, fowls sewed up, are testimonies of our outrageous luxury. Those who (as Seneca expresses it) divide their lives betwixt an anxious conscience, and a nauseated stomach, have a just reward of their gluttony in the diseases it brings with it: for human savages, like other wild beasts, find snares and poison in the provisions of life, and are allured by their appetite to their destruction. I know nothing more shocking, or horrid, than the prospect of one of their kitchens covered with blood, and filled with the cries of the creatures expiring in tortures. It gives one an image of a giant's den in a romance, bestrewed with the scattered heads and mangled limbs of those who were slain by his cruelty. *Pope.*

§ 23. *Halfpenny, its Adventures.*

" Sir,

" I shall not pretend to conceal from you the illegitimacy of my birth, or the baseness of my extraction: and though I seem to bear the venerable marks of old age, I received my being at Birmingham not six months ago. From thence I was transported, with many of my brethren of different dates, characters, and configurations, to a Jew pedlar in Duke's-place, who paid for us in specie scarce a fifth part of our nominal and extrinsic value. We were soon after separately disposed of, at a more moderate profit, to coffee-houses, chop-houses, chandlers-shops, and gin-shops. I had not been long in the world, before an ingenious transmuter of metals laid violent hands on me; and observing my thin shape and flat surface, by the help of a little quicksilver exalted me into a shilling. Use, however, soon degraded me again to my native low station; and I unfortunately fell into the possession of an urchin just breeched, who received me as a Christmas-box of his god-mother.

" A love of money is ridiculously instilled into children so early, that before they can possibly comprehend the use of it, they consider it it as of great value: I loſt therefore the very eſſence of my being, in the cuſtody of this hopeful diſciple of avarice and folly; and was kept only to be looked at and admired: but a bigger boy after a while ſnatched me from him, and releaſed me from my confinement.

"I now underwent various hardſhips among his play-fellows, and was kicked about, huſtled, toſſed up, and chucked into holes; which very much battered and impaired me: but I ſuffered moſt by the pegging of toys, the marks of which I have borne about me to this day. I was in this ſtate the unwitting cauſe of rapacity, ſtrife, envy, rancour, malice, and revenge, among the little apes of mankind; and became the object and the nurſe of thoſe paſſions which diſgrace human nature, while I appeared only to engage children in innocent paſtimes. At length I was diſmiſſed from their ſervice by a throw with a barrow-woman for an orange.

"From her it is natural to conclude, I poſted to the gin-ſhop; where, indeed, it is probable I ſhould have immediately gone, if her huſband, a foot-ſoldier, had not wreſted me from her, at the expence of a bloody noſe, black eye, ſcratched face, and torn regimentals. By him I was carried to the Mall in St. James's Park, where I am aſhamed to tell how I parted from him—let it ſuffice that I was ſoon after depoſited in a night-cellar.

"From hence I got into the coat-pocket of a blood, and remained there with ſeveral of my brethren for ſome days unnoticed. But one evening as he was reeling home from the tavern, he jerked a whole handful of us through a ſaſh-window into the dining-room of a tradeſman, who he remembered had been ſo unmannerly to him the day before, as to deſire payment of his bill. We repoſed in ſoft eaſe on a fine Turkey carpet till the next morning, when the maid ſwept us up; and ſome of us were allotted to purchaſe tea, ſome to buy ſnuff, and I myſelf was immediately trucked away at the door for the Sweethearts Delight.

"It is not my deſign to enumerate every little accident that has befallen me, or to dwell upon trivial and indifferent circumſtances, as is the practice of thoſe important egotiſts, who write narratives, memoirs, and travels. As uſeleſs to community as my ſingle ſelf may appear to be, I have been the inſtrument of much good and evil in the intercourſe of mankind: I have contributed no ſmall ſum to the revenues of the crown, by my ſhare in each news-paper; and in the conſumption of tobacco, ſpirituous liquors, and other taxable commodities. If I have encouraged debauchery, or ſupported extravagance; I have alſo rewarded the labours of induſtry, and relieved the neceſſities of indigence. The poor acknowledge me as their conſtant friend; and the rich, though they affect to ſlight me, and treat me with contempt, are often reduced by their follies to diſtreſſes, which it is even in my power to relieve.

"The preſent exact ſcrutiny into our conſtitution has, indeed, very much obſtructed and embarraſſed my travels; tho' I could not but rejoice in my condition laſt Tueſday, as I was debarred having any ſhare in maiming, bruiſing, and deſtroying the innocent victims of vulgar barbarity: I was happy in being confined to the mock encounters with feathers and ſtuffed leather; a childiſh ſport, rightly calculated to initiate tender minds in acts of cruelty, and prepare them for the exerciſe of inhumanity on helpleſs animals.

"I shall conclude, Sir, with informing you by what means I came to you in the condition you see. A choice spirit, a member of the kill-care club, broke a link-boy's pate with me last night, as a reward for lighting him across the channel; the lad wasted half his tar flambeau in looking for me, but I escaped his search, being lodged snugly against a post. This morning a parish girl picked me up, and carried me with raptures to the next baker's shop to purchase a roll. The master, who was church-warden, examined me with great attention, and then gruffly threatening her with Bridewell for putting off bad money, knocked a nail through my middle, and fastened me to the counter: but the moment the poor hungry child was gone, he whipt me up again, and sending me away with others in change to the next customer, gave me this opportunity of relating my adventures to you." *Adventurer.*

§ 24. *Patience exemplified in the Story of an Ass.*

I was just receiving the dernier compliments of Monsieur Le Blanc, for a pleasant voyage down the Rhône——when I was stopped at the gate——

'Twas by a poor ass, who had just turned in with a couple of large panniers upon his back, to collect eleemosinary turnip-tops and cabbage-leaves; and stood dubious, with pleads so mightily for him, that it always disarms me; and to that degree, that I do not like to speak unkindly to him: on the contrary, meet him where I will—whether in town or country—in cart or under panniers—whether in liberty or bondage——I have ever something civil to say to him on my part; and as one word begets another (if he has as little to do as I)—I generally fall into conversation with him; and surely never is my imagination so busy as in framing his responses from the etchings of his countenance—and where those carry me not deep enough——in flying from my own heart into his, and seeing what is natural for an ass to think—as well as a man, upon the occasion. In truth, it is the only creature of all the classes of beings below me, with whom I can do this: for parrots, jack-daws, &c.——I never exchange a word with them——nor with the apes, &c. for pretty near the same reason; they act by rote, as the others speak by it, and equally make me silent: nay, my dog and my cat, though I value them both——(and for my dog, he would speak if he could)—yet, somehow or other, they neither of them possess the talents for conversation—I can make nothing of a discourse with them, beyond the proposition, the reply, and rejoinder, which terminated my father's and my mother's conversations, in his beds of justice—and those uttered—there's an end of the dialogue——

——But with an ass, I can commune for

——— He turned his head thoughtful about, and looked wiſtfully the oppoſite way——

I underſtand thee perfectly, anſwered I—if thou takeſt a wrong ſtep in this affair, he will cudgel thee to death——Well! a minute is but a minute, and if it ſaves a fellow-creature a drubbing, it ſhall not be ſet down as ill-ſpent.

He was eating the ſtem of an artichoke as this diſcourſe went on, and in the little peeviſh contentions of nature betwixt hunger and unſavourineſs, had dropt it out of his mouth half a dozen times, and pick'd it up again.——God help thee, Jack! ſaid I, thou haſt a bitter breakfaſt on't—and many a bitter day's labour—and many a bitter blow, I fear, for its wages—'tis all—all bitterneſs to thee, whatever life is to others.——And now thy mouth, if one knew the truth of it, is as bitter, I dare ſay, as ſoot—(for he had caſt aſide the ſtem) and thou haſt not a friend perhaps in all this world, that will give thee a macaroon.——In ſaying this, I pulled out a paper of them, which I had juſt purchaſed, and gave him one—and at this moment that I am telling it, my heart ſmites me, that there was more of pleaſantry in the conceit, of ſeeing how an aſs would eat a macaroon——than of benevolence in giving him one, which preſided in the act.

When the aſs had eaten his macaroon, I preſs'd him to come in—the poor beaſt was heavy loaded—his legs ſeem'd to tremble under him—he hung rather backwards, and, as I pulled at his halter, it broke ſhort in my hand—he look'd up penſive in my face—"Don't thraſh me with it—but if you will, you may."——If I do, ſaid I, I'll be d——d.

The word was but one half of it pronounced, like the abbeſs of Andoüillets—(ſo there was no ſin in it)—when a perſon coming in, let fall a thundering baſtinado upon the poor devil's crupper, which put an end to the ceremony.

Out upon it!

cried I——but the interjection was equivocal——and, I think, wrong placed too—for the end of an oſier, which had ſtarted out from the contexture of the aſs's pannier, had caught hold of my breeches pocket as he ruſhed by me, and rent it in the moſt diſaſtrous direction you can imagine—ſo that the *Out upon it!* in my opinion, ſhould have come in here. *Sterne.*

§ 25. *An Enumeration of Superſtitions obſerved in the Country.*

You muſt know, Mr. Town, that I am juſt returned from a viſit of a fortnight to an old aunt in the North; where I was mightily diverted with the traditional ſuperſtitions, which are moſt religiouſly preſerved in the family, as they have been delivered down (time out of mind) from their ſagacious grandmothers.

When I arrived, I found the miſtreſs of the houſe very buſily employed, with her two daughters, in nailing an horſeſhoe to the threſhold of the door. This, they told me, was to guard againſt the ſpiteful deſigns of an old woman, who was a witch, and had threatened to do the family a miſchief, becauſe one of my young couſins laid two ſtraws acroſs, to ſee if the old hag could walk over them. The young lady aſſured me, that ſhe had ſeveral times heard Goody Cripple muttering to herſelf; and to be ſure ſhe was ſaying the Lord's Prayer backwards. Beſides, the old woman had very often aſked them for a pin: but they took care never to give her any thing that was ſharp, b.cauſe ſhe ſhould not bewitch them. They afterwards told me many other particulars of this kind, the ſame as are mentioned with infinite humour by the **Spectator**: and to confirm them, they aſſured me, that the eldeſt miſs, when ſhe was little, uſed to have fits, till the mother flung a knife at another old witch (whom the devil had carried off in an high wind), and fetched blood from her.

When I was to go to bed, my aunt made a thouſand apologies for not putting me in the beſt room in the houſe; which (ſhe ſaid) had never been lain in ſince the death of an old waſherwoman, who walked every night, and haunted that room in particular. They fancied that the old woman had hid money ſomewhere, and could not reſt till ſhe had told ſomebody; and my couſin aſſured me, that ſhe might have had it all to herſelf; for the ſpirit came one night to her bed-ſide, and wanted to tell her, but ſhe had not courage to ſpeak to it. I learned alſo, that they had a footman once, who hanged himſelf for love; and he walked for a great while, till they got the parſon to lay him in the Red Sea.

I had not been here long, when an accident happened, which very much alarmed the whole family. Towzer one night howled moſt terribly; which was a ſure ſign, that ſomebody belonging to them would die. The youngeſt miſs declared, that ſhe had heard the hen crow that morning; which was another fatal prognoſtic. They told me, that, juſt before uncle died, Towzer howled ſo for ſeveral nights together, that they could not quiet him; and my aunt heard the death-watch tick as plainly as if there had been a clock in the room: the maid too, who ſat up with him, heard a bell toll at the top of the ſtairs, the very moment the breath went out of his body. During this diſcourſe, I overheard one of my couſins whiſper the other, that ſhe was afraid their mamma would not live long; for ſhe ſmelt an ugly ſmell, like a dead carcaſe. They had a dairy-maid, who died the very week after an hearſe had ſtopt at their door in its way to church: and the eldeſt miſs, when ſhe was but thirteen, ſaw her own brother's ghoſt (who was gone to the Weſt Indies) walking in the garden; and to be ſure, nine months after, they had an account, that he died on board the ſhip, the very ſame day, and hour of the day, that miſs ſaw his apparition.

I need not mention to you the common incidents, which were accounted by them no leſs prophetic. If a cinder popped from the fire, they were in haſte to examine whether it was a purſe or a coffin. They were aware of my coming long before I arrived, becauſe they had ſeen a ſtranger on the grate. The youngeſt miſs will let nobody uſe the poker but herſelf; becauſe, when ſhe ſtirs the fire, it always burns bright, which is a ſign ſhe will have a briſk huſband: and ſhe is no leſs ſure of a good one, becauſe ſhe generally has ill luck at cards. Nor is the candle leſs oracular than the fire: for the 'ſquire of the pariſh came one night to pay them a viſit, when the tallow winding-ſheet pointed towards him; and he broke his neck ſoon after in a fox-chaſe. My aunt one night obſerved with great pleaſure a letter in the candle; and the very next day one came from her ſon in London. We knew when a ſpirit was in the room, by the candle burning blue: but poor couſin Nancy was ready to cry one time, when ſhe ſnuffed it out, and could not blow it in again; though her ſiſter did it at a whiff,

whiff, and consequently triumphed in her superior virtue.

We had no occasion for an almanack or the weather-glass, to let us know whether it would rain or shine. One evening I proposed to ride out with my cousins the next day to see a gentleman's house in the neighbourhood; but my aunt assured us it would be wet, she knew very well, from the shooting of her corn. Besides, there was a great spider crawling up the chimney, and the blackbird in the kitchen began to sing; which were both of them as certain forerunners of rain. But the most to be depended on in these cases is a tabby cat, which usually lies basking on the parlour hearth. If the cat turned her tail to the fire, we were to have an hard frost; if the cat licked her tail, rain would certainly ensue. They wondered what stranger they should see; because puss washed her face over her left ear. The old lady complained of a cold, and her eldest daughter remarked, it would go through the family; for she observed that poor Tab had sneezed several times. Poor Tab, however, once flew at one of my cousins: for which she had like to have been destroyed, as the whole family began to think she was no other than a witch.

It is impossible to tell you the several tokens by which they know whether good or ill luck will happen to them. Spilling the salt, or laying knives across, are every where accounted ill omens; but a pin with the head turned towards you, or to be followed by a strange dog, I found were very lucky. I heard one of my cousins tell the cook-maid, that she boiled away all her sweethearts, because she had let her dish-water boil over. The same young lady one morning came down to breakfast with her cap the wrong side out; which the mother observing, charged her not to alter it all day, for fear she should turn luck.

But, above all, I could not help remarking the various prognostics which the old lady and her daughters used to collect from almost every part of the body. A white speck upon the nails made them as sure of a gift as if they had it already in their pockets. The elder sister is to have one husband more than the youngest, because she has one wrinkle more in her forehead; but the other will have the advantage of her in the number of children, as was plainly proved by snapping their finger-joints. It would take up too much room to set down every circumstance, which I observed of this sort during my stay with them: I shall therefore conclude my letter with the several remarks on other parts of the body, as far as I could learn them from this prophetic family: for, as I was a relation, you know, they had less reserve.

If the head itches, it is a sign of rain. If the head aches, it is a profitable pain. If you have the tooth-ache, you don't love true. If your eye-brow itches, you will see a stranger. If your right eye itches, you will cry; if your left, you will laugh: but left or right is good at night. If your nose itches, you will shake hands with or kiss a fool, drink a glass of wine, run against a cuckold's door, or miss them all four. If your right ear or cheek burns, your left friends are talking of you; if your left, your right friends are talking of you. If your elbow itches, you will change your bedfellow. If your right hand itches, you will pay away money; if your left, you will receive. If your stomach itches, you will eat pudding. If your back itches, butter will be cheap when grass grows there. If your side itches, somebody

ſomebody is wiſhing for you. If your gartering-place itches, you will go to a ſtrange place. If your foot itches, you will tread upon ſtrange ground. Laſtly, If you ſhiver, ſomebody is walking over your grave.

Connoiſſeur.

§ 26. *Painting diſagreeable in Women.*

A lady's face, like the coat in the Tale of a Tub, if left alone, will wear well; but if you offer to load it with foreign ornaments, you deſtroy the original ground.

Among other matter of wonder on my firſt coming to town, I was much ſurpriſed at the general appearance of youth among the ladies. At preſent there is no diſtinction in their complexions between a beauty in her teens and a lady in her grand climacteric; yet at the ſame time I could not but take notice of the wonderful variety in the face of the ſame lady. I have known an olive beauty on Monday grow very ruddy and blooming on Tueſday; turn pale on Wedneſday; come round to the olive hue again on Thurſday; and in a word, change her complexion as often as her gown. I was amazed to find no old aunts in this town, except a few unfaſhionable people, whom no body knows; the reſt ſtill continuing in the zenith of their youth and health, and falling off, like timely fruit, without any previous decay. All this was a myſtery that I could not unriddle, till on being introduced to ſome ladies, I unluckily improved the hue of my lips at the expence of a fair-one, who unthinkingly had turned her cheek; and found that my kiſſes were given (as is obſerved in the epigram) like thoſe of Pyramus, through a wall. I then diſcovered, that this ſurpriſing youth and beauty was all counterfeit; and that (as Hamlet ſays) "God had given them one face, and they had made themſelves another."

I have mentioned the accident of my carrying off half a lady's face by a ſalute, that your courtly dames may learn to put on their faces a little tighter; but as for my own daughters, while ſuch faſhions prevail, they ſhall ſtill remain in Yorkſhire. There, I think, they are pretty ſafe; for this unnatural faſhion will hardly make its way into the country, as this vamped complexion would not ſtand againſt the rays of the ſun, and would inevitably melt away in a country-dance. The ladies have, indeed, been always the greateſt enemies to their own beauty, and ſeem to have a deſign againſt their own faces. At one time the whole countenance was eclipſed in a black velvet maſk; at another it was blotted with patches; and at preſent it is cruſted over with plaiſter of Paris. In thoſe battered belles who ſtill aim at conqueſt, this practice is in ſome ſort excuſable; but it is ſurely as ridiculous in a young lady to give up beauty for paint, as it would be to draw a good ſet of teeth merely to fill their places with a row of ivory.

Indeed ſo common is this faſhion among the young as well as the old, that when I am in a group of beauties, I conſider them as ſo many pretty pictures; looking about me with as little emotion as I do at Hudſon's: and if any thing fills me with admiration, it is the judicious arrangement of the tints, and delicate touches of the painter. Art very often ſeems almoſt to vie with nature: but my attention is too frequently diverted by conſidering the texture and hue of the ſkin beneath; and the picture fails to charm, while my thoughts are engroſſed by the wood and canvaſs.

Connoiſſeur.

§ 27.

§ 27. *The study of Astronomy peculiarly delightful.*

In fair weather, when my heart is cheared, and I feel that exaltation of spirits which results from light and warmth, joined with a beautiful prospect of nature, I regard myself as one placed by the hand of God in the midst of an ample theatre, in which the sun, moon, and stars, the fruits also and vegetables of the earth, perpetually changing their positions or their aspects, exhibit an elegant entertainment to the understanding as well as to the eye.

Thunder and lightning, rain and hail, the painted bow and the glaring comet, are decorations of this mighty theatre; and the sable hemisphere studded with spangles, the blue vault at noon, the glorious gildings and the rich colours in the horizon, I look on as so many successive scenes.

When I consider things in this light, methinks it is a sort of impiety to have no attention to the course of nature, and the revolutions of the heavenly bodies. To be regardless of those phænomena that are placed within our view, on purpose to entertain our faculties, and display the wisdom and power of our Creator, is an affront to Providence of the same kind (I hope it was not impious to make such a simile) as it would be to a good poet to sit out his play without minding the plot or beauties of it. And yet how few are there who attend to the drama of nature, its artificial structure, and those admirable scenes whereby the passions of a philosopher are gratefully agitated, and his soul affected with the sweet emotions of joy and surprise!

How many fox-hunters and rural squires are to be found all over Great Britain, who are ignorant that they have lived all this time in a planet; that the sun is several thousand times bigger than the earth; and that there are several other worlds within our view, greater and more glorious than our own! "Ay, but," says some illiterate fellow, "I enjoy the world, and leave it to others to contemplate it." Yes, you eat, and drink, and run about upon it; that is, you enjoy as a brute; but to enjoy as a rational being is to know it, to be sensible of its greatness and beauty, to be delighted with its harmony, and by these reflections to obtain just sentiments of the almighty mind that framed it.

The man who, unembarrassed with vulgar cares, leisurely attends to the flux of things in heaven and things on earth, and observes the laws by which they are governed, hath secured to himself an easy and convenient seat, where he beholds with pleasure all that passes on the stage of nature, while those about him are, some fast asleep, and others struggling for the highest places, or turning their eyes from the entertainment prepared by Providence, to play at push-pin with one another.

Within this ample circumference of the world, the glorious lights that are hung on high, the meteors in the middle region, the various livery of the earth, and the profusion of good things that distinguish the seasons, yields a prospect which annihilates all human grandeur. *Tatler.*

§ 28. *The Character of Toby Bumper.*

It is one of the greatest advantages of education, that it encourages an ingenuous spirit, and cultivates a liberal disposition. We do not wonder that a lad who has never been sent to school, and whose faculties have been suffered to rust at the hall-house, should form too close an intimacy with his best friends, the groom and the game-keeper; but it would amaze us to see a boy well educated cherish this ill-placed pride, of being, as it is called, the head of the company. A person of this humble ambition will be very well content to pay the reckoning, for the honour of being distinguished by the title of 'the gentleman,' while he is unwilling to associate with men of fashion, lest they should be his superiors in rank or fortune; or with men of parts, lest they should excel him in abilities. Sometimes indeed it happens that a person of genius and learning will stoop to receive the incense of mean and illiterate flatterers in a porter-house and cyder-cellar; and I remember to have heard of a poet, who was once caught in a brothel, in the very fact of reading his verses to the good old mother, and and a circle of her daughters.

There are some few, who have been led into low company, merely from an affectation of humour, and, from a desire of seeing the droller scenes of life, have descended to associate with the meanest of the mob, and picked their cronies from lanes and alleys. The most striking instance I know of this low passion for drollery, is Toby Bumber, a young fellow of family and fortune, and not without talents, who has taken more than ordinary pains to degrade himself; and is now become almost as low a character, as any of those whom he has chosen for his companions. Toby will drink purl in a morning, smoke his pipe in a night-cellar, dive for a dinner, or eat black-puddings at Bartholomew-fair, for the humour of the thing. He has also studied, and practises, all the plebeian arts and exercises, under the best masters; and has disgraced himself with every unpolite accomplishment. He has had many a set-to with Buckhorse; and has now and then the honour of receiving a fall from the great Broughton himself. Nobody is better known among the hackney-coachmen, as a brother whip: at the noble game of prison-bars, he is a match even for the natives of Essex and Cheshire; and he is frequently engaged at the Artillery-ground with Faulkner and Dingate at cricket; and is himself esteemed as good a bat as either of the Bennets. Another of Toby's favourite amusements is, to attend the executions at Tyburn; and it once happened, that one of his familiar intimates was unfortunately brought thither; when Toby carried his regard to his deceased friend so far, as to get himself knocked down in endeavouring to rescue the body from the surgeons.

As Toby affects to mimic, in every particular, the art and manners of the vulgar, he never fails to enrich his conversation with their emphatic oaths and expressive dialect, which recommends him as a man of excellent humour and high fun, among the Choice Spirits at Comus's court, or at the meeting of the *Sons of sound Sense and Satisfaction*. He is also particularly famous for singing those cant songs, drawn up in the barbarous dialect of sharpers and pickpockets; the humour of which he often heightens, by screwing up his mouth, and rolling about a large quid of tobacco between his jaws. These and other like accomplishments frequently promote him to the chair in these facetious societies.

Toby has indulged the same notions of humour even in his amours; and is well-known to every street-walker from Cheapside to Charing-cross. This has given several shocks to his constitution, and often involved him in unlucky scrapes. He has been frequently bruised, beaten, and kicked, by the bullies of Wapping and Fleet-ditch; and was once soundly drubbed by a soldier for engaging with

with his trull. The laſt time I ſaw him he was laid up with two black eyes, and a broken pate, which he got in a midnight ſkirmiſh, about a miſtreſs, in a night-cellar.

Connoiſſeur.

§ 29. *The Characters of Gameſters.*

The whole tribe of gameſters may be ranked under two diviſions: Every man who makes carding, dicing, and betting his daily practice, is either a dupe or a ſharper; two characters equally the objects of envy and admiration. The dupe is generally a perſon of great fortune and weak intellects,

"Who will as tenderly be led by th' noſe,
"As aſſes are." SHAKESPEARE.

He plays, not that he has any delight in cards and dice, but becauſe it is the faſhion; and if whiſt or hazard are propoſed, he will no more refuſe to make one at the table, than among a ſet of hard drinkers he would object drinking his glaſs in turn, becauſe he is not dry.

There are ſome few inſtances of men of ſenſe, as well as family and fortune, who have been dupes and bubbles. Such an unaccountable itch of play has ſeized them, that they have ſacrificed every thing to it, and have ſeemed wedded to ſeven's the main, and the odd trick. There is not a more melancholy object than a gentleman of ſenſe thus infatuated. He makes himſelf and family a prey to a gang of villains more infamous than highwaymen; and perhaps, when his ruin is completed, he is glad to join with the very ſcoundrels that deſtroyed him, and live upon the ſpoil of others, whom he can draw into the ſame follies that proved ſo fatal to himſelf.

Here we may take a ſurvey of the character of a ſharper; and that he may have no room to complain of foul play, let us begin with his excellencies. You will perhaps be ſtartled, Mr. Town, when I mention the excellencies of a ſharper; but a gameſter, who makes a decent figure in the world, muſt be endued with many amiable qualities, which would undoubtedly appear with great luſtre, were they not eclipſed by the odious character affixed to his trade. In order to carry on the common buſineſs of his profeſſion, he muſt be a man of quick and lively parts, attended with a ſtoical calmneſs of temper, and a conſtant preſence of mind. He muſt ſmile at the loſs of thouſands; and is not to be diſcompoſed, though ruin ſtares him in the face. As he is to live among the great, he muſt not want politeneſs and affability; he muſt be ſubmiſſive, but not ſervile; he muſt be maſter of an ingenuous liberal air, and have a ſeeming openneſs of behaviour.

Theſe muſt be the chief accompliſhments of our hero: but leſt I ſhould be accuſed of giving too favourable a likeneſs of him, now we have ſeen his outſide, let us take a view of his heart. There we ſhall find avarice the main ſpring that moves the whole machine. Every gameſter is eaten up with avarice; and when this paſſion is in full force, it is more ſtrongly predominant than any other. It conquers even luſt; and conquers it more effectually than age. At ſixty we look at a fine woman with pleaſure; but when cards and dice have engroſſed our attention, women and all their charms are ſlighted at five-and-twenty. A thorough gameſter renounces Venus and Cupid for Plutus and Ames-ace, and owns no miſtreſs of his heart except the queen of trumps. His inſatiable avarice can only be gratified by hypocriſy; ſo that all thoſe ſpecious virtues already mentioned, and which, if real, might be turned to the benefit of mankind, muſt be directed in a gameſter towards the deſtruction of his fellow-creatures. His quick and lively parts ſerve only to inſtruct and aſſiſt him in the moſt dexterous method of packing the cards and cogging the dice; his fortitude, which enables him to loſe thouſands without emotion, muſt often be practiſed againſt the ſtings and reproaches of his conſcience, and his liberal deportment and affected openneſs is a ſpecious veil to recommend and conceal the blackeſt villainy.

It is now neceſſary to take a ſecond ſurvey of his heart; and as we have ſeen its vices, let us conſider its miſeries. The covetous man, who has not ſufficient courage or inclination to increaſe his fortune by bets, cards, or dice, but is contented to hoard up thouſands by thefts leſs public, or by cheats leſs liable to uncertainty, lives in a ſtate of perpetual ſuſpicion and terror: but the avaricious fears of the gameſter are infinitely greater. He is conſtantly to wear a maſk; and like Monſieur St. Croix, *coadjuteur* to that famous *empoiſonneuſe*, Madame Brinvillier, if his maſk falls off, he runs the hazard of being ſuffocated by the ſtench of his own poiſons. I have ſeen ſome examples of this ſort not many years ago at White's. I am uncertain whether the wretches are ſtill alive; but if they are ſtill alive, they breathe like toads under ground, crawling amidſt old walls, and paths long ſince unfrequented.

But ſuppoſing that the Sharper's hypocriſy remains undetected, in what a ſtate of mind muſt that man be, whoſe fortune depends upon the inſincerity of his heart, the diſingenuity of his behaviour, and the falſe bias of his dice! What ſenſations muſt he ſuppreſs, when he is obliged to ſmile, although he is provoked; when he muſt look ſerene in the height of deſpair: and when he muſt act the ſtoic, without the conſolation of one virtuous ſentiment, or one moral principle! How unhappy muſt he be, even in that ſituation from which he hopes to reap moſt benefit; I mean amidſt ſtars, garters, and the various herds of nobility! Their lordſhips are not always in a humour for play: they chooſe to laugh; they chooſe to joke; in the mean while our hero muſt patiently await the good hour, and muſt not only join in the laugh, and applaud the joke, but muſt humour every turn and caprice to which that ſet of ſpoiled children, called bucks of quality, are liable. Surely his brother Thicket's employment, of ſauntering on horſeback in the wind and rain till the Reading coach paſſes through Smallberry-green, is the more eligible, and no leſs honeſt occupation.

The Sharper has alſo frequently the mortification of being thwarted in his deſigns. Opportunities of fraud will not for ever preſent themſelves. The falſe dice cannot be conſtantly produced, nor the packed cards always be placed upon the table. It is then our gameſter is in the greateſt danger. But even then, when he is in the power of fortune, and has nothing but mere luck and fair play on his ſide, he muſt ſtand the brunt, and perhaps give away his laſt guinea, as coolly as he would lend a nobleman a ſhilling.

Our hero is now going off the ſtage, and his cataſtrophe is very tragical. The next news we hear of him is his death, atchieved by his own hand, and with his own piſtol. An inqueſt is bribed, he is buried at midnight—and forgotten before ſun-riſe.

Theſe two portraits of a Sharper, wherein I have endeavoured to ſhew different likeneſſes in in the ſame man, put me in mind of an old print, which I remember at Oxford, of Count Guiſcard. At firſt ſight he was exhibited in a full-bottomed wig, a hat and feather, embroidered cloaths, diamond buttons, and the full court dreſs of thoſe days; but by pulling a ſtring the folds of the paper were ſhifted, the face only remained, a new body came forward, and Count Guiſcard appeared to be a devil. *Connoiſſeur.*

§ 30. *The various Faults in Converſation and Behaviour pointed out.*

I ſhall not attempt to lay down any particular rules for converſation, but rather point out ſuch faults in diſcourſe and behaviour, as render the company of half mankind rather tedious than amuſing. It is in vain, indeed, to look for converſation, where we might expect to find it in the greateſt perfection, among perſons of faſhion: there it is almoſt annihilated by univerſal card-playing; inſomuch that I have heard it given as a reaſon, why it is impoſſible for our preſent writers to ſucceed in the dialogue of genteel comedy, that our people of quality ſcarce ever meet but to game. All their diſcourſe turns upon the odd trick and the four honours: and it is no leſs a maxim with the votaries of whiſt than with thoſe of Bacchus, that talking ſpoils company.

Every one endeavours to make himſelf as agreeable to ſociety as he can: but it often happens, that thoſe, who moſt aim at ſhining in converſation, over-ſhoot their mark. Though a man ſucceeds, he ſhould not (as is frequently the caſe) engroſs the whole talk to himſelf; for that deſtroys the very eſſence of converſation, which is talking together. We ſhould try to keep up converſation like a ball bandied to and fro from one to the other, rather than ſeize it all to ourſelves, and drive it before us like a foot-ball. We ſhould likewiſe be cautious to adapt the matter of our diſcourſe to our company; and not talk Greek before ladies, or of the laſt new furbelow to a meeting of country juſtices.

But nothing throws a more ridiculous air over our whole converſation, than certain peculiarities, eaſily acquired, but very difficultly conquered and diſcarded. In order to diſplay theſe abſurdities in a truer light, it is my preſent purpoſe to enumerate ſuch of them, as are moſt commonly to be met with; and firſt to take notice of thoſe buffoons in ſociety, the Attitudinarians and Face-makers. Theſe accompany every word with a particular grimace or geſture: they aſſent with a ſhrug, and contradict with a twiſting of the neck; are angry by a wry mouth, and pleaſed in a caper of a minuet-ſtep. They may be conſidered as ſpeaking harlequins; and their rules of eloquence are taken from the poſture-maſter. Theſe ſhould be condemned to converſe only in dumb-ſhew with their own perſons in the looking-glaſs; as well as the Smirkers and Smilers, who ſo prettily ſet off their faces, together with their words, by a *je-ne-ſçai-quoi* between a grin and a dimple. With theſe we may likewiſe rank the affected tribe of Mimics, who are conſtantly taking off the peculiar tone of voice or geſture of their acquaintance: though they are ſuch wretched imitators, that (like bad painters) they are frequently forced to write the name under the picture, before we can diſcover any likeneſs.

Next to thoſe, whoſe elocution is abſorbed in action, and who converſe chiefly with their arms and legs, we may conſider the profeſſed Speakers. And firſt, the emphatical; who ſqueeze, and preſs, and ram down every ſyllable

ſyllable with exceſſive vehemence and energy These orators are remarkable for their diſtinct elocution and force of expreſſion: they dwell on the important particles *of* and *the*, and the ſignificant conjunctive *and*; which they ſeem to hawk up, with much difficulty, out of their own throats, and to cram them, with no leſs pain, into the ears of their auditors. Theſe ſhould be ſuffered only to ſyringe (as it were) the ears of a deaf man, through an hearing-trumpet: though I muſt confeſs, that I am equally offended with the Whiſperers or Low Speakers, who ſeem to fancy all their acquaintance deaf, and come up ſo cloſe to you, that they may be ſaid to meaſure noſes with you, and frequently overcome you with the full exhalations of a ſtinking breath. I would have theſe oracular gentry obliged to talk at a diſtance through a ſpeaking-trumpet, or apply their lips to the walls of a whiſpering-gallery. The Wits, who will not condeſcend to utter any thing but a *bon mot*, and the Whiſtlers or Tune-hummers, who never articulate at all, may be joined very agreeably together in concert; and to theſe tinkling cymbals I would alſo add the ſounding braſs, the Bawler, who enquires after your health with the bellowing of a town-crier.

The Tatlers, whoſe pliable pipes are admirably adapted to the "ſoft parts of converſation," and ſweetly "prattling out of faſhion" make very pretty muſic from a beautiful face and a female tongue; but from a rough manly voice and coarſe features, mere nonſenſe is as harſh and diſſonant as a jig from a hurdy-gurdy. The Swearers I have ſpoken of in a former paper; but the Half-ſwearers, who ſplit, and mince, and fritter their oaths into *gad's bud, ad's fiſh*, and *demme*; the gothic humbuggers, and thoſe who "nick-name God's creatures," and call a man a cabbage, a crab, a queer cub, an odd fiſh, and an unaccountable *muſkin*, ſhould never come into company without an interpreter. But I will not tire my reader's patience by pointing out all the peſts of converſation; nor dwell particularly on the Senſibles, who pronounce dogmatically on the moſt trivial points, and ſpeak in ſentences; the Wonderers, who are always wondering what o'clock it is, or wondering whether it will rain or no, or wondering when the moon changes; the Phraſeologiſts, who explain a thing by *all that*, or enter into particulars with *this and that and t'other*; and laſtly, the Silent Men, who ſeem afraid of opening their mouths, leſt they ſhould catch cold, and literally obſerve the precept of the goſpel, by letting their converſation be only yea yea, and nay nay.

The rational intercourſe kept up by converſation, is one of our principal diſtinctions from brutes. We ſhould therefore endeavour to turn this peculiar talent to our advantage, and conſider the organs of ſpeech as the inſtruments of underſtanding: we ſhould be very careful not to uſe them as the weapons of vice, or tools of folly, and do our utmoſt to unlearn any trivial or ridiculous habits, which tend to leſſen the value of ſuch an ineſtimable prerogative. It is, indeed, imagined by ſome philoſophers, that even birds and beaſts (though without the power of articulation) perfectly underſtand one another by the ſounds they utter; and that dogs, cats, &c. have each a particular language to themſelves, like different nations. Thus it may be ſuppoſed, that the nightingales of Italy have as fine an ear for their own native wood-notes, as any ſignor or ſignora for an Italian air; that the boars of Weſtphalia gruntle as expreſſively through the noſe as the inhabitants in High-Germany;

German; and that the frogs in the dykes of Holland croak as intelligibly as the natives jabber their Low-Dutch. However this may be, we may consider those, whose tongues hardly seem to be under the influence of reason, and do not keep up the proper conversation of human creatures, as imitating the language of different animals. Thus, for instance, the affinity between chatterers and monkeys, and praters and parrots, is too obvious not to occur at once: Grunters and growlers may be justly compared to hogs: Snarlers are curs, that continually shew their teeth, but never bite; and the *spitfire* passionate are a sort of wild cats, that will not bear stroking, but will purr when they are pleased. Complainers are screech-owls; and story-tellers, always repeating the same dull note, are cuckoos. Poets that prick up their ears at their own hideous braying, are no better than asses: Critics in general are venemous serpents, that delight in hissing; and some of them, who have got by heart a few technical terms without knowing their meaning, are no other than magpies. *Connoisseur.*

§ 31. *A Citizen's Country House described.*

Sir,

I remember to have seen a little French novel giving an account of a citizen of Paris making an excursion into the country. He imagines himself about to undertake a long voyage to some strange region, where the natives were as different from the inhabitants of his own city as the most distant nations. He accordingly takes boat, and is landed at a village about a league from the capital. When he is set on shore, he is amazed to see the people speak the same language, wear the same dress, and use the same customs with himself. He, who had spent all his life within the sight of Pont Neuf, looked upon every one that lived out of Paris as a foreigner; and though the utmost extent of his travels was not three miles, he was as much surprised, as he would have been to meet with a colony of Frenchmen on the Terra Incognita.

In your late paper on the amusements of Sunday, you have set forth in what manner our citizens pass that day, which most of them devote to the country; but I wish you had been more particular in your descriptions of those elegant rural mansions, which at once shew the opulence and the taste of our principal merchants, mechanics, and artificers.

I went last Sunday, in compliance with a most pressing invitation from a friend, to spend the whole day with him at one of these little seats, which he had fitted out for his retirement once a week from business. It is pleasantly situated about three miles from London, on the side of a public road, from which it is separated by a dry ditch, over which is a little bridge, consisting of two narrow planks, leading to the house. From the lower part of the house there is no prospect; but from the garrets, indeed, one may see two men hanging in chains on Kennington-common, with a distant view of St. Paul's cupola enveloped in a cloud of smoke. I set out in the morning with my friend's book-keeper, who was my guide. When I came to the house, I found my friend in a black velvet cap sitting at the door smoking: he welcomed me into the country; and after having made me observe the turnpike on my left, and the Golden Sheaf on my right, he conducted me into his house, where I was received by his lady, who made a thousand apologies for being catched in such a dishabille.

The hall (for so I was taught to call it) had

had its white wall almost hid by a curious collection of prints and paintings. On one side was a large map of London, a plan and elevation of the Mansion House, with several lesser views of the public buildings and halls: on the other, was the Death of the Stag, finely coloured by Mr. Overton: close by the parlour-door there hung a pair of stag's horns; over which there was laid across a red roccelo, and an amber-headed cane. Over the chimney-piece was my friend's picture, who was drawn bolt upright in a full-bottomed perriwig, a laced cravat with the fringed ends appearing through a button-hole, a snuff-coloured velvet coat with gold buttons, a red velvet waistcoat trimmed with gold, one hand stuck in the bosom of his shirt, and the other holding out a letter with this superscription: "To Mr. ——, common-council-man of Farringdon-ward without." My eyes were then directed to another figure in a scarlet gown, who I was informed was my friend's wife's great great uncle, and had been sheriff and knighted in the reign of king James the First. Madam herself filled up a pannel on the opposite side, in the habit of a shepherdess, smelling to a nosegay, and stroking a ram with gilt horns.

I was then invited by my friend to see what he has pleased to call his garden, which was nothing more than a yard about thirty feet in length, and contained about a dozen little pots ranged on each side with lilies and coxcombs, supported by some old laths painted green, with bowls of tobacco-pipes on their tops. At the end of this garden he bade me take notice of a little square building surrounded with filleroy, which he told me an alderman of great taste had turned into a temple, by erecting some battlements and spires of painted wood on the front of it: but concluded with a hint, that I might retire to it upon occasion.

As the riches of a country are visible in the number of its inhabitants, and the elegance of their dwellings, we may venture to say that the present state of England is very flourishing and prosperous; and if our taste for building encreases with our opulence, for the next century, we shall be able to boast of finer country-seats belonging to our shopkeepers, artificers, and other plebeians, than the most pompous descriptions of Italy or Greece have ever recorded. We read, it is true, of country-seats belonging to Pliny, Hortensius, Lucullus, and other Romans. They were Patricians of great rank and fortune: there can therefore be no doubt of the excellence of their villas. But who has ever read of a Chinese-bridge belonging to an Attic tallow-chandler, or a Roman pastry cook? Or could any of their shoe-makers or taylors boast a villa with his tin cascades, paper statutes, and Gothic root-houses? Upon the above principles we may expect, that posterity will perhaps see a cheese-monger's *apiarium* at Brentford, a poulterer's *theriotrophium* at Chiswick, and an *ornithon* in a fishmonger's garden at Putney.

Connoisseur.

§ 32. *The two Bees.*

On a fine morning in May, two bees set forward in quest of honey; the one wise and temperate, the other careless and extravagant. They soon arrived at a garden enriched with aromatic herbs, the most fragrant flowers, and the most delicious fruits. They regaled themselves for a time on the various dainties that were spread before them: the one loading his thigh at intervals with provisions for the hive against the distant winter; the other revelling in sweets without regard to any thing

but

but his present gratification. At length they found a wide mouthed phial, that hung beneath the bough of a peach tree, filled with honey ready tempered, and exposed to their taste in the most alluring manner. The thoughtless epicure, spite of all his friends remonstrances, plunged headlong into the vessel, resolving to indulge himself in all the pleasures of sensuality. The philosopher, on the other hand, sipped a little with caution; but being suspicious of danger, flew off to fruits and flowers; where, by the moderation of his meals, he improved his relish for the true enjoyment of them. In the evening, however, he called upon his friend, to enquire whether he would return to the hive; but found him surfeited in sweets, which he was as unable to leave, as to enjoy. Clogged in his wings, enfeebled in his feet, and his whole frame totally enervated, he was but just able to bid his friend adieu, and to lament with his latest breath, that, though a taste of pleasure might quicken the relish of life, an unrestrained indulgence is inevitably destruction.

§ 33. *Pleasant Scene of Anger, and the Disappointment of it.*

There came into a bookseller's shop a very learned man, with an erect solemn air; who, though a person of great parts otherwise, is slow in understanding any thing which makes against himself. After he had turned over many volumes, said the seller to him—Sir, you know I have long asked you to send me back the first volume of French Sermons I formerly lent you. Sir, said the chapman, I have often looked for it, but cannot find it: it is certainly lost; and I know not to whom I lent it, it is so many years ago. Then, Sir, here is the other volume; I'll send you home that, and please to pay for both. My friend, replied he, can'st thou be so senseless, as not to know, that one volume is as imperfect in my library, as in your shop? Yes, Sir; but it is you have lost the first volume; and, to be short, I will be paid. Sir, answered the chapman, you are a young man; your book is lost; and learn, by this little loss, to bear much greater adversities, which you must expect to meet with. Yes, Sir, I'll bear when I must; but I have not lost now, for I say you have it, and shall pay me. Friend, you grow warm: I tell you, the book is lost; and I foresee, in the course even of a prosperous life, that you will meet afflictions to make you mad, if you cannot bear this trifle. Sir, there is, in this case, no need of bearing, for you have the book. I say, Sir, I have not the book; but your passion will not let you hear enough to be informed that I have it not. Learn resignation betimes to the distresses of this life: nay, do not fret and fume; it is my duty to tell you that you are of an impatient spirit; and an impatient spirit is never without woe. Was ever any thing like this?—Yes, Sir, there have been many things like this. The loss is but a trifle; but your temper is wanton, and incapable of the least pain; therefore, let me advise you, be patient: the book is lost, but do not you, for that reason, lose yourself. *Spectator.*

§ 34. *Falstaff's Encomiums on Sack.*

A good sherris-sack hath a two-fold operation in it—It ascends me into the brain: dries me, there, all the foolish, dull, and crudy vapours which environ it; makes it apprehensive, quick, inventive; full of nimble, fiery, and delectable shapes, which, delivered over to the voice, the tongue, which is the birth, becomes excellent wit.—The second property of of your excellent sherris, is, the warming of the blood; which, before, cold and settled, left the liver white and pale, which is the badge of pusillanimity and cowardice. But the sherris warms it, and makes it course from the inwards to the parts extreme. It illuminateth the face, which, as a beacon, gives warning to all the rest of this little kingdom, man, to arm: and, then, the vital commoners, and inland petty spirits, muster me all to their captain, the heart; who, great, and puffed up with this retinue, doth any deed of courage—and this valour comes of sherris. So that skill in the weapon is nothing without sack, for that sets it awork; and learning a mere hoard of gold kept by a devil, till sack commences it, and sets it in act and use. Hereof comes it that Prince Harry is valiant; for the cold blood he did naturally inherit of his father he hath, like lean, sterile, and bare land, manured, husbanded, and tilled, with drinking good, and good store of fertile sherris.—If I had a thousand sons, the first human principle I would teach them, should be — To forswear thin potations, and to addict themselves to sack. *Shakespeare.*

§ 35. *Falstaff's Soliloquy on Honour.*

Owe Heaven a death! 'Tis not due yet; and I would be loth to pay him before his day. What need I be so forward with him that calls not on me?—Well, 'tis no matter, honour pricks me on. But how if honour prick me off when I come on? how then? Can honour set to a leg? no: or an arm? no: or take away the grief of a wound? no. Honour hath no skill in surgery, then? no. What is honour? a word. What is that word honour? air; a trim reckoning. Who hath it? he that died a Wednesday. Doth he feel it? no. Doth he hear it? no. Is it insensible then? yea to the dead. But will it not live with the living? no. Why? detraction will not suffer it; therefore, I'll none of it: honour is a mere 'scutcheon: and so ends my catechism. *Ibid.*

§ 36. *Distempers of the Mind cured.*

Sir,

Being bred to the study of physic, and having observed, with sorrow and regret, that whatever success the faculty may meet with in bodily distempers, they are generally baffled by distempers of the mind, I have made the latter the chief subject of my attention, and may venture to affirm, that my labour has not been thrown away. Though young in my profession, I have had a tolerable share of experience, and have a right to expect, that the credit of some extraordinary cures I have performed will furnish me with opportunities of performing more. In the mean time, I require it of you, not as a favour to myself, but as an act of justice to the public, to insert the following in your Chronicle.

Mr. Abraham Buskin, taylor, was horribly infected with the itch of stage-playing, to the grievous discomfiture of his wife, and the great detriment of nine small children. I prevailed with the manager of one of the theatres to admit him for a single night in the character of Othello, in which it may be remembered that a button-maker had formerly distinguished himself; when, having secured a seat in a convenient corner of the gallery, by the dexterous application of about three pecks of potatoes to the *sinciput* and *occiput* of the patient, I entirely cured him of his delirium; and he has ever since betaken himself quietly to his needle and thimble.

Mr. Edward Snap was of so choleric a temper,

temper, and ſo extremely apt to think himſelf affronted, that it was reckoned dangerous even to look at him. I tweaked him by the noſe, and adminiſtered the proper application behind; and he is now ſo good-humoured, that he will take the groſſeſt affront imaginable without ſhewing the leaſt reſentment.

The reverend Mr. Puff, a methodiſt preacher, was ſo extravagantly zealous and laborious in his calling, that his friends were afraid he would bawl himſelf into a conſumption. By my intereſt with a noble lord, I procured him a living with a reaſonable income; and he now behaves himſelf like a regular divine of the eſtabliſhed church, and never gets into a pulpit.

Mrs. Diana Bridle, a maiden lady, about forty years of age, had a conceit that ſhe was with child. I adviſed her to convert her imaginary pregnancy into a real one, by taking a huſband; and ſhe has never been troubled with any *fancies* of that kind ſince.

Mr. William Moody, an elderly gentleman, who lived in a ſolitary part of Kent, was apt to be very low-ſpirited in an eaſterly wind. I nailed his weather-cock to a weſterly point; and at preſent, whichſoever way the wind blows, he is equally cheerful.

Alexander Stingo, Eſq; was ſo ſtrongly poſſeſſed by the ſpirit of witticiſm, that he would not condeſcend to open his lips for any thing leſs than an epigram. Under the influence of this malady he has been ſo deplorably dull, that he has often been ſilent a whole week together. I took him into my own houſe: inſtead of laughing at his jeſts, I either pronounced them to be puns, or paid no attention to them at all. In a month I perceived a wonderful alteration in him for the better: from thinking without ſpeaking, he began to ſpeak without thinking; at preſent never ſays a good thing, and is a very agreeable companion.

I likewiſe cured a lady of a longing for ortolans, by a dozen of Dunſtable larks; and could ſend you many other remarkable inſtances of the efficacy of my preſcriptions; but theſe are ſufficient for a ſpecimen.

I am, &c.

Bonnel Thornton.

§ 37. *Character of a Choice Spirit.*

Sir,

That a tradeſman has no buſineſs with humour, unleſs perhaps in the way of his dealing; or with writing, unleſs in his ſhop-book, is a truth, which I believe nobody will diſpute with me. I am ſo unfortunate however as to have a nephew, who, not contented with being a grocer, is in danger of abſolute ruin by his ambition of being a wit; and having forſaken his counter for Comus's Court, and dignified himſelf with the appellation of a Choice Spirit, is upon the point of becoming a bankrupt. Inſtead of diſtributing his ſhop-bills as he ought, he waſtes a dozen in a morning, by ſcribbling ſhreds of his nonſenſe upon the back of them; and a few days ſince affronted an alderman, his beſt cuſtomer, by ſending him a pound of prunes wrapt up in a ballad he had juſt written, called, The Citizen outwitted, or a Bob for the Manſion-Houſe.

He is likewiſe a regular frequenter of the play-houſes, and being acquainted with every underling of each theatre, is at an annual expence of ten pounds in tickets for their reſpective benefits. They generally adjourn together from the play to the tavern; and there is hardly a watchman, within a mile of Covent-garden, but has had his head or his lantern

lantern broke by one or other of the ingenious fraternity.

I turned into his ſhop this morning, and had no ſooner ſet my foot upon the threſhold, than he leaped over the counter, threw himſelf into an attitude, as he calls it, and aſked me, in the words of ſome play that I remember to have ſeen formerly, "Whether I was a ſpirit "of health, or a goblin damn'd?" I told him he was an undutiful young dog for daring to accoſt his uncle in that irreverent manner; and bid him ſpeak like a Chriſtian, and a reaſonable perſon. Inſtead of being ſenſible of my rebuke, he took off his wig, and having very deliberately given it two or three twirls upon his fiſt, and pitched it upon his head again, ſaid I was a dry old fellow, and ſhould certainly afford them much entertainment at the club, to which he had the impudence to invite me: at the ſame time he thruſt a card into my hand, containing a bill of fare for the evening's entertainment; and as a farther inducement, aſſured me that Mr. Twiſter himſelf would be in the chair; that he was a great creature, and ſo prodigiouſly droll, that though he had heard him ſing the ſame ſongs, and repeat the ſame ſtories, a thouſand times, he could ſtill attend to him with as much pleaſure as at firſt. I caſt my eye over the liſt, and can recollect the following items:

"*To all true Lovers of Fun and Jocularity.*

"Mr. Twiſter will this evening take off a "cat, worried by two bull-dogs; ditto mak-"ing love in a gutter; the knife-grinder "and his wheel; High-Dutch ſquabble; and "a hog in a ſlaughter-houſe."

I aſſured him, that ſo far from having any reliſh for theſe deteſtable noiſes, the more they reſembled the originals the leſs I ſhould like them; and, if I could ever be fool enough to go, ſhould at leaſt be wiſe enough to ſtop my ears till I came out again.

Having lamented my deplorable want of taſte, by the elevation of his eye-brows, and a ſignificant ſhrug of his ſhoulders, he thruſt his fore-finger againſt the inſide of his cheek, and plucking it out of his mouth with a jerk, made a noiſe which very much reſembled the drawing of a cork: I found, that by this ſignal he meant to aſk me, if I choſe a whet? I gave my conſent by a ſulky kind of nod, and walked into the back-room, as much aſhamed of my nephew, as he ought to have been of himſelf. While he was gone to fetch a pint of mountain from the other ſide of the ſtreet, I had an opportunity to minute down a few of the articles of which the litter of his apartment conſiſted, and have ſelected theſe, as the moſt material from among them:

On one of the ſconces by the chimney, a ſmart grizzle bob-wig, well oiled and powdered, feather-topt, and bag-fronted.

On the oppoſite ſconce, a ſcratch.

On the window-ſeat, a Nankin waiſtcoat, bound with ſilver twiſt, without ſkirts or pockets, ſtained with red wine, and pretty much ſhrunk.

Item, A pair of buck-ſkin breeches, in one pocket a cat-call, in the other the mouth of a quart-bottle chipt and ground into a ſmooth ring, very fit to be uſed as a ſpying-glaſs by thoſe who never want one.

Item, A red pluſh frock lapelled with ditto, one pocket ſtuffed with orange-peel, and the other with ſquare bits of white paper ready cut and dried for a ſhower.

In the corner, a walking-ſtaff, not portable.

Item, A ſmall ſwitch.

On the head of the bureau, a letter-caſe, containing a play-bill, and a quack-bill; a copy of verſes, being an encomium upon

upon Mr. Twister; another of four lines, which he calls a distich; and a third, very much blotted and scratched, and yet not finished, entitled, An Extempore Epigram.

Having taken this inventory of his goods and furniture, I sat down before the fire, to devise, if possible, some expedient to reclaim him; when, on a sudden, a sound like the braying of an ass, at my elbow, alarmed me to such a degree, that I started from my seat in an instant, and, to my farther astonishment, beheld my nephew, almost black in the face, covering his ear with the hollow of his hand, and exerting the whole force of his lungs in imitating that respectable animal: I was so exasperated at this fresh instance of his folly, that I told him hastily, he might drink his wine alone, and that I would never see his face again, till he should think proper to appear in a character more worthy of himself and his family. He followed me to the door without making any reply; and, having advanced into the middle of the street, fell to clapping his sides, and crowing like a cock, with the utmost vehemence; and continued his triumphant ejaculations till I was fairly out of hearing.

Having reached my lodgings, I immediately resolved to send you an account of his absurdities; and shall take this opportunity to inform him, that as he is blest with such a variety of useful talents, and so completely accomplished as a Choice Spirit, I shall not do him the injury to consider him as a tradesman, or mortify him hereafter by endeavouring to give him any assistance in his business.

I am, &c.

B. Thornton.

§ 38. *Character of a mighty good Kind of Man.*

Sir,

I have always thought your mighty good kind of man to be a very good-for-nothing fellow; and whoever is determined to think otherwise may as well pass over what follows.

The good qualities of a mighty good kind of a man (if he has any) are of the negative kind. He does very little harm; but you never find him do any good. He is very decent in appearance, and takes care to have all the externals of sense and virtue; but you never perceive the heart concerned in any word, thought, or action. Not many love him, though very few think ill of him: to him every body is his "Dear Sir," though he cares not a farthing for any body but himself. If he writes to you, though you have but the slightest acquaintance with him, he begins with "Dear Sir," and ends with "I "am, good Sir, your ever sincere and affec- "tionate friend, and most obedient humble "servant." You may generally find him in company with older persons than himself, but always with richer. He does not talk much; but he has a "Yes," or a "True, Sir," or "You observe very right, Sir," for every word that is said; which, with the old gentry, that love to hear themselves talk, makes him pass for a mighty sensible and discerning, as well as a mighty good kind of man. It is so familiar to him to be agreeable, and he has got such a habit of assenting to every thing advanced in company, that he does it without the trouble of thinking what he is about. I have known such a one, after having approved an observation made by one of the company, assent

assent with "What you say is very just," to an opposite sentiment from another; and I have frequently made him contradict himself five times in a minute. As the weather is a principal and favourite topic of a mighty good kind of man, you may make him agree, that it is very hot, very cold, very cloudy, a fine sunshine, or it rains, snows, hails, or freezes, all in the same hour. The wind may be high, or not blow at all; it may be East, West, North, or South, South East and by East, or in any point in the compass, or any point not in the compass, just as you please. This, in a stage coach, makes him a mighty agreeable companion, as well as a mighty good kind of man. He is so civil, and so well-bred, that he would keep you standing half an hour, uncovered, in the rain, rather than he would step into your chariot before you; and the dinner is in danger of growing cold, if you attempt to place him at the upper end of the table. He would not suffer a glass of wine to approach his lips, till he had drank the health of half the company, and would sooner rise hungry from table, than not drink to the other half before dinner is over, lest he should offend any by his neglect. He never forgets to hob or nob with the lady of the family, and by no means omits to toast her fire-side. He is sure to take notice of little master and miss, when they appear after dinner, and is very assiduous to win their little hearts, by almonds and raisins, which he never fails to carry about him for that purpose. This of course recommends hi to mamma's esteem; and he is not only a mighty good kind of man, but she is certain he would make a mighty good husband.

No man is half so happy in his friendships. Almost every one he names is a friend of his, and every friend a mighty good kind of man. I had the honour of walking lately with one of these good creatures from the Royal Exchange to Piccadilly; and, I believe, he pulled off his hat to every third person we met, with a "How do you do, my dear Sir?" though, I found he hardly knew the names of five of these intimate acquaintances. I was highly entertained with the greeting between my companion, and another mighty good kind of man that we met in the Strand. You would have thought they were brothers, and that they had not seen one another for many years, by their mutual expressions of joy at meeting. They both talked together, not with a design of opposing each other, but through eagerness to approve what each other said. I caught them frequently, crying, "Yes," together, and "Very true,"—"You are very right, my dear Sir;" and at last, having exhausted their favourite topic of what news, and the weather, they concluded with each begging to have the vast pleasure of an agreeable evening with the other very soon; but parted without naming either time or place.

I remember, at Westminster, a mighty good kind of boy, though he was generally hated by his schoolfellows, was the darling of the dame where he boarded, as by his means she knew who did all the mischief in the house. He always finished his exercise before he went to play: you could never find a false concord in his prose, or a false quantity in his verse; and he made huge amends for the want of sense and spirit in his compositions, by having very few grammatical errors. If you could not call him a scholar, you must allow he took great pains not to appear a dunce. At the university he never failed attending his tutor's lectures, was constant at prayers night and morning, never missed gates, or or the hall at meal-times, was regular in his academical exercises, and took pride in appearing, on all occasions, with masters of arts; and he was happy, beyond measure, in being acquainted with some of the heads of houses, who were glad through him to know what passed among the under-graduates. Though he was not reckoned, by the college, to be a Newton, a Locke, or a Bacon, he was universally esteemed by the senior part, to be a mighty good kind of young man; and this even placid turn of mind has recommended him to no small preferment in the church.

We may observe, when these mighty good kind of young men come into the world, their attention to appearances and externals, beyond which the generality of people seldom examine, procures them a much better subsistence, and a more reputable situation in life, than ever their abilities, or their merit, could otherwise entitle them to. Though they are seldom advanced very high, yet, if such a one is in orders, he gets a tolerable living, or is appointed tutor to a dunce of quality, or is made companion to him on his travels; and then, on his return, he is a mighty polite, as well as a mighty good kind of man. If he is to be a lawyer, his being such a mighty good kind of man will make the attornies supply him with special pleadings, or bills and answers to draw, as he is sufficiently qualified by his slow genius to be a dray-horse of the law. But though he can never hope to be a chancellor, or an archbishop, yet, if he is admitted of the medical college in Warwick-lane, he will have a good chance to be at the top of their profession, as the success of the faculty depends chiefly on old women, fanciful and hysterical young ones, whimsical men, and young children, among the generality of whom, nothing recommends a person so much as his being a mighty good kind of man.

I must own, that a good man, and a man of sense, certainly should have every thing that this kind of man has; yet, if he possesses no more, much is wanting to finish and complete his character. Many are deceived by French paste: it has the lustre and brilliancy of a real diamond; but the want of hardness, the essential property of this valuable jewel, discovers the counterfeit, and shews it to be of no intrinsic value whatsoever. If the head and the heart are left out in the character of any man, you might as well look for a perfect beauty in a female face without a nose, as to expect to find a valuable man without sensibility and understanding. But it often happens, that these mighty good kind of men are wolves in sheep's cloathing; that their want of parts is supplied by an abundance of cunning, and the outward behaviour and deportment calculated to entrap the short-sighted and unwary.

Where this is not the case, I cannot help thinking that these kind of men are no better than blanks in the creation: if they are not unjust stewards, they are certainly to be reckoned unprofitable servants; and I would recommend, that this harmless, inoffensive, insipid, mighty good kind of man should be married to a character of a very different stamp, the mighty good sort of woman—an account of whom I shall give you in a day or two.

I am your humble servant, &c.

B. Thornton.

§ 39. *Character of a mighty good Sort of Woman.*

I suppose the female part of my readers are very impatient to see the character of a mighty good ſort of woman; and doubtleſs every mighty good kind of man is anxious to know what ſort of a wife I have picked out for him.

The mighty good ſort of woman is civil without good-breeding, kind without good-nature, friendly without affection, and devout without religion. She wiſhes to be thought every thing ſhe is not, and would have others looked upon to be every thing ſhe really is. If you will take her word, ſhe deteſts ſcandal from her heart: yet, if a young lady happens to be talked of as being too gay, with a ſignificant ſhrug of her ſhoulders, and ſhake of her head, ſhe confeſſes, "It is too true, and "the whole town ſays the ſame thing." She is the moſt compaſſionate creature living, and is ever *pitying* one perſon, and *ſorry* for another. She is a great dealer in *buts*, and *ifs*, and half ſentences, and does more miſchief with a *may be*, and *I'll ſay no more*, than ſhe could do by ſpeaking out. She confirms the truth of any ſtory more by her fears and doubts, than if ſhe had given proof poſitive; though ſhe always concludes with a "Let us "hope otherwiſe."

One principal buſineſs of a mighty good ſort of woman is the regulation of families; and ſhe extends a viſitatorial power over all her acquaintance. She is the umpire in all differences between man and wife, which ſhe is ſure to foment and increaſe by pretending to ſettle them; and her great impartiality and regard for both leads her always to ſide with one againſt the other. She has a moſt penetrating and diſcerning eye into the faults of the family, and takes care to pry into all their ſecrets, that ſhe may reveal them. If a man happens to ſtay out too late in the evening, ſhe is ſure to rate him handſomely the next time ſhe ſees him, and takes ſpecial care to tell him, in the hearing of his wife, what a bad huſband he is: or if the lady goes to Ranelagh, or is engaged in a party at cards, ſhe will keep the poor huſband company, that he might not be dull, and entertains him all the while with the imperfections of his wife. She has alſo the entire diſpoſal of the children in her own hands, and can diſinherit them, provide for them, marry them, or confine them to a ſtate of celibacy, juſt as ſhe pleaſes: ſhe fixes the lad's pocket-money at ſchool, and allowance at the univerſity; and has ſent many an untoward boy to ſea for education. But the young ladies are more immediately under her eye, and, in the grand point of matrimony, the choice or refuſal depends ſolely upon her. One gentleman is too young, another too old; one will run out his fortune, another has too little; one is a profeſſed rake, another a ſly ſinner; and ſhe frequently tells the girl, "'Tis time enough to "marry yet," till at laſt there is nobody will have her. But the moſt favourite occupation of a mighty good ſort of woman is, the ſuperintendance of the ſervants: ſhe proteſts, there is not a good one to be got; the men are idle, and thieves, and the maids are ſluts, and good-for-nothing huſſies. In her own family ſhe takes care to ſeparate the men from the maids, at night, by the whole height of the houſe; theſe are lodged in the garret, while John takes up his rooſting-place in the kitchen, or is ſtuffed into the turn-up ſeat in the paſſage, cloſe to the ſtreet-door. She riſes at five in the ſummer, and at day-light in the winter, to detect them in giving away broken victuals, coals, candles, &c. and her own footman is employed the whole morning in carrying letters of information to the maſters and miſtreſſes, wherever ſhe ſees, or rather imagines, this to be practiſed. She has cauſed

 many

many a man-ſervant to loſe his place for romping in the kitchen; and many a maid has been turned away, upon her account, for *dreſſing at the men*, as ſhe calls it, looking out at the window, or ſtanding at the ſtreet-door, in a ſummer's evening. I am acquainted with three maiden-ſiſters, all mighty good ſort of women, who, to prevent any ill conſequences, will not keep a footman at all; and it is at the riſk of their place, that the maids have any *comers after them*, nor will, on any account, a brother, or a male couſin, be ſuffered to viſit them.

A diſtinguiſhing mark of a mighty good ſort of woman is, her extraordinary pretenſions to religion: ſhe never miſſes church twice a-day, in order to take note of thoſe who are abſent; and ſhe is always lamenting the decay of piety in theſe days. With ſome of them, the good Dr. Whitefield, or the good Dr. Romaine, is ever in their mouths: and they look upon the whole bench of biſhops to be very Jews in compariſon of theſe ſaints. The mighty good ſort of woman is alſo very charitable in outward appearance; for, though ſhe would not relieve a family in the utmoſt diſtreſs, ſhe deals out her halfpence to every common beggar, particularly at the church door; and ſhe is eternally ſoliciting other people to contribute to this or that public charity, though ſhe herſelf will not give ſix pence to any one of them. An univerſal benevolence is another characteriſtic of a mighty good ſort of woman, which renders her (as ſtrange as it may ſeem) of a moſt unforgiving temper. Heaven knows, ſhe bears nobody any ill-will; but if a tradeſman has diſobliged her, the honeſteſt man in all the world becomes the moſt arrant rogue; and ſhe cannot reſt till ſhe has perſuaded all her acquaintance to turn him off as well as herſelf. Every one is with her "The beſt "creature in the univerſe," while they are intimate; but upon any ſlight difference—— "Oh—ſhe was vaſtly miſtaken in the per- "ſons;—ſhe thought them good ſort of bo- "dies——but—ſhe has done with them;— "other people will find them out as well as "herſelf:——that's all the harm ſhe wiſhes "them."——

As the mighty good ſort of women differ from each other, according to their age and ſituation in life, I ſhall endeavour to point out their ſeveral marks, by which we may diſtinguiſh them. And firſt, for the moſt common character:—If ſhe happens to be of that neutral ſex, an old maid, you may find her out by her prim look, her formal geſture, and the ſee-ſaw motion of her head in converſation. Though a moſt rigid Proteſtant, her religion ſavours very much of the Roman Catholic, as ſhe holds that almoſt every one muſt be damned except herſelf. But the leaven that runs moſtly through her whole compoſition, is a deteſtation of that odious creature, man, whom ſhe affects to loath as much as ſome people do a rat or a toad; and this affectation ſhe cloaks under a pretence of a love of God, at a time of life when it muſt be ſuppoſed, that ſhe can love nobody, or rather nobody loves her. If the mighty good ſort of body is young and unmarried, beſides the uſual tokens, you may know her by her quarrelling with her brothers, thwarting her ſiſters, ſnapping her father, and over-ruling her mother, though it is ten to one ſhe is the favourite of both. All her acquaintance cry her up as a mighty diſcreet kind of body; and as ſhe affects an indifference for the men, though not a total antipathy, it is a wonder if the giddy girls, her ſiſters, are not married before her, which ſhe would look upon as the greateſt mortification that could happen to her. Among the mighty good ſort of women in wedlock, we muſt not reckon the tame domeſtic animal, who thinks it her duty to take care of her houſe, and be obliging to her huſband. On the contrary, ſhe is negligent of her home-affairs, and ſtudies to recommend herſelf more abroad than in her own houſe. If ſhe pays a regular round of viſits, if ſhe behaves decently at the card-table, if ſhe is ready to come into any party of pleaſure, if ſhe pays no regard to her huſband, and puts her children out to nurſe, ſhe is not a good wife, or a good mother, perhaps; but ſhe is——a mighty good ſort of woman.

As I diſpoſed of the mighty good kind of man in marriage, it may be expected, that I ſhould find out a proper match alſo for the mighty good ſort of woman. To tell you my opinion then—if ſhe is old, I would give her to a young rake, being the character ſhe loves beſt at her heart:—or, if ſhe is mighty young, mighty handſome, mighty rich, as well as a mighty good ſort of woman, I will marry her myſelf, as I am unfortunately a batchelor.

Your very humble ſervant, &c.

B. Thornton.

§ 40. *A Sunday in the Country.*

Sir, Aug. 8, 1761.

As life is ſo ſhort, you will agree with me, that we cannot afford to loſe any of that precious time, every moment of which ſhould be employed in ſuch gratifications as are ſuitable to our ſtations and diſpoſitions. For this reaſon we cannot but lament, that the year ſhould be curtailed of almoſt a ſeventh part, and that, out of three hundred and ſixty-five days, fifty-two of them ſhould be allotted, with reſpect to many perſons, to dullneſs and inſipidity. You will eaſily conceive, that, by what I have ſaid, I allude to that enemy to all mirth and gaiety, Sunday, whoſe impertinent intruſion puts a check on our amuſements, and caſts a gloom over our cheerful thoughts. Perſons, indeed, of high faſhion regard it no more than the other part of the week, and would no more be reſtrained from their pleaſures on this day, than they would keep faſt on a faſt-day; but others, who have the ſame taſte and ſpirit, though leſs fortunes, are conſtrained, in order to ſave appearances, to debar themſelves of every amuſement except that of going to church, which they can only enjoy in common with the vulgar. The vulgar, it is true, have the happy privilege of converting this holy-day into a day of extraordinary feſtivity; and the mechanic is allowed to get drunk on this day, if on no other, becauſe he has nothing elſe to do. It is true, that the citizen on this day gets looſe from his counter, to which he had been faſtened all the reſt of the week like a bad ſhilling, and riots in the luxuries of Iſlington or Mile-end. But what ſhall be ſaid of thoſe who have no buſineſs to follow but the bent of their inclinations? on whoſe hands, indeed, all the days of their life would hang as heavy as Sundays, if they were not enlivened by the dear variety of amuſements and diverſions. How can a woman of any ſpirit paſs her time on this diſmal day, when the playhouſes, and Vauxhall, and Ranelagh, are ſhut, and no places of public meeting are open, but the churches? I talk not of thoſe in higher life, who are ſo much above the world, that they are out of the reach of its cenſures; I mean thoſe who are confined in a narrower ſphere, ſo as to be obliged to pay ſome regard to reputation. But if people in town

town have reason to complain of this weekly bar put upon their pleasures, how unhappy must they be who are immured in the old mansion-house in the country, and cloistered up (as it were) in a nunnery? This is my hard case: my aunt, who is a woman of the last age, took me down with her this summer to her house in Northamptonshire; nor shall I be released from my prison till the time of the coronation, which will be as joyful to me as the act of grace to an insolvent debtor. My time, however, is spent agreeably enough, as far as any thing can be agreeable in the country, as we live in a good neighbourhood, see a good deal of company, pay a good many visits, and are near enough Astrop-Wells for me to play at cards at all the public breakfastings, and to dance at the assemblies. But, as I told you, my aunt is an old-fashioned lady, and has got queer notions of I know not what. I dread nothing so much as the coming round of Sunday, which is sure to prove, to me at least, a day of penance and mortification. In the morning we are dragged, in the old family coach, to the parish-church, not a stone's throw off the house, for grandeur-sake; and, though I dress me ever so gay, the ignorant bumkins take no more notice of me than they do of my aunt, who is muffled up to the chin. At dinner we never see a creature but the parson, who never fails coming for his customary fee of roast-beef and plumb-pudding; in the afternoon the same dull work of church-going is repeated; and the evening is as melancholy as it is to a criminal who is to be executed the next morning. When I first came down, I proposed playing a game at whist, and invited the doctor to make a fourth; but my aunt looked upon the very mention of it as an abomination. I thought there could be no harm in a little innocent music; and therefore, one morning, while she was getting ready for church, I began to tune my guitar, the sound of which quickly brought her down stairs, and she vowed she would break it all to pieces, if I was so wicked as to touch it; though I offered to compromise the matter with her, by playing nothing but psalm-tunes to please her. I hate reading any thing, but especially good books, as my aunt calls them, which are dull at any time, but much duller on a Sunday; yet my aunt wonders I will not employ myself, when I have nothing to do, in reading Nelson on the Feasts and Fasts, or a chapter in the Bible. You must know, that the day I write this on is Sunday; and it happens to be so very rainy, that my aunt is afraid to venture herself in the damp church, for fear of encreasing her rheumatism; she has therefore put on her spectacles, ordered the great family-bible into the hall, and is going to read prayers herself to the servants. I excused myself from being present, by pretending an head-ach, and stole into my closet in order to divert myself in writing to you. How I shall be able to go through the rest of the day, I know not; as the rain, I believe, will not suffer us to stir out, and we shall sit moping and yawning at one another, and looking stupidly at the rain out of the Gothic window in the little parlour, like the clean and unclean beasts in Noah's ark. It is said, that the gloomy weather in November induces Englishmen commonly to make away with themselves; and, indeed, considering the weather, and all together, I believe I shall be tempted to drown myself at once in the pond before the door, or fairly tuck myself up in my own garters.

I am your very humble servant,

DOROTHY THURSDAY

B. Thornton.

§ 41. *A circumstantial Detail of every Particular that passed at the Coronation.*

[In a Letter from a Gentleman to his Friend in the Country.]

Dear Sir,

Though I regret leaving you so soon, especially as the weather has since proved so fine, that it makes me long to be with you in the country, yet I honestly confess, that I am heartily glad I came to town as I did. As I have seen it, I declare I would not have missed the sight upon any consideration. The friendship of Mr. Rolles, who procured me a pass-ticket, as they call it, enabled me to be present both in the Hall and the Abbey; and as to the procession out of doors, I had a fine view of it from a one-pair of stairs room, which your neighbour, Sir Edward, had hired, at the small price of one hundred guineas, on purpose to oblige his acquaintance. I wish you had been with me; but as you have been deprived of a sight, which probably very few that were present will ever see again, I will endeavour to describe it to you as minutely as I can, while the circumstances are fresh in my memory, though my description must fall very short of the reality. First, then, conceive to yourself the fronts of the houses, in all the streets that could command the least point of view, lined with scaffolding, like so many galleries or boxes raised one above another to the very roofs. These were covered with carpets and cloths of different colours, which presented a pleasing variety to the eye; and if you consider the brilliant appearance of the spectators who were seated in them (many being richly dressed) you will easily imagine that this was no indifferent part of the show. The mob underneath made a pretty contrast to the rest of the company. Add to this, that though we had nothing but wet and cloudy weather for some time before, the day cleared up, and the sun shone auspiciously, as it were in compliment to the grand festival. The platform, on account of the uncertainty of the weather, had a shelving roof, which was covered with a kind of sail-cloth; but near the place where I was, an honest Jack Tar climbed up to the top and stripped off the covering, which gave us not only a more extensive view, but let the light in upon every part of the procession. I should tell you, that a rank of foot-soldiers was placed on each side within the platform; and it was not a little surprising to see the officers familiarly conversing and walking arm and arm with many of them, till we were let into the secret that they were gentlemen who had put on the dresses of common soldiers, for what purpose I need not mention. On the outside were stationed, at proper distances, several parties of horse-guards, whose horses, indeed, somewhat incommoded the people, that pressed incessantly upon them, by their prancing and capering; though, luckily, I do not hear of any great mischief being done. I must confess, it gave me much pain, to see the soldiers, both horse and foot, most unmercifully belabouring the heads of the mob with their broad-swords, bayonets, and musquets; but it was not unpleasant to observe several tipping the horse-soldiers slily from time to time (some with halfpence, and some with silver, as they could muster up the cash) to let them pass between the horses to get nearer the platform; after which these unconscionable gentry drove them back again. As soon as it was day-break (for I chose to go to my place over-night) we were diverted with seeing the coaches and chairs of the nobility and gentry passing along with much ado; and several

persons

persons, very richly dressed, were obliged to quit their equipages, and be escorted by the soldiers through the mob to their respective places. Several carriages, I am told, received great damage: Mr. Jennings, whom you know, had his chariot broke to pieces; but providentially neither he nor Mrs. Jennings, who were in it, received any hurt.

Their majesties (to the shame of those be it spoken who were not so punctual) came in their chairs from St. James's through the Park to Westminster about nine o'clock. The king went into a room which they call the Court of Wards, and the queen into that belonging to the gentleman-usher of the black-rod. The nobility and others, who were to walk in the procession, were mustered and ranged by the officers of arms in the Court of Requests, Painted Chamber, and House of Lords, from whence the cavalcade was conducted into Westminster-hall. As you know all the avenues and places about the Hall, you will not be at a loss to understand me. My pass-ticket would have been of no service, if I had not prevailed on one of the guards, by the irresistible argument of half-a-crown, to make way for me through the mob to the Hall-gate, where I got admittance just as their majesties were seated at the upper end, under magnificent canopies. Her majesty's chair was on the left hand of his majesty; and they were attended by the great chamberlain, lord high constable, earl marshal, and other great officers. Four swords, I observed, and as many spurs, were presented in form, and then placed upon a table before the king.

There was a neglect, it seems, somewhere, in not sending for the dean and prebendaries of Westminster, &c. who, not finding themselves summoned, came of their own accord, preceded by the choristers, singers, &c. among whom was your favourite, as indeed he is of every one, Mr. Beard. The Hall-gate was now thrown open to admit this lesser procession from the Abbey, when the bishop of Rochester (that is, the dean) and his attendants brought the Bible and the following regalia of the king, *viz.* St. Edward's crown, rested on a cushion of gold-cloth, the orb with the cross, a sceptre with the dove on the top, another tipt with a cross, and what they call St. Edward's staff. The queen's regalia were brought at the same time, *viz.* her crown upon a cushion, a sceptre with a cross, and a rod of ivory with a dove. These were severally laid before their majesties, and afterwards delivered to the respective officers who were to bear them in the procession.

Considering the length of the cavalcade, and the numbers that were to walk, it is no wonder that there should be much confusion in marshalling the ranks. At last, however, every thing was regularly adjusted, and the procession began to quit the Hall between eleven and twelve. The platform leading to the west door of the Abbey was covered with blue baize for the train to walk on; but there seemed to me a defect in not covering the upright posts that supported the awning, as it is called, (for they looked mean and naked) with that or some other coloured cloth. As I carry you along, I shall wave mentioning the minute particulars of the procession, and only observe that the nobility walked two by two. Being willing to see the procession pass along the platform through the streets, I hastened from the Hall, and by the assistance of a soldier made my way to my former station at the corner of Bridge-street, where the windows commanded a double view at the turning. I shall not attempt to describe the splendor and magnificence of the whole; and words must fall short of that innate joy and satisfaction which the spectators felt and expressed, especially as their majesties passed by; on whose countenances a dignity suited to their station, tempered with the most amiable complacency, was sensibly impressed. It was observable, that as their majesties and the nobility passed the corner which commanded a prospect of Westminster-bridge, they stopped short, and turned back to look at the people, whose appearance, as they all had their hats off, and were thick planted on the ground, which rose gradually, I can compare to nothing but a pavement of heads and faces.

I had the misfortune not to be able to get to the Abbey time enough to see all that passed there; nor, indeed, when I got in, could I have so distinct a view as I could have wished. But our friend Harry Whitaker had the luck to be stationed in the first row of the gallery behind the seats allotted for the nobility, close to the square platform which was erected by the altar, with an ascent of three steps, for their majesties to be crowned on. You are obliged to him, therefore, for several particulars which I could not otherwise have informed you of. He tells me, as soon as their majesties entered the church, the choir struck up with an anthem; and, after they were seated, and the usual recognition and oblations were made, the litany was chanted by the bishops of Chester and Chichester, and the responses made by the whole choir, accompanied by the whole band of music. Then the first part of the communion-service was read; after which a sermon was preached by the bishop of Salisbury, now archbishop of York. I was not near enough to hear it, nor, perhaps you will say, did I much desire it; but, by my watch, it lasted only fifteen minutes. This done, Harry says he saw very distinctly his majesty subscribe the declaration, and take the coronation oath, the solemnity of which struck him with an unspeakable awe and reverence; and he could not help reflecting on the glorious privilege which the English enjoy, of binding their kings by the most sacred ties of conscience and religion. The king was then anointed by his grace of Canterbury on the crown of his head, his breast, and the palms of his hands; after which he was presented with the spurs, and girt with the sword, and was then invested with the coronation-robes, the armills, as they are called, and the imperial pall. The orb with the cross was also presented, and the ring was put upon the fourth finger of his majesty's right hand by the archbishop, who then delivered the sceptre with the cross, and the other with the dove; and being assisted by several bishops, he lastly placed the crown reverently upon his majesty's head. A profound awful silence had reigned till this moment, when, at the very instant the crown was let fall on the king's head, a fellow having been placed on the top of the Abbey-dome, from whence he could look down into the chancel, with a flag which he dropt as a signal; the Park and Tower guns began to fire, the Trumpets sounded, and the Abbey echoed with the repeated shouts and acclamations of the people. The peers, who before this time had their coronets in their hands, now put them on, as the bishops did their caps, and the representatives of the dukes of Aquitaine and Normandy their hats. The knights of the Bath in particular made a most splendid figure, when they put on their caps, which were adorned with large plumes of white feathers. It is to be observed, that there were no commoners knights of the Garter; consequently, instead of caps and vestments peculiar to their order, they, being all peers, wore the robes and coronets of their respective ranks. I should mention, that the kings of arms also put on coronets.

Silence again assumed her reign, and the shouts ceasing, the archbishop proceeded with the rest of the divine service; and after he had presented the Bible to his majesty, and solemnly read the benedictions, his majesty kissed the archbishops and bishops one after another as they knelt before him. The *Te Deum* was now performed, and this being ended, his majesty was elevated on a superb throne, which all the peers approached in their order, and did their homages.

The coronation of the queen was performed in nearly the same manner with that of his majesty; the archbishop anointed her with the holy oil on the head and breast, and after he had put the crown upon her head, it was a signal for princess Augusta and the peeresses to put on their coronets. Her majesty then received the sceptre with the cross, and the ivory rod with the dove, and was conducted to a magnificent throne on the left hand of his majesty.

I cannot but lament that I was not near enough to observe their majesties going thro' the most serious and solemn acts of devotion; but I am told, that the reverent attention which both paid, when (after having made their second oblations) the next ceremony was, their receiving the holy communion, it brought to the mind of every one near them, a proper recollection of the consecrated place in which they were. Prayers being over, the king and queen retired into St. Edward's chapel, just behind the altar. You must remember it—it is where the superstition of the Roman Catholics has robbed the tomb of that royal confessor of some of its precious ornaments; here their majesties received each of them a crown of state, as it is called, and a procession was made in the same manner as before, except in some trifling instances, back again to Westminster-hall, all wearing their coronets, caps, *&c.* You know I have often said, that if one loses an hour in the morning, one may ride after it the whole day without being able to overtake it. This was the case in the present instance; for, to whatever causes it might be owing, the procession most assuredly set off too late: besides, according to what Harry observed, there were such long pauses between some of the ceremonies in the Abbey, as plainly shewed all the actors were not perfect in their parts. However it be, it is impossible to conceive the chagrin and disappointment which the late return of the procession occasioned; it being so late indeed, that the spectators, even in the open air, had but a very dim and gloomy view of it, while to those who had sat patiently in Westminster-hall, waiting its return for six hours, scarce a glimpse of it appeared, as the branches were not lighted till just upon his majesty's entrance. I had flattered myself that a new scene of splendid grandeur would have been presented to us in the return of the procession, from the reflection of the lights, *&c.* and had therefore posted back to the Hall with all possible expedition: but not even the brilliancy of the ladies jewels, or the greater lustre of their eyes, had the power to render our *darkness visible*; the whole was confusion, irregularity, and disorder.

However, we were afterwards amply recompensed for this partial eclipse by the bright picture which the lighting of the chandeliers presented to us. Your unlucky law-suit has made you too well acquainted with Weſtminſter-hall for me to think of deſcribing it to you; but I aſſure you the face of it was greatly altered from what it was when you attended to hear the verdict given againſt you. Inſtead of the incloſures for the courts of Chancery and King's Bench at the upper end, which were both removed, a platform was raiſed with ſeveral aſcents of ſteps, where their majeſties in their chairs of ſtate, and the royal family, ſat at table. On each ſide, down the whole length of the Hall, the reſt of the company were ſeated at long tables, in the middle of which were placed, on elevations painted to repreſent marble, the deſerts, &c. Conceive to yourſelf, if you can conceive, what I own I am at a loſs to deſcribe, ſo magnificent a building as that of Weſtminſter-hall, lighted up with near three thouſand wax-candles in moſt ſplendid branches; our crowned heads, and almoſt the whole nobility, with the prime of our gentry, moſt ſuperbly arrayed, and adorned with a profuſion of the moſt brilliant jewels; the galleries on every ſide crowded with company for the moſt part elegantly and richly dreſſed: but to conceive it in all its luſtre, I am conſcious that it is abſolutely neceſſary one muſt have been preſent. To proceed in my narration—Their majeſties table was ſerved with three courſes, at the firſt of which earl Talbot, as ſteward of his majeſty's houſhold, rode up from the Hall-gate to the ſteps leading to where their majeſties ſat; and on his returning the ſpectators were preſented with an unexpected ſight, in his lordſhip's backing his horſe, that he might keep his face ſtill towards the king. A loud clapping and huzzaing conſequently enſued from the people preſent. The ceremony of the champion, you may remember we laughed at, at its repreſentation laſt winter; but I aſſure you it had a very ſerious effect on thoſe ladies who were near him (though his horſe was very gentle) as he came up, accompanied by lord Effingham as earl marſhal, and the duke of Bedford as lord high conſtable, likewiſe on horſeback: it is needleſs to repeat what paſſed on this occaſion. I am told, that the horſe which the champion rode was the ſame that his late majeſty was mounted on at the glorious and memorable battle of Dettingen. The beaſt, as well as the rider, had his head adorned with a plume of white, red, and blue feathers.

You cannot expect that I ſhould give you a bill of fare, or enumerate the number of diſhes that were provided and ſent from the temporary kitchens erected in Cotton-garden for this purpoſe. No leſs than ſixty haunches of veniſon, with a ſurpriſing quantity of all ſorts of game, were laid in for this grand feaſt: but that which chiefly attracted our eyes, was their majeſties deſert, in which the confectioner had laviſhed all his ingenuity in rock-work and emblematical figures. The other deſerts were no leſs admirable for their expreſſive devices. But I muſt not forget to tell you, than when the company came to be ſeated, the poor knights of the Bath had been overlooked, and no table provided for them: an airy apology, however, was ſerved up to them inſtead of a ſubſtantial dinner; but the two junior knights, in order to preſerve their rank of precedency to their ſucceſſors, were placed at the head of the judges table, above all the learned brethren of the coif. The peers were placed on the outermoſt ſide of the tables, and the peereſſes within, neareſt to the walls. You cannot ſuppoſe that there was the greateſt order imaginable obſerved during the dinner, but muſt conclude, that ſome of the company were as eager and impatient to ſatisfy

ſatisfy the craving of their appetites as any of your country 'ſquires at a race or aſſize ordinary.

It was pleaſant to ſee the various ſtratagems made uſe of by the company in the galleries to come in for a ſnack of the good things below. The ladies clubbed their handkerchiefs to be tied together to draw up a chicken or a bottle of wine; nay, even garters (I will not ſay of a different ſex) were united for the ſame purpoſe. Some had been ſo provident as to bring baſkets with them, which were let down, like the priſoners boxes at Ludgate or the Gate-houſe, with a *Pray, remember the poor.*

You will think it high time that I ſhould bring this long letter to a concluſion. Let it ſuffice then to acquaint you, that their majeſties returned to St. James's a little after ten o'clock at night; but they were pleaſed to give time for the peereſſes to go firſt, that they might not be incommoded by the preſſure of the mob to ſee their majeſties. After the nobility were departed, the illuſtrious *mobility* were (according to cuſtom) admitted into the Hall, which they preſently cleared of all the moveables, ſuch as the victuals, cloths, plates, diſhes, *&c.* and, in ſhort, every thing that could ſtick to their fingers.

I need not tell you, that ſeveral coronation medals, in ſilver, were thrown among the populace at the return of the proceſſion. One of them was pitched into Mrs. Dixon's lap, as ſhe ſat upon a ſcaffold in Palace-yard. Some, it is ſaid, were alſo thrown among the peereſſes in the Abbey juſt after the king was crowned; but they thought it below their dignity to ſtoop to pick them up.

My wife deſires her compliments to you: ſhe was *hugeouſly* pleaſed with the ſight. All friends are well, except that little Nancy Green has got a ſwelled face, by being up all night; and Tom Moffat has his leg laid up on a ſtool, on account of a broken ſhin, which he got by a kick from a trooper's horſe, as a reward for his mobbing it. I ſhall ſay nothing of the illuminations at night: the newspapers muſt have told you of them, and that the Admiralty in particular was remarkably lighted up. I expect to have from you an account of the rejoicings at your little town; and deſire to know whether you was able to get a ſlice of the ox which was roaſted whole on this occaſion.

I am, dear Sir,
Yours moſt heartily,
James Hemming.

P. S. The Princeſs Dowager of Wales, with the younger branches of the royal family, did not walk in the grand proceſſion, but made up a leſſer proceſſion of their own; of which you will find a ſufficient account in the public prints. They had a box to ſee the coronation in the Abbey, and afterwards dined in an apartment by themſelves adjoining to the Hall.

Since my writing the above, I have been informed for certain, that the ſword of ſtate, by ſome miſtake, being left behind at St. James's, the Lord Mayor's ſword was carried before the king by the earl of Huntingdon, in its ſtead; but when the proceſſion came into the Abbey, the ſword of ſtate was found placed upon the altar.

Our friend Harry, who was upon the ſcaffold, at the return of the proceſſion cloſed in with the rear; at the expence of half a guinea was admitted into the Hall; got brim-full of his majeſty's claret; and, in the univerſal plunder, brought off the glaſs her majeſty drank in, which is placed in the beaufait as a valuable curiosity. *B. Thornton.*

§ 42. *Curiosity.*

The love of variety, or curiosity of seeing new things, which is the same or at least a sister passion to it,—seems wove into the frame of every son and daughter of Adam; we usually speak of it as one of nature's levities, though planted within us for the solid purposes of carrying forward the mind to fresh enquiry and knowledge: strip us of it, the mind (I fear) would doze for ever over the present page; and we should all of us rest at ease with such objects as presented themselves in the parish or province where we first drew breath.

It is to this spur which is ever in our sides, that we owe the impatience of this desire for travelling: the passion is no ways bad,—but as others are—in its mismanagement or excess;—order it rightly, the advantages are worth the pursuit; the chief of which are—to learn the languages, the laws and customs, and understand the government and interest of other nations,—to acquire an urbanity and confidence of behaviour, and fit the mind more easily for conversation and discourse;—to take us out of the company of our aunts and grandmothers, and from the tracks of nursery mistakes; and by shewing us new objects, or old ones in new lights, to reform our judgments—by tasting perpetually the varieties of nature, to know what is good—by observing the address and arts of men, to conceive what is sincere,—and by seeing the difference of so many various humours and manners—to look into ourselves, and form our own.

This is some part of the cargo we might return with; but the impulse of seeing new sights, augmented with that of getting clear from all lessons both of wisdom and reproof at home—carries our youth too early out, to turn this venture to much account; on the contrary, if the scene painted of the prodigal in his travels, looks more like a copy than an original—will it not be well if such an adventurer, with so unpromising a setting-out,—without care,—without compass,—be not cast away for ever;—and may he not be said to escape well—if he returns to his country only as naked as he first left it?

But you will send an able pilot with your son—a scholar—

If wisdom could speak no other language but Greek or Latin—you do well—or if mathematics will make a gentleman,—or natural philosophy but teach him to make a bow,—he may be of some service in introducing your son into good societies, and supporting him in them when he has done—but the upshot will be generally this, that in the most pressing occasions of address, if he is a mere man of reading, the unhappy youth will have the tutor to carry,—and not the tutor to carry him.

But you will avoid this extreme; he shall be escorted by one who knows the world, not merely from books—but from his own experience:—a man who has been employed on such services, and thrice made the tour of Europe with success.

—That is, without breaking his own, or his pupil's neck;—for if he is such as my eyes have seen! some broken Swiss valet-de-chambre——some general undertaker, who will perform the journey in so many months, "if God permit,"—much knowledge will not accrue;—some profit at least,—he will learn the amount to a halfpenny, of every stage from Calais to Rome;—he will be carried to the

the beſt inns,—inſtructed where there is the beſt wine, and ſup a livre cheaper, than if the youth had been left to make the tour and bargain himſelf. Look at our governor! I beſeech you:—ſee, he is an inch taller as he relates the advantages.—

—And here endeth his pride—his knowledge, and his uſe.

But when your ſon gets abroad, he will be taken out of his hand, by his ſociety with men of rank and letters, with whom he will paſs the greateſt part of his time.

Let me obſerve, in the firſt place,—that company which is really good is very rare—and very ſhy: but you have ſurmounted this difficulty, and procured him the beſt letters of recommendation to the moſt eminent and reſpectable in every capital.

And I anſwer, that he will obtain all by them, which courteſy ſtrictly ſtands obliged to pay on ſuch occaſions,—but no more.

There is nothing in which we are ſo much deceived, as in the advantages propoſed from our connections and diſcourſe with the literati, &c. in foreign parts; eſpecially if the experiment is made before we are matured by years or ſtudy.

Converſation is a traffic; and if you enter into it without ſome ſtock of knowledge, to balance the account perpetually betwixt you,—the trade drops at once: and this is the reaſon,—however it may be boaſted to the contrary, why travellers have ſo little (eſpecially good) converſation with natives,—owing to their ſuſpicion,—or perhaps conviction, that there is nothing to be extracted from the converſation of young itinerants, worth the trouble of their bad language,—or the interruption of their viſits.

The pain on theſe occaſions is uſually reciprocal; the conſequence of which is, that the diſappointed youth ſeeks an eaſier ſociety; and as bad company is always ready,—and ever laying in wait—the career is ſoon finiſhed; and the poor prodigal returns the ſame object of pity, with the prodigal in the goſpel. *Sterne's Sermons.*

§ 43. *On Pedantry.*

Sir,

To diſplay the leaſt ſymptom of learning, or to ſeem to know more than your footman, is become an offence againſt the rules of politeneſs, and is branded with the name of pedantry and ill-breeding. The very ſound of a Roman or a Grecian name, or a hard name, as the ladies call it, though their own perhaps are harder by half, is enough to diſconcert the temper of a dozen counteſſes, and to ſtrike a whole aſſembly of fine gentlemen dumb with amazement.

This ſqueamiſhneſs of theirs is owing to their averſion to pedantry, which they underſtand to be a ſort of muſtineſs that can only be contracted in a recluſe and a ſtudious life, and a foible peculiar to men of letters. But if a ſtrong attachment to a particular ſubject, a total ignorance of every other, an eagerneſs to introduce that ſubject upon all occaſions, and a confirmed habit of declaiming upon it without either wit or diſcretion, be the marks of a pedantic character, as they certainly are, it belongs to the illiterate as well as the learned; and St. James's itſelf may boaſt of producing as arrant pedants as were ever ſent forth from a college.

I know a woman of faſhion who is perpetually employed in remarks upon the weather, who obſerves from morning to noon that it is likely to rain, and from noon to night that it ſpits, that it miſſes, that it is ſet in for a wet evening; and, being incapable of any other discourse, is as insipid a companion and just as pedantic, as he who quotes Aristotle over his tea, or talks Greek at a card-table.

A gentleman of my acquaintance is a constant attendant upon parliamentary business, and I have heard him entertain a large circle, by the hour, with the speeches that were made in a debate upon mum and perry. He has a wonderful memory, and a kind of oratorical tune in his elocution, that serves him instead of an emphasis. By those means he has acquired the reputation of having a deal to say for himself; but as it consists entirely of what others have said for themselves before him, and if he should be deaf during the Sessions, he would certainly be dumb in the intervals, I must needs set him down for a pedant.

But the most troublesome, as well as most dangerous character of this sort that I am so unhappy as to be connected with, is a stripling who spends his whole life in a fencing-school. This athletic young pedant is, indeed, a most formidable creature; his whole conversation lies in *Quart* and *Tierce*; if you meet him in the street, he salutes you in the gymnastic manner, throws himself back upon his left hip, levels his cane at the pit of your stomach, and looks as fierce as a prize-fighter. In the midst of a discourse upon politics, he starts from the table on a sudden, and splits himself into a monstrous lounge against the wainscot; immediately he puts a foil into your hand, insists upon teaching you his murthering thrust, and if, in the course of his instructions, he pushes out an eye or a fore-tooth, he tells you that you *flapp'd your point*, or *dropp'd your wrist*, and imputes all the mischief to the awkwardness of his pupil.

The musical pedant, who, instead of attending to the discourse, diverts himself with humming an air, or, if he speaks, expresses himself in the language of the orchestra: the Newmarket pedant, who has no knowledge but what he gathers upon the turf; the female pedant, who is an adept in nothing but the patterns of silks and flounces; and the coffee-house pedant, whose whole erudition lies within the margin of a news-paper, are nuisances so extremely common, that it is almost unnecessary to mention them. Yet, pedants as they are, they shelter themselves under the fashionableness of their foible, and with all the properties of the character, generally escape the imputation of it. In my opinion, however, they deserve our censure more than the merest book-worm imaginable. The man of letters is usually confined to his study, and having but little pleasure in conversing with men of the world, does not often intrude himself into their company: these unlearned pedants, on the contrary, are to be met with every where: they have nothing to do but to run about and be troublesome, and are universally the bane of agreeable conversation. I am, Sir, &c.

B. Thornton.

§ 44. *The faint-hearted Lover.*

Sir,

I do not doubt but every one of your readers will be able to judge of my case, as without question, every one of them either has been, or is at present, as much in love as your humble servant. You must know, Sir, I am the very Mr. *Faint-heart* described in the proverb, who *never won fair lady*: for though I have paid my addresses to several of the sex, I have gone about it in so meek and pitiful a manner, that it might fairly be a question, whether I was in earnest. One of my Dulcineas was taken, as we catch mackerel, by a bit of scarlet; another was seduced from

from me by a ſuit of embroidery; and another ſurrendered, at the firſt attack, to the long ſword of an Iriſhman. My preſent ſuit and ſervice is paid to a certain lady who is as fearful of receiving any tokens of my affection as I am of offering them. I am only permitted to admire her at a diſtance; an ogle or a leer are all the advances I dare make; if I move but a finger it puts her all in a ſweat; and, like the ſenſitive plant, ſhe would ſhrink and die away at a touch. During our long courtſhip I never offered to ſalute her but once; and then ſhe made ſuch a wriggling with her body, ſuch a ſtruggling with her arms, and ſuch a toſſing and twirling of her head to and fro, that, inſtead of touching her lips, I was nearly in danger of carrying off the tip of her noſe. I even dared at another time to take her round the waiſt; but ſhe bounced away from me, and ſcreamed out as if I had actually been going to commit a rape upon her. I alſo once plucked up courage ſufficient to attempt ſqueezing her by the hand, but ſhe reſiſted my attack by ſo cloſe a clench of her fiſt, that my graſp was preſented with nothing but ſharp-pointed knuckles, and a long thumb-nail; and I was directly after ſaluted with a violent ſtroke on my jaw-bone. If I walk out with her, I uſe all my endeavours to keep cloſe at her ſide; but ſhe whiſks away from me as though I had ſome catching diſtemper about me: if there are but three of us, ſhe eludes my deſign by ſkipping ſometimes on one ſide and ſometimes on t'other as I approach her; but when there are more of us in company, ſhe takes care to be ſheltered from me by placing herſelf the very midmoſt of the rank. If we ride in a coach together, I am not only debarred from ſitting on the ſame ſide, but I muſt be ſeated on the furthermoſt corner of the ſeat oppoſite to her, that our knees may not meet. We are as much at diſtance from one another at dinner, as if we were really man and wife, whom cuſtom has directed to be kept aſunder the whole length of the table; and when we drink tea, ſhe would ſooner run the riſk of having the contents ſpilt over her, than take the cup and ſaucer from me any nearer than at both our arms length. If I mention a ſyllable that in the leaſt borders upon love, ſhe immediately reddens at it as much as if I had let drop a looſe or indelicate expreſſion; and when I deſire to have a little private converſation with her, ſhe wonders at my impudence, to think that ſhe could truſt herſelf with a man alone. In ſhort, Sir, I begin to deſpair of ever coming to cloſe contact with her: but what is ſtill more provoking, though ſhe keeps me at ſo reſpectful a diſtance, ſhe tamely permits a ſtrapping fellow of the guards to pat her on the cheek, play with her hand, and even approach her lips, and that too in my preſence. If you, or any of your readers, can adviſe me what to do in this caſe, it will be a laſting obligation conferred on

Your very humble ſervant

TIMOTHY MILDMAN.

B. Thornton.

§ 45. *A Letter from a ſucceſsful Adventurer in the Lottery.*

Sir,

You will not be at all ſurpriſed when I tell you that I have had very ill-luck in the lottery; but you will ſtare when I further tell you, it is becauſe unluckily I have got a conſiderable prize in it. I received the glad tidings of my misfortune laſt Saturday night from your Chronicle, when, on looking over the liſt of the prizes, as I was got behind my pipe at the club, I found that my ticket was

come

come up a 2000l. In the pride as well as joy of my heart, I could not help proclaiming to the company—my good luck, as I then foolishly thought it, and as the company thought it too, by insisting that I should treat them that evening. Friends are never so merry, or stay longer, than when they have nothing to pay: they never care too how extravagant they are on such an occasion. Bottle after bottle was therefore called for, and that too of claret, though not one of us, I believe, but had rather had port. In short, I reeled home as well as I could about four in the morning; when thinking to pacify my wife, who began to rate me (as usual) for staying out so long, I told her the occasion of it; but instead of rejoicing, as I thought she would, she cried—"Pish, ONLY two thousand pounds!" However, she was at last reconciled to it, taking care to remind me, that she had chosen the ticket herself, and she was all along sure it would come up a prize, because the number was an odd one. We neither of us got a wink of sleep, though I was heartily inclined to it; for my wife kept me awake—by telling me of this, that, and t'other thing which he wanted, and which she would now purchase, as we could afford it.

I know not how the news of my success spread so soon among my other acquaintance, except that my wife told it to every one she knew, or not knew, at church. The consequence was, that I had no less than seven very hearty friends came to dine with us by way of wishing us joy; and the number of these hearty friends was increased to above a dozen by supper-time. It is kind in one's friends to be willing to partake of one's success; they made themselves very merry literally at my expence; and, at parting, told me they would bring some more friends, and have another jolly evening with me on this happy occasion.

When they were gone, I made shift to get a little rest, though I was often disturbed by my wife talking in her sleep. Her head, it seems, literally ran upon wheels, that is, the lottery-wheels; she frequently called out that she had got the ten thousand pounds; she muttered several wild and incoherent expressions about gowns, and ruffles, and ear-rings, and necklaces; and I once heard her mention the word *coach*. In the morning, when I got up, how was I surprised to find my good fortune published to all the world in the news-paper! though I could not but smile (and madam was greatly pleased) at the printer's exalting me to the dignity of *Esquire*, having been nothing but plain Mr. all my life before. And now the misfortunes arising from my good fortune began to pour in thick upon me. In consequence of the information given in the news-paper, we were no sooner sat down to breakfast than we were complimented with a rat-a-tatoo from the drums, as if we had been just married: after these had been silenced by the usual method, another band of music saluted us with a peal from the marrow-bones and cleavers to the same tune. I was harassed the whole day with petitions from the hospital boys who drew the ticket, the commissioners clerks who wrote down the ticket, and the clerks of the office where I bought the ticket, all of them praying, "That my *Honour* would consider them." I should be glad you would inform me what these people would have given me if I had had a blank.

My acquaintance in general called to know, when they should wait upon me to *wet* my good fortune. My own relations, and my wife's wife's relations, came in ſuch ſhoals to congratulate me, that I hardly knew the faces of many of them. One inſiſted on my giving a piece of plate to his wife; another recommended to me to put his little boy (my two-and-fortieth couſin) out 'prentice; another, lately *white-waſhed*, propoſed to me my ſetting him up again in buſineſs; and ſeveral of them very kindly told me, they would borrow three or four hundred pounds of me, as they knew I could now ſpare it.

My wife in the mean time, you may be ſure, was not idle in contriving how to diſpoſe of this new acquiſition. She found out, in the firſt place, (according to the complaint of moſt women) that ſhe had not got a gown to her back, at leaſt not one fit for her *now* to appear in. Her wardrobe of linen was no leſs deficient; and ſhe diſcovered ſeveral chaſms in our furniture, eſpecially in the articles of plate and china. She is alſo determined to *ſee a little pleaſure*, as ſhe calls it, and has actually made a party to go to the next opera. Now, in order to ſupply theſe immediate wants and neceſſities, ſhe has prevailed on me (though at a great loſs) to turn the prize into ready money; which I dared not refuſe her, becauſe the number was her own chooſing: and ſhe has further perſuaded me (as we have had ſuch good luck) to lay out a great part of the produce in purchaſing more tickets, all of her own chooſing. To me it is indifferent which way the money goes; for, upon my making out the balance, I already find I ſhall be a loſer by my gains: and all my fear is, that one of the tickets may come up a five thouſand or ten thouſand.

I am
Your very humble ſervant,
JEOFFREY CHANCE.

P. S. I am juſt going to club—I hope they won't deſire me to treat them again.

B. Thornton.

§ 46. *Characters of* CAMILLA *and* FLORA.

Camilla is really what writers have ſo often imagined; or rather ſhe poſſeſſes a combination of delicacies, which they have ſeldom had minuteneſs of virtue and taſte enough to conceive; to ſay ſhe is beautiful, ſhe is accompliſhed, ſhe is generous, ſhe is tender, is talking in general, and it is the particular I would deſcribe. In her perſon ſhe is almoſt tall, and almoſt thin; graceful, commanding, and inſpiring a kind of tender reſpect; the tone of her voice is melodious, and ſhe can neither look nor move without expreſſing ſomething to her advantage. Poſſeſſed of almoſt every excellence, ſhe is unconſcious of any, and this heightens them all: ſhe is modeſt and diffident of her own opinion, yet always perfectly comprehends the ſubject on which ſhe gives it, and ſees the queſtion in its true light: ſhe has neither pride, prejudice, nor precipitancy to miſguide her; ſhe is true, and therefore judges truly. If there are ſubjects too intricate, too complicated for the feminine ſimplicity of her ſoul, her ignorance of them ſerves only to diſplay a new beauty in her character, which reſults from her acknowledging, nay, perhaps from her poſſeſſing that very ignorance. The great characteriſtic of Camilla's underſtanding is taſte; but when ſhe ſays moſt upon a ſubject, ſhe ſtill ſhews that ſhe has much more to ſay, and by this unwillingneſs to triumph, ſhe perſuades the more. With the moſt refined ſentiments, ſhe poſſeſſes the ſofteſt ſenſibility, and it lives and ſpeaks in every feature of her face. Is Camilla

Camilla melancholy? does ſhe ſigh? Every body is affected: they enquire whether any misfortune has happened to Camilla; they find that ſhe ſighed for the misfortune of another, and they are affected ſtill more. Young, lovely, and high born, Camilla graces every company, and heightens the brilliancy of courts; wherever ſhe appears, all others ſeem by a natural impulſe to feel her ſuperiority; and yet when ſhe converſes, ſhe has the art of inſpiring others with an eaſe which they never knew before: ſhe joins to the moſt ſcrupulous politeneſs a certain feminine gaiety, free both from reſtraint and boldneſs; always gentle, yet never inferior; always unaſſuming, yet never aſhamed or awkward; for ſhame and awkwardneſs are the effects of pride, which is too often miſcalled modeſty: nay, to the moſt critical diſcernment, ſhe adds ſomething of a bluſhing timidity, which ſerves but to give a meaning and piquancy even to her looks, an admirable effect of true ſuperiority! by this ſilent unaſſuming merit ſhe over-awes the turbulent and the proud, and ſtops the torrent of that indecent, that overbearing noiſe, with which inferior natures in ſuperior ſtations overwhelm the ſlaviſh and the mean. Yes, all admire, and love, and reverence Camilla.

You ſee a character that you admire, and you think it perfect; do you therefore conclude that every different character is imperfect? what, will you allow a variety of beauty almoſt equally ſtriking in the art of a Corregio, a Guido, and a Raphael, and refuſe it to the infinity of nature! How different from lovely Camilla is the beloved Flora! In Camilla, nature has diſplayed the beauty of exact regularity, and the elegant ſoftneſs of female propriety: in Flora, ſhe charms with a certain artleſs poignancy, a graceful negligence, and an uncontrouled, yet blameleſs freedom. Flora has ſomething original and peculiar about her, a charm which is not eaſily defined; to know her and to love her is the ſame thing; but you cannot know her by deſcription. Her perſon is rather touching than majeſtic, her features more expreſſive than regular, and her manner pleaſes rather becauſe it is reſtrained by no rule, than becauſe it is conformable to any that cuſtom has eſtabliſhed. Camilla puts you in mind of the moſt perfect muſic that can be compoſed; Flora, of the wild ſweetneſs which is ſometimes produced by the irregular play of the breeze upon the Æolian harp. Camilla reminds you of a lovely young queen; Flora, of her more lovely maid of honour. In Camilla you admire the decency of the Graces; in Flora, the attractive ſweetneſs of the Loves. Artleſs ſenſibility, wild, native feminine gaiety, and the moſt touching tenderneſs of ſoul, are the ſtrange characteriſtics of Flora. Her countenance glows with youthful beauty, which all art ſeems rather to diminiſh than increaſe, rather to hide than adorn, and while Camilla charms you with the choice of her dreſs, Flora enchants you with the neglect of hers. Thus different are the beauties which nature has manifeſted in Camilla and Flora! yet while ſhe has, in this contrariety, ſhewn the extent of her power to pleaſe, ſhe has alſo proved, that truth and virtue are always the ſame. Generoſity and tenderneſs are the firſt principles in the minds of both favourites, and were never poſſeſſed in an higher degree than they are poſſeſſed by Flora: ſhe is juſt as attentive to the intereſt of others, as ſhe is negligent of her own; and tho' ſhe could ſubmit to any misfortune that could befal herſelf, yet ſhe hardly knows how to to bear the misfortunes of another. Thus does Flora unite the ſtrongeſt ſenſibility with the moſt lively gaiety; aud both are expreſſed with the moſt bewitching mixture in her countenance. While Camilla inſpires a reverence that keeps you at a reſpectful, yet admiring diſtance, Flora excites the moſt ardent, yet moſt elegant deſire. Camilla reminds you of the dignity of Diana, Flora of the attractive ſenſibility of Caliſto: Camilla almoſt elevates you to the ſenſibility of angels, Flora delights you with the lovelieſt idea of woman.

Greville.

§ 47. *A Fable by the celebrated Linnæus, tranſlated from the Latin.*

Once upon a time the ſeven wiſe men of Greece were met together at Athens, and it was propoſed that every one of them ſhould mention what he thought the greateſt wonder in the creation. One of them, of higher conceptions than the reſt, propoſed the opinion of ſome of the aſtronomers about the fixed ſtars, which they believed to be ſo many ſuns, that had each their planets rolling about them, and were ſtored with plants and animals like this earth. Fired with this thought, they agreed to ſupplicate Jupiter, that he would at leaſt permit them to take a journey to the moon, and ſtay there three days, in order to ſee the wonders of that place, and give an account of them at their return. Jupiter conſented, and ordered them to aſſemble on a high mountain, where there ſhould be a cloud ready to convey them to the place they deſired to ſee. They picked out ſome choſen companions, who might aſſiſt them in deſcribing and painting the objects they ſhould meet with. At length they arrived at the moon, and found a palace there well fitted up for their reception. The next day, being very much fatigued with their journey, they kept quiet at home till noon; and being ſtill faint, they refreſhed themſelves with a moſt delicious entertainment, which they reliſhed ſo well, that it overcame their curioſity. This day they only ſaw through the window that delightful ſpot, adorned with the moſt beautiful flowers, to which the beams of the ſun gave an uncommon luſtre, and heard the ſinging of moſt melodious birds till evening came on. The next day they roſe very early in order to begin their obſervations; but ſome very beautiful young ladies of that country coming to make them a viſit, adviſed them firſt to recruit their ſtrength before they expoſed themſelves to the laborious taſk they were about to undertake.

The delicate meats, the rich wines, the beauty of theſe damſels, prevailed over the reſolution of theſe ſtrangers. A fine concert of muſic is introduced, the young ones begin to dance, and all is turned to jollity; ſo that this whole day was ſpent in gallantry, till ſome of the neighbouring inhabitants, growing envious at their mirth, ruſhed in with ſwords. The elder part of the company tried to appeaſe the younger, promiſing the very next day they would bring the rioters to juſtice. This they performed, and the third day the cauſe was heard; and what with accuſations, pleadings, exceptions, and the judgment itſelf, the whole day was taken up, on which the term ſet by Jupiter expired. On their return to Greece, all the country flocked in upon them to hear the wonders of the moon deſcribed, but all they could tell was, for that was all they knew, that the ground was covered with green, intermixed with flowers, and that the birds ſung among the branches of the trees; but what kind of flowers they ſaw, or what kind of birds

birds they heard, they were totally ignorant. Upon which they were treated every where with contempt.

If we apply this fable to men of the present age, we ſhall perceive a very juſt ſimilitude. By theſe three days the fable denotes the three ages of man. Firſt, youth, in which we are too feeble in every reſpect to look into the works of the Creator: all that ſeaſon is given up to idleneſs, luxury, and paſtime. Secondly, manhood, in which men are employed in ſettling, marrying, educating children, providing fortunes for them, and raiſing a family. Thirdly, old age, in which after having made their fortunes, they are overwhelmed with law-ſuits and proceedings relating to their eſtates. Thus it frequently happens that men never conſider to what end they were deſtined, and why they were brought into the world. *B. Thornton.*

§ 48. *Mercy recommended.*

My uncle Toby was a man patient of injuries;—not from want of courage,—where juſt occaſions preſented, or called it forth,—I know no man under whoſe arm I would ſooner have taken ſhelter;—nor did this ariſe from any inſenſibility or obtuſeneſs of his intellectual parts;—he was of a peaceful, placid nature,—no jarring element in it,—all was mixed up ſo kindly within him: my uncle Toby had ſcarce a heart to retaliate upon a fly:——Go,—ſays he, one day at dinner, to an overgrown one which had buzzed about his noſe, and tormented him cruelly all dinner-time,—and which, after infinite attempts, he had caught at laſt, as it flew by him;—I'll not hurt thee, ſays my uncle Toby, riſing from his chair, and going acroſs the room, with the fly in his hand,—I'll not hurt a hair of thy head:—Go, ſays he, lifting up the ſaſh, and opening his hand as he ſpoke, to let it eſcape;—go, poor devil,—get thee gone, why ſhould I hurt thee?—This world, ſurely, is wide enough to hold both thee and me.

*** This is to ſerve for parents and governors inſtead of a whole volume upon the ſubject. *Sterne.*

§ 49. *The Starling.*

——Beſhrew the *ſombre* pencil! ſaid I vauntingly—for I envy not its powers, which paints the evils of life with ſo hard and deadly a colouring. The mind ſits terrified at the objects ſhe has magnified herſelf and blackened: reduce them to their proper ſize and hue, ſhe overlooks them.——'Tis true, ſaid I, correcting the propoſition—the Baſtile is not an evil to be deſpiſed—but ſtrip it of its towers—fill up the foſſe—unbarricade the doors—call it ſimply a confinement, and ſuppoſe 'tis ſome tyrant of a diſtemper—and not of a man—which holds you in it—the evil vaniſhes, and you bear the other half without complaint.

I was interrupted in the hey-day of this ſoliloquy, with a voice which I took to be of a child, which complained, "it could not get out."——I looked up and down the paſſage, and ſeeing neither man, woman, nor child, I went out without further attention.

In my return back through the paſſage, I heard the ſame words repeated twice over; and looking up, I ſaw it was a Starling hung in a little cage——"I can't get out—I can't get out," ſaid the Starling.

I ſtood looking at the bird; and to every perſon who came through the paſſage, it ran fluttering to the ſide towards which they approached it, with the ſame lamentations of its captivity—"I can't get out," ſaid the Starling—God help thee! ſaid I, but I will let thee

thee out, coſt what it will; ſo I turned about the cage to get at the door; it was twiſted and double twiſted ſo faſt with wire, there was no getting it open without pulling the cage to pieces—I took both hands to it.

The bird flew to the place where I was attempting his deliverance, and thruſting his head through the trellis, preſſed his breaſt againſt it, as if impatient.—I fear, poor creature! ſaid I, I cannot ſet thee at liberty—"No," ſaid the Starling.—"I can't get out, I can't get out," ſaid the Starling.

I vow I never had my affections more tenderly awakened; nor do I remember an incident in my life, where the diſſipated ſpirits, to which my reaſon had been a bubble, were ſo ſuddenly called home. Mechanical as the notes were, yet ſo true in tune to nature were they chanted, that in one moment they overthrew all my ſyſtematic reaſonings upon the Baſtile; and I heavily walked up ſtairs, unſaying every word I had ſaid in going down them.

Diſguiſe thyſelf as thou wilt, ſtill, ſlavery! ſaid I—ſtill thou art a bitter draught! and though thouſands in all ages have been made to drink of thee, thou art no leſs bitter on that account. 'Tis thou, thrice ſweet and gracious goddeſs, addreſſing myſelf to Liberty, whom all in public or in private worſhip, whoſe taſte is grateful, and ever will be ſo, till Nature herſelf ſhall change—no tint of words can ſpot thy ſnowy mantle, or chymic power turn thy ſceptre into iron——with thee to ſmile upon him as he eats his cruſt, the ſwain is happier than his monarch, from whoſe court thou art exiled!—Gracious Heaven! cried I, kneeling down upon the laſt ſtep but one in my aſcent——Grant me but health, thou great Beſtower of it, and give me but this fair goddeſs as my companion—and ſhower down thy mitres, if it ſeems good unto thy Divine providence, upon thoſe heads which are aching for them! *Sterne.*

§ 50. *The Captive.*

The bird in his cage purſued me into my room; I ſat down cloſe by my table, and leaning my head upon my hand, I began to figure to myſelf the miſeries of confinement: I was in a right frame for it, and ſo I gave full ſcope to my imagination.

I was going to begin with the millions of my fellow-creatures born to no inheritance but ſlavery; but finding, however affecting the picture was, that I could not bring it near me, and that the multitude of ſad groupes in it did but diſtract me——

I took a ſingle captive, and having firſt ſhut him up in his dungeon, I then looked through the twilight of his grated door to take his picture.

I beheld his body half waſted away with long expectation and confinement, and felt what kind of ſickneſs of the heart it was which ariſes from hope deferred. Upon looking nearer, I ſaw him pale and feveriſh: in thirty years the weſtern breeze had not once fanned his blood—he had ſeen no ſun, no moon, in all that time—nor had the voice of friend or kinſman breathed through his lattice—his children——

—But here my heart began to bleed—and I was forced to go on with another part of the portrait.

He was ſitting upon the ground upon a little ſtraw, in the furtheſt corner of his dungeon, which was alternately his chair and bed: a little calendar of ſmall ſticks were laid at the head, notched all over with the diſmal days and nights he had paſſed there—he had one of theſe little ſticks in his hand, and with

a ruſty

a rusty nail he was etching another day of misery to add to the heap. As I darkened the little light he had, he lifted up a hopeless eye towards the door, then cast it down—shook his head, and went on with his work of affliction. I heard his chains upon his legs, as he turned his body to lay his little stick upon the bundle—He gave a deep sigh—I saw the iron enter into his soul—I burst into tears—I could not sustain the picture of confinement which my fancy had drawn.

Sterne.

§ 51. *Trim's Explanation of the Fifth Commandment.*

———Pr'ythee, Trim, quoth my father,—What dost thou mean, by "honouring thy father and mother?"

Allowing them, an't please your honour, three halfpence a day out of my pay, when they grow old.—And didst thou do that, Trim? said Yorick. —He did indeed, replied my uncle Toby.—Then, Trim, said Yorick, springing out of his chair, and taking the Corporal by the hand, thou art the best commentator upon that part of the Decalogue; and I honour thee more for it, Corporal Trim, than if thou hadst had a hand in the Talmud itself.

Ibid.

§ 52. *Health.*

O blessed health! thou art above all gold and treasure; 'tis thou who enlargest the soul,—and openest all its powers to receive instruction, and to relish virtue.—He that has thee, has little more to wish for! and he that is so wretched as to want thee,—wants every thing with thee.

Ibid.

§ 53. *Detached Sentences.*

To be ever active in laudable pursuits, is the distinguishing characteristic of a man of merit.

There is an heroic innocence, as well as an heroic courage.

There is a mean in all things. Even virtue itself hath its stated limits; which not being strictly observed, it ceases to be virtue.

It is wiser to prevent a quarrel beforehand, than to revenge it afterwards.

It is much better to reprove, than to be angry secretly.

No revenge is more heroic, than that which torments envy by doing good.

The discretion of a man deferreth his anger, and it is his glory to pass over a transgression.

Money, like manure, does no good till it is spread. There is no real use of riches, except in the distribution; the rest is all conceit.

A wise man will desire no more than what he may get justly, use soberly, distribute cheerfully, and live upon contentedly.

A contented mind, and a good conscience, will make a man happy in all conditions. He knows not how to fear, who dares to die.

There is but one way of fortifying the soul against all gloomy presages and terrors of mind; and that is, by securing to ourselves the friendship and protection of that Being, who disposes of events, and governs futurity.

Philosophy is then only valuable, when it serves for the law of life, and not for the ostentation of science.

Without a friend, the world is but a wilderness.

A man may have a thousand intimate acquaintances, and not a friend among them all. If you have one friend, think yourself happy.

When

When once you profess yourself a friend, endeavour to be always such. He can never have any true friends, that will be often changing them.

Prosperity gains friends, and adversity tries them.

Nothing more engages the affections of men, than a handsome address, and graceful conversation.

Complaisance renders a superior amiable, an equal agreeable, and an inferior acceptable.

Excess of ceremony shews want of breeding. That civility is best, which excludes all superfluous formality.

Ingratitude is a crime so shameful, that the man was never yet found, who would acknowledge himself guilty of it.

Truth is born with us; and we must do violence to nature to shake off our veracity.

There cannot be a greater treachery, than first to raise a confidence, and then deceive it.

By others faults wise men correct their own.

No man hath a thorough taste of prosperity, to whom adversity never happened.

When our vices leave us, we flatter ourselves that we leave them.

It is as great a point of wisdom to hide ignorance, as to discover knowledge.

Pitch upon that course of life which is the most excellent; and habit will render it the most delightful.

Custom is the plague of wise men, and the idol of fools.

As, to be perfectly just, is an attribute of the Divine nature; to be so to the utmost of our abilities, is the glory of man.

No man was ever cast down with the injuries of fortune, unless he had before suffered himself to be deceived by her favours.

Anger may glance into the breast of a wise man, but rests only in the bosom of fools.

None more impatiently suffer injuries, than those that are most forward in doing them.

By taking revenge, a man is but even with his enemy; but in passing it over he is superior.

To err is human; to forgive, divine.

A more glorious victory cannot be gained over another man, than this, that when the injury began on his part, the kindness should begin on ours.

The prodigal robs his heir, the miser robs himself.

We should take a prudent care for the future, but so as to enjoy the present. It is no part of wisdom to be miserable to-day, because we may happen to be so to-morrow.

To mourn without measure, is folly; not to mourn at all, insensibility.

Some would be thought to do great things, who are but tools and instruments; like the fool who fancied he played upon the organ, when he only blew the bellows.

Though a man may become learned by another's learning, he can never be wise but by his own wisdom.

He who wants good sense is unhappy in having learning; for he has thereby more ways of exposing himself.

It is ungenerous to give a man occasion to blush at his own ignorance in one thing, who perhaps may excel us in many.

No object is more pleasing to the eye, than the sight of a man whom you have obliged; nor any music so agreeable to the ear, as the voice of one that owns you for his benefactor.

The

The coin that is most current among mankind is flattery; the only benefit of which is, that by hearing what we are not, we may be instructed what we ought to be.

The character of the person who commends you, is to be considered before you set a value on his esteem. The wise man applauds him whom he thinks most virtuous; the rest of the world, him who is most wealthy.

The temperate man's pleasures are durable, because they are regular; and all his life is calm and serene, because it is innocent.

A good man will love himself too well to lose, and all his neighbours too well to win, an estate by gaming. The love of gaming will corrupt the best principles in the world.

An angry man who suppresses his passions, thinks worse than he speaks; and an angry man that will chide, speaks worse than he thinks.

A good word is an easy obligation; but not to speak ill, requires only our silence, which costs us nothing.

It is to affectation the world owes its whole race of coxcombs. Nature in her whole drama never drew such a part; she has sometimes made a fool, but a coxcomb is always of his own making.

It is the infirmity of little minds, to be taken with every appearance, and dazzled with every thing that sparkles; but great minds have but little admiration, because few things appear new to them.

It happens to men of learning, as to ears of corn: they shoot up, and raise their heads high, while they are empty: but when full and swelled with grain, they begin to flag and droop.

He that is truly polite, knows how to contradict with respect, and to please without adulation; and is equally remote from an insipid complaisance, and a low familiarity.

The failings of good men are commonly more published in the world than their good deeds; and one fault of a deserving man shall meet with more reproaches, than all his virtues praise: such is the force of ill-will and ill-nature.

It is harder to avoid censure, than to gain applause; for this may be done by one great or wise action in an age; but to escape censure, a man must pass his whole life without saying or doing one ill or foolish thing.

When Darius offered Alexander ten thousand talents to divide Asia equally with him, he answered, The earth cannot bear two suns, nor Asia two kings.—Parmenio, a friend of Alexander's, hearing the great offers Darius had made, said, Were I Alexander I would accept them. So would I, replied Alexander, were I Parmenio.

Nobility is to be considered only as an imaginary distinction, unless accompanied with the practice of those generous virtues by which it ought to be obtained. Titles of honour conferred upon such as have no personal merit, are at best but the royal stamp set upon base metal.

Though an honourable title may be conveyed to posterity, yet the ennobling qualities which are the soul of greatness are a sort of incommunicable perfections, and cannot be transferred. If a man could bequeath his virtues by will, and settle his sense and learning upon his heirs, as certainly as he can his lands, a noble descent would then indeed be a valuable privilege.

Truth

Truth is always consistent with itself, and needs nothing to help it out. It is always near at hand, and sits upon our lips, and is ready to drop out before we are aware: whereas a lye is troublesome, and sets a man's invention upon the rack; and one trick needs a great many more to make it good.

The pleasure which affects the human mind with the most lively and transporting touches, is the sense that we act in the eye of infinite wisdom, power, and goodness, that will crown our virtuous endeavours here with a happiness hereafter, large as our desires, and lasting as our immortal souls: without this the highest state of life is insipid, and with it the lowest is a paradise.

Honourable age is not that which standeth in length of time, nor that is measured by number of years; but wisdom is the grey hair unto man, and unspotted life is old age.

Wickedness, condemned by her own witness, is very timorous, and being pressed with conscience, always forecasteth evil things; for fear is nothing else but a betraying of the succours which reason offereth.

A wise man will fear in every thing. He that contemneth small things, shall fall by little and little.

A rich man beginning to fall, is held up of his friends: but a poor man being down, is thrust away by his friends: when a rich man is fallen, he hath many helpers; he speaketh things not to be spoken, and yet men justify him: the poor man slipt, and they rebuked him; he spoke wisely, and could have no place. When a rich man speaketh, every man holdeth his tongue, and, look, what he saith they extol it to the clouds; but if a poor man speaks, they say, What fellow is this?

Many have fallen by the edge of the sword, but not so many as have fallen by the tongue. Well is he that is defended from it, and hath not passed through the venom thereof; who hath not drawn the yoke thereof, nor been bound in her bonds; for the yoke thereof is a yoke of iron, and the bands thereof are bands of brass; the death thereof is an evil death.

My son, blemish not thy good deeds, neither use uncomfortable words, when thou givest any thing. Shall not the dew asswage the heat? so is a word better than a gift. Lo, is not a word better than a gift? but both are with a gracious man.

Blame not, before thou hast examined the truth; understand first, and then rebuke.

If thou wouldest get a friend, prove him first, and be not hasty to credit him; for some men are friends for their own occasions, and will not abide in the day of thy trouble.

Forsake not an old friend, for the new is not comparable to him: a new friend is as new wine; when it is old, thou shalt drink it with pleasure.

A friend cannot be known in prosperity; and an enemy cannot be hidden in adversity.

Admonish thy friend; it may be he hath not done it; and if he have, that he do it no more. Admonish thy friend; it may be he hath not said it; or if he have, that he speak it not again. Admonish a friend; for many times it is a slander; and believe not every tale. There is one that slippeth in his speech, but not from his heart; and who is he that hath not offended with his tongue?

Whoso discovereth secrets loseth his credit, and shall never find a friend to his mind.

Honour thy father with thy whole heart, and forget not the sorrows of thy mother; how

how canſt thou recompenſe them the things that they have done for thee?

There is nothing ſo much worth as a mind well inſtructed.

The lips of talkers will be telling ſuch things as pertain not unto them; but the words of ſuch as have underſtanding are weighed in the balance. The heart of fools is in their mouth, but the tongue of the wiſe is in their heart.

To labour, and to be content with that a man hath, is a ſweet life.

Be at peace with many; nevertheleſs, have but one counſellor of a thouſand.

Be not confident in a plain way.

Let reaſon go before every enterprize, and counſel before every action.

The latter part of a wiſe man's life is taken up in curing the follies, prejudices, and falſe opinions he had contracted in the former.

Cenſure is the tax a man pays to the public for being eminent.

Very few men, properly ſpeaking, live at preſent, but are providing to live another time.

Party is the madneſs of many, for the gain of a few.

To endeavour to work upon the vulgar with fine ſenſe, is like attempting to hew blocks of marble with a razor.

Superſtition is the ſpleen of the ſoul.

He who tells a lye is not ſenſible how great a taſk he undertakes; for he muſt be forced to invent twenty more to maintain that one.

Some people will never learn any thing, for this reaſon, becauſe they underſtand every thing too ſoon.

There is nothing wanting, to make all rational and diſintereſted people in the world of one religion, but that they ſhould talk together every day.

Men are grateful, in the ſame degree that they are reſentful.

Young men are ſubtle arguers; the cloak of honour covers all their faults, as that of paſſion all their follies.

Œconomy is no diſgrace; it is better living on a little, than outliving a great deal.

Next to the ſatisfaction I receive in the proſperity of an honeſt man, I am beſt pleaſed with the confuſion of a raſcal.

What is often termed ſhyneſs, is nothing more than refined ſenſe, and an indifference to common obſervations.

The higher character a perſon ſupports, the more he ſhould regard his minuteſt actions.

Every perſon inſenſibly fixes upon ſome degree of refinement in his diſcourſe, ſome meaſure of thought which he thinks worth exhibiting. It is wiſe to fix this pretty high, although it occaſions one to talk the leſs.

To endeavour all one's days to fortify our minds with learning and philoſophy, is to ſpend ſo much in armour, that one has nothing left to defend.

Deference often ſhrinks and withers as much upon the approach of intimacy, as the ſenſitive plant does upon the touch of one's finger.

Men are ſometimes accuſed of pride, merely becauſe their accuſers would be proud themſelves if they were in their places.

People frequently uſe this expreſſion, I am inclined to think ſo and ſo, not conſidering that they are then ſpeaking the moſt literal of all truths.

Modeſty makes large amends for the pain it

it gives the persons who labour under it, by the prejudice it affords every worthy person in their favour.

The difference there is betwixt honour and honesty seems to be chiefly in the motive. The honest man does that from duty, which the man of honour does for the sake of character.

A liar begins with making falsehood appear like truth, and ends with making truth itself appear like falsehood.

Virtue should be considered as a part of taste; and we should as much avoid deceit, or sinister meanings in discourse, as we would puns, bad language, or false grammar.

Deference is the most complicate, the most indirect, and the most elegant of all compliments.

He that lies in bed all a summer's morning, loses the chief pleasure of the day: he that gives up his youth to indolence, undergoes a loss of the same kind.

Shining characters are not always the most agreeable ones; the mild radiance of an emerald is by no means less pleasing than the glare of the ruby.

To be at once a rake, and to glory in the character, discovers at the same time a bad disposition and a bad taste.

How is it possible to expect that mankind will take advice, when they will not so much as take warning?

Although men are accused for not knowing their own weakness, yet perhaps as few know their own strength. It is in men as in soils, where sometimes there is a vein of gold which the owner knows not of.

Fine sense, and exalted sense, are not half so valuable as common sense. There are forty men of wit for one man of sense; and he that will carry nothing about him but gold, will be every day at a loss for want of ready change.

Learning is like mercury, one of the most powerful and excellent things in the world in skilful hands; in unskilful, most mischievous.

A man should never be ashamed to own he has been in the wrong; which is but saying in other words, that he is wiser to-day than he was yesterday.

Wherever I find a great deal of gratitude in a poor man, I take it for granted there would be as much generosity if he were a rich man.

Flowers of rhetoric in sermons or serious discourses, are like the blue and red flowers in corn, pleasing to those who come only for amusement, but prejudicial to him who would reap the profit.

It often happens that those are the best people, whose characters have been most injured by slanderers: as we usually find that to be the sweetest fruit which the birds have been pecking at.

The eye of a critic is often like a microscope, made so very fine and nice, that it discovers the atoms, grains, and minutest articles, without ever comprehending the whole, comparing the parts, or seeing all at once the harmony.

Men's zeal for religion is much of the same kind as that which they shew for a foot-ball; whenever it is contested for, every one is ready to venture their lives and limbs in the dispute; but when that is once at an end, it is no more thought on, but sleeps in oblivion, buried in rubbish, which no one thinks it worth his pains to rake into, much less to remove.

Honour is but a fictious kind of honesty; a mean but a necessary substitute for it, in societies who have none; it is a sort of paper-credit, with which men are obliged to trade who are deficient in the sterling cash of true morality and religion.

Persons of great delicacy should know the certainty of the following truth——There are abundance of cases which occasion suspence, in which, whatever they determine, they will repent of their determination; and this through a propensity of human nature to fancy happiness in those schemes which it does not pursue.

The chief advantage that ancient writers can boast over modern ones, seems owing to simplicity. Every noble truth and sentiment was expressed by the former in a natural manner, in word and phrase simple, perspicuous, and incapable of improvement. What then remained for later writers, but affectation, witticism, and conceit?

What a piece of work is man! how noble in reason! how infinite in faculties! in form and moving, how express and admirable! in action, how like an angel! in apprehension, how like a God!

If to do were as easy as to know what were good to do, chapels had been churches, and poor men's cottages princes palaces. He is a good divine that follows his own instructions: I can easier teach twenty what were good to be done, than to be one of the twenty to follow my own teaching.

Men's evil manners live in brass; their virtues we write in water.

The web of our life is of a mingled yarn, good and ill together; our virtues would be proud, if our faults whipped them not; and our crimes would despair, if they were not cherished by our virtues.

The sense of death is most in apprehension;
and the poor beetle that we tread upon,

In corporal sufferance feels a pang as great,
As when a giant dies.

---

§ 54. PROVERBS.

As PROVERBS *are allowed to contain a great deal of Wisdom forcibly expressed, it has been judged proper to add a Collection of English, Italian, and Spanish Proverbs. They will tend to exercise the powers of Judgment and Reflection. They may also furnish Subjects for Themes, Letters, &c. at Schools. They are so easily retained in the memory that they may often occur in an emergency, and serve a young man more effectually than more formal and elegant sentences.*

Old English Proverbs.

In every work begin and end with God.

The grace of God is worth a fair.

He is a fool who cannot be angry; but he is a wise man who will not.

So much of passion, so much of nothing to the purpose.

'Tis wit to pick a lock, and steal a horse; but 'tis wisdom to let him alone.

Sorrow is good for nothing but for sin.

Love thy neighbour; yet pull not down thy hedge.

Half an acre is good land.

Chear up, man, God is still where he was.

Of little meddling comes great ease.

Do well, and have well.

He who perishes in a needless danger is the devil's martyr.

Better

Better ſpare at the brim, than at the bottom.

He who ſerves God is the true wiſe man.

The haſty man never wants woe.

There is God in the almonry.

He who will thrive muſt riſe at five.

He who hath thriven may ſleep till ſeven.

Prayer brings down the firſt bleſſing, and praiſe the ſecond.

He plays beſt who wins.

He is a proper man who hath proper conditions.

Better half a loaf than no bread.

Beware of *Had-I-wiſt*.

Froſt and fraud have always foul ends.

Good words coſt nought.

A good word is as ſoon ſaid as a bad one.

Little ſaid ſoon amended.

Fair words butter no parſnips.

That penny is well ſpent that ſaves a groat to its maſter.

Penny in pocket is a good companion.

For all your kindred make much of your friends.

He who hath money in his purſe, cannot want an head for his ſhoulders.

Great cry and little wool, quoth the devil when he ſhear'd his hogs.

'Tis ill gaping before an oven.

Where the hedge is loweſt all men go over.

When ſorrow is aſleep wake it not.

Up ſtarts a churl that gathered good,
From whence did ſpring his noble blood.

Provide for the worſt, the beſt will ſave itſelf.

A covetous man, like a dog in a wheel, roaſts meat for others to eat.

Speak me fair, and think what you will.

Serve God in thy calling; 'tis better than always praying.

A child may have too much of his mother's bleſſing.

He who gives alms makes the very beſt uſe of his money.

A wiſe man will neither ſpeak, nor do,
Whatever anger would provoke him to.

Heaven once named, all other things are trifles.

The patient man is always at home.

Peace with heaven is the beſt friendſhip.

The worſt of croſſes is never to have had any.

Croſſes are ladders that do lead up to heaven.

Honour buys no beef in the market.

Care-not would have.

When it rains pottage you muſt hold up your diſh.

He that would thrive muſt aſk leave of his wife.

A wonder laſts but nine days.

The ſecond meal makes the glutton: and
The ſecond blow, or ſecond ill word, makes the quarrel.

A young ſerving man an old beggar.

A pennyworth of eaſe is worth a penny at all times.

As proud comes behind as goes before.

Bachelor's wives and maid's children are well taught.

Beware of the geeſe when the fox preaches.

Rich men ſeem happy, great, and wiſe,
All which the good man only is.

Look not on pleaſures as they come, but go.

Love me little, and love me long.

He that buys an houſe ready wrought,
Hath many a pin and nail for nought.

Fools build houſes, and wiſe men buy them, or live in them.

Opportunity makes the thief.

Out of debt, out of deadly ſin.

Pride goes before, and ſhame follows after.

That groat is ill ſaved that ſhames its maſter.

Quick believers need broad ſhoulders.

Three may keep counſel, if two be away.

He who weddeth ere he be wiſe, ſhall die ere he thrives.

He who moſt ſtudies his content, wants it moſt.

God hath often a great ſhare in a little houſe, and but a little ſhare in a great one.

When prayers are done my lady is ready.

He that is warm thinks all are ſo.

If every man will mend one, we ſhall all be mended.

Marry your ſon when you will, your daughter when you can.

None is a fool always, every one ſometimes.

Think of eaſe, but work on.

He that lies long in bed his eſtate feels it.

The child ſaith nothing but what it heard by the fire-ſide.

A gentleman, a grey-hound, and a ſalt-box, look for at the fire-ſide.

The ſon full and tattered, the daughter empty and fine..

He who riſeth betimes hath ſomething in his head.

Fine dreſſing is a foul houſe ſwept before the doors.

Diſcontent is a man's worſt evil.

He who lives well ſees afar off.

Love is not to be found in the market.

My houſe, my houſe, though thou art ſmall,
Thou art to me the Eſcurial.

He who ſeeks trouble never miſſeth it.

Never was ſtrumpet fair in a wiſe man's eye.

He that hath little is the leſs dirty.

Good counſel breaks no man's head.

Fly the pleaſure that will bite to-morrow.

Woe be to the houſe where there is no chiding.

The greateſt ſtep is that out of doors.

Poverty is the mother of health.

Wealth, like rheum, falls on the weakeſt parts.

If all fools wore white caps, we ſhould look like a flock of geeſe.

Living well is the beſt revenge we can take on our enemies.

Fair words make me look to my purſe.

The ſhorteſt anſwer is doing the thing.

He who would have what he hath not, ſhould do what he doth not.

He who hath horns in his boſom, needs not put them upon his head.

Good and quickly ſeldom meet.

God is at the end when we think he is fartheſt off.

He who contemplates hath a day without night.

Time is the rider that breaks youth.

Better ſuffer a great evil than do a little one.

Talk much, and err much.

The perſuaſion of the fortunate ſways the doubtful.

True praiſe takes root, and ſpreads.

Happy is the body which is bleſt with a mind not needing.

Fooliſh tongues talk by the dozen.

Shew a good man his error, and he turns it into a virtue; a bad man doubles his fault.

When either ſide grows warm in arguing, the wiſeſt man gives over firſt.

Wiſe men with pity do behold
Fools worſhip mules that carry gold.

In the huſband wiſdom, in the wife gentleneſs.

A wiſe

A wiſe man cares not much for what he cannot have.

Pardon others but not thyſelf.

If a good man thrives, all thrive with him.

Old praiſe dies unleſs you feed it.

That which two will takes effect.

He only is bright who ſhines by himſelf.

Proſperity lets go the bridle.

Take care to be what thou would'ſt ſeem.

Great buſineſſes turn on a little pin.

He that will not have peace, God gives him war.

None is ſo wiſe but the fool overtakes him.

That is the beſt gown that goes moſt up and down the houſe.

Silks and ſattins put out the fire in the kitchen.

The firſt diſh pleaſeth all.

God's mill grinds ſlow, but ſure.

Neither praiſe nor diſpraiſe thyſelf, thy actions ſerve the turn.

He who fears death lives not.

He who preaches gives alms.

He who pitieth another thinks on himſelf.

Night is the mother of counſels.

He who once hits will be ever ſhooting.

He that cockers his child provides for his enemy.

The faulty ſtands always on his guard.

He that is thrown would ever wreſtle.

Good ſwimmers are drowned at laſt.

Courteſy on one ſide only laſts not long.

Wine counſels ſeldom proſper.

Set good againſt evil.

He goes not out of his way who goes to a good inn.

It is an ill air where we gain nothing.

Every one hath a fool in his ſleeve.

Too much taking heed is ſometimes loſs.

'Tis eaſier to build two chimneys than to maintain one.

He hath no leiſure who uſeth it not.

The wife is the key of the houſe.

The life of man is a winter way.

The leaſt fooliſh is accounted wiſe.

Life is half ſpent before we know what it is to live.

Wine is a turn-coat; firſt a friend, then an enemy.

Wine ever pays for his lodging.

Time undermines us all.

Converſation makes a man what he is.

The dainties of the great are the tears of the poor.

The great put the little on the hook.

Lawyers houſes are built on the heads of fools.

Among good men two ſuffice.

The beſt bred have the beſt portion.

To live peaceably with all breeds good blood.

He who hath the charge of ſouls tranſports them not in bundles.

Pains to get, care to keep, fear to loſe.

When a lackey comes to hell, the devil locks the gates.

He that tells his wife news is but newly married.

He who will make a door of gold, muſt knock in a nail every day.

If the brain ſows not corn, it plants thiſtles.

A woman conceals what ſhe knows not.

Some evils are cured by contempt.

God deals his wrath by weight, but without weight his mercy.

Follow not truth too near at the heels, leſt it daſh out your teeth.

Say to pleaſure, gentle Eve, I will have none of your apple.

Marry your daughters betimes, leſt they marry themſelves.

Every man's cenſure is uſually firſt moulded in his own nature.

Suſpicion is the virtue of a coward.

Stay a while, that we may make an end the ſooner.

Let us ride fair and ſoftly that we may get home the ſooner.

Debtors are liars.

Knowledge (or cunning) is no burthen.

Dearths foreſeen come not.

A penny ſpared is twice got.

Penſion never enriched young man.

If things were to be done twice, all would be wiſe.

If the mother had never been in the oven, ſhe would not have looked for her daughter there.

The body is ſooner well dreſſed than the ſoul.

Every one is a maſter, and a ſervant.

No profit to honour, no honour to virtue or religion.

Every ſin brings its puniſhment along with it.

The devil divides the world between atheiſm and ſuperſtition.

Good huſbandry is good divinity.

Be reaſonable and you will be happy.

It is better to pleaſe a fool than to anger him.

A fool, if he ſaith he will have a crab, he will not have an apple.

Take heed you find not what you do not ſeek.

The highway is never about.

He lives long enough who hath lived well.

Mettle is dangerous in a blind horſe.

Winter never rots in the ſky.

God help the rich, the poor can beg.

He that ſpeaks me fair, and loves me not,
I will ſpeak him fair, and truſt him not.

He who preaches war is the devil's chaplain.

The trueſt wealth is contentment with a little.

A man's beſt fortune, or his worſt, is a wife.

Marry in haſte, and repent at leiſure.

Sir John Barley-Corn is the ſtrongeſt knight.

Like blood, like good, and like age,
Make the happieſt marriage.

Every aſs thinks himſelf worthy to ſtand with the king's horſes.

A good beginning makes a good ending.

One ounce of diſcretion, or of wiſdom, is worth two pound of wit.

The devil is good, or kind, when he is pleaſed.

A fair face is half a portion.

To forget a wrong is the beſt revenge.

Manners make the man.

Man doth what he can, God doth what he pleaſes.

Gold goes in at any gate except that of heaven.

Knaves and fools divide the world.

No great loſs but may bring ſome little profit.

When poverty comes in at the door, love leaps out at the window.

That ſuit is beſt that beſt fits me.

If I had revenged every wrong,
I had not worn my ſkirts ſo long.

Self-love is a mote in every man's eye.

That which is well done is twice done.

Uſe ſoft words and hard arguments.

There is no coward to an ill conſcience.

He who makes other men afraid of his wit, had need be afraid of their memories.

Riches are but the baggage of virtue.

He who defers his charities till his death, is

is rather liberal of another man's than of his own.

A wiſe man hath more ballaſt than ſail.

Great men's promiſes, courtier's oaths, and dead men's ſhoes, a man may look for, but not truſt to.

Be wiſe on this ſide heaven.

The devil tempts others, an idle man tempts the devil.

Good looks buy nothing in the market.

He who will be his own maſter often hath a fool for his ſcholar.

That man is well bought who coſts you but a compliment.

The greateſt king muſt at laſt go to bed with a ſhovel or ſpade.

He only truly lives who lives in peace.

If wiſe men never erred, it would go hard with the fool.

Great virtue ſeldom deſcends.

One wiſe (in marriage) and two happy.

Almſgiving never made any man poor, nor robbery rich, nor proſperity wiſe.

A fool and his money are ſoon parted.

Fear of hell is the true valour of a chriſtian.

For ill do well, then fear not hell.

The beſt thing in this world is to live above it.

Happy is he who knows his follies in his youth.

A thouſand pounds and a bottle of hay,
Will be all one at Doomſday.

One pair of heels is ſometimes worth two pair of hands.

'Tis good ſleeping in a whole ſkin.

Enough is as good as a feaſt.

A fool's bolt is ſoon ſhot.

All is well that ends well.

Ever drink, ever dry.

He who hath an ill name is half-hanged.

Harm watch, harm catch.

A friend's frown is better than a fool's ſmile.

The eaſieſt work and way is, To beware.

If the beſt man's faults were written in his forehead, it would make him pull his hat over his eyes.

A man may be great by chance; but never wiſe, or good, without taking pains for it.

Succeſs makes a fool ſeem wiſe.

All worldly joys go leſs
To that one joy of doing kindneſſes.

What fools ſay doth not much trouble wiſe men.

Money is a good ſervant, but an ill maſter.

Pleaſure gives law to fools, God to the wiſe.

He lives indeed who lives not to himſelf alone.

Good to begin well, better to end well.

There would be no ill language if it were not ill taken.

Induſtry is fortune's right-hand, and frugality is her left.

We ſhall lie all alike in our graves.

When flatterers meet, the devil goes to dinner.

'Tis a ſmall family that hath neither a thief nor an harlot in it.

To give and to keep there is need of wit.

A man never ſurfeits of too much honeſty.

Honour and eaſe are ſeldom bedfellows.

Thoſe huſbands are in heaven whoſe wives do not chide.

He can want nothing who hath God for his friend.

Young men's knocks old men feel.

He who is poor when he is married, shall be rich when he is buried.

Of all tame beasts, I hate sluts.

Giving much to the poor doth increase a man's store.

That is my good that doth me good.

An idle brain is the devil's shop.

God send us somewhat of our own when rich men go to dinner.

Let your purse still be your master.

Young men think old men fools; but old men know that young men are fools.

Wit once bought is worth twice taught.

A wise head makes a close mouth.

All foolish fancies are bought much too dear.

Women's and children's wishes are the aim and happiness of the more weak men.

Ignorance is better than pride with greater knowledge.

The charitable man gives out at the door, and God puts in at the window.

Every man is a fool where he hath not considered or thought.

He who angers others is not himself at ease.

He dies like a beast who hath done no good while he lived.

Heaven is not to be had by men's barely wishing for it.

Patch and long sit, build and soon flit.

One hour's sleep before midnight is worth two hours sleep after it.

Wranglers never want words.

War is death's feast.

Idle lazy folks have most labour.

Knavery may serve a turn, but honesty is best at the long-run.

A quick landlord makes a careful tenant.

Look ever to the main chance.

Will is the cause of woe.

Welcome is the best chear.

I will keep no more cats than what will catch mice.

Reprove others, but correct thyself.

Once a knave and ever a knave.

Planting of trees is England's old thrift.

It is more painful to do nothing than something.

Any thing for a quiet life.

'Tis great folly to want when we have it, and when we have it not too.

Fly pleasure, and it will follow thee.

God's Providence is the surest and best inheritance.

That is not good language which all understand not.

Much better lose a jest than a friend.

Ill-will never said well.

He that hath some land must have some labour.

Shew me a liar, and I will shew you a thief.

We must wink at small faults.

Use legs and have legs.

Keep your shop, and your shop will keep you.

Every one should sweep before his own door.

Much coin usually much care.

Good take-heed doth always speed.

He who gets doth much, but he who keeps doth more.

A pound of gold is better than an ounce of honour.

We think lawyers to be wise men, and they know us to be fools.

Eaten bread is soon forgotten.

When you see your friend, trust to yourself.

Let my friend tell my tale.

Mention not a rope in the house of one whose father was hanged.

Speak the truth and ſhame the devil.

God help the fool, quoth Pedly. (*An Ideot.*)

Lend, and loſe my money; ſo play fools.

Early to go to bed, and then early to riſe, makes men more holy, more healthy, wealthy, and wiſe.

Anger dies ſoon with a wiſe and good man.

✗ He who will not be counſelled, cannot be helped.

God hath provided no remedy for wilful obſtinacy.

All vice infatuates, and corrupts the judgment.

He who converſes with nobody, knows nothing.

There is no fool to the old fool.

A good wife makes a good huſband.

'Tis much better to be thought a fool, than to be a knave.

One fool makes many.

Penny, whence cameſt thou? Penny, whither goeſt thou? and, Penny, when wilt thou come again?

'Tis worſe to be an ill man than to be thought to be one.

A fool comes alway ſhort of his reckoning.

A young ſaint an old ſaint; and a young devil an old devil.

Wit is folly unleſs a wiſe man hath the keeping of it.

Knowledge of God and of ourſelves is the mother of true devotion, and the perfection of wiſdom.

Afflictions are ſent us from God for our good.

Confeſſion of a fault makes half amends.

Every man can tame a ſhrew but he who hath her.

'Tis better to die poor than to live poor.

Craft brings nothing home at the laſt.

Diſeaſes are the intereſt of pleaſures.

All covet, all loſe.

Plain-dealing is a jewel; but he who uſeth it will die a beggar.

Honour bought is temporal ſimony.

Live, and let live, *i. e.* be a kind landlord.

Children are certain cares, but very uncertain comforts.

Giving begets love, lending uſually leſſens it.

He is the wiſe, who is the honeſt man.

Take part with reaſon againſt thy own will or humour.

Wit is a fine thing in a wiſe man's hand.

Speak not of my debts except you mean to pay them.

Words inſtruct, but examples perſuade effectually.

He who lives in hopes dies a fool.

He who gives wiſely ſells to advantage.

Years know more than books.

Live ſo as you do mean to die.

Go not to hell for company.

All earthly joys are empty bubbles, and do make men boys.

Better unborn than untaught.

If thou do ill, the joy fades, not the pains: if well, the pains do fade, the joy remains.

Always refuſe the advice which paſſion gives.

Nor ſay nor do that thing which anger prompts you to.

Bear and forbear is ſhort and good philoſophy.

Set out wiſely at firſt; cuſtom will make every virtue more eaſy and pleaſant to you than any vice can be.

The beſt and nobleſt conqueſt is that of a man's own reaſon over his paſſions and follies.

Religion hath true lasting joys; weigh all, and so
If any thing have more, or such, let heaven go.
Whatever good thou dost, give God the praise;
Who both the power and will first gave to thee.

§ 55. *Old Italian Proverbs.*

He who serves God hath the best master in the world. Where God is there nothing is wanting. No man is greater in truth than he is in God's esteem. He hath a good judgement who doth not rely on his own. Wealth is not his who gets it, but his who enjoys it. He who converses with nobody, is either a brute or an angel. Go not over the water where you cannot see the bottom. He who lives disorderly one year, doth not enjoy himself for five years after. Friendships are cheap, when they are to be bought with pulling off your hat. Speak well of your friend, of your enemy neither well nor ill. The friendship of a great man is a lion at the next door. The money you refuse will never do you good. A beggar's wallet is a mile to the bottom. I once had, is a poor man. There are a great many asses without long ears. An iron anvil should have a hammer of feathers. He keeps his road well enough who gets rid of bad company. You are in debt, and run in farther; if you are not a liar yet, you will be one. The best throw upon the dice is to throw them away. 'Tis horribly dangerous to sleep near the gates of hell. He who thinks to cheat another, cheats himself most. Giving is going a fishing. Too much prosperity makes most men fools. Dead men open the eyes of the living. No man's head akes while he comforts another. Bold and shameless men are masters of half the world. Every one hath enough to do to govern himself well. He who is an ass, and takes himself to be a stag, when he comes to leap the ditch finds his mistake. Praise doth a wise man good, but a fool harm. No sooner is a law made, but an evasion of it is found out. He who gives fair words, feeds you with an empty spoon. Three things cost dear; the caresses of a dog, the love of a miss, and the invitation of an host, Hunger never fails of a good cook. A man is valued as he makes himself valuable Three littles make a man rich on a sudden; little wit, little shame, and little honesty. He who hath good health is a rich man, and doth not know it. Give a wise man a hint, and he will do the business well enough. A bad agreement is better than a good law-suit. The best watering is that which comes from heaven. When your neighbour's house is on fire carry water to your own. Spare diet and no trouble keep a man in good health. He that will have no trouble in this world must not be born in it. The maid is such as she is bred, and tow as it is spun. He that would believe he hath a great many friends, must try but few of them. Love bemires young men, and drowns the old. Once in every ten years every man needs his neighbour. Aristotle saith, When you can have any good thing take it: and Plato saith, If you do not take it, you are a great coxcomb. From an ass you can get nothing but kicks and stench. Either say nothing of the absent, or speak like a friend. One man forewarned (or apprised of a thing) is worth two. He is truly happy who can make others happy too. A fair woman without virtue is like palled wire. Tell a woman she is wondrous fair, and she will soon turn fool. Paint and

and patches give offence to the husband, hopes to her gallant. He that would be well spoken of himself, must not speak ill of others. He that doth the kindness hath the noblest pleasure of the two. He who doth a kindness to a good man, doth a greater to himself. A man's hat in his hand never did him harm. One cap or hat more or less, and one quire of paper in a year, cost but little, and will make you many friends. He who blames grandees endangers his head, and he who praises them must tell many a lie. A wise man goes not on board without due provision. Keep your mouth shut, and your eyes open. He who will stop every man's mouth must have a great deal of meal. Wise men have their mouth in their heart, fools their heart in their mouth. Shew not to all the bottom either of your purse or of your mind. I heard one say so, is half a lie. Lies have very short legs. One lie draws ten more after it. Keep company with good men, and you'll increase their number. He is a good man who is good for himself, but he is good indeed who is so for others too. When you meet with a virtuous man, draw his picture. He who keeps good men company may very well bear their charges. He begins to grow bad who takes himself to to be a good man. He is far from a good man who strives not to grow better. Keep good men company, and fall not out with the bad. He who throws away his estate with his hands, goes afterwards to pick it up on his feet. 'Tis a bad house that hath not an old man in it. To crow well and scrape ill is the devil's trade. Be ready with your hat, but slow with your purse. A burthen which one chuses is not felt. The dearer such a thing is, the better pennyworth for me. Suppers kill more than the greatest doctor ever cured. All the wit in the world is not in one head. Let us do what we can and ought, and let God do his pleasure. 'Tis better to be condemned by the college of physicians than by one judge. Skill and assurance are an invincible couple. The fool kneels to the distaff. Knowing is worth nothing, unless we do the good we know. A man is half known when you see him, when you hear him speak you know him all out. Write down the advice of him who loves you, tho' you like it not at present. Be slow to give advice, ready to do any service. Both anger and haste hinder good counsel. Give neither counsel nor salt till you are asked for it. The fool never thinks higher than the top of his house. A courtier is a slave in a golden chain. A little kitchen makes a large house. Have money, and you will find kindred enough. He that lends his money hath a double loss. Of money, wit, and virtue, believe one fourth part of what you hear men say. Money is his servant who knows how to use it as he should, his master who doth not. 'Tis better to give one shilling than to lend twenty. Wise distrust is the parent of security. Mercy or goodness alone makes us like to God. So much only is mine, as I either use myself or give for God's sake. He who is about to speak evil of another, let him first well consider himself. Speak not of me unless you know me well; think of yourself ere aught of me you tell. One day of a wise man is worth the whole life of a fool. What you give shines still, what you eat smells ill next day. Asking costs no great matter. A woman that loves to be at the window is like a bunch of grapes in the highway. A woman and a glass are never out of danger. A woman and a cherry are painted for their own harm. The best furniture in the house is a virtuous woman. The first wife is matrimony, the second company, the third heresy. A doctor

 and

and a clown know more than a doctor alone. Hard upon hard never makes a good wall. The example of good men is visible philosophy. One ill example spoils many good laws. Every thing may be, except a ditch without a bank. He who throws a stone against God, it falls upon his own head. He who plays me one trick shall not play me a second. Do what you ought, and let what will come on it. By making a fault you may learn to do better. The first faults are theirs who commit them, all the following are his who doth not punish them. He who would be ill served, let him keep good store of servants. To do good still make no delay; for life and time slide fast away. A little time will serve to do ill. He who would have trouble in this life, let him get either a ship or a wife. He who will take no pains, will never build a house three stories high. The best of the game is, to do one's business and talk little of it. The Italian is wise before he undertakes a thing, the German while he is doing it, and the Frenchman when it is over. In prosperity we need moderation, in adversity patience. Prosperous men sacrifice not, i. e. they forget God. Great prosperity and modesty seldom go together. Women, wine, and horses, are ware men are often deceived in. Give your friend a fig, and your enemy a peach. He who hath no children doth not know what love means. He who spins hath one shirt, he who spins not hath two. He who considers the end, restrains all evil inclinations. He who hath the longest sword is always thought to be in the right. There lies no appeal from the decision of fortune. Lucky men need no counsel. Three things only are well done in haste; flying from the plague, escaping quarrels, and catching fleas. 'Tis better it should be said, Here he ran away, than Here he was slain. The sword from heaven above falls not down in haste. The best thing in gaming is, that it be but little used, Play, women, and wine, make a man laugh till he dies of it. Play or gaming hath the devil at the bottom. The devil goes shares in gaming. He who doth not rise early never does a good day's work. He who hath good health is young, and he is rich who owes nothing. If young men had wit, and old men strength enough, every thing might be well done. He who will have no judge but himself, condemns himself. Learning is folly, unless a good judgment hath the management of it. Every man loves justice at another man's house; nobody cares for it at his own. He who keeps company with great men is the last at the table, and the first at any toil or danger. Every one hath his cricket in his head, and makes it sing as he pleases. In the conclusion, even sorrows with bread are good. When war begins, hell gates are set open. He that hath nothing knows nothing, and he that hath nothing is nobody. He who hath more, hath more care, still desires more, and enjoys less. At a dangerous passage give the precedency. The sickness of the body may prove the health of the soul. Working in your calling is half praying. An ill book is the worst of thieves. The wise hand doth not all which the foolish tongue saith. Let not your tongue say what your head may pay for. The best armour is to keep out of gun-shot. The good woman doth not say, Will you have this? but gives it you. That is a good misfortune which comes alone. He who doth no ill hath nothing to fear. No ill befalls us but what may be for our good. He that would be master of his own must not be bound for another. Eat after your own fashion, clothe yourself as others do. A fat physician, but a lean monk. Make yourself

yourſelf all honey, and the flies will eat you up. Marry a wife, and buy a horſe from your neighbour. He is maſter of the world who deſpiſes it; its ſlave who values it. This world is a cage of fools. He who hath moſt patience beſt enjoys the world. If veal (or mutton) could fly, no wild fowl could come near it. He is unhappy who wiſhes to die; but more ſo he who fears it. The more you think of dying, the better you will live. He who oft thinks on death provides for the next life. Nature, time, and patience, are the three great phyſicians. When the ſhip is ſunk every man knows how ſhe might have been ſaved. Poverty is the worſt guard for chaſtity. Affairs, like ſalt-fiſh, ought to lie a good while a ſoaking. He who knows nothing is confident in every thing. He who lives as he ſhould, has all that he needs. By doing nothing, men learn to do ill. The beſt revenge is to prevent the injury. Keep yourſelf from the occaſion, and God will keep you from the ſins it leads to. One eye of the maſter ſees more than four eyes of his ſervant. He who doth the injury never forgives the injured man. Extravagant offers are a kind of denial. Vice is ſet off with the ſhadow or reſemblance of virtue. The ſhadow of a lord is an hat or cap for a fool. Large trees give more ſhade than fruit. True love and honour go always together. He who would pleaſe every body in all he doth, troubles himſelf, and contents nobody. Happy is the man who doth all the good he talks of. That is beſt or fineſt which is moſt fit or ſeaſonable. He is a good orator who prevails with himſelf. One pair of ears will drain dry an hundred tongues. A great deal of pride obſcures, or blemiſhes, a thouſand good qualities. He who hath gold hath fear, who hath none, hath ſorrow. An Arcadian aſs, who is laden with gold, and eats but ſtraw. The hare catched the lion in a net of gold. Obſtinacy is the worſt, the moſt incurable of all ſins. Lawyers gowns are lined with the wilfulneſs of their clients. Idleneſs is the mother of vice, the ſtep-mother to all virtues. He who is employed is tempted by one devil; he who is idle, by an hundred. An idle man is a bolſter for the devil. Idleneſs buries a man alive. He that makes a good war hath a good peace. He who troubles not himſelf with other men's buſineſs, gets peace and eaſe thereby. Where peace is, there God is or dwells. The world without peace is the ſoldier's pay. Arms carry peace along with them. A little in peace and quiet is my heart's wiſh. He bears with others, and ſaith nothing, who would live in peace. One father is ſufficient to govern an hundred children, and an hundred children are not ſufficient to govern one father. The maſter is the eye of the houſe. The firſt ſervice a bad child doth his father, is to make him a fool; the next is, to make him mad. A rich country and a bad road. A good lawyer is a bad neighbour. He who pays well is maſter of every body's purſe. Another man's bread coſts very dear. Have you bread and wine? ſing and be merry. If there is but little bread, keep it in your hand; if but a little wine, drink often; if but a little bed, go to bed early, and clap yourſelf down in the middle. 'Tis good keeping his cloaths who goes to ſwim. A man's own opinion is never in the wrong. He who ſpeaks little, needs but half ſo much brains as another man. He who knows moſt, commonly ſpeaks leaſt. Few men take his advice who talks a great deal. He that is going to ſpeak ill of another, let him conſider himſelf well, and he will hold his peace. Eating little, and ſpeaking little,

can

can never do a man hurt. A civil anſwer to a rude ſpeech coſts not much, and is worth a great deal. Speaking without thinking is ſhooting without taking aim. He doth not loſe his labour who counts every word he ſpeaks. One mild word quenches more heat than a whole bucket of water. Yes, good words to put off your rotten apples. Give every man good words, but keep your purſe ſtrings cloſe. Fine words will not keep a cat from ſtarving. He that hath no patience, hath nothing at all. No patience, no true wiſdom. Make one bargain with other men, but make four with yourſelf. There is no fool to a learned fool. The firſt degree of folly is to think one's ſelf wiſe; the next to tell others ſo; the third to deſpiſe all counſel. If wiſe men play the fool, they do it with a vengeance. One fool in one houſe is enough in all conſcience. He is not a thorough wiſe man who cannot play the fool on a juſt occaſion. A wiſe man doth that at the firſt which a fool muſt do at the laſt. Men's years and their faults are always more than they are willing to own. Men's ſins and their debts are more than they take them to be. Puniſhment, though lame, overtakes the ſinner at the laſt. He conſiders ill, that conſiders not on both ſides. Think much and often, ſpeak little, and write leſs. Conſider well, Who you are, What you do, Whence you came, and Whither you are to go. Keep your thoughts to yourſelf, let your mien be free and open. Drink wine with pears, and water after figs. When the pear is ripe, it muſt fall of courſe. He that parts with what he ought, loſes nothing by the ſhift. Forgive every man's faults except your own. To forgive injuries is a noble and God-like revenge. 'Tis a mark of great proficiency, to bear eaſily the failings of other men. Fond love of a man's ſelf ſhews that he doth not know himſelf. That which a man likes well is half done. He who is uſed to do kindneſſes, always finds them when he ſtands in need. A wiſe lawyer never goes to law himſelf. A ſluggard takes an hundred ſteps becauſe he would not take one in due time. When you are all agreed upon the time, quoth the curate, I will make it rain. I will do what I can, and a little leſs, that I may hold out the better. Truſt ſome few, but beware of all men. He who knows but little preſently outs with it. He that doth not mind ſmall things will never get a great deal. John Do-little was the ſon of Good-wiſe Spin-little. To know how to be content with a little, is not a morſel for a fool's mouth. That is never to be called little, which a man thinks to be enough. Of two cowards, he hath the better who firſt finds the other out. The worſt pig often gets the beſt pear. The devil turns his back when he finds the door ſhut againſt him. The wiſer man yields to him who is more than his match. He who thinks he can do moſt, is moſt miſtaken. The wiſe diſcourſes of a poor man go for nothing. Poor folks have neither any kindred nor any friends. Good preachers give their hearers fruit, not flowers. Woe to thoſe preachers who liſten not to themſelves. He who quakes for cold, either wants money to buy him cloaths, or wit to put them on. Poverty is a good hated by all men. He that would have a thing done quickly and well, muſt do it himſelf. He who knows moſt is the leaſt preſuming or confident. 'Tis more noble to make yourſelf great, than to be born ſo. The beginning of an amour (or gallantry) is fear, the middle ſin, and the end ſorrow or repentance. The beginning only of a thing is hard, and coſts dear. A fair promiſe catches the fool. He who is bound for another goes

in

in at the wide end of the horn, and muſt come out at the narrow if he can. Promiſing is not with deſign to give, but to pleaſe fools. Give no great credit to a great promiſer. Proſperity is the worſt enemy men uſually have. Proverbs bear age, and he who would do well may view himſelf in them as in a looking-glaſs. A proverb is the child of experience. He that makes no reckoning of a farthing, will not be worth an half-penny. Avoid carefully the firſt ill or miſchief, for that will breed an hundred more. Reaſon governs the wiſe man, and a cudgel the fool. Suffering is the mother of fools, reaſon of wiſe men. If you would be as happy as any king, conſider not the few that are before, but the many that come behind you. Our religion and our language we ſuck in with our milk. Love, knavery, and neceſſity, make men good orators. There is no fence againſt what comes from Heaven. Good huſbandry is the firſt ſtep towards riches. A ſtock once gotten, wealth grows up of its own accord. Wealth hides many a great fault. Good ware was never dear, nor a miſs ever worth the money ſhe coſts. The fool's eſtate is the firſt ſpent. Wealth is his that enjoys it, and the world is his who ſcrambles for it. A father with very great wealth, and a ſon with no virtue at all. Little wealth, and little care and trouble. The Roman conquers by ſitting ſtill at home. Between robbing and reſtoring, men commonly get thirty in the hundred. He is learned enough who knows how to live well. The more a man knows, the leſs credulous he is. There is no harm in deſiring to be thought wiſe by others, but a great deal in a man's thinking himſelf to be ſo. Bare wages never made a ſervant rich. Loſing much breeds bad blood. Health without any money is half ſickneſs. When a man is tumbling down, every ſaint lends a hand. He that unſeaſonably plays the wiſe man is a fool. He that pretends too much to wiſdom is counted a fool. A wiſe man never ſets his heart upon what he cannot have. A lewd batchelor makes a jealous huſband. That crown is well ſpent which ſaves you ten. Love can do much, but ſcorn or diſdain can do more. If you would have a thing kept ſecret, never tell it to any one; and if you would not have a thing known of you, never do it. Whatever you are going to do or ſay, think well firſt what may be the conſequence of it. They are always ſelling wit to others who have leaſt of it for themſelves. He that gains time gains a great point. Every ditch is full of after-wit. A little wit will ſerve a fortunate man. The favour of the court is like fair weather in winter. Neither take for a ſervant him who you muſt entreat, nor a kinſman, nor a friend, if you would have a good one. A man never loſes by doing good offices to others. He that would be well ſerved, muſt know when to change his ſervants. Ignorance and proſperity make men bold and confident. He who employs one ſervant in any buſineſſes, hath him all there; who employs two, hath half a ſervant; who three, hath never a one. Either a civil grant, or a civil denial. When you have any buſineſs with a man give him title enough. The covetous man is the bailiff, not the maſter, of his own eſtate. Trouble not your head about the weather, or the government. Like with like looks well, and laſts long. All worldly joy is but a ſhort-lived dream. That is a curſed pleaſure that makes a man a fool. The ſoldier is well paid for doing miſchief. A ſoldier, fire, and water, ſoon make room for themſelves. A conſidering careful man is half a conjurer. A man would not be alone even

even in paradise. One nap finds out, or draws on another. Have good luck, and you may lie in bed. He that will maintain every thing must have his sword always ready drawn. That house is in an ill case where the distaff commands the sword. One sword keeps another in the scabbard. He that speaks ill of other men, burns his own tongue. He that is most liberal where he should be so, is the best husband. He is gainer enough who gives over a vain hope. A mighty hope is a mighty cheat. Hope is a pleasant kind of deceit. A man cannot leave his experience or wisdom to his heirs. Fools learn to live at their own cost, the wise at other men's. He is master of the whole world who hath no value for it. He who saith Woman, saith Wo to man. One enemy is too much for a man in a great post, and an hundred friends are too few. Let us enjoy the present, we shall have trouble enough hereafter. Men toil and take pains in order to live easily at last. He that takes no care of himself, must not expect it from others. Industry makes a gallant man, and breaks ill fortune. Study, like a staff of cotton, beats without noise. Mother-in-law and daughter-in-law are a tempest and hail-storm. If pride were a deadly disease, how many would be now in their graves! He who cannot hold his peace will never live at ease. A fool will be always talking, right or wrong. In silence there is many a good morsel. Pray hold your peace, or you will make me fall asleep. The table, a secret thief, sends its master to the hospital. Begin your web, and God will supply you with thread. Too much fear is an enemy to good deliberation. As soon as ever God hath a church built for him, the devil gets a tabernacle set up for himself. Time is a file that wears, and makes no noise. Nothing is so hard to bear well as prosperity. Patience, time, and money, set every thing to rights. The true art of making gold is to have a good estate, and to spend but little of it. Abate two thirds of all the reports you hear. A fair face, or a fine head, and very little brains in it. He who lives wickedly lives always in fear. A beautiful face is a pleasing traitor. If three know it, all the world will know it too. Many have too much, but nobody hath enough. An honest man hath half as much more brains as he needs, a knave hath not half enough. A wise man changes his mind when there is reason for it. From hearing, comes wisdom; and from speaking, repentance. Old age is an evil desired by all men, and youth an advantage which no young man understands. He that would have a good revenge, let him leave it to God. Would you be revenged on your enemy? live as you ought, and you have done it to purpose. He that will revenge every affront, either falls from a good post, or never gets up to it. Truth is an inhabitant of heaven. That which seems probable is the greatest enemy to the truth. A thousand probabilities cannot make one truth. 'Tis no great pains to speak the truth. That is most true which we least care to hear. Truth hath the plague in his house (*i. e.* is carefully avoided). A wise man will not tell such a truth as every one will take for a lie. Long voyages occasion great lies. The world makes men drunk as much as wine doth. Wine and youth are fire upon fire. Enrich your younger age with virtue's lore. 'Tis virtue's picture which we find in books. Virtue must be our trade and study, not our chance. We shall have a house without a fault in the next world. Tell me what life you lead, and I will tell you how

how you ſhall die. He is in a low form who never thinks beyond this ſhort life. Vices are learned without a teacher. Wicked men are dead whilſt they live. He is rich who deſires nothing more. To recover a bad man is a double kindneſs or virtue. Who are you for? I am for him whom I get moſt by. He who eats but of one diſh never wants a phyſician. He hath lived to ill purpoſe who cannot hope to live after his death Live as they did of old; ſpeak as men do now. The mob is a terrible monſter. Hell is very full of good meanings and intentions. He only is well kept whom God keeps. Break the legs of an evil cuſtom. Tyrant cuſtom makes a ſlave of reaſon. Experience is the father, and memory the mother of wiſdom. He who doeth every thing he has a mind to do, doth not what he ſhould do. He who ſays all that he has a mind to ſay, hears what he hath no mind to hear. That city thrives beſt where virtue is moſt eſteemed and rewarded. He cannot go wrong whom virtue guides. The ſword kills many, but wine many more. 'Tis truth which makes the man angry. He who tells all the truth he knows, muſt lie in the ſtreets. Oil and truth will get uppermoſt at the laſt. A probable ſtory is the beſt weapon of calumny. He counts very unſkilfully who leaves God out of his reckoning. Nothing is of any great value but God only. All is good that God ſends us. He that hath children, all his morſels are not his own. Thought is a nimble footman. Many know every thing elſe, but nothing at all of themſelves. We ought not to give the fine flour to the devil, and the bran to God. Six foot of earth make all men of one ſize. He that is born of a hen muſt ſcrape for his living. Afflictions draw men up towards heaven. That which does us good is never too late. Since my houſe muſt be burnt, I will warm myſelf at it. Tell every body your buſineſs, and the devil will do it for you. A man was hanged for ſaying what was true. Do not all that you can do; ſpend not all that you have; believe not all that you hear; and tell not all that you know. A man ſhould learn to ſail with all winds. He is the man indeed who can govern himſelf as he ought. He that would live long, muſt ſometimes change his courſe of life. When children are little they make their parents heads ake; and when they are grown up, they make their hearts ake. To preach well, you muſt firſt practiſe what you teach others. Uſe or practice of a thing is the beſt maſter. A man that hath learning is worth two who have it not. A fool knows his own buſineſs better than a wiſe man doth another's. He who underſtands moſt is other men's maſter. Have a care of—Had I known this before.—— Command your ſervant, and do it yourſelf, and you will have leſs trouble. You may know the maſter by his man. He who ſerves the public hath but a ſcurvy maſter. He that would have good offices done to him, muſt do them to others. 'Tis the only true liberty to ſerve our good God. The common ſoldier's blood makes the general a great man. An huge great houſe is an huge great trouble. Never adviſe a man to go to the wars, nor to marry. Go to the war with as many as you can, and with as few to counſel. 'Tis better keeping out of a quarrel, than to make it up afterward. Great birth is a very poor diſh on the table. Neither buy any thing of, nor ſell to, your friend. Sickneſs or diſeaſes are viſits from God. Sickneſs is a perſonal citation before our Judge. Beauty and folly do not often part company.

Beauty beats a call upon a drum. Teeth placed before the tongue give good advice. A great many pair of shoes are worn out before men do all they say. A great many words will not fill a purse. Make a slow answer to an hasty question. Self-praise is the ground of hatred. Speaking evil of one another is the fifth element men are made up of. When a man speaks you fair, look to your purse. Play not with a man till you hurt him, nor jest till you shame him. Eating more than you should at once, makes you eat less afterward. He makes his grief light who thinks it so. He thinks but ill who doth not think twice of a thing. He who goes about a thing himself, hath a mind to have it done; who sends another, cares not whether it be done or no. There is no discretion in love, nor counsel in anger. Wishes never can fill a sack. The first step a man makes towards being good, is to know he is not so already. He who is bad to his relations is worst to himself. 'Tis good to know our friends failings, but not to publish them. A man may see his own faults in those which others do. 'Tis the virtue of saints to be always going on from one kind and degree of virtue to another. A man may talk like a wise man, and yet act like a fool. Every one thinks he hath more than his share of brains. The first chapter (or point) of fools is to think they are wise men. Discretion, or a true judgment of things, is the parent of all virtue. Chastity is the chief and most charming beauty. Little conscience and great diligence make a rich man. Never count four except you have them in your bag. Open your door to a fair day, but make yourself ready for a foul one. A little too late is too late still. A good man is ever at home wherever he chance to be. Building is a word that men pay dear for. If you would be healthful, clothe yourself warm, and eat sparingly. Rich men are slaves condemned to the mines. Many men's estates come in at the door, and go out at the chimney. Wealth is more dear to men than their blood or life is. Foul dirty water makes the river great. That great saint interest rules the world alone. Their power and their will are the measures princes take of right and wrong. In governing others you must do what you can do, not all you would do. A wise man will stay for a convenient season, and will bend a little, rather than be torn up by the roots. Ever buy your wit at other men's charges. You must let your phlegm subdue your choler, if you would not spoil your business. Take not physic when you are well, lest you die to be better. Do not do evil to get good by it, which never yet happened to any. That pleasure's much too dear which is bought with any pain. To live poor that a man may die rich, is to be the king of fools, or a fool in grain. Good wine makes a bad head, and a long story. Be as easy as you can in this world, provided you take good care to be happy in the next. Live well, and be chearful. A man knows no more to any purpose than he practises. He that doth most at once, doth least. He is a wretch whose hopes are all below. Thank you, good puss, starved my cat. No great good comes without looking after it. Gather the rose, and leave the thorn behind. He who would be rich in one year is hanged at six months end. He who hath a mouth will certainly eat. Go early to the market, and as late as ever you can to a battle. The barber learns to shave at the beards of fools. He who is lucky (or rich) passes for a wise man too. He commands enough who is ruled by a wise man. He who reveals his se-

cret

cret makes himſelf a ſlave. Gaming ſhews what metal a man is made of. How can the cat help it if the maid be a fool? Fools grow up apace without any watering. God ſupplies him with more who lays out his eſtate well. The printing-preſs is the mother of errors. Let me ſee your man dead, and I will tell you how rich he is. Men live one half of the year with art and deceit, and the other half with deceit and art. Do yourſelf a kindneſs, Sir. [The beggar's phraſe for Give alms.] I was well, would be better; took phyſic, and died. [On a monument.] All row galley-wiſe; every man draws towards himſelf. He who hath money and capers is provided for Lent. A proud man hath vexation or fretting enough. He who buys by the penny keeps his own houſe and other men's too. Tell me what company you keep, and I will tell you what you do. At a good pennyworth pauſe awhile. He who doth his own buſineſs doth not foul his fingers. 'Tis good feaſting at other men's houſes. A wiſe man makes a virtue of what he cannot help. Talk but little, and live as you ſhould do.

§ 56. *Old Spaniſh Proverbs.*

He is a rich man who hath God for his friend. He is the beſt ſcholar who hath learned to live well. A handful of mother wit is worth a buſhel of learning. When all men ſay you are an aſs, 'tis time to bray. Change of weather finds diſcourſe for fools. A pound of care will not pay an ounce of debt. The ſorrow men have for others hangs upon one hair. A wiſe man changes his mind, a fool never will. That day on which you marry you either mar or make yourſelf. God comes to ſee, or look upon us, without a bell. You had better leave your enemy ſomething when you die, than live to beg of your friend. That's a wiſe delay which makes the road ſafe. Cure your ſore eyes only with your elbow. Let us thank God, and be content with what we have. The foot of the owner is the beſt manure for his land. He is my friend who grinds at my mill. Enjoy that little you have while the fool is hunting for more. Saying and doing do not dine together. Money cures all diſeaſes. A life ill-ſpent makes a ſad old-age. 'Tis money that makes men lords. We talk, b.* God doth what he pleaſes. May you have good luck, my ſon, and a little wit will ſerve your turn. Gifts break through ſtone walls. Go not to your doctor for every ail, nor to your lawyer for every quarrel, nor to your pitcher for every thirſt. There is no better looking-glaſs than an old true friend. A wall between both beſt preſerves friendſhip. The ſum of all is, to ſerve God well, and to do no ill thing. The creditor always hath a better memory than the debtor. Setting down in writing is a laſting memory. Repentance always coſts very dear. Good-breeding and money make our ſons gentlemen. As you uſe your father, ſo your children will uſe you. There is no evil, but ſome good uſe may be made of it. No price is great enough for good counſel. Examine not the pedigree nor patrimony of a good man. There is no ill thing in Spain but that which can ſpeak. Praiſe the man whoſe bread you eat. God keep me from him whom I truſt, from him whom I truſt not I ſhall keep myſelf. Keep out of an haſty man's way for a while, out of a ſullen man's all days of your life. If you love me, John, your deeds will tell me ſo. I defy all fetters, though they were made of gold. Few die of hunger, an hundred thouſand of ſurfeits. Govern yourſelf by reaſon, though ſome like it, it, others do not. If you would know the worth of a ducat, go and borrow one. No companion like money. A good wife is the workmanſhip of a good huſband. The fool fell in love with the lady's laced apron. The friar who aſks for God's ſake, aſks for himſelf too. God keeps him who takes what care he can of himſelf. Nothing is valuable in this world, except as it tends to the next. Smoke, raining into the houſe, and a talking wife, make a man run out of doors. There is no to-morrow for an aſking friend. God keep me from ſtill-water, from that which is rough I will keep myſelf. Take your wife's firſt advice, not her ſecond. Tell not what you know, judge not what you ſee, and you will live in quiet. Hear reaſon, or ſhe will make herſelf be heard. Gifts enter every where without a wimble. A great fortune with a wife is a bed full of brambles. One pin for your purſe, and two for your mouth. There was never but one man who never did a fault. He who promiſes runs into debt. He who holds his peace gathers ſtones. Leave your ſon a good reputation and an employment. Receive your money before you give a receipt for it, and take a receipt before you pay it. God doth the cure, and the phyſician takes the money for it. Thinking is very far from knowing the truth. Fools make great feaſts, and wiſe men eat of them. June, July, Auguſt, and Carthagena, are the four beſt ports of Spain. A gentle calf ſucks her own mother, and four cows more (between two own brothers, two witneſſes, and a notary). The devil brings a modeſt man to the court. He who will have a mule without any fault, muſt keep none. The wolves eat the poor aſs that hath many owners. Viſit your aunt, but not every day in the year. In an hundred years time princes are peaſants, and in an hundred and ten peaſants grow princes. The poor cat is whipped becauſe our dame will not ſpin. Leave your jeſt whilſt you are moſt pleaſed with it. Whither goeſt thou, grief? Where I am uſed to go. Leave a dog and a great talker in the middle of the ſtreet. Never truſt a man whom you have injured. The laws go on the king's errands. Parents love indeed, others only talk of it. Three helping one another will do as much as ſix men ſingle. She ſpins well who breeds her children well. You cannot do better for your daughter than to breed her virtuouſly, nor for your ſon than to fit him for an employment. Lock your door, that ſo you may keep your neighbour honeſt. Civil obliging language coſts but little, and doth a great deal of good. One "Take it" is better than two "Thou ſhalt have it's." Prayers and provender never hindered any man's journey. There is a fig at Rome for him who gives another advice before he aſks it. He who is not more, or better than another, deſerves not more than another. He who hath no wiſdom hath no worth. 'Tis better to be a wiſe than a rich man. Becauſe I would live quietly in the world, I hear, and ſee, and ſay nothing. Meddle not between two brothers. The dead and the abſent have no friends left them. Who is the true gentleman, or nobleman? He whoſe actions make him ſo. Do well to whom you will; do any man harm, and look to yourſelf. Good courage breaks ill luck to pieces. Great poverty is no fault or baſeneſs, but ſome inconvenience. The hard-hearted man gives more than he who has nothing at all. Let us not fall out, to give the devil a dinner. Truths too fine ſpun are ſubtle fooleries. If you would always have money, keep it when you have it. I ſuſpect that ill in others which I know by myſelf.

myſelf. Sly knavery is too hard for honeſt wiſdom. He who reſolves to amend hath God on his ſide. Hell is crowded up with ungrateful wretches. Think of yourſelf, and let me alone. He can never enjoy himſelf one day who fears he may die at night. He who hath done ill once, will do it again. No evil happens to us but what may do us good. If I have broke my leg, who knows but 'tis beſt for me. The more honour we have, the more we thirſt after it. If you would be pope, you muſt think of nothing elſe. Make the night night, and the day day, and you will be merry and wiſe. He who eats moſt eats leaſt. If you would live in health be old betimes. I will go warm, and let fools laugh on. Chuſe your wife on a Saturday, not on a Sunday. Drinking water neither makes a man ſick nor in debt, nor his wife a widow. No pottage is good without bacon, no ſermon without St. Auguſtin. Have many acquaintance, and but a few friends. A wondrous fair woman is not all her huſband's own. He who marries a widow, will have a dead man's head often thrown in his diſh. Away goes the devil when he finds the door ſhut againſt him, 'Tis great courage to ſuffer, and great wiſdom to hear patiently. Doing what I ought ſecures me againſt all cenſures. I wept when I was born, and every day ſhews why. Experience and wiſdom are the two beſt fortune-tellers. The beſt ſoldier comes from the plough. Wine wears no breeches. The hole in the wall invites the thief. A wiſe man doth not hang his wiſdom on a peg. A man's love and his belief are ſeen by what he does. A covetous man makes a halfpenny of a farthing, and a liberal man makes ſix-pence of it. In December keep yourſelf warm and ſleep. He who will revenge every affront, means not to live long. Keep your money, niggard, live miſerably that your heir may ſquander it away. In war, hunting, and love, you have a thouſand ſorrows for every joy or pleaſure. Honour and profit will not keep both in one ſack. The anger of brothers is the anger of devils. A mule and a woman do beſt by fair means. A very great beauty is either a fool or proud. Look upon a picture and a battle at a good diſtance. A great deal is ill waſted, and a little would do as well. An eſtate well got is ſpent, and that which is ill got deſtroys its maſter too. That which is bought cheap is the deareſt. 'Tis more trouble to do ill than to do well. The huſband muſt not ſee, and the wife muſt be blind. While the tall maid is ſtooping the little one hath ſwept the houſe. Neither ſo fair as to kill, nor ſo ugly as to fright a man. May no greater ill befal you than to have many children, and but a little bread for them. Let nothing affright you but ſin. I am no river, but can go back when there is reaſon for it. Do not make me kiſs, and you will not make me ſin. Vain-glory is a flower which never comes to fruit. The abſent are always in the fault. A great good was never got with a little pains. Sloth is the key to let in beggary. I left him I knew, for him who was highly praiſed, and I found reaſon to repent it. Do not ſay I will never drink of this water, however dirty it is. He who trifles away his time, perceives not death which ſtands upon his ſhoulders. He who ſpits againſt heaven, it falls upon his face. He who ſtumbles, and falls not, mends his pace. He who is ſick of folly recovers late or never. He who hath a mouth of his own ſhould not bid another man blow. He who hath no ill fortune is tired out with good. He who depends wholly upon another's providing for him, hath but an ill breakfaſt, and

and a worſe ſupper. A chearful look, and forgiveneſs, is the beſt revenge of an affront. The requeſt of a grandee is a kind of force upon a man. I am always for the ſtrongeſt ſide. If folly were pain, we ſhould have great crying out in every houſe. Serve a great man, and you will know what ſorrow is. Make no abſolute promiſes, for nobody will help you to perform them. Every man is a fool in another man's opinion. Wiſdom comes after a long courſe of years. Good fortune comes to him who takes care to get her. They have a fig at Rome for him who refuſes any thing that is given him. One love drives out another. Kings go as far as they are able, not ſo far as they deſire to go. So play fools—I muſt love you, and you love ſomebody elſe. He who thinks what he is to do, muſt think what he ſhould ſay too. A miſchief may happen which will do me (or make me) good. Threatened men eat bread ſtill, *i. e.* live on. Get but a good name and you may lie in bed. Truth is the child of God. He who hath an ill cauſe, let him ſell it cheap. A wiſe man never ſays, I did not think of that. Reſpect a good man that he may reſpect you, and be civil to an ill man that he may not affront you. A wiſe man only knows when to change his mind. The wiſe's counſel is not worth much, but he who takes it not is a fool. When two friends have a common purſe, one ſings and the other weeps. I loſt my reputation by ſpeaking ill of others, and being worſe ſpoken of. He who loves you will make you weep, and who hates you may make you laugh. Good deeds live and flouriſh when all other things are at an end. At the end of liſe La Gloria is ſung. By yielding you make all your friends; but if you will tell all the truth you know, you will have your head broke. Since you know every thing, and I know nothing, pray tell me what I dreamed this morning. Your looking-glaſs will tell you what none of your friends will. The clown was angry, and he paid dear for it. If you are vexed or angry, you will have two troubles inſtead of one. The laſt year was ever better than the preſent. That wound that was never given is beſt cured of any other. Afflictions teach much, but they are a hard cruel maſter. Improve rather by other men's errors, than find fault with them. Since you can bear with your own, bear with other men's failings too. Men lay out all their underſtanding in ſtudying to know one another, and ſo no man knows himſelf. The applauſe of the mob or multitude is but a poor comfort. Truths and roſes have thorns about them. He loves you better who ſtrives to make you good, than he who ſtrives to pleaſe you. You know not what may happen, is the hope of fools. Sleep makes every man as great and rich as the greateſt. Follow, but do not run after good fortune. Anger is the weakneſs of the underſtanding. Great poſts and offices are like ivy on the wall, which makes it look fine, but ruins it. Make no great haſte to be angry; for if there be occaſion, you will have time enough for it. Riches, which all applaud, the owner feels the weight or care of. A competency leaves you wholly at your diſpoſal. Riches make men worſe in their latter days. He is the only rich man who underſtands the uſe of wealth. He is a great fool who ſquanders rather than doth good with his eſtate. To heap freſh kindneſſes upon ungrateful men, is the wiſeſt, but withal the moſt cruel revenge. The fool's pleaſures coſt him very dear. Contempt of a man is the

the ſharpeſt reproof. Wit without diſcretion is a ſword in the hand of a fool. Other virtues without prudence are a blind beauty. Neither enquire after, nor hear of, nor take notice of the faults of others when you ſee them. Years paſs not over men's heads for nothing. An halter will ſooner come without taking any care about it, than a canonry. If all aſſes wore packſaddles, what a good trade would the packſadlers have. The uſual forms of civility oblige no man. There is no more faithful nor pleaſant friend than a good book. He who loves to employ himſelf well can never want ſomething to do. A thouſand things are well forgot for peace and quietneſs ſake. A wiſe man avoids all occaſions of being angry. A wiſe man aims at nothing which is out of his reach. Neither great poverty nor great riches will hear reaſon. A good man hath ever good luck. No pleaſure is a better penny-worth than that which virtue yields. No old age is agreeable but that of a wiſe man. A man's wiſdom is no where more ſeen than in his marrying himſelf. Folly and anger are but two names for the ſame thing. Fortune knocks once at leaſt at every one's door. The father's virtue is the beſt inheritance a child can have. No ſenſual pleaſure ever laſted ſo much as for a whole hour. Riches and virtue do not often keep one another company. Ruling one's anger well, is not ſo good as preventing it. The moſt uſeful learning in the world is that which teaches us how to die well. The beſt men come worſe out of company than they went into it. The moſt mixed or allayed joy is that men take in their children. Find money and marriage to rid yourſelf of an ill daughter. There is no better advice than to look always at the iſſue of things. Compare your griefs with other men's, and they will ſeem leſs. Owe money to be paid at Eaſter, and Lent will ſeem ſhort to you. He who only returns home, doth not run away. He can do nothing well who is at enmity with his God. Many avoid others becauſe they ſee not and know not themſelves. God is always opening his hand to us. Let us be friends, and put out the devil's eye. 'Tis true there are many very good wives, but they are under ground. Talking very much, and lying, are couſin-germans. With all your learning be ſure to know yourſelf. One error breeds twenty more. I will never jeſt with my eye nor with my religion. Do what you have to do juſt now, and leave it not for to-morrow. Ill tongues ſhould have a pair of ſciſſors. Huge long hair, and very little brains. Speak little, hear much, and you will ſeldom be much out. Give me a virtuous woman, and I will make her a fine woman. He who truſts nobody is never deceived. Drink water like an ox, wine like a king of Spain. I am not ſorry that my ſon loſes his money, but that he will have his revenge, and play on ſtill. My mother bid me be confident, but lay no wagers. A good fire is one half of a man's life. Covetouſneſs breaks the ſack; *i. e.* loſes a great deal. That meat reliſhes beſt which coſts a man nothing. The aſs bears his load, but not an over-load. He who eats his cock alone, muſt catch his horſe ſo too. He who makes more of you than he uſed to do, either would cheat you or needs you. He that would avoid the ſin, muſt avoid the occaſion of it. Keep yourſelf from the anger of a great man, from a tumult of the mob, from fools in a narrow way, from a man that is marked, from a widow that hath been thrice married, from wind that comes in at at a hole, and from a reconciled enemy. One ounce of mirth is worth more than ten thousand weight of melancholy. A contented mind is a great gift of God. He that would cheat the devil must rise early in the morning. Every fool is in love with his own bauble. Every ill man will have an ill time. Keep your sword between you and the strength of a clown. Be ye last to go over a deep river. He who hath a handsome wife, or a castle on the frontier, or a vineyard near the highway, never wants a quarrel. Never deceive your physician, your confessor, nor your lawyer. Make a bridge of silver for a flying enemy. Never trust him whom you have wronged. Seek for good, and be ready for evil. What you can do alone by yourself, expect not from another. Idleness in youth makes way for a painful and miserable old age. He who pretends to be every body's particular friend is nobody's. Consider well before you tie that knot you never can undo. Neither praise nor dispraise any before you know them. A prodigal son succeeds a covetous father. He is fool enough himself who will bray against another ass. Though old and wise, yet still advise. Happy is he that mends of himself, without the help of others. A wise man knows his own ignorance, a fool thinks he knows every thing. What you eat yourself never gains you a friend. Great house-keeping makes but a poor will. Fair words and foul deeds deceive wise men as well as fools. Eating too well at first makes men eat ill afterwards. Let him speak who received, let the giver hold his peace. An house built by a man's father, and a vineyard planted by his grandfather. A dapple-grey horse will die sooner than tire. No woman is ugly when she is dressed. The best remedy against an evil man is to keep at a good distance from him. A man's folly is seen by his singing, his playing, and riding full speed. Buying a thing too dear is no bounty. Buy at a fair, and sell at home. Keep aloof from all quarrels, be neither a witness nor party. God doth us more and more good every hour of our lives. An ill blow, or an ill word, is all you will get from a fool. He who lies long in bed his estate pays for it. Consider well of a business, and dispatch it quickly. He who hath children hath neither kindred nor friends. May I have a dispute with a wise man, if with any. He who hath lost shame is lost to all virtue. Being in love brings no reputation to any man, but vexation to all. Giving to the poor lessens no man's store. He who is idle is always wanting somewhat. Evil comes to us by ells, and goes away by inches. He whose house is tiled with glass must not throw stones at his neighbours. The man is fire, the woman tow, and the devil comes to blow the coals. He who doth not look forward, finds himself behind other men. The love of God prevails for ever, all other things come to nothing. He who is to give an account of himself and others, must know both himself and them. A man's love and his faith appear by his works or deeds. In all contention put a bridle upon your tongue. In a great frost a nail is worth a horse. I went a fool to the court, and came back an ass. Keep money when you are young, that you may have it when you are old. Speak but little, and to the purpose, and you will pass for somebody. If you do evil, expect to suffer evil. Sell cheap, and you will sell as much as four others. An ill child is better sick than well. He who rises early in the morning hath somewhat in his head. The gallows will have its own

own at laſt. A lie hath no legs. Women, wind, and fortune, are ever changing. Fools and wilful men make the lawyers great. Never ſign a writing till you have read it, nor drink water till you have ſeen it. Neither is any barber dumb, nor any ſongſter very wiſe. Neither give to all, nor contend with fools. Do no ill, and fear no harm. He doth ſomething who ſets his houſe on fire; he ſcares away the rats, and warms himſelf. I ſell nothing on truſt till to-morrow. [Written over the ſhop doors.] The common people pardon no fault in any man. The fidler of the ſame town never plays well at their feaſt. Either rich, or hanged in the attempt. The feaſt is over, but here is the fool ſtill. To divide as brothers uſe to do: that which is mine is all my own, that which is yours I go halves in. There will be no money got by loſing your time. He will ſoon be a loſt man himſelf who keeps ſuch men company. By courteſies done to the meaneſt men, you get much more than you can loſe. Trouble not yourſelf about news, it will ſoon grow ſtale and you will have it. That which is well ſaid, is ſaid ſoon enough. When the devil goes to his prayers he means to cheat you. When you meet with a fool, pretend buſineſs to get rid of him. Sell him for an aſs at a fair, who talks much and knows little. He who buys and ſells doth not feel what he ſpends. He who ploughs his land, and breeds cattle, ſpins gold. He who will venture nothing muſt never get on horſeback. He who goes far from home for a wife, either means to cheat, or will be cheated. He who ſows his land, truſts in God. He who leaves the great road for a by-path, thinks to ſave ground, and he loſes it. He who ſerves the public obliges nobody. He who keeps his firſt innocency eſcapes a thouſand ſins. He who abandons his poor kindred, God forſakes him. He who is not handſome at twenty, nor ſtrong at thirty, nor rich at forty, nor wiſe at fifty, will never be handſome, ſtrong, rich, nor wiſe. He who reſolves on the ſudden, repents at leiſure. He who riſes late loſes his prayers, and provides not well for his houſe. He who peeps through a hole may ſee what will vex him. He who amends his faults puts himſelf under God's protection. He who loves well ſees things at a diſtance. He who hath ſervants hath enemies which he cannot well be without. He who pays his debts begins to make a ſtock. He who gives all before he dies will need a great deal of patience. He who ſaid nothing had the better of it, and had what he deſired. He who ſleeps much gets but little learning. He who ſins like a fool, like a fool goes to hell. If you would have your buſineſs well done, do it yourſelf. 'Tis the wiſe man only who is content with what he hath. Delay is odious, but it makes things more ſure. He is always ſafe who knows himſelf well. A good wife by obeying commands in her turn. Not to have a mind to do well, and to put it off at the preſent, are much the ſame. Italy to be born in, France to live in, and Spain to die in. He loſes the good of his afflictions who is not the better for them. 'Tis the moſt dangerous vice which looks like virtue. 'Tis great wiſdom to forget all the injuries we may receive. Proſperity is the thing in the world we ought to truſt the leaſt. Experience without learning does more good than learning without experience. Virtue is the beſt patrimony for children to inherit. 'Tis much more painful to live ill than to live well. An hearty good-will never wants time to ſhew itſelf. To have done well obliges us to do ſo ſtill. He hath a great opinion of himſelf who

R makes

makes no comparison with others. He only is rich enough who hath all that he desires. The best way of instruction is to practise that which we teach others. 'Tis but a little narrow soul which earthly things can please. The reason why parents love the younger children best, is because they have so little hopes that the elder will do well. The dearest child of all is that which is dead. He who is about to marry should consider how it is with his neighbours. There is a much shorter cut from virtue to vice, than from vice to virtue. He is the happy man, not whom other men think, but who thinks himself to be so. Of sinful pleasures repentance only remains. He who hath much wants still more, and then more. The less a man sleeps the more he lives. He can never speak well who knows not when to hold his peace. The truest content is that which no man can deprive you of. The remembrance of wise and good men instructs as well as their presence. 'Tis wisdom in a doubtful case, rather to take another man's judgment than our own. Wealth betrays the best resolved mind into one vice or other. We are usually the best men when we are worst in health. Learning is wealth to the poor, an honour to the rich, and a support and comfort to old age. Learning procures respect to good fortune, and helps out the bad. The master makes the house to be respected, not the house the master. The shortest and sure way to reputation, is to take care to be in truth what we would have others think us to be. A good reputation is a second, or half an estate. He is the better man who comes nearest to the best. A wrong judgment of things is the most mischievous thing in the world. The neglect or contempt of riches makes a man more truly great than the possession of them. That only is true honour which he gives who deserves it himself. Beauty and chastity have always a mortal quarrel between them. Look always upon life, and use it as a thing that is lent you. Civil offers are for all men, and good offers for our friends. Nothing in the world is stronger than a man but his own passions. When a man comes into troubles, money is one of his best friends. He only is the great learned man who knows enough to make him live well. An empty purse and a new house finished make a man wise, but 'tis somewhat too late.

§ 57. *The Way to Wealth, as clearly shewn in the Preface of an old Pennsylvanian Almanack, intitled, "Poor Richard improved." Written by Dr. Benjamin Franklin.*

Courteous Reader,

I have heard, that nothing gives an author so great pleasure, as to find his works, respectfully quoted by others. Judge, then, how much I must have been gratified by an incident I am going to relate to you. I stopped my horse, lately, where a great number of people were collected at an auction of merchants goods. The hour of the sale not being come, they were conversing on the badness of the times; and one of the company called to a plain, clean old man, with white locks, 'Pray, father Abraham, what think you of the times? Will not those heavy taxes quite ruin the country? how shall we be ever able to pay them? What would you advise us to?' ——Father Abraham stood up, and replied, 'If you would have my advice, I will give it you in short; "for a word to the wise is "enough," as poor Richard says.' They joined in desiring him to speak his mind, and gathering round him, he proceeded as follows *:

'Friends,' says he, 'the taxes are, indeed, very heavy; and, if those laid on by the government were the only ones we had to pay, we might more easily discharge them; but we have many others, and much more grievous to some of us. We are taxed twice as much by our idleness, three times as much by our pride, and four times as much by our folly; and from these taxes the commissioners cannot ease or deliver us by allowing an abatement. However, let us hearken to good advice, and something may be done for us; "God helps them that help themseves," as Poor Richard says.

I. 'It would be thought a hard government that should tax its people one-tenth part of their time to be employed in its service: but idleness taxes many of us much more; sloth, by bringing on diseases, absolutely shortens life. "Sloth, like rust, consumes faster than labour wears, while the used key is always bright," as Poor Richard says— "But dost thou love life, then do not squander time, for that is the stuff life is made of," as Poor Richard says.—How much more than is necessary do we spend in sleep! forgetting that "The sleeping fox catches no poultry, and that there will be sleeping enough in the grave," as Poor Richard says.

"If time be of all things the most precious, wasting time must be," as Poor Richard says, "the greatest prodigality;" since, as he elsewhere tells us, "Lost time is never found ag.in; and what we call time enough always proves little enough." Let us then up and be doing, and doing to the purpose: so by diligence shall we do more with less perplexity. "Sloth makes all things difficult, but industry all easy; and he that riseth late, must trot all day, and shall scarce overtake his business at night; while laziness travels so slowly, that poverty soon overtakes him. Drive thy business, let not that drive thee; and early to bed, and early to rise, makes a man healthy, wealthy, and wise," as Poor Richard says.

'So what signifies wishing and hoping for better times? We may make these times better, if we bestir ourselves. "Industry need not wish, and he that lives upon hope will die fasting. There are no gains without pains; then help hands, for I have no lands," or, if I have, they are smartly taxed. "He that hath a trade, hath an estate; and he that hath a calling, hath an office of profit and honour," as Poor Richard says; but then the trade must be worked at, and the calling well followed, or neither the estate nor the office will enable us to pay our taxes—If we are industrious we shall never starve; for, "at the working man's house hunger looks in, but dares not enter." Nor will the bailiff or the constable enter, for "industry pays debts, while despair encreaseth them." What though you have found no treasure, nor has any rich relation left you a legacy, "Di-

* Dr. Franklin, wishing to collect into one piece all the sayings upon the following subjects, which he had dropped in the course of publishing the Almanacks called Poor Richard, introduces father Abraham for this purpose. Hence it is, that Poor Richard is so often quoted, and that, in the present title, he is said to be improved.—Notwithstanding the stroke of humour in the concluding paragraph of this address, Poor Richard (Saunders) and father Abraham have proved, in America, that they are no common preachers.—And shall we, brother Englishmen, refuse good sense and saving knowledge, because it comes from the other side of the water?

gence is the mother of good luck, and God gives all things to induſtry. Then plow deep, while ſluggards ſleep, and you ſhall have corn to ſell and to keep." Work while it is called to-day, for you know not how much you may be hindered to-morrow. "One to-day is worth two to-morrows," as Poor Richard ſays; and farther, "Never leave that till to-morrow, which you can do to-day."—If you were a ſervant, would you not be aſhamed that a good maſter ſhould catch you idle? Are you then your own maſter? be aſhamed to catch yourſelf idle, when there is ſo much to be done for yourſelf, your family, your country, and your king. Handle your tools without mittens: remember, that "The cat in gloves catches no mice," as Poor Richard ſays. It is true, there is much to be done, and, perhaps, you are weak-handed; but ſtick to it ſteadily, and you will ſee great effects; for "Conſtant dropping wears away ſtones: and by diligence and patience the mouſe ate in two the cable; and little ſtrokes fell great oaks."

'Methinks I hear ſome of you ſay, "Muſt a man afford himſelf no leiſure?" I will tell thee, my friend, what Poor Richard ſays; "Employ thy time well, if thou meaneſt to gain leiſure; and, ſince thou art not ſure of a minute, throw not away an hour." Leiſure is time for doing ſomething uſeful; this leiſure the diligent man will obtain, but the lazy man never; for, "A life of leiſure and a life of lazineſs are two things. Many, without labour, would live by their wits only, but they break for want of ſtock;" whereas induſtry gives comfort, and plenty, and reſpect. "Fly pleaſures, and they will follow you. The diligent ſpinner has a large ſhift; and now I have a ſheep and a cow, every body bids me good-morrow."

II. 'But with our induſtry we muſt likewiſe be ſteady, ſettled, and careful, and overſee our own affairs with our own eyes, and not truſt too much to others; for, as Poor Richard ſays,

"I never ſaw an oft-removed tree,
Nor yet an oft-removed family,
That throve ſo well as thoſe that ſettled be."

'And again, "Three removes is as bad as a fire:" and again, "Keep thy ſhop, and thy ſhop will keep thee:" and again, "If you would have your buſineſs done, go; if not, ſend." And again,

"He that by the plough would thrive,
Himſelf muſt either hold or drive."

'And again, "The eye of the maſter will do more work than both his hands:" and again, "Want of care does us more damage than want of knowledge:" and again, "Not to overſee workmen, is to leave them your purſe open." Truſting too much to others care is the ruin of many; for, "In the affairs of this world, men are ſaved, not by faith, but by the want of it:" but a man's own care is profitable; for, "If you would have a faithful ſervant, and one that you like,—ſerve yourſelf. A little neglect may breed great miſchief; for want of a nail the ſhoe was loſt; for want of a ſhoe the horſe was loſt; and for want of a horſe the rider was loſt," being overtaken and ſlain by the enemy; all for want of a little care about a horſeſhoe nail.

III. 'So much for induſtry, my friends, and attention to one's own buſineſs; but to theſe we muſt add frugality, if we would make our induſtry more certainly ſucceſsful. A man may, if he knows not how to ſave as he gets, "keep his noſe all his life to the grindſtone, and die not worth a groat at laſt. A fat kitchen makes a lean will;" and,

" Many eſtates are ſpent in the getting,
Since women for tea forſook ſpinning and knitting,
And men for punch forſook hewing and ſplitting.'

" If you would be wealthy, think of ſaving, as well as of getting. The Indies have not made Spain rich, becauſe her out-goes are greater than her in-comes."

' Away, then, with your expenſive follies, and you will not then have ſo much cauſe to complain of hard times, heavy taxes, and chargeable families; for

" Women, and wine, game and deceit,
Make the wealth ſmall, and the want great."

And farther, " What maintains one vice, would bring up two children." You may think, perhaps, that a little tea, or a little punch now and then, diet a little more coſtly, cloaths a little finer, and a little entertainment now and then, can be no great matter; but remember, " Many a little makes a mickle." Beware of little expences; " A ſmall leak will ſink a great ſhip," as Poor Richard ſays; and again, " Who dainties love, ſhall beggars prove;" and moreover, " Fools make feaſts, and wiſe men eat them." Here you are all got together to this ſale of fineries and nick-nacks. You call them goods: but, if you do not take care, they will prove evils to ſome of you. You expect they will be ſold cheap, and, perhaps, they may for leſs than they coſt; but, if you have no occaſion for them, they muſt be dear to you. Remember what Poor Richard ſays, " Buy what thou haſt no need of, and ere long thou ſhalt ſell thy neceſſaries." And again, " At a great pennyworth pauſe a while:" he means, that perhaps the cheapneſs is apparent only, and not real; or the bargain, by ſtraitening thee in thy buſineſs, may do thee more harm than good. For in another place he ſays; " Many have been ruined by buying good pennyworths." Again, " It is fooliſh to lay out money in a purchaſe of repentance;" and yet this folly is practiſed every day at auctions, for want of minding the Almanack. Many a one, for the ſake of finery on the back, have gone with a hungry belly, and half ſtarved their families; " Silks and ſattins, ſcarlet and velvets, put out the kitchen-fire," as Poor Richard ſays. Theſe are not the neceſſaries of life; they can ſcarcely be called the conveniences: and yet only becauſe they look pretty, how many want to have them?—By theſe, and other extravagancies, the genteel are reduced to poverty, and forced to borrow of thoſe whom they formerly deſpiſed, but who, through induſtry and frugality, have maintained their ſtanding; in which caſe it appears plainly, that " A ploughman on his legs is higher than a gentleman on his knees," as Poor Richard ſays. Perhaps they have had a ſmall eſtate left them, which they knew not the getting of; they think " It is day, and will never be night:" that a little to be ſpent out of ſo much is not worth minding; but " Always taking out of the meal-tub, and never putting in, ſoon comes to the bottom," as Poor Richard ſays; and then. " When the well is dry, they know the worth of water." But this they might have known before, if they had taken his advice. " If you would know the value of money, go and try to borrow ſome; for he that goes a borrowing, goes a ſorrowing," as Poor Richard ſays;

 and,

and, indeed, ſo does he that lends to ſuch people, when he goes to get it in again. Poor Dick farther adviſes, and ſays.

> "Fond pride of dreſs is ſure a very curſe,
> Ere fancy you conſult, conſult your purſe."

And again, "Pride is as loud a beggar as Want, and a great deal more ſaucy." When you have bought one fine thing, you muſt buy ten more, that your appearance may be all of a piece; but Poor Dick ſays, "It is eaſier to ſuppreſs the firſt deſire, than to ſatisfy all that follow it." And it is as truly folly for the poor to ape the rich, as for the frog to ſwell, in order to equal the ox.

> "Veſſels large may venture more,
> But little boats ſhould keep near ſhore."

It is, however, a folly ſoon puniſhed; for, as Poor Richard ſays, "Pride that dines on vanity, ſups on contempt;—Pride breakfaſted with Plenty, dined with Poverty, and ſupped with Infamy." And, after all, of what uſe is this pride of appearance, for which ſo much is riſked, ſo much is ſuffered? It cannot promote health, nor eaſe pain; it makes no increaſe of merit in the perſon, it creates envy, it haſtens misfortune.

'But what madneſs it muſt be to run in debt for theſe ſuperfluities? We are offered, by the terms of this ſale, ſix months credit; and that, perhaps, has induced ſome of us to attend it, becauſe we cannot ſpare the ready money, and hope now to be fine without it. But, ah! think what you do when you run in debt; you give to another power over your liberty. If you cannot pay at the time, you will be aſhamed to ſee your creditor; you will be in fear when you ſpeak to him; you will make poor pitiful ſneaking excuſes, and, by degrees, come to loſe your veracity, and ſink into baſe, downright lying; for, "The ſecond vice is lying, the firſt is running in debt," as Poor Richard ſays; and again, to the ſame purpoſe, "Lying rides upon Debt's back:" whereas a free-born Engliſhman ought not to be aſhamed nor afraid to ſee or ſpeak to any man living. But poverty often deprives a man of all ſpirit and virtue. "It is hard for an empty bag to ſtand upright." —What would you think of that prince, or of that government, who ſhould iſſue an edict forbidding you to dreſs like a gentleman or gentlewoman, on pain of impriſonment or ſervitude? Would you not ſay that you were free, have a right to dreſs as you pleaſe, and that ſuch an edict would be a breach of your privileges, and ſuch a government tyrannical? and yet you are about to put yourſelf under that tyranny, when you run in debt for ſuch dreſs! Your creditor has authority, at his pleaſure, to deprive you of your liberty, by confining you in gaol for life, or by ſelling you for a ſervant, if you ſhould not be able to pay him. When you have got your bargain, you may, perhaps, think little of payment; but, as Poor Richard ſays, "Creditors have better memories than debtors; creditors are a ſuperſtitious ſect, great obſervers of ſet days and times." The day comes round before you are aware, and the demand is made before you are prepared to ſatisfy it; or, if you bear your debt in mind, the term, which at firſt ſeemed ſo long, will, as it leſſens, appear extremely ſhort: Time will ſeem to have added wings to his heels as well as his ſhoulders. "Thoſe have a ſhort Lent, who owe money to be paid at Eaſter." At preſent, perhaps, you may think yourſelves in in thriving circumftances, and that you can bear a little extravagance without injury; but

> For age and want fave while you may,
> No morning-fun lafts a whole day."

Gain may be temporary and uncertain; but ever, while you live, expence is conftant and certain; and "It is eafier to build two chimneys, than to keep one in fuel," as Poor Richard fays: So, "Rather go to bed fupperlefs, than rife in debt.

> Get what you can, and what you get hold,
> 'Tis the ftone that will turn all your lead into gold."

And when you have got the philofopher's ftone, fure you will no longer complain of bad times, or the difficulty of paying taxes.

IV. 'This doctrine, my friends, is reafon and wifdom: but, after all, do not depend too much upon your own induftry, and frugality, and prudence, though excellent things; for they may all be blafted without the blef-fing of Heaven; and therefore afk that blef-fing humbly, and be not uncharitable to thofe that at prefent feem to want it, but comfort and help them. Remember, Job fuffered, and was afterwards profperous.

'And now to conclude, "Experience keeps a dear fchool, but fools will learn in no other," as Poor Richard fays, and fcarce in that; for it is true, "We may give advice, but we cannot give conduct." However, remember this, "They that will not be counfelled cannot be helped," and farther, that "If you will not hear Reafon, fhe will furely rap your knuckles," as Poor Richard fays.'

Thus the old gentleman ended his harangue. The people heard it, and approved the doctrine, and immediately practifed the contrary, juft as if it had been a common fermon; for the auction opened, and they began to buy extravagantly.—I found the good man had thoroughly ftudied my Almanacks, and digefted all I had dropt on thofe topics during the courfe of twenty-five years. The frequent mention he made of me muft have tired any one elfe; but my vanity was wonderfully delighted with it, though I was confcious that not a tenth part of the wifdom was my own, which he afcribed to me; but rather the gleanings that I had made of the fenfe of all ages and nations. However, I refolved to be the better for the echo of it; and though I had at firft determined to buy ftuff for a new coat, I went away, refolved to wear my old one a little longer. Reader, if thou wilt do the fame, thy profit will be as great as mine.—I am, as ever, thine to ferve thee.

RICHARD SAUNDERS.

§ 58. *In Praife of Virtue.*

Virtue is of intrinfic value and good defert, and of indifpenfable obligation; not the creature of will, but neceffary and immutable: not local or temporary, but of equal extent and antiquity with the divine mind; not a mode of fenfation, but everlafting truth; not dependent on power, but the guide of all power. Virtue is the foundation of honour and efteem, and the fource of all beauty, order, and happinefs, in nature. It is what confers value on all the other endowments and qualities of a reafonable being, to which they ought to be abfolutely fubfervient, and without which the more eminent they are, the more hideous deformities and the greater curfes they become. The ufe of it is not confined to any one ftage of of our existence, or to any particular situation we can be in, but reaches through all the periods and circumstances of our beings. Many of the endowments and talents we now possess, and of which we are too apt to be proud, will cease entirely with the present state; but this will be our ornament and dignity in every future state to which we may be removed. Beauty and wit will die, learning will vanish away, and all the arts of life be soon forgot; but virtue will remain for ever. This unites us to the whole rational creation, and fits us for conversing with any order of superior natures, and for a place in any part of God's works. It procures us the approbation and love of all wise and good beings, and renders them our allies and friends. —But what is of unspeakably greater consequence is, that it makes God our friend, assimilates and unites our minds to his, and engages his almighty power in our defence. Superior beings of all ranks are bound by it no less than ourselves. It has the same authority in all worlds that it has in this. The further any being is advanced in excellence and perfection, the greater is his attachment to it, and the more he is under its influence. To say no more, 'tis the law of the whole universe; it stands first in the estimation of the Deity; its original is his nature; and it is the very object that makes him lovely.

Such is the importance of virtue.—Of what consequence, therefore, is it that we practise it!—There is no argument or motive, which is at all fitted to influence a reasonable mind, which does not call us to this. One virtuous disposition of soul is preferable to the greatest natural accomplishments and abilities, and of more value than all the treasures of the world. If you are wise, then, study virtue, and contemn every thing that can come in competition with it. Remember, that nothing else deserves one anxious thought or wish. Remember, that this alone is honour, glory, wealth, and happiness. Secure this, and you secure every thing; lose this, and all is lost. *Price.*

§ 59. *On Cruelty to inferior Animals.*

Man is that link of the chain of universal existence, by which spiritual and corporeal beings are united: as the numbers and variety of the latter his inferiors are almost infinite, so probably are those of the former his superiors; and as we see that the lives and happiness of those below us are dependant on our wills, we may reasonably conclude, that our lives and happiness are equally dependant on the wills of those above us; accountable, like ourselves, for the use of this power, to the Supreme Creator and Governor of all things. Should this analogy be well founded, how criminal will our account appear, when laid before that just and impartial Judge! How will man, that sanguinary tyrant, be able to excuse himself from the charge of those innumerable cruelties inflicted on his unoffending subjects committed to his care, formed for his benefit, and placed under his authority by their common Father? whose mercy is over all his works, and who expects that his authority should be exercised not only with tenderness and mercy, but in conformity to the laws of justice and gratitude.

But to what horrid deviations from these benevolent intentions are we daily witnesses! no small part of mankind derive their chief amusements from the deaths and sufferings of inferior animals; a much greater, consider them only as engines of wood, or iron, useful in in their ſeveral occupations. The carman drives his horſe, and the carpenter his nail, by repeated blows; and ſo long as theſe produce the deſired effect, and they both go, they neither reflect or care whether either of them have any ſenſe of feeling. The butcher knocks down the ſtately ox, with no more compaſſion than the blackſmith hammers a horſeſhoe; and plunges his knife into the throat of the innocent lamb, with as little reluctance as the taylor ſticks his needle into the collar of a coat.

If there are ſome few, who, formed in a ſofter mould, view with pity the ſufferings of theſe defenceleſs creatures, there is ſcarce one who entertains the leaſt idea, that juſtice or gratitude can be due to their merits, or their ſervices. The ſocial and friendly dog is hanged without remorſe, if, by barking in defence of his maſter's perſon and property, he happens unknowingly to diſturb his reſt: the generous horſe, who has carried his ungrateful maſter for many years with eaſe and ſafety, worn out with age and infirmities, contracted in his ſervice, is by him condemned to end his miſerable days in a duſt-cart, where the more he exerts his little remains of ſpirit, the more he is whipped to ſave his ſtupid driver the trouble of whipping ſome other leſs obedient to the laſh. Sometimes, having been taught the practice of many unnatural and uſeleſs feats in a riding-houſe, he is at laſt turned out, and conſigned to the dominion of a hackney-coachman, by whom he is every day corrected for performing thoſe tricks, which he has learned under ſo long and ſevere a diſcipline. The ſluggiſh bear, in contradiction to his nature, is taught to dance, for the diverſion of a malignant mob, by placing red-hot irons under his feet: and the majeſtic bull is tortured by every mode which malice can invent, for no offence, but that he is gentle, and unwilling to aſſail his diabolical tormentors. Theſe, with innumerable other acts of cruelty, injuſtice, and ingratitude, are every day committed, not only with impunity, but without cenſure, and even without obſervation; but we may be aſſured, that they cannot finally paſs away unnoticed and unretaliated.

The laws of ſelf-defence undoubtedly juſtify us in deſtroying thoſe animals who would deſtroy us, who injure our properties, or annoy our perſons; but not even theſe, whenever their ſituation incapacitates them from hurting us. I know of no right which we have to ſhoot a bear on an inacceſſible iſland of ice, or an eagle on the mountain's top; whoſe lives cannot injure us, nor deaths procure us any benefit. We are unable to give life, and therefore ought not wantonly to take it away from the meaneſt inſect, without ſufficient reaſon; they all receive it from the ſame benevolent hand as ourſelves, and have therefore an equal right to enjoy it.

God has been pleaſed to create numberleſs animals intended for our ſuſtenance; and that they are ſo intended, the agreeable flavour of their fleſh to our palates, and the wholeſome nutriment which it adminiſters to our ſtomachs, are ſufficient proofs: theſe, as they are formed for our uſe, propagated by our culture, and fed by our care, we have certainly a right to deprive of life, becauſe it is given and preſerved to them on that condition; but this ſhould always be performed with all the tenderneſs and compaſſion which ſo diſagreeable an office will permit; and no circumſtances ought to be omitted, which can render their executions as quick and eaſy as poſſible. For this, Providence has wiſely and benevolently provided, by forming them in ſuch a manner, that their fleſh becomes rancid and unpalateable by a painful and lingering death; and has thus compelled us to be merciful without compaſſion, and cautious of their ſuffering, for the ſake of ourſelves: but, if there are any whoſe taſtes are ſo vitiated, and whoſe hearts are ſo hardened, as to delight in ſuch inhuman ſacrifices, and to partake of them without remorſe, they ſhould be looked upon as dæmons in human ſhapes, and expect a retaliation of thoſe tortures which they have inflicted on the innocent, for the gratification of their own depraved and unnatural appetites.

So violent are the paſſions of anger and revenge in the human breaſt, that it is not wonderful that men ſhould perſecute their real or imaginary enemies with cruelty and malevolence; but that there ſhould exiſt in nature a being who can receive pleaſure from giving pain, would be totally incredible, if we were not convinced, by melancholy experience, that there are not only many, but that this unaccountable diſpoſition is in ſome manner inherent in the nature of man; for, as he cannot be taught by example, nor led to it by temptation, or prompted to it by intereſt, it muſt be derived from his native conſtitution; and is a remarkable confirmation of what revelation ſo frequently inculcates — that he brings into the world with him an original depravity, the effects of a fallen and degenerate ſtate; in proof of which we need only obſerve, that the nearer he approaches to a ſtate of nature, the more predominant this diſpoſition appears, and the more violent it operates. We ſee children laughing at the miſeries which they inflict on every unfortunate animal which comes within their power; all ſavages are ingenious in contriving, and happy in executing, the moſt exquiſite tortures; and the common people of all countries are delighted with nothing ſo much as bull-baitings, prize-fightings, executions, and all ſpectacles of cruelty and horror. Though civilization may in ſome degree abate this native ferocity, it can never quite extirpate it: the moſt poliſhed are not aſhamed to be pleaſed with ſcenes of little leſs barbarity, and, to the diſgrace of human nature, to dignify them with the name of ſports. They arm cocks with artificial weapons, which nature had kindly denied to their malevolence, and, with ſhouts of applauſe and triumph, ſee them plunge them into each other's hearts: they view with delight the trembling deer and defenceleſs hare, flying for hours in the utmoſt agonies of terror and deſpair, and at laſt, ſinking under fatigue, devoured by their merciless purſuers: they ſee with joy the beautiful pheaſant and harmleſs partridge drop from their flight, weltering in their blood, or perhaps periſhing with wounds and hunger, under the cover of ſome friendly thicket to which they have in vain retreated for ſafety: they triumph over the unſuſpecting fiſh, whom they have decoyed by an inſidious pretence of feeding, and drag him from his native element by a hook fixed to and tearing out his entrails: and, to add to all this, they ſpare neither labour nor expence to preſerve and propagate theſe innocent animals, for no other end but to multiply the objects of their perſecution.

What name ſhould we beſtow on a ſuperior being, whoſe whole endeavours were employed, and whoſe whole pleaſure conſiſted, in terrifying, enſnaring, tormenting, and deſtroying mankind? whoſe ſuperior faculties were exerted in fomenting animoſities amongſt them, in contriving engines of deſtruction, and inciting them to uſe them in maiming

and

and murdering each other? whose power over them was employed in aſſiſting the rapacious, deceiving the ſimple, and oppreſſing the innocent? who, without provocation or advantage, ſhould continue from day to day, void of all pity and remorſe, thus to torment mankind for diverſion, and at the ſame time endeavour with his utmoſt care to preſerve their lives, and to propagate their ſpecies, in order to increaſe the number of victims devoted to his malevolence, and be delighted in proportion to the miſeries he occaſioned? I ſay, what name deteſtable enough could we find for ſuch a being? yet if we impartially conſider the caſe, and our intermediate ſituation, we muſt acknowledge, that, with regard to inferior animals, juſt ſuch a being is a ſportſman. *Jenyns.*

§ 60. *On the Duties of School Boys, from the pious and judicious* ROLLIN.

Quinctilian ſays, that he has included almoſt all the duty of ſcholars in this one piece of advice which he gives them, to love thoſe who teach them, as they love the ſciences which they learn of them; and to look upon them as fathers, from whom they derive not the life of the body, but that inſtruction which is in a manner the life of the ſoul. Indeed this ſentiment of affection and reſpect ſuffices to make them apt to learn during the time of their ſtudies, and full of gratitude all the reſt of their lives. It ſeems to me to include a great part of what is to be expected from them.

Docility, which conſiſts in ſubmitting to directions, in readily receiving the inſtructions of their maſters, and reducing them to practice, is properly the virtue of ſcholars, as that of maſters is to teach well. The one can do nothing without the other; and as it is not ſufficient for a labourer to ſow the ſeed, unleſs the earth, after having opened its boſom to receive it, in a manner hatches, warms, and moiſtens it; ſo likewiſe the whole fruit of inſtruction depends upon a good correſpondence between the maſters and the ſcholars.

Gratitude for thoſe who have laboured in our education, is the character of an honeſt man, and the mark of a good heart. Who is there among us, ſays Cicero, that has been inſtructed with any care, that is not highly delighted with the ſight, or even the bare remembrance of his preceptors, maſters, and the place where he was taught and brought up? Seneca exhorts young men to preſerve always a great reſpect for their maſters, to whoſe care they are indebted for the amendment of their faults, and for having imbibed ſentiments of honour and probity. Their exactneſs and ſeverity diſpleaſe ſometimes at an age when we are not in a condition to judge of the obligations we owe to them; but when years have ripened our underſtanding and judgment, we then diſcern that what made us diſlike them, I mean admonitions, reprimands, and a ſevere exactneſs in reſtraining the paſſions of an imprudent and inconſiderate age, is expreſsly the very thing which ſhould make us eſteem and love them. Thus we ſee that Marcus Aurelius, one of the wiſeſt and moſt illuſtrious emperors that Rome ever had, thanked the gods for two things eſpecially—for his having had excellent tutors himſelf, and that he had found the like for his children.

Quinctilian, after having noted the different characters of the mind in children, draws, in a few words, the image of what he judged to be a perfect ſcholar; and certainly it is a very amiable one: "For my part," ſays he, "I like a child who is encouraged by commen-

 dation,

dation, is animated by a ſenſe of glory, and weeps when he is outdone. A noble emulation will always keep him in exerciſe, a reprimand will touch him to the quick, and honour will ſerve inſtead of a ſpur. We need not fear that ſuch a ſcholar will ever give himſelf up to ſullenneſs." Mihi ille detur puer, quem laus excitet, quem gloria juvet, qui victus fleat. Hic erit alendus ambitu: hunc mordebit objurgatio: hunc honor excitabit: in hoc deſidiam nunquam verebor.

How great a value ſoever Quinctilian ſets upon the talents of the mind, he eſteems thoſe of the heart far beyond them, and looks upon the others as of no value without them. In the ſame chapter from whence I took the preceding words, he declares, he ſhould never have a good opinion of a child, who placed his ſtudy in occaſioning laughter, by mimicking the behaviour, mien, and faults of others; and he preſently gives an admirable reaſon for it: " A child," ſays he, " cannot be truly ingenious, in my opinion, unleſs he be good and virtuous; otherwiſe, I ſhould rather chooſe to have him dull and heavy than of a bad diſpoſition." Non dabit ſpem bonæ indolis, qui hoc imitandi ſtudio petit, ut rideatur. Nam probus quoque imprimis erit ille vere ingenioſus: alioqui non pejus duxerim tardi eſſe ingenii, quam mali.

He diſplays to us all theſe talents in the eldeſt of his two children, whoſe character he draws, and whoſe death he laments in ſo eloquent and pathetic a ſtrain, in the beautiful preface to his ſixth book. I ſhall beg leave to inſert here a ſmall extract of it, which will not be uſeleſs to the boys, as they will find it a model which ſuits well with their age and condition.

After having mentioned his younger ſon, who died at five years old, and deſcribed the graces and beauties of his countenance, the prettineſs of his expreſſions, the vivacity of his underſtanding, which began to ſhine through the veil of childhood; " I had ſtill left me, ſays he, my ſon Quinctilian, in whom I placed all my pleaſure and all my hopes, and comfort enough I might have found in him: for, having now entered into his tenth year, he did not produce only bloſſoms like his younger brother, but fruits already formed, and beyond the power of diſappointment.—I have much experience; but I never ſaw in any child, I do not ſay only ſo many excellent diſpoſitions for the ſciences, nor ſo much taſte, as his maſters know, but ſo much probity, ſweetneſs, good-nature, gentleneſs, and inclination to pleaſe and oblige, as I diſcerned in him.

" Beſides this, he had all the advantages of nature, a charming voice, a pleaſing countenance, and a ſurpriſing facility in pronouncing well the two languages, as if he had been equally born for both of them.

" But all this was no more than hopes. I ſet a greater value upon his admirable virtues, his equality of temper, his reſolution, the courage with which he bore up againſt fear and pain; for, how were his phyſicians aſtoniſhed at his patience under a diſtemper of eight months continuance, when at the point of death he comforted me himſelf, and bade me not to weep for him! and delirious as he ſometimes was at his laſt moments, his tongue ran of nothing elſe but learning and the ſciences: O vain and deceitful hopes!" &c.

Are there many boys amongſt us, of whom we can truly ſay ſo much to their advantage, as Quinctilian ſays here of his ſon? What a ſhame would it be for them, if, born and brought up in a Chriſtian country, they had not even the virtues of Pagan children! I make

make no ſcruple to repeat them here again—docility, obedience, reſpect for their maſters, or rather a degree of affection, and the ſource of an eternal gratitude; zeal for ſtudy, and a wonderful thirſt after the ſciences, joined to an abhorrence of vice and irregularity; an admirable fund of probity, goodneſs, gentleneſs, civility, and liberality; as alſo patience, courage, and greatneſs of ſoul in the courſe of a long ſickneſs. What then was wanting to all theſe virtues?—That which alone could render them truly worthy the name, and muſt be in a manner the ſoul of them, and conſtitute their whole value, the precious gift of faith and piety; the ſaving knowledge of a Mediator; a ſincere deſire of pleaſing God, and referring all our actions to him.

NATURAL HISTORY.

Extracts from Mr. PENNANT'*s British Zoology.*

§ 1. *The* HORSE.

THE breed of horſes in Great Britain is as mixed as that of its inhabitants: the frequent introduction of foreign horſes has given us a variety, that no ſingle country can boaſt of: moſt other kingdoms produce only one kind, while ours, by a judicious mixture of the ſeveral ſpecies, by the happy difference of our ſoils, and by our ſuperior ſkill in management, may triumph over the reſt of Europe, in having brought each quality of this noble animal to the higheſt perfection.

In the annals of Newmarket, may be found inſtances of horſes that have literally out-ſtripped the wind, as the celebrated M. Condamine has lately ſhewn in his remarks on thoſe of Great Britain. Childers is an amazing inſtance of rapidity, his ſpeed having been more than once exerted equal to 82½ feet in a ſecond, or near a mile in a minute: the ſame horſe has alſo run the round courſe at Newmarket (which is about 400 yards leſs than 4 miles) in ſix minutes and forty ſeconds; in which caſe his fleetneſs is to that of the ſwifteſt Barb, as four to three; the former, according to Doctor Maty's computation, covering at every bound a ſpace of ground equal in length to twenty-three feet royal, the latter only that of eighteen feet and a half royal.

Horſes of this kind, derive their origin from Arabia; the ſeat of the pureſt, and moſt generous breed.

The ſpecies uſed in hunting, is a happy combination of the former with others ſuperior in ſtrength, but inferior in point of ſpeed and lineage: an union of both is neceſſary; for the fatigues of the chace muſt be supported by the spirit of the one, as well as by the vigour of the other.

No country can bring a parallel to the strength and size of our horses destined for the draught; or to the activity and strength united, of those that form our cavalry.

In our capital there are instances of single horses that are able to draw on a plain, for a small space, the weight of three tons; but could with ease, and for a continuance draw half that weight. The pack horses of Yorkshire, employed in conveying the manufactures of that county to the most remote parts of the kingdom, usually carry a burden of 420 pounds; and that indifferently over the highest hills of the north, as well as the most level roads; but the most remarkable proof of the strength of our British horses, is to be drawn from that of our mill-horses: some of these will carry at one load thirteen measures, which at a moderate computation of 70 pounds each, will amount to 910; a weight superior to that which the lesser sort of camels will bear: this will appear less surprising, as these horses are by degrees accustomed to the weight; and the distance they travel no greater than to and from the adjacent hamlets.

Our cavalry in the late campaigns (when they had opportunity) shewed over those of our allies, as well as of the French, a great superiority both of strength and activity: the enemy was broken through by the impetuous charge of our squadrons; while the German horses, from their great weight, and inactive make, were unable to second our efforts; though those troops were actuated by the noblest ardour.

The present cavalry of this island only supports its ancient glory; it was eminent in the earliest times: our scythed chariots, and the activity and good discipline of our horses, even struck terror into Cæsar's legions: and the Britains, as soon as they became civilized enough to coin, took care to represent on their money the animal for which they were so celebrated. It is now impossible to trace out this species; for those which exist among the *indigenæ* of Great Britain, such as the little horses of Wales and Cornwall, the hobbies of Ireland, and the shelties of Scotland, though admirably well adapted to the uses of those countries, could never have been equal to the work of war; but probably we had even then a larger and stronger breed in the more fertile and luxuriant parts of the island. Those we employ for that purpose, or for the draught, are an offspring of the German or Flemish breed, meliorated by our soil, and a judicious culture:

The English were ever attentive to an exact culture of these animals; and in very early times set a high value on their breed. The esteem that our horses were held in by foreigners so long ago as the reign of Athelstan, may be collected from a law of that monarch prohibiting their exportation, except they were designed as presents. These must have been the native kind, or the prohibition would have been needless, for our commerce was at that time too limited to receive improvement from any but the German kind, to which country their own breed could be of no value.

But when our intercourse with the other parts of Europe was enlarged, we soon laid hold of the advantage this gave of improving our breed. Roger de Belesme, Earl of Shrewsbury, is the first that is on record: he introduced the Spanish stallions into his estate in Powisland, from which that part of Wales was for many ages celebrated for a swift and generous race of horses. Giraldus Cambrensis, who lived in the reign of Henry II. takes notice

notice of it; and Michael Drayton, cotemporary with Shakespeare, sings their excellence in the sixth part of his Polyolbion. This kind was probably destined to mount our gallant nobility, or courteous knights for feats of chivalry, in the generous contests of the tilt-yard. From these sprung, to speak the language of the times, the Flower of Coursers, whose elegant form added charms to the rider; and whose activity and managed dexterity gained him the palm in that field of gallantry and romantic honour.

Notwithstanding my former supposition, races were known in England in very early times. Fitz-Stephen who wrote in the days of Henry II. mentions the great delight that the citizens of London took in the diversion. But by his words, it appears not to have been designed for the purposes of gaming, but merely to have sprung from a generous emulation of shewing a superior skill in horsemanship.

Races appear to have been in vogue in the reign of Queen Elizabeth, and to have been carried to such excess as to injure the fortunes of the nobility. The famous George Earl of Cumberland is recorded to have wasted more of his estate than any of his ancestors; and chiefly by his extreme love to horse-races, tiltings, and other expensive diversions. It is probable that the parsimonious queen did not approve of it; for races are not among the diversions exhibited at Kennelworth by her favourite Leicester. In the following reign, were places allotted for the sport: Croydon in the South, and Garterly in Yorkshire, were celebrated courses. Camden also says, that in 1607 there were races near York, and the prize was a little golden bell.

Not that we deny this diversion to be known in these kingdoms in earlier times; we only assert a different mode of it, gentlemen being then their own jockies, and riding their own horses. Lord Herbert of Cherbury enumerates it among the sports that gallant philosopher thought unworthy of a man of honour. "The exercise (says he) I do not "approve of, is running of horses, there "being much cheating in that kind; neither "do I see why a brave man should delight in "a creature whose chief use is to help him to "run away."

The increase of our inhabitants, and the extent of our manufactures, together with the former neglect of internal navigation to convey those manufactures, multiplied the number of our horses: an excess of wealth, before unknown in these islands, increased the luxury of carriages, and added to the necessity of an extraordinary culture of these animals: their high reputation abroad, has also made them a branch of commerce, and proved another cause of their vast increase.

As no kingdom can boast of parallel circumstances, so none can vie with us in the number of these noble quadrupeds; it would be extremely difficult to guess at the exact amount of them, or to form a periodical account of their increase: the number seems very fluctuating: William Fitz-Stephen relates, that in the reign of King Stephen, London alone poured out 20,000 horsemen in the wars of those times: yet we find that in the beginning of Queen Elizabeth's reign, the whole kingdom could not supply 2000 horses to form our cavalry; and even in the year 1588, when the nation was in the most imminent danger from the Spanish invasion, all the cavalry which the nation could then furnish amounted only to 3000: to account for this difference we must imagine, that the number of horses which took the field in Stephen's reign was

no

no more than an undisciplined rabble; the few that appeared under the banners of Elizabeth, a corps well formed, and such as might be opposed to so formidable an enemy as was then expected: but such is their present increase, that in the late war, the number employed was 13,575; and such is our improvement in the breed of horses, that most of those which are used in our waggons and carriages of different kinds, might be applied to the same purpose: of those, our capital alone employs near 22,000.

The learned M. de Buffon has almost exhausted the subject of the natural history of the horse, and the other domestic animals; and left very little for after writers to add. We may observe, that this most noble and useful quadruped is endowed with every quality that can make it subservient to the uses of mankind, and those qualities appear in a more exalted, or in a less degree, in proportion to our various necessities.

Undaunted courage, added to a docility half reasoning, is given to some, which fits them for military services. The spirit and emulation so apparent in others, furnish us with that species, which is admirably adapted for the course; or, the more noble and generous pleasure of the chace.

Patience and perseverance appear strongly in that most useful kind destined to bear the burdens we impose on them; or that employed in the slavery of the draught.

Though endowed with vast strength, and great powers, they very rarely exert either to their master's prejudice; but on the contrary, will endure fatigues, even to death, for our benefit. Providence has implanted in them a benevolent disposition, and a fear of the human race, together with a certain consciousness of the services we can render them. Most of the hoofed quadrupeds are domestic, because necessity compels them to seek our protection: wild beasts are provided with feet and claws, adapted to the forming dens and retreats from the inclemency of the weather; but the former, destitute of these advantages, are obliged to run to us for artificial shelter, and harvested provisions: as nature, in these climates, does not throughout the year supply them with necessary food.

But still, many of our tame animals must by accident endure the rigour of the season: to prevent which inconvenience, their feet (for the extremities suffer first by cold) are protected by strong hoofs of a horny substance.

The tail too is guarded with long bushy hair that protects it in both extremes of weather; during the summer it serves, by its pliancy and agility, to brush off the swarms of insects which are perpetually attempting either to sting them, or to deposit their eggs in the *rectum*; the same length of hair contributes to guard them from the cold in winter. But we, by the absurd and cruel custom of docking, a practice peculiar to our country, deprive these animals of both advantages: in the last war our cavalry suffered so much on that account, that we now seem sensible of the error, and if we may judge from some recent orders in respect to that branch of the service, it will for the future be corrected.

Thus is the horse provided against the two greatest evils he is subject to from the seasons: his natural diseases are few; but our ill usage, or neglect, or, which is very frequent, our over care of him, bring on a numerous train, which are often fatal. Among the distempers he is naturally subject to, are the worms, the bots,

bots, and the ſtone: the ſpecies of worms that infeſt him are the *lumbrici*, and *aſcarides*; both theſe reſemble thoſe found in human bodies, only larger: the bots are the *erucæ*, or caterpillars of the *oeſtrus*, or gad-fly: theſe are found both in the *rectum*, and in the ſtomach, and when in the latter bring on convulſions, that often terminate in death.

The ſtone is a diſeaſe the horſe is not frequently ſubject to; yet we have ſeen two examples of it; the one in a horſe near High-wycombe, that voided ſixteen *calculi*, each of an inch and a half diameter; the other was of a ſtone taken out of the bladder of a horſe, and depoſited in the cabinet of the late Dr. Mead; weighing eleven ounces. Theſe ſtones are formed of ſeveral cruſts, each very ſmooth and gloſſy; their form triangular; but their edges rounded, as if by colliſion againſt each other.

The all-wiſe Creator hath finely limited the ſeveral ſervices of domeſtic animals towards the human race; and ordered that the parts of ſuch, which in their lives have been the moſt uſeful, ſhould after death contribute the leaſt to our benefit. The chief uſe that the *exuviæ* of the horſe can be applied to, is for collars, traces, and other parts of the harneſs; and thus, even after death, he preſerves ſome analogy with his former employ. The hair of the mane is of uſe in making wigs; of the tail in making the bottoms of chairs, floor-cloths, and cords; and to the angler in making lines.

§ 2. *The* OX.

The climate of Great Britain is above all others productive of the greateſt variety and abundance of wholeſome vegetables, which, to crown our happineſs, are almoſt equally diffuſed through all its parts: this general fertility is owing to thoſe clouded ſkies, which foreigners miſtakenly urge as a reproach on our country; but let us cheartully endure a temporary gloom, which cloaths not only our meadows but our hills with the richeſt verdure. To this we owe the number, variety, and excellence of our cattle, the richneſs of our dairies, and innumerable other advantages. Cæſar (the earlieſt writer who deſcribes this iſland of Great Britain) ſpeaks of the numbers of our cattle, and adds that we neglected tillage, but lived on milk and fleſh. Strabo takes notice of our plenty of milk, but ſays we were ignorant of the art of making cheeſe. Mela informs us, that the wealth of the Britons conſiſted in cattle: and in his account of Ireland reports that ſuch was the richneſs of the paſtures in that kingdom, that the cattle would even burſt if they were ſuffered to feed in them long at a time.

This preference of paſturage to tillage was delivered down from our Britiſh anceſtors to much later times; and continued equally prevalent during the whole period of our feodal government: the chieftain, whoſe power and ſafety depended on the promptneſs of his vaſſals to execute his commands, found it his intereſt to encourage thoſe employments that favoured that diſpoſition; that vaſſal, who made it his glory to fly at the firſt call to the ſtandard of his chieftain, was ſure to prefer that employ, which might be tranſacted by his family with equal ſucceſs during his abſence. Tillage would require an attendance incompatible with the ſervices he owed the baron, while the former occupation not only gave leiſure for thoſe duties, but furniſhed the hoſpitable board of his lord with ample proviſion, of which the vaſſal was equal partaker. The reliques of the larder of the elder Spencer are evident

evident proofs of the plenty of cattle in his days; for after his winter provisions may have been supposed to have been mostly consumed, there were found, so late as the month of May, in salt, the carcases of not fewer than 80 beeves, 600 bacons, and 600 muttons. The accounts of the several great feasts in after times, afford amazing instances of the quantity of cattle that were consumed in them. This was owing partly to the continued attachment of the people to grazing; partly to the preference that the English at all times gave to animal food. The quantity of cattle that appear from the latest calculation to have been consumed in our metropolis, is a sufficient argument of the vast plenty of these times; particularly when we consider the great advancement of tillage, and the numberless variety of provisions, unknown to past ages; that are now introduced into these kingdoms from all parts of the world.

Our breed of horned cattle has in general been so much improved by a foreign mixture, that it is difficult to point out the original kind of these islands. Those which may be supposed to have been purely British, are far inferior in size to those on the northern part of the European continent: the cattle of the highlands of Scotland are exceeding small, and many of them, males as well as females, are hornless: the Welsh runts are much larger: the black cattle of Cornwall are of the same size with the last. The large species that is now cultivated through most parts of Great Britain are either entirely of foreign extraction, or our own improved by a cross with the foreign kind. The Lincolnshire kind derive their size from the Holstein breed; and the large hornless cattle that are bred in some parts of England come originally from Poland.

About two hundred and fifty years ago there was found in Scotland a wild race of cattle, which were of a pure white colour, and had (if we may credit Boethius) manes like lions. I cannot but give credit t[illegible] tion; having seen in the woods of Dru[illegible] rig in North Britain, and in the park belonging to Chillingham castle in Northumberland, herds of cattle probably derived from the savage breed. They have lost their manes; but retain their colour and fierceness: they were of a middle size; long legg'd; and had black muzzles, and ears: their horns fine, and with a bold and elegant bend. The keeper of those at Chillingham said, that the weight of the ox was 38 stones: of the cow 28: that their hides were more esteemed by the tanners than those of the tame; and they would give six-pence per stone more for them. These cattle were wild as any deer, on being approached would instantly take to flight and gallop away at full speed: never mix with the tame species; nor come near the house unless constrained by hunger in very severe weather. When it is necessary to kill any they are always shot: if the keeper only wounds the beast, he must take care to keep behind some tree, or his life would be in danger from the furious attacks of the animal; which will never desist till a period is put to his life.

Frequent mention is made of our savage cattle by historians. One relates that Robert Bruce was (in chasing these animals) preserved from the rage of a wild Bull by the intrepidity of one of his courtiers, from which he and his lineage acquired the name of Turn-Bull. Fitz-Stephen names these animals *(Uri-Sylvestres)* among those that harboured in the great forest that in his time lay adjacent to London. Another enumerates, among the provisions at the great feast of Nevil archbishop of York, six wild Bulls; and Sibbald assures

aſſures us that in his days a wild and white ſpecies was found in the mountains of Scotland, but agreeing in form with the common ſort. I believe theſe to have been the *Biſontes jubati* of Pliny, found then in Germany, and might have been common to the continent and our iſland: the loſs of their ſavage vigour by confinement might occaſion ſome change in the external appearance, as is frequent with wild animals deprived of liberty; and to that we may aſcribe their loſs of mane. The Urus of the Hercynian foreſt, deſcribed by Cæſar, book VI. was of this kind, the ſame which is called by the modern Germans, *Aurochs*, i. e. *Bos ſylveſtris*.

The ox is the only horned animal in theſe iſlands that will apply his ſtrength to the ſervice of mankind. It is now generally allowed, that in many caſes oxen are more profitable in the draught than horſes; their food, harneſs, and ſhoes being cheaper, and ſhould they be lamed or grow old, an old working beaſt will be as good meat, and fatten as well as a young one.

There is ſcarce any part of this animal without its uſe. The blood, fat, marrow, hide, hair, horns, hoofs, milk, cream, butter, cheeſe, whey, urine, liver, gall, ſpleen, bones, and dung, have each their particular uſe in manufactures, commerce, and medicine.

The ſkin has been of great uſe in all ages. The ancient Britons, before they knew a better method, built their boats with oſiers, and covered them with the hides of bulls, which ſerved for ſhort coaſting voyages.

Primum cana ſalix madefacto vimine parvam
Texitur in Puppim, cæſoque induta juvenco,
Vectoris patiens, tumidum ſuper emicat amnem:
Sic Venetus ſtagnante Pado, fuſoque Britannus
Navigat oceano. LUCAN. lib. iv. 131.

The bending willow into barks they twine;
Then line the work with ſpoils of ſlaughter'd kine.
Such are the floats Venetian fiſhers know,
Where in dull marſhes ſtands the ſettling Po;
On ſuch to neighbouring Gaul, allured by gain,
The bolder Britons croſs the ſwelling main.
ROWE.

Veſſels of this kind are ſtill in uſe on the Iriſh lakes; and on the Dee and Severn: in Ireland they are called *Curach*, in England *Coracles*, from the Britiſh *Cwrwgl*, a word ſignifying a boat of that ſtructure.

At preſent, the hide, when tanned and curried, ſerves for boots, ſhoes, and numberleſs other conveniences of life.

Vellum is made of calves ſkin, and goldbeaters ſkin is made of a thin vellum, or a finer part of the ox's guts. The hair mixed with lime is a neceſſary article in building. Of the horns are made combs, boxes, handles for knives, and drinking veſſels; and when ſoftened by water, obeying the manufacturer's hand, they are formed into pellucid laminæ for the ſides of lanthorns. Theſe laſt conveniences we owe to our great king Alfred, who firſt invented them to preſerve his candle time meaſurers from the wind; or (as other writers will have it) the tapers that were ſet up before the reliques in the miſerable tattered churches of that time.

In medicine, the horns were employed as alexipharmics or antidotes againſt poiſon, the plague, or the ſmall pox; they have been dignified with the title of Engliſh bezoar; and are ſaid to have been found to anſwer the end of the oriental kind; the chips of the hoofs, and paring of the raw hides, ſerve to make carpenters glue.

The bones are uſed by mechanics, where ivory is too expenſive; by which the common people

people are ſerved with many neat conveniences at an eaſy rate. From the tibia and carpus bones is procured an oil much uſed by coach-makers and others in dreſſing and cleaning harneſs, and all trappings belonging to a coach; and the bones calcined afford a fit matter for teſts for the uſe of the refiner in the ſmelting trade.

The blood is uſed as an excellent manure for fruit-trees; and is the baſis of that fine colour, the Pruſſian blue.

The fat, tallow, and ſuet, furniſh us with light; and are alſo uſed to precipitate the ſalt that is drawn from briny ſprings. The gall, liver, ſpleen, and urine, have alſo their place in the *materia medica.*

The uſes of butter, cheeſe, cream, and milk, in domeſtic œconomy; and the excellence of the latter, in furniſhing a palatable nutriment for moſt people, whoſe organs of digeſtion are weakened, are too obvious to be inſiſted on.

§ 3. *The* Sheep.

It does not appear from any of the early writers, that the breed of this animal was cultivated for the ſake of the wool among the Britons; the inhabitants of the inland parts of this iſland either went entirely naked, or were only clothed with ſkins. Thoſe who lived on the ſea-coaſts, and were the moſt civilized, affected the manners of the Gauls, and wore like them a ſort of garments made of coarſe wool, called *Brachæ.* Theſe they probably had from Gaul, there not being the leaſt traces of manufactures among the Britons, in the hiſtories of thoſe times.

On the coins or money of the Britons are ſeen impreſſed the figures of the horſe, the bull, and the hog, the marks of the tributes exacted from them by the conquerors. The Reverend Mr. Pegge was ſo kind as to inform me that he has ſeen on the coins of Cunobelin that of a ſheep. Since that is the caſe, it is probable that our anceſtors were poſſeſſed of the animal, but made no farther uſe of it than to ſtrip off the ſkin and wrap themſelves in it, and with the wool inmoſt obtain a comfortable protection againſt the cold of the winter ſeaſon.

This neglect of manufacture, may be eaſily accounted for, in an uncivilized nation whoſe wants were few, and thoſe eaſily ſatisfied; but what is more ſurpriſing, when after a long period we had cultivated a breed of ſheep, whoſe fleeces were ſuperior to thoſe of other countries, we ſtill neglected to promote a woollen manufacture at home. That valuable branch of buſineſs lay for a conſiderable time in foreign hands; and we were obliged to import the cloth manufactured from our own materials. There ſeems indeed to have been many unavailing efforts made by our monarchs to preſerve both the wool and the manufacture of it among ourſelves: Henry the Second, by a patent granted to the weavers in London, directed that if any cloth was found made of a mixture of Spaniſh wool, it ſhould be burnt by the mayor: yet ſo little did the weaving buſineſs advance, that Edward the Third was obliged to permit the importation of foreign cloth in the beginning of his reign; but ſoon after, by encouraging foreign artificers to ſettle in England, and inſtruct the natives in their trade, the manufacture increaſed ſo greatly as to enable him to prohibit the wear of foreign cloth. Yet, to ſhew the uncommercial genius of the people, the effects of this prohibition were checked by another law, as prejudicial to trade as the former was ſalutary; this was an act of the ſame reign, againſt exporting woollen

len goods manufactured at home, under heavy penalties; while the exportation of wool was not only allowed but encouraged. This oversight was not so soon rectified, for it appears that, on the alliance that Edward the Fourth made with the king of Arragon, he presented the latter with some ewes and rams of the Coteswold kind; which is a proof of their excellency, since they were thought acceptable to a monarch, whose dominions were so noted for the fineness of their fleeces.

In the first year of Richard the Third, and in the two succeeding reigns, our woollen manufactures received some improvements; but the grand rise of all its prosperity is to be dated from the reign of queen Elizabeth, when the tyranny of the duke of Alva in the Netherlands drove numbers of artificers for refuge into this country, who were the founders of that immense manufacture we carry on at present. We have strong inducements to be more particular on the modern state of our woollen manufactures; but we desist, from a fear of digressing too far; our enquiries must be limited to points that have a more immediate reference to the study of Zoology.

No country is better supplied with materials, and those adapted to every species of the clothing business, than Great Britain; and though the sheep of these islands afford fleeces of different degrees of goodness, yet there are not any but what may be used in some branch of it. Herefordshire, Devonshire, and Cotesvold downs are noted for producing sheep with remarkable fine fleeces; the Lincolnshire and Warwickshire kind, which are very large, exceed any for the quantity and goodness of their wool. The former county yields the largest sheep in these islands, where it is no uncommon thing to give fifty guineas for a ram, and a guinea for the admission of a ewe to one of the valuable males; or twenty guineas for the use of it for a certain number of ewes during one season. Suffolk also breeds a very valuable kind. The fleeces of the northern parts of this kingdom are inferior in fineness to those of the south; but still are of great value in different branches of our manufactures. The Yorkshire hills furnish the looms of that county with large quantities of wool; and that which is taken from the neck and shoulders is used (mixed with Spanish wool) in some of their finest cloths.

Wales yields but a coarse wool; yet it is of more extensive use than the finest Segovian fleeces; for rich and poor, age and youth, health and infirmities, all confess the universal benefit of the flannel manufacture.

The sheep of Ireland vary like those of Great Britain. Those of the south and east being large, and their flesh rank. Those of the north, and the mountainous parts, small, and their flesh sweet. The fleeces in the same manner differ in degrees of value.

Scotland breeds a small kind, and their fleeces are coarse. Sibbald (after Boethius) speaks of a breed in the isle of Rona, covered with blue wool; of another kind in the isle of Hirta, larger than the biggest he-goat, with tails hanging almost to the ground, and horns as thick, and longer than those of an ox. He mentions another kind, which is clothed with a mixture of wool and hair; and a fourth species, whose flesh and fleeces are yellow, and their teeth of the colour of gold; but the truth of these relations ought to be enquired into, as no other writer has mentioned them, except the credulous Boethius. Yet the last particular is not to be rejected: for notwith-

standing

ſtanding I cannot inſtance the teeth of ſheep, yet I ſaw in the ſummer of 1772, at Athol houſe, the jaws of an ox, with teeth thickly incruſted with a gold-coloured pyrites; and the ſame might have happened to thoſe of ſheep had they fed in the ſame grounds, which were in the valley beneath the houſe.

Beſides the fleece, there is ſcarce any part of this animal but what is uſeful to mankind. The fleſh is a delicate and wholeſome food. The ſkin dreſſed, forms different parts of our apparel; and is uſed for covers of books. The entrails, properly prepared and twiſted, ſerve for ſtrings for various muſical inſtruments. The bones calcined (like other bones in general) form materials for teſts for the refiner. The milk is thicker than that of cows, and conſequently yields a greater quantity of butter and cheeſe; and in ſome places is ſo rich, that it will not produce the cheeſe without a mixture of water to make it part from the whey. The dung is a remarkably rich manure; inſomuch that the folding of ſheep is become too uſeful a branch of huſbandry for the farmer to neglect. To conclude, whether we conſider the advantages that reſult from this animal to individuals in particular, or to theſe kingdoms in general, we may with Columella conſider this in one one ſenſe, as the firſt of the domeſtic animals. *Poſt majores quadrupedes ovilli pecoris ſecunda*

it will make ſome ſhew of defence, by ſtamping with its feet, and puſhing with its head: it is a gregarious animal, is fond of any jingling noiſe, for which reaſon the leader of the flock has in many places a bell hung round its neck, which the others will conſtantly follow: it is ſubject to many diſeaſes: ſome ariſe from inſects which depoſit their eggs in different parts of the animal; others are cauſed by their being kept in wet paſtures; for as the ſheep requires but little drink, it is naturally fond of a dry ſoil. The dropſy, vertigo (the *pendro* of the Welſh) the phthiſic, jaundice, and worms in the liver, annually make great havock among our flocks: for the firſt diſeaſe the ſhepherd finds a remedy by turning the infected into fields of broom; which plant has been alſo found to be very efficacious in the ſame diſorder among the human ſpecies.

The ſheep is alſo infeſted by different ſorts of inſects: like the horſe it has its peculiar *oeſtrus* or gadfly, which depoſits its eggs above the noſe in the frontal ſinuſes; when thoſe turn into maggots they become exceſſive painful, and cauſe thoſe violent agitations that we ſo often ſee the animal in. The French ſhepherds make a common practice of eaſing the ſheep, by trepanning and taking out the maggot; this practice is ſometimes uſed by the Engliſh ſhepherds, but not always

tural hiſtory, one written expreſsly on the ſpecies of Britiſh dogs: they were wrote for the uſe of his learned friend Geſner; with whom he kept a ſtrict correſpondence; and whoſe death he laments in a very elegant and pathetic manner.

Beſides a brief account of the variety of dogs then exiſting in this country, he has added a ſyſtematic table of them: his method is ſo judicious, that we ſhall make uſe of the ſame; explain it by a brief account of each kind; and point out thoſe that are no longer in uſe among us.

SYNOPSIS OF BRITISH DOGS.

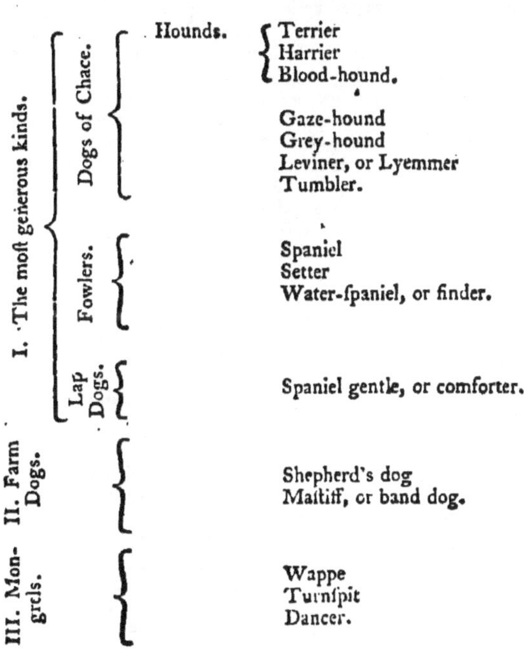

The

The firſt variety is the Terrarius or Terrier, which takes its name from its ſubterraneous employ; being a ſmall kind of hound, uſed to force the fox, or other beaſts of prey, out of their holes; and (in former times) rabbets out of their burrows into nets.

The Leverarius, or Harrier, is a ſpecies well known at preſent; it derives its name from its uſe, that of hunting the hare; but under this head may be placed the fox-hound, which is only a ſtronger and fleeter variety, applied to a different chaſe.

The Sanguinarius, or Bloodhound, or the Sleuthounde of the Scots, was a dog of great uſe, and in high eſteem with our anceſtors: its employ was to recover any game that had eſcaped wounded from the hunter; or been killed and ſtole out of the foreſt. It was remarkable for the acuteneſs of its ſmell, tracing the loſt beaſt by the blood it had ſpilt; from whence the name is derived: This ſpecies could, with the utmoſt certainty, diſcover the thief by following his footſteps, let the diſtance of his flight be ever ſo great; and through the moſt ſecret and thickeſt coverts: nor would it ceaſe its purſuit, till it had taken the felon. They were likewiſe uſed by Wallace and Bruce during the civil wars. The poetical hiſtorians of the two heroes frequently relate very curious paſſages on this ſubject; of the ſervice theſe dogs were of to their maſters, and the eſcapes they had from thoſe of the enemy. The bloodhound was in great requeſt on the confines of England and Scotland; where the borderers were continually preying on the herds and flocks of their neighbours. The true bloodhound was large, ſtrong, muſcular, broad-breaſted, of a ſtern countenance, of a deep tan colour, and generally marked with a black ſpot above each eye.

The next diviſion of this ſpecies of dogs, comprehends thoſe that hunt by the eye; and whoſe ſucceſs depends either upon the quickneſs of their ſight, their ſwiftneſs, or their ſubtilty.

The Agaſæus, or Gazehound, was the firſt: it chaſed indifferently the fox, hare, or buck. It would ſelect from the herd the fatteſt and faireſt deer; purſue it by the eye; and if loſt for a time, recover it again by its ſingular diſtinguiſhing faculty; and ſhould the beaſt rejoin the herd, this dog would fix unerringly on the ſame. This ſpecies is now loſt, or at leaſt unknown to us.

It muſt be obſerved that the Agaſæus of Dr. Caius, is a very different ſpecies from the Agaſſeus of Oppian, for which it might be miſtaken from the ſimilitude of names: this he deſcribes as a ſmall kind of dog, peculiar to Great Britain; and then goes on with theſe words;

Γυρὸν, ἀσαρκότατον, λασιότριχον, ὄμμασι νωθές.

Curvum, macilentum, hiſpidum, oculis pigrum.

what he adds afterwards, ſtill marks the difference more ſtrongly.

Ῥίνεσι δ' αὖτε μάλιστα πανέξοχος ἐστὶν ἀγασσεύς.

Naribus autem longè præſtantiſſimus eſt agaſſeus.

From Oppian's whole deſcription, it is plain he meant our Beagle.

The next kind is the Leporarius, or Grehound. Dr. Caius informs us, that it takes its name *quod præcipui gradus ſit inter canes*, the firſt in rank among dogs: that it was formerly eſteemed ſo, appears from the foreſt laws of king Canute; who enacted, that no one under the degree of a gentleman ſhould preſume to keep a gre-hound; and ſtill more ſtrongly from an old Welſh ſaying; *Wrth ei Walch, ei Farch, a'i Filgi, yr adwaenir Bonheddig:* which ſignifies, that you may know a gentleman by his hawk, his horſe, and his gre-hound.

Froiſſart relates a fact not much to the credit of the fidelity of this ſpecies: when that unhappy prince, Richard the Second, was taken in Flint caſtle, his favourite gre-hound immediately deſerted him, and fawned on his rival Bolingbroke; as if he underſtood and foreſaw the misfortunes of the former.

The variety called the Highland gre-hound, and now become very ſcarce, is of a very great ſize, ſtrong, deep-cheſted, and covered with long and rough hair. This kind was much eſteemed in former days, and uſed in great numbers by the powerful chieftains in their magnificent hunting matches. It had as ſagacious noſtrils as the Blood-hound, and was as fierce. This ſeems to be the kind Boethius ſtyles *genus venaticum cum celerrimum tum audaciſſimum: nec modo in feras, ſed in hoſtes etiam latroneſque; præſertim ſi dominum ductoremve injuriam affici cernat aut in eos concitetur.*

The third ſpecies is the Levinarius or Lorarius; the Leviner or Lyemmer: the firſt name is derived from the lightneſs of the kind, the other from the old word *Lyemme*, a thong; this ſpecies being uſed to be led in a thong, and ſlipped at the game. Our author ſays, that this dog was a kind that hunted both by ſcent and ſight; and in the form of its body obſerved a medium between the hound and the gre-hound. This probably is the kind now known to us by the name of the Iriſh gre-hound, a dog now extremely ſcarce in that kingdom, the late king of Poland having procured from them as many as poſſible. I have ſeen two or three in the whole iſland: they were of the kind called by M. de Buffon *Le grand Danois*, and probably imported there by the Danes, who long poſſeſſed that kingdom. Their uſe ſeems originally to have been for the chaſe of wolves, with which Ireland ſwarmed till the latter end of the laſt century. As ſoon as thoſe animals were extirpated, the numbers of the dogs decreaſed; for from that period they were kept only for ſtate.

The Vertagus, or Tumbler, is a fourth ſpecies; which took its prey by mere ſubtilty, depending neither on the ſagacity of its noſe, nor its ſwiftneſs: if it came into a warren, it neither barked, nor ran on the rabbets; but by a ſeeming neglect of them, or attention to ſomething elſe, deceived the object till it got within reach, ſo as to take it by a ſudden ſpring. This dog was leſs than the hound; more ſcraggy, and had prickt-up ears; and by Dr. Caius's deſcription ſeems to anſwer to the modern lurcher.

The third diviſion of the more generous dogs, comprehends thoſe which were uſed in fowling; firſt the Hiſpaniolus, or ſpaniel: from the name it may be ſuppoſed that we were indebted to Spain for this breed: there were two varieties of this kind, the firſt uſed in hawking, to ſpring the game, which are the ſame with our ſtarters.

The other variety was uſed only for the net, and was called Index, or the ſetter; a kind well known at preſent. This kingdom has long been remarkable for producing dogs of this ſort, particular care having been taken to preſerve the breed in the utmoſt purity. They are ſtill diſtinguſhed by the name of Engliſh ſpaniels; ſo that notwithſtanding the derivation of the name, it is probable they are natives of Great Britain. We may ſtrengthen our ſuſpicion by ſaying that the ſirſt who broke a dog to the net was an Engliſh nobleman of a moſt diſtinguiſhed character, the great Robert Dudley, duke of Northumberland. The Pointer, which is a dog of a foreign extraction, was unknown to our anceſtors.

The Aquaticus, or Fynder, was another ſpecies uſed in fowling; was the ſame as our water ſpaniel; and was uſed to find or recover the game that was ſhot.

The Melitæus, or Fotor; the ſpaniel gentle or comforter of Dr. Caius (the modern lap-dog) was the laſt of this diviſion. The Malteſe little dogs were as much eſteemed by the fine ladies of paſt times, as thoſe of Bologna are among the modern. Old Hollingſhed is ridiculouſly ſevere on the fair of his days, for their exceſſive paſſion for theſe little animals; which is ſufficient to prove it was in his time a novelty.

The ſecond grand diviſion of dogs, comprehends the Ruſtici; or thoſe that were uſed in the country.

The firſt ſpecies is the Paſtoralis, or ſhepherd's dog; which is the ſame that is uſed at preſent, either in guarding our flocks, or in driving herds of cattle. This kind is ſo well trained for thoſe purpoſes, as to attend to every part of the herd be it ever ſo large; confine them to the road, and force in every ſtraggler without doing it the leaſt injury.

The next is the Villaticus, or Catenarius; the maſtiff or band dog; a ſpecies of great ſize and ſtrength, and a very loud barker. Manwood ſays, it derives its name from *maſe theſeſe*, being ſuppoſed to frighten away robbers by its tremendous voice. Caius tells us that three of theſe were reckoned a match for a bear; and four for a lion: but from an experiment made in the tower by James the Firſt, that noble quadruped was found an unequal match to only three. Two of the dogs were diſabled in the combat, but the third forced the lion to ſeek for ſafety by flight. The Engliſh bull-dog ſeems to belong to this ſpecies; and probably is the dog our author mentions under the title of Laniarius. Great Britain was ſo noted for its maſtiffs, that the Roman emperors appointed an officer in this iſland with the title of *Procurator Cynegii*, whoſe ſole buſineſs was to breed, and tranſmit from hence to the amphitheatre, ſuch as would prove equal to the combats of the place,

Magnaque taurorum fracturi colla Britanni.

And Britiſh dogs ſubdue the ſtouteſt bulls.

Gratius ſpeaks in high terms of the excellency of the Britiſh dogs,

Atque ipſos libeat penetrare Britannos?
O quanta eſt merces et quantum impendia ſupra!
Si non ad ſpeciem mentituroſque decores
Protinus: hæc una eſt catulis jactura Britannis.
At magnum cum venit opus, promendaque virtus,
Et vocat extremo præceps diſcrimine Mavors,
Non tunc egregios tantum admirere Moloſſos.

If Britain's diſtant coaſt we dare explore,
How much beyond the coſt the valued ſtore;
If ſhape and beauty not alone we prize,
Which nature to the Britiſh hound denies:
But when the mighty toil the huntſman warms,
And all the ſoul is rous'd by fierce alarms,
When Mars calls furious to th' enſanguin'd field,
Even bold Moloſſians then to theſe muſt yield.

Strabo tells us, that the maſtiffs of Britain were trained for war, and were uſed by the Gauls in their battles: and it is certain a well-trained maſtiff might be of conſiderable uſe in diſtreſſing ſuch half-armed and irregular combatants as the adverſaries of the Gauls ſeem feem generally to have been before the Romans conquered them.

The laft divifion is that of the Degeneres, or Curs. The firft of thefe was the Wappe, a name derived from its note: its only ufe was to alarm the family by barking, if any perfon approached the houfe. Of this clafs was the Verfator, or turnfpit; and laftly the Saltator, or dancing dog, or fuch as was taught variety of tricks, and carried about by idle people as a fhew. Thofe Degeneres were of no certain fhape, being mongrels or mixtures of all kinds of dogs.

We fhould now, according to our plan, after enumerating the feveral varieties of Britifh dogs, give its general natural hiftory; but fince Linnæus has already performed it to our hand, we fhall adopt his fenfe, tranflating his very words (wherever we may) with literal exactnefs.

" The dog eats flefh, and farinaceous ve-" getables, but not greens: its ftomach di-" gefts bones: it ufes the tops of grafs as a " vomit. It voids its excrements on a ftone: " the *album græcum* is one of the greateft en-" couragers of putrefaction. It laps up its " drink with its tongue: it voids its urine " fideways, by lifting up one of its hind " legs; and is moft diuretic in the company " of a ftrange dog. *Odorat anum alterius:* " its fcent is moft exquifite, when its nofe is " moift: it treads lightly on its toes; fcarce " ever fweats; but when hot lolls out its " tongue. It generally walks frequently " round the place it intends to lie down on: " its fenfe of hearing is very quick when " afleep: it dreams. *Procis rixantibus cru-" delis: catulit cum variis: mordet illa illos:* " *cohæret copula junctus*: it goes with young " fixty-three days; and commonly brings " from four to eight at a time: the male pup-" pies refemble the dog, the female the bitch. " It is the moft faithful of all animals: is " very docible: hates ftrange dogs: will fnap " at a ftone thrown at it: will howl at certain " mufical notes: all (except the South Ame-" rican kind) will bark at ftrangers: dogs " are rejected by the Mahometans."

§ 5. *The* Wild Cat.

This animal does not differ fpecifically from the tame cat; the latter being originally of the fame kind, but altered in colour, and in fome other trifling accidents, as are common to animals reclaimed from the woods and domefticated.

The cat in its favage ftate is three or four times as large as the houfe-cat; the head larger, and the face flatter. The teeth and claws tremendous: its mufcles very ftrong, as being formed for rapine: the tail is of a moderate length, but very thick, marked with alternate bars of black and white, the end always black: the hips and hind part of the lower joints of the leg, are always black: the fur is very foft and fine. The general colour of thefe animals is of a yellowifh white, mixed with a deep grey: thefe colours, though they appear at firft fight confufedly blended together, yet on a clofe infpection will be found to be difpofed like the ftreaks on the fkin of the tiger, pointing from the back downwards, rifing from a black lift that runs from the head along the middle of the back to the tail.

This animal may be called the Britifh tiger; it is the fierceft and moft deftructive beaft we have; making dreadful havock among our poultry, lambs, and kids. It inhabits the moft mountainous and woody parts of thefe iflands, living moftly in trees, and feeding only by night. It multiplies as faft as our common cats; and often the females of the latter will quit their domestic mates, and return home pregnant by the former.

They are taken either in traps, or by shooting: in the latter case it is very dangerous only to wound them, for they will attack the person who injured them, and have strength enough to be no despicable enemy. Wild cats were formerly reckoned among the beasts of chace; as appears by the charter of Richard the Second, to the abbot of Peterborough, giving him leave to hunt the hare, fox, and wild cat. The use of the fur was in lining of robes; but it was esteemed not of the most luxurious kind; for it was ordained 'that 'no abbess or nun should use more costly 'apparel than such as is made of lambs 'or cats skins.' In much earlier times it was also the object of the sportsman's diversion.

> Felemque minacem
> Arboris in trunco longis præfigere telis.
> *Nemesiani Cynegeticon*, L. 55.

§ 6. *The* Domestic Cat.

This animal is so well known as to make a description of it unnecessary. It is an useful, but deceitful domestic; active, neat, sedate, intent on its prey. When pleased purrs and moves its tail: when angry spits, hisses, and strikes with its foot. When walking, it draws in its claws: it drinks little: is fond of fish: it washes its face with its fore-foot, (Linnæus says at the approach of a storm:) the female is remarkably salacious; a piteous, squalling, jarring lover. Its eyes shine in the night: its hair when rubbed in the dark emits fire: it is even proverbially tenacious of life: always lights on its feet: is fond of perfumes, marum, cat-mint, valerian, &c.

Our ancestors seem to have had a high sense of the utility of this animal. That excellent prince *Hoel dda*, or Howel the Good, did not think it beneath him (among his laws relating to the prices, &c. of animals) to include that of the cat; and to describe the qualities it ought to have. The price of a kitling before it could see, was to be a penny; till it caught a mouse two-pence; when it commenced mouser four-pence. It was required besides, that it should be perfect in its senses of hearing and seeing, be a good mouser, have the claws whole, and be a good nurse: but if it failed in any of these qualities, the seller was to forfeit to the buyer the third part of its value. If any one stole or killed the cat that guarded the prince's granary, he was to forfeit a milch ewe, its fleece and lamb; or as much wheat as when poured on the cat suspended by its tail (the head touching the floor) would form a heap high enough to cover the tip of the former. This last quotation is not only curious, as being an evidence of the simplicity of ancient manners, but it almost proves to a demonstration that cats are not aborigines of these islands; or known to the earliest inhabitants. The large prices set on them, (if we consider the high value of specie at that time) and the great care taken of the improvement and breed of an animal that multiplies so fast, are almost certain proofs of their being little known at that period.

§ 7. Explanation *of ſome* technical Terms *in* Ornithology.

Fig.		
1.	*Cere. Cera*	The naked ſkin that covers the baſe of the bill in the *Hawk* kind.
2.	*Capiſtrum*	A word uſed by *Linnæus* to expreſs the ſhort feathers on the fore-head juſt above the bill. In *Crows* theſe fall forwards over the noſtrils.
3.	*Lorum*	The ſpace between the bill and the eye, generally covered with feathers, but in ſome birds naked, as in the black and white *Grebe*.
4.	*Orbits. Orbita*	The ſkin that ſurrounds the eye, which is generally bare, particularly in the *Heron* and *Parrot*.
5.	*Emarginatum*	A bill is called *roſtrum emarginatum* when there is a ſmall notch near the end: this is conſpicuous in that of *Butcher-birds* and *Thruſhes*.
6.	*Vibriſſæ*	*Vibriſſæ pectinatæ*, ſtiff hairs that grow on each ſide the mouth, formed like a double comb, to be ſeen in the *Goatſucker*, *Fly-catcher*, &c.
7.	*Baſtard wing. Alula ſpuria*	A ſmall joint riſing at the end of the middle part of the wing, or the *cubitus*; on which are three or five feathers.
8.	*Leſſer coverts of the wings. Tectrices primæ*	The ſmall feathers that lie in ſeveral rows on the bones of the wings. The *under coverts* are thoſe that line the inſide of the wings.
9.	*Greater coverts. Tectrices ſecundæ*	The feathers that lie immediately over the quill-feathers and ſecondary feathers.
10.	*Quill-feathers. Primores*	The largeſt feathers of the wings, or thoſe that riſe from the firſt bone.
11.	*Secondary feathers. Secondariæ*	Thoſe that riſe from the ſecond.
12.	*Coverts of the tail. Uropygium*	Thoſe that cover the baſe of the tail.
13.	*Vent-feathers*	Thoſe that lie from the vent to the tail. *Criſſum Linnæi.*
14.	*The tail. Rectrices*	
15.	*Scapular feathers*	That riſe from the ſhoulders, and cover the ſides of the back.
16.	*Nucha*	The hind part of the head.
17.	*Roſtrum ſubulatum*	A term *Linnæus* uſes for a ſtraight and ſlender bill.
18.		To ſhew the ſtructure of the feet of the *Kingfiſher*.

19.	*Pes ſcanſorius*	The foot of the *Woodpecker* formed for climbing. Climbing feet.
20.	*Finned foot. Pes lobatus, pinnatus*	Such as thoſe of the *Grebes*, &c. Such as are indented are called ſcalloped; ſuch are thoſe of *Coots* and ſcallop-toed *Sandpipers*.
22.	*Pes tridactylus*	Such as want the back toe.
23.	*Semi-palmated. Pes ſemi-palmatus*	When the webs only reach half way of the toes.
24.	*Ungue poſtico ſeſſili*	When the hind claw adheres to the leg without any toe, as in the *Petrels*.
25.	*Digitis 4 omnibus palmatis.*	All the four toes connected by webs, as in the *Corvorants*.

Explanation *of other* Linnæan Terms.

Roſtrum cultratum	When the edges of the bill are very ſharp, ſuch as in that of the *Crow*.
Unguiculatum	A bill with a nail at the end, as in thoſe of the *Gooſanders* and *Ducks*.
Lingua ciliata	When the tongue is edged with fine briſtles, as in *Ducks*.
Integra	When quite plain or even.
Lumbriciformis	When the tongue is long, round, and ſlender, like a worm, as that of the *Woodpecker*.
Pedes compedes	When the legs are placed ſo far behind as to make the bird walk with difficulty, or as if *in fetters*; as is the caſe with the *Auks*, *Grebes*, and *Divers*.
Nares Lineares	When the noſtrils are very narrow, as in *Sea Gulls*.
Marginatæ	With a rim round the noſtrils, as in the *Stare*.

§ 8. *The* Pigeon.

The tame pigeon, and all its beautiful varieties, derive their origin from one ſpecies, the Stock Dove: the Engliſh name implying its being the *ſtock* or *ſtem* from whence the other domeſtic kinds ſprung. Theſe birds, as Varro obſerves, take their (Latin) name, *Columba*, from their voice or cooing; and had he known it, he might have added the Britiſh, &c. for *Klommen*, *Kylobman*, *Kulm*, and *Kolm* ſignify the ſame bird. They were, and ſtill are in moſt parts of our iſland, in a ſtate of nature; but probably the Romans taught us the method of making them domeſtic, and conſtructing pigeon-houſes. Its characters in the ſtate neareſt that of its origin, is a deep bluiſh aſh-colour; the breaſt daſhed with a fine changeable green and purple; the ſides of the neck with ſhining copper colour; its wings marked with two black bars, one on the coverts of the wings, the other on the quill-

quill-feathers. The back white, and the tail barred near the end with black. The weight fourteen ounces.

In the wild ſtate it breeds in holes of rocks, and hollows of trees, for which reaſon ſome writers ſtile it *columba cavernalis*, in oppoſition to the Ring Dove, which makes its neſt on the boughs of trees. Nature ever preſerves ſome agreement in the manners, characters, and colours of birds reclaimed from their wild ſtate. This ſpecies of pigeon ſoon takes to build in artificial cavities, and from the temptation of a ready proviſion becomes eaſily domeſticated. The drakes of the tame duck, however they may vary in colour, ever retain the mark of their origin from our Engliſh mallard, by the curled feathers of the tail: and the tame gooſe betrays its deſcent from the wild kind, by the invariable whiteneſs of its rump, which they always retain in both ſtates.

Multitudes of theſe birds are obſerved to migrate into the ſouth of England; and while the beech woods were ſuffered to cover large tracts of ground, they uſed to haunt them in myriads, reaching in ſtrings of a mile in length, as they went out in the morning to feed. They viſit us the lateſt of any bird of paſſage, not appearing till November; and retire in the ſpring. I imagine that the ſummer haunts of theſe are in Sweden, for Mr. Eckmark makes their retreat thence coincide with their arrival here. But many breed here, as I have obſerved, on the cliffs of the coaſt of Wales, and of the Hebrides.

The varieties produced from the domeſtic pigeon are very numerous, and extremely elegant; theſe are diſtinguiſhed by names expreſſive of their ſeveral properties, ſuch as Tumblers, Carriers, Jacobines, Croppers, Powters, Runts, Turbits, Owls, Nuns, &c. The moſt celebrated of theſe is the Carrier, which, from the ſuperior attachment that pigeon ſhews to its native place, is employed in many countries as the moſt expeditious courier: the letters are tied under its wing, it is let looſe, and in a very ſhort ſpace returns to the home it was brought from, with its advices. This practice was much in vogue in the Eaſt; and at Scanderoon, till of late years, uſed on the arrival of a ſhip, to give the merchants at Aleppo a more expeditious notice than could be done by any other means. In our own country, theſe aerial meſſengers have been employed for a very ſingular purpoſe, being let looſe at Tyburn at the moment the fatal cart is drawn away, to notify to diſtant friends the departure of the unhappy criminal.

In the Eaſt, the uſe of theſe birds ſeem to have been improved greatly, by having, if we may uſe the expreſſion, relays of them ready to ſpread intelligence to all parts of the country. Thus the governor of Damiata circulated the news of the death of Orrilo:

> Toſto che'l Caſtellan di Damiata
> Certificoſſi, ch'era morto Orrilo,
> La Colomba laſciò, ch'avea legata
> Sotto l'ala la lettera col filo.
> Quella andò al Cairo, ed indi fu laſciata
> Un' altra altrove, come quivi e ſtilo:
> Si, che in pochiſſime ore andò l'avviſo
> Per tutto Egitto, ch'era Orrilo ucciſo *.

* 'As ſoon as the commandant of Damiata 'heard that Orrilo was dead, he let looſe a pi'geon, under whoſe wing he had tied a letter; 'this fled to Cairo, from whence a ſecond was 'diſpatched to another place, as is uſual; ſo that 'in a very few hours all Egypt was acquainted with 'the death of Orrilo.' ARIOSTO, canto 15.

But

But the ſimple uſe of them was known in very early times: Anacreon tells us, he conveyed his billet-doux to his beautiful Bathyllus by a dove.

> Εγὼ δ' Ἀνακρέοντι
> Διάκονῶ τοσαῦτα·
> Και νῦν οἷας ἐκείνȣ
> Ἐπιςολας κομίζω *.

> I am now Anacreon's ſlave,
> And to me entruſted have
> All the o'erflowings of his heart
> To Bathyllus to impart:
> Each ſoft line, with nimble wing,
> To the lovely boy I bring.

Tauroſthenes alſo, by means of a pigeon he he had decked with purple, ſent advice to his father, who lived in the iſle of Ægina, of his victory in the Olympic games, on the very day he had obtained it. And, at the ſiege of Modena, Hirtius without, and Brutus within the walls, kept, by the help of pigeons, a conſtant correſpondence; baffling every ſtratagem of the beſieger Antony to intercept their couriers. In the times of the cruſades there are many more inſtances of theſe birds of peace being employed in the ſervice of war: Joinville relates one during the cruſade of Saint Louis; and Taſſo another, during the ſiege of Jeruſalem.

The nature of pigeons is to be gregarious; to lay only two eggs; to breed many times in the year; to bill in their courtſhip; for the male and female to ſit by turns, and alſo to feed their young; to caſt the proviſion out of their craw into the young one's mouths; to drink, not like other birds by ſipping, but by continual draughts like quadrupeds; and to have notes mournful or plaintive.

* Anacreon, ode 9. εἰς περιςεράν.

§ 9. *The* Blackbird.

This bird is of a very retired and ſolitary nature; frequents hedges and thickets, in which it builds earlier than any other bird: the neſt is formed of moſs, dead graſs, fibres, &c. lined or plaiſtered with clay, and that again covered with hay or ſmall ſtraw. It lays four or five eggs of a bluiſh green colour, marked with irregular duſky ſpots. The note of the male is extremely fine, but too loud for any place except the woods; it begins to ſing early in the ſpring, continues its muſic part of the ſummer, deſiſts in the moulting ſeaſon; but reſumes it for ſome time in September, and the firſt winter months.

The colour of the male, when it has attained its full age, is of a fine deep black, and the bill of a bright yellow; the edges of the eyelids yellow. When young the bill is duſky, and the plumage of a ruſty black, ſo that they are not to be diſtinguiſhed from the females; but at the age of one year they attain their proper colour.

§ 10. *The* Bullfinch.

The wild note of this bird is not in the leaſt muſical; but when tamed it becomes remarkably docile, and may be taught any tune after a pipe, or to whiſtle any notes in the juſteſt manner: it ſeldom forgets what it has learned; and will become ſo tame as to come at call, perch on its maſter's ſhoulders, and (at command) go through a difficult muſical leſſon. They may be taught to ſpeak, and ſome thus inſtructed are annually brought to London from Germany.

The male is diſtinguiſhed from the female by the ſuperior blackneſs of its crown, and by the rich crimſon that adorns the cheeks, breaſt,

breast, belly, and throat of the male; those of the female being of a dirty colour: the bill is black, short, and very thick: the head large: the hind part of the neck and the back are grey: the coverts of the wings are black; the lower crossed with a white line: the quill-feathers dusky, but part of their inner webs white: the coverts of the tail and vent-feathers white: the tail black.

In the spring these birds frequent our gardens, and are very destructive to our fruit-trees, by eating the tender buds. They breed about the latter end of May, or beginning of June, and are seldom seen at that time near houses, as they chuse some very retired place to breed in. These birds are sometimes wholly black; I have heard of a male bullfinch which had changed its colours after it had been taken in full feather, and with all its fine teints. The first year it began to assume a dull hue, blackening every year, till in the fourth it attained the deepest degree of that colour. This was communicated to me by the Reverend Mr. White of Selborne. Mr. Morton, in his History of Northamptonshire, gives another instance of such a change, with this addition, that the year following, after moulting, the bird recovered its native colours. Bullfinches fed entirely on hemp-seed are aptest to undergo this change.

§ 11. *The* Goldfinch.

This is the most beautiful of our hard-billed small birds; whether we consider its colours, the elegance of its form, or the music of its note. The bill is white, tipt with black; the base is surrounded with a ring of rich scarlet feathers: from the corners of the mouth to the eyes is a black line: the cheeks are white: the top of the head is black; and the white on the cheeks is bounded almost to the fore part of the neck with black: the hind part of the head is white: the back, rump, and breast are of a fine pale tawny brown, lightest on the two last: the belly is white: the covert feathers of the wings, in the male, are black: the quill-feathers black, marked in their middle with a beautiful yellow; the tips white: the tail is black, but most of the feathers marked near their ends with a white spot: the legs are white.

The female is distinguished from the male by these notes; the feathers at the end of the bill in the former are brown; in the male black: the lesser coverts of the wings are brown: and the black and yellow in the wings of the female are less brilliant. The young bird, before it moults, is grey on the head; and hence it is termed by the bird-catchers a *grey pate*.

There is another variety of goldfinch, which is, perhaps, not taken above once in two or three years, which is called by the London bird-catchers a *cheverel*, from the manner in which it concludes its jerk: when this sort is taken, it sells at a very high price: it is distinguished from the common sort by a white streak, or by two, and sometimes three white spots under the throat.

Their note is very sweet, and they are much esteemed on that account, as well as for their great docility. Towards winter they assemble in flocks, and feed on seeds of different kinds, particularly those of the thistle. It is fond of orchards, and frequently builds in an apple or pear-tree: its nest is very elegantly formed of fine moss, liverworts, and bents on the outside; lined first with wool and hair, and then with the goslin or cotton of the sallow. It lays five white eggs,

eggs, marked with deep purple spots on the upper end.

This bird seems to have been the χρυσομίτρις * of Aristotle; being the only one that we know of, that could be distinguished by a golden fillet round its head, feeding on the seeds of prickly plants. The very ingenious translator (Dr. Martyn) of Virgil's Eclogues and Georgics, gives the name of this bird to the *acalanthis* or *acanthis*:

Littoraque *alcyonen* resonant, *acanthida* dumi.

In our account of the *Halcyon* of the ancients, we followed his opinion; but having since met with a passage in Aristotle, that clearly proves that *acanthis* could not be used in that sense, we beg, that, till we can discover what it really is, the word may be rendered *linnet*; since it is impossible the philosopher could distinguish a bird of such striking and brilliant colours as the *goldfinch*, by the epithet κακόχροος, or bad coloured; and as he celebrates his *acanthis* for a fine note, φωνὴν μέν τοι λιγυρὰν ἔχουσι, both characters will suit the linnet, being a bird as remarkable for the sweetness of its note, as for the plainness of its plumage.

§ 12. *The* LINNET.

The bill of this species is dusky, but in the spring assumes a bluish cast: the feathers on the head are black, edged with ash-colour: the sides of the neck deep ash-colour: the throat marked in the middle with a brown line, bounded on each side with a white one: the back black, bordered with reddish brown: the bottom of the breast is of a fine blood red, which heightens in colour as the spring advances: the belly white: the vent-feathers yellowish: the sides under the wings spotted with brown: the quill-feathers are dusky; the lower part of the nine first white: the coverts incumbent on them black; the others of a reddish brown; the lowest order tipt with a paler colour: the tail is a little forked, of a brown colour, edged with white; the two middle feathers excepted, which are bordered with dull red. The females and young birds want the red spot on the breast; in lieu of that, their breasts are marked with short streaks of brown pointing downwards: the females have also less white in their wings.

These birds are much esteemed for their song: they feed on seeds of different kinds, which they peel before they eat: the seed of the *linum* or *flax* is their favourite food; from whence the name of the linnet tribe.

They breed among furze and white thorn: the outside of their nest is made with moss and bents; and lined with wool and hair. They lay five whitish eggs, spotted like those of the goldfinch.

§ 13. *The* CANARY BIRD.

This bird is of the finch tribe. It was originally peculiar to those isles, to which it owes its name; the same that were known to the ancients by the addition of the *fortunate*. The happy temperament of the air; the spontaneous productions of the ground in the varieties of fruits; the sprightly and chearful disposition of the inhabitants; and the harmony arising from the number of the birds found there, procured them that romantic distinction. Though the ancients celebrate the isle of *Canaria* for the multitude of birds, they

* Which he places among the ἀκανθοφάγα. Scaliger reads the word χυσομίτρις, which has no meaning; neither does the critic support his alteration with any reason. *Hist. an.* 887.

they have not mentioned any in particular. It is probable then, that our ſpecies was not introduced into Europe till after the ſecond diſcovery of theſe iſles, which was between the thirteenth and fourteenth centuries. We are uncertain when it firſt made its appearance in this quarter of the globe. Belon, who wrote in 1555, is ſilent in reſpect to theſe birds: Geſner is the firſt who mentions them; and Aldrovand ſpeaks of them as rarities; that they were very dear on account of the difficulty attending the bringing them from ſo diſtant a country, and that they were purchaſed by people of rank alone. Olina ſays, that in his time there was a degenerate ſort found on the iſle of Elba, off the coaſt of Italy, which came there originally by means of a ſhip bound from the Canaries to Leghorn, and was wrecked on that iſland. We once ſaw ſome ſmall birds brought directly from the Canary Iſlands, that we ſuſpect to be the genuine ſort: they were of a dull green colour; but as they did not ſing, we ſuppoſed them to be hens. Theſe birds will produce with the goldfinch and linnet, and the offspring is called a mule-bird, becauſe, like that animal, it proves barren.

They are ſtill found on the ſame ſpot to which we were firſt indebted for the production of ſuch charming ſongſters; but they are now become ſo numerous in our country, that we are under no neceſſity of croſſing the ocean for them.

§ 14. *The* Sky Lark.

The length of this ſpecies is ſeven inches one-fourth: the breadth twelve and a half: the weight one ounce and a half: the tongue broad and cloven: the bill ſlender: the upper mandible duſky, the lower yellow: above the eyes is a yellow ſpot: the crown of the head a reddiſh brown ſpotted with deep black: the hind part of the head aſh-colour: chin white. It has the faculty of erecting the feathers of the head. The feathers on the back, and coverts of the wings, duſky edged with reddiſh brown, which is paler on the latter: the quill-feathers duſky: the exterior web edged with white, that of the others with reddiſh brown: the upper part of the breaſt yellow ſpotted with black: the lower part of the body of a pale yellow: the exterior web, and half of the interior web next to the ſhaft of the firſt feather of the tail, are white; of the ſecond only the exterior web; the reſt of thoſe feathers duſky; the others are duſky edged with red; thoſe in the middle deeply ſo, the reſt very ſlightly: the legs duſky: ſoles of the feet yellow: the hind claw very long and ſtrait.

This and the wood lark are the only birds that ſing as they fly; this raiſing its note as it ſoars, and lowering it till it quite dies away as it deſcends. It will often ſoar to ſuch a height, that we are charmed with the muſic when we loſe ſight of the ſongſter; it alſo begins its ſong before the earlieſt dawn. Milton, in his Allegro, moſt beautifully expreſſes theſe circumſtances: and Biſhop Newton obſerves, that the beautiful ſcene that Milton exhibits of rural chearfulneſs, at the ſame time gives us a fine picture of the regularity of his life, and the innocency of his own mind; thus he deſcribes himſelf as in a ſituation

> To hear the lark begin his flight,
> And ſinging ſtartle the dull night,
> From his watch tower in the ſkies,
> 'Till the dappled dawn doth riſe.

It continues its harmony ſeveral months, beginning early in the ſpring, on pairing. In the

the winter they assemble in vast flocks, grow very fat, and are taken in great numbers for our tables. They build their nest on the ground, beneath some clod; forming it of hay, dry fibres, &c. and lay four or five eggs.

The place these birds are taken in the greatest quantity, is the neighbourhood of Dunstable: the season begins about the fourteenth of September, and ends the twenty-fifth of February; and during that space about 4000 dozen are caught, which supply the markets of the metropolis. Those caught in the day are taken in clap-nets of fifteen yards length, and two and a half in breadth; and are enticed within their reach by means of bits of looking-glass, fixed in a piece of wood, and placed in the middle of the nets, which are put in a quick whirling motion, by a string the larker commands; he also makes use of a decoy lark. These nets are used only till the fourteenth of November, for the larks will not *dare*, or frolick in the air, except in fine sunny weather; and of course cannot be inveigled into the snare. When the weather grows gloomy, the larker changes his engine, and makes use of a trammel-net twenty-seven or twenty-eight feet long, and five broad; which is put on two poles eighteen feet long, and carried by men under each arm, who pass over the fields and quarter the ground as a setting dog; when they hear or feel a lark hit the net, they drop it down, and so the birds are taken.

§ 15. *The* Nightingale.

The nightingale takes its name from *night*, and the Saxon word *galan*, to sing; expressive of the time of its melody. In size it is equal to the redstart; but longer bodied, and more elegantly made. The colours are very plain. The head and back are of a pale tawny, dashed with olive: the tail is of a deep tawny red: the throat, breast, and upper part of the belly, of a light glossy ash-colour: the lower belly almost white: the exterior webs of the quill-feathers are of a dull reddish brown; the interior of brownish ash-colour: the irides are hazel, and the eyes remarkably large and piercing: the legs and feet a deep ash-colour.

This bird, the most famed of the feathered tribe, for the variety, length, and sweetness of its notes, visits England the beginning of April, and leaves us in August. It is a species that does not spread itself over the island. It is not found in North Wales; or in any of the English counties north of it, except Yorkshire, where they are met with in great plenty about Doncaster. They have been also heard, but rarely, near Shrewsbury. It is also remarkable, that this bird does not migrate so far west as Devonshire and Cornwall; counties where the seasons are so very mild, that myrtles flourish in the open air during the whole year: neither are they found in Ireland. Sibbald places them in his list of Scotch birds; but they certainly are unknown in that part of Great Britain, probably from the scarcity and the recent introduction of hedges there. Yet they visit Sweden, a much more severe climate. With us they frequent thick hedges, and low coppices; and generally keep in the middle of the bush, so that they are very rarely seen. They form their nest of oak-leaves, a few bents, and reeds. The eggs are of a deep brown. When the young first come abroad, and are helpless, the old birds make a plaintive and jarring noise with a sort of snapping as if in menace, pursuing along the hedge the passengers.

They begin their song in the evening, and continue

continue it the whole night. These their vigils did not pass unnoticed by the antients: the slumbers of these birds were proverbial; and not to rest as much as the nightingale, expressed a very bad sleeper *. This was the favourite bird of the British poet, who omits no opportunity of introducing it, and almost constantly noting its love of solitude and night. How finely does it serve to compose part of the solemn scenery of his Penseroso; when he describes it

In her saddest sweetest plight,
Smoothing the rugged brow of night;
While Cynthia checks her dragon yoke,
Gently o'er th' accustom'd oak;
Sweet bird, that shunn'st the noise of folly,
Most musical, most melancholy!
Thee, chauntress, oft the woods among,
I woo to hear thy evening song.

In another place he styles it the *solemn bird*; and again speaks of it,

As the wakeful bird
Sings darkling, and in shadiest covert hid,
Tunes her nocturnal note.

The reader must excuse a few more quotations from the same poet, on the same subject: the first describes the approach of evening, and the retiring of all animals to their repose.

Silence accompanied; for beast and bird,
They to their grassy couch, these to their nests
Were slunk; all but the wakeful nightingale,
She all night long her amorous descant sung.

When Eve passed the irksome night preceding her fall, she, in a dream, imagines herself thus reproached with losing the beauties of the night by indulging too long a repose:

Why sleep'st thou, Eve? now is the pleasant time,
The cool, the silent, save where silence yields
To the night-warbling bird, that now awake
Tunes sweetest his love-labour'd song.

The same birds sing their nuptial song, and lull them to rest. How rapturous are the following lines! how expressive of the delicate sensibility of our Milton's tender ideas!

The earth
Gave sign of gratulation, and each hill;
Joyous the birds; fresh gales and gentle airs
Whisper'd it to the woods, and from their wings
Flung rose, flung odours from the spicy shrub,
Disporting, till the amorous bird of night
Sung spousal, and bid haste the evening star
On his hill-top to light the bridal lamp.

These, lull'd by nightingales, embracing slept;
And on their naked limbs the flowery roof
Shower'd roses, which the morn repair'd.

These quotations from the best judge of melody, we thought due to the sweetest of our feathered choiristers; and we believe no reader of taste will think them tedious.

Virgil seems to be the only poet among the ancients, who hath attended to the circumstance of this bird's singing in the night time.

Qualis populeâ mœrens Philomela sub umbrâ
Amissos queritur fœtus, quos durus arator
Observans nido implumes detraxit: at illa
Flet noctem, ramoque sedens miserabile carmen
Integrat, et mœstis late loca questibus implet.
GEORG. IV. l. 511.

As Philomel in poplar shades, alone,
For her lost offspring pours a mother's moan,
Which

* Ælian var. hist. 577. both in the text and note. It must be remarked, that nightingales sing also in the day.

Which some rough ploughman marking for his prey,
From the warm nest, unfledg'd hath dragg'd away;
Percht on a bow, she all night long complains,
And fills the grove with sad repeated strains.

F. WARTON.

Pliny has described the warbling notes of this bird, with an elegance that bespeaks an exquisite sensibility of taste: notwithstanding that his words have been cited by most other writers on natural history, yet such is the beauty, and in general the truth of his expressions, that they cannot be too much studied by lovers of natural history. We must observe notwithstanding, that a few of his thoughts are more to be admired for their vivacity than for strict philosophical reasoning; but these few are easily distinguishable.

§ 16. *The* RED BREAST.

This bird, though so very petulant as to be at constant war with its own tribe, yet is remarkably sociable with mankind: in the winter it frequently makes one of the family; and takes refuge from the inclemency of the season even by our fire-sides. Thomson * has prettily described the annual visits of this guest.

The RED-BREAST, sacred to the houshold gods,
Wisely regardful of th' embroiling sky,
In joyless fields, and thorny thickets, leaves
His shivering mates, and pays to trusted Man
His annual visit. Half afraid, he first
Against the window beats; then, brisk, alights
On the warm hearth; then, hopping o'er the floor,
Eyes all the smiling family askance,
And pecks and starts, and wonders where he is:
'Till more familiar grown, the table-crumbs
Attract his slender feet.

* In his Seasons, vide Winter, line 246.

The great beauty of that celebrated poet consists in his elegant and just descriptions of the œconomy of animals; and the happy use he hath made of natural knowledge, in descriptive poetry, shines through almost every page of his Seasons. The affection this bird has for mankind, is also recorded in that antient ballad, *The babes in the wood*; a composition of a most beautiful and pathetic simplicity. It is the first trial of our humanity: the child that refrains from tears on hearing that read, gives but a bad presage of the tenderness of his future sensations.

In the spring this bird retires to breed in the thickest covers, or the most concealed holes of walls and other buildings. The eggs are of a dull white, sprinkled with reddish spots. Its song is remarkably fine and soft; and the more to be valued, as we enjoy it the greatest part of the winter, and early in the spring, and even through great part of the summer, but its notes are part of that time drowned in the general warble of the season. Many of the autumnal songsters seem to be the young cock red-breasts of that year.

The bill is dusky: the forehead, chin, throat and breast are of a deep orange-colour: the head, hind part of the neck, the back and tail are of a deep ash-colour, tinged with green: the wings rather darker; the edges inclining to yellow: the legs and feet dusky.

§ 17. *The* WREN.

The wren may be placed among the finest of our singing birds. It continues its song throughout the winter, excepting during the frosts. It makes its nest in a very curious manner; of an oval shape, very deep, with a small hole in the middle for egress and regress: the external material is moss, within it is lined with hair and feathers. It lays from

from ten to eighteen eggs; and as often brings up as many young; which, as Mr. Ray obſerves, may be ranked among thoſe daily miracles that we take no notice of; that it ſhould feed ſuch a number without paſſing over one, and that too in utter darkneſs.

The head and upper part of the body of the wren are of a deep reddiſh brown: above each eye is a ſtroke of white: the back, and coverts of the wings, and tail, are marked with ſlender tranſverſe black lines: the quill-feathers with bars of black and red. The throat is of a yellowiſh white. The belly and ſides croſſed with narrow duſky and pale reddiſh brown lines. The tail is croſſed with duſky bars.

§ 18. *The* SWIFT.

This ſpecies is the largeſt of our ſwallows; but the weight is moſt diſproportionately ſmall to its extent of wing of any bird; the former being ſcarce one ounce, the latter eighteen inches. The length near eight. The feet of this bird are ſo ſmall, that the action of walking and of riſing from the ground is extremely difficult; ſo that nature hath made it full amends, by furniſhing it with ample means for an eaſy and continual flight. It is more on the wing than any other ſwallows; its flight is more rapid, and that attended with a ſhrill ſcream. It reſts by clinging againſt ſome wall, or other apt body; from whence Klein ſtyles this ſpecies *Hirundo muraria.* It breeds under the eaves of houſes, in ſteeples, and other lofty buildings; makes its neſt of graſſes and feathers; and lays only two eggs, of a white colour. It is entirely of a gloſſy dark ſooty colour, only the chin is marked with a white ſpot: but by being ſo conſtantly expoſed to all weathers, the gloſs of the plumage is loſt before it retires. I cannot trace them to their winter quarters, unleſs in one inſtance of a pair found adhering by their claws and in a torpid ſtate, in February 1766, under the roof of Longnor chapel, Shropſhire: on being brought to a fire, they revived and moved about the room. The feet are of a particular ſtructure, all the toes ſtanding forward; the leaſt conſiſts of only one bone; the others of an equal number, viz. two each; in which they differ from thoſe of all other birds.

This appears in our country about fourteen days later than the ſand martin; but differs greatly in the time of its departure, retiring invariably about the tenth of Auguſt, being the firſt of the genus that leaves us.

The fabulous hiſtory of the Manucodiata, or bird of Paradiſe, is in the hiſtory of this ſpecies in great meaſure verified. It was believed to have no feet, to live upon the celeſtial dew, to float perpetually on the Indian air, and to perform all its functions in that element.

The Swift actually performs what has been in theſe enlightened times diſproved of the former; except the ſmall time it takes in ſleeping, and what it devotes to incubation, every other action is done on wing. The materials of its neſt it collects either as they are carried about by the winds, or picks them up from the ſurface in its ſweeping flight. Its food is undeniably the inſects that fill the air. Its drink is taken in tranſient ſips from the water's ſurface. Even its amorous rites are performed on high. Few perſons who have attended to them in a fine ſummer's morning, but muſt have ſeen them make their aerial courſes at a great height, encircling a certain ſpace with an eaſy ſteady motion. On a ſudden they fall into each other's embraces, then drop precipitate with a loud ſhriek

shriek for numbers of yards. This is the critical conjuncture, and to be no more wondered at, than that insects (a familiar instance) should discharge the same duty in the same element.

These birds and swallows are inveterate enemies to hawks. The moment one appears, they attack him immediately: the swifts soon desist; but the swallows pursue and persecute those rapacious birds, till they have entirely driven them away.

Swifts delight in sultry thundry weather, and seem thence to receive fresh spirits. They fly in those times in small parties with particular violence; and as they pass near steeples, towers, or any edifices where their mates perform the office of incubation, emit a loud scream, a sort of serenade, as Mr. White supposes, to their respective females.

To the curious monographies on the swallow tribe, of that worthy correspondent, I must acknowledge myself indebted for numbers of the remarks abovementioned.

§ 19. *Of the Disappearance of Swallows.*

There are three opinions among naturalists concerning the manner the swallow tribe dispose of themselves after their disappearance from the countries in which they make their summer residence. Herodotus mentions one species that resides in Egypt the whole year: Prosper Alpinus asserts the same; and Mr. Loten, late governor of Ceylon, assured us, that those of Java never remove. These excepted, every other known kind observe a periodical migration, or retreat. The swallows of the cold Norway, and of North America, of the distant Kamtschatka, of the temperate parts of Europe, of Aleppo, and of the hot Jamaica, all agree in this one point.

In cold countries, a defect of insect food on the approach of winter, is a sufficient reason for these birds to quit them: but since the same cause probably does not subsist in the warm climates, recourse should be had to some other reason for their vanishing.

Of the three opinions, the first has the utmost appearance of probability; which is, that they remove nearer the sun, where they can find a continuance of their natural diet, and a temperature of air suiting their constitutions. That this is the case with some species of European swallows, has been proved beyond contradiction (as above cited) by M. Adanson. We often observe them collected in flocks innumerable on churches, on rocks, and on trees, previous to their departure hence; and Mr. Collinson proves their return here in perhaps equal numbers, by two curious relations of undoubted credit: the one communicated to him by Mr. Wright, master of a ship; the other by the late Sir Charles Wager; who both described (to the same purpose) what happened to each in their voyages. "Returning home (says Sir "Charles) in the spring of the year, as I "came into sounding in our channel, a great "flock of swallows came and settled on all "my rigging; every rope was covered; they "hung on one another like a swarm of bees; "the decks and carving were filled with "them. They seemed almost famished and "spent, and were only feathers and bones; "but being recruited with a night's rest, took "their flight in the morning." This vast fatigue, proves that their journey must have been very great, considering the amazing swiftness of these birds: in all probability they had crossed the Atlantic ocean, and were returning from the shores of Senegal, or other parts of Africa; so that this account from that most able and honest seaman, confirms

firms the later information of M. Adanson.

Mr. White, on Michaelmas-day 1768, had the good fortune to have ocular proof of what may reasonably be supposed an actual migration of swallows. Travelling that morning very early between his house and the coast, at the beginning of his journey he was environed with a thick fog, but on a large wild heath the mist began to break, and discovered to him numberless swallows, clustered on the standing bushes, as if they had roosted there: as soon as the sun burst out, they were instantly on wing, and with an easy and placid flight proceeded towards the sea. After this he saw no more flocks, only now and then a straggler*.

This rendezvous of swallows about the same time of year is very common on the willows, in the little isles in the Thames. They seem to assemble for the same purpose as those in Hampshire, notwithstanding no one yet has been eye-witness of their departure. On the 26th of September last, two gentlemen who happened to lie at Maidenhead bridge, furnished at least a proof of the multitudes there assembled: they went by torch-light to an adjacent isle, and in less than half an hour brought ashore fifty dozen; for they had nothing more to do than to draw the willow twigs through their hands, the birds never stirring till they were taken.

* In Kalm's Voyage to America, is a remarkable instance of the distant flight of swallows; for one lighted on the ship he was in, September 2d, when he had passed only over two-thirds of the Atlantic ocean. His passage was uncommonly quick, being performed from Deal to Philadelphia in less than six weeks; and when this accident happened, he was fourteen days sail from Cape Hinlopen.

The northern naturalists will perhaps say, that this assembly met for the purpose of plunging into their subaqueous winter quarters; but was that the case, they would never escape discovery in a river perpetually fished as the Thames, some of them must inevitably be brought up in the nets that harass that water.

The second notion has great antiquity on its side. Aristotle and Pliny give, as their belief, that swallows do not remove very far from their summer habitation, but winter in the hollows of rocks, and during that time lose their feathers. The former part of their opinion has been adopted by several ingenious men; and of late, several proofs have been brought of some species, at least, having been discovered in a torpid state. Mr. Collinson favoured us with the evidence of three gentlemen, eye-witnesses to numbers of sand martins being drawn out of a cliff on the Rhine, in the month of March 1762. And the honourable Daines Barrington communicated to us the following fact, on the authority of the late Lord Belhaven, that numbers of swallows have been found in old dry walls, and in sandhills near his lordship's seat in East Lothian; not once only, but from year to year; and that when they were exposed to the warmth of a fire, they revived. We have also heard of the same annual discoveries near Morpeth in Northumberland, but cannot speak of them with the same assurance as the two former: neither in the two last instances are we certain of the particular species.

Other witnesses crowd on us to prove the residence of those birds in a torpid state during the severe season.

First, In the chalky cliffs of Sussex; as was seen on the fall of a great fragment some years ago.

Secondly, In a decayed hollow tree that was

was cut down, near Dolgelli, in Merionethshire.

Thirdly, In a cliff near Whitby, Yorkshire; where, on digging out a fox, whole bushels of swallows were found in a torpid condition. And,

Lastly, The Reverend Mr. Conway, of Sychton, Flintshire, was so obliging as to communicate the following fact: A few years ago, on looking down an old leadmine in that county, he observed numbers of swallows clinging to the timbers of the shaft, seemingly asleep; and on flinging some gravel on them, they just moved, but never attempted to fly or change their place; this was between All Saints and Christmas.

These are doubtless the lurking-places of the latter hatches, or of those young birds, who are incapable of distant migrations. There they continue insensible and rigid; but like flies, may sometimes be re-animated by an unseasonable hot day in the midst of winter: for very near Christmas a few appeared on the moulding of a window of Merton College, Oxford, in a remarkably warm nook, which prematurely set their blood in motion, having the same effect as laying them before the fire at the same time of year. Others have been known to make this premature appearance; but as soon as the cold natural to the season returns, they withdraw again to their former retreats.

I shall conclude with one argument drawn from the very late hatches of two species.

On the twenty-third of October 1767, a martin was seen in Southwark, flying in and out of its nest: and on the twenty-ninth of the same month, four or five swallows were observed hovering round and settling on the county hospital at Oxford. As these birds must have been of a late hatch, it is highly improbable that at so late a season of the year they would attempt, from one of our midland counties, a voyage almost as far as the equator to Senegal or Goree: we are therefore confirmed in our notion, that there is only a partial migration of these birds; and that the feeble late hatches conceal themselves in this country.

The above are circumstances we cannot but assent to, though seemingly contradictory to the common course of nature in regard to other birds. We must, therefore, divide our belief relating to these two so different opinions, and conclude, that one part of the swallow tribe migrate, and that others have their winter quarters near home. If it should be demanded, why swallows alone are found in a torpid state, and not the other many species of soft billed birds, which likewise disappear about the same time? The following reason may be assigned:

No birds are so much on the wing as swallows, none fly with such swiftness and rapidity, none are obliged to such sudden and various evolutions in their flight, none are at such pains to take their prey, and we may add, none exert their voice more incessantly; all these occasion a vast expence of strength, and of spirits, and may give such a texture to the blood, that other animals cannot experience; and so dispose, or we may say, necessitate, this tribe of birds, or part of them, at least, to a repose more lasting than that of any others.

The third notion is, even at first sight, too amazing and unnatural to merit mention, if it was not that some of the learned have been credulous enough to deliver, for fact, what has the strongest appearance of impossibility; we mean the relation of swallows passing the winter immersed under ice, at the bottom of lakes, or lodged beneath the water of the sea

at

at the foot of rocks. The first who broached this opinion, was Olaus Magnus, Archbishop of Upsal, who very gravely informs us, that these birds are often found in clustered masses, at the bottom of the northern lakes, mouth to mouth, wing to wing, foot to foot; and that they creep down the reeds in autumn to their subaqueous retreats. That when old fishermen discover such a mass, they throw it into the water again; but when young inexperienced ones takes it, they will, by thawing the birds at a fire, bring them indeed to the use of their wings, which will continue but a very short time, being owing to a premature and forced revival.

That the good Archbishop did not want credulity, in other instances, appears from this, that after having stocked the bottoms of the lakes with birds, he stores the clouds with mice, which sometimes fall in plentiful showers on Norway and the neighbouring countries.

Some of our own countrymen have given credit to the submersion of swallows; and Klein patronises the doctrine strongly, giving the following history of their manner of retiring, which he received from some countrymen and others. They asserted, that sometimes the swallows assembled in numbers on a reed, till it broke and sunk with them to the bottom; and their immersion was preluded by a dirge of a quarter of an hour's length. That others would unite in laying hold of a straw with their bills, and so plunge down in society. Others again would form a large mass, by clinging together with their feet, and so commit themselves to the deep.

Such are the relations given by those that are fond of this opinion, and though delivered without exaggeration, must provoke a smile. They assign not the smallest reason to account for these birds being able to endure so long a submersion without being suffocated, or without decaying, in an element so unnatural to so delicate a bird; when we know that the otter *, the corvorant, and the grebes, soon perish, if caught under ice, or entangled in nets; and it is well known, that those animals will continue much longer under water than any others, to whom nature hath denied that particular structure of heart, necessary for a long residence beneath that element.

---

§ 20. *Of the* Small Birds *of* Flight.

In the suburbs of London (and particularly about Shoreditch) are several weavers and other tradesmen, who during the months of October and March, get their livelihood by an ingenious, and we may say, a scientific method of bird-catching, which is totally unknown in other parts of Great Britain.

The reason of this trade being confined to so small a compass, arises from there being no considerable

* Though entirely satisfied in our own mind of the impossibility of these relations; yet, desirous of strengthening our opinion with some better authority, we applied to that able anatomist, Mr. John Hunter; who was so obliging to inform us, that he had dissected many swallows, but found nothing in them different from other birds as to the organs of respiration. That all those animals which he had dissected of the class that sleep during winter, such as lizards, frogs, &c. had a very different conformation as to those organs. That all these animals, he believes, do breathe in their torpid state; and as far as his experience reaches, he knows they do: and that therefore he esteems it a very wild opinion, that terrestrial animals can remain any long time under water without drowning.

considerable sale for singing-birds except in the metropolis: as the apparatus for this purpose is also heavy, and at the same time must be carried on a man's back, it prevents the bird catchers going to above three or four miles distance.

This method of bird-catching must have been long practised, as it is brought to a most systematical perfection, and is attended with a very considerable expence.

The nets are a most ingenious piece of mechanism, are generally twelve yards and a half long, and two yards and a half wide; and no one on bare inspection would imagine that a bird (who is so very quick in all its motions) could be catched by the nets flapping over each other, till he becomes eye-witness of the pullers seldom failing *.

The wild birds *fly* (as the bird-catchers term it) chiefly during the month of October, and part of September and November; as the flight in March is much less considerable than that of Michaelmas. It is to be noted also, that the several species of birds of flight do not make their appearance precisely at the same time, during the months of September, October, and November. The Pippet †, for example, begins to fly about Michaelmas, and then the Woodlark, Linnet, Goldfinch, Chaffinch, Greenfinch, and other birds of flight succeed; all of which are not easily to be caught, or in any numbers, at any other time, and more particularly the Pippet and the Woodlark.

* These nets are known in most parts of England by the name of day-nets or clap-nets; but all we have seen are far inferior in their mechanism to those used near London,

† A small species of Lark, but which is inferior to other birds of that genus in point of song.

These birds, during the Michaelmas and March flights, are chiefly on the wing from day-break to noon, though there is afterwards a small flight from two till night; but this however is so inconsiderable, that the bird-catchers always take up their nets at noon.

It may well deserve the attention of the naturalist whence these periodical flights of certain birds can arise. As the ground however is ploughed during the months of October and March for sowing the winter and lent corn, it should seem that they are thus supplied with a great profusion both of seeds and insects, which they cannot so easily procure at any other season.

It may not be improper to mention another circumstance, to be observed during their flitting, viz. that they fly always against the wind; hence, there is great contention amongst the bird-catchers who shall gain that point; if (for example) it is westerly, the bird-catcher who lays his nets most to the east, is sure almost of catching every thing, provided his call-birds are good: a gentle wind to the south-west generally produces the best sport.

The bird-catcher who is a substantial man, and hath a proper apparatus for this purpose, generally carries with him five or six linnets (of which more are caught than any singing bird) two goldfinches, two greenfinches, one woodlark, one redpoll, a yellowhammer, titlark, and aberdavine, and perhaps a bullfinch; these are placed at small distances from the nets in little cages. He hath, besides, what are called flur-birds, which are placed within the nets, are raised upon the flur ‡, and gently

‡ A moveable perch to which the bird is tied, and which the bird-catcher can raise at pleasure, by means of a long string fastened to it.

let down at the time the wild bird approaches them. These generally consist of the linnet, the goldfinch, and the greenfinch, which are secured to the flur by what is called a *brace* *; a contrivance that secures the birds without doing any injury to their plumage.

It having been found that there is a superiority between bird and bird, from the one being more in song than the other; the bird-catchers contrive that their call-birds should moult before the usual time. They, therefore, in June or July, put them into a close box, under two or three folds of blankets, and leave their dung in the cage to raise a greater heat; in which state they continue, being perhaps examined but once a week to have fresh water. As for food, the air is so putrid, that they eat little during the whole state of confinement, which lasts about a month. The birds frequently die under the operation †; and hence the value of a stopped bird rises greatly.

When the bird hath thus prematurely moulted, he is in song, whilst the wild birds are out of song, and his note is louder and more piercing than that of a wild one; but it is not only in his note he receives an alteration, the plumage is equally improved. The black and yellow in the wings of the goldfinch, for example, become deeper and more vivid, together with a most beautiful gloss, which is not to be seen in the wild bird. The bill, which in the latter is likewise black at the end, in the stopped bird becomes white and more taper, as do its legs: in short, there is as much difference between a wild and a stopped bird, as there is between a horse which is kept in body clothes, or at grass.

When the bird-catcher hath laid his nets, he disposes of his call-birds at proper intervals. It must be owned, that there is a most malicious joy in these call-birds to bring the wild ones into the same state of captivity; which may likewise be observed with regard to the decoy ducks.

Their sight and hearing infinitely excels that of the bird-catcher. The instant that the ‡ wild birds are perceived, notice is given by one to the rest of the call-birds (as it is by the first hound that hits on the scent to the rest of the pack) after which follows the same sort of tumultuous ecstacy and joy. The call-birds, while the bird is at a distance, do not sing as a bird does in a chamber; they invite the wild ones by what the bird-catchers call short jerks, which when the birds are good, may be heard at a great distance. The ascendancy by this call or invitation is so great, that the wild bird is stopped in its course of flight, and if not already acquainted with the nets §, lights boldly within twenty yards of

* A sort of bandage, formed of a slender silken string that is fastened round the bird's body, and under the wings, in so artful a manner as to hinder the bird from being hurt, let it flutter ever so much in the raising.

† We have been lately informed by an experienced bird-catcher, that he pursues a cooler regimen in stopping his birds, and that he therefore seldom loses one: but we suspect that there is not the same certainty of making them moult.

‡ It may be also observed, that the moment they see a hawk, they communicate the alarm to each other by a plaintive note; nor will they then jerk or call though the wild birds are near.

§ A bird, acquainted with the nets, is by the bird-catchers termed a sharper, which they endeavour to drive away, as they can have no sport whilst it continues near them.

perhaps

perhaps three or four bird-catchers, on a ſpot which otherwiſe it would not have taken the leaſt notice of. Nay, it frequently happens, that if half a flock only are caught, the remaining half will immediately afterwards light in the nets, and ſhare the ſame fate; and ſhould only one bird eſcape, that bird will ſuffer itſelf to be pulled at till it is caught, ſuch a faſcinating power have the call birds.

While we are on this ſubject of the jerking of birds, we cannot omit mentioning, that the bird-catchers frequently lay conſiderable wagers whoſe call-bird can jerk the longeſt, as that determines the ſuperiority. They place them oppoſite to each other, by an inch of candle, and the bird who jerks the ofteneſt, before the candle is burnt out, wins the wager. We have been informed, that there have been inſtances of a bird's giving a hundred and ſeventy jerks in a quarter of an hour; and we have known a linnet, in ſuch a trial, perſevere in its emulation till it ſwooned from the perch: thus, as Pliny ſays of the nightingale, *victa morte finit ſæpe vitam, ſpiritu prius deficiente quàm cantu.* Lib. x. c. 29.

It may be here obſerved, that birds when near each other, and in ſight, ſeldom jerk or ſing. They either fight, or uſe ſhort and wheedling calls; the jerking of theſe call-birds, therefore, face to face, is a moſt extraordinary inſtance of contention for ſuperiority in ſong.

It may be alſo worthy of obſervation, that the female of no ſpecies of birds ever ſings: with birds, it is the reverſe of what occurs in human kind: among the feathered tribe, all the cares of life fall to the lot of the tender ſex: theirs is the fatigue of incubation; and the principal ſhare in nurſing the helpleſs brood: to alleviate theſe fatigues, and to ſupport her under them, nature hath given to the male the ſong, with all the little blandiſhments and ſoothing arts; theſe he fondly exerts (even after courtſhip) on ſome ſpray contiguous to the neſt, during the time his mate is performing her parental duties. But that ſhe ſhould be ſilent, is alſo another wiſe proviſion of nature, for her ſong would diſcover her neſt; as would a gaudineſs of plumage, which, for the ſame reaſon, ſeems to have been denied her.

To theſe we may add a few particulars that fell within our notice during our enquiries among the bird-catchers, ſuch as, that they immediately kill the hens of every ſpecies of birds they take, being incapable of ſinging, as alſo being inferior in plumage; the pippets likewiſe are indiſcriminately deſtroyed, as the cock does not ſing well: they ſell the dead birds for three-pence or four-pence a dozen.

Theſe ſmall birds are ſo good, that we are ſurpriſed the luxury of the age neglects ſo delicate an acquiſition to the table. The modern Italians are fond of ſmall birds, which they eat under the common name of Beccaficos: and the dear rate a Roman tragedian paid for one diſh of ſinging birds * is well known.

Another particular we learned, in converſation with a London bird-catcher, was, the vaſt price that is ſometimes given for a ſingle ſong-bird, which had not learned to whiſtle tunes. The greateſt ſum we heard of, was five guineas for a chaffinch, that had

* *Maximè tamen inſignis eſt in hac memoria,* Clodii Æſopi *tragici hiſtrionis patina ſexcentis H. S. taxata; in quo poſuit aves cantu aliquo, aut humano ſermone, vocales.* Plin. lib. x. c. 51. The price of this expenſive diſh was about 6843 *l.* 10 *s.* according to Arbuthnot's Tables. This ſeems to have been a wanton caprice, rather than a tribute to epicuriſm.

a particular and uncommon note, under which it was intended to train others: and we alſo heard of five pounds ten ſhillings being given for a call-bird linnet.

A third ſingular circumſtance, which confirms an obſervation of Linnæus, is, that the male chaffinches fly by themſelves, and in the flight precede the females; but this is not peculiar to the chaffinches. When the titlarks are caught in the beginning of the ſeaſon, it frequently happens, that forty are taken and not one female among them: and probably the ſame would be obſerved with regard to other birds (as has been done with relation to the wheat-ear) if they were attended to.

An experienced and intelligent bird-catcher informed us, that ſuch birds as breed twice a year, generally have in their firſt brood a majority of males, and in their ſecond, of females, which may in part account for the above obſervation.

We muſt not omit mention of the bullfinch, though it does not properly come under the title of a ſinging bird, or a bird of flight, as it does not often move farther than from hedge to hedge; yet, as the bird ſells well on account of its learning to whiſtle tunes, and ſometimes flies over the fields where the nets are laid; the bird-catchers have often a call-bird to enſnare it, though moſt of them can imitate the call with their mouths. It is remarkable with regard to this bird, that the female anſwers the purpoſe of a call-bird as well as the male, which is not experienced in any other bird taken by the London bird-catchers.

It may perhaps ſurpriſe, that under this article of ſinging-birds, we have not mentioned the nightingale, which is not a bird of flight, in the ſenſe the bird-catchers uſe this term. The nightingale, like the robin, wren, and many other ſinging birds, only moves from hedge to hedge, and does not take the periodical flights in October and March. The perſons who catch theſe birds, make uſe of ſmall trap-nets, without call-birds, and are conſidered as inferior in dignity to other bird-catchers, who will not rank with them.

The nightingale being the firſt of ſinging-birds, we ſhall here inſert a few particulars relating to it.

Its arrival is expected, by the trappers in the neighbourhood of London, the firſt week in April; at the beginning none but cocks are taken, but in a few days the hens make their appearance, generally by themſelves, though ſometimes a few males come along with them.

The latter are diſtinguiſhed from the females not only by their ſuperior ſize, but by a great ſwelling of their vent, which commences on the firſt arrival of the hens.

They do not build till the middle of May, and generally chuſe a quickſet to make their neſt in.

If the nightingale is kept in a cage, it often begins to ſing about the latter end of November, and continues its ſong more or leſs till June.

A young canary bird, linnet, ſkylark, or robin (who have never heard any other bird) are ſaid beſt to learn the note of a nightingale.

They are caught in a net-trap; the bottom of which is ſurrounded with an iron ring; the net itſelf is rather larger than a cabbage-net.

When the trappers hear or ſee them, they ſtrew ſome freſh mould under the place, and bait the trap with a meal-worm from the baker's ſhop.

Ten

Ten or a dozen nightingales have been thus caught in a day. *Barrington.*

§ 21. *Experiments and Obſervations on the* Singing *of* Birds.

From the Philoſophical Tranſactions, Vol. lxiii.

As the experiments and obſervations I mean to lay before the Royal Society relate to the ſinging of birds, which is a ſubject that hath never before been ſcientifically treated of *, it may not be improper to prefix an explanation of ſome uncommon terms, which I ſhall be obliged to uſe, as well as others which I have been under a neceſſity of coining.

To *chirp*, is the firſt ſound which a young bird utters, as a cry for food, and is different in all neſtlings, if accurately attended to; ſo that the hearer may diſtinguiſh of what ſpecies the birds are, though the neſt may hang out of his ſight and reach.

This cry is, as might be expected, very weak and querulous; it is dropped entirely as the bird grows ſtronger, nor is afterwards intermixed with its ſong, the chirp of a nightingale (for example) being hoarſe and diſagreeable.

To this definition of the chirp, I muſt add, that it conſiſts of a ſingle ſound, repeated at very ſhort intervals, and that it is common to neſtlings of both ſexes.

The *call* of a bird, is that ſound which it is able to make when about a month old; it is, in moſt inſtances (which I happen to recollect) a repetition of one and the ſame note, is retained by the bird as long as it lives, and is common, generally, to both the cock and hen †.

The next ſtage in the notes of a bird is termed, by the bird-catchers, *recording*, which word is probably derived from a muſical inſtrument, formerly uſed in England, called a recorder ‡.

This attempt in the neſtling to ſing, may be compared to the imperfect endeavour in a child to babble. I have known inſtances of birds beginning to record when they were not a month old.

This firſt eſſay does not ſeem to have the leaſt rudiments of the future ſong; but as the bird grows older and ſtronger, one may begin to perceive what the neſtling is aiming at.

Whilſt the ſcholar is thus endeavouring to form his ſong, when he is once ſure of a paſſage, he commonly raiſes his tone, which he drops again, when he is not equal to what he

* Kircher, indeed, in his Muſurgia, hath given us ſome few paſſages in the ſong of the nightingale, as well as the call of a quail and cuckow, which he hath engraved in muſical characters. Theſe inſtances, however, only prove that ſome birds have in their ſong notes which correſpond

† For want of terms to diſtinguiſh the notes of birds, Bellon applies the verb *chantent*, or ſing, to the gooſe and crane, as well as the nightingale. « Pluſieurs oiſeaux *chantent* la nuit, comme eſt l'oye, la grue, & le roſſignol." Bellon's Hiſt. of Birds, p. 50.

‡ It ſeems to have been a ſpecies of flute, and was probably uſed to teach young birds to pipe tunes.

Lord Bacon deſcribes this inſtrument to have been ſtrait, to have had a leſſer and greater bore, both above and below, to have required very little breath from the blower, and to have had what he

is attempting; juſt as a ſinger raiſes his voice, when he not only recollects certain parts of a tune with preciſion, but knows that he can execute them.

What the neſtling is not thus thoroughly maſter of, he hurries over, lowering his tone, as if he did not wiſh to be heard, and could not yet ſatisfy himſelf.

I have never happened to meet with a paſſage in any writer, which ſeems to relate to this ſtage of ſinging in a bird, except, perhaps, in the following lines of Statius:

———" Nunc volucrum novi
" Queſtus, inexpertumque carmen,
" Quod tacitâ ſtatuere brumâ."
Stat. Sylv. L. IV. Ecl. 5.

A young bird commonly continues to record for ten or eleven months, when he is able to execute every part of his ſong, which afterwards continues fixed, and is ſcarcely ever altered *.

When the bird is thus become perfect in his leſſon, he is ſaid to ſing his ſong round, or in all its varieties of paſſages, which he connects together, and executes without a pauſe.

I would therefore define a bird's ſong to be a ſucceſſion of three or more different notes, which are continued without interruption during the ſame interval with a muſical bar of four crotchets in an adagio movement, or whilſt a pendulum ſwings four ſeconds.

By the firſt requiſite in this definition, I mean to exclude the call of a cuckow, or clucking of a hen †, as they conſiſt of only two notes; whilſt the ſhort burſts of ſinging-birds, contending with each other (called *jerks* by the bird-catchers) are equally diſtinguiſhed from what I term ſong, by their not continuing for four ſeconds.

As the notes of a cuckow and hen, therefore, though they exceed what I have defined the call of a bird to be, do not amount to its ſong, I will, for this reaſon, take the liberty of terming ſuch a ſucceſſion of two notes as we hear in theſe birds the *varied call*.

Having thus ſettled the meaning of certain words, which I ſhall be obliged to make uſe of, I ſhall now proceed to ſtate ſome general principles with regard to the ſinging of birds, which ſeem to reſult from the experiments I have been making for ſeveral years, and under a great variety of circumſtances.

Notes in birds are no more innate, than language is in man, and depend entirely upon the maſter under which they are bred, as far as their organs will enable them to imitate the ſounds which they have frequent opportunities of hearing.

Moſt of the experiments I have made on this ſubject have been tried with cock linnets, which were fledged and nearly able to leave their neſt, on account not only of this bird's docility, and great powers of imitation, but becauſe the cock is eaſily diſtinguiſhed from the hen at that early period, by the ſuperior whiteneſs in the wing ‡.

* The bird called a Twite by the bird-catchers commonly flies in company with linnets, yet theſe two ſpecies of birds never learn each other's notes, which always continue totally different.

† The common hen, when ſhe lays, repeats the ſame note, very often, and concludes with the ſixth above, which ſhe holds for a longer time.

‡ The white reaches almoſt to the ſhaft of the quill feathers, and in the hen does not exceed more than half of that ſpace: it is alſo of a brighter hue.

T In

In many other sorts of singing birds the male is not at the age of three weeks so certainly known from the female; and if the pupil turns out to be a hen,

> ——— " ibi omnis
> " Effusus labor."

The Greek poets made a songster of the τεττιξ, whatever animal that may be, and it is remarkable, that they observed the female was incapable of singing as well as hen birds:

> Ειτ' εισιν οι τεττιγες ουκ ευδαιμονες,
> Ων ταις γυναιξιν ουδ' οτιουν φωνης ενι;
>
> Comicorum Græcorum Sententiæ, p. 452. Ed. Steph.

I have indeed known an instance or two of a hen's making out something like the song of her species; but these are as rare as the common hen's being heard to crow.

I rather suspect also, that those parrots, magpies, &c. which either do not speak at all, or very little, are hens of those kinds.

I have educated nestling linnets under the three best singing larks, the skylark, woodlark, and titlark, every one of which, instead of the linnet's song, adhered entirely to that of their respective instructors.

When the note of the titlark-linnet * was thoroughly fixed, I hung the bird in a room with two common linnets, for a quarter of a year, which were full in song; the titlark-linnet, however, did not borrow any passages from the linnet's song, but adhered stedfastly to that of the titlark.

I had some curiosity to find out whether an European nestling would equally learn the note of an African bird: I therefore educated a young linnet under a vengolina †, which imitated its African master so exactly, without any mixture of the linnet song, that it was impossible to distinguish the one from the other.

This vengolina-linnet was absolutely perfect, without ever uttering a single note by which it could have been known to be a linnet. In some of my other experiments, however, the nestling linnet retained the call of its own species, or what the bird-catchers term the linnet's chuckle, from some resemblance to that word when pronounced.

I have before stated, that all my nestling linnets were three weeks old, when taken from the nest; and by that time they frequently learn their own call from the parent birds, which I have mentioned to consist of only a single note.

To be certain, therefore, that a nestling will not have even the call of its species, it should be taken from the nest when only a day or two old; because, though nestlings cannot see till the seventh day, yet they can hear from the instant they are hatched, and probably,

* I thus call a bird which sings notes he would not have learned in a wild state; thus by a skylark-linnet, I mean a linnet with the skylark song; a nightingale-robin, a robin with the nightingale song, &c.

† This bird seems not to have been described by any of the ornithologists; it is of the finch tribe, and about the same size with our aberdavine (or siskin). The colours are grey and white, and the cock hath a bright yellow spot from the rump. It is a very familiar bird, and sings better than any of those which are not European, except the American mocking bird. An instance hath lately happened, in an aviary at Hampstead, of a vengolina's breeding with a Canary bird.

probably, from that circumſtance, attend to ſounds more than they do afterwards, eſpecially as the call of the parents announces the arrival of their food.

I muſt own, that I am not equal myſelf, nor can I procure any perſon to take the trouble of breeding up a bird of this age, as the odds againſt its being reared are almoſt infinite. The warmth indeed of incubation may be, in ſome meaſure, ſupplied by cotton and fires; but theſe delicate animals require in this ſtate, being fed almoſt perpetually, whilſt the nouriſhment they receive ſhould not only be prepared with great attention, but given in very ſmall portions at a time.

Though I muſt admit, therefore, that I have never reared myſelf a bird of ſo tender an age, yet I have happened to ſee both a linnet and a goldfinch which were taken from their neſts when only two or three days old.

The firſt of theſe belonged to Mr. Matthews, an apothecary at Kenſington, which, from a want of other ſounds to imitate, almoſt articulated the words pretty boy, as well as ſome other ſhort ſentences: I heard the bird myſelf repeat the words pretty boy; and Mr. Matthews aſſured me, that he had neither the note or call of any bird whatſoever.

This talking linnet died laſt year, before which, many people went from London to hear him ſpeak.

The goldfinch I have before mentioned, was reared in the town of Knighton in Radnorſhire, which I happened to hear, as I was walking by the houſe where it was kept.

I thought indeed that a wren was ſinging; and I went into the houſe to inquire after it, as that little bird ſeldom lives long in a cage.

The people of the houſe, however, told me, that they had no bird but a goldfinch, which they conceived to ſing its own natural note, as they called it; upon which I ſtaid a conſiderable time in the room, whilſt its notes were merely thoſe of a wren, without the leaſt mixture of goldfinch.

On further inquiries, I found that the bird had been taken from the neſt when only a day or two old, that it was hung in a window which was oppoſite to a ſmall garden, whence the neſtling had undoubtedly acquired the notes of the wren, without having had any opportunity of learning even the call of the goldfinch.

Theſe facts, which I have ſtated, ſeem to prove very deciſively, that birds have not any innate ideas of the notes which are ſuppoſed to be peculiar to each ſpecies. But it will poſſibly be aſked, why, in a wild ſtate, they adhere ſo ſteadily to the ſame ſong, inſomuch, that it is well known, before the bird is heard, what notes you are to expect from him.

This, however, ariſes entirely from the neſtling's attending only to the inſtruction of the parent bird, whilſt it diſregards the notes of all others, which may perhaps be ſinging round him.

Young Canary birds are frequently reared in a room where there are many other ſorts; and yet I have been informed, that they only learn the ſong of the parent cock.

Every one knows, that the common houſe-ſparrow, when in a wild ſtate, never does any thing but chirp: this, however, does not ariſe from want of powers in this bird to imitate others; but becauſe he only attends to the parental note.

But, to prove this decisively, I took a common sparrow from the nest when it was fledged, and educated him under a linnet: the bird, however, by accident, heard a goldfinch also, and his song was, therefore, a mixture of the linnet and goldfinch.

I have tried several experiments, in order to observe, from what circumstances birds fix upon any particular note when taken from the parents; but cannot settle this with any sort of precision, any more than at what period of their recording they determine upon the song to which they will adhere.

I educated a young robin under a very fine nightingale; which, however, began already to be out of song, and was perfectly mute in less than a fortnight.

This robin afterwards sung three parts in four nightingale; and the rest of his song was what the bird-catchers call rubbish, or no particular note whatsoever.

I hung this robin nearer to the nightingale than to any other bird; from which first experiment I conceived that the scholar would imitate the master which was at the least distance from him.

From several other experiments, however, which I have since tried, I find it to be very uncertain what notes the nestlings will most attend to, and often their song is a mixture; as in the instance which I before stated of the sparrow.

I must own also, that I conceived, from the experiment of educating the robin under a nightingale, that the scholar would fix upon the note which it first heard when taken from the nest; I imagined likewise, that, if the nightingale had been fully in song, the instruction for a fortnight would have been sufficient.

I have, however, since tried the following experiment, which convinces me, so much depends upon circumstances, and perhaps caprice in the scholar, that no general inference, or rule, can be laid down with regard to either of these suppositions.

I educated a nestling robin under a woodlark-linnet, which was full in song, and hung very near to him for a month together: after which, the robin was removed to another house, where he could only hear a skylark-linnet. The consequence was, that the nestling did not sing a note of woodlark (though I afterwards hung him again just above the woodlark-linnet) but adhered entirely to the song of the skylark-linnet.

Having thus stated the result of several experiments, which were chiefly intended to determine, whether birds had any innate ideas of the notes, or song, which is supposed to be peculiar to each species, I shall now make some general observations on their singing; though perhaps the subject may appear to many a very minute one.

Every poet, indeed, speaks with raptures of the harmony of the groves; yet those even, who have good musical ears, seem to pay little attention to it, but as a pleasing noise.

I am also convinced (though it may seem rather paradoxical) that the inhabitants of London distinguish more accurately, and know more on this head, than of all the other parts of the island taken together.

This seems to arise from two causes.

The first is, that we have not more musical ideas which are innate, than we have of language; and therefore those even, who have the happiness to have organs which are capable of receiving a gratification from this sixth sense (as it hath been called by some) require, however, the best instruction.

The orchestra of the opera, which is confined to the metropolis, hath diffused a good style of playing over the other bands of the capital, which is, by degrees, communicated to the fidler and ballad-singer in the streets; the organs in every church, as well as those of the Savoyards, contribute likewise to this improvement of musical faculties in the Londoners.

If the singing of the ploughman in the country is therefore compared with that of the London blackguard, the superiority is infinitely on the side of the latter; and the same may be observed in comparing the voice of a country girl and London house-maid, as it is very uncommon to hear the former sing tolerably in tune.

I do not mean by this, to assert that the inhabitants of the country are not born with as good musical organs; but only, that they have not the same opportunities of learning from others, who play in tune themselves.

The other reason for the inhabitants of London judging better in relation to the song of birds, arises from their hearing each bird distinctly, either in their own or their neighbours shops; as also from a bird continuing much longer in song whilst in a cage than when at liberty; the cause of which I shall endeavour hereafter to explain.

They who live in the country, on the other hand, do not hear birds sing in their woods for above two months in the year, when the confusion of notes prevents their attending to the song of any particular bird; nor does he continue long enough in a place, for the hearer to recollect his notes with accuracy.

Besides this, birds in the spring sing very loud indeed; but they only give short jerks, and scarcely ever the whole compass of their song.

For these reasons, I have never happened to meet with any person, who had not resided in London, whose judgment or opinion on this subject I could the least rely upon; and a stronger proof of this cannot be given, than that most people, who keep Canary birds, do not know that they sing chi [illegible] her the titlark or nightingale notes *.

Nothing, however, can be [illegible]re marked than the note of a nightingale called its jug, which most of the Canary birds brought from the Tyrol commonly have, as well as several nightingale strokes, or particular passages in the song of that bird.

I mention this superior knowledge in the inhabitants of the capital, because I am convinced, that, if others are consulted in relation to the singing of birds, they will only mislead, instead of giving any material or useful information †.

Birds

* I once saw two of these birds which came from the Canary Islands, neither of which had any song at all; and I have been informed that a ship brought a great many of them not long since, which sung as little.

Most of those Canary birds, which are imported from the Tyrol, have been educated by parents, the progenitor of which was instructed by a nightingale; our English Canary birds have commonly more of the titlark note.

The traffick in these birds makes a small article of commerce, as four Tyroleze generally bring over to England sixteen hundred every year; and though they carry them on their backs one thousand miles, as well as pay 20*l.* duty for such a number, yet, upon the whole, it answers to sell these birds at 5 *s.* apiece.

The chief place for breeding Canary birds is Inspruck and its environs, from whence they are sent to Constantinople, as well as every part of Europe.

† As it will not answer to catch birds with

 clap-

Birds in a wild ſtate do not commonly ſing above ten weeks in the year? which is then alſo confined to the cocks of a few ſpecies; I conceive that this laſt circumſtance ariſes from the ſuperior ſtrength of the muſcles of the larynx.

I procured a cock nightingale, a cock and hen blackbird, a cock and hen rook, a cock linnet, as alſo a cock and hen chaffinch, which that very eminent anatomiſt, Mr. Hunter, F. R. S. was ſo obliging as to diſſect for me, and begged, that he would particularly attend to the ſtate of the organs in the different birds, which might be ſuppoſed to contribute to ſinging.

Mr. Hunter found the muſcles of the larynx to be ſtronger in the nightingale than in any other bird of the ſame ſize; and in all thoſe inſtances (where he diſſected both cock and hen) that the ſame muſcles were ſtronger in the cock.

I ſent the cock and hen rook, in order to ſee whether there would be the ſame difference in the cock and hen of a ſpecies which did not ſing at all. Mr. Hunter, however, told me, that he had not attended ſo much to their comparative organs of voice, as in the other kinds; but that, to the beſt of his recollection, there was no difference at all.

Strength, however, in theſe muſcles, ſeems not to be the only requiſite; the birds muſt have alſo great plenty of food, which ſeems to

wild ones do not (as I obſerved before) continue in ſong above ten weeks.

The food of ſinging birds conſiſts of plants, inſects, or ſeeds, and of the two firſt of theſe there is infinitely the greateſt profuſion in the ſpring.

As for ſeeds, which are to be met with only in the autumn, I think they cannot well find any great quantities of them in a country ſo cultivated as England is; for the ſeeds in meadows are deſtroyed by mowing; in paſtures, by the bite of the cattle; and in arable, by the plough, when moſt of them are buried too deep for the bird to reach them †.

I know well that the ſinging of the cock-bird in the ſpring is attributed by many to the motive only of pleaſing its mate during incubation.

They, however, who ſuppoſe this, ſhould recollect, that much the greater part of birds do not ſing at all, why ſhould their mate therefore be deprived of this ſolace and amuſement?

The bird in a cage, which, perhaps, ſings nine or ten months in a year, cannot do ſo from this inducement: and, on the contrary, it ariſes chiefly from contending with another bird, or indeed againſt almoſt any ſort of continued noiſe.

Superiority in ſong gives to birds a moſt amazing aſcendency over each other; as is well know to the bird-catchers by the faſci-

contrive ſhould moult prematurely for this purpoſe.

But, to ſhew deciſively that the ſinging of a bird in the ſpring does not ariſe from any attention to its mate, a very experienced catcher of nightingales hath informed me, that ſome of theſe birds have jerked the inſtant they were caught. He hath alſo brought to me a nightingale, which had been but a few hours in a cage, and which burſt forth in a roar of ſong.

At the ſame time this bird is ſo ſulky on its firſt confinement, that he muſt be crammed for ſeven or eight days, as he will otherwiſe not feed himſelf; it is alſo neceſſary to tye his wings, to prevent his killing himſelf againſt the top or ſides of the cage

I believe there is no inſtance of any bird's ſinging which exceeds our black-bird in ſize: and poſſibly this may ariſe from the difficulty of its concealing itſelf, if it called the attention of its enemies, not only by bulk, but by the proportionable loudneſs of its notes *.

I ſhould rather conceive, it is for the ſame reaſon that no hen-bird ſings, becauſe this talent would be ſtill more dangerous during incubation; which may poſſibly alſo account for the inferiority in point of plumage.

Barrington.

* For the ſame reaſon, moſt large birds are wilder than the ſmaller ones.

FISHES.

§ 22. *The* Eel.

The eel is a very ſingular fiſh in ſeveral things that relate to its natural hiſtory, and in ſome reſpects borders on the nature of the reptile tribe.

It is known to quit its element, and during night to wander along the meadows, not only for change of habitation, but alſo for the ſake of prey, feeding on the ſnails it finds in its paſſage.

During winter it beds itſelf deep in the mud, and continues in a ſtate of reſt like the ſerpent kind. It is very impatient of cold, and will eagerly take ſhelter in a whiſp of ſtraw flung into a pond in ſevere weather, which has ſometimes been practiſed as a method of taking them. Albertus goes ſo far as to ſay, that he has known eels to ſhelter in an hay-rick, yet all periſhed through exceſs of cold.

It has been obſerved, that in the river Nyne there is a variety of ſmall eel, with a leſſer head and narrower mouth than the common kind; that it is found in cluſters in the bottom of the river, and is called the bed-eel; theſe are ſometimes rouſed up by violent floods, and are never found at that time with meat in their ſtomachs. This bears ſuch an analogy with the cluſtering of blindworms in their quieſcent ſtate, that we cannot but conſider it as a further proof of a partial agreement in the nature of the two genera.

The ancients adopted a moſt wild opinion about the generation of theſe fiſh, believing them to be either created from the mud, or that the ſcrapings of their bodies which they left on the ſtones were animated and became young eels. Some moderns gave into theſe opinions, and into others that were equally extravagant. They could not account for the appearance of theſe fiſh in ponds that never were ſtocked with them, and that were even ſo remote as to make their being met with in ſuch places a phænomenon that they could not ſolve. But there is much reaſon to believe, that many waters are ſupplied with theſe fiſh by the aquatic fowl of prey, in the ſame manner as vegetation is ſpread by many of the land birds, either by being dropped as they carry them to feed their young, or by paſſing quick through their bodies, as is the caſe with herons; and ſuch may be the occaſion of the appearance of theſe fiſh in places where they were never ſeen before. As to their immediate generation, it has been ſufficiently proved to be effected in the ordinary courſe of nature, and that they are viviparous.

They are extremely voracious, and very deſtructive to the fry of fiſh.

No fiſh lives ſo long out of water as the eel: it is extremely tenacious of life, as its parts will move a conſiderable time after they are flayed and cut into pieces.

The eel is placed by Linnæus in the genus of *muræna*, his firſt of the apodal fiſh, or ſuch which want the ventral fins.

The eyes are placed not remote from the end of the noſe: the irides are tinged with red: the under jaw is longer than the upper; the teeth are ſmall, ſharp, and numerous: beneath each eye is a minute orifice: at the end of the noſe two others, ſmall and tubular.

The fiſh is furniſhed with a pair of pectoral fins, rounded at their ends. Another narrow fin on the back, uniting with that of the tail; and the anal fin joins it in the ſame manner beneath.

Behind the pectoral fins is the orifice to the gills, which are concealed in the ſkin.

Eels vary much in their colours, from a ſooty hue to a light olive green; and thoſe which are called ſilver eels, have their bellies white, and a remarkable clearneſs throughout.

Beſides theſe, there is another variety of this fiſh, known in the Thames by the name of grigs, and about Oxford by that of grigs or gluts. Theſe are ſcarce ever ſeen near Oxford in the winter, but appear in ſpring, and bite readily at the hook, which common eels in that neighbourhood will not. They have a larger head, a blunter noſe, thicker ſkin, and leſs fat than the common ſort; neither are they ſo much eſteemed, nor do they often exceed three or four pounds in weight.

Common eels grow to a large ſize, ſometimes ſo great as to weigh fifteen or twenty pounds, but that is extremely rare. As to inſtances brought by Dale and others, of theſe fiſh increaſing to a ſuperior magnitude, we have much reaſon to ſuſpect them to have been congers, ſince the enormous fiſh they deſcribe have all been taken at the mouths of the Thames or Medway.

The eel is the moſt univerſal of fiſh, yet is ſcarce ever found in the Danube, though it is very common in the lakes and rivers of Upper Auſtria.

The Romans held this fiſh very cheap, probably from its likeneſs to a ſnake.

Vos anguilla manet longæ cognata colubræ,
Vernula riparum pinguis torrente cloaca.
Juvenal, Sat. v.

For you is kept a ſink-fed ſnake-like eel.

On the contrary, the luxurious Sybarites were ſo fond of theſe fiſh, as to exempt from every kind of tribute the perſons who ſold them.

§ 23. *The* Perch.

The perch of Ariſtotle and Auſonius is the ſame with that of the moderns. That mentioned by Oppian, Pliny, and Athenæus, is is a ſea-fiſh, probably of the *Labrus* or *Sparus* kind, being enumerated by them among ſome congenerous ſpecies. Our perch was much eſteemed by the Romans:

> Nec te delicias menſarum Perca, ſilebo
> Amnigenos inter piſces dignande marinis.
>
> Ausonius.

It is not leſs admired at preſent as a firm and delicate fiſh; and the Dutch are particularly fond of it when made into a diſh called water ſouchy.

It is a gregarious fiſh, and loves deep holes and gentle ſtreams. It is a moſt voracious fiſh, and eager biter: if the angler meets with a ſhoal of them, he is ſure of taking every one.

It is a common notion that the pike will not attack this fiſh, being fearful of the ſpiny fins which the perch erects on the approach of the former. This may be true in reſpect to large fiſh; but it is well known the ſmall ones are the moſt tempting bait that can be laid for the pike.

The perch is a fiſh very tenacious of life: we have known them carried near ſixty miles in dry ſtraw, and yet ſurvive the journey.

Theſe fiſh ſeldom grow to a large ſize: we once heard of one that was taken in the Serpentine river, Hyde Park, that weighed nine pounds; but that is very uncommon.

The body is deep: the ſcales very rough: the back much arched: ſide-line near the back.

The irides golden: the teeth ſmall, diſpoſed in the jaws and on the roof of the mouth: the edges of the covers of the gills ſerrated: on the lower end of the largeſt is a ſharp ſpine.

The firſt dorſal fin conſiſts of fourteen ſtrong ſpiny rays: the ſecond of ſixteen ſoft ones: the pectoral fins are tranſparent, and conſiſt of fourteen rays; the ventral of ſix; the anal of eleven.

The tail is a little forked.

The colours are beautiful: the back and part of the ſides being of a deep green, marked with five broad black bars pointing downwards: the belly is white, tinged with red: the ventral fins of a rich ſcarlet; the anal fins and tail of the ſame colour, but rather paler.

In a lake called Llyn Raithlyn, in Merionethſhire, is a very ſingular variety of perch: the back is quite hunched, and the lower part of the back bone, next the tail, ſtrangely diſtorted: in colour, and in other reſpects, it reſembles the common kind, which are as numerous in the lake as theſe deformed fiſh. They are not peculiar to this water; for Linnæus takes notice of a ſimilar variety found at Fahlun, in his own country. I have alſo heard that it is to be met with in the Thames near Marlow.

§ 24. *The* Trout.

It is matter of ſurpriſe that this common fiſh has eſcaped the notice of all the ancients, except Auſonius: it is alſo ſingular, that ſo delicate a ſpecies ſhould be neglected at a time when the folly of the table was at its height; and that the epicures ſhould overlook a fiſh that is found in ſuch quantities in the lakes of their neighbourhood, when they ranſacked the univerſe for dainties. The milts of *murænæ* were brought from one place; the livers of *ſcari* from another *; and oyſters even

* Suetonius, vita Vitellii.

from ſo remote a ſpot as our Sandwich *: but there was, and is a faſhion in the article of good living. The Romans ſeem to have deſpiſed the trout, the piper, and the doree; and we believe Mr. Quin himſelf would have reſigned the rich paps of a pregnant ſow †, the heels of camels ‡, and the tongues of *flamingos* ||, though dreſſed by Heliogabalus's cooks, for a good jowl of ſalmon with lobſter-ſauce.

When Auſonius ſpeaks of this fiſh, he makes no euloge on its goodneſs, but celebrates it only for its beauty.

> Purpureiſque Salar ſtellatus tergore guttis.
>
> With purple ſpots the Salar's back is ſtain'd.

Theſe marks point out the ſpecies he intended: what he meant by his *fario* is not ſo eaſy to determine: whether any ſpecies of trout, of a ſize between the *ſalar* and the ſalmon; or whether the ſalmon itſelf, at a certain age, is not very evident.

> Teque inter geminos ſpecies, neutrumque et utrumque,
> Qui nec dum Salmo, nec Salar ambiguuſque,
> Amborum medio Fario intercepte ſub ævo.
>
> Salmon or Salar, I'll pronounce thee neither;
> A doubtful kind, that may be none or either,
> Fario, when ſtopt in middle growth.

In fact, the colours of the trout, and its ſpots, vary greatly in different waters, and in different ſeaſons; yet each may be reduced to one ſpecies. In Llyndivi, a lake in South Wales, are trouts called *coch y dail*, marked with red and black ſpots as big as ſix-pences; others unſpotted, and of a reddiſh hue, that ſometimes weigh near ten pounds, but are bad taſted.

In Lough Neagh, in Ireland, are trouts called there *buddaghs*, which I was told ſometimes weighed thirty pounds; but it was not my fortune to ſee any during my ſtay in the neighbourhood of that vaſt water.

Trouts (probably of the ſame ſpecies) are alſo taken in Hulſe-water, a lake in Cumberland, of a much ſuperior ſize to thoſe of Lough Neagh. Theſe are ſuppoſed to be the ſame with the trout of the lake of Geneva, a fiſh I have eaten more than once, and think but a very indifferent one.

In the river Eynion, not far from Machynleth, in Merionethſhire, and in one of the Snowdon lakes, are found a variety of trout, which are naturally deformed, having a ſtrange crookedneſs near the tail, reſembling that of the perch before deſcribed. We dwell the leſs on theſe monſtrous productions, as our friend the Hon. Daines Barrington, has already given an account of them in an ingenious diſſertation on ſome of the Cambrian fiſh, publiſhed in the Philoſophical Tranſactions of the year 1767.

The ſtomachs of the common trouts are uncommonly thick and muſcular. They feed on the ſhell-fiſh of lakes and rivers, as well as on ſmall fiſh. They likewiſe take into their ſtomachs gravel, or ſmall ſtones, to aſſiſt in comminuting the teſtaceous parts of their food. The trouts of certain lakes in Ireland, ſuch as thoſe of the province of Galway, and ſome others, are re-

that has them, *Gillaroo* trouts. These stomachs are sometimes served up to table, under the former appellation. It does not appear to me, that the extraordinary strength of stomach in the Irish fish, should give any suspicion that it is a distinct species: the nature of the waters might increase the thickness; or the superior quantity of shell-fish, which may more frequently call for the use of its comminuting powers than those of our trouts, might occasion this difference. I had opportunity of comparing the stomach of a great *Gillaroo* trout, with a large one from the Uxbridge river. The last, if I recollect, was smaller, and out of season; and its stomach (notwithstanding it was very thick) was much inferior in strength to that of the former: but on the whole, there was not the least specific difference between the two subjects.

Trouts are most voracious fish, and afford excellent diversion to the angler: the passion for the sport of angling is so great in the neighbourhood of London, that the liberty of fishing in some of the streams in the adjacent counties, is purchased at the rate of ten pounds per annum.

These fish shift their quarters to spawn, and, like salmon, make up towards the heads of rivers to deposit their roes. The under jaw of the trout is subject, at certain times, to the same curvature as that of the salmon.

A trout taken in Llynallet, in Denbighshire, which is famous for an excellent kind, measured seventeen inches, its depth three and three quarters, its weight one pound ten ounces: the head thick; the nose rather sharp: the upper jaw a little longer than the lower; both jaws, as well as the head, were of a pale brown, blotched with black: the teeth sharp and strong, disposed in the jaws, roof of the mouth and tongue, as is the case with the whole genus, except the gwyniad, which is toothless, and the grayling, which has none on its tongue.

The back was dusky; the sides tinged with a purplish bloom, marked with deep purple spots, mixed with black, above and below the side line which was strait: the belly white.

The first dorsal fin was spotted; the spurious fin brown, tipped with red; the pectoral, ventral, and anal fins, of a pale brown; the edges of the anal fin white, the tail very little forked when extended.

§ 25. *The* Pike *or* Jack.

The pike is common in most of the lakes of Europe, but the largest are those taken in Lapland, which, according to Schæffer, are sometimes eight feet long. They are taken there in great abundance, dried, and exported for sale. The largest fish of this kind which we ever heard of in England, weighed thirty-five pounds.

According to the common saying, these fish were introduced into England in the reign of Henry VIII. in 1537. They were so rare, that a pike was sold for double the price of a house-lamb in February, and a pickerel for more than a fat capon.

All writers who treat of this species bring instances of its vast voraciousness. We have known one that was choaked by attempting to swallow one of its own species that proved too large a morsel. Yet its jaws are very loosely connected; and have on each side an additional bone like the jaw of a viper, which renders them capable of greater distention when it swallows its prey. It does not confine it-

 self

ſelf to feed on fiſh and frogs; it will devour the water rat, and draw down the young ducks as they are ſwimming about. In a manuſcript note which we found, p. 244, of our copy of Plott's Hiſtory of Staffordſhire, is the following extraordinary fact: "At Lord "Gower's canal at Trentham, a pike ſeized "the head of a ſwan as ſhe was feeding under "water, and gorged ſo much of it as killed "them both. The ſervants perceiving the "ſwan with its head under water for a longer "time than uſual, took the boat, and found "both ſwan and pike dead *."

But there are inſtances of its fierceneſs ſtill more ſurpriſing, and which indeed border a little on the marvellous. Geſner † relates, that a famiſhed pike in the Rhone ſeized on the lips of a mule that was brought to water, and that the beaſt drew the fiſh out before it could diſengage itſelf. That people have been bit by theſe voracious creatures while they were waſhing their legs, and that they will even contend with the otter for its prey, and endeavour to force it out of its mouth.

Small fiſh ſhew the ſame uneaſineſs and deteſtation at the preſence of this tyrant, as the little birds do at the ſight of the hawk or owl, When the pike lies dormant near the ſurface (as is frequently the caſe) the leſſer fiſh are often obſerved to ſwim around it in vaſt numbers, and in great anxiety. Pike are often haltered in a nooſe, and taken while they lie thus aſleep, as they are often found in the ditches near the Thames, in the month of May.

* This note we afterwards diſcovered was wrote by Mr. Plott, of Oxford, who aſſured me he inſerted it on good authority.

† Geſner piſc, 503.

In the ſhallow water of the Lincolnſhire fens they are frequently taken in a manner peculiar, we believe, to that country, and the iſle of Ceylon. The fiſhermen make uſe of what is called a crown-net, which is no more than a hemiſpherical baſket, open at top and bottom. He ſtands at the end of one of the little fenboats, and frequently puts his baſket down to the bottom of the water, then poking a ſtick into it, diſcovers whether he has any booty by the ſtriking of the fiſh; and vaſt numbers of pike are taken in this manner.

The longevity of this fiſh is very remarkable, if we may credit the accounts given of it. Rzaczynſki tells us of one that was ninety years old; but Geſner relates, that in the year 1497, a pike was taken near Hailbrun, in Suabia, with a brazen ring affixed to it, on which were theſe words in Greek characters: *I am the fiſh which was firſt of all put into this lake by the hands of the governor of the univerſe*, Frederick *the ſecond, the 5th of October*, 1230: ſo that the former muſt have been an infant to this Methuſalem of a fiſh.

Pikes ſpawn in March or April, according to the coldneſs or warmth of the weather. When they are in high ſeaſon their colours are very fine, being green, ſpotted with bright yellow; and the gills are of a moſt vivid and full red. When out of ſeaſon, the green changes to grey, and the yellow ſpots turn pale.

The head is very flat; the upper jaw broad, and is ſhorter than the lower: the under jaw turns up a little at the end, and is marked with minute punctures.

The teeth are very ſharp, diſpoſed only in the front of the upper jaw, but in both ſides of the lower, in the roof of the mouth, and often the

the tongue. The ſlit of the mouth, or the gape, is very wide; the eyes ſmall.

The dorſal fin is placed very low on the back, and conſiſts of twenty-one rays; the pectoral of fifteen; the ventral of eleven; the anal of eighteen.

The tail is bifurcated.

§ 26. *The* Carp.

This is one of the naturalized fiſh of our country, having been introduced here by Leonard Maſchal, about the year 1514* to whom we were alſo indebted for that excellent apple the pepin. The many good things that our iſland wanted before that period, are enumerated in this old diſtich:

Turkies, carps, hops, pickerel, and beer,
Came into England all in one year.

As to the two laſt articles we have ſome doubts, the others we believe to be true. Ruſſia wants theſe fiſh at this day; Sweden has them only in the ponds of the people of faſhion; Poliſh Pruſſia is the chief ſeat of the carp; they abound in the rivers and lakes of that country, particularly in the Friſch and Curiſch-haff, where they are taken of a vaſt ſize. They are there a great article of commerce, and ſent in well-boats to Sweden and Ruſſia. The merchants purchaſe them out of the waters of the nobleſſe of the country, who draw a good revenue from this article. Neither are there wanting among our gentry, inſtances of ſome who make good profit of their ponds.

The ancients do not ſeparate the carp from the ſea fiſh. We are credibly informed that they are ſometimes found in the harbour of Dantzick, between the town and a ſmall place called Hela.

Carp are very long lived. Geſner brings an inſtance of one that was an hundred years old. They alſo grow to a very great ſize. On our own knowledge we can ſpeak of none that exceeded twenty pounds in weight; but Jovius ſays, that they were ſometimes taken in the Lacus Larius (the Lago di Como) of two hundred pounds weight; and Rzaczynſki mentions others taken in the Dnieſter that were five feet in length.

They are alſo extremely tenacious of life, and will live for a moſt remarkable time out of water. An experiment has been made by placing a carp in a net, well wrapped up in wet moſs, the mouth only remaining out, and then hung up in a cellar, or ſome cool place: the fiſh is frequently fed with white bread and milk, and is beſides often plunged into water. Carp thus managed have been known, not only to have lived above a fortnight, but to grow exceedingly fat, and far ſuperior in taſte to thoſe that are immediately killed from the pond †.

The carp is a prodigious breeder: its quantity of roe has been ſometimes found ſo great, that when taken out and weighed againſt the fiſh itſelf, the former has been found to preponderate. From the ſpawn of this fiſh caviare is made for the Jews, who hold the ſturgeon in abhorrence.

Theſe fiſh are extremely cunning, and on that

* Fuller's Britiſh Worthies, Suſſex. 113.

† This was told me by a gentleman of the utmoſt veracity, who had twice made the experiment. The ſame fact is related by that pious philoſopher Doctor Derham, in his Phyſico-Theology, edit. 9th. 1737. ch. 1. p. 7. n. *a*.

that account are by ſome ſtyled the *river fox*. They will ſometimes leap over the nets, and eſcape that way; at others, will immerſe themſelves ſo deep in the mud, as to let the net paſs over them. They are alſo very ſhy of taking a bait; yet at the ſpawning time they are ſo ſimple, as to ſuffer themſelves to be tickled, handled, and caught by any body that will attempt it.

This fiſh is apt to mix its milt with the roe of other fiſh, from which is produced a ſpurious breed: we have ſeen the offspring of the carp and tench, which bore the greateſt reſemblance to the firſt: have alſo heard of the ſame mixture between the carp and bream.

The carp is of a thick ſhape: the ſcales very large, and when in beſt ſeaſon of a fine gilded hue,

The jaws are of equal length; there are two teeth in the jaws, or on the tongue; but at the entrance of the gullet, above and below, are certain bones that act on each other, and comminute the food before it paſſes down.

On each ſide of the mouth is a ſingle beard; above thoſe on each ſide another, but ſhorter: the dorſal fin extends far towards the tail, which is a little bifurcated; the third ray of the dorſal fin is very ſtrong, and armed with ſharp teeth, pointing downwards; the third ray of the anal fin is conſtructed in the ſame manner.

§ 27. *The* Barbel.

This fiſh was ſo extremely coarſe, as to be overlooked by the ancients till the time of Auſonius, and what he ſays is no panegyric on it; for he lets us know it loves deep waters, and that when it grows old it was not abſolutely bad.

> Laxos exerces Barbe natatus,
> Tu melior pejore ævo, tibi contigit uni
> Spirantum ex numero non inlaudata ſenectus.

It frequents the ſtill and deep parts of rivers, and lives in ſociety, rooting like ſwine with their noſes in the ſoft banks. It is ſo tame as to ſuffer itſelf to be taken with the hand; and people have been known to take numbers by diving or them. In ſummer they move about during night in ſearch of food but towards autumn, and during winter, confine themſelves to the deepeſt holes.

They are the worſt and coarſeſt of freſh water fiſh, and ſeldom eat but by the poorer ſort of people, who ſometimes boil them with a bit of bacon to give them a reliſh. The roe is very noxious, affecting thoſe who unwarily eat of it with a nauſea, vomiting, purging, and a ſlight ſwelling.

It is ſometimes found of the length of three feet, and eighteen pounds in weight: it is of a long and rounded form: the ſcales not large.

Its head is ſmooth: the noſtrils placed near the eyes; the mouth is placed below: on each corner is a ſingle beard, and another on each ſide the noſe.

The dorſal fin is armed with a remarkable ſtrong ſpine, ſharply ſerrated, with which it can inflict a very ſevere wound on the incautious handler, and even do much damage to the nets.

The pectoral fins are of a pale brown colour; the ventral and anal tipped with yellow: the tail a little bifurcated, and of a deep purple: the ſide line is ſtrait.

The ſcales are of a pale gold colour, edged with black: the belly is white.

§ 28.

§ 28. *The* Tench.

The tench underwent the same fate with the barbel, in respect to the notice taken of it by the early writers: and even Ausonius, who first mentions it, treats it with such disrespect, as evinces the great capriciousness of taste; for that fish, which at present is held in such good repute was, in his days the repast only of the canaille.

> Quis non et virides vulgi solatia Tincas
> Norit?

It has been by some called the Physician of the fish, and that the slime is so healing, that the wounded apply it as a styptic. The ingenious Mr. Diaper, in his piscatory eclogues, says, that even the voracious pike will spare the tench on account of its healing powers:

> The Tench he spares a medicinal kind:
> For when by wounds distrest, or sore disease,
> He courts the salutary fish for ease;
> Close to his scales the kind physician glides,
> And sweats a healing balsam from his sides.
>
> Ecl. II.

Whatever virtue its slime may have to the inhabitants of the water, we will not vouch for, but its flesh is a wholesome and delicious food to those of the earth. The Germans are of a different opinion. By way of contempt, they call it Snoemaker. Gesner even says, that it is insipid and unwholesome.

It does not commonly exceed four or five pounds in weight, but we have heard of one that weighed ten pounds; Salvianus speaks of some that arrived at twenty pounds.

They love still waters, and are rarely found in rivers: they are very foolish, and easily caught.

The tench is thick and short in proportion to its length: the scales are very small, and covered with slime.

The irides are red: there is sometimes, but not always, a small beard at each corner of the mouth.

The colour of the back is dusky; the dorsal and ventral fins of the same colour: the head, sides, and belly, of a greenish cast, most beautifully mixed with gold, which is in its greatest splendor when the fish is in the highest season.

The tail is quite even at the end, and very broad.

§ 29. *The* Gudgeon.

Aristotle mentions the gudgeon in two places; once as a river fish, and again as a species that was gregarious: in a third place he describes it as a sea fish; we must therefore consider the Κωβιος he mentions lib. ix. c. 2. and lib. viii. c. 19. as the same with our species.

This fish is generally found in gentle streams, and is of a small size: those few, however, that are caught in the Kennet, and Cole, are three times the weight of those taken elsewhere. The largest we ever heard of was taken near Uxbridge, and weighed half a pound.

They bite eagerly, and are assembled by raking the bed of the river; to this spot they immediately crowd in shoals, expecting food from this disturbance.

The shape of the body is thick and round: the irides tinged with red: the gill covers with green and silver: the lower jaw is shorter than the upper: at each corner of the mouth is a single beard: the back olive, spotted with black: the side line strait; the sides beneath that silvery: the belly white.

The

The tail is forked; that, as well as the dorfal fin, is fpotted with black.

§ 30. *The* Bream.

The bream is an inhabitant of lakes, or the deep parts of ftill rivers. It is a fifh that is very little efteemed, being extremely infipid.

It is extremely deep, and thin in proportion to its length. The back rifes very much, and is very fharp at the top. The head and mouth are fmall: on fome we examined in the fpring, were abundance of minute whitifh tubercles; an accident which Pliny feems to have obferved befals the fifh of the Lago Maggiore, and Lago di Como. The fcales are very large: the fides flat and thin.

The dorfal fin has eleven rays, the fecond of which is the longeft: that fin, as well as all the reft, are of a dufky colour; the back of the fame hue: the fides yellowifh.

The tail is very large, and of the form of a crefcent.

§ 31. *The* Crucian.

This fpecies is common in many of the fifh-ponds about London, and other parts of the fouth of England; but I believe is not a native fifh.

It is very deep and thick: the back is much arched: the dorfal fin confifts of nineteen rays; the two firft ftrong and ferrated. The pectoral fins have (each) thirteen rays; the ventral nine; the anal feven or eight: the lateral line parallel with the belly: the tail almoft even at the end.

The colour of the fifh in general is a deep yellow: the meat is coarfe, and little efteemed.

§ 32. *The* Roach.

'Sound as a roach,' is a proverb that appears to be but indifferently founded, that fifh being not more diftinguifhed for its vivacity than many others; yet it is ufed by the French as well as us, who compare people of ftrong health to their *gardon*, our roach.

It is a common fifh, found in many of our deep ftill rivers, affecting, like the others of this genus, quiet waters. It is gregarious, keeping in large fhoals. We have never feen them very large. Old Walton fpeaks of fome that weighed two pounds. In a lift of fifh fold in the London markets, with the greateft weight of each, communicated to us by an intelligent fifhmonger, is mention of one whofe weight was five pounds.

The roach is deep but thin, and the back is much elevated, and fharply ridged: the fcales large and fall off very eafily. Side line bends much in the middle towards the belly.

§ 33. *The* Dace.

This, like the roach, is gregarious, haunts the fame places, is a great breeder, very lively, and during fummer is very fond of frolicing near the furface of the water. This fifh and the roach are coarfe and infipid meat.

Its head is fmall: the irides of a pale yellow: the body long and flender: its length feldom above ten inches, though in the abovementioned lift is an account of one that weighed a pound and a half: the fcales fmaller than thofe of the roach.

The back is varied with dufky, with a caft of a yellowifh green: the fides and belly filvery: the dorfal fin dufky: the ventral, anal, and caudal fins red, but lefs fo than thofe of the former: the tail is very much forked.

§ 34. *The* CHUB.

Salvianus imagines this fish to have been the *squalus* of the ancients, and grounds his opinion on a supposed error in a certain passage in Columella and Varro, where he would substitute the word *squalus* instead of *scarus*: Columella says no more than that the old Romans paid much attention to their stews, and kept even the sea-fish in fresh water, paying as much respect to the *mullet* and *scarus*, as those of his days did to the *muræna* and *bass*.

That the *scarus* was not our *chub*, is very evident; not only because the chub is entirely an inhabitant of fresh waters, but likewise it seems improbable that the Romans would give themselves any trouble about the worst of river fish, when they neglected the most delicious kinds; all their attention was directed towards those of the sea: the difficulty of procuring them seems to have been the criterion of their value, as is ever the case with effete luxury.

The chub is a very coarse fish, and full of bones: it frequents the deep holes of rivers, and during summer commonly lies on the surface, beneath the shade of some tree or bush. It is a very timid fish, sinking to the bottom on the least alarm, even at the passing of a shadow, but they will soon resume their situation. It feeds on worms, caterpillars, grasshoppers, beetles, and other coleopterous insects that happen to fall into the water; and it will even feed on cray-fish. This fish will rise to a fly.

This fish takes its name from its head, not only in our own, but in other languages: we call it *chub*, according to Skinner, from the old English, *cop*, a head; the French, *testard*; the Italians, *capitone*.

It does not grow to a large size; we have known some that weighed above five pounds, but Salvianus speaks of others that were eight or nine pounds in weight.

The body is oblong, rather round, and of a pretty equal thickness the greatest part of the way: the scales are large.

The irides silvery; the cheeks of the same colour: the head and back of a deep dusky green; the sides silvery, but in the summer yellow: the belly white: the pectoral fins of a pale yellow: the ventral and anal fins red: the tail a little forked, of a brownish hue, but tinged with blue at the end.

§ 35. *The* BLEAK.

The taking of these, Ausonius lets us know, was the sport of children,

ALBURNOS prædam puerilibus hamis.

They are very common in many of our rivers, and keep together in large shoals. These fish seem at certain seasons to be in great agonies; they tumble about near the surface of the water, and are incapable of swimming far from the place, but in about two hours recover, and disappear. Fish thus affected the Thames fishermen call *mad bleaks*. They seem to be troubled with a species of *gordius* or hair-worm, of the same kind with those which Aristotle * says that the *ballerus* and *tillo* are infested with, which torments them so that they rise to the surface of the water and then die.

Artificial pearls are made with the scales of this fish, and we think of the dace. They are beat into a fine powder, then diluted with water, and introduced into a thin glass bub-

*. Hist. an. lib. viii. c. 20.

ble,

ble, which is afterwards filled with wax. the French were the inventors of this art. Doctor Lister * tells us, that when he was at Paris, a certain artist used in one winter thirty hampers full of fish in this manufacture.

The bleak seldom exceeds five or six inches in length: their body is slender, greatly compressed sideways, not unlike that of the sprat.

The eyes are large: the irides of a pale yellow: the under jaw the longest: the lateral line crooked: the gills silvery: the back green: the sides and belly silvery: the fins pellucid: the scales fall off very easily: the tail much forked.

The White Bait.

During the month of July there appear in the Thames, near Blackwall and Greenwich, innumerable multitudes of small fish, which are known to the Londoners by the name of White Bait. They are esteemed very delicious when fried with fine flour, and occasion, during the season, a vast resort of the lower order of epicures to the taverns contiguous to the places they are taken at.

There are various conjectures about this species, but all terminate in a supposition that they are the fry of some fish, but few agree to which kind they owe their origin. Some attribute it to the shad, others to the sprat, the smelt, and the bleak. That they neither belong to the shad, nor the sprat, is evident from the number of branchiostegous rays, which in those are eight, in this only three. That they are not the young of smelts is as clear, because they want the *pinna adiposa*, or rayless fin; and that they are not the offspring of the bleak is extremely probable, since we never heard of the white bait being found in any other river, notwithstanding the bleak is very common in several of the British streams: but as the white bait bears a greater similarity to this fish than to any other we have mentioned, we give it a place here as an appendage to the bleak, rather than form a distinct article of a fish which it is impossible to class with certainty.

It is evident that it is of the carp or *cyprinus* genus: it has only three branchiostegous rays, and only one dorsal fin; and in respect to the form of the body, is compressed like that of the bleak.

Its usual length is two inches: the under jaw is the longest: the irides silvery, the pupil black: the dorsal fin is placed nearer to the head than to the tail, and consists of about fourteen rays: the side line is strait: the tail forked, the tips black.

The head, sides, and belly, are silvery; the back tinged with green.

* Journey to Paris, 142.

§ 36. *The* Minow.

This beautiful fish is frequent in many of our small gravelly streams, where they keep in shoals.

The body is slender and smooth, the scales being extremely small. It seldom exceeds three inches in length.

The lateral line is of a golden colour: the back flat, and of a deep olive: the sides and belly vary greatly in different fish; in a few are of a rich crimson, in others bluish, in others white. The tail is forked, and marked near the base with a dusky spot.

§ 37.

§ 37. *The* Gold Fish.

These fish are now quite naturalized in this country, and breed as freely in the open waters as the common carp.

They were first introduced into England about the year 1691, but were not generally known till 1728, when a great number were brought over, and presented first to Sir Mathew Dekker, and by him circulated round the neighbourhood of London, from whence they have been distributed to most parts of the country.

In China the most beautiful kinds are taken in a small lake in the province of Che-Kyang. Every person of fashion keeps them for amusement, either in porcelaine vessels, or in the small basons that decorate the courts of the Chinese houses. The beauty of their colours, and their lively motions, give great entertainment, especially to the ladies, whose pleasures, by reason of the cruel policy of that country, are extremely limited.

In form of the body they bear a great resemblance to a carp. They have been known in this island to arrive at the length of eight inches; in their native place they are said * to grow to the size of our largest herring.

The nostrils are tubular, and form sort of appendages above the nose: the dorsal fin and the tail vary greatly in shape: the tail is naturally bifid, but in many is trifid, and in some even quadrifid: the anal fins are the strongest characters of this species, being placed not behind one another like those of other fish, but opposite each other like the ventral fins.

The colours vary greatly; some are marked with a fine blue, with brown, with bright silver; but the general predominant colour is gold, of a most amazing splendor; but their colours and form need not be dwelt on, since those who want opportunity of seeing the living fish, may survey them expressed in the most animated manner, in the works of our ingenious and honest friend Mr. George Edwards.

Pennant.

* Du Halde, 316.

END OF THE FOURTH BOOK.

A NEW

A NEW CHRONOLOGICAL TABLE

OF

REMARKABLE EVENTS, DISCOVERIES, AND INVENTIONS.

Alſo, the Æra, the Country, and Writings of Learned Men.

The whole comprehending in one View, the Analyſis or Outlines of General Hiſtory from the Creation to the preſent Time.

Before Chriſt.

4004 THE creation of the world, and Adam and Eve.

4003 The birth of Cain, the firſt who was born of a woman.

3017 Enoch, for his piety, is tranſlated into Heaven.

2348 The old world is deſtroyed by a deluge which continued 377 days.

2247 The tower of Babel is built about this time by Noah's poſterity, upon which God miraculouſly confounds their language, and thus diſperſes them into different nations.

About the ſame time Noah is, with great probability, ſuppoſed to have parted from his rebellious offspring, and to have led a colony of ſome of the more tractable into the Eaſt, and there either he or one of his ſucceſſors to have founded the ancient Chineſe monarchy.

2234 The celeſtial obſervations are begun at Babylon, the city which firſt gave birth to learning and the ſciences.

2188 Miſraim, the ſon of Ham, founds the kingdom of Egypt, which laſted 1663 years, down to the conqueſt of Cambyſes, in 525 before Chriſt.

2059 Ninus, the ſon of Belus, founds the kingdom of Aſſyria, which laſted above 1000 years, and out of its ruins were formed the Aſſyrians of Babylon, thoſe of Nineveh, and the kingdom of the Medes.

1921 The covenant of God made with Abram, when he leaves Haran to go into Canaan, which begins the 430 years of ſojourning.

1897 The

1897 The cities of Sodom and Gommorrah are destroyed for their wickedness, by fire from Heaven.

1856 The kingdom of Argos, in Greece, begins under Inachus.

1822 Memnon, the Egyptian, invents the letters.

1715 Prometheus first struck fire from flints.

1635 Joseph dies in Egypt, which concludes the book of Genesis, containing a period of 2369 years.

1574 Aaron born in Egypt: 1490, appointed by God first high-priest of the Israelites.

1571 Moses, brother to Aaron, born in Egypt, and adopted by Pharaoh's daughter, who educates him in all the learning of the Egyptians.

1556 Cecrops brings a colony of Saites from Egypt into Attica, and begins the kingdom of Athens, in Greece.

1546 Scamander comes from Crete into Phrygia, and begins the kingdom of Troy.

1493 Cadmus carried the Phœnician letters into Greece, and built the citadel of Thebes.

1491 Moses performs a number of miracles in Egypt, and departs from that kingdom, together with 600,000 Israelites, besides children; which completed the 430 years of sojourning. They miraculously pass through the Red Sea, and come to the desert of Sinai, where Moses receives from God, and delivers to the people, the Ten Commandments, and the other laws, and sets up the tabernacle, and in it the ark of the covenant.

1485 The first ship that appeared in Greece was brought from Egypt by Danaus, who arrived at Rhodes, and brought with him his fifty daughters.

1453 The first Olympic games celebrated at Olympia, in Greece.

1452 The Pentateuch, or five first books of Moses, are written in the land of Moab, where he died the year following, aged 110.

1451 The Israelites, after sojourning in the wilderness forty years, are led under Joshua into the land of Canaan, where they fix themselves, after having subdued the natives; and the period of the sabbatical year commences.

1406 Iron is found in Greece from the accidental burning of the woods.

1198 The rape of Helen, by Paris, which, in 1193, gave rise to the Trojan war, and siege of Troy by the Greeks, which continued ten years, when that city was taken and burnt.

1048 David is sole king of Israel.

1004 The Temple is solemnly dedicated by Solomon.

896 Elijah, the prophet, is translated to Heaven.

894 Money first made of gold and silver at Argos.

869 The city of Carthage, in Africa, founded by queen Dido.

814 The kingdom of Macedon begins.

753 Æra of the building of Rome in Italy by Romulus, first king of the Romans.

720 Samaria taken, after three years siege, and the kingdom of Israel finished, by Salmanasar, king of Assyria, who carries the ten tribes into captivity.
The first eclipse of the moon on record.
658 Byzantium (now Constantinople) built by a colony of Athenians.
604 By order of Necho, king of Egypt, some Phœnicians sailed from the Red Sea round Africa, and returned by the Mediterranean.
600 Thales, of Miletus, travels into Egypt, consults the priests of Memphis, acquires the knowledge of geometry, astronomy, and philosophy; returns to Greece, calculates eclipses, gives general notions of the universe, and maintains that one Supreme Intelligence regulates all its motions.
600 Maps, Globes, and the signs of the Zodiac, invented by Anaximander, the scholar of Thales.
597 Jehoiakin, king of Judah, is carried away captive, by Nebuchadnezzar, to Babylon.
587 The city of Jerusalem taken, after a siege of eighteen months.
562 The first comedy at Athens acted upon a moveable scaffold.
559 Cyrus the first king of Persia.
538 The kingdom of Babylon finished; that city being taken by Cyrus, who, in 536, issues an edict for the return of the Jews.
534 The first tragedy was acted at Athens, on a waggon, by Thespis.
526 Learning is greatly encouraged at Athens, and a public library first founded.
515 The second Temple at Jerusalem is finished under Darius.
509 Tarquin, the seventh and last king of the Romans, is expelled, and Rome is governed by two consuls, and other republican magistrates, till the battle of Pharsalia, being a space of 461 years.
504 Sardis taken and burnt by the Athenians, which gave occasion to the Persian invasion of Greece.
486 Æscylus, the Greek poet, first gains the prize of tragedy.
481 Xerxes the Great, king of Persia, begins his expedition against Greece.
458 Ezra is sent from Babylon to Jerusalem, with the captive Jews, and the vessels of gold and silver, &c. being seventy weeks of years, or 490 years before the crucifixion of our Saviour.
454 The Romans send to Athens for Solon's laws.
451 The Decemvirs created at Rome, and the laws of the twelve tables compiled and ratified.
430 The history of the Old Testament finishes about this time.
Malachi, the last of the prophets.
400 Socrates, the founder of moral philosophy among the Greeks, believes the immortality of the soul, and a state of rewards and punishments, for which, and other sublime doctrines, he is put to death by the Athenians, who soon after repent, and erect to his memory a statue of brass.

331 Alexander

331 Alexander the Great, king of Macedon, conquers Darius king of Persia, and other nations of Asia. 323, Dies at Babylon, and his empire is divided by his generals into four kingdoms.

285 Dionysius, of Alexandria, began his astronomical æra on Monday, June 26, being the first who found the exact solar year to consist of 365 days, 5 hours, and 49 minutes.

284 Ptolemy Philadelphus, king of Egyyt, employs seventy-two interpreters to translate the Old Testament into the Greek language, which is called the Septuagint.

269 The first coining of silver at Rome.

264 The first Punic war begins, and continues 23 years. The chronology of the Arundelian marbles composed.

260 The Romans first concern themselves in naval affairs, and defeat the Carthaginians at sea.

237 Hamilcar, the Carthaginian, causes his son Hannibal, at nine years old, to swear eternal enmity to the Romans.

218 The second Punic war begins, and continues 17 years. Hannibal passes the Alps, and defeats the Romans in several battles; but, being amused by his women, does not improve his victories by the storming of Rome.

190 The first Roman army enters Asia, and from the spoils of Antiochus brings the Asiatic luxury first to Rome.

168 Perseus defeated by the Romans, which ends the Macedonian kingdom.

167 The first library erected at Rome, of books brought from Macedonia.

163 The government of Judea under the Maccabees begins, and continues 126 years.

146 Carthage, the rival to Rome, is razed to the ground by the Romans.

135 The history of the Apocrypha ends.

52 Julius Cæsar makes his first expedition into Britain.

47 The battle of Pharsalia between Cæsar and Pompey, in which the latter is defeated.
The Alexandrian library, consisting of 400,000 valuable books, burnt by accident.

45 The war of Africa, in which Cato kills himself.
The solar year introduced by Cæsar.

44 Cæsar, the greatest of the Roman conquerors, after having fought fifty pitched battles, and slain 1,192,000 men, and overturned the liberties of his country, is killed in the senate-house.

35 The battle of Actium fought, in which Mark Antony and Cleopatra are totally defeated by Octavius nephew to Julius Cæsar.

30 Alexandria, in Egypt, is taken by Octavius, upon which Antony and Cleopatra put themselves to death, and Egypt is reduced to a Roman province.

27 Octavius, by a decree of the senate, obtains the title of Augustus Cæsar, and an absolute exemption from the laws, and is properly the first Roman emperor.

8 Rome at this time is fifty miles in circumference, and contains 463,000 men fit to bear arms.
The temple of Janus is ſhut by Auguſtus, as an emblem of univerſal peace, and JESUS CHRIST is born on Monday, December 25.

A. C.

12 ——— diſputes with the doctors in the Temple;
27 ——— is baptized in the Wilderneſs by John;
33 ——— is crucified on Friday, April 3, at 3 o'clock P. M.
His Reſurrection on Sunday, April 5: his Aſcenſion, Thurſday, May 14.
36 St. Paul converted.
39 St. Matthew writes his Goſpel.
Pontius Pilate kills himſelf.
40 The name of Chriſtians firſt given at Antioch to the followers of Chriſt.
43 Claudius Cæſar's expedition into Britain.
44 St. Mark writes his Goſpel.
49 London is founded by the Romans; 368, ſurrounded by ditto with a wall, ſome parts of which are ſtill obſervable.
51 Caractacus, the Britiſh king, is carried in chains to Rome.
52 The council of the Apoſtles at Jeruſalem.
55 St. Luke writes his Goſpel.
59 The emperor Nero puts his mother and brothers to death.
——— perſecutes the Druids in Britain.
61 Boadicea, the Britiſh queen, defeats the Romans; but is conquered ſoon after by Suetonius, governor of Britain.
62 St. Paul is ſent in bonds to Rome—writes his Epiſtles between 51 and 66.
63 The Acts of the Apoſtles written.
Chriſtianity is ſuppoſed to be introduced into Britain by St. Paul, or ſome of his diſciples, about this time.
64 Rome ſet on fire, and burned for ſix days; upon which began (under Nero) the firſt perſecution againſt the Chriſtians.
67 St. Peter and St. Paul put to death.
70 Whilſt the factious Jews are deſtroying one another with mutual fury, Titus, the Roman general, takes Jeruſalem, which is razed to the ground, and the plough made to paſs over it.
83 The philoſophers expelled Rome by Domitian.
85 Julius Agricola, governor of South Britain, to protect the civilized Britons from the incurſions of the Caledonians, builds a line of forts between the rivers Forth and Clyde; defeats the Caledonians under Galgacus on the Grampian hills; and firſt ſails round Britain, which he diſcovers to be an iſland.
96 St. John the Evangeliſt wrote his Revelation—his Goſpel in 97.

121 The

121 The Caledonians reconquer from the Romans all the southern parts of Scotland; upon which the emperor Adrian builds a wall between Newcastle and Carlisle; but this also proving ineffectual, Pollius Urbicus, the Roman general, about the year 144, repairs Agricola's forts, which he joins by a wall four yards thick.
135 The second Jewish war ends, when they were all banished Judæa.
139 Justin writes his first Apology for the Christians.
141 A number of heresies appear about this time.
152 The emperor Antoninus Pius stops the persecution against the Christians.
217 The Septuagint said to be found in a cask.
222 About this time the Roman empire begins to sink under its own weight. The Barbarians begin their irruptions, and the Goths have annual tribute not to molest the empire.
260 Valerius is taken prisoner by Sapor, king of Persia, and flayed alive.
274 Silk first brought from India: the manufactory of it introduced into Europe by some monks, 551; first worn by the clergy in England, 1534.
291 Two emperors, and two Cæsars, march to defend the four quarters of the empire.
306 Constantine the Great begins his reign.
308 Cardinals first began.
313 The tenth persecution ends by an edict of Constantine, who favours the Christians, and gives full liberty to their religion.
314 Three bishops, or fathers, are sent from Britain to assist at the council of Arles.
325 The first general council at Nice, when 318 fathers attended, against Arius, where was composed the famous Nicene Creed, which we attribute to them.
328 Constantine removes the seat of empire from Rome to Byzantium, which is thence-forwards called Constantinople.
331 ——— orders all the heathen temples to be destroyed.
363 The Roman emperor Julian, surnamed the Apostate, endeavours in vain to rebuild the temple of Jerusalem.
364 The Roman empire is divided into the eastern (Constantinople the capital) and western (of which Rome continued to be the capital) each being now under the government of different emperors.
400 Bells invented by bishop Paulinus, of Campagnia.
404 The kingdom of Caledonia, or Scotland, revives under Fergus.
406 The Vandals, Alans, and Suevi, spread into France and Spain, by a concession of Honorius, emperor of the West.
410 Rome taken and plundered by Alaric, king of the Visi-Goths.
412 The Vandals begin their kingdom in Spain.
420 The kingdom of France begins upon the Lower Rhine, under Pharamond.
426 The Romans, reduced to extremities at home, withdraw their troops from Britain, and never return; advising the Britons to arm in their own defence, and trust to their own valour.

446 The Britons, now left to themſelves, are greatly haraſſed by the Scots and Picts, upon which they once more make their complaint to the Romans, but receive no aſſiſtance from that quarter.
447 Attila (ſurnamed the Scourge of God) with his Huns, ravages the Roman empire.
449 Vortigern, king of the Britons, invites the Saxons into Britain, againſt the Scots and Picts.
455 The Saxons having repulſed the Scots and Picts, invite over more of their countrymen, and begin to eſtabliſh themſelves in Kent, under Hengiſt.
476 The weſtern empire is finiſhed, 523 years after the battle of Pharſalia; upon the ruins of which ſeveral new ſtates ariſe in Italy and other parts, conſiſting of Goths, Vandals, Huns, and other Barbarians, under whom literature is extinguiſhed, and the works of the learned are deſtroyed.
496 Clovis, king of France, baptized, and Chriſtianity begins in that kingdom.
508 Prince Arthur begins his reign over the Britons.
513 Conſtantinople beſieged by Vitalianus, whoſe fleet is burned by a ſpeculum of braſs.
516 The computing of time by the Chriſtian æra is introduced by Dionyſius the monk.
529 The code of Juſtinian, the eaſtern emperor, is publiſhed.
557 A terrible plague all over Europe, Aſia, and Africa, which continues near 50 years.
581 Latin ceaſed to be ſpoken about this time in Italy.
596 Auguſtine the monk comes into England with forty monks.
606 Here begins the power of the popes, by the conceſſions of Phocas, emperor of the Eaſt.
622 Mahomet, the falſe prophet, flies from Mecca to Medina, in Arabia, in the 44th year of his age, and 10th of his miniſtry, when he laid the foundation of the Saracen empire, and from whom the Mahometan princes to this day claim their deſcent. His followers compute their time from this æra, which in Arabic is called Hegira, i. e. the Flight.
637 Jeruſalem is taken by the Saracens, or followers of Mahomet.
640 Alexandria in Egypt is taken by ditto, and the grand library there burnt by order of Omar, their caliph or prince.
653 The Saracens now extend their conqueſts on every ſide, and retaliate the barbarities of the Goths and Vandals upon their poſterity.
664 Glaſs invented in England by Benalt, a monk.
685 The Britons, after a brave ſtruggle of near 150 years, are totally expelled by the Saxons, and driven into Wales and Cornwall.
713 The Saracens conquer Spain.
726 The controverſy about images begins, and occaſions many inſurrections in the eaſtern empire.
748 The computing of years from the birth of Chriſt began to be uſed in hiſtory.
749 The race of Abbas became caliphs of the Saracens, and encourage learning.

 762 The

762 The city of Bagdad upon the Tigris is made the capital for the caliphs of the houſe of Abbas.

800 Charlemagne, king of France, begins the empire of Germany, afterwards called the weſtern empire; gives the preſent names to the winds and months; endeavours to reſtore learning in Europe; but mankind are not yet diſpoſed for it, being ſolely engroſſed in military enterprizes.

826 Harold, king of Denmark, dethroned by his ſubjects, for being a Chriſtian.

828 Egbert, king of Weſſex, unites the Heptarchy, by the name of England.

836 The Flemings trade to Scotland for fiſh.

838 The Scots and Picts have a deciſive battle, in which the former prevail, and both kingdoms are united by Kenneth, which begins the ſecond period of the Scottiſh hiſtory.

867 The Danes begin their ravages in England.

896 Alfred the Great, after ſubduing the Daniſh invaders (againſt whom he fought 56 battles by ſea and land), compoſes his body of laws; divides England into counties, hundreds, and tythings; erects county courts, and founds the univerſity of Oxford, about this time.

915 The univerſity of Cambridge founded.

936 The Saracen empire is divided by uſurpation into ſeven kingdoms.

975 Pope Boniface VII. is depoſed and baniſhed for his crimes.

979 Coronation oaths ſaid to be firſt uſed in England.

991 The figures in arithmetic are brought into Europe by the Saracens from Arabia. Letters of the Alphabet were hitherto uſed.

996 Otho III. makes the empire of Germany elective.

999 Boleſlaus, the firſt king of Poland.

1000 Paper made of cotton rags was in uſe; that of linen rags in 1170: the manufactory introduced into England at Dartford, 1588.

1005 All the old churches are rebuilt about this time in a new manner of architecture.

1015 Children forbidden by law to be ſold by their parents in England.

1017 Canute, king of Denmark, gets poſſeſſion of England.

1040 The Danes, after ſeveral engagements with various ſucceſs, are about this time driven out of Scotland, and never again return in a hoſtile manner.

1041 The Saxon line reſtored under Edward the Confeſſor.

1043 The Turks (a nation of adventurers from Tartary, ſerving hitherto in the armies of contending princes) become formidable, and take poſſeſſion of Perſia.

1054 Leo IX. the firſt pope that kept up an army.

1057 Malcolm III. king of Scotland, kills the tyrant Macbeth at Dunſinane, and marries the princeſs Margaret, ſiſter to Edgar Atheling.

1065 The Turks take Jeruſalem from the Saracens.

1066 The battle of Haſtings fought, between Harold and William (ſurnamed the Baſtard)

 duke

duke of Normandy, in which Harold is conquered and slain, after which William becomes king of England.

1070 William introduces the feudal law.
Musical notes invented.

1075 Henry IV. emperor of Germany, and the pope, quarrel about the nomination of the German bishops. Henry, in penance, walks barefooted to the pope, towards the end of January.

1076 Justices of peace first appointed in England.

1080 Doomsday-book began to be compiled by order of William, from a survey of all the estates in England, and finished in 1086.
The Tower of London built by ditto, to curb his English subjects; numbers of whom fly to Scotland, where they introduce the Saxon or English language, are protected by Malcolm, and have lands given them.

1091 The Saracens in Spain, being hard pressed by the Spaniards, call to their assistance Joseph, king of Morocco; by which the Moors get possession of all the Saracen dominions in Spain.

1096 The first crusade to the Holy Land is begun under several Christian princes, to drive the infidels from Jerusalem.

1110 Edgar Atheling, the last of the Saxon princes, dies in England, where he had been permitted to reside as a subject.

1118 The order of the Knights Templars instituted, to defend the Sepulchre at Jerusalem, and to protect Christian strangers.

1151 The canon law collected by Gratian, a monk of Bologna.

1163 London bridge, consisting of 19 small arches, first built of stone.

1164 The Teutonic order of religious knights begins in Germany.

1172 Henry II. king of England (and first of the Plantagenets) takes possession of Ireland; which, from that period, has been governed by an English viceroy, or lord-lieutenant.

1176 England is divided, by Henry, into six circuits, and justice is dispensed by itinerant judges.

1180 Glass windows began to be used in private houses in England.

1181 The laws of England are digested about this time by Glanville.

1182 Pope Alexander III. compelled the kings of England and France to hold the stirrups of his saddle when he mounted his horse.

1186 The great conjunction of the sun and moon, and all the planets in Libra, happened in September.

1192 The battle of Ascalon, in Judæa, in which Richard, king of England, defeats Saladine's army, consisting of 300,000 combatants.

1194 *Dieu et mon Droit* first used as a motto by Richard, on a victory over the French.

1200 Chimnies were not known in England.
Surnames now began to be used; first among the nobility.

1208 London

1208 London incorporated, and obtained their first charter, for electing their Lord Mayor and other magistrates, from king John.

1215 Magna Charta is signed by king John and the barons of England.

Court of Common Pleas established.

1227 The Tartars, a new race of heroes, under Gingis-Kan, emerge from the northern parts of Asia, over-run all the Saracen empire, and, in imitation of former conquerors, carry death and desolation wherever they march.

1233 The Inquisition, begun in 1204, is now trusted to the Dominicans.

The houses of London, and other cities in England, France, and Germany, still thatched with straw.

1253 The famous astronomical tables are composed by Alonzo, king of Castile.

1258 The Tartars take Bagdad, which finishes the empire of the Saracens.

1263 Acho, king of Norway, invades Scotland with 160 sail, and lands 20,000 men at the mouth of the Clyde, who are cut to pieces by Alexander III. who recovers the western isles.

1264 According to some writers, the commons of England were not summoned to parliament till this period.

1269 The Hamburgh company incorporated in England.

1273 The empire of the present Austrian family begins in Germany.

1282 Llewellyn, prince of Wales, defeated and killed by Edward I. who unites that principality to England.

1284 Edward II. born at Caernarvon, is the first prince of Wales.

1285 Alexander III. king of Scotland, dies, and that kingdom is disputed by twelve candidates, who submit their claims to the arbitration of Edward, king of England; which lays the foundation of a long and desolating war between both nations.

1293 There is a regular succession of English parliaments from this year, being the 22d of Edward I.

1298 The present Turkish empire begins in Bithynia under Ottoman.

Silver-hafted knives, spoons, and cups, a great luxury.

Tallow candles so great a luxury, that splinters of wood were used for lights.

Wine sold by apothecaries as a cordial.

1302 The mariner's compass invented, or improved, by Givia, of Naples.

1307 The beginning of the Swiss cantons.

1308 The popes remove to Avignon, in France, for 70 years.

1310 Lincoln's Inn society established.

1314 The battle of Bannockburn, between Edward II. and Robert Bruce, which establishes the latter on the throne of Scotland.

The cardinals set fire to the conclave, and separate. A vacancy in the papal chair for two years.

1320 Gold first coined in Christendom; 1344, ditto in England.

1336 Two Brabant weavers ſettle at York, which, ſays Edward III. may prove of great benefit to us and our ſubjects.
1337 The firſt comet whoſe courſe is deſcribed with an aſtronomical exactneſs.
1340 Gunpowder and guns firſt invented by Swartz, a monk of Cologn; 1346, Edward III. had four pieces of cannon, which contributed to gain him the battle of Creſſy; 1346, bombs and mortars were invented.
Oil-painting firſt made uſe of by John Vaneck.
Heralds college inſtituted in England.
1344 The firſt creation to titles by patents uſed by Edward III.
1346 The battle of Durham, in which David, king of Scots, is taken priſoner.
1349 The order of the Garter inſtituted in England by Edward III. altered in 1557, and conſiſts of 26 knights.
1352 The Turks firſt enter Europe.
1354 The money in Scotland till now the ſame as in England.
1356 The battle of Poictiers, in which king John of France, and his ſon, are taken priſoners by Edward the Black Prince.
1357 Coals firſt brought to London.
1358 Arms of England and France firſt quartered by Edward III.
1362 The law pleadings in England changed from French to Engliſh, as a favour of Edward III. to his people.
John Wickliffe, an Engliſhman, begins about this time to oppoſe the errors of the church of Rome with great acuteneſs and ſpirit. His followers are called Lollards.
1386 A company of linen-weavers, from the Netherlands, eſtabliſhed in London.
Windſor caſtle built by Edward III.
1388 The battle of Otterburn, between Hotſpur and the earl of Douglas.
1391 Cards invented in France for the king's amuſement.
1399 Weſtminſter abbey built and enlarged—Weſtminſter hall ditto.
Order of the Bath inſtituted at the coronation of Henry IV.; renewed in 1725, conſiſting of 38 knights.
1410 Guildhall, London, built.
1411 The univerſity of St. Andrew's in Scotland founded.
1415 The battle of Agincourt gained over the French by Henry V. of England.
1428 The ſiege of Orleans, the firſt blow to the Engliſh power in France.
1430 About this time Laurentius of Harleim invented the art of printing, which he practiſed with ſeparate wooden types. Guttemburgh afterwards invented cut metal types: but the art was carried to perfection by Peter Schoeffer, who invented the mode of caſting the types in matrices. Frederick Corſellis began to print at Oxford, in 1468, with wooden types; but it was William Caxton who introduced into England the art of printing with fuſile types, in 1474.
1446 The Vatican library founded at Rome.
The ſea breaks in at Dort, in Holland, and drowns 100,000 people.

1453 Conſtantinople

1453 Conftantinople taken by the Turks, which ends the eaftern empire, 1123 years from its dedication by Conftantine the Great, and 2206 years from the foundation of Rome.
1454 The univerfity of Glafgow, in Scotland, founded.
1460 Engraving and etching in copper invented.
1477 The univerfity of Aberdeen, in Scotland, founded.
1483 Richard III. king of England, and laft of the Plantagenets, is defeated and killed at the battle of Bofworth, by Henry (Tudor) VII. which puts an end to the civil wars between the houfes of York and Lancafter, after a conteft of 30 years, and the lofs of 100,000 men.
1486 Henry eftablifhes fifty yeomen of the guards, the firft ftanding army.
1489 Maps and fea-charts firft brought to England by Barth. Columbus.
1491 William Grocyn publicly teaches the Greek language at Oxford.
The Moors, hitherto a formidable enemy to the native Spaniards, are entirely fubdued by Ferdinand, and become fubjects to that prince on certain conditions, which are ill obferved by the Spaniards, whofe clergy employ the powers of the Inquifition, with all its tortures; and in 1609, near one million of the Moors are driven from Spain to the oppofite coaft of Africa, from whence they originally came.
1492 America firft difcovered by Columbus, a Genoefe, in the fervice of Spain.
1494 Algebra firft known in Europe.
1497 The Portuguefe firft fail to the Eaft Indies by the Cape of Good Hope.
South America difcovered by Americus Vefpufius, from whom it has its name.
1499 North America ditto, for Henry VII. by Cabot.
1500 Maximilian divides the empire of Germany into fix circles, and adds four more in 1512.
1505 Shillings firft coined in England.
1509 Gardening introduced into England from the Netherlands, from whence vegetables were imported hitherto.
1513 The battle of Flowden, in which James IV. of Scotland is killed, with the flower of his nobility.
1517 Martin Luther began the Reformation.
Egypt is conquered by the Turks.
1518 Magellan, in the fervice of Spain, firft difcovers the ftraits of that name in South America.
1520 Henry VIII. for his writings in favour of popery, receives the title of Defender of the Faith from his Holinefs.
1529 The name of Proteftant takes its rife from the Reformed protefting againft the church of Rome, at the diet of Spires in Germany.
1534 The Reformation takes place in England, under Henry VIII.
1537 Religious houfes diffolved by ditto.

1539 The first English edition of the Bible authorized; the present translation finished 1611.
About this time cannon began to be used in ships.
1543 Silk stockings first worn by the French king; first worn in England by queen Elizabeth, 1561; the steel frame for weaving invented by the Rev. Mr. Lee, of St. John's College, Cambridge, 1589.
Pins first used in England, before which time the ladies used skewers.
1544 Good lands let in England at one shilling per acre.
1545 The famous council of Trent begins, and continues 18 years.
1546 First law in England, establishing the interest of money at ten *per cent.*
1549 Lords lieutenants of counties instituted in England.
1550 Horse guards instituted in England.
1555 The Russian company established in England.
1558 Queen Elizabeth begins her reign.
1560 The Reformation in Scotland completed by John Knox.
1563 Knives first made in England.
1569 Royal Exchange first built.
1572 The great massacre of Protestants at Paris.
1579 The Dutch shake off the Spanish yoke, and the republic of Holland begins.
English East India company incorporated—established 1600.
——— Turkey company incorporated.
1580 Sir Francis Drake returns from his voyage round the world, being the first English circumnavigator.
Parochial register first appointed in England.
1582 Pope Gregory introduces the New Style in Italy; the 5th of October being counted 15.
1583 Tobacco first brought from Virginia into England.
1587 Mary queen of Scots is beheaded by order of Elizabeth, after 18 years imprisonment.
1588 The Spanish Armada destroyed by Drake and other English admirals.
Henry IV. passes the edict of Nantes, tolerating the Protestants.
1589 Coaches first introduced into England; hackney act 1693; increased to 1000, in 1770.
1590 Band of pensioners instituted in England.
1591 Trinity College, Dublin, founded.
1597 Watches first brought into England from Germany.
1602 Decimal arithmetic invented at Bruges.
1603 Queen Elizabeth (the last of the Tudors) dies, and nominates James VI. of Scotland (and first of the Stuarts) as her successor; which unites both kingdoms under the name of Great Britain.
1605 The gunpowder-plot discovered at Westminster; being a project of the Roman catholics to blow up the king and both houses of parliament.
1606 Oaths of allegiance first administered in England.

1608 Galileo,

1608 Galileo, of Florence, firſt diſcovers the ſatellites about the planet Saturn, by the teleſcope, then juſt invented in Holland.
1610 Henry IV. is murdered at Paris, by Ravaillac, a prieſt.
1611 Baronets firſt created in England, by James I.
1614 Napier, of Marcheſton, in Scotland, invents the logarithms.
Sir Hugh Middleton brings the New River to London from Ware.
1616 The firſt permanent ſettlement in Virginia.
1619 Dr. W. Harvey, an Engliſhman, diſcovers the doctrine of the circulation of the blood.
1620 The broad ſilk manufactory from raw ſilk introduced into England.
1621 New England planted by the Puritans.
1625 King James dies, and is ſucceeded by his ſon, Charles I.
The iſland of Barbadoes, the firſt Engliſh ſettlement in the Weſt Indies, is planted.
1632 The battle of Lutzen, in which Guſtavus Adolphus, king of Sweden, and head of the Proteſtants in Germany, is killed.
1635 Province of Maryland planted by lord Baltimore.
Regular poſts eſtabliſhed from London to Scotland, Ireland, &c.
1640 King Charles diſobliges his Scottiſh ſubjects, on which their army, under general Leſley, enters England, and takes Newcaſtle, being encouraged by the malcontents in England.
The maſſacre in Ireland, when 40,000 Engliſh Proteſtants were killed.
1642 King Charles impeaches five members, who had oppoſed his arbitrary meaſures, which begins the civil war in England.
1643 Exciſe on beer, ale, &c. firſt impoſed by parliament.
1649 Charles I. beheaded at Whitehall, January 30, aged 49.
1654 Cromwell aſſumes the protectorſhip.
1655 The Engliſh, under admiral Penn, take Jamaica from the Spaniards.
1658 Cromwell dies, and is ſucceeded in the protectorſhip by his ſon Richard.
1660 King Charles II. is reſtored by Monk, commander of the army, after an exile of twelve years in France and Holland.
Epiſcopacy reſtored in England and Scotland.
The people of Denmark, being oppreſſed by the nobles, ſurrender their privileges to Frederic III. who becomes abſolute.
1662 The Royal Society eſtabliſhed at London, by Charles II.
1663 Carolina planted; 1728, divided into two ſeparate governments.
1664 The New Netherlands, in North America, conquered from the Swedes and Dutch, by the Engliſh.
1665 The plague rages in London, and carries off 68,000 perſons.
1666 The great fire of London began Sept. 2, and continued three days, in which were deſtroyed 13,000 houſes, and 400 ſtreets.
Tea firſt uſed in England.

1667 The peace of Breda, which confirms to the English the New Netherlands, now known by the names of Pennſylvania, New York, and New Jerſey.

1668 ——— ditto, Aix-la-Chapelle.

St. James's Park planted, and make a thoroughfare for public uſe, by Charles II.

1670 The Engliſh Hudſon's Bay company incorporated.

1672 Lewis XIV. over-runs great part of Holland, when the Dutch open their ſluices, being determined to drown their country, and retire to their ſettlements in the Eaſt Indies.

African company eſtabliſhed.

1678 The peace of Nimeguen.

The habeas corpus act paſſed.

1680 A great comet appeared, and from its nearneſs to our earth, alarmed the inhabitants. It continued viſible from Nov. 3, to March 9.

William Penn, a Quaker, receives a charter for planting Pennſylvania.

1683 India ſtock ſold from 360 to 500 per cent.

1685 Charles II. dies, aged 55, and is ſucceeded by his brother, James II.

The duke of Monmouth, natural ſon to Charles II. raiſes a rebellion, but is defeated at the battle of Sedgmoor, and beheaded.

The edict of Nantes infamouſly revoked by Lewis XIV. and the Proteſtants cruelly perſecuted.

1687 The palace of Verſailles, near Paris, finiſhed by Lewis XIV.

1688 The Revolution in Great Britain begins, Nov. 5. King James abdicates, and retires to France, December 3.

King William and queen Mary, daughter and ſon-in-law to James, are proclaimed, February 16.

Viſcount Dundee ſtands out for James in Scotland, but is killed by general Mackey, at the battle of Killycrankie; upon which the Highlanders, wearied with repeated misfortunes, diſperſe.

1689 The land-tax paſſed in England.

The toleration act paſſed in Ditto.

Several biſhops are deprived for not taking the oath to king William.

William Fuller, who pretended to prove the prince of Wales ſpurious, was voted by the commons to be a notorious cheat, impoſtor, and falſe accuſer.

1690 The battle of the Boyne, gained by William againſt James in Ireland.

1691 The war in Ireland finiſhed, by the ſurrender of Limerick to William.

1692 The Engliſh and Dutch fleets, commanded by admiral Ruſſel, defeat the French fleet off La Hogue.

1693 Bayonets at the end of loaded muſkets firſt uſed by the French againſt the Confederates in the battle of Turin.

The duchy of Hanover made the ninth electorate.

Bank of England eſtabliſhed by king William.

1693 The

1693 The first public lottery was drawn this year.
Massacre of Highlanders at Glencoe, by king William's troops.
1694 Queen Mary dies at the age of 33, and William reigns alone.
Stamp duties instituted in England.
1696 The peace of Ryswick.
1699 The Scots settled a colony at the isthmus of Darien, in America, and called it Caledonia.
1700 Charles XII. of Sweden begins his reign.
King James II. dies at St. Germain's, in the 68th year of his age.
1701 Prussia erected into a kingdom.
Society for the propagation of the Gospel in foreign parts established.
1702 King William dies, aged 50, and is succeeded by Queen Anne, daughter to James II. who, with the emperor and States General, renews the war against France and Spain.
1704 Gibraltar taken from the Spaniards, by admiral Rooke.
The battle of Blenheim won by the duke of Marlborough and allies, against the French.
The court of Exchequer instituted in England.
1706 The treaty of Union betwixt England and Scotland, signed July 22.
The battle of Ramillies won by Marlborough and the allies.
1707 The first British parliament.
1708 Minorca taken from the Spaniards by general Stanhope.
The battle of Oudenarde won by Marlborough and the allies.
Sardinia erected into a kingdom, and given to the duke of Savoy.
1709 Peter the Great, czar of Muscovy, defeats Charles XII. at Pultowa, who flies to Turkey.
The battle of Malplaquet won by Marlborough and the allies.
1710 Queen Anne changes the Whig Ministry for others more favourable to the interest of her brother, the late Pretender.
The cathedral church of St. Paul, London, rebuilt by Sir Christopher Wren, in 37 years, at one million expence, by a duty on coals.
The English South-Sea company began.
1712 Duke of Hamilton and lord Mohun killed in a duel in Hyde-Park.
1713 The peace of Utrecht, whereby Newfoundland, Nova Scotia, New Britain, and Hudson's Bay, in North America, were yielded to Great Britain; Gibraltar and Minorca, in Europe, were also confirmed to the said crown by this treaty.
1714 Queen Anne dies, at the age of fifty, and is succeeded by George I.
Interest reduced to five *per cent.*
1715 Lewis XIV. dies, and is succeeded by his great-grandson, Lewis XV. the late king of France.
The rebellion in Scotland begins in September, under the earl of Mar, in favour of the Pretender.

Pretender. The action of Sheriff-muir, and the surrender of Preston, both in November, when the rebels disperse.

1716 The Pretender married to the princess Sobieski, grand-daughter of John Sobieski, late king of Poland.

An act passed for septennial parliaments.

1719 The Mississipi scheme at its height in France.

Lombe's silk-throwing machine, containing 26,586 wheels, erected at Derby; takes up one-eighth of a mile; one water-wheel moves the rest; and in 24 hours it works 318,504,960 yards of organzine silk thread.

The South-Sea scheme in England begun April 7; was at its height at the end of June; and quite sunk about September 29.

1727 King George I. dies, in the 68th year of his age; and is succeeded by his only son, George II.

Inoculation first tried on criminals with success.

Russia, formerly a dukedom, is now established as an empire.

1732 Kouli Khan usurps the Persian throne, conquers the Mogul empire, and returns with two hundred and thirty-one millions sterling.

Several public-spirited gentlemen begin the settlement of Georgia, in North America.

1736 Capt. Porteus, having ordered his soldiers to fire upon the populace at the execution of a smuggler, is himself hanged by the mob at Edinburgh.

1738 Westminster Bridge, consisting of fifteen arches, begun; finished in 1750, at the expence of 389,000l. defrayed by parliament.

1739 Letters of marque issued out in Britain against Spain, July 21, and war declared, October 23.

1743 The battle of Dettingen won by the English and allies, in favour of the queen of Hungary.

1744 War declared against France.

Commodore Anson returns from his voyage round the world.

1745 The allies lose the battle of Fontenoy.

The rebellion breaks out in Scotland, and the Pretender's army defeated by the duke of Cumberland, at Culloden, April 16, 1746.

1746 British Linen Company erected.

1748 The peace of Aix-la-Chapelle, by which a restitution of all places, taken during the war, was to be made on all sides.

1749 The interest of the British funds reduced to three *per cent.*

British herring fishery incorporated.

1751 Frederic, prince of Wales, father to his present majesty, died.

Antiquarian society at London incorporated.

1752 The new style introduced into Great Britain, the third of September being counted the fourteenth.

1753 The

1753 The British Museum erected at Montagu-house.
Society of Arts, Manufactures, and Commerce, instituted in London.
1755 Lisbon destroyed by an earthquake.
1756 146 Englishmen are confined in the black hole at Calcutta, in the East Indies, by order of the Nabob, and 123 found dead next morning.
Marine society established at London.
1757 Damien attempted to assassinate the French king.
1759 General Wolfe is killed in the battle of Quebec, which is gained by the English.
1760 King George II. dies, October 25, in the 77th year of his age, and is succeeded by his present majesty, who, on the 22d of September, 1761, married the princess Charlotte of Mecklenburgh Strelitz.
Black-Friars bridge, consisting of nine arches, begun; finished 1770, at the expence of 52,840l. to be discharged by a toll. Toll taken off 1785.
1762 War declared against Spain.
Peter III. emperor of Russia, is deposed, imprisoned, and murdered.
American Philosophical Society established in Philadelphia.
George Augustus Frederic, prince of Wales, born August 12.
1763 The definitive treaty of peace between Great Britain, France, Spain, and Portugal, concluded at Paris, February 10, which confirms to Great Britain the extensive provinces of Canada, East and West Florida, and part of Louisiana, in North America; also the islands of Grenada, St. Vincent, Dominica, and Tobago, in the West Indies.
1764 The parliament granted 10,000l. to Mr. Harrison, for his discovery of the longitude by his time-piece.
1765 His majesty's royal charter passed for incorporating the Society of Artists.
An act passed annexing the sovereignty of the island of Man to the crown of Great Britain.
1766 April 21, a spot or macula of the sun, more than thrice the bigness of our earth, passed the sun's centre.
1768 Academy of painting established in London.
The Turks imprison the Russian ambassador, and declare war against that empire.
1771 Dr. Solander and Mr. Banks, in his majesty's ship the Endeavour, lieut. Cook, return from a voyage round the world, having made several important discoveries in the South Seas.
1772 The king of Sweden changes the constitution of that kingdom.
The Pretender marries a princess of Germany, grand-daughter of Thomas, late earl of Aylesbury.
The emperor of Germany, empress of Russia, and the king of Prussia, strip the king of Poland of great part of his dominions, which they divide among themselves, in violation of the most solemn treaties.
1773 Captain Phipps is sent to explore the North Pole, but having made eighty-one degrees,

i-is in danger of being locked up by the ice, and his attempt to discover a passage in that quarter proves fruitless.

1773 The Jesuits expelled from the Pope's dominions.

The English East India company having, by conquest or treaty, acquired the extensive provinces of Bengal, Orixa, and Bahar, containing fifteen millions of inhabitants, great irregularities are committed by their servants abroad; upon which government interferes, and sends out judges, &c. for the better administration of justice.

The war between the Russians and Turks proves disgraceful to the latter, who lose the islands in the Archipelago, and by sea are every where unsuccessful.

1774 Peace is proclaimed between the Russians and Turks.

The British parliament having passed an act, laying a duty of three pence per pound upon all teas imported into America, the Colonists, considering this as a grievance, deny the right of the British parliament to tax them.

Deputies from the several American colonies meet at Philadelphia, as the first General Congress, Sept. 5.

First petition of Congress to the King, November.

1775 April 19. The first action happened in America between the king's troops and the provincials at Lexington.

May 20, Articles of confederation and perpetual union between the American provinces.

June 17, A bloody action at Bunker's Hill, between the royal troops and the Americans.

1776 March 17, The town of Boston evacuated by the King's troops.

An unsuccessful attempt, in July, made by commodore Sir Peter Parker, and lieutenant-general Clinton, upon Charles Town, in South Carolina.

The Congress declare the American colonies free and independent states, July 4.

The Americans are driven from Long Island, New York, in August, with great loss, and great numbers of them taken prisoners; and the city of New York is afterwards taken possession of by the king's troops.

December 25, General Washington takes 900 of the Hessians prisoners at Trenton.

Torture abolished in Poland.

1777 General Howe takes possession of Philadelphia.

Lieutenant-general Burgoyne is obliged to surrender his army at Saratoga, in Canada, by convention, to the American army under the command of the generals Gates and Arnold, October 17.

1778 A treaty of alliance concluded at Paris between the French king and the thirteen united American colonies, in which their independence is acknowledged by the court of France, February 6.

The remains of the earl of Chatham interred at the public expence in Westminster Abbey, June 9, in consequence of a vote of parliament.

1778 The

1778 The earl of Carlisle, William Eden, Esq; and George Johnstone, Esq; arrive at Philadelphia the beginning of June, as commissioners for restoring peace between Great Britain and America.

Philadelphia evacuated by the king's troops, June 18.

The Congress refuse to treat with the British commissioners, unless the independence of the American colonies were first acknowledged, or the king's fleets and armies withdrawn from America.

An engagement fought off Brest between the English fleet under the command of admiral Keppel, and the French fleet under the command of the count d'Orvilliers, July 27.

Dominica taken by the French, Sept. 7.

Pondicherry surrenders to the arms of Great Britain, Oct. 17.

St. Lucia taken from the French, Dec. 28.

1779 St. Vincent's taken by the French.

Grenada taken by the French, July 3.

1780 Torture in courts of justice abolished in France.

The Inquisition abolished in the duke of Modena's dominions.

Admiral Rodney takes twenty-two sail of Spanish ships, Jan. 8.

The same admiral also engages a Spanish fleet under the command of Don Juan de Langara, near Cape St. Vincent, and takes five ships of the line, one more being driven on shore, and another blown up, Jan. 16.

Three actions between admiral Rodney and the count de Guichen, in the West Indies, in the months of April and May; but none of them decisive.

Charles Town, South Carolina, surrenders to Sir Henry Clinton, May 4.

Pensacola, and the whole province of West Florida, surrender to the arms of the king of Spain, May 9.

The Protestant Association, to the number of 50,000, go up to the House of Commons, with their petition, for the repeal of an act passed in favour of the Papists, June 2.

That event followed by the most daring riots, in the city of London, and in Southwark, for several successive days, in which some Popish chapels are destroyed, together with the prisons of Newgate, the King's Bench, the Fleet, several private houses, &c. These alarming riots are at length suppressed by the interposition of the military, and many of the rioters tried and executed for felony.

Five English East Indiamen, and fifty English merchant ships bound for the West Indies, taken by the combined fleets of France and Spain, Aug. 8.

Earl Cornwallis obtains a signal victory over general Gates, near Camden, in South Carolina, in which above 1,000 American prisoners are taken, Aug. 16.

Mr. Laurens, late president of the Congress, taken in an American packet, near Newfoundland, Sept. 3.

1780 General

1780 General Arnold deserts the service of the Congress, escapes to New York, and is made a brigadier-general in the royal service, Sept. 24.

Major André, adjutant-general to the British army, hanged as a spy at Tappan, in the province of New York, Oct. 2.

Mr. Laurens is committed prisoner to the Tower, on a charge of high treason, October 4.

Dreadful hurricanes in the West Indies, by which great devastation is made in Jamaica, Barbadoes, St. Lucia, Dominica, and other islands, Oct. 3 and 10.

A declaration of hostilities published against Holland, Dec. 20.

1781 The Dutch island of St. Eustatia taken by admiral Rodney and general Vaughan, Feb. 3. Retaken by the French, Nov. 27.

Earl Cornwallis obtains a victory, but with considerable loss, over the Americans under general Green, at Guildford, in North Carolina, March 15.

The island of Tobago taken by the French, June 2.

A bloody engagement fought between an English squadron under the command of admiral Parker, and a Dutch squadron under the command of admiral Zoutman, off the Dogger-bank, Aug. 5.

Earl Cornwallis, with a considerable British army, surrendered prisoners of war to the American and French troops, under the command of general Washington and count Rochambeau, at York-town, in Virginia, Oct. 19.

1782 Trincomale, on the island of Ceylon, taken by admiral Hughes, Jan. 11.

Minorca surrendered to the arms of the king of Spain, Feb 5.

The island of St. Christopher taken by the French, Feb. 12.

The island of Nevis, in the West Indies, taken by the French, Feb. 14.

Montserrat taken by the French, Feb. 22.

The house of commons address the king against any further prosecution of offensive war on the continent of North America, Mar. 4; and resolve, That that house would consider all those as enemies to his majesty, and this country, who should advise, or by any means attempt, the farther prosecution of offensive war on the continent of North America, for the purpose of reducing the revolted colonies to obedience by force.

Admiral Rodney obtains a signal victory over the French fleet under the command of count de Grasse, near Dominica, in the West Indies, April 12.

Admiral Hughes, with eleven ships, beat off, near the island of Ceylon, by the French admiral Suffrein, with twelve ships of the line, after a severe engagement, in which both fleets lost a great number of men, April 13.

The resolution of the house of commons relating to John Wilkes, Esq. and the Middlesex election, passed Feb. 17, 1769, rescinded, May 3.

The bill to repeal the declaratory act of George I. relative to the legislation of Ireland, received the royal assent, June 20.

The French took and destroyed the forts and settlements in Hudson's Bay, Aug. 24.

1782 The

1782 The Spaniards defeated in their grand attack on Gibraltar, Sept. 13.

Treaty concluded betwixt the republic of Holland and the United States of America, Oct. 8.

Provisional articles of peace signed at Paris between the British and the American commissioners, by which the Thirteen United American colonies are acknowledged by his Britannic majesty to be free, sovereign, and independent states, Nov. 30.

1783 Preliminary articles of peace between his Britannic majesty and the kings of France and Spain, signed at Versailles, Jan. 20.

The order of St. Patrick instituted, Feb. 5.

Three earthquakes in Calabria Ulterior and Sicily, destroying a great number of towns and inhabitants, Feb. 5th, 7th, and 28th.

Armistice betwixt Great Britain and Holland, Feb. 10.

Ratification of the definitive treaty of peace between Great Britain, France, Spain, and the United States of America, Sept. 3.

1784 The city of London wait on the king, with an address of thanks for dismissing the coalition ministry, Jan. 16.

The great seal stolen from the lord chancellor's house in Great Ormond-street, March 24.

The ratification of the peace with America arrived, April 7.

The definitive treaty of peace between Great Britain and Holland, May 24.

The memory of Handel commemorated by a grand jubilee at Westminster-abbey, May 26.—Continued annually for decayed musicians, &c.

Proclamation for a public thanksgiving, July 2.

Mr. Lunardi ascended in a balloon from the Artillery-ground, Moorfields, the first attempt of the kind in England, Sept. 15.

1785 Dr. Seabury, an American missionary, was consecrated bishop of Connecticut by five nonjuring Scotch prelates, Nov.

1786 The king of Sweden prohibited the use of torture in his dominions.

Cardinal Turlone, high inquisitor at Rome, was publicly dragged out of his carriage by an incensed multitude, for his cruelty, and hung on a gibbet 50 feet high.

Sept. 26, Commercial treaty signed between England and France.

Nov. 21. £. 471,000 3 *per cent.* stock transferred to the landgrave of Hesse, for Hessian soldiers lost in the American war, at £. 30 a man.

Dec. 4. Mr. Adams, the American ambassador, presented to the archbishop of Canterbury Dr. White, of Pennsylvania, and Dr. Provost, of New York, to be consecrated bishops for the United States. They were consecrated Feb. 4, 1787.

1787 May 21. Mr. Burke, at the bar of the house of lords, in the name of all the commons of Great Britain, impeached Warren Hastings, late governor-general of Bengal, of high crimes and misdemeanors.

1787 Aug. 11. The king, by letters patent, erected the province of Nova Scotia into a bishop's see, and appointed Dr. Charles Inglis to be the bishop.

1788 In the early part of October, the first symptoms appeared of a severe disorder which afflicted our gracious Sovereign. On the 6th of November they were very alarming, and on the 13th a form of prayer for his recovery was ordered by the privy council.

1789 Feb. 17. His Majesty was pronounced to be in a state of convalescence, and on the 26th to be free from complaint.

April 23. A general thanksgiving for the King's recovery, who attended the service at St. Paul's with a great Procession.

July 14. Revolution in France—capture of the Bastile, execution of the governor, &c.

1790 July 14. Grand French confederation in the Champ de Mars.

1791 July 14. Great riot at Birmingham, in consequence of celebrating the French confederation.

MEN of LEARNING and GENIUS.

N. B. *By the Dates is implied the Time when the above Writers died; but when that Period happens not to be known, the Age in which they flourished is signified by* fl. *The names in Italics, are those who have given the best English Translations, exclusive of School-Books.*

Bef: Ch.

907 HOMER, the first prophane writer and Greek poet, flourished. *Pope.*
Hesiod, the Greek poet, supposed to live near the time of Homer. *Cooke.*
884 Lycurgus, the Spartan lawgiver.
600 Sappho, the Greek lyric poetess, fl. *Fawkes.*
558 Solon, lawgiver of Athens.
556 Æsop, the first Greek fabulist. *Croxal.*
548 Thales, the first Greek astronomer and geographer.
497 Pythagoras, founder of the Pythagorean philosophy in Greece. *Rowe.*
474 Anacreon, the Greek lyric poet. *Fawkes, Addison.*
456 Æschylus, the first Greek tragic poet. *Potter.*
435 Pindar, the Greek lyric poet. *West.*
413 Herodotus, of Greece, the first writer of prophane history. *Littlebury.*
407 Aristophanes, the Greek comic poet. fl. *White.*
Euripides, the Greek tragic poet, *Woodhull.*

406 Sophocles,

406 Sophocles, ditto. *Franklin, Potter.*
Confucius, the Chinese philosopher, fl.
400 Socrates, the founder of moral philosophy in Greece.
391 Thucydides, the Greek historian. *Smith, Hobbes.*
361 Hippocrates, the Greek physician. *Clifton.*
Democritus, the Greek philosopher.
359 Xenophon, the Greek philosopher and historian. *Smith, Spelman, Ashly, Fielding.*
348 Plato, the Greek philosopher, and disciple of Socrates. *Sydenham.*
336 Isocrates, the Greek orator. *Dimsdale.*
332 Aristotle, the Greek philosopher, and disciple of Plato. *Hobbes.*
313 Demosthenes, the Athenian orator, poisoned himself. *Leland, Francis.*
288 Theophrastus, the Greek philosopher, and scholar of Aristotle. *Budgel.*
285 Theocritus, the first Greek pastoral poet, fl. *Fawkes.*
277 Euclid, of Alexandria, in Egypt, the mathematician, fl. *R. Simpson.*
270 Epicurus, founder of the Epicurean philosophy in Greece. *Digby.*
264 Xeno, founder of the Stoic philosophy in ditto.
244 Callimachus, the Greek elegiac poet.
208 Archimedes, the Greek geometrician.
184 Plautus, the Roman comic poet. *Thornton.*
159 Terence, of Carthage, the Latin comic poet. *Colman.*
155 Diogenes, of Babylon, the Stoic philosopher.
124 Polibius, of Greece, the Greek and Roman historian. *Hampton.*
54 Lucretius, the Roman poet. *Creech.*
44 Julius Cæsar, the Roman historian and commentator, killed. *Duncan.*
Diodorus Siculus, of Greece, the universal historian, fl. *Booth.*
Vitruvius, the Roman architect, fl.
43 Cicero, the Roman orator and philosopher, put to death. *Guthrie, Melmoth.*
Cornelius Nepos, the Roman biographer, fl. *Rowe.*
34 Sallust, the Roman historian. *Gordon, Rose.*
30 Dionysius of Halicarnassus, the Roman historian, fl. *Spelman.*
19 Virgil, the Roman epic poet. *Dryden, Pitt, Warton,*
11 Catullus, Tibullus, and Propertius. Roman poets. *Grainger, Dart.*
8 Horace, the Roman lyric and satyric poet. *Francis.*

A. C.

17 Livy, the Roman historion. *Ray.*
19 Ovid, the Roman elegiac poet. *Garth.*
20 Celsus, the Roman philosopher and physician, fl. *Grieve.*
25 Strabo, the Greek geographer.
33 Phædrus, the Roman fabulist. *Smart.*
45 Paterculus, the Roman historian, fl. *Newcombe.*
62 Persius, the Roman satiric poet. *Brewster.*

64 Quintius Curtius, a Roman, hiſtorian of Alexander the Great, fl. *Digby.*
Seneca, of Spain, the philoſopher and tragic poet, put to death. *L'Eſtrange.*
65 Lucan, the Roman epic poet, ditto. *Rowe.*
79 Pliny the elder, the Roman natural hiſtorian. *Holland.*
93 Joſephus, the Jewiſh hiſtorian. *Whiſton.*
94 Epictetus, the Greek ſtoic philoſopher, fl. Mrs. *Carter.*
95 Quinctilian, the Roman orator and advocate. *Guthrie.*
96 Statius, the Roman epic poet. *Lewis.*
Lucius Florus, of Spain, the Roman hiſtorian, fl.
99 Tacitus, the Roman hiſtorian. *Gordon.*
104 Martial, of Spain, the epigrammatic poet. *Hay.*
Valerius Flaccus, the Roman epic poet.
116 Pliny the younger, hiſtorical letters. *Melmoth, Orrery.*
117 Suetonius, the Roman hiſtorian. *Hughes.*
119 Plutarch, of Greece, the biographer. *Dryden, Langhorne.*
128 Juvenal, the Roman ſatiric poet. *Dryden.*
140 Ptolemy, the Egyptian geographer, mathematician, and aſtronomer, fl.
150 Juſtin, the Roman hiſtorian, fl. *Turnbul.*
161 Arrian, the Roman hiſtorian and philoſopher, fl. *Rooke.*
167 Juſtin, of Samaria, the oldeſt Chriſtian author after the apoſtles.
180 Lucian, the Roman philologer. *Dimſdale, Dryden, Franklin.*
Marcus Aur. Antoninus, Roman emperor and philoſopher. *Collier, Elphinſtone.*
193 Galen, the Greek philoſopher and phyſician.
200 Diogenes Laertius, the Greek biographer, fl.
229 Dion Caſſius, of Greece, the Roman hiſtorian, fl.
254 Origen, a Chriſtian father of Alexandria.
Herodian, of Alexandria, the Roman hiſtorian, fl. *Hart.*
258 Cyprian, of Carthage, ſuffered martyrdom. *Marſhal.*
273 Longinus, the Greek orator, put to death by Aurelian. *Smith.*
320 Lactantius, a father of the church, fl.
336 Arius, a prieſt of Alexandria, founder of the ſect of Arians.
342 Euſebius, the eccleſiaſtical hiſtorian and chronologer. *Hanmer.*
379 Bazil, biſhop of Cæſaria.
389 Gregory Nazianzen, biſhop of Conſtantinople.
397 Ambroſe, biſhop of Milan.
415 Macrobius, the Roman grammarian.
428 Eutropius, the Roman hiſtorian.
524 Boethius, the Roman poet, and Platonic philoſopher. *Bellamy, Preſton.*
529 Procopius of Cæſarea, the Roman hiſtorian. *Holcroft.*

Here ends the illuſtrious liſt of ancient, or, as they are ſtyled, Claſſic authors, for mankind are indebted to Greece and Rome, thoſe two great theatres of glory: but it will ever be regretted, that a ſmall part only of their writings have come to our hands. This was owing to the barbarous policy of thoſe fierce illiterate pagans, who, in the fifth century, ſubverted the Roman empire, and in which practices they were joined ſoon after by the Saracens, or followers of Mahomet. Conſtantinople alone had eſcaped the ravages of the Barbarians; and to the few literati who ſheltered themſelves within its walls, is chiefly owing the preſervation of thoſe valuable remains of antiquity. To learning, civility, and refinement, ſucceeded worſe than Gothic ignorance—the ſuperſtition and buffoonery of the church of Rome: Europe therefore produces few names worthy of record during the ſpace of a thouſand years; a period which hiſtorians, with great propriety, denominate the dark or Gothic ages.

The invention of printing contributed to the revival of learning in the ſixteenth century, from which memorable æra a race of men have ſprung up in a new ſoil, France, Germany, and Britain; who, if they do not exceed, at leaſt equal, the greateſt geniuſes of antiquity. Of theſe our own countrymen have the reputation of the firſt rank, with whoſe names we ſhall finiſh our liſt.

A. C.

735 Bede, a prieſt of Northumberland; Hiſtory of the Saxons, Scots, &c.
901 King Alfred; hiſtory, philoſophy, and poetry.
1259 Matthew Paris, monk of St. Alban's; Hiſtory of England.
1292 Roger Bacon, Somerſetſhire; natural philoſophy.
1308 John Fordun, a prieſt of Mearns-ſhire; Hiſtory of Scotland.
1400 Geoffry Chaucer, London; the father of Engliſh poetry.
1402 John Gower, Wales; the poet.
1535 Sir Thomas More, London; hiſtory, politics, divinity.
1552 John Leland, London; lives and antiquities.
1568 Roger Aſcham, Yorkſhire; philology and polite literature.
1572 Rev. John Knox, the Scotch reformer; hiſtory of the church of Scotland.
1582 George Buchanan, Dumbartonſhire; Hiſtory of Scotland, Pſalms of David, politics, &c.
1598 Edmund Spenſer, London; Fairy Queen, and other poems.
1615—25 Beaumont and Fletcher; 53 Dramatic pieces.
1616 William Shakeſpeare, Stratford; 42 tragedies and comedies.
1622 John Napier, of Marcheſton, Scotland; diſcoverer of logarithms.
1623 William Camden, London; hiſtory and antiquities.
1626 Lord Chancellor Bacon, London; natural philoſophy, literature in general.
1634 Lord Chief Juſtice Coke, Norfolk; laws of England.
1638 Ben Jonſon, London; 53 dramatic pieces.
1641 Sir Henry Spelman, Norfolk; laws and antiquities.
1654 John Selden, Suſſex: antiquities and laws.
1657 Dr. William Harvey, Kent, diſcovered the circulation of the blood.

1667 Abraham

1667 Abraham Cowley, London; miscellaneous poetry.
1674 John Milton, London; Paradise Lost, Regained, and various other pieces in verse and prose.
Hyde, earl of Clarendon, Wiltshire; History of the Civil Wars in England.
1675 James Gregory, Aberdeen; mathematics, geometry, and optics.
1677 Reverend Dr. Isaac Barrow, London; natural philosophy, mathematics, and sermons.
1680 Samuel Butler, Worcestershire; Hudibras, a burlesque poem.
1685 Thomas Otway, London; 10 tragedies and comedies, with other poems.
1687 Edmund Waller, Bucks; poems, speeches, letters, &c.
1688 Dr. Ralph Cudworth, Somersetshire; Intellectual System.
1689 Dr. Thomas Sydenham, Dorsetshire; History of Physic.
1690 Nathinel Lee, London; 11 tragedies.
Robert Barclay, Edinburgh; Apology for the Quakers.
1691 Hon Robert Boyle; natural and experimental philosophy and theology.
Sir George M'Kenzie, Dundee; Antiquities and Laws of Scotland.
1694 John Tillotson, archbishop of Canterbury, Halifax; 254 sermons.
1697 Sir William Temple, London; politics, and polite literature.
1701 John Dryden, Northamptonshire; 27 tragedies and comedies, satiric poems, Virgil.
1704 John Locke, Somersetshire; philosophy, government, and theology.
1705 John Ray, Essex; botany, natural philosophy, and divinity.
1707 George Farquhar, Londonderry; eight comedies.
1713 Ant. Ash. Cowper, earl of Shaftesbury; Characteristics.
1714 Gilbert Burnet, Edinburgh, bishop of Salisbury; history, biography, divinity, &c.
1718 Nicholas Rowe, Devonshire; 7 tragedies, translation of Lucan's Pharsalia.
1719 Reverend John Flamsteed, Derbyshire; mathematics and astronomy.
Joseph Addison, Wiltshire; Spectator, Guardian, poems, politics.
Dr. John Keil, Edinburgh; mathematics and astronomy.
1721 Matthew Prior, London; poems and politics.
1724 William Wollaston, Staffordshire; Religion of Nature delineated.
1727 Sir Isaac Newton, Lincolnshire; mathematics, geometry, astronomy, optics.
1729 Reverend Dr. Samuel Clarke, Norwich; mathematics, divinity, &c.
Sir Richard Steele, Dublin; four comedies, papers in Tatler, &c.
William Congreve, Staffordshire; seven dramatic pieces.
1732 John Gay, Exeter; poems, fables, and eleven dramatic pieces.
1734 Dr. John Arbuthnot, Mearns-shire; medicine, coins, politics.
1742 Dr. Edmund Halley; natural philosophy, astronomy, navigation.
Dr. Richard Bentley, Yorkshire; classical learning, criticism.
1744 Alexander Pope, London; poems, letters, translation of Homer.

1745 Reverend Dr. Jonathan Swift, Dublin; poems, politics, and letters.
1746 Colin M'Laurin, Argyleshire; Algebra, View of Newton's Philosophy.
1748 James Thomson, Roxburghshire; Seasons, and other poems, five tragedies.
Reverend Dr. Isaac Watts, Southampton; logic, philosophy, psalms, hymns, sermons, &c.
Dr. Francis Hutcheson, Airshire; System of Moral Philosophy.
1750 Reverend Dr. Conyers Middleton, Yorkshire; Life of Cicero, &c.
Andrew Baxter, Old Aberdeen; metaphysics, and natural philosophy.
1751 Henry St. John, Lord Bolingbroke, Surrey; philosophy, metaphysics, and politics.
Dr. Alexander Monro, Edinburgh; Anatomy of the Human Body.
1754 Dr. Richard Mead, London, on poisons, plague, small-pox, medicine, precepts.
Henry Fielding, Somersetshire; Tom Jones, Joseph Andrews, &c.
1757 Colley Cibber, London; 25 tragedies and comedies.
1761 Thomas Sherlock, bishop of London; 69 sermons, &c.
Benjamin Hoadley, bishop of Winchester; sermons and controversy.
Samuel Richardson, London; Grandison, Clarissa, Pamela.
Reverend Dr. John Leland, Lancashire, Answer to Deistical Writers.
1765 Reverend Dr. Edward Young; Night Thoughts, and other poems, three tragedies
Robert Simson, Glasgow; Conic Sections, Euclid, Apollonius.
1768 Reverend Lawrence Sterne; 45 sermons, Sentimental Journey, Tristram Shandy.
1769 Robert Smith, Lincolnshire; harmonics and optics.
1770 Reverend Dr. Jortin; Life of Erasmus, Ecclesiastical History, and sermons.
Dr. Mark Akenside, Newcastle upon Tyne; poems.
Dr. Tobias Smollet, Dumbartonshire; History of England, novels, translations.
1771 Thomas Gray, Professor of Modern History, Cambridge; poems.
1773 Philip Dormer Stanhope, earl of Chesterfield; letters.
George Lord Lyttleton, Worcestershire; History of England.
1774 Oliver Goldsmith; poems, essays, and other pieces.
Zachary Pearce, bishop of Rochester; Annotations on the New Testament, &c.
1775 Dr. John Hawkesworth; essays.
1776 David Hume, Merse; History of England, and essays.
James Ferguson, Aberdeenshire; astronomy.
1777 Samuel Foote, Cornwall; plays.
1779 David Garrick, Hereford; plays, &c.
William Warburton, bishop of Gloucester; Divine Legation of Moses, and various other works.
1780 Sir William Blackstone, Judge of the court of Common Pleas, London; Commentaries on the Laws of England.

1780 Dr.

1780 Dr. John Fothergill, Yorkshire; philosophy and medicine.
James Harris; Hermes, Philological Inquiries, and Philosophical Arrangements.

1782 Thomas Newton, bishop of Bristol, Litchfield; Discourses on the Prophecies, and other works.

1782 Sir John Pringle, Bart. Roxburghshire; Diseases of the Army.
Henry Home, Lord Kaimes, Scotland; Elements of Criticism, Sketches of the History of Man.

1783 Dr. William Hunter, Lanerkshire; anatomy.
Dr. Benjamin Kennicott; Hebrew Version of the Bible, theological tracts.

1784 Dr. Thomas Morell; Editor of Ainsworth's Dictionary, Hedericus's Lexicon, and some Greek tragedies.
Dr. Samuel Johnson, Litchfield; English Dictionary, biography, essays, poetry. Died December 13, aged 71.

1785 William Whitehead, Poet Laureat; poems and plays. Died April 14.
Reverend Richard Burn, LL.D. author of the Justice of Peace, Ecclesiastical Laws, &c. Died Nov. 20.
Richard Glover, Esq; Leonidas, Medea, &c. Died Nov. 25.

1786 Jonas Hanway, Esq; travels, miscellaneous. Died Sept. 5, aged 74.

1787 Dr. Robert Lowth, bishop of London; criticism, divinity, grammar. Died Nov. 3.
Soame Jenyns, Esq; Internal Evidence of the Christian Religion, and other pieces. Died Dec. 18.

1788 James Stuart, Esq; celebrated by the name of "Athenian Stuart." Died Feb. 1.
Thomas Gainsborough, Esq; the celebrated painter. Died Aug. 2.
Thomas Sheridan, Esq; English Dictionary, works on education, elocution, &c. Died Aug. 14.
William Julius Mickle, Esq; translator of the Lusiad. Died Oct. 25.

1789 Dr. William Cullen; Practice of Physic, Materia Medica, &c. Died Feb. 5.

1790 Benjamin Franklin, Esq; electricity, natural philosophy, miscellanies. Died April 17.
Reverend Thomas Warton, B.D. Poet Laureat; History of English Poetry.
Dr. Adam Smith; Moral Sentiments, Inquiry into the Wealth of Nations.
John Howard, Esq. Account of Prisons and Lazarettos, &c.

1791 Dr. Richard Price, Annuities, &c.
John Wesley, a popular preacher amongst the Methodists.
Catharine Macaulay Graham, History of England, Political Tracts, &c.

www.ingramcontent.com/pod-product-compliance
Lightning Source LLC
Chambersburg PA
CBHW031814270326
41932CB00008B/414

* 9 7 8 3 7 4 4 6 9 6 4 6 3 *